CONTENTS AT A GLANCE

EXPERT

PHP and MySQL®

EXPERT

PHP and MySQL®

Andrew Curioso
Ronald Bradford
Patrick Galbraith

Wiley Publishing, Inc.

Expert PHP and MySQL®

Published by
Wiley Publishing, Inc.
10475 Crosspoint Boulevard
Indianapolis, IN 46256
www.wiley.com

Copyright © 2010 by Wiley Publishing, Inc., Indianapolis, Indiana

Published simultaneously in Canada

ISBN: 978-0-470-56312-0

Manufactured in the United States of America

10 9 8 7 6 5 4 3 2 1

For general information on our other products and services please contact our Customer Care Department within the United States at (877) 762-2974, outside the United States at (317) 572-3993 or fax (317) 572-4002.

Wiley also publishes its books in a variety of electronic formats. Some content that appears in print may not be available in electronic books.

Library of Congress Control Number: 2010920658

This book is dedicated to my wife, Laura. Without your support this book wouldn't be possible. Thank you for being by my side and planning the wedding while I was doing my writing!

—ANDREW CURIOSO

For MySQL Culture, past, present, and future. To many in the MySQL community: you are more than colleagues, you are great friends.

—RONALD BRADFORD

This book is dedicated to my son, Kiran Patrick. "Kiran" means "ray of light" in Sanskrit, and you are a ray of light in my life!

—PATRICK GALBRAITH

ABOUT THE AUTHORS

ANDREW CURIOSO has been coding in PHP and MySQL for a decade. His experience includes developing professional-grade PHP and MySQL based web applications for MIT Lincoln Laboratory (part of the Massachusetts Institute of Technology) and being at the ground floor of the state-of-the-art web-publishing platform Webon at Lycos (currently the page builder technology for `Angelfire.com`). Aside from software engineering, Andrew takes interest in software usability, business, the semantic web, and robotics. He currently works at MyVBO, a virtual business office that provides powerful tools to help small to medium sized business manage their companies online. Over the years, he's had the opportunity to work on exciting projects and specializes in data portability, linked data, social media, and Rich Internet Applications. His home on the web can be found at `http://andrewcurioso.com/`.

RONALD BRADFORD has more than two decades of professional IT industry experience in a broad range of disciplines. His core expertise is in relational database management systems (RDBMS) including MySQL, Oracle and Ingres. His technical software development skills include working in Java (J2EE), PHP, Perl, Python, Web (HTML/CSS/XML/JSON), and Linux/Unix operating systems. He is a professional speaker, educational curriculum developer, and writer who specializes in technical presentations, workshops, online content publishing, and knowledge transfer. More information on his related MySQL writings, presentations and useful tools can be found at `http://ronaldbradford.com`.

PATRICK GALBRAITH lives up in the sticks of southwestern New Hampshire near Mt. Monadnock with his wife Ruth and son Kiran. Since 1993, he has been using and developing Open Source software. He has worked on various Open Source projects including MySQL, federated storage engine, memcached Functions for MySQL, Drizzle, Narada Search Engine Slashcode, and is the maintainer of DBD::mysql. He has worked at a number of companies throughout his career, including MySQL AB, `Classmates.com`, OSDN/Slashdot, and Lycos. He currently works at NorthScale, a leading provider of scale-out infrastructure software for web applications. He is also part owner of a wireless broadband company, Radius North, which provides Internet service to underserved rural areas of New Hampshire. His website, which comes by way of a 5.8GHz Alvarion access unit up in a pine tree, is `http://patg.net`.

ABOUT THE TECHNICAL EDITORS

ALAN COLLISON is a software engineer with more than a dozen years of experience developing scalable PHP applications. His expertise ranges from the design and development of front end GUIs to the implementation of core server side application business logic.

JAY COSKEY is a software developer and software development manager who lives in Seattle, and has worked for companies including Cray Inc. and Amazon.com. He has used numerous languages on Linux, Unix, and Windows platforms, in environments ranging from OS development, to web and enterprise systems. When not involved in mathematics or software, he can sometimes be found woodworking.

ERIC DAY has been writing high-performance servers and databases for most of his career and currently works on open source projects such as Drizzle and Gearman. He has also written a number of extensions for higher level languages such as PHP. When not hacking on code, he can be found running, enjoying a good vegan meal, or blogging at http://oddments.org/.

KEN MACKE is a systems architect, developer, and owner of RockIP Networks — a provider of web hosting and IT consulting services. Ken has over 15 years of experience creating cutting-edge software with technologies such as PHP, C++, C#, and .NET. You can find Ken online at twitter.com/kmacke.

ELIZABETH NARAMORE has been a web developer since 1997, with a focus in PHP and E-commerce. In addition to being a web developer, she is an author, editor, speaker, and educator, and active member of communities such as the PHP Community, PHPWomen, and her local PHP Users Group.

TROND NORBYE is a Senior Software Engineer specializing in databases and distributed caching. He currently works at NorthScale designing and implementing scale out data systems. Prior to joining NorthScale, Trond was a key member of Sun Microsystems' Web Scale Infrastructure group where he worked on Drizzle, Gearman and Memcached. In his copious free time he is a core contributor on the Memcached, Libmemcached and OpenGrok Open Source projects.

KARL WILBUR is an enterprise consultant, PHP developer and Linux guru with more than a decade of LAMP experience and a passion for the bleeding-edge. When not out motorcycling the Midwest he can be found lurking on the Internet at http://karlwilbur.net/.

CREDITS

EXECUTIVE EDITOR
Robert Elliott

PROJECT EDITOR
Maureen Spears

TECHNICAL EDITORS
Alan Collison
Jay Coskey
Eric Day
Ken Macke
Elizabeth Naramore
Trond Norbye
Karl Wilbur

PRODUCTION EDITOR
Eric Charbonneau

COPY EDITOR
Kim Cofer

EDITORIAL DIRECTOR
Robyn B. Siesky

EDITORIAL MANAGER
Mary Beth Wakefield

MARKETING MANAGER
Ashley Zurcher

PRODUCTION MANAGER
Tim Tate

VICE PRESIDENT AND EXECUTIVE GROUP PUBLISHER
Richard Swadley

VICE PRESIDENT AND EXECUTIVE PUBLISHER
Barry Pruett

ASSOCIATE PUBLISHER
Jim Minatel

PROJECT COORDINATOR, COVER
Lynsey Stanford

COMPOSITOR
Jeff Lytle, Happenstance Type-o-Rama

PROOFREADER
Nancy Bell

INDEXER
Johnna VanHoose Dinse

COVER DESIGNER
Michael E. Trent

COVER IMAGE
©Gavin Hellier/Photographer's Choice RF/
Getty Images

ACKNOWLEDGMENTS

IT WAS THANKS TO MY BROTHER RAY CURIOSO JR. that I was really able to get a head start. He started an embroidery business in the 90s out of my parents' garage. It has since moved to its own place but there was that time in-between where, thanks to his company, I was one of the only people that I knew with Internet access. It was slow and it took days to download software development kits and it wasn't as easy to find programming help for a beginner as it is today. But I made do with what I had. It was also because of him and his business — it needed an ecommerce site — that I put down the C code and the ASP and got my start with PHP and MySQL.

I'd like to thank my parents too for being a constant source of support for me. It was my father who taught me the value of hard work. And, of course, thank my wife who put up with me spending long nights working for a start up and writing a book at the same time. We were married during the writing and without her hard work planning the wedding, supporting me, and standing by my side this book would not have been possible.

I'd like to thank my teammates at Lycos. It was truly a pleasure working with each of them. I'd particularly like to thank my managers. Don Kosak for inspiring me, Neal Shanske for keeping me on my toes. I'd like to thank Derek Bruneau since everything I learned about good software design and usability I learned thanks to him. And I'd like to thank my fellow engineers Lisa Wallmark, Chandra Yadav, and Kevin Harrington. I'd like to also thank my team at MyVBO, in particular Robert (Bob) Wilkins and Matthew Sheppard for their understanding as I juggled work and writing.

Finally, I would also like to take a minute to thank the team that worked tirelessly to make this book happen. Bob Elliott who made this book happen, Maureen Spears who edited this whole thing cover to cover, and my co-authors Patrick and Ronald. Patrick in particular has been a good friend and deserves credit for putting the team together. He is the one thread that connects us all. Which brings me to the tech editors. They all did an amazing job and the book is much better because of each of them.

There are countless people who have helped me along the way. I am sure that I forgot someone. To anyone who has ever encouraged me to follow my dreams or supported me in any way: thank you.

—Andrew Curioso

TODAY, I AM A WELL RESPECTED AUTHORITY in the MySQL field. This was not possible without a lot of hard work and great mentorship. I would first like to thank the late Frank Jarvis from DDIAE (now USQ) who in 1988 introduced me to the works of C.J. Date, M. Stonebraker and E.F. Codd during my university studies.

My first relational database experience started with Ingres and led to immediate work with systems design and software development in the database field. In the early 90's, as a young, energetic and knowledgeable database architect with several successful government projects, my work alongside my now good friend Bruce Turner helped in my understanding and appreciation of more formal processes in the management and success of large scale deployments. We worked together again for Oracle Corporation in the late 90s where Bruce still works today. To Bruce, thank you for your support and mentoring. Those TAFE days with Mike and Laurie still rate as some of my favorites. From my first use of MySQL over ten years ago until today I still seek input, advice and encouragement from the MySQL community. Many of you from the MySQL community I consider as great friends.

Finally, to my fiance Cindy who has been supportive throughout the entire process of my first book in MySQL with compromises that have enabled me to complete this work on schedule.

—Ronald Bradford

ONE WEEKEND IN 1993, I had the chance to go on a getaway to San Diego. Instead, I opted to stay home and download, onto 26 floppies, Slackware Linux, which I promptly installed onto my Packard Bell 386. I could never get the built-in video card to work with X, so I ended up buying a separate video card and had to edit my XConfig file to get it to work. How much more interesting this was to do than editing a config.sys and an autoexec.bat! From then on, I was hooked. I worked at Siemens Ultrasound Group in Issaquah, Washington, at the time. An engineer there named Debra, when asked what was a good thing to learn, said something I'll never forget: "Learn Perl." Debra — you were right! I always wanted to be a C ++ graphics programmer. That didn't happen because of this thing called the World Wide Web. I remember Ray Jones and Randy Bentson of Celestial Software showing me a program called Mosaic, which allowed you to view text over the Internet. Images would be launched using XV. Everywhere I worked, I had to write programs that ran on the Web, which required me to write CGI in Perl. So much for my goal of being a C ++ programmer — but I consider this a great trade for a great career. (I did eventually get to write C ++ for MySQL!) I would first like to thank my wife, Ruth, for being patient and supportive of me for numerous lost weekends with this book and my previous book Developing Web Applications with Perl, memcached, MySQL and Apache, as well as accepting me working on yet another book so soon after the first! Next in line for thanks, our editor, Maureen Spears, who is not only a great editor, but also a friend. Not only did she edit this current work, but she was my editor for my previous book. Next, I would like to thank my co-authors, Andrew and Ronald. It's been a whole different experience co-authoring versus being a sole author, having learned a bit about putting together something — as a team.

A special thanks goes to our tech editors as well as to Trond Norbye (memcached, libmemcached), Eric Day (Gearman, Drizzle) and Andrew Aksyonoff (Sphinx) for stepping up as tech editors when we were in a crunch and reviewing the material I wrote about their projects!

Thank you to Bob Elliott, who gave us the opportunity to work as a team to write this book! Thanks to Monty Widenius for creating MySQL and for being a mentor as well as a good friend who worked hard to include FederatedX into MariaDB while I was working on this book. Thanks also to Brian Aker for being another great mentor and friend, as well as being a software-producing machine with a scrolling page full of open source software projects that he's created, including Drizzle and libmemcached.

I **WOULD LIKE TO THANK MY CURRENT COLLEAGUES** at Northscale — Steve Yen, Dustin Sallings, James Phillips, Matt Ingenthron, Rod Ebrahimi, Eric Lambert and Trond Norbye — it's a real privilege to work with guys who have so much expertise. Also thanks go to my former colleagues at Lycos who encouraged me while writing my previous book — Don Kosak, Chandra Yadav, Tristan Escalada, others, as well as Andrew Curioso! Also to former colleagues at Grazr and MySQL. Last but not least, thanks to the team members of MariaDB and Drizzle for integrating projecs I worked on while writing this book. Thanks also to anyone I forgot to mention. I know I probably forgot someone!

—PATRICK GALBRAITH

CONTENTS

INTRODUCTION

PHP AND MYSQL HAVE BEEN USED FOR YEARS to power some of the most popular websites and open source applications anywhere. It's no secret that the Web has evolved. Modern web sites are expected to be dynamic and the user count for popular sites is now measured in the millions.

This book examines some of the technologies and techniques needed to make robust and scalable applications perform in today's high-demand world. Early chapters focus on essential concepts. For example:

- ➤ Object Oriented Programming
- ➤ Design Patterns
- ➤ Advanced MySQL queries

Later chapters get down into the trenches and focus on ways to improve application performance through caching with memcached (and others), full-text search with Sphinx, and multitasking with Gearman.

Today's PHP programmer can't be afraid to get their hands dirty. By the time this book is done you will be well on your way to extending PHP and MySQL using C. In PHP we cover extension writing. In MySQL we cover User Defined Functions.

The book focuses on critical skills and best practices in the areas of security, optimization, and software architecture. The examples are written with the assumption that you already know the basics so common code is occasionally stripped out to make the examples more readable and focused. And as such you will see examples in the book that don't check the return value of a function for errors. Don't put code like that onto your live server; fix it first! You know how.

This book will give you the tools that you need to write mission critical applications with PHP and MySQL — including high-traffic ones. The hope is that you can use some of the skills covered in this book to create your own open source projects and eventually contribute to the PHP and MySQL communities. Or perhaps you just use this book to help you create the next PHP and MySQL powered success story

WHO THIS BOOK IS FOR

This book is designed to cover some of the most advanced topics in the PHP and MySQL worlds. It is intended for advanced PHP and MySQL users who have significant experience and have already worked on several projects. Some people who should read this book include:

- ➤ Programmers creating mission-critical applications
- ➤ Programmers creating websites or applications that need to support thousands (if not millions) of users

➤ Programmers who create applications that need to store and access large amounts of data or requires lots of processing

➤ Programmers who just find things like design patterns, PHP extensions, and MySQL UDFs interesting and who want to learn more

This book assumes that you also have a working knowledge of C as well and that you have at least compiled a C programmer or two (PHP and MySQL count). PHP extensions and MySQL User Defined Functions are both written in C.

This book starts off easy but quickly dives into many advanced topics. It's all right if you're not already an advanced PHP, MySQL, and C programmer but you'll probably want to keep some other Wrox books handy for reference.

WHAT THIS BOOK COVERS

PHP and MySQL are both well established with many libraries and extensions available. It would be impossible to cover every expert topic in a single book. Likewise, this book doesn't try to cover beginner level topics at all. The authors did, however, hand pick topics that they think are essential for any expert PHP and MySQL programmer to know.

The book is laid out like this:

➤ Chapters 1 through 3 are intended as a crash course in concepts that you absolutely must know before reading the rest of the book. They cover topics like design patters, iterators, and the difference between the MySQL storage engines.

➤ Chapters 4 and 5 take a brief break from the essentials and focuses on one of the most important concepts for creating scalable applications: caching.

➤ Chapter 6 revisits the essentials and touches on some advanced MySQL topics.

➤ Chapters 7 and 8 dive into extending PHP and MySQL with C. They are the only chapters in the book where you're not writing code in just PHP or SQL.

➤ Chapter 9 goes over full-text search and introduces Sphinx.

➤ Chapter 10 covers multitasking and discusses Gearman.

➤ Chapters 11 and 12 cover essentials including advanced rewrite rules, custom session handling and user security.

➤ Chapter 13 goes over MySQL INFORMATION_SCHEMA.

➤ Chapter 14 touches on security some more.

➤ Chapters 15 and 16 wrap up the book with other uses of PHP and MySQL besides web applications and optimizing and debugging.

WHAT YOU NEED TO USE THIS BOOK

Apart from a willingness to learn and all the skills listed in "Whom This Book Is For" you will also need:

➤ PHP 5.3 or newer with MySQL and MySQLi enabled. Preferably compiled from source (for Chapter 8). However, some examples will run in older versions as well.

➤ MySQL 5.1 or higher. You can also substitute MariaDB or Drizzle for most examples.

➤ Apache 2.0 web server configured for PHP with mod_rewrite enabled.

Using Linux

If you are using Linux for your PHP and MYSQL development (highly recommended):

➤ An ANSI C compiler (Ex: GCC) to compile PHP extensions and MySQL User Defined Functions

➤ flex: Version 2.5.4

➤ bison: Version 1.28 (preferred), 1.35, or 1.75

Using Windows

If you are using Windows you will need:

➤ Microsoft Visual Studio 2008 or newer

➤ Windows SDK 6.1

You can also substitute Microsoft IIS in place of Apache. However, some of the content in this book is Apache specific.

CONVENTIONS

To help you get the most from the text and keep track of what's happening, we've used a number of conventions throughout the book.

Boxes like this one hold important, not-to-be forgotten information that is directly relevant to the surrounding text.

Tips, hints, tricks, and asides to the current discussion look like this.

As for other conventions in the text:

➤ New terms and important words are highlighted *in italics* when first introduced.

➤ Keyboard combinations are treated like this: Ctrl+R.

➤ Filenames, URLs, and code within the text are treated like so: `persistence.properties`.

```
This book uses monofont type with no highlighting for most code examples.
This book uses bolding to emphasize code that is of particular importance in the
present context.
```

SOURCE CODE

As you work through the examples in this book, you may choose either to type in all the code manually or to use the source-code files that accompany the book. All of the source code used in this book is available for download at `www.wrox.com`. Once at the site, simply locate the book's title (either by using the Search box or by using one of the title lists) and click the Download Code link on the book's detail page to obtain all the source code for the book.

 Because many books have similar titles, you may find it easiest to search by ISBN; this book's ISBN is 978-0-470-56312-0.

Once you download the code, just decompress it with your favorite compression tool. Alternately, you can go to the main Wrox code download page at `www.wrox.com/dynamic/books/download.aspx` to see the code available for this book and all other Wrox books.

ERRATA

We make every effort to ensure that there are no errors in the text or in the code. However, no one is perfect, and mistakes do occur. If you find an error in one of our books, like a spelling mistake or faulty piece of code, we would be very grateful for your feedback. By sending in errata, you may save another reader hours of frustration, and at the same time you will be helping us provide even higher-quality information.

To find the errata page for this book, go to `www.wrox.com` and locate the title using the Search box or one of the title lists. Then, on the book details page, click the Book Errata link. On this page you can view all errata that have been submitted for this book and posted by Wrox editors. A complete book list, including links to each book's errata, is also available at `www.wrox.com/misc-pages/booklist.shtml`.

If you don't spot "your" error on the Book Errata page, go to www.wrox.com/contact/ techsupport.shtml and complete the form there to send us the error you have found. We'll check the information and, if appropriate, post a message to the book's errata page and fix the problem in subsequent editions of the book.

P2P.WROX.COM

For author and peer discussion, join the P2P forums at p2p.wrox.com. The forums are a web-based system on which you can post messages relating to Wrox books and related technologies and interact with other readers and technology users. The forums offer a subscription feature to e-mail you topics of interest of your choosing when new posts are made to the forums. Wrox authors, editors, other industry experts, and your fellow readers are present on these forums.

At http://p2p.wrox.com you will find a number of different forums that will help you not only as you read this book, but also as you develop your own applications. To join the forums, just follow these steps:

1. Go to p2p.wrox.com and click the Register link.

2. Read the terms of use and click Agree.

3. Complete the required information to join as well as any optional information you wish to provide, and click Submit.

4. You will receive an e-mail with information describing how to verify your account and complete the joining process.

 You can read messages in the forums without joining P2P, but in order to post your own messages, you must join.

Once you join, you can post new messages and respond to messages other users post. You can read messages at any time on the Web. If you would like to have new messages from a particular forum e-mailed to you, click the Subscribe to this Forum icon by the forum name in the forum listing.

For more information about how to use the Wrox P2P, be sure to read the P2P FAQs for answers to questions about how the forum software works, as well as many common questions specific to P2P and Wrox books. To read the FAQs, click the FAQ link on any P2P page.

1

Techniques Every Expert Programmer Needs to Know

WHAT'S IN THIS CHAPTER?

➤ Understanding Object-oriented fundamentals in PHP

➤ Understanding INNER and OUTER JOINs

➤ Other JOIN syntax you should know

➤ Using MySQL Unions

➤ Using GROUP BY in MySQL queries

➤ Implementing MySQL Logical Operations and flow control

➤ Maintaining MySQL relational integrity

➤ Using subqueries in MySQL

➤ Utilizing advanced PHP regular expressions

This chapter covers the techniques that you, the proficient PHP and MySQL developer, should know and use before you tackle more advanced domain features in PHP and MySQL. The chapter starts with an in-depth overview of object-oriented programming techniques in PHP and object-oriented design patterns. As a PHP developer, you then become familiar with a number of core MySQL requirements for retrieving data including the different types of joins, UNION, GROUP BY, and subqueries syntax. This chapter also details the logic operators and flow control and techniques for maintaining relational integrity in MySQL. The chapter concludes with an in-depth review of advanced regular expressions in both PHP and MySQL.

OBJECT-ORIENTED PHP

Object-orientation has become a key concept behind proper PHP software design. This book follows the idea that in properly designed software, all business logic (the rules that drive how an application behaves) should be object oriented. The only exception is when small scripts act as a view or a way to display data returned from other objects.

Taking this approach solves a few problems because it:

➤ Makes it easy to extend the functionality of existing code.

➤ Allows for type hinting, which gives greater control over what variables are passed into functions.

➤ Allows for established design patterns to be used to solve common software design problems and makes debugging much easier.

This section covers object-oriented PHP and key design patterns in depth. Later chapters cover even more advanced object-oriented topics.

Instantiation and Polymorphism

The two key benefits of object-oriented programming in PHP are the ability to abstract data into classes and for the application to act on those structures. It is important to understand polymorphism, which is when one object appears and can be used in the same way as another object of a related type. It stands to reason that if B is a descendant of A and a function can accept A as a parameter, it can also accept B.

Three classes are used in this chapter while covering polymorphism:

➤ `Node`

➤ `BlogEntry`

➤ `ForumTopic`

In this application both `BlogEntry` and `ForumTopic` are siblings of each other and descendants of `Node`. This is a good time to become familiar with the example code that comes with the book. The code archive contains a folder for every chapter. Each folder has a `.class.php` file and a `.test.php` file for every class. SQL files aren't used in this section, but when they are, they have a `.sql` extension.

The typical class looks a lot like this:

```
class ClassNameHere extends AnotherClass {
  public function someFunction() {
    parent::someFunction();
  }
};
```

The `parent` keyword is used to directly reference a variable or method in the parent class, bypassing any variables or methods of the same name in the current class. The method is marked as `public`, which is a familiar concept for object-oriented programming but relatively new to PHP.

Older PHP applications will not define a visibility for the member methods. When the visibility is not defined it is assumed to be public. A member variable or method (function inside a class) can have one of three visibilities:

➤ **public** indicates that the member is accessible globally across all of PHP.

➤ **private** indicates that a member can be accessed only from within the class in which it is defined. Private members cannot be overridden in later classes because those classes too do not have access to the member.

➤ **protected** indicates that the member can be accessed only by the class in which it is defined and all descending classes.

Additionally, three other keywords can augment `private`, `public`, and `protected`. They are `static`, `abstract`, and `final`:

➤ **static** members are not tied to particular instances of a class and can be accessed by any instance. They should be used sparingly but are very useful for shared variables across all instances. The `static` keyword can also be used inside methods and functions to define a variable that is global to all calls to that function. Both uses are relied upon by later examples in this chapter.

➤ **abstract** methods must be implemented in all classes that descend from that class that defines it. Abstract methods can only be defined in classes that are marked as abstract. It is not possible to directly instantiate an abstract class because of the nature of abstraction.

➤ **final** methods can never be redefined in descending classes and therefore their functionality cannot be changed.

Variables inside a class can also be declared constant using `const`. Constants are always `public static` and their value can never be changed at run time. Unlike normal variables, constants cannot have a dollar sign in front of them and by convention are always capitalized.

Each and every type of visibility is used throughout this book. The next section covers most of them by using the three classes described previously.

Polymorphism in Action

The three classes mentioned previously need to be defined in order to be useful. The goal of this section is not to create a fully functioning application but rather to demonstrate techniques that are the core of the rest of the book. The first class to be defined is the `Node` class as shown in Listing 1-1.

LISTING 1-1: NODE.CLASS.PHP

Available for download on Wrox.com

```php
<?php
abstract class Node {
  private $debugMessages;

  public function __construct() {
    $this->debugMessages = array();
    $this->debug(__CLASS__." constructor called.");
```

```php
  }

  public function __destruct() {
    $this->debug(__CLASS__." destructor called.");
    $this->dumpDebug();
  }

  protected function debug( $msg ) {
    $this->debugMessages[] = $msg;
  }

  private function dumpDebug( ) {
    echo implode( "\n", $this->debugMessages);
  }

  public abstract function getView();
}
?>
```

The Node class is abstract and therefore cannot be instantiated. However, it can have private members. The descendant classes will not be able to access the private members directly but the members can be accessed from other more visible methods inside of Node. In the node class, the member variable $debugMessage is being accessed from several methods and dumpDebug() is a private method being called from the destructor. For the purpose of this example, both ForumTopic and BlogEntry are identical in all regards except name. The magic constant __CLASS__ will be used to tell them apart as shown in Listing 1-2.

LISTING 1-2: ForumTopic.class.php

```php
<?php
class ForumTopic extends Node {
  private $debugMessages;

  public function __construct() {
    parent::__construct();
    $this->debug(__CLASS__." constructor called.");
  }

  public function __destruct() {
    $this->debug(__CLASS__." destructor called.");
    parent::__destruct();
  }

  public function getView() {
    return "This is a view into ".__CLASS__;
  }
}
?>
```

Now it is time to run some tests and see what happens. The first test is to create an instance of each subclass and observe the debug output. The entire test is just one line of code but has a several lines of output:

```
$forum = new ForumTopic();
/* Output:
Node constructor called.
ForumTopic constructor called.
ForumTopic destructor called.
Node destructor called.
*/
```

The output shows that the constructor for each class is called and that it bubbles down appropriately to the parent class before adding its own debug message. The opposite is true for the destructor. Whether the parent class is called first, last, or in the middle of a method can be determined at design time for each specific class. However, in general, because the constructors and destructors for descendant classes often reference the variables from the parent, it is a good practice to call the parent at the beginning of the constructor and end of the destructor.

Almost as important is the output demonstrating that the __CLASS__ variable is always equal to the name of the class in which the function being called is defined. It is not necessarily the same as the output of get_class($this). The get_class() method returns the name of the class that was instantiated. In non-technical terms this method always returns the class name that directly follows the new keyword when instantiating the object.

A WORD ON THE DESTRUCTOR

The destructor, in this case, was never explicitly called. Unless the script ends in a fatal error, the destructor for any remaining objects will always be executed when the script completes. The garbage collector will also fire the destructor immediately if the number of references to an object goes to zero. In this case the destructor is what dumps the debug output to the screen, so it is simple to test to see if the garbage collector is doing its job:

```
$topic = new ForumTopic();

echo "--------------------\n";
$topic = null;
echo "--------------------\n";

/* Output:
--------------------
Node constructor called.
ForumTopic constructor called.
ForumTopic destructor called.
Node destructor called.
--------------------
*/
```

continues

However, if there is another variable thrown into the mix the situation becomes much different:

```
$topic = new ForumTopic();
$reference = $topic;

echo "--------------------\n";
$topic = null;
echo "--------------------\n";

/* Output:
--------------------
--------------------
Node constructor called.
ForumTopic constructor called.
ForumTopic destructor called.
Node destructor called.
*/
```

Class instances are always passed by reference unless explicitly cloned. Using the reference operator on a class variable like $reference = &$topic; will not increase the reference count for the object and will therefore not prevent it from being garbage collected. The code, in effect, is creating a reference to a reference.

Handling Terminal Types and Type Hinting

One practical application of get_class() is explored later in this book; however, it is not always helpful to determine just the terminal type of an object. For example, in almost every case it is wrong to execute code only if the output of get_class() matches a string. After all, what happens if the class is subclassed? Shouldn't the subclasses also pass the test?

The keyword that solves the issue is instanceof. It evaluates to true if the operand on the left is of the type on the right or any subclasses of that type. For example, if a method takes an arbitrary parameter but should execute specific code if the variable is a Node object, it can be written like this:

```
if ( $foo instanceof Node ) ...
```

In this case $foo can be an instance of ForumTopic or BlogEntry. It cannot be an instance of Node only because Node is abstract and cannot be instantiated. PHP also supports type hinting, which allows a method or function to take only an object of a set type or its descendants. Type hinting, unfortunately, is not available for primitive types such as string and integer:

```
function print_view( Node $node ) {
  echo "Printing the view for ".get_class($node)."\n";
  echo $node->getView()."\n";
}
```

Class methods should use type hinting whenever possible to improve the maintainability of the code. Code that uses type hinting is less error-prone and partially self-documenting.

Interfaces

Interfaces are structures for defining functionality that a class must implement. An interface does not dictate the inner workings of that functionality. Think of interfaces as templates that classes need to adhere to. Chapter 2 makes heavy use of some of PHP's built-in interfaces.

Classes do not inherit interfaces because only the method signatures and return types are defined within them. Instead they *implement* the interface. However, it is occasionally useful to derive one interface from another. For example, an interface called `Iterator` may be used as the base interface for a new interface called `RecursiveIterator` that defines all the functionality of the standard `Iterator` interface but also defines new functionality.

An interface is never instantiated directly. However, variables can be tested against interfaces. Testing against an interface ensures that an object implements all the methods of the interface before attempting to call a method. For example, say the interface `PageElement` defines a `getXML()` method:

```
if ( $object instanceof PageElement )
  $body->appendChild( $object->getXML( $document ) );
```

Interfaces are defined in a similar way to classes. Instead of `class` the keyword `interface` is used. Two other important distinctions are that all methods inside an interface must always be defined as public and methods do not have a body. Consider Listing 1-3 which shows a new interface called `ReadableNode`:

LISTING 1-3: ReadableNode.interface.php

```php
<?php
interface ReadableNode {
  public function isRead();
  public function markAsRead();
  public function markAsUnread();
};
?>
```

You can then create a reusable utility function `markNodeAsRead()` to check if a node is readable and to call the `markAsRead()` method if it is.

```php
function markNodeAsRead( $node ) {
  if ( $node instanceof ReadableNode )
    $node->markAsRead();
}
```

Interfaces are useful for defining sets of functionality when it is not important how the methods are implemented. Because PHP doesn't have multi-inheritance they are also useful for defining classes that have a collection of disparate functionality but still need the benefits of polymorphism and type hinting. Unlike inheritance, a class can implement as many interfaces as it desires. Also, an interface can extend multiple other interfaces. For example, if a class is both `Readable` and `Deletable`:

```php
<?php
interface MessagingNode extends Readable, Deletable {
```

```
};

class ForumTopic extends Node implements Readable, Deletable {
  …
};

class BlogEntry extends Node implements MessagingNode {
  …
}
?>
```

In this case both the classes `ForumTopic` and `BlogEntry` must implement every method found in both the interface `Readable` and `Deletable`. In this case the new `MessagingNode` interface is little more than shorthand.

Magic Methods and Constants

Before diving into design patterns it is necessary to review magic methods inside PHP. *Magic methods* are specially named methods that can be defined in any class and are executed via built-in PHP functionality. Magic methods always begin with a double underscore. In fact, the magic methods `__destruct()` and `__construct()` have already been used several times in this chapter. It is not good practice to write user-defined functions and methods that begin with the double underscore in case PHP implements methods with those names in future versions.

Magic constants are used to access certain read-only properties inside PHP. Magic constants both begin and end with a double underscore and are always capitalized. The constant `__CLASS__` has been used several times in this chapter to output the name of the class in which the code is defined.

Practical Use of Magic Constants

It is often useful to determine where in the code output originates. This is the purpose of all of the magic constants and is particularly useful when writing custom logging functions. The seven magic constants are as follows:

➤ `__CLASS__` equates to the class in which the constant is referenced. As noted earlier, this variable is always equal to the class in which it is defined, which is not always the class that was instantiated. In the previous example, `__CLASS__` as defined inside `Node` always returns `Node` even if the method is part of an object that was instantiated as a descendant class. In addition to debugging, the class constant is also useful for static callback functions.

➤ `__FILE__` is always equal to the filename where the constant is referenced.

➤ `__LINE__` is used in conjunction with `__FILE__` in order to output a location in code. For example:

```
error_log('Notice: Placeholder class. Don't forget to change before
    release! In '.__FILE__.' on line '.__LINE__);
```

 Both _FILE_ and _LINE_ are relative to the file currently executing regardless of whether that file was included or required from a different file.

➤ **__DIR__** functions exactly like `dirname(__FILE__)` and returns the absolute directory in which the file is located. It is useful for specifying absolute paths, which are sometimes faster than relative paths; particularly when including scripts.

➤ **__FUNCTION__** and **__METHOD__** make it possible to determine the function or method name, respectively, using magic constants. When possible, these constants should be used in place of hard-coding the function name.

➤ **__NAMESPACE__** is the seventh and final magic constant. As the name suggests, it is equal to the current namespace.

As a debugging mechanism using the magic constants is very basic. More advanced techniques for debugging are discussed in depth in Chapter 16.

Adding Magic Functionality to Classes

Although the magic methods `__construct()` and `__destruct()` are the most commonly used, several more exist. When using design patterns it becomes necessary to expand on certain built-in functionality of PHP. This section first covers the cases where each magic method is useful and then illustrates the use of the method. The first set of methods has to do with data representation.

In many cases it is useful to have a string representation of an object so you can output it to the user or another process. Referencing an object as a string will, by default, evaluate to the object's ID in memory, which in most cases is less than ideal. PHP provides a standard way of overriding this default functionality and returning any desirable string representation. A numeric class might return the number as a string, a user class might return a username, a node class might return a node title, an XML node might return the text content of the node, and so on. The magic method used for this functionality is `__toString()`. The method is triggered in any situation where an object is used as a string, for example: `echo "Hello $obj";`. It can also be called directly like any other normal public method, which is preferable to hacks such as appending an empty string to force coercion.

Serialization is another process integral to PHP applications that store state or cache entire objects. It generates a string representation of an object. Serialization is done manually by calling `serialize()` and is reversed with `unserialize()`. Both methods work on any PHP variable (except a resource such as a MySQL handle) without any modification. However, sometimes it is necessary to clean up a complex object prior to serialization.

Classes can implement the magic method `__sleep()`, which is called immediately before serialization. It is expected to return an array where the values are the member variables that should be saved. Member variables can be `public`, `private`, or `protected`. Likewise, `__wakeup()` is called when you restore the object. One use for these functions is to ignore a resource handle on sleep and to then reopen the handle on restoration as shown in Listing 1-4.

LISTING 1-4: FileLog.class.php

```php
<?php
class FileLog {
  private $fpointer;
```

```php
      private $filename;

      function __construct( $filename ) {
        $this->filename = $filename;
        $this->fpointer = fopen($filename,'a');
      }

      function __destruct() {
        fclose($this->fpointer);
      }

      function __sleep() {
        return array( "filename" );
      }

      function __wakeup() {
        $this->fpointer = fopen($this->filename,'a');
      }

      public function write( $line ) {
        fwrite( "$line\n", $this->fpointer );
      }
  };

  /*
    Example usage:
      $log = new FileLog( "debug.txt" );
      $data = serialize( $log );
      $log = null;
      $log = unserialize($data);
      echo $data;
    Example output:
      O:7:"FileLog":1:{s:17:"FileLogfilename";s:9:"debug.txt"}
  */
  ?>
```

The serialized data, as seen in the comments of the previous example, contains the data type followed by the length of the data and then the data itself. A semicolon separates multiple members and each member has two variables. The first variable is the name and the second is the value.

When serializing, private member variables have the class name prepended to them, whereas protected variables have an asterisk prepended. In both cases the prefix is surrounded by two null bytes. The bytes cannot be seen in print, however. Looking closely at the string `s:17:"FileLogfilename"` it becomes apparent that the string is only 15 printable characters in length. The remaining two characters are the null bytes before and after the word `FileLog`.

The next four magic methods have to do with retrieving, inspecting, and storing inaccessible member variables. They are `__set()`, `__unset()`, `__get()`, and `__isset()`. Each is invoked when trying to access a member variable that is not available to the context that is requesting it. That can mean that a variable marked as private or protected and accessed outside the scope or that a member variable does not exist. Both `__unset()` and `__isset()` are triggered by the functions with the same name (sans the underscores) in PHP. All these methods are used extensively in the section "Design Patterns" so they won't be covered in any more detail in this section.

Similarly, the method __call() is invoked when you try to call a method that is either undefined or inaccessible. A similar method named __callStatic() is called for static methods.

Three magic methods won't be covered in this chapter. __set_state() is used when you import a class via a call to var_export() and is worth looking into if an application does a lot of dynamic code evaluation. __clone() is invoked if you try to make a clone of an object and you can use it for various processes. The third method, __invoke(), is used when an object is being called as if it were a function; it is covered more in Chapter 2.

The next section discusses the eight design patterns that you can use in applications for cleaner and more readable code as well as to solve common problems in software design.

Design Patterns

This section covers design patterns in PHP. The eight patterns that are covered in this section are:

- ➤ Singleton
- ➤ Multiton
- ➤ Proxy
- ➤ Façade
- ➤ Decorator
- ➤ Factory
- ➤ Observer Pattern
- ➤ Publisher/subscriber

Singleton and Multiton Patterns

The singleton and less common multiton patterns control the number of instances of a class in an application. As the names imply, a *singleton* can be instantiated only once and a *multiton* any number of times. In the case of the latter, there can be only one instance for any given key.

Because of the nature of singletons they are often used for configuration and for variables that need to be accessed from anywhere in the application. Using singletons is sometimes considered poor practice because it creates a global state and does not encapsulate all the functionality of the system in a single root object. In many cases this can make unit testing and debugging more difficult. This book leaves the reader to make his or her own decision regarding these patterns. In general, some object orientation is better than none. Listing 1-5 shows an example of a singleton pattern.

LISTING 1-5: SingletonExample.class.php

```php
<?php
class SingletonExample {
  public static function getInstance() {
    static $instance = null;
    if ( $instance == null ) {
```

```
            $instance = new SingletonExample();
        }
        return $instance;
    }
};
?>
```

The singleton class makes use of both functions of the keyword `static`. The first is in the method definition, indicating that the method is not associated with any particular instance of the class. The second is in the method itself. The keyword `static`, when placed in front of a local variable in a function or method indicates that all calls to that method, regardless of what object the call is made to, will share that variable.

In the case of the singleton, the variable `$instance` is initialized to `null` and retains whatever value is set to it across all calls to the method. On first execution it is always `null`. On later executions it is always the same instance of the `SingletonExample` object. Making a single static method call ensures retrieval of the same instance every time:

```
$singleton = SingletonExample::getInsance();
```

A multiton is similar except that it requires a key to be passed to the `getInstance()` function. For a given key there can be only one instance of the object. This pattern is useful when dealing with many nodes that have unique identifiers that can appear multiple times in a single execution (such as a node in a Content Management System). Multitons save memory and ensure that there aren't multiple conflicting instances of the same object. The `SingletonExample` class can be quickly modified to be a multiton instead as shown in Listing 1-6.

LISTING 1-6: MultitonExample.class.php

```
<?php
class MultitonExample {
  public static function getInstance( $key ) {
    static $instances = array();
    if ( !array_key_exists( $key, $instances ) ) {
      $instances[$key] = new MultitonExample();
    }
    return $instance[$key];
  }
};
?>
```

Because PHP objects are always passed by reference it is ensured that each instance returned from a multiton or singleton object is consistent throughout the application. You must be careful when using these patterns with serialization or with the `clone` keyword because either action may result in multiple versions of what should be the same object.

Multitons and singletons are similar in concept to lazy initialization. In *lazy initialization*, object initialization that requires a significant amount of processing or memory is delayed until the object is needed. This usually consists of a conditional to check to see if the object exists, followed by a return of either the existing object or a new one — much like in the two previous patterns. The book sometimes uses lazy initialization for database handles or data sets to avoid spending resources that are not needed by the application.

Proxy and Façade Patterns

Proxy and façade patterns are grouped together because they each provide abstraction for more complex functionality. How abstraction is achieved differs for both patterns.

In the case of a proxy, all methods and member variables are routed to the destination object. The proxy can, if it is desirable, modify or inspect the data as it passes through. The magic methods make implementing this pattern very easy in PHP. One use for this pattern is to log method access. It could also be used to determine code coverage or to just debug an issue (see Listing 1-7):

LISTING 1-7: LoggingProxy.class.php

```php
<?php

class LoggingProxy {
  private $target;

  function __construct( $target ) {
    $this->target = $target;
  }

  protected function log( $line ) {
    error_log($line);
  }

  public function __set( $name, $value ) {
    $this->target->$name = $value;
    $this->log("Setting value for $name: $value");
  }

  public function __get( $name ) {
    $value = $this->target->$name;
    $this->log( "Getting value for $name: $value" );
    return $value;
  }

  public function __isset( $name ) {
    $value = isset($this->target->$name);
    $this->log( "Checking isset for $name: ".($value?"true":"false") );
    return $value;
  }

  public function __call( $name, $arguments ) {
    $this->log( "Calling method $name with: ".implode(",",$arguments) );
    return call_user_func_array( array($this->target,$name), $arguments );
  }

};

?>
```

The `LoggingProxy` example uses callback functions in the `__call()` method. The purpose of the method is to call a defined function within the target class. The class also makes liberal use of variable member names. Variable member names and callbacks are covered in greater detail in Chapter 2.

A proxy can be as simple as the preceding one or as complex as needed. In most cases a proxy should not change the behavior of the class that it is a proxy for; however, it is possible to do that as well. It is also possible for the proxy to be an interface into an entirely different system. For example, it may be useful to have a MySQL database proxy that executes stored procedures or a proxy that is an interface to XML Remote Procedure Calls.

One disadvantage of a proxy is that it is not of the same type as the class it is a proxy for. Therefore it cannot be used in situations where type hinting is necessary or when the code checks to ensure that an object is of a certain type.

The façade pattern serves a different purpose. It is meant to abstract complex functionality so that the application does not need to know the details around which subsystem handles each request. For example, if making a typical API request requires that a user be authenticated via a user subsystem, the request is made to a remote server with an API subsystem, and then the response is decoded via a function from a different API, the resulting façade method looks like this:

```
public function apiRequestJson( $method, $parameters ) {
  $user = User::getAuthenticatedUser();
  if ( $user->hasPermission( $method ) ) {
    $result = $this->api->$method( $parameters );
    return json_decode( $result );
  }
}
```

Façades do not add new functionality but rather delegate the responsibilities to the appropriate subsystem. The subsystems do not need to know of the existence of a façade and the application does not need to know about the existence of the subsystems.

Sometimes it becomes necessary to extend the functionality of a class while maintaining object integrity and allowing for type hinting. The ideal pattern for that is the decorator pattern.

Decorator Pattern

The decorator pattern extends the functionality of a class similar to standard inheritance. Unlike standard inheritance, the decorator pattern can add functionality dynamically at run time if an object has already been instantiated. This action is referred to as *decorating* the object. One benefit of decoration is that it allows any combination of decorators to extend the same object. For example, a car might have an option for an in-car navigation system and an option for leather seats. A customer may want just the seats or may want just the navigation system. Using this pattern the combination can be dynamic.

Taking the car example a step further, you can create a series of classes for decorating the car. To make things easier, all car decorations will extend from a `CarDecorator` class. It is also possible for decorators to extend other decorators. For instance, the user may be able to upgrade from a basic radio to a CD player/radio combination to a multi-disc CD player with radio. A chain of inheritance can be created because a multi-disk CD player with radio shares all the functionality of a basic radio. For simplicity, the following examples assume that the only two methods in the class Car are getPrice() and getManufacturer() as shown in Listing 1-8:

LISTING 1-8: AbstractCar.class.php

```php
<?php

abstract class AbstractCar {
  public abstract function getPrice();
  public abstract function getManufacturer();
};

?>
```

The car class extends the AbstractCar class and must implement all the methods in the abstract class. The result is the car without any decorators added as shown in Listing 1-9.

LISTING 1-9: Car.class.php

```php
<?php

class Car extends AbstractCar {
  private var $price = 16000;
  private var $manufacturer = "Acme Autos";

  public function getPrice() { return $this->price; }
  public function getManufacturer() { return $this->manufacturer; }
};

?>
```

The CarDecorator class also extends AbstractCar. It serves as the base class for all future decorators. The purpose of the class is to act as a proxy into the real implementation, which in this case is called the target. Because the base price for the car exists not in the decorator object but in the target, it is necessary for getPrice() to query the price from the target object as shown in Listing 1-10.

LISTING 1-10: CarDecorator.class.php

```php
<?php

class CarDecorator extends AbstractCar {
  private var $target;

  function __construct( Car $target ) { $this->target = $target; }

  public function getPrice() { return $target->getPrice(); }
  public function getManufacturer() { return $target->getManufacturer(); }
};

?>
```

The first step is complete, creating a `CarDecorator` class that extends from `AbstractCar`. The car decorator could be used directly but it wouldn't serve much purpose. For now all it does is forward all requests to the target `Car` object. Extending both `Car` and its decorator from an abstract class allows the decorators to avoid the overhead of extending a complete `Car` object but still maintain its polymorphic properties.

The next step is to define a *concrete decorator*. Once the base decorator is created it becomes easy to implement new decorators as shown in Listing 1-11:

LISTING 1-11: NavigationSystem.class.php

```php
<?php

class NavigationSystem extends CarDecorator {
  public function getPrice() { return parent::getPrice()+1000; }
};

?>
```

The pattern can be particularly useful in ecommerce applications but it is also commonly used in graphical applications. An icon may decorate a text box; or a scroll bar may decorate a canvas. In the previous example getting the price of a car that has a navigation system and leather seats is just three lines of code:

```php
<?php

$car = new Car();
$car = new NavigationSystem( $car );
$car = new LeatherSeats( $car );
echo $car->getPrice();

?>
```

When using decorators in this manner, it is technically possible for multiple instances of the same decorator to decorate an object. Having two navigation systems in one car doesn't make any sense. A simple function can be added to the `CarDecorator` class to check to see if a decorator is being used:

```php
public function hasDecoratorNamed( $name ) {
  if ( get_class($this) == $name )
    return true;
  else if ( $this->target instanceof CarDecorator )
    return $this->target->hasDecoratorNamed( $name );
  else
    return false;
}
```

The decorator can be combined with a proxy pattern to create additional functionality at run time. For example, if the code were to implement all the functionality of a car, the `NavigationSystem` class may add a `turnOnNavigation()` method. Because the method to turn on navigation would only be available in the navigation decorator it becomes necessary to proxy call to unknown methods through to the target.

Factory Method

The factory method pattern is a creational pattern much like singletons, multitons, and lazy initialization. *Factory methods* are used to return an instance of an object that is a subclass of the object containing the factory method. One simple example is a class called GDImage that will take a valid image filename and return an appropriate image object as shown in Listing 1-12.

Available for
download on
Wrox.com

LISTING 1-12: GDImage.class.php

```php
<?php

abstract class GDImage {
  public static function createImage( $filename ) {
    $info = getimagesize( $filename );
    $type = $info[2];

    switch ( $type ) {
      case IMAGETYPE_JPEG:
        new new JPEGImage( $filename );

      case IMAGETYPE_PNG:
        new new PNGImage( $filename );

      case IMAGETYPE_GIF:
        new new GIFImage( $filename );
    }

    return null;
  }
};

?>
```

In the GD example, the classes PNGImage, GIFImage, and JPEGImage would all descend from the common class GDImage. Pure implementations of the factory design pattern will always define factory methods as static. Additionally, GDImage should be treated as an abstract class and never be directly instantiated.

Another use for factory methods is for unit testing. A factory might return a working valid object under normal conditions but return a dummy object under test conditions. This is useful because using a live object both requires a fully functional data service and can possibly modify real data. For example, a class called User may return an AuthenticatedUser if the system is not in testing mode or a TestUser if the system is in testing mode and AuthenticatedUser is not the direct subject of the test.

The factory method can be implemented in nearly any situation where a different class needs to be instantiated depending on the type of data. There can also be more than one factory method per class. For example, the GDImage class in the previous example may have a second factory method called createFromString() that returns the appropriate object based on a binary input.

Observer and Publisher/Subscriber Patterns

The observer pattern and the publisher/subscriber pattern are more common in event-based architectures than they are in most stateless server-side Internet applications; however they do have uses in PHP. The observer pattern is simpler to implement and is sufficient in most cases so it is covered first.

In the observer pattern the observer must know what objects are broadcasting the events that they want to listen for. It is a sniper rifle approach to event handling. When an event happens on the publisher object, it notifies all observers at once. But if another object fires the same event, it is not broadcasted unless the observer is also watching that object. In Listing 1-13, a simple reusable observer system can be defined with one class and one interface:

LISTING 1-13: Observer.interface.php

```php
<?php
interface Observer {
  public function notify( $event );
};
?>
```

The observable object then contains a method that can be used to register an observer as shown in Listing 1-14.

LISTING 1-14:OBSERVABLEOBJECT.CLASS.PHP

```php
<?php
class ObservableObject {
  private function $observers = array();

  public function observe( Observer $observer ) {
    $this->observers[] = $observer;
  }

  public function dispatch( $event ) {
    foreach ( $this->observers as $observer )
      $observer->notify( $event );
  }
};
?>
```

A class that wants to broadcast events extends `ObservableObject` and any class that wants to listen to events can simply implement the interface `Observer`. In a more complex system the observer can specify the type of event that it wants to listen for.

The publisher/subscriber pattern is similar except that it decouples the subscribers (observers) from the publishers (observable objects). Instead a new class is introduced called an `Event`. The observer subscribes for notification whenever the event is triggered anywhere in the application instead of observing events on just a single class. The observer does not know or care what classes can publish the event.

Some systems implement the publisher/subscriber pattern using a controller as a delegate for all events. That method requires that all events be registered in a central location. For simplicity, the event object itself will act as a delegate (Listing 1-15):

LISTING 1-15: BroadcastingEvent.class.php

```php
<?php
class BroadcastingEvent {
  private static $observers = array();

  public static function subscribe( Observer $observer ) {
    self::$observers[] = $observer;
  }

  public function publish() {
    foreach ( self::$observers as $observer )
      $observer->notify( $this );
  }
};
?>
```

The `BroadcastingEvent` class and the `ObservableObject` class both look very similar. Two changes are that the array of observers is now a static variable in the class instead of an instance variable and the event type no longer needs to be passed to the dispatching function because dispatching is a method of the event itself.

The major paradigm shift is that the observers and the dispatching object no longer need to have any knowledge of each other. This decoupling allows for an observer/subscriber to listen for all events of that type without needing specific application knowledge.

In a PHP application, this pattern is used in systems that can be dynamically extended such as Content Management Systems. For example, an object can listen for a user load event and take specific actions. A CMS should not require implementation-level knowledge of all its modules.

USING MYSQL JOINS

Retrieving data from a normalized relational database that contains many tables generally involves the use of joins in a SELECT statement. A join in MySQL queries enables you to select or manipulate data from multiple tables in a single SQL statement.

The SQL standard provides various different join operations such as INNER JOIN, OUTER JOIN, STRAIGHT_JOIN, and NATURAL JOIN. MySQL implements most common join syntax; however, your expectation may differ between different relational database products.

The following examples use two simple base tables to demonstrate various different joins. The first table contains colors, and second table contains the colors of country flags. The sample data includes the following rows:

For simplicity, this data is de-normalized to demonstrate the various possible MySQL join syntax. These table structures may not necessarily represent optimal database schema design (see Table 1-1). To construct this table and data for all examples in this section, see the code file create-tables.sql

TABLE 1-1: Schema Tables

TABLE	VALUES
Colors	Red, White, Blue, Green, Black
Flags	USA, Australia, Canada, Japan, Sweden

To understand joins with multiple tables, you can use the concept of sets and the mathematical visual approach of Venn diagrams. This shows the interaction between various sets and therefore the types of joins that can be used to retrieve information. See http://en.wikipedia.org/wiki/Venn_diagram for more background information on Venn diagrams.

Figure 1-1 shows the Venn diagram of two individual sets of information.

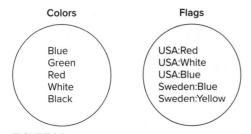

FIGURE 1-1

If you wanted to know the colors that are in the USA flag, you could use the following SELECT statement to retrieve the necessary rows as described in Figure 1-1. This is shown in Listing 1-16.

LISTING 1-16: simple-select.sql

```
SELECT color
FROM flags
WHERE country='USA';

+-------+
| color |
+-------+
| Blue  |
| Red   |
| White |
+-------+
```

Note the following from the previous listing:

➤ In line 1 you specify the column(s) you want to retrieve.

➤ In line 2 you specify which table you want to retrieve these column(s) from.

➤ In line 3 you specify any criteria or condition where you want to restrict the types of rows you want to retrieve.

Figure 1-2 shows the Venn diagram of the intersection of these two sets, and also two exception sets of information.

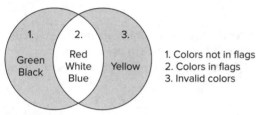

1. Colors not in flags
2. Colors in flags
3. Invalid colors

FIGURE 1-2

INNER JOIN

If you want to know more about the attributes of the colors for the USA flag, you can use an INNER JOIN, as shown in Listing 1-17, with the colors table to retrieve more information.

LISTING 1-17: inner-join.sql

```
SELECT flags.color, colors.is_primary, colors.is_dark, colors.is_rainbow
FROM    flags
INNER JOIN colors ON flags.color = colors.color
WHERE   flags.country='USA';

+-------+------------+---------+------------+
| color | is_primary | is_dark | is_rainbow |
+-------+------------+---------+------------+
| Blue  | yes        | yes     | yes        |
| Red   | yes        | no      | yes        |
| White | yes        | no      | no         |
+-------+------------+---------+------------+
```

Note the following for the previous Listing:

➤ Line 1 selects additional columns from the colors table.

➤ Line 3 specifies an INNER JOIN with the colors table and the flags table, and states that you want to join on the color column in flags with the color column in colors.

The Table Alias

When working with joins in MySQL it is common practice to alias tables used in the SQL query. You can very easily rewrite the previous example as shown in Listing 1-18.

LISTING 1-18: inner-join-alias.sql

```
SELECT f.color, c.is_primary, c.is_dark, c.is_rainbow
FROM    flags f
INNER JOIN colors c ON f.color = c.color
WHERE   f.country='USA';
```

For each table, you can optionally specify an alias after the table in the FROM clause. There are no general restrictions on the length of the alias; however it is best practice to use appropriate naming standards for your application. A table alias in MySQL has a maximum 256 characters in length, whereas a table name has only 64 characters.

ON and USING

For a join command, the ON syntax is of the format `table1.column_name = table2.column_name`.

When your schema design names columns in an identical fashion between join tables, you can shortcut the ON syntax with the USING syntax in the format `USING(column_name)`. For an example see Listing 1-19.

LISTING 1-19: inner-join-using.sql

```
SELECT f.color, c.is_primary, c.is_dark, c.is_rainbow
FROM    flags f
INNER JOIN colors c USING (color)
WHERE   f.country='USA';
```

In line 3 you will see the USING syntax as an alternative to the ON syntax in the previous SQL example.

> *When the column name between two tables is the same, you can simply use the* ON *syntax with the* USING *syntax. It is a good practice to use appropriate database naming standards, and specify columns with the same name when they contain the same data in different tables.*

An Alternative INNER JOIN Syntax

You can also use the comma (,) syntax for specifying an INNER JOIN as shown in Listing 1-20.

LISTING 1-20: inner-join-comma.sql

```sql
SELECT  f.color, c.is_primary, c.is_dark, c.is_rainbow
FROM    flags f, colors c
WHERE   f.country='USA'
AND     f.color = c.color;
```

This comma syntax is a common and well-used approach; however, it does not provide the best readability for a software developer. With this comma syntax the join columns and restriction criteria are all specified in the WHERE clause, unlike with the INNER JOIN syntax where the ON or USING defines the join between each table when the table is specified, and the WHERE restricts the rows of results based on the table join. Overall this improves readability and decreases the possibility of missing a join column in a more complex multitable statement.

Listing 1-21 shows an example where you miss a join between two tables because it is not defined in the WHERE clause:

LISTING 1-21: missing-where-join.sql

```sql
SELECT  f.color, c.is_primary, c.is_dark, c.is_rainbow
FROM    flags f, colors c
WHERE   f.country='USA';
```

```
+-------+------------+---------+------------+
| color | is_primary | is_dark | is_rainbow |
+-------+------------+---------+------------+
| Blue  | no         | yes     | no         |
| Red   | no         | yes     | no         |
| White | no         | yes     | no         |
| Blue  | yes        | yes     | yes        |
| Red   | yes        | yes     | yes        |
| White | yes        | yes     | yes        |
| Blue  | yes        | yes     | yes        |
| Red   | yes        | yes     | yes        |
| White | yes        | yes     | yes        |
| Blue  | yes        | no      | yes        |
| Red   | yes        | no      | yes        |
| White | yes        | no      | yes        |
| Blue  | yes        | no      | no         |
| Red   | yes        | no      | no         |
| White | yes        | no      | no         |
+-------+------------+---------+------------+
```

Without the correct table join you are effectively retrieving a cartesian product of both tables.

OUTER JOIN

As you probably noticed with the Venn diagram in Figure 1-2, when looking at a cartesian product between two intersecting sets, you will see there are indeed three different possible sets of data. The first set is the intersection of both sets and retrieving these rows using the INNER JOIN syntax has been demonstrated with Listing 1-17. The other two sets are the exclusions, that is, the colors that are not in flags, and the countries that have colors that are not defined in the set of recorded colors. You can retrieve these rows using the OUTER JOIN syntax as shown in Listing 1-22.

LISTING 1-22: outer-join.sql

```
SELECT f.country, f.color
FROM   flags f
LEFT OUTER JOIN colors c USING (color)
WHERE  c.color IS NULL;

+---------+--------+
| country | color  |
+---------+--------+
| Sweden  | Yellow |
+---------+--------+

SELECT c.color, c.is_primary
FROM   colors c
LEFT OUTER JOIN  flags f USING (color)
WHERE f.country IS NULL;

+-------+------------+
| color | is_primary |
+-------+------------+
| Black | no         |
| Green | yes        |
+-------+------------+
```

As you have noticed in these queries, the syntax is not just OUTER JOIN, but it also includes the keyword LEFT. You should also note that OUTER is an optional keyword and it is generally a best practice to reduce the SQL syntax to just use LEFT JOIN.

> *An OUTER JOIN is used for two primary reasons. The first is when a set of data values may be unknown yet you want to retrieve a full set of rows that match part of your criteria. The second reason is when a normalized database does not enforce referential integrity. In the preceding example, it's* logical *that colors may exist and are not a flag color. It is not logical that flag colors do not exist in the colors table. In this situation the use of an OUTER JOIN is identifying data that constitutes a lack of data integrity.*

RIGHT JOIN

If you were wondering if there was a companion RIGHT OUTER JOIN syntax, there is. It is possible to return the same results as shown in the preceding example using a RIGHT JOIN as shown in Listing 1-23.

LISTING 1-23: right-join.sql

```sql
SELECT c.color, c.is_primary
FROM    colors c
LEFT JOIN  flags f USING (color)
WHERE f.country IS NULL;
```

...can be written as

```sql
SELECT c.color, c.is_primary
FROM    flags f
RIGHT JOIN colors c USING (color)
WHERE f.country IS NULL;
```

```
+-------+------------+
| color | is_primary |
+-------+------------+
| Black | no         |
| Green | yes        |
+-------+------------+
```

LEFT JOIN

It is generally considered a good practice to write queries as LEFT JOIN, and to be consistent throughout all your SQL statements for your application.

In review of these two join examples you can conclude the following conditions:

➤ A join using INNER JOIN can be considered a mandatory condition, where a row in the left-side table must match a corresponding row in the right-side table.

➤ A join using OUTER JOIN can be considered an optional condition, where a row in the LEFT or RIGHT table as specified may or may not correspond to a row in the associated table.

Other JOIN Syntax

MySQL provides a number of other varieties of joins. For the CROSS JOIN in MySQL this is considered identical in operation to an INNER JOIN.

MySQL provides a STRAIGHT_JOIN, which is considered equivalent to the JOIN command. However, this acts more as a hint to the MySQL optimizer to determine processing tables in a given order. The NATURAL [LEFT|RIGHT] JOIN is similar to the corresponding [INNER|LEFT|RIGHT] JOIN; however, all matching column names between both tables are implied. In the previous INNER JOIN example with both the ON and USING syntax, you could have simply written:

LISTING 1-24: natural-join.sql

```sql
SELECT f.color, c.is_primary, c.is_dark, c.is_rainbow
FROM    flags f
NATURAL JOIN colors c
WHERE  f.country='USA';
```

The NATURAL JOIN can be dangerous because the columns are not specified, additional join columns may actually exist in your database design intentionally or unintentionally, and your table structures may change over time; the results of the query may in fact result in different rows returned. For more information on joins you can review the MySQL Reference Manual, which includes several different sections:

➤ Join Syntax http://dev.mysql.com/doc/refman/5.1/en/join.html

➤ Left Join and Right Join Optimization http://dev.mysql.com/doc/refman/5.1/en/left-join-optimization.html

➤ Outer Join Simplification http://dev.mysql.com/doc/refman/5.1/en/outer-join-simplification.html

➤ Join Types Index http://dev.mysql.com/doc/refman/5.1/en/dynindex-jointype.html

UPDATE and DELETE JOIN Syntax

Joins are not limited to SELECT statements in MySQL. You can use a join in MySQL UPDATE and DELETE statements as well. Listing 1-25 shows an example.

LISTING 1-25: update.sql

```
UPDATE flags INNER JOIN colors USING (color)
SET    flags.color = UPPER(color)
WHERE  colors.is_dark = 'yes';

SELECT color
FROM   flags
WHERE  country = 'USA';

+-------+
| color |
+-------+
| BLUE  |
| Red   |
| White |
+-------+
```

Case Sensitivity

MySQL by default performs case-insensitive comparison for string columns in a table join ON, USING, or WHERE comparison. This differs from other popular relational databases. In this case 'USA' is equal to 'usa', for example. It is possible via either defining your table column with a case-sensitive collation or using a specific prequalifier to implement case-sensitive comparison. Listing 1-26 shows an example.

LISTING 1-26: case-sensitivity.sql

```
SELECT 'USA' = 'USA', 'USA' = 'Usa', 'USA' = 'usa',
       'USA' = 'usa' COLLATE latin1_general_cs AS different;
```

```
+---------------+---------------+---------------+-----------+
| 'USA' = 'USA' | 'USA' = 'Usa' | 'USA' = 'usa' | different |
+---------------+---------------+---------------+-----------+
|             1 |             1 |             1 |         0 |
+---------------+---------------+---------------+-----------+
```

Complex Joins

Although the basics of joins in MySQL have been described, to become a real expert is to understand the possibilities of joins. It is possible to write rather obfuscated SQL statements including subqueries and derived tables. However, the disadvantage is the lack of readability and maintainability of your SQL. Listing 1-27 is a simple multi-table join that combines joining to the same table multiple times, and combines INNER JOIN and LEFT JOIN syntax to return the population, state, and capital of all countries that have at least Red, White, and Blue in the flag:

LISTING 1-27: complex-join.sql

Available for download on Wrox.com

```sql
SELECT f1.country, c.population,
       IFNULL(ci.city,'Not Recorded') AS city, s.abbr, s.state
FROM   flags f1
INNER JOIN flags f2 ON f1.country = f2.country
INNER JOIN flags f3 ON f1.country = f3.country
INNER JOIN countries c ON f1.country = c.country
LEFT JOIN cities ci ON f1.country = ci.country AND ci.is_country_capital = 'yes'
LEFT JOIN states s  ON f1.country = s.country AND ci.state = s.state
WHERE f1.color = 'Red'
AND    f2.color = 'White'
AND    f3.color = 'Blue';
```

```
+-----------+------------+---------------+------+-------+
| country   | population | city          | abbr | state |
+-----------+------------+---------------+------+-------+
| Australia |   21888000 | Not Recorded  | NULL | NULL  |
| USA       |  307222000 | Washington DC | NULL | NULL  |
+-----------+------------+---------------+------+-------+
```

In this example, if you were to replace the LEFT JOIN with an INNER JOIN, the results of the data would change accordingly based on the recorded data.

> When it is possible to write complex joins, in MySQL the combination of joins, subqueries, and derived tables can result in SQL statements that do not perform optimally. There must always be a balance between returning a result set in a single query and performance of the statement. Although writing multiple statements in MySQL, combined with the use of temporary tables, may introduce more SQL code, this may be more optimal for the speed of your web site.

MYSQL UNIONS

A UNION statement is used to combine the results of more than one SELECT statement into the results for one SQL query. For a valid UNION statement, all SELECT statements must have the same number of columns, and these columns must be of the same data type for each column in the SELECT statement. MySQL supports the UNION and UNION ALL constructs for joining SELECT results.

When learning to use UNION, you can first consider writing individual SELECT statements. All individual SELECT statements within a UNION statement are valid SELECT statements, except for the ORDER BY clause, which can be defined only once in a UNION statement and is used to order the results of all combined queries. Listing 1-28 shows an example.

LISTING 1-28: union.sql

```
SELECT f.country
FROM    flags f
INNER JOIN colors c USING (color)
WHERE c.is_dark = 'yes'
UNION
SELECT f.country
FROM    flags f
INNER JOIN colors c USING (color)
WHERE c.is_primary = 'yes';


+-----------+
| country   |
+-----------+
| Australia |
| Sweden    |
| USA       |
| Canada    |
| Japan     |
+-----------+
```

The UNION also supports the additional keywords ALL or DISTINCT. By default, the UNION syntax returns a unique set of rows for all SELECT sets, removing any duplicates. The ALL syntax, however, returns all rows from each SELECT statement combined, and the DISTINCT syntax returns all DISTINCT rows for each SELECT. Listing 1-29 shows an example of this.

LISTING 1-29: union-all.sql

```
SELECT f.country, 'Dark'
FROM    flags f
INNER JOIN colors c USING (color)
WHERE c.is_dark = 'yes'
UNION ALL
SELECT f.country, 'Primary'
FROM    flags f
INNER JOIN colors c USING (color)
```

```
WHERE c.is_primary = 'yes';
```

```
+-----------+---------+
| country   | Dark    |
+-----------+---------+
| Australia | Dark    |
| Sweden    | Dark    |
| USA       | Dark    |
| Australia | Primary |
| Sweden    | Primary |
| USA       | Primary |
| Australia | Primary |
| Canada    | Primary |
| Japan     | Primary |
| USA       | Primary |
| Australia | Primary |
| Canada    | Primary |
| Japan     | Primary |
| USA       | Primary |
+-----------+---------+
```

In Listing 1-30 you will see a different set of results using the DISTINCT keyword.

LISTING 1-30: union-distinct.sql

```
SELECT f.country, 'Dark'
FROM    flags f
INNER JOIN colors c USING (color)
WHERE c.is_dark = 'yes'
UNION DISTINCT
SELECT f.country, 'Primary'
FROM    flags f
INNER JOIN colors c USING (color)
WHERE c.is_primary = 'yes';
```

```
+-----------+---------+
| country   | Dark    |
+-----------+---------+
| Australia | Dark    |
| Sweden    | Dark    |
| USA       | Dark    |
| Australia | Primary |
| Sweden    | Primary |
| USA       | Primary |
| Canada    | Primary |
| Japan     | Primary |
+-----------+---------+
```

MySQL does not support the INTERSECT or MINUS syntax that are additional UNION related constructs that can be found in other relational database products. Refer to http://dev.mysql.com/doc/refman/5.1/en/union.html *for more information.*

GROUP BY IN MYSQL QUERIES

The GROUP BY syntax allows for the aggregation of rows selected and the use of scalar functions. In MySQL, it is possible to use scalar functions without a GROUP BY and produce what can be considered inconsistent results. Listing 1-31 shows an example.

LISTING 1-31: count-no-group.sql

```
SELECT country, COUNT(*)
FROM    flags;
+-----------+----------+
| country   | COUNT(*) |
+-----------+----------+
| Australia |       12 |
+-----------+----------+
```

MySQL provides the expected ANSI SQL syntax requiring a GROUP BY statement to contain all non-scalar function columns with the use of sql_mode. Listing 1-32 shows an example of this.

LISTING 1-32: count-group.sql

```
SET SESSION sql_mode=ONLY_FULL_GROUP_BY;

SELECT country, COUNT(*)
FROM    flags;
ERROR 1140 (42000): Mixing of GROUP columns (MIN(),MAX(),COUNT(),...)
    with no GROUP columns is illegal if there is no GROUP BY clause

SELECT country, COUNT(*) AS color_count
FROM    flags
GROUP  BY country;
+-----------+-------------+
| country   | color_count |
+-----------+-------------+
| Australia |           3 |
| Canada    |           2 |
| Japan     |           2 |
| Sweden    |           2 |
| USA       |           3 |
+-----------+-------------+
```

One scalar function exists that does not return a numeric value; this is the GROUP_CONCAT() function shown in Listing 1-33.

LISTING 1-33: count-group-concat.sql

```
SELECT country, GROUP_CONCAT(color) AS colors
FROM    flags
GROUP BY country;
```

```
+-----------+---------------+
| country   | colors        |
+-----------+---------------+
| Australia | Blue,Red,White |
| Canada    | Red,White     |
| Japan     | Red,White     |
| Sweden    | Blue,Yellow   |
| USA       | Blue,Red,White |
+-----------+---------------+

SELECT country, GROUP_CONCAT(color) AS colors, COUNT(*) AS color_count
FROM    flags
GROUP BY country;
+-----------+---------------+-------------+
| country   | colors        | color_count |
+-----------+---------------+-------------+
| Australia | Blue,Red,White |           3 |
| Canada    | Red,White     |           2 |
| Japan     | Red,White     |           2 |
| Sweden    | Blue,Yellow   |           2 |
| USA       | Blue,Red,White |           3 |
+-----------+---------------+-------------+
5 rows in set (0.00 sec)
```

WITH ROLLUP

A feature of the GROUP BY syntax is the additional keywords WITH ROLLUP. With this syntax, the
rows returned include aggregated rows for each GROUP BY column. This is represented by NULL. The
output in Listing 1-34 shows a single-column and two-column example:

**Available for
download on
Wrox.com**

LISTING 1-34: count-with-rollup.sql

```
SELECT country, COUNT(*) AS color_count
FROM    flags
GROUP  BY country WITH ROLLUP;
+-----------+-------------+
| country   | color_count |
+-----------+-------------+
| Australia |           3 |
| Canada    |           2 |
| Japan     |           2 |
| Sweden    |           2 |
| USA       |           3 |
| NULL      |          12 |
+-----------+-------------+

SELECT c.color, c.is_dark, COUNT(*)
FROM    colors c, flags f
WHERE c.color = f.color
GROUP BY c.color, c.is_dark WITH ROLLUP;
+-------+---------+----------+
| color | is_dark | COUNT(*) |
```

```
+-------+---------+----------+
| Blue  | yes     |        3 |
| Blue  | NULL    |        3 |
| Red   | no      |        4 |
| Red   | NULL    |        4 |
| White | no      |        4 |
| White | NULL    |        4 |
| NULL  | NULL    |       11 |
+-------+---------+----------+
```

HAVING

To restrict the list of aggregated rows returned when using GROUP BY for any scalar functions, you use the HAVING clause to define the condition and not the WHERE clause. Listing 1-35 shows an example.

LISTING 1-35: having.sql

```sql
SELECT country, GROUP_CONCAT(color) AS colors
FROM    flags
GROUP BY country
HAVING COUNT(*) = 2;
```

```
+---------+-------------+
| country | colors      |
+---------+-------------+
| Canada  | Red,White   |
| Japan   | Red,White   |
| Sweden  | Blue,Yellow |
+---------+-------------+
```

You can use scalar functions that are not defined in the SELECT clause as shown in the preceding example. Unlike ORDER BY you must specify the name of the column; the numeric column order is not a permitted syntax.

LOGICAL OPERATIONS AND FLOW CONTROL IN MYSQL

MySQL has three states for any logic, TRUE, FALSE, or NULL:

```
mysql> SELECT TRUE,FALSE,NULL;
+------+-------+------+
| TRUE | FALSE | NULL |
+------+-------+------+
|    1 |     0 | NULL |
+------+-------+------+
```

Comparison operations such as =, <>, IS, IS NOT, IN, ISNULL, and so on will result in one of these three states:

```
mysql> SELECT 'A' IS NOT NULL, 'A' IS NULL, NULL = NULL, NULL IS NULL;
+----------------+-------------+-------------+--------------+
| 'A' IS NOT NULL | 'A' IS NULL | NULL = NULL | NULL IS NULL |
```

```
+-----------------+-------------+-------------+-------------+
|               1 |           0 |        NULL |           1 |
+-----------------+-------------+-------------+-------------+
```

MySQL always returns 1 for a TRUE state, and any non-zero value evaluates to TRUE.

```
mysql> SELECT 5 IS TRUE, 0 IS FALSE, 10 IS NOT NULL;
+-----------+------------+-----------------+
| 5 IS TRUE | 0 IS FALSE | 10 IS NOT NULL  |
+-----------+------------+-----------------+
|         1 |          1 |               1 |
+-----------+------------+-----------------+
```

Logic Operators

MySQL has four logic control operators: AND, OR, NOT, and XOR. Three of these operators also have shorthand notations: && (AND), || (OR), ! (NOT). These shorthand notations should not be confused with the Bit operators, which are single characters of & and |.

```
mysql> SELECT TRUE AND TRUE, TRUE AND FALSE, TRUE AND NULL, NULL AND NULL;
+---------------+----------------+---------------+---------------+
| TRUE AND TRUE | TRUE AND FALSE | TRUE AND NULL | NULL AND NULL |
+---------------+----------------+---------------+---------------+
|             1 |              0 |          NULL |          NULL |
+---------------+----------------+---------------+---------------+

mysql> SELECT TRUE OR TRUE, TRUE OR FALSE, TRUE OR NULL, NULL OR NULL;
+--------------+---------------+--------------+--------------+
| TRUE OR TRUE | TRUE OR FALSE | TRUE OR NULL | NULL OR NULL |
+--------------+---------------+--------------+--------------+
|            1 |             1 |            1 |         NULL |
+--------------+---------------+--------------+--------------+

mysql> SELECT TRUE XOR TRUE, TRUE XOR FALSE, TRUE XOR NULL, NULL XOR NULL;
+---------------+----------------+---------------+---------------+
| TRUE XOR TRUE | TRUE XOR FALSE | TRUE XOR NULL | NULL XOR NULL |
+---------------+----------------+---------------+---------------+
|             0 |              1 |          NULL |          NULL |
+---------------+----------------+---------------+---------------+
```

Unlike AND, OR, and XOR, the NOT operator does not evaluate two values; it simply returns the inverse of the provided value:

```
mysql> SELECT NOT TRUE, NOT FALSE, NOT NULL;
+----------+-----------+----------+
| NOT TRUE | NOT FALSE | NOT NULL |
+----------+-----------+----------+
|        0 |         1 |     NULL |
+----------+-----------+----------+
```

You can change the || shorthand operator of MySQL using sql_mode=PIPES_AS_CONCAT, which will give unexpected results as shown in Listing 1-36.

LISTING 1-36: logic-operators.sql

```
mysql> SELECT TRUE OR FALSE, TRUE || FALSE;
+---------------+---------------+
| TRUE OR FALSE | TRUE || FALSE |
+---------------+---------------+
|             1 |             1 |
+---------------+---------------+

mysql> SET SESSION sql_mode=PIPES_AS_CONCAT;
mysql> SELECT TRUE OR FALSE, TRUE || FALSE;
+---------------+---------------+
| TRUE OR FALSE | TRUE || FALSE |
+---------------+---------------+
|             1 | 10            |
+---------------+---------------+
```

Flow Control

MySQL provides four functions for control flow: `IF()`, `CASE`, `IFNULL()`, and `NULLIF()`. The `IF()` function provides the syntax of a ternary operator with two possible outcomes for a given condition:

```
mysql> SELECT IF (2 > 1,'2 is greater than 1','2 is not greater than 1') AS answer;
+--------------------+
| answer             |
+--------------------+
| 2 is greater than 1 |
+--------------------+
```

The MySQL `CASE` statement operates in similar fashion to the PHP switch syntax where a single given condition of multiple options results in a true assignment. The `CASE` statement also includes a special default case when no conditions equate to a `TRUE` value.

```
mysql> SET @value=CONVERT(RAND()* 10, UNSIGNED INTEGER);

mysql> SELECT @value,
    -> CASE
    ->   WHEN @value < 3 THEN 'Value is < 3'
    ->   WHEN @value > 6 THEN 'Value is > 6'
    ->   WHEN @value = 3 OR @value = 6 THEN 'Value is 3 or 6'
    ->   ELSE 'Value is 4 or 5'
    ->   END;

+--------+------------------+
|      3 | Value is 3 or 6  |
+--------+------------------+
```

Though it is possible to perform complex flow control functions via SQL, the MySQL database is designed for storing and retrieving data. Where possible, complex rules should be written in the application layer to enable greater performance.

The remaining two functions `IFNULL()` and `NULLIF()` support conditional expressions for handling `NULL`. `IFNULL()` returns `NULL` if the provided expression equates to `NULL`, or the value of the expression. `NULLIF()` returns a `NULL` result if the two expressions result in a `TRUE` condition. Listing 1-37 shows an example of this.

LISTING 1-37: flow-control.sql

```
mysql> SELECT IFNULL(NULL,'Value is NULL') AS result1,
              IFNULL(1 > 2, 'NULL result') AS result2;
+---------------+---------+
| result1       | result2 |
+---------------+---------+
| Value is NULL | 0       |
+---------------+---------+

mysql> SELECT NULLIF(TRUE,TRUE) AS istrue,
              NULLIF(TRUE,FALSE) AS isfalse,
              NULLIF(TRUE,NULL) AS isnull;
+--------+---------+--------+
| istrue | isfalse | isnull |
+--------+---------+--------+
|   NULL |       1 |      1 |
+--------+---------+--------+
```

MAINTAINING RELATIONAL INTEGRITY

Although many developers consider relational integrity as using foreign keys to maintain referential integrity of your data, i.e. the Consistency part of the ACID properties, relational integrity in MySQL is available via a variety of means and at various different levels. These can be specified at the table structure level syntax of `CREATE TABLE`, `ALTER TABLE` or at the MySQL `SESSION` or `GLOBAL VARIABLES` level. MySQL can also provide a level of integrity that is storage engine specific.

Constraints

A constraint restricts the type of value that is stored in a given table column. There are various options for single column values including `NOT NULL`, `UNSIGNED`, `ENUM`, and `SET`. A `UNIQUE KEY` constraint applies to one or more columns of a single table. A `FOREIGN KEY` constraint involves a mandatory relationship between two tables.

NOT NULL

To ensure a column must contain a value, you can specify the `NOT NULL` constraint. It is important that the use of `DEFAULT` is not specified to enforce `NOT NULL` constraints. The `DEFAULT` attribute, as the name suggests, provides a default value when one is not specified. With a column definition of `col1 CHAR(5) NOT NULL DEFAULT ''`, when `col1` is not specified in an `INSERT` statement, an error is not returned for not specifying a mandatory column. Instead a blank value `''` — not to be confused with a `NULL` value — is inserted into the column. This is even more confusing when the column is defined as nullable. In this instance, you have `NULL` and `''` as possible values. These are not equal and this leads to confusion in your application. Should they be equal? When searching `col1` `LIKE NULL` you would also need to include `OR col1 = ''`.

UNSIGNED

When an integer column only requires a non-negative number, the specification of the `UNSIGNED` constraint will ensure the column can only contain 0 or a positive value. For example:

LISTING 1-38: unsigned.sql

```
mysql> DROP TABLE IF EXISTS example;
mysql> CREATE TABLE example (
    ->    int_signed        INT NOT NULL,
    ->    int_unsigned      INT UNSIGNED NOT NULL
    -> ) ENGINE=InnoDB DEFAULT CHARSET latin1;

mysql> INSERT INTO example (int_signed, int_unsigned) VALUES ( 1, 1);
mysql> INSERT INTO example (int_signed, int_unsigned) VALUES ( 0, 0);
mysql> INSERT INTO example (int_signed, int_unsigned) VALUES ( -1, 1);
mysql> INSERT INTO example (int_signed, int_unsigned) VALUES ( 1, -1);

ERROR 1264 (22003): Out of range value for column 'int_unsigned' at row 1

mysql> SELECT * FROM example;

+------------+--------------+
| int_signed | int_unsigned |
+------------+--------------+
|          1 |            1 |
|          0 |            0 |
|         -1 |            1 |
+------------+--------------+
```

ENUM and SET

The `ENUM` data column and supporting `SET` column data types enable you to enforce integrity by enabling only a specific set of possible values. This can be of benefit when only a set range of values are possible for a column. Listing 1-39 shows an example.

LISTING 1-39: enum.sql

```
mysql> CREATE TABLE example (
    ->    currency   ENUM('USD','CAD','AUD') NOT NULL
    -> ) ENGINE=InnoDB DEFAULT CHARSET latin1;

mysql> INSERT INTO example (currency) VALUES ('AUD');
mysql> INSERT INTO example (currency) VALUES ('EUR');
```

```
ERROR 1265 (01000): Data truncated for column 'currency' at row 1

mysql> SELECT * FROM example;
+----------+
| currency |
+----------+
| AUD      |
+----------+
```

The SET data type operates similarly to ENUM except that one or more of the defined values are permitted as a valid value. The disadvantage of using ENUM or SET is that a DDL statement is required to change the range of possible values.

UNIQUE KEY

The UNIQUE KEY constraint ensures that all values in a given column are actually unique. A UNIQUE KEY constraint may also involve more than one column. It is possible for a UNIQUE KEY constraint to contain a nullable column, because NULL is considered a unique value. Listing 1-40 shows an example.

LISTING 1-40: unique-key.sql

```
mysql> CREATE TABLE example (
    ->   int_unique           INT UNSIGNED NOT NULL,
    ->   int_nullable_unique  INT UNSIGNED NULL,
    ->   UNIQUE KEY (int_unique),
    ->   UNIQUE KEY(int_nullable_unique)
    -> ) ENGINE=InnoDB DEFAULT CHARSET latin1;

mysql> INSERT INTO example (int_unique, int_nullable_unique) VALUES (1, 1);
mysql> INSERT INTO example (int_unique, int_nullable_unique) VALUES (2, NULL);
mysql> INSERT INTO example (int_unique, int_nullable_unique) VALUES (3, NULL);
mysql> INSERT INTO example (int_unique, int_nullable_unique) VALUES (1, NULL);
ERROR 1062 (23000): Duplicate entry '1' for key 'int_unique'

mysql> INSERT INTO example (int_unique, int_nullable_unique) VALUES (4, 1);
ERROR 1062 (23000): Duplicate entry '1' for key 'int_nullable_unique'

mysql> SELECT * FROM example;
+------------+---------------------+
| int_unique | int_nullable_unique |
+------------+---------------------+
|          2 |                NULL |
|          3 |                NULL |
|          1 |                   1 |
+------------+---------------------+
```

FOREIGN KEY

Developers will generally consider foreign keys as the basis of relational integrity; however, as shown in this chapter, other important factors exist for maintaining integrity. Foreign keys can ensure the Consistency portion of ACID compliance. Though it is possible to use manual procedures to maintain data integrity, this is a less than an ideal approach.

In the current production MySQL 5.1, foreign keys are supported only with the InnoDB storage engine. Some additional third-party storage engines do support foreign keys. Refer to Chapter 3 for additional information.

The MySQL Reference Manual defines the syntax for a FOREIGN KEY that can be used in CREATE TABLE or ALTER TABLE as:

```
[CONSTRAINT [symbol]] FOREIGN KEY
    [index_name] (index_col_name, ...)
    REFERENCES tbl_name (index_col_name,...)
    [ON DELETE reference_option]
    [ON UPDATE reference_option]

reference_option:
    RESTRICT | CASCADE | SET NULL | NO ACTION
```

As you've seen from earlier join examples, the countries table contains an invalid color. If you had defined the tables using foreign keys, you would not have experienced this data integrity problem. This provides a code example of what is necessary to correct bad data. First, you should attempt to create the missing foreign key integrity constraint as shown in Listing 1-41.

LISTING 1-41: foreign-key-alter.sql

```
mysql> ALTER TABLE flags
    -> ADD FOREIGN KEY (color)
    -> REFERENCES colors (color)
    -> ON DELETE CASCADE;
ERROR 1452 (23000): Cannot add or update a child row:a foreign key constraint fails
('chapter1'.'#sql-86f_1928bd', CONSTRAINT '#sql-86f_1928bd_ibfk_1' FOREIGN KEY
('color') REFERENCES 'colors' ('color') ON DELETE CASCADE)
```

Due to the error, you now need to identify the problem data in either the parent or child table. You could identify with a subquery or, as shown previously, an outer join to retrieve the invalid data. We know because of the small sample data that the color Yellow is the cause of the failure. Do you:

➤ Delete the offending row that contains the invalid data? This would then in turn produce invalid consistent data for the Swedish flag.

➤ Delete all flag data for Sweden? This would delete potentially valid data that you may use or that may be valuable elsewhere.

➤ Add the missing data to the colors base table?

These are important design decisions that affect how your application will run. In Listing 1-42, we make the decision to use the last option and add the missing color Yellow to the colors table to successfully add the foreign key.

LISTING 1-42: foreign-key-yellow.sql

```
mysql> INSERT INTO colors (color,is_primary,is_dark,is_rainbow)
                    VALUES ('Yellow','no','no','yes');

mysql> ALTER TABLE flags
        ADD FOREIGN KEY (color)
        REFERENCES colors (color)
        ON DELETE CASCADE;

mysql> SELECT *
        FROM colors
        WHERE color='Yellow';
+--------+------------+---------+------------+
| color  | is_primary | is_dark | is_rainbow |
+--------+------------+---------+------------+
| Yellow | no         | no      | yes        |
+--------+------------+---------+------------+

mysql> SELECT *
        FROM flags
        WHERE country IN (SELECT country
                          FROM flags
                          WHERE color='Yellow');
+---------+--------+
| country | color  |
+---------+--------+
| Sweden  | Blue   |
| Sweden  | Yellow |
+---------+--------+
```

You have now defined a FOREIGN KEY between the colors table and the flags table where the color for the flag must exist in the colors tables. You have also defined this rule to have a cascade DELETE rule, which states that if you delete a color, you will also delete all rows that use this color. Listing 1-43 shows an example:

LISTING 1-43: foreign-key-delete.sql

```
mysql> DELETE FROM colors WHERE color='Yellow';
mysql> SELECT * FROM flags WHERE color='Yellow';
Empty set (0.00 sec)

mysql> SELECT *
        FROM flags
        WHERE country IN (SELECT country
                          FROM flags
                          WHERE color='Yellow');

mysql> SELECT *
```

```
        FROM flags
        WHERE country = 'Sweden';
+---------+-------+
| country | color |
+---------+-------+
| Sweden  | Blue  |
+---------+-------+
```

Although the FOREIGN KEY constraint has ensured data integrity at the row level, it has not performed the type of integrity you would expect. The use of the FOREIGN KEY constraint will not ensure the level of application integrity you ideally wish to have.

> *Defining your foreign key definitions is a very important architectural design decision that should be performed before you add any data. It is far easier to remove a constraint later than to add it later.*

A further benefit of InnoDB foreign key constraints is the requirement that both columns in the from table and the to table must use an identical data type. This improves the data integrity of the database.

You can find additional information on foreign keys in InnoDB at http://dev.mysql.com/doc/refman/5.0/en/innodb-foreign-key-constraints.html.

It is possible for foreign key constraints to be disabled within MySQL with the SET foreign_key_checks = 0|1 option. This can further confuse the integrity of your database because permission to manipulate data via a DML statement can be overridden via the SET command at both the SESSION or GLOBAL level.

> *When using cascading foreign key constraints and the REPLACE command, your database may exhibit unexpected behavior or performance. The REPLACE command is generally understood and described as an UPDATE for the matching row. If no row is found then the INSERT command inserts the row. In implementation, however, REPLACE is actually a DELETE of the existing row, and then an INSERT of the new row. Be aware of this execution path of REPLACE when adding constraints that use cascading syntax.*

Using Server SQL Modes

Introduced first in 4.1 and enhanced in 5.0, the Server SQL mode provides various features including different types of relational integrity. MySQL, by default, is very lax with data integrity and this can have unexpected results. For example, look at Listing 1-44.

LISTING 1-44: no-sql-mode.sql

```
mysql> CREATE TABLE example (
    ->  i TINYINT UNSIGNED NOT NULL,
    ->  c CHAR(2) NULL
    -> ) ENGINE=InnoDB DEFAULT CHARSET latin1;

mysql> INSERT INTO example (i) VALUES (0), (-1),(255), (9000);
Query OK, 4 rows affected, 2 warnings (0.00 sec)

mysql> SHOW WARNINGS;
+---------+------+------------------------------------------+
| Level   | Code | Message                                  |
+---------+------+------------------------------------------+
| Warning | 1264 | Out of range value for column 'i' at row 2 |
| Warning | 1264 | Out of range value for column 'i' at row 4 |
+---------+------+------------------------------------------+
2 rows in set (0.00 sec)

mysql> INSERT INTO example (c) VALUES ('A'),('BB'),('CCC');
Query OK, 3 rows affected, 2 warnings (0.00 sec)

mysql> SHOW WARNINGS;
+---------+------+-----------------------------------+
| Level   | Code | Message                           |
+---------+------+-----------------------------------+
| Warning | 1364 | Field 'i' doesn't have a default value |
| Warning | 1265 | Data truncated for column 'c' at row 3 |
+---------+------+-----------------------------------+
2 rows in set (0.00 sec)

mysql> SELECT * FROM example;
+-----+------+
| i   | c    |
+-----+------+
|   0 | NULL |
|   0 | NULL |
| 255 | NULL |
| 255 | NULL |
|   0 | A    |
|   0 | BB   |
|   0 | CC   |
+-----+------+
7 rows in set (0.00 sec)
```

In these preceding SQL statements you find numerous actual errors in the data, yet no errors actually occurred.

MySQL issues only warnings, and most application developers actually ignore these warnings, never executing a SHOW WARNINGS to identify these silent data truncations. You expected to insert a value of 9,000; however, only 255 was stored. You expected to insert a string of three characters, yet only two characters were recorded. You didn't specify a value for a NOT NULL column, yet a default value was recorded.

The solution is to use a strict SQL mode available since MySQL 5.0. MySQL provides two strict types: STRICT_ALL_TABLES and STRICT_TRANS_TABLES. For the purposes of ensuring data integrity for all tables, this section only discusses STRICT_ALL_TABLES. When you re-run the previous SQL statements, you see the code in Listing 1-45:

LISTING 1-45: sql-mode-traditional.sql

```
mysql> TRUNCATE TABLE example;
Query OK, 0 rows affected (0.00 sec)

mysql> SET SESSION sql_mode='TRADITIONAL';
Query OK, 0 rows affected (0.00 sec)

mysql> INSERT INTO example (i) VALUES (0), (-1),(255), (9000);
ERROR 1264 (22003): Out of range value for column 'i' at row 2
mysql> INSERT INTO example (c) VALUES ('A'),('BB'),('CCC');
ERROR 1364 (HY000): Field 'i' doesn't have a default value
mysql> SELECT * FROM example;
Empty set (0.00 sec)

mysql> INSERT INTO example (i) VALUES (0);
mysql> INSERT INTO example (i) VALUES (-1);
ERROR 1264 (22003): Out of range value for column 'i' at row 1
mysql> INSERT INTO example (i) VALUES (255);
mysql> INSERT INTO example (i) VALUES (9000);
ERROR 1264 (22003): Out of range value for column 'i' at row 1
mysql> INSERT INTO example (c) VALUES ('A');
ERROR 1364 (HY000): Field 'i' doesn't have a default value
mysql> INSERT INTO example (i,c) VALUES (1,'A');
mysql> INSERT INTO example (i,c) VALUES (1,'BB');
mysql> INSERT INTO example (i,c) VALUES (1,'CCC');
ERROR 1406 (22001): Data too long for column 'c' at row 1
mysql> SELECT * FROM example;
+-----+------+
| i   | c    |
+-----+------+
|   0 | NULL |
| 255 | NULL |
|   1 | A    |
|   1 | BB   |
+-----+------+
4 rows in set (0.00 sec)
```

You will notice now the expected errors of a more traditional relational database system. You will also notice that the multiple INSERT VALUES statements fail unconditionally. It is possible to alter this behavior by using a nontransactional storage engine such as MyISAM and further confuse the possible lack of data integrity. Listing 1-46 shows an example.

LISTING 1-46: sql-mode-traditional-myisam.sql

```
mysql> ALTER TABLE example ENGINE=MyISAM;
mysql> TRUNCATE TABLE example;
```

```
mysql> SET SESSION sql_mode='TRADITIONAL';
mysql> INSERT INTO example (i) VALUES (0), (-1),(255), (9000);
ERROR 1264 (22003): Out of range value for column 'i' at row 2
mysql> INSERT INTO example (i,c) VALUES (1,'A'),(1,'BB'),(1,'CCC');
ERROR 1406 (22001): Data too long for column 'c' at row 3
mysql> SELECT * FROM example;
+---+------+
| i | c    |
+---+------+
| 0 | NULL |
| 1 | A    |
| 1 | BB   |
+---+------+
3 rows in set (0.00 sec)
```

sql_mode=TRADITIONAL

The use of `sql_mode` is essential in application development to providing an acceptable level of data integrity. Systems should ideally be defined with a minimum of `sql_mode=TRADITIONAL`. The MySQL Reference Manual provides the following description for `TRADITIONAL`.

> *"Make MySQL behave like a 'traditional' SQL database system. A simple description of this mode is 'give an error instead of a warning' when inserting an incorrect value into a column.*
>
> *Equivalent to STRICT_TRANS_TABLES, STRICT_ALL_TABLES, NO_ZERO_IN_DATE, NO_ZERO_DATE, ERROR_FOR_DIVISION_BY_ZERO, NO_AUTO_CREATE_USER."*

`TRADITIONAL` provides additional modes including important data integrity for date values.

> *It is important that changing the* `sql_mode` *for an application requires appropriate testing. It is dangerous to change* `sql_mode` *on a production system because functionality that may have operated previously may now operate differently.*

sql_mode=NO_ENGINE_SUBSTITUTION

When using relational integrity that is engine specific, such as the InnoDB `FOREIGN KEY` constraint, it is important that a table is created with the intended storage engine as specified with the `CREATE TABLE` statement. Unfortunately, MySQL does not enforce this by default. Listing 1-47 shows an example.

LISTING 1-47: sql-mode-engine-myisam.sql

Available for
download on
Wrox.com

```
mysql> CREATE TABLE example (
    ->    col1 INT UNSIGNED NOT NULL,
    ->    col2 INT UNSIGNED NOT NULL
```

```
    -> ) ENGINE=InnoDB DEFAULT CHARSET latin1;
Query OK, 0 rows affected, 2 warnings (0.01 sec)

mysql> SHOW WARNINGS;
+---------+------+-----------------------------------------------+
| Level   | Code | Message                                       |
+---------+------+-----------------------------------------------+
| Warning | 1286 | Unknown table engine 'InnoDB'                 |
| Warning | 1266 | Using storage engine MyISAM for table 'example' |
+---------+------+-----------------------------------------------+
2 rows in set (0.00 sec)

mysql> SHOW CREATE TABLE example\G
*************************** 1. row ***************************
       Table: example
Create Table: CREATE TABLE `example` (
  `col1` int(10) unsigned NOT NULL,
  `col2` int(10) unsigned NOT NULL
) ENGINE=MyISAM DEFAULT CHARSET=latin1
1 row in set (0.00 sec)
```

 The table has been successfully created, yet the created storage of MyISAM is not the specified storage engine of InnoDB.

To ensure this does not occur, you need to use the `sql_mode` in Listing 1-48.

LISTING 1-48: sql-mode-engine-error.sql

```
mysql> SET SESSION sql_mode='NO_ENGINE_SUBSTITUTION';

mysql> CREATE TABLE example (
    ->   col1 INT UNSIGNED NOT NULL,
    ->   col2 INT UNSIGNED NOT NULL
    -> ) ENGINE=InnoDB DEFAULT CHARSET latin1;
ERROR 1286 (42000): Unknown table engine 'InnoDB'
```

Storage Engine Integrity

The ARCHIVE storage engine provides a unique feature that can be considered a level of integrity. In Listing 1-49, DELETE and UPDATE are not supported and they return an error:

LISTING 1-49: archive-engine.sql

```
mysql> CREATE TABLE example (
    ->   pk INT UNSIGNED NOT NULL AUTO_INCREMENT,
    ->   col2 VARCHAR(10) NOT NULL,
    ->   PRIMARY KEY(pk)
```

```
    -> ) ENGINE=ARCHIVE DEFAULT CHARSET latin1;

mysql> INSERT INTO example (col2) VALUES ('a'),('b'),('c');

mysql> UPDATE example SET col2='x' WHERE pk=1;
ERROR 1031 (HY000): Table storage engine for 'example' doesn't have this option

mysql> DELETE FROM example  WHERE pk=1;
ERROR 1031 (HY000): Table storage engine for 'example' doesn't have this option
```

What MySQL Does Not Tell You

You should also be aware that MySQL may perform silent column changes when you create a table in MySQL. Though subtle, it is important that you know about these changes because they may reflect an impact on relational integrity. The following is a summary of several important points; however, you should always refer to the MySQL manual for a complete list of version specific changes: `http://dev.mysql.com/doc/refman/5.1/en/silent-column-changes.html`.

> ➤ VARCHAR columns specified less than four characters are silently converted to CHAR.

> ➤ All TIMESTAMP columns are converted to NOT NULL.

> ➤ String columns defined with a binary CHARACTER SET are converted to the corresponding binary data type; for example, VARCHAR is converted to VARBINARY.

What's Missing?

MySQL does not support any check constraints on columns, for example the popular Oracle syntax that can restrict the range of values that can be recorded in a column:

```
CONSTRAINT country_id  CHECK (country_id BETWEEN 100 and 999)
```

SUBQUERIES IN MYSQL

The *subquery* is a powerful means of retrieving additional data in a single MySQL SELECT statement. With subqueries, it is possible to introduce other sets of information for varying purposes. The following examples show three different and popular forms of subqueries.

Subquery

A true subquery, also known as *dependent query*, is a standalone SELECT statement that you can execute independently to produce a set of results that are then used with the parent query. In this form, the subquery is executed first, and the results are used for comparison with the parent query.

LISTING 1-50: subquery.sql

```
SELECT color
FROM colors
```

```
WHERE color IN
  (SELECT color
   FROM flags);

+-------+
| color |
+-------+
| Blue  |
| Red   |
| White |
+-------+
```

Correlated Subquery

A *correlated subquery* performs a join between the parent query and the subquery resulting in a dependency during the process of retrieving results. In this situation, both sets of data must be determined independently, then compared to return the matching results:

LISTING 1-51: correlated-sub-query.sql

```
SELECT DISTINCT f.color
FROM flags f
WHERE EXISTS
  (SELECT 1
   FROM colors c
   WHERE c.color = f.color);

+-------+
| color |
+-------+
| Blue  |
| Red   |
| White |
+-------+
```

Derived Table

Though SELECT statements shown in this chapter have used tables and columns, it is possible for any table or column within a SELECT statement to actually be the result of a SELECT statement. This is known as a *derived table*.

You can use a SELECT statement to create a derived table that acts in the position as a normal table. For example:

LISTING 1-52: derived-table.sql

```
SELECT r.color, r.countries, c.is_dark, c.is_primary
FROM colors c,
     (SELECT color, GROUP_CONCAT(country) AS countries
      FROM   flags
```

```
        GROUP BY color) r
        WHERE c.color = r.color;
+-------+--------------------------+---------+------------+
| color | countries                | is_dark | is_primary |
+-------+--------------------------+---------+------------+
| Blue  | Australia,Sweden,USA     | yes     | yes        |
| Red   | Australia,Canada,Japan,USA | no    | yes        |
| White | Australia,Canada,Japan,USA | no    | yes        |
+-------+--------------------------+---------+------------+
```

An earlier example used a GROUP BY statement to return a concatenated list of colors per country. This can also be retrieved using a column-based derived table as shown in Listing 1-53.

LISTING 1-53: derived-column.sql

```sql
SELECT DISTINCT f.country,
       (SELECT GROUP_CONCAT(color)
        FROM flags f2
        WHERE f2.country = f.country) AS colors
FROM    flags f;
```

```
+-----------+----------------+
| country   | colors         |
+-----------+----------------+
| Australia | Blue,Red,White |
| Sweden    | Blue,Yellow    |
| USA       | Blue,Red,White |
| Canada    | Red,White      |
| Japan     | Red,White      |
+-----------+----------------+
```

You can find a great example of the complexity of SQL and derived tables in the Blog Post by Shlomi Noach at http://code.openark.org/blog/mysql/sql-pie-chart.

Complex Sub Queries

Listing 1-54 is a 66-line SQL statement that includes combined examples of UNION, GROUP BY, IF() and CASE() flow control, and multiple subqueries including table and column derived tables:

LISTING 1-54: complex-sql.sql

```sql
SELECT
   group_concat(
     IF(round(sqrt(pow(col_number/@stretch-0.5-(@size-1)/2, 2) +
        pow(row_number-(@size-1)/2, 2))) BETWEEN @radius*2/3 AND @radius,
     (SELECT SUBSTRING(@colors, name_order, 1) FROM
       (
       SELECT
         name_order,
         name_column,
         value_column,
```

```
              accumulating_value,
              accumulating_value/@accumulating_value AS accumulating_value_ratio,
              @aggregated_data := CONCAT(@aggregated_data, name_column, ': ',
                value_column, ' (', ROUND(100*value_column/@accumulating_value), '%)',
                '|') AS aggregated_name_column,
              2*PI()*accumulating_value/@accumulating_value AS accumulating_value_radians
            FROM (
              SELECT
                name_column,
                value_column,
                @name_order := @name_order+1 AS name_order,
                @accumulating_value := @accumulating_value+value_column
                  AS accumulating_value
              FROM (
                <strong>SELECT name AS name_column, value AS value_column
                  FROM sample_values2 LIMIT 4</strong>
                ) select_values,
                (SELECT @name_order := 0) select_name_order,
                (SELECT @accumulating_value := 0) select_accumulating_value,
                (SELECT @aggregated_data := '') select_aggregated_name_column
              ) select_accumulating_values
            ) select_for_radians
          WHERE accumulating_value_radians &gt;= radians LIMIT 1
          ), ' ')
        order by col_number separator '') as pie
FROM (
  SELECT
    t1.value AS col_number,
    t2.value AS row_number,
    @dx := (t1.value/@stretch - (@size-1)/2) AS dx,
    @dy := ((@size-1)/2 - t2.value) AS dy,
    @abs_radians := IF(@dx = 0, PI()/2, (atan(abs(@dy/@dx)))) AS abs_radians,
    CASE
      WHEN SIGN(@dy) &gt;= 0 AND SIGN(@dx) &gt;= 0 THEN @abs_radians
      WHEN SIGN(@dy) &gt;= 0 AND SIGN(@dx) &lt;= 0 THEN PI()-@abs_radians
      WHEN SIGN(@dy) &lt;= 0 AND SIGN(@dx) &lt;= 0 THEN PI()+@abs_radians
      WHEN SIGN(@dy) &lt;= 0 AND SIGN(@dx) &gt;= 0 THEN 2*PI()-@abs_radians
    END AS radians
  FROM
    tinyint_asc t1,
    tinyint_asc t2,
    (select @size := 23) sel_size,
    (select @radius := (@size/2 - 1)) sel_radius,
    (select @stretch := 4) sel_stretch,
    (select @colors := '#;o:X"@+-=123456789abcdef') sel_colors
  WHERE
    t1.value &lt; @size*@stretch
    AND t2.value &lt; @size) select_combinations
  GROUP BY row_number
UNION ALL
  SELECT
    CONCAT(
      REPEAT(SUBSTRING(@colors, value, 1), 2),
      ' ',
      SUBSTRING_INDEX(SUBSTRING_INDEX(@aggregated_data, '|', value), '|', -1)
    )
```

```
FROM
  tinyint_asc
WHERE
  value BETWEEN 1 AND @name_order
;
```

 Subqueries in MySQL were first available in version 5.0. In prior versions, the use of joins was necessary and in many instances they were able to achieve the same result.

USING REGULAR EXPRESSIONS

Regular expressions become indispensable as soon as application requirements include validation or parsing of complicated text data. This book does a lot of that and it all builds on the foundations in this chapter. It is vital for a developer to have a good working knowledge of the regular expression language in order to increase productivity and to save time by avoiding the need to write special-purpose text parsers.

This section starts with general practices regarding regular expressions and then finishes with some examples. The expressions in the book can sometimes be complicated and difficult to read. This is one of the downsides of using regular expressions, but when they are used properly they can replace hundreds of lines of traditional text-parsing code and will outperform native PHP on long or complex strings.

General Patterns

Regular expressions in PHP start and end with a boundary character. This is usually a slash but it can be any character as long as it is the first character of the expression. Regular expressions in MySQL, by contrast, do not have a boundary character. For ease of reading, this book uses slash as a boundary character for all regular expressions unless they appear directly in a MySQL query. It is also common to use a hash character as a boundary in PHP. When an expression has many slashes the hash effectively avoids the need to escape every single non-terminal slash. In web applications this approach is very useful for URIs. These two lines are both functionally identical and valid regular expressions:

```
/yin\/yang/i
#yin/yang#i
```

In all cases a regular expression will match the pattern inside the boundaries. Modifiers can be placed after the closing boundary to alter the behavior of the regular expression. In the previous example, the modifier "i" is used to make the expression case-insensitive.

The pattern can range from simple (a tiny set of possible strings) to complex (an infinite number of possible matches). Complex regular expressions should always be commented to avoid confusion down the road. It is not uncommon for developers to come across a regular expression and ask, "What is that supposed to be doing?" even if they wrote it themselves just a few days earlier.

Matching a Range of Characters

Regular expressions are often used to match a string where a finite character set is expected to occur (or not occur). This is where regular expressions save a lot of time. Enclosing a set of characters in square brackets [like this] will match any of the characters in the set. The example in the preceding sentence will match the letters l, i, k, e, t, h, and s as well as a space (ASCII 0x20). Putting a caret (^) after the opening bracket will give you any character that is not one of those seven. Using a dash inside the brackets can specify ranges, for example: a valid username contains only letters A-Z, numbers, dashes, and underscores. There are also several short codes for predefined and frequently used character sets. These two regular expressions both match the username:

```
/^[A-Za-z0-9_\-]{3,15}$/
/^[\w\-]{3,15}$/
```

By design, those regular expressions will also ensure that the username is between three and fifteen characters long as indicated by the braces. They force the regular expression to match that many instances of the pattern preceding them. The brackets, combined with the numbers inside of them, are called a *quantifier*.

This is the first time in the book that \w *is used.* \w *will match word characters in a regular expression. So* [A-Za-z0-9_] *can be simplified into just* \w. *Two other useful and related shorthand characters are:*

➤ \s *matches whitespace characters such as spaces, line feeds, and carriage returns:* [\t\n\r]

➤ \d *matches digits:* [0-9]

Using the uppercase version of a shorthand character will negate it. For example: \S *will match any character that is not whitespace.*

Even slightly changing the regular expression alters the meaning dramatically. Changing the braces to {3,} instead of {3,15} will match usernames that are at least three characters long but can be any length. Likewise, changing it to {3} will only allow usernames that are exactly three characters long.

The expression is anchored by a caret at the front and a dollar sign at the end. This ensures that the entire string is matched. Remove both of them and the resulting regular expression would match any substring that has at least three consecutive characters and matches the pattern (allowing bogus usernames). Removing the dollar sign will match any string that starts with at least three of the allowed characters. The inverse is true if just the caret sign is removed.

A more complex task would be to match an email address. Matching an email address is useful for dumb validation of input. The application can ensure that the user at least tried to enter valid data (but not that the data is actually valid). RFC 5322 documents the proper format for an email address. The task can be as easy as /\w@\w/ or very difficult.

The email address is divided into a local-part and a domain-part. The local-part can contain almost any printable ASCII character. It excludes all brackets except curly brackets. It also excludes the

@ sign, colon, semicolon, and commas, with the exception being if the local-part is surrounded by quotes, it can contain the excluded characters. These first two addresses have valid local-parts and the third does not (note the commas):

```
Boston.MA@example.com
"Boston,MA"@example.com
Boston,MA@example.com
```

The quote syntax is rarely seen and the RFC for the Simple Mail Transfer Protocol (RFC 5321) warns against it in section 4.2.1. Two possible regular expressions for the local-part of the domain (with and without quotes) look like this:

```
/"[\w!#$%&'*+\/=?^`{|}~.@()[\]\\;:,<>-]+"/
/[\w!#$%&'*+\/=?^`{|}~.-]+/
```

The plus sign is a quantifier that tells the regular expression engine to look for one or more of the previous expressions. Using an asterisk as a quantifier tells the engine to look for zero or more.

The domain-part has more strict rules to follow (and thus is a little easier to validate against). The domain can be any number of subdomains separated by dots. The subdomain can contain alphanumeric characters and dashes as long as it doesn't start or end with a dash. The domain can also be an IP address enclosed in square brackets. The resulting regular expressions for the domain portion might look like this:

```
/([A-Za-z0-9-]+\.)+[A-Za-z0-9-]+/
/\[([0-9]{1,3}\.){3}[0-9]{1,3}\]/
```

Complex groups can be enclosed in parentheses like they are in the previous example for matching a valid IP address. The expression will match the first three octets followed by a dot and then the final octet (which does not have a trailing dot).

Now that all the pieces are there they need to be put together using *alternation*. Using the pipe character to separate parts of the regular expression tells the engine that it can accept any of the parts as input. You can group alternations together using parentheses. The almost final regular expression looks like this:

```
/^(
  "[\w!#$%&'*+\/=?^`{|}~.@()[\]\\;:,<>-]+"
| [\w!#$%&'*+\/=?^`{|}~.-]+
) @ (
  ([A-Za-z0-9-]+\.)+[A-Za-z0-9-]+
| \[([0-9]{1,3}\.){3}[0-9]{1,3}\]
)$/x
```

The x modifier in the preceding example can be used to indicate that whitespace should be ignored. It is useful for making long expressions easier to read by making them span multiple lines.

The regular expressions for both parts have glaring errors. The local-part allows for a dot at the beginning and the end as well as consecutive dots, and the domain-part of the regular expression allows for hyphens at the beginning and end of subdomains, none of which is allowed by the RFC. Those errors need to be fixed for the regular expression to be accurate.

Expert Regular Expressions

The errors in the email expression can be fixed using simple regular expression syntax to detect a more limited character set for the beginning and end. Ironically that will produce a more complicated and difficult to read expression. Instead, lookarounds can be used.

Lookaheads and Lookbehinds

Lookaheads and *lookbehinds* (collectively called *lookarounds*) can be used to assert the presence or absence of characters in a string. In the email example they can be used to assert that the first character in the local-part is not a dot and neither is the last character. They are each special types of groups. When the start of a group (opening parenthesis) is followed by a question mark, it indicates to the engine that the type for that group will follow. There are many types of groups, all of which are covered in this chapter.

Lookaheads use an equal sign and lookbehinds use a less-than sign followed by an equal sign. Using both, the engine can match the letter b that is immediately preceded by a and followed by c:

```
/(?<=a)b(?=c)/
```

Lookaheads and lookbehinds can also be negated using an exclamation point instead of an equal sign. The preceding regular expression can easily be modified to be the letter b that is not preceded by a or followed by c:

```
/(?<!a)b(?!c)/
```

> *The entire string will not match if any negative lookahead or negative lookbehind matches. So* abx *and* xbc *both fail to match. A slightly more complicated regular expression that succeeds for both those strings but still fails for* abc *would be:*
>
> ```
> /(?<!a)b|b(?!c)/
> ```

All lookarounds are zero-width, which means that they do not count toward the match. This can be useful for string replacement where you do not want the beginning or end of a string to be replaced. They can then be used to help out with the email problem as well. The problem can be simplified by ignoring the complexity of the local-part for now and saying that the expression only needs to match a word containing dots that does not start or end with a dot. The expression [\w.]+ will match alphanumeric characters and dots. A negative lookahead and a negative lookbehind can be used together so that it doesn't match words that start or end with a dot:

```
/^(?!\.)[\w.]+(?<!\.)$/
```

Caution must be taken when using the dot character. It does not need to be escaped inside the character set, but outside it must be. Removing the slash before the first or last dot will read "not ending/beginning with any character," which is clearly not desirable. Changing the last exclamation point to an equal sign will only match strings that do end in a dot. Using negative lookarounds to catch leading and trailing dots in the local-part and hyphens in the domain-part lead to a new completed regular expression:

```
/^(
    "[\w!#$%&'*+\/=?^`{|}~.@()[\]\\;:,<>-]+"
|   (?!\.)[\w!#$%&'*+\/=?^`{|}~.-]+(?<!\.)
) @ (
    ((?!-)[\w-]+(?<!-)\.)+(?!-)[\w-]+(?<!-)
|   \[([0-9]{1,3}\.){3}[0-9]{1,3}\]
)$/x
```

The new expression will match any valid email address and will fail on an address that does not follow the rules outlined in the RFCs. Lookarounds are just one type of group. There is an entirely different type called capture groups that is also very common.

Capturing Data

Regular expressions have the ability to capture data. Starting a group without providing a type (a parenthesis that is not followed by unescaped question mark) will cause that group to be captured. Data from the capture group can be referenced both from inside the regular expression and PHP. When referenced from within the same expression it is referred to as a *back-reference*. Backreferences can be achieved by using \# where # is the number of the captured groups. You can use back-references to match both a single and double-quoted string with the same regular expression:

```
/('|")[^\1]*?\1/
```

The back-references (\1) ensure that the end quote is of the same type as the opening quote and that the quoted string can contain other quotes as long as they are not the same type. It is important that the asterisk is made lazy using the question mark. Otherwise if there are multiple quoted strings inside the subject, the expression will match it as if it contains only one giant quoted string.

Any quantifier can be made lazy using the question mark (even the question mark quantifier itself). The question mark serves several purposes in regular expressions:

➤ *To mark the previous character, group, or character class as optional.*

➤ *To mark the previous quantifier as lazy. A lazy quantifier will quit matching as soon as it can. It will continue on to the next part of the regular expression if it can. In contrast, a greedy quantifier (no question mark) will keep matching as long as it can.*

➤ *To indicate the type of a group (if placed immediately after the opening parenthesis).*

Most programmers are accustomed to escaping quotes inside a quoted string to prevent the string from terminating. The previous regular expression does not behave properly in that situation.

By using a negative lookbehind and alternation the top example string can be matched using the bottom regular expression:

```
"Hello \"my\" world"
/('|")([^\1]|\\\1)*?(?<!\\)\1/
```

The alternation ensures that the engine behaves as intended when it encounters a backslash followed by the quote type. The negative lookbehind then ensures that the expression keeps looking for a closing quote instead of terminating lazily when it finds the first inner quote.

Sometimes it is undesirable to capture data. In those cases it can be avoided by putting `?:` at the beginning of the group. The colon turns it into a non-capturing group. Non-capturing groups are extremely useful for keeping the number of back-references available down to a minimum and makes writing code much easier and cleaner. Sometimes it is desirable to have a lot of back-references. In these cases it is useful to name them so as to avoid confusion ("Is that group `\4` or is it `\5`?").

Naming a capture group is as easy as putting `P<name_here>` after the question mark. A named group can then be back-referenced using `(?=name_here)` in the expression. A simple example pattern will discover Pseudo-Shakespearean questions in the subject text. The regular expression on the first line will match all subsequent subjects:

```
/(?P<word>(?:\w+\s?)+) or not (?P=word)\?$/i
To be or not to be?
PHP or not PHP?
Sleep or not sleep?
```

Named capture groups are used later in this chapter when writing a PHP script that verifies an email address. For now it is useful to go over documenting regular expressions.

Documenting Regular Expressions

Regular expressions can also be commented. The comment syntax is rarely used in this book. An alternative method is to use PHP comments above the regular expression. However, it is a good practice to comment individual alternations and subpatterns when the code contains complex regular expressions (like the email expression).

Comments are a special type of non-capturing group that starts with a `?#`. A comment can very easily be added into any expression but they are easiest to read in expressions where the x modifier is used and whitespace can be utilized liberally. A comment inside a regular expression will look like this:

```
(?# comment goes here)
```

The completed email regular expression from before is altered to include comments when it is used in the next section and in the code examples that accompany this book.

Putting It All Together in PHP

PHP uses Perl-style regular expressions via its `preg_` family of functions. PHP has also supported POSIX-style regular expressions via `ereg_`; however, those functions are deprecated in PHP 5.3 and should not be used anymore.

The PHP example in this section completely validates an email address. It supports two types of validation: lazy and complete. The lazy method simply returns true if the regular expression matches and if the string appears to be a valid email. However, that only serves to make using a fake email more difficult but not impossible. The complete method also checks DNS to make sure the domain name exists and then uses SMTP to connect to the Mail Transfer Agent (MTA) and make sure the user exists.

Each DNS zone for a domain can contain one or more Mail Exchange (MX) records that tell mail clients and transfer agents what server to connect to in order to send and retrieve mail. RFC 2810 states that a domain can receive email even if no MX records are found or valid for it. In that case, the mail client will attempt to connect to the hostname itself. PHP has a handy function called getmxrr() that will get the MX records. Prior to PHP 5.3 the function would only work on UNIX/Linux-based systems. As of PHP 5.3 it will also work on Windows without any messy hacks. The getMX() method looks like this:

```
private function getMX( $hostname ) {
  $hosts = array();
  $weights = array();
  getmxrr( $hostname, $hosts, $weights );
  $results = array();
  foreach ( $hosts as $i => $host )
    $results[ $host ] = $weights[$i];
  arsort($results, SORT_NUMERIC);
  $results[$hostname] = 0;
  return $results;
}
```

As mentioned earlier, RFC 2810 states that the domain itself is a valid location to look for an email server, so the code appends the domain to the end of the result array but gives it zero weight and adds it after the sort so that it will be lighter (lower priority) than any MX records that were returned from the DNS server.

The second method takes the MX records and tries to connect to them on port 25 (SMTP) in order until one succeeds. If it reaches the end of the list and still doesn't have a valid connection, either the host — and therefore the entire email address — is bogus or the server is down. This example assumes the server should be up and returns false under the case where it is unreachable.

The new method called openSMTPSocket() takes a host name, uses it to call getMX(), loops through all the hosts, and returns a valid socket pointer if it can:

```
private function openSMTPSocket( $hostname ) {
  $hosts = $this->getMX($hostname);
  foreach ( $hosts as $host => $weight ) {
    if ( $sock = @fsockopen($host, self::SMTP_PORT,
         $errno, $errstr, self::CONN_TIMEOUT) ) {
      stream_set_timeout($sock, self::READ_TIMEOUT);
      return $sock;
    }
  }
  return null;
}
```

With a valid socket pointer the example can then say "hello" to the MTA (telling it what host you are looking for in case there is more than one host on that server) and then ask if the email is valid. If it is valid it returns true. In all cases, it closes the socket handle when it is done with it:

```php
private function validateUser( $hostname, $user ) {
  if ( $sock = $this->openSMTPSocket($hostname) ) {
    $this->smtpSend("HELO $hostname");
    $this->smtpSend("MAIL FROM: <$user@$hostname>");
    $resp = $this->smtpSend("RCPT TO: <$user@$hostname>");

    $valid = (preg_match('/250|45(1|2)\s/') == 1);
    fclose($fp);
    return $valid;
  } else {
    return false;
  }
}

private function smtpSend( $sock, $data ) {
  fwrite($sock, "$data\r\n")
  return fgets($sock, 1024);
}
```

The email address may be definitively valid (response 250) or gray-listed (responses 451 and 451) on the MTA. The method uses a regular expression to test the response and returns true in any of those cases. In a completed application it makes sense to return a confidence score instead of a Boolean. The score may be zero if the regular expression doesn't match or the MTA returns negative when asking if the user exists. It may be one if the MTA verifies the user and the user is not gray-listed, and 0.25 and 0.75 might be used for "the SMTP server is unreachable" and "the user is gray-listed," respectively. That way an application can choose to only allow a user to register if the score is 0.5 or higher.

The final piece of the puzzle is the class that holds it all together — the rest of the email address verification class looks like the code in Listing 1-55.

LISTING 1-55: EmailValidator.class.php

```php
<?php

class EmailValidator {
  const CONN_TIMEOUT = 10;
  const READ_TIMEOUT = 5;
  const SMTP_PORT = 25;
  private $email;

  public function __construct( $email ) { $this->email = $email; }

  private function getParts() {
    $regex = <<<__REGEX__
/^(?P<user>
  "[\w!#$%&'*+\/=?^`{|}~.@()[\]\\;:,<>-]+" (?# quoted username )
| (?!\.)[\w!#$%&'*+\/=?^`{|}~.-]+(?<!\.) (?# non-quoted username )
```

```
)   @ (?P<host>
    (?:(?!-)[\w-]+(?<!-)\.)+(?!-)[\w-]+(?<!-)  (?# host )
|   \[([0-9]{1,3}\.){3}[0-9]{1,3}\]  (?# host IP address )
)$/x
__REGEX__;

    return ( preg_match($regex, $this->email, $matches) ? $matches : null);
}

public function isValid( $lazy ) {
  static $valid = null;

  if ( $lazy ) return ( $this->getParts() != null );
  if ( $valid !== null ) return $valid;
  $valid = false;

  if ( $parts = $this->getParts() ) {
    $valid = $this->validateUser( $parts['host'], $parts['user'] );
  }
  return $valid;
}

private function validateUser( $hostname, $user ) { ... }
private function openSMTPSocket( $hostname ) { ... }
private function smtpSend( $sock, $data ) { ... }
private function getMX( $hostname ) { ... }
};
?>
```

It is common for ISPs to block outgoing connections on port 25. This tactic forces the customer to use the ISP's mail relay and makes it easier to thwart people who are trying to use the network for spam. Unfortunately, it also means that if the example application in this section is being run on a home network it is likely that the port will be blocked and the application will always return false *for every email address. The only two solutions are to get the ISP to unblock the port (much more likely on hosting providers than consumer ISPs) or run the PHP from a computer living on a different ISP's network.*

Lazy validation (regular expression only) will always work regardless of the ISP's firewall settings but does not have as high a confidence factor.

The email regular expression changed slightly between the previous section and this. It now captures the hostname and user in named groups so that they can be easily referenced by PHP. It also makes the host pattern non-capturing so the matches don't end up with extra data that isn't needed. Passing a third parameter to preg_match() captures the matches and capture groups in an array. The output of the $matches array on the input andrew@example.com looks like this:

```
Array
(
    [0] => Array
```

```
(
    [0] => andrew@example.com
    [user] => andrew
    [1] => andrew
    [host] => example.com
    [2] => example.com
)

)
```

Notice how the numbered matches are still kept in the result so each named group can be referenced two different ways. It also means that changing a group from unnamed to named will not affect the ordering of the unnamed groups. The first index (index zero) always equals the entire match string. The email testing class is now complete; however, it is just one of the uses for regular expressions in PHP.

Replacing Strings

The email regular expression can also be used to replace all valid emails in a string with an HTML link to send a mail to the user. To make things more interesting the next example replaces each email address username with a mailto link and each domain with a link directly to the domain. Assume that $emailRegex is filled with the entire email regular expression from the previous example but with the anchors removed so it can match a partial string:

```php
preg_replace( $emailRegex,
              '<a href="mailto:\1">\1</a>@<a href="http://\2">\2</a>'
              $testString );
```

This example shows a simple replacement. For more complex replacements a callback function can be used to replace the string with a computed value. Callback functions are used extensively in later chapters. Listing 1-56 is a utility class can be used to replace all email addresses in a given text with obfuscated links that can then be clicked to open the email client but won't give away the email to data miners:

LISTING 1-56: EmailLinker.php

```php
<?php
class EmailLinker {

    public function getJavascript() {
        return <<<__JS__
<script type="text/javascript" language="javascript">
function mailDecode( url ) {
  var script=document.createElement('script');
  script.src = '?mail='+url;
  document.body.appendChild(script);
}
</script>
__JS__;
    }

    public function redirectIfNeeded() {
        if ( array_key_exists('mail', $_GET) ) {
```

```
          header("Location: mailto:".base64_decode($_GET['mail']));
          exit;
      }
  }

  private function emailReplaceCallback( $matches ) {
    $encoded = base64_encode($matches[0]);
    return '<a href="?mail='.urlencode($encoded).'"'.
           ' onclick="mailDecode(\''.$encoded.'\'); return false;">'.
           'email '.$matches['user'].'</a>';
  }

  public function link( $text ) {
    $emailRegex = <<<__REGEX__
/(?P<user>
   "[\w!#$%&'*+\/=?^`{|}~.@()[\]\\;:,<>-]+" (?# quoted username )
 | (?!\.)[\w!#$%&'*+\/=?^`{|}~.-]+(?<!\.)    (?# non-quoted username )
 ) @ (?P<host>
   (?:(?!-)[\w-]+(?<!-)\.)+(?!-)[\w-]+(?<!-) (?# host )
 | \[([0-9]{1,3}\.){3}[0-9]{1,3}\] (?# host IP address )
 )/x
__REGEX__;

    return preg_replace_callback($emailRegex,
           array($this,'emailReplaceCallback'), $text );
  }
}
?>
```

The `preg_replace()` callback line and the callback function that is used are both highlighted. The class has corresponding JavaScript that can be retrieved using `getJavascript()` and echoed into the header of the document. The class will work without the JavaScript, but it works much better with it. It also relies on the method `redirectIfNeeded()` being called before any output. The redirect will detect if the user clicked an email link and will send the user to the properly formatted `mailto:` URL.

The resulting text does not include the email address anywhere in it but still allows users to be emailed. It is not completely secure: if spammers or malicious users went through the trouble of Base 64 decoding the string or following the link they could get the users' email addresses. But it does prevent all but the most sophisticated email data mining techniques to the point where a data miner would have to write a script specifically for this example.

PHP has been the primary focus for regular expressions up to this point. It is also possible to perform basic regular expression matches in MySQL in order to filter the data before it even gets to the PHP.

Regular Expressions in MySQL

MySQL has extremely limited support for the now familiar Perl-style regular expressions. It uses a modified POSIX format so support is limited to basic character classes, alternations, anchors, and quantifiers. Lookarounds, back-references, and capture groups are not allowed. However, regular expressions in MySQL can be useful for matching simple strings and for narrowing down a result set for later culling in PHP.

Regular expressions in MySQL are referenced using the REGEXP and REGEXP BINARY operations. The latter is case-sensitive whereas the former is not. Expression can also be negated using the NOT operation. For example, a links table can be queried for all links that point to example.com or its subdomains:

```
SELECT  *
   FROM  `links`
  WHERE  `url` REGEXP 'https?://([a-z0-9-]*\.)*example\.com';
```

MySQL doesn't have the escaped characters that many other regular expression engines have. Instead it has special keywords that can be used in the expression to match a range of characters. Table 1-2 shows the MySQL character classes and their PHP equivalents.

TABLE 1-2: MySQL Character Classes with PHP Equivalents

MYSQL (POSIX)	PHP	LONG FORM (EITHER)
[:alpha:]		[A-Za-z]
[:alnum:]		[A-Za-z0-9]
[:blank:]		[\t\r\n]
[:cntrl:]		[\x00-\x1F\x7F]
[:digit:]	\d	[0-9]
[:graph:]		[\x21-\x7E]
[:lower:]		[a-z]
[:print:]		[\x20-\x7E]
[:punct:]		[!"#$%&'()*+,\-./:;<=>?@[\\\]^_`{|}~]
[:space:]	\s	[\t\r\n\v\f]
[:upper:]		[A-Z]
[:xdigit:]		[A-Fa-f0-9]

It is worth noting that [:print:] will match any character that can be printed to the screen and that [:graph:] is identical except that it will not match a space character (because space is not graphical).

The special character classes can be combined with other characters or classes. Because the subdomain of the previous regular expression consists of alphanumeric characters or hyphens it can be rewritten as:

```
SELECT  *
   FROM  `links`
  WHERE  `url` REGEXP 'https?://([:alnum:-]*\.)*example\.com';
```

The word boundary shorthand (\b) is replaced in MySQL by two character classes. One matches the end of a word and the other matches the beginning. Like \b they are both zero-width. To match all messages in a forum that contain the word HTML but not XHTML, a simple regular expression could be used:

```
SELECT * FROM `forum` WHERE `body` REGEXP '[[:<:]]HTML[[:>:]]'
```

The regular expression functionality built into MySQL is sufficient under almost all circumstances. However, if a PHP program ends up doing a lot of post-filtering of the result set based on the output of a complex regular expression, it may be time to extend MySQL.

Using LIB_MYSQLUDF_PREG

The LIB_MYSQLUDF_PREG library is a set of MySQL User Defined Functions that allow Perl-compatible regular expressions (same as PHP) to be executed in a MySQL query. Besides allowing for back-references and lookarounds it also allows capture groups to be selected by the query.

The library must be installed from source. Chapter 7 on MySQL UDFs provides more details on installing from source code. If you are already familiar with the typical build process, it can be installed in three lines:

```
./configure
make
make installdb
```

It requires the libpcre headers and MySQL to be on the system. If they are installed in unusual locations there are a few extra steps. The location of either can be easily specified manually:

```
./configure --with-pcre=/path/to/libpcre --with-mysql=/path/to/mysql/config
```

Almost anything that PHP is capable of can also be done in MySQL once the library is installed.

Capturing Data

It is often useful to capture part of a complex string in a data set. One example is to query the database for a list of all domains that have registered users and return the number of users from each. There is no need for a complicated email matching expression like the one used in previous examples because the application can assume that if the email made its way into the database, it is already valid. The query looks like this:

```
SELECT
   PREG_CAPTURE('/@([^@]+)$/' , `email`, 1) AS `domain`,
   COUNT(*) AS `count`
FROM `users`
GROUP BY `domain`
```

However, if the application does this often for the same string it is a sign that a new column should be added to the table. Because a column cannot be returned as an array, the PREG_CAPTURE function takes a third parameter that is the group to return. If PREG_CAPTURE is replaced by PREG_POSITION, then instead of the domain it will return the index of the start of the first group. In MySQL the index is one-based so when querying for the position of the first character it is index 1, not 0. The default for the group parameter is 0, which returns the entire match, 1 returns the first match, and so on, like in PHP.

String Replacement

When selecting from or updating a table, it is useful to modify an existing column. For example, the application may need to display a sample report that blanks out certain information such as revenue numbers. MySQL can replace the data at query time instead of having to loop through the entire data set in PHP when displaying it:

```
SELECT
    PREG_REPLACE('/\$[:digit:]*(\.[:digit:]+)?/',
                '[subscriber-only]', `body`)
  AS `body`
FROM `reports`;
```

String replacements are also useful when doing updates to a table. Because the library supports back-references it is easy to make complex replacements.

Filtering a Query Based on a Regular Expression

The built-in MySQL regular expression functionality is primarily useful for returning a Boolean or filtering an entire result set. LIB_MYSQLUDF_PREG can do that too.

One alias for REGEXP in MySQL is RLIKE. Similarly, the UDF includes a function PREG_RLIKE that returns 1 if the pattern matched and 0 if there isn't any match. The behavior is identical to the built-in MySQL functionality except that it allows for more complex Perl-compatible regular expressions. The syntax is also slightly different because the latter is a UDF. The following two queries have identical output:

```
SELECT *
  FROM `links`
  WHERE `url` REGEXP 'https?://([:alnum:-]*\.)*example\.com';

SELECT *
  FROM `links`
  WHERE PREG_RLIKE('https?://([\w-]*\.)*example\.com',`url`);
```

Regular expressions are slower than other methods of string matching because they need to compile the expression in order to match against it and each position in the string may take several passes to look for a match. For those reasons a developer should always opt to use basic string matching such as LIKE to filter results. However, when more complex string matching and replacements are needed Regular Expressions are the only way to go.

SUMMARY

This chapter covered both PHP and MySQL essentials for the expert developer.

It covered the object-oriented design approach now available in PHP including a number of key design patterns. It is impossible to master PHP without first having a complete understanding of class instantiation, interfaces, class methods, and constants.

This chapter also went over the foundations of MySQL. Being able to use MySQL joins is essential in a normalized relational database design where data is maintained in multiple tables. Combined with the ability to aggregate and group results, and leverage subqueries and derived tables, you can master all the power and flexibility that MySQL has to offer in retrieving your information.

Though MySQL provides options for flow control and logic within SQL, as a developer you should always determine what is best performed at the database level and what is best performed within your PHP code.

The chapter concluded with regular expressions — the cornerstone of string manipulation — and parsing in any programming language, including PHP and MySQL.

2

Advanced PHP Concepts

WHAT'S IN THIS CHAPTER?

➤ Using `iterators`

➤ Making classes behave like arrays

➤ Understanding Lambda-style functions

➤ Using True lambda functions and closures

This chapter covers several concepts that can lead to better coding practices and cleaner, more manageable code. They are used in various chapters throughout the rest of the book and several of the concepts take advantage of the built-in functionality of the Standard PHP Library (SPL). Specifically, the four interfaces provided by the SPL allow programmers to easily utilize PHP's ability to iterate through data and create a data structure that behaves exactly like a PHP array.

This chapter also uses standard language constructs available in PHP 5.3.0 called **lambda functions**. Lambda functions are useful when they are used as closures to create dynamic functionality.

A fictitious book club database is used as the example for this chapter. The application is simple; it provides the minimal functionality and keeps the least amount of information about the books possible. This chapter goes over simple use cases.

A PROBLEM THAT NEEDS SOLVING

Loops are used in a typical PHP application to iterate directly through result sets fetched from MySQL:

```php
<?php
$conn = mysql_connect( 'localhost', 'mysql_user',
                       'mysql_password', 'database' );
$result = mysql_query('SELECT * FROM `example_table`', $conn);
```

```
if ( $result )
  while ( $row = mysql_fetch_assoc($result) ) {
    // Execute logic or display row
}
?>
```

The highlighted approach is beneficial only for the most basic of PHP applications. Issues come into the picture when you start dealing with more expansive date sets. Consider some casual use cases:

USE CASES

The following use cases illustrate two users: one who manages inventory versus one who wants to browse a list.

Sue Needs to Manage Books

Sue has been running a book club for eight years and wants to display all her books online so that her members can view them. She needs to manage her inventory by going to a book management page where she can read the first 20 books. On the top of the page she can see that there are 75 books total. There are four pages total. On the bottom she can click and go directly to any of the pages. To the right of each book she can click Delete or Edit.

Jane Wants to Browse Book Club Books

Jane is a member of the book club and wants to browse through the list of books. She navigates to a page with 10 book results on it. On the top of the page she can see that there are 75 total results. On the bottom of the page she can jump to any page from one to eight or click Next to go directly to the next page.

The basic procedural code that is commonly used to query MySQL is too simple to be useful. Much more code must be added to the example to support Jane's use case. The simple example can become unmanageable very quickly. For a one-person team this may be acceptable. However, a larger team will run into significant problems. It requires that the developer who designs the view know the details of how the books are stored in the database, and it makes changing the underlying storage mechanism difficult.

Sue's use case introduces a slightly different page but one that shares many of the same functions. On that page, she is also viewing a list of books. However, she has 20 books listed per page instead of the 10 that Jane had and she has a couple of additional management options presented to her. Using these two use cases you can get a list of requirements for the example application:

➤ The application must facilitate browsing through a variable-length collection of books.

➤ The results must be paginated by an arbitrary number of results per page. You can default to 10.

➤ You should not be fetching results from the database if they are not needed yet. Not all books are being displayed at the same time. Conversely, you should not be fetching less data than is required so that you can avoid excessive database calls.

➤ The business logic should be separated into classes that can be easily reused by both views.

➤ It must be easy for a developer to loop through the list and retrieve data from each of the books.

➤ A developer does not need to worry about the details of how to paginate the list or of the underlying database. The storage mechanism can be changed at any time without breaking either of the views.

The last two items aren't actually from the use case. However, they are equally as important when you're dealing with a medium to large team or an open source project. As a rule, logical business units should always be separated into classes. By doing this, you create a standard and easily understood method to access and modify the data. This approach can cut development time, lessen maintenance costs, and shorten the learning curve for new developers coming on the team. It is always easier to take these goals into consideration at the beginning of the project rather than waiting until the code base becomes larger. You will be using iterators and closures to accomplish each of these goals.

ITERATORS AND THE SPL

Iterators provide a way for PHP to loop through an arbitrary data set using a `foreach` loop. Predefined iterators exist in the SPL to loop through arrays, directories, and XML. Another common use of iterators, and one that you will be implementing in this chapter, is to loop through a MySQL result set. You will also be using several other interfaces from the SPL to create array-like functionality for your object.

You will also create three new classes:

➤ A class that retrieves the data

➤ A class that extends one of the SPL classes to provide pagination functionally

➤ A `Book` class that stores, modifies, and accesses the book information

A Sample View for the Application

You will be using MySQL as the database connector in order to simplify the application requirements. The application does require that the server is running PHP 5.3 and is compiled using the MySQL Native Driver (covered in the next chapter). The view for this application may look something like this:

```php
<?php
$dbConn = new mysqli('localhost', 'mysql_user', 'mysql_password', 'bookclub');

$booksPerPage = 10;
$page = ( isset($_GET['page']) ? $_GET['page']: 1 );

$bookList = new BookList($dbConn);
$bookPage = new Page($bookList, $page, $booksPerPage);
?>
```

```
<!DOCTYPE html PUBLIC "-//W3C//DTD XHTML 1.0 Strict//EN"
  "http://www.w3.org/TR/xhtml1/DTD/xhtml1-strict.dtd">
<html xmlns="http://www.w3.org/1999/xhtml">
<head> <title>Book Club List</title> </head>
<body>
  <p>
    Showing books
  <?php
    printf('%d-%d of %d', $page->getFirstIndex(),
           $page->getLastIndex(), count($bookList) );
  ?>
  </p>
  <table>
    <thead>
      <th>Title</th>
      <th>Author</th>
      <th>Publisher</th>
    </thead>
    <tbody>
<?php
foreach ( $bookPage as $key => $book ) {
  printf('    <tr><td>%s</td>%s</td><td>%s</td></tr>\n',
         $book->title, $book->authors, $book->publisher);
}
?>
    </tbody>
  </table>
  <ul class="pages">
<?php
$totalPages = ceil(count($bookList)/$booksPerPage);
if ( $page > 1 )
  printr('    <li><a href="?page=%d">Prev</a></li>\n', $page-1);

for ( $i=1; $i <= $totalPages; $i++ ) {
  if ( $i == $page )
    printr('    <li>%d</li>\n', $i);
  else
    printr('    <li><a href="?page=%d">%d</a></li>\n', $i, $i);
}

if ( $page < $totalPages )
  printr('    <li><a href="?page=%d">Next</a></li>\n', $page+1);
?>
  </ul>
  </body>
</html>
```

This view satisfies all the major requirements for this application. It displays the total number of results at the top, followed by a table of book results, and then finishes off with a list of pages and a Next button if the visitor is not already on the last page. It also produces valid XHTML. Following markup standards helps designers create better-looking pages and keeps code quality high. It also has the benefit of being able to open pages with a PHP DOM object if needed. All of the examples in this book validate to XHTML 1.0 Strict if their output is intended for a web browser.

The developer coding the view for this book club doesn't need to have any understanding of how the data is stored and can use a standard `foreach` loop to print out a row for each book. It is common to populate applications with dummy data early on in the development of a project before access to the real data is completed. This is particularly true in larger teams where multiple groups might be writing closely related pieces of code. Using standard design patterns available in PHP ensures that each team is on the same page.

Another benefit that the example view demonstrates is the ability to use `count($bookList)` to retrieve the total number of books returned by the underlying query. The `Page` and `BookList` classes can both look and behave exactly like a standard array in PHP. That ability is part of what makes the SPL so powerful.

The first iterator that you will be building is the `BookList` class as illustrated in Listing 2-1. It will be a wrapper for all the MySQL selecting functionality. Before you begin, you need to create the table to store the books and design a query to fetch all the books in a format that you can use:

LISTING 2-1: bookclub.sql

```sql
CREATE TABLE books ( id INT AUTO_INCREMENT PRIMARY KEY,
                     ISBN VARCHAR(20) UNIQUE,
                     title VARCHAR(50), publisher INT );
CREATE TABLE book_authors ( bookid INT, authorid INT,
                            PRIMARY KEY (bookid,authorid) );
CREATE TABLE authors ( id INT AUTO_INCREMENT PRIMARY KEY, name VARCHAR(20) );
CREATE TABLE publishers ( id INT AUTO_INCREMENT PRIMARY KEY, name VARCHAR(20) );

SELECT `ISBN`, `title`, (
  SELECT GROUP_CONCAT( `name` )
    FROM `book_authors` AS t2
    JOIN `authors` AS t3 ON t2.authorid = t3.id
    WHERE t2.bookid = t1.id
    GROUP BY `bookid`
) AS `author`, `t4`.`name` AS publisher
FROM `books` AS t1
JOIN `publishers` AS t4 ON t1.publisher = t4.id;
```

Now that the database tables are created it is time to write more PHP code. As mentioned earlier, much of the functionality in the SPL is provided by interfaces. `BookList` will need to implement three of the interfaces for this simple application. The new class, once done, will be both robust and reusable in just about any situation where a list of books would be needed in the application. The same patterns can be applied to any type of data.

The Iterator Interface

The first interface to implement is the aptly named Iterator interface. The Iterator interface provides a set of five methods that must be implemented in order for iteration to work with built-in PHP constructs. The Iterator design pattern itself is well established and is not exclusive to PHP. The SPL interface is simply a standardization of the methods so that they can be reliably implemented across all PHP applications.

All iterators, in any language, must be able to perform four actions:

➤ Rewind the iterator to the first element.

➤ Advance to the next element.

➤ Check to see if the iterator has reached the last element.

➤ Get the current item pointed to by the iterator's internal pointer.

The PHP interface defines these four methods as well as a fifth (bolded in the code) to replicate PHP's treatment of arrays as hash tables. Here is the basic layout of a class that implements the interface:

```php
<?php
class BookList implements Iterator {
  public function current() { .. }
  public function key() { .. }
  public function next() { .. }
  public function rewind() { .. }
  public function valid() { .. }
}
?>
```

The class has everything it needs in order to be traversed in a `foreach` loop just by combining these methods. At the same time, they are the bare minimum. You will be implementing two more interfaces over the course of this chapter to add some important but missing functionality. For now, it may be helpful to consider this: the following two pieces of code are identical to each other:

```php
foreach ( $bookList as $key => $book ) { }

for ( $bookList->rewind(); $bookList->valid(); $bookList->next() ) {
  $key = $bookList->key();
  $book = $bookList->current();
}
```

You need your data before either of those will function. A good first place to start is by writing the constructor and defining the variables that the class will need. The design makes one assumption. If the application requests any book on the page it is extremely likely that it will be requesting all the books on the page (if it wasn't then it probably wouldn't be using a class called `BookList` and would be using `Book` instead). The consequence is that the class can load all the records with just one trip to the database. You are not going to assume that the developer will only be requesting one page at a time. Instead the class will be built so that it is very easy for the developer to loop from the first book all the way through to the last on a single page. It will, however, make multiple database calls if it isn't configured correctly.

The most direct way to do this is by having an associative array inside your class and using the page number as the key to that array. The data in the array will be a set of additional arrays that include the actual books. You will also need to store the current page that the user is on.

In the sample view for the application a MySQL object was passed to the constructor. The class will also store that resource so that you can fetch new values from the database as needed. Your new constructor and variable definitions look like this:

```
class BookList implements Iterator {
  private $pages = array();
  private $currentPage = 1;
  private $database = null;
  private  $booksPerPage = 10;

  public function __construct( $database ) { $this->database = $database; }
}
```

Once you have all the variable definitions in place you can start to write your iterator methods. There isn't a particular order to implement these because all of them must be fully working in order for the foreach loop to be able to do its job. You might as well start with the first one that is called for any loop.

Rewinding an Iterator

The rewind() method needs to set or reset the iterator to the very first item of the data set. Pagination will be ignored for the purpose of this method. The first item is always book zero on page one regardless of what page the view is currently displaying. The method does not return any values (and if it does they will be completely ignored by PHP) so you can write it in as few as three lines of code:

```
public function rewind() {
  $this->currentPage = 1;
  if ( array_key_exists(1,$this->pages) )
    reset( $this->pages[$i] );
}
```

The first thing the method does after setting the current page is to check to make sure the page exists inside of the pages array before proceeding. The constructor does not initialize any page data so when the rewind method is called for the first time it is likely the actual array may be empty. Your class will be doing delayed loading of the data from MySQL so the array will not be there until it is actually needed. It is possible that the first page will never be needed so fetching it now could be unnecessarily costly. The remaining methods do require accessing the data from the database at this stage of the application; they will each be covered in the next section.

 The rewind() *method does have an analog in procedural PHP and arrays. However, it is named differently. There is a built-in function that shares its name with the iterator method but it will return a file pointer to the beginning of the file and throw an error if you pass an array to it. The equivalent operation on an array is actually* reset($array).

Validating and Returning the Current Record

The valid() method is used to check to see if the iterator's internal pointer is referencing a legitimate entry. It always returns a Boolean value. It will typically return a value of false when the iterator has reached the last item in the collection or if the collection does not contain any items.

The key() method returns an identifier for the current item. Its complement is the current() method, which returns the data that corresponds to the key. It is not technically required that the key be unique; however, in practice there should be only one value per key. A unique key allows for a much wider range of applications. Later in the chapter you will be using the key to access books and conflicting keys would introduce ambiguity.

Because all three methods need to use the data from the page array you'll write a helper method to retrieve the data for the current page. Each call to the method would need to be preceded by a check to see if the data for the page has already been fetched. You can simply move the check into the method. UNIX and Linux users will be familiar with the touch program that can be used to set the access time of a file or create it if it doesn't exist. Your new method follows this approach. It can — and should — be declared as a private member because it will only be used internally. The new method and the validation and retrieval methods that use it look like this:

```php
private function &touchPage( $pageNo=false ) {
  if ( $pageNo === false ) $pageNo = $this->currentPage;

  if ( !array_key_exists($pageNo,$this->pages) ) {
    $start = ($pageNo-1)*$this->itemsPerPage;
    $query = <<<__QUERY
      SELECT `ISBN`, `title`, (
        SELECT GROUP_CONCAT( `name` )
        FROM `book_authors` AS t2
        JOIN `authors` AS t3 ON t2.authorid = t3.id
        WHERE t2.bookid = t1.id
        GROUP BY `bookid`
      ) AS `author`, `t4`.`name` AS publisher
      FROM `books` AS t1
      JOIN `publishers` AS t4 ON t1.publisher = t4.id
      LIMIT $start, {$this->booksPerPage}
__QUERY;

    $result = $this->database->query($query);
    $this->pages[$pageNo] = $result->fetch_all(MYSQLI_ASSOC);
  }

  $tmp = &$this->pages[$pageNo];
  return $tmp;
}

public function valid() {
  $page = &$this->touchPage();
  return ( key($page) !== null );
}

public function current() {
  return current( $this->touchPage() );
```

```
      }

      public function key() {
        return key( $this->touchPage() )+$this->booksPerPage*($this->currentPage-1);
      }
```

Without the last of the methods it is impossible to read any values from the iterator except the first. The `next()` method will advance the internal pointer by one and return the current element. The new pointer may or may not refer to a valid value. The `next()` method is more complicated than some of the other methods of the class because the books are stored in multiple arrays. It needs to detect if the internal pointer for the inner array has reached the end and attempt to advance to the next page if it has. First, the method also checks if the page is full. Each page has a fixed number of elements and a partially full page cannot have a next page.

```
      public function next() {
        $page = &$this->touchPage();
        next($page);
        if ( key($page) === null && count($page) == $this->booksPerPage ) {
          $this->currentPage++;
          $page = &$this->touchPage();
          reset($page);
        }
        return current($page);
      }
```

The newly completed class loops through every book in the database. Every 10 records (or however many records are defined in `$booksPerPage`) it will fetch a new set from the database until they are exhausted. Unfortunately, there will be one extra database query in the case where the last page is full. You will fix that next. The `Iterator` interface gets you most of the way to meeting the business requirements. Two more interfaces need to be implemented in order to completely satisfy the requirements.

The Countable Interface

Going back to the view, you can see that the total number of results is obtained by calling `count($bookList)`. In order for the `count()` function to work, you need to implement the `Countable` interface. The interface defines only one method. However, to obtain the results you must store the total number of records in the table. You will use the constructor for that:

```
      ..
      private $totalBooks = 0;

      public function __constructor( $database ) {
        ..
        if ( $result = $database->query("SELECT count(*) FROM books") )
          if ( $row = $result->fetch_row() )
            $this->totalBooks = $row[0];
      }

      public function count() {
        return $this->totalBooks;
      }
```

The validity function can be optimized now that the class has the ability to report its count. The method can assume that if the page being fetched is greater than the maximum number of pages, it must be empty. In that case, an empty array can be returned instead of executing a SELECT from the database. The bold lines of code were added in this revision of the method:

```
private function &touchPage( $pageNo=false ) {
   if ( $pageNo === false ) $pageNo = $this->currentPage;

   if ( !array_key_exists($pageNo,$this->pages) ) {
     if ( $pageNo > ceil($this->count()/$this->booksPerPage) ) {
       $this->pages[$pageNo] = array();
     } else {
       ..
     }
   }

   $tmp = &$this->pages[$pageNo];
   return $tmp;
}
```

In a more complex application with expensive queries, using count(*) on every page may be prohibitive. Caching yields better performance and avoids database hits. Caching is covered extensively in both Chapters 4 and 5.

It is a good idea to stop and examine some of the implications of the code thus far. It is likely that in some cases, the count may become invalid while looping because it is calculated only once. If accuracy is necessary, it might be a good idea to do a write-lock on the table in the constructor and unlock it in the destructor. This will stall any scripts attempting to do a write to the table, so it is important that caution be taken when performing locks.

Another condition exists when the user moves to the next page. If a record has been added or deleted, the user may end up missing entries and possibly see the same entry on two consecutive pages. This can be avoided several ways:

➤ Passing the first entry on the next page via the query string along with the page number that is already being sent

➤ Caching the search results, either in a file, memory, or a temporary table in MySQL

However, in situations where the data is non-critical or updated infrequently (such as the book club application) it is acceptable to paginate using only the methods in this chapter.

The SeekableIterator Interface and Pagination

The final feature that the class is missing is seeking a specific record. Without that ability, it is not possible to paginate and still stay within the parameters of the SPL. The SeekableIterator interface extends Iterator so a class does not need to indicate that it implements both of them. It also adds an additional method called seek(), which takes an integer as a parameter.

The seek() method will move the internal pointer for the object to the record that exists at a particular index. Seeking is unlike other methods that you have implemented thus far. Instead of waiting for a validity call it will immediately throw an OutOfBoundsException when trying to access a record that doesn't exist. Because you have implemented Countable it can easily check against those bounds. Seeking is also the only method that doesn't have an analog when dealing with arrays. Instead it must reset the array, then loop until the internal pointer hits the appropriate item:

```
public function seek( $index ) {
  if ( $index < 0 || $index > $this->totalBooks )
    throw new OutOfBoundsException();

  $this->currentPage = (int)floor($index/$this->booksPerPage)+1;
  $page = &$this->touchPage();
  reset($page);
  for ( $i= $index % $this->booksPerPage; $i>0; $i--) next($page);
}
```

Now that you have the ability to seek you can implement your Pagination class. The Pagination class is an extension of the IteratorIterator class that is also a part of the SPL. IteratorIterator implements OuterIterator, which, as the name implies, provides a wrapper around a second unseen iterator.

IteratorIterator provides you with one useful method: getInnerIterator(). Aside from that, every method needs to be rewritten. The new class is an iterator that loops through only the elements on a given page. Each method in the Iterator interface — which is also implemented by IteratorIterator — must know the bounds and act accordingly. In simple applications the inherited functionality of the other methods are acceptable and don't need to be re-implemented. Listing 2-2 shows this in action.

LISTING 2-2: Page.class.php

```php
<?php
class Page extends IteratorIterator {
  private $page;
  private $currentItem;
  public $itemsPerPage;

  public function __construct( Iterator $iterator, $page, $itemsPerPage) {
    parent::__construct($iterator);
```

```php
        $this->page = $page;
        $this->itemsPerPage = $itemsPerPage;
        $this->rewind();
    }

    public function valid() {
        return ( $this->currentItem != $this->itemsPerPage &&
                $this->getInnerIterator()->key() !== null );
    }

    public function rewind() {
        $currentItem = 0;
        $this->getInnerIterator()->seek( ($this->page-1)*$this->itemsPerPage);
    }

    public function next() {
        if ( $this->currentItem < $this->itemsPerPage) {
            $this->currentItem++;
            $this->getInnerIterator()->next();
        }
    }

    public function current() {
        return ( $this->currentItem != $this->itemsPerPage
                ? $this->getInnerIterator()->current()
                : null );
    }
    public function key() {
        return ( $this->currentItem != $this->itemsPerPage
                ? $this->getInnerIterator()->key()
                : null );
    }
}
?>
```

Each method checks to make sure that the iterator is still within the bounds of the page. The current page and the number of records per page are passed to the constructor and then the rewind() method is called. The method is different than previous implementations because instead of going to the front of the inner iterator it goes to the first item on the selected page.

The new Page class can be extended to also implement the Countable and Seekable interfaces. For this application they are not needed so they are not covered in this chapter. If the new Page class is used in other applications, it is worth the time to implement the two additional interfaces. Each has only one method and can be written in under five lines of code.

You have now fully implemented everything you need to satisfy your use cases, but the application is far from being ready to deploy. It has a robust and easy-to-use reporting system but it still lacks the ability to insert, update, or delete records and the security that comes with those abilities. The next step is to create a Book class that has all the necessary operations. You can find full versions of the classes described in this chapter, as well as a Book class, on the Wiley web site. Chapter 12 covers adding authentication and user management. Before you go into that there is one more interface that you can add to the BookList class.

The ArrayAccess Interface

The new application behaves almost exactly like an array. It implements every feature of an array that is needed for the use case. There is one piece of functionality missing that could conceivably be needed in future cases. That is the ability to access elements of the BookList using array notation. By implementing the ArrayAccess interface the BookList can be accessed randomly using a familiar $bookList[$i] notation and without changing the internal pointer to the current record.

If the keys returned by the key() method in the BookList class were not unique, this technique would not be able to function properly and you would only be able to access some of the books.

The ArrayAccess interface defines four methods that must be implemented. Three of the methods can be programmed easily. They are the methods to access, update, and check the validity of records based on a given key:

```
public function offsetExists( $offset ) {
  return ( $offset > 0 && $offset < count($this) );
}

public function offsetGet( $offset ) {
  $pageOfOffset = (int)floor($offset/$this->booksPerPage)+1;
  $page = &$this->touchPage( $pageOfOffset );
  return $page[ $offset % $this->booksPerPage ];
}

public function offsetSet( $offset, $newValue ) {
  $pageOfOffset = (int)floor($offset/$this->booksPerPage)+1;
  $page = &$this->touchPage( $pageOfOffset );
  $page[ $offset % $this->booksPerPage ] = $newValue;
}
```

The fourth method provides the ability to unset an element. This is problematic because there are a fixed number of elements on each page and you keep a hash table for all the book records. You can't simply shift the entire result set downward. You also need to refill any partially filled pages and make sure that future calls to touchPage() are properly limited. You can accomplish this by using an array to track unlinks.

In this case, the new lower bound of the LIMIT in your query is now the total number of unlinks in all pages prior to the page currently being fetched subtracted from the original offset:

```
public function offsetUnset( $offset ) {
  $pageOfOffset = (int)floor($offset/$this->booksPerPage)+1;
  $page = &$this->touchPage( $pageOfOffset );

  $this->deletions[$pageOfOffset]++;
  ksort($this->deletions);
  unset( $page[ $offset % $this->booksPerPage ] );
  $page = array_values($page);
  while ( is_array($this->pages[$pageOfOffset+1]) ) {
    $this->pages[$pageOfOffset][] = array_shift($this->pages[++$pageOfOffset]);
```

```
        }

        $record = ($pageOfOffset-1)*$this->booksPerPage +
                count($this->pages[$pageOfOffset]) +
                $this->getAdjustmentForPage($pageOfOffset);
        if ( $result = $this->database->query("SELECT * FROM books LIMIT $record,1") )
          $this->pages[$pageOfOffset][] = $result->fetch_object();

         $this->totalBooks--;
    }

    private function getAdjustmentForPage( $pageNo ) {
      $adjust = 0;
      for ( reset($this->deletions);
            key($this->deletions) !== null && key($this->deletions) < $pageNo;
            next($this->deletions) )
        $adjust += current($this->deletions);
      return $adjust;
    }
}
```

The new `$deletions` member variable must be defined and initialized to an empty array. It is used to get an adjustment for when the database is queried for new pages and when filling pages that were left partially filled after calling `unset()`. The `touchPage()` method must then be updated to account for the change.

An acceptable alternative in many situations is to throw an exception stating that the method is not implemented, especially because making `unlink()` work as it does with arrays can pose some design questions. For example: does calling `unlink()` on a book in a `BookList` cause the book to then be removed from the database? In this example it does not.

The SPL offers much more functionality in addition to the interfaces covered in this chapter. Some of the functionality not covered in this chapter is discussed in later chapters, specifically exception handling.

LAMBDA FUNCTIONS AND CLOSURES

A *lambda function* (also commonly referred to as an *anonymous function*) is, as its alternative name implies, a function that does not require a name when it is defined. Instead, lambda functions are assigned to a variable that can then be used to call that function. They are used as callback functions and in other situations where it is unnecessary or undesirable to define a function in the global scope.

The Old Way: Lambda-Style Functions

Lambda-style functions are something that has been part of PHP since version 4.0.1 via the `create_function()` call. They are called *lambda-style* functions because they are not truly anonymous. The function will find a unique name that is not currently being used as an identifier elsewhere in the script and then use that as the name for the newly created function. Usually the generated function will be called lambda_N where N is an integer starting at one and lambda_N is not yet defined. The new function's name is returned as a string.

The function `create_function()` *relies on the ability for variable notation to be used in almost any atomic part of an identifier, including as the name of a function and the name of a method or member variable inside a class. Some examples of this type of notation are:*

```php
<?php
$x = "hello";

function hello($name) { echo "Hello $name\n"; }
$x("Andrew"); // Output: "Hello Andrew"

$obj = new StdClass();
$obj->$x = "Test Hello";
echo "{$obj->hello}\n"; // Output: "Test Hello"

class say {
   public static function hello($name) { echo "Hello $name\n"; }
}
say::$x("Boston"); // Output: "Hello Boston"
?>
```

The ability to create new functions dynamically via a built-in PHP function does solve some non-trivial problems. It allows the programmer to write one-time-use functions without needing a constant name in the class or global scopes. What it does not do is provide any functionality that cannot be accomplished using different means. It does save time and avoids bloating the code for extremely simple functions. A common use of lambda-style functions is as a callback to pass to a `preg_replace_callback()` function call. Consider that you use the notation `{table_name}` to represent a table in your query and you want to add the prefix "foo_" to the front of every table name while simultaneously removing the brackets (see Listing 2-3):

LISTING 2-3: CreateFunctionDemo.php

```php
<?php
$temp = create_function( '$match', 'return '.
        '(preg_match(\'/^{(.*)}$/\',$match[1],$m) '.
        '? "foo_$m[1]": $match[1]);');
$query = 'SELECT * FROM {books}';
$regExp = '/([^{"\']+|\'(?:\\\\\'.|[^\'])*\'|"(?:\\\\"|[^"])*"|{[^}{]+})/';
echo preg_replace_callback($regExp, $temp, $query);
?>
```

The second regular expression only looks complicated because it must account for a bracketed string inside of single or double quotes that is not a table name. When parsing quoted strings, it is important to ensure that quotes inside the string can be escaped. Because escaping of quotes is done with a backslash, there are a significant number of slashes in the regular expression. After all the slashes are parsed out by PHP you end up with a slightly simplified regular expression:

```
/([^{"']+|'(?:\\'.|[^'])*'|"(?:\\"|[^"])*"|{[^}{]+})/
```

The expression will match free text, single-quoted strings, double-quoted strings, and your table names. A more simple expression would result in matching of bracketed strings that are not intended to be table names; for instance, a bracketed string inside quotation marks or a bracketed string inside of quotation marks with other escaped quotation marks inside. The resulting code is not very readable but it covers all the cases.

The result achieved by lambda-style functions can also be accomplished by defining a function or method. The benefit of not needing a unique name when writing the code is lost in exchange for syntax checking by the byte code compiler, ease of reading, and the ability to include the callback function inside of a class. Your new query builder might look something like Listing 2-4.

LISTING 2-4: QueryBuilder.class.php

```php
<?php
class QueryBuilder {
  private $query;
  private $prefix;

  public function __construct($prefix='' ) {
    $this->query = $query;
    $this->prefix = $prefix;
  }

  public function replaceCallback( $match ) {
    return ( preg_match('/^{(.*)}$/',$match[1],$m)
      ? ( empty($this->prefix) ? $m[1]: "{$this->prefix}_$m[1]" )
      : $match[1]
    );
  }

  public function build($query) {
    static $regExp = '/([^{"\']+|\'(?:\\\\\'.|[^\'])*\'|'.
              '"(?:\\\\"|[^"])*"|{[^}{]+})/';
    return preg_replace_callback($regExp,
                array(&$this, "replaceCallback"), $query);
  }
};

$builder = new QueryBuilder('foo');
echo $builder->build("SELECT * FROM {books}");
?>
```

Any function in PHP that takes a parameter of type Callback can be one of four types:

➤ *A string with the name of the function to call. The* `create_function()` *example uses this method.*

➤ *An array of two elements with the first element as an object and the second element as the name of a method in the object. The highlighted code in the preceding example uses this method.*

➤ *A string representing a static method (example:* "`hello::world`"*).*

➤ *A certain type of object (more on this one next).*

Doing the extra work and putting the functions directly inside the class as methods makes for much easier-to-read and more manageable code. PHP 5.3 and future versions provide true lambda functions as a method for maintaining code manageability while still providing the benefit of using `create_function()` to define functions without needing to give them a name. However, if that were all lambda functions did, they would just be syntactic sugar without providing any new functionality. The killer application that they bring to the table is the ability to have closures.

Understanding Closures

Closures are a concept that should be very familiar to JavaScript programmers as well as programmers for many other modern languages. A *closure* is a function that wraps (or closes around) the current scope. It has the implication that the scope in which the function is defined will remain accessible for at least as long as the closure itself. To create a closure, first, create a new lambda function in PHP:

```php
<?php
$x = function($number) {
  return $number * 10;
};
echo $x(8); // Output: 80
?>
```

Notice how the function isn't given a name and the result is assigned to a variable. Lambda functions created this way are returned as objects of type `closure`. This can be a source of confusion. Although closure is created transparently in this situation it does not take advantage of any of the properties of a closure.

Lambda functions take advantage of new functionality in PHP 5.3: the ability to call an object as if it were a function. It is possible to emulate the functionality of the `closure` *class by using a new magic method called* `__invoke()`. *The* `__invoke()` *method will be called whenever the class is called as a function.*

Because closures are stored in variables they can be returned from functions and executed outside the scope of the function in which they are defined. The similarities between PHP and many languages with closure end here. Variables are not accessible inside functions unless they are declared as global. In much the same way, variables from the child scope are not accessible from within the closure unless explicitly stated using the use keyword.

One of the benefits of closures is that variables inside of the closure are not necessarily bound to copies of the variables in the parent scope, but can be bound to the actual variables themselves. In a true closure such as JavaScript the latter is usually the case. In PHP, variables are copied into the closure by value. The default behavior can be modified by explicitly typing an ampersand before the variable in the use statement as shown in Listing 2-5.

LISTING 2-5: ClosureTest.class.php

```php
<?php
class ClosureTest {
  public $multiplier;
  public function __construct( $multilier ) {
    $this->multiplier = $multilier;
  }
  public function getClosure() {
    $mul = &$this->multiplier;
    return function( $number ) use( &$mul ) {
      return $mul * $number;
    };
  }
}

$test = new ClosureTest(10);
$x = $test->getClosure();

echo $x(8); // Output: 80
$test->multiplier = 2;
echo $x(8); // Output: 16
?>
```

If either of the ampersands in the getClosure() method are deleted, both outputs will be 80 because the variable $mul inside of the closure will be a copy and not a reference. This can be further illustrated in Listing 2-6, which uses a simple for loop:

LISTING 2-6: ClosureLoop.php

```php
<?php
$i = 0;

$lambda1 = function() use ($i) { echo "$i"; };
$lambda2 = function() use (&$i) { echo "$i"; };

for ( $i=1; $i<=5; $i++ ) {
  $lambda1();
  $lambda2();
```

```
    }
    // Output: 0102030405
    ?>
```

The first closure passes a copy and the second passes by reference. By combining all the new techniques from this chapter you can extend your previous query generation class. The new class will return closure objects that can be passed an arbitrary number of parameters. You will use `sprintf()` for variable replacement but the code, shown in Listing 2-7, will escape all input before inserting it into the query.

LISTING 2-7: QueryBuilderImproved.class.php

```php
<?php
class QueryBuilderImproved extends QueryBuilder {

  public function getQueryObject($query) {
    $self = $this;
    return function() use ($self,$query) {
      $argv = func_get_args();
      foreach ( $argv as $i => $arg )
        $argv[$i] = mysql_escape_string($arg);
      array_unshift($argv, $self->build($query));
      return call_user_func_array( "sprintf", $argv);
    };
  }

};

// Example usage
$builder = new QueryBuilderImproved();
$deleteBook = $builder->getQueryObject("DELETE FROM {books} WHERE id=%d");

$deleteBook( $_GET['id'] );
?>
```

One of the restrictions of closures in PHP is that you cannot pass the keyword `$this` to it. It is not uncommon for languages to have this restriction. The workaround is to assign `$this` to a temporary variable and pass that variable through to the closure instead. `$self` is easy to remember and understand. It is also common practice in other languages with support for closure. `$self` is used throughout this book when using closures. Objects in PHP do not need to be explicitly declared as "by reference"; they are always by reference unless explicitly copied. There isn't any need for an ampersand in front of the operator.

Using the Query Builder for Prototyping

The query builder can be used to generate quick book class that is useful for rapid prototyping. It is not a good idea to release code using this method to production systems. For that, you should separate the methods into completely defined functions. You will be using a static property inside your page class as an array of pointers to closures. Each closure represents a data operation. Only the delete method is used in Listing 2-8, but other methods can be quickly inserted as well.

LISTING 2-8: Book.class.php

```php
<?php
class Book{
  private static $methods = null;
  private static $builder;

  private $database;

  public $id;
  public $authors;
  public $title;
  public $publisher;

  public function __construct( $database ) { $this->database = $database; }

  public function __call($name, $params) {
    if ( !is_array(self::$methods) ) self::init();

    if ( array_key_exists($name, self::$methods) ) {
      array_unshift($params, $this->id);
      $query = call_user_func_array( self::$methods[$name], $params );
      return $this->database->query( $query );
    }
  }

  private static function init() {
    self::$builder = new QueryBuilderImproved();
    self::$methods = array(
      'delete' => self::$builder->getQueryObject("DELETE FROM {books} WHERE id=%d")
    );
  }
}
?>
```

The `BookList` class will need to be updated to use the new page object. The `mysqli_result` object has a `fetch_object()` method, which can be used to automatically load a MySQL result into a class. By passing the name of the class in as the first parameter you can create and load the page object: `$result->fetch_object('Page')`. The method will work as intended regardless of whether the member variables are public or private.

> *Variables that do not exist will be created automatically. The default behavior can be overridden by using the `__set()` magic method. A simple empty setter will disallow creation of any variables that do not exist:*
>
> ```php
> public function __set( $name, $value ) {
>   /* intentionally empty */
> }
> ```

The next steps are to create the update and insert functionality, test the application, and finally convert any prototype class members to complete methods. Both can be done easily using the techniques covered earlier in this chapter.

SUMMARY

This chapter covered one method for separating display and business logic by using the Iterator design pattern. The pattern is defined in PHP by an interface in the Standard PHP Library. The SPL contains several useful interfaces that can be utilized by standard PHP functionality, including:

➤ **Iterator** is used to enable a data set to be easily traversed by standard `foreach` loops. It defines the methods `next()`, `current()`, `rewind()`, `valid()`, and `key()`.

➤ **SeekableIterator** extends the basic `Iterator` interface and adds a definition for a `seek()` method. The `seek()` method should throw an `OutOfBoundsException` if the index being sought is not valid.

➤ **Countable** allows any class that implements it to be enumerated via the PHP `count()` function, which bears the same name as the interface's only method definition.

➤ **ArrayAccess** is an interface that allows the class to be accessed via standard array notation. It specifies the methods needed to read, update, delete, and check the validity of data at specific keys.

You looked at the disadvantages of having business logic in the view and saw how pagination, data access, and reporting can be quickly implemented for specific data sets by combining an iterator with an outer iterator that extends `IteratorIterator` to only show records from a specific page. You also saw how functionality can be generically implemented using lambda functions and closures.

Lambda — dynamic unnamed — functions can be created at run time. Lambda-style functions can be created in any version of PHP greater than 4.0.1 by calling `create_function()` but as of PHP 5.3 you can create true lambda functions. Lambda functions along with closures can be used to create functionality that would be difficult to create otherwise.

Variables from the initiating scope can be passed into the closures by using the `use` keyword. They are passed by value unless they are objects. However, by using an ampersand any variable can also be passed by reference. The keyword `$this` cannot be passed directly into a closure; it must be assigned to a temporary variable first. `$self` is commonly used for this practice. The same technique must be used for any class member.

So far you haven't looked deeply into the inner workings of MySQL. The next chapter goes into detail about the two MySQL drivers available to PHP and the various storage engines that programmers can choose for their MySQL database.

3

MySQL Drivers and Storage Engines

WHAT'S IN THIS CHAPTER?

➤ Understanding the available PHP drivers for MySQL access

➤ Learning about MySQL storage engines

➤ Identifying features of specific storage engines for your application requirements

➤ Learning about the underlying disk layouts, formats, and space requirements of different storage engines

➤ Learning about additional MySQL-related products and specialized storage engines

While it is possible to program in PHP to produce web pages with static data, and with MySQL to create tables and manage data directly, accessing MySQL information via PHP completes the integration of LAMP stack functionality and provides a data-driven dynamic web site.

MySQL can be accessed in PHP by two different MySQL drivers. This chapter looks at these various options and the different features for drivers.

MySQL is a unique database that allows for different approaches to storing and accessing data via the concept of a storage engine. With different MySQL storage engines comes a variety of different features that can dramatically affect the application experience. As a developer, it is important to understand the differences between features, including transactional and non-transactional support, various table- and row-level locking strategies, and data integrity with foreign keys as well as different index types including btree, hash, and full-text. This chapter discusses the default built-in storage engines with MySQL and describes the variety of different engines and associated products that can operate like a MySQL database, but provide a wide variety of features and different performance.

MYSQL DRIVERS

As of PHP 5.3 there are two different libraries available for interfacing PHP with MySQL. Traditionally PHP is compiled against libmysql. It is an external C library that implements the low-level protocol for communicating with MySQL servers. But it does have a few drawbacks:

➤ It is difficult to compile against because it is necessary to first download the MySQL distribution onto the PHP server.

➤ The GPL license that is used for libmysql is not compatible with the PHP license.

➤ Persistent connections are not supported in MySQLi using libmysql.

Fortunately PHP 5.3 came along and with it: mysqlnd. The name mysqlnd stands for *MySQL Native Driver (for PHP)*, and it is an implementation of the MySQL protocol written completely with PHP in mind. It is also licensed under the PHP license. Solving the licensing issues means that it can be distributed with PHP so you no longer need to download a copy of MySQL on the same machine.

The improved library also adds persistent connections to MySQLi but the benefits don't stop there:

➤ It is reported that mysqlnd has better performance.

➤ The function `mysqli_fetch_all()` works with mysqlnd.

➤ Performance statistics calls were added to MySQLi.

The fact that it is a native PHP extension also means that it makes use of PHP memory management routines and libraries. Thus making it tightly integrated with PHP and providing better memory performance and resource limiting.

Both extensions conform to the MySQL API so it is transparent to the other extensions that use it. You can compile against either library, just don't use any of the new functionality with the old library. To compile against mysqlnd simple configure PHP with:

```
./configure --with-mysql=mysqlnd \
            --with-mysqli=mysqlnd
```

It is possible to use either of the MySQL libraries in your installation. However, it is a good idea to use mysqlnd. It has all the benefits of the non-native MySQL driver and then some and in the future it will be better maintained.

 This book does not explicitly take advantage of any of the functionality of mysqlnd. It also uses the original MySQL extension instead of MySQLi in many cases. This is to make code easier to read and quicker to get up and running. In a production environment it is recommended that you use the mysqlnd library and MySQLi or PDO for data access.

ABOUT MYSQL STORAGE ENGINES

MySQL as a relational database offers a unique feature in the management of data — it offers different storage engines that define different characteristics for the persistence and retrieval of your information.

Each storage engine has relative strengths and weaknesses; the choice of one engine for one task may not be ideal for another. MySQL supports the use of multiple storage engines in a single schema; however, complexity in execution and functionality such as transaction support and backup strategy are all affected.

Beginning with MySQL 5.1, MySQL offers the *pluggable storage engine architecture (PSEA)*, where it is possible for a vendor to provide a runtime storage engine that can be loaded dynamically in an operational environment. While the theory enables this, in practice only a few engines have been able to achieve it. Limitations with the customization of internal MySQL features including parsing and optimizing SQL statements, and the changes in the specification in point releases leading to incompatibilities, has made it impossible for creative solutions with optimized data management to work seamlessly. Many providers have been forced to produce custom MySQL binaries.

Some of the different features of storage engines include:

➤ Transactional and non-transactional

➤ Persistent and non-persistent

➤ Table and row level locking

➤ Different index methods such as btree, hash, and rtree

➤ Clustered indexes, primary and secondary

➤ Data compression

➤ Full-text searching

Obtaining Storage Engine Information

This section covers the various ways to obtain information about storage engines for the tables that you have defined in your database schemas.

Available Engines

The SHOW.ENGINES command and the INFORMATION_SCHEMA.ENGINES table provide information on what engines are available in your current MySQL instance. This includes details of whether the engine is supported (for example, look at FEDERATED section in the code that follows) and whether the engine is transactional or non-transactional.

```
mysql> SHOW ENGINES\G
*************************** 1. row ***************************
      Engine: InnoDB
     Support: YES
     Comment: Supports transactions, row-level locking, and foreign keys
Transactions: YES
```

```
            XA: YES
    Savepoints: YES
...
*************************** 5. row ***************************
        Engine: MEMORY
       Support: YES
       Comment: Hash based, stored in memory, useful for temporary tables
  Transactions: NO
            XA: NO
    Savepoints: NO
*************************** 6. row ***************************
        Engine: FEDERATED
       Support: NO
       Comment: Federated MySQL storage engine
  Transactions: NULL
            XA: NULL
    Savepoints: NULL
...
*************************** 8. row ***************************
        Engine: MyISAM
       Support: DEFAULT
       Comment: Default engine as of MySQL 3.23 with great performance
  Transactions: NO
            XA: NO
    Savepoints: NO
```

Defining the Storage Engine

The default storage engine for official MySQL binaries is the `MyISAM` engine. You can alter this with the system variable `default-storage-engine` when defined in the MySQL configuration my.cnf file.

Generally you will specify the storage engine in a `CREATE TABLE` or `ALTER TABLE` command. This occurs after the column definitions, and is specified with the `ENGINE` option, as shown in Listing 3-1.

LISTING 3-1: simple-examples.sql

```
mysql> CREATE TABLE example_myisam(
    > id INT UNSIGNED NOT NULL AUTO_INCREMENT PRIMARY KEY,
    > c  VARCHAR(100) NOT NULL)
    > ENGINE=MyISAM;

mysql> SHOW CREATE TABLE example_myisam\G
*************************** 1. row ***************************
        Table: example_myisam
Create Table: CREATE TABLE `example_myisam` (
  `id` int(10) unsigned NOT NULL AUTO_INCREMENT,
  `c` varchar(100) NOT NULL,
  PRIMARY KEY (`id`)
```

```
) ENGINE=MyISAM DEFAULT CHARSET=latin1

mysql> CREATE TABLE example_memory(
    > id INT UNSIGNED NOT NULL AUTO_INCREMENT PRIMARY KEY,
    > c  VARCHAR(100) NOT NULL)
    > ENGINE=MEMORY;

mysql> SHOW CREATE TABLE example_memory\G
*************************** 1. row ***************************
       Table: example_memory
Create Table: CREATE TABLE `example_memory` (
  `id` int(10) unsigned NOT NULL AUTO_INCREMENT,
  `c` varchar(100) NOT NULL,
  PRIMARY KEY (`id`)
) ENGINE=MEMORY DEFAULT CHARSET=latin1
```

If you do not specify a storage engine with the CREATE TABLE command, the default is used as shown in Listing 3-2.

LISTING 3-2: noengine-example.sql

```
mysql> SELECT @@storage_engine\G
*************************** 1. row ***************************
@@storage_engine: MyISAM

mysql> CREATE TABLE example_noengine(
    > id INT UNSIGNED NOT NULL AUTO_INCREMENT PRIMARY KEY,
      c  VARCHAR(100) NOT NULL);

mysql> SHOW CREATE TABLE example_noengine\G
*************************** 1. row ***************************
       Table: example_noengine
Create Table: CREATE TABLE `example_noengine` (
  `id` int(10) unsigned NOT NULL AUTO_INCREMENT,
  `c` varchar(100) NOT NULL,
  PRIMARY KEY (`id`)
) ENGINE=MyISAM DEFAULT CHARSET=latin1
```

Storage engines may also have specific settings. For example, MAX_ROWS is applicable only to MyISAM. The MySQL parser is generally incapable of determining which options are storage engine–specific, so while a table structure definition may include additional options, they may not apply. Refer to the MySQL Reference Manual for more information.

Confirming a Table Storage Engine

You have three ways to determine the storage engine of a table with the mysql client. You can use the SHOW CREATE TABLE command to find the full table structure, including all table options:

```
mysql> SHOW CREATE TABLE mysql.db\G
*************************** 1. row ***************************
       Table: db
```

```
Create Table: CREATE TABLE `db` (
  `Host` char(60) COLLATE utf8_bin NOT NULL DEFAULT '',
  `Db` char(64) COLLATE utf8_bin NOT NULL DEFAULT '',
  `User` char(16) COLLATE utf8_bin NOT NULL DEFAULT '',
...
  PRIMARY KEY (`Host`,`Db`,`User`),
  KEY `User` (`User`)
) ENGINE=MyISAM DEFAULT CHARSET=utf8 COLLATE=utf8_bin
```

You can use the SHOW TABLE STATUS command to obtain table statistics and engine-specific details:

```
mysql> USE mysql
mysql> SHOW TABLE STATUS LIKE 'db'\G
*************************** 1. row ***************************
           Name: db
         Engine: MyISAM
        Version: 10
     Row_format: Fixed
           Rows: 2
  ...
        Comment: Database privileges
```

You can use the INFORMATION_SCHEMA to obtain the same information from the SHOW CREATE TABLE and SHOW TABLE STATUS commands (see Listing 3-3):

LISTING 3-3: show-tables.sql

Available for
download on
Wrox.com

```
SELECT table_schema, table_name, engine, version, row_format
FROM information_schema.tables;
+--------------------+------------------------+--------+---------+------------+
| table_schema       | table_name             | engine | version | row_format |
+--------------------+------------------------+--------+---------+------------+
...
| information_schema | COLUMNS                | MyISAM |      10 | Dynamic    |
| information_schema | TABLES                 | MEMORY |      10 | Fixed      |
...
| mysql              | db                     | MyISAM |      10 | Fixed      |
| mysql              | event                  | MyISAM |      10 | Dynamic    |
| mysql              | func                   | MyISAM |      10 | Fixed      |
| mysql              | general_log            | CSV    |      10 | Dynamic    |
| mysql              | slow_log               | CSV    |      10 | Dynamic    |
| mysql              | user                   | MyISAM |      10 | Dynamic    |
...
+--------------------+------------------------+--------+---------+------------+
```

Storage engines have three important characteristics:

➤ Engine name

➤ Version

➤ Row format

These are discussed in more detail with the individual engines.

DEFAULT STORAGE ENGINES

By default, MySQL official binaries include a number of different built-in storage engines. The following are supplied and enabled by default in a MySQL 5.1 binary distribution:

➤ MyISAM

➤ InnoDB

➤ Memory

➤ Blackhole

➤ Archive

➤ Merge

➤ CSV

 The Federated *engine is provided in MySQL 5.1 source code but is not enabled by default. As of 5.1.38, the* InnoDB *plugin version 1.04 is included in the binary distribution but is not enabled by default.*

MyISAM

MyISAM is the default storage engine of MySQL 5.1. This engine is an implementation of the well-defined database storage ISAM architecture and has been available since MySQL 3.x.

Key Features

➤ Non-transactional

➤ Fast insert rate

➤ Btree based indexes

➤ Supports FULLTEXT index

➤ 16k data pages

➤ 4k index pages

Limitations

➤ Non-transactional

➤ Fast insert rate

➤ Btree based indexes

➤ Supports FULLTEXT index

➤ 16k data pages

➤ 4k index pages

Important Parameters

➤ `key_buffer_size`: This buffer is used for holding data from MyISAM indexes. MyISAM can also support the definition of multiple index caches and enables the ability for pinning of specific table indexes per named buffer.

➤ `table_cache`: This buffer holds information of open tables that are used when running queries. While applicable to all storage engines, due to additional files, it is important to tune this parameter when there are a lot of tables and complex queries.

➤ `bulk_insert_buffer_size`: This buffer is used for improving INSERT statements with a large number of VALUES or INSERT…SELECT as well as LOAD DATA INFILE.

➤ `myisam_recover`: This parameter defines the storage engine default recovery mode. A recommended value is FORCE, BACKUP.

Examples

A MyISAM table is represented as three separate files in the file system located in the defined data directory for the MySQL instance. These files are:

➤ `table.frm`: This is the table format definition file.

➤ `table.MYD`: This is the MyISAM data file.

➤ `table.MYI`: This is the MyISAM index file.

MyISAM has three different row formats. By default, MyISAM determines whether to use Fixed or Dynamic format based on the column definitions specified in the table. The Fixed row format provides a calculation to determine the offset of the row within the data file, and can provide a small improvement in performance. You can force MyISAM to used Fixed format; however, this can lead to an increased disk footprint (see Listing 3-4).

LISTING 3-4: myisam-examples.sql

```
CREATE TABLE example_myisam_fixed(
    id INT UNSIGNED NOT NULL AUTO_INCREMENT PRIMARY KEY,
    c  CHAR(100) NOT NULL)
ENGINE=MyISAM;

CREATE TABLE example_myisam_dynamic(
    id INT UNSIGNED NOT NULL AUTO_INCREMENT PRIMARY KEY,
    c  VARCHAR(100) NOT NULL)
ENGINE=MyISAM;

CREATE TABLE example_myisam_fixed2(
    id INT UNSIGNED NOT NULL AUTO_INCREMENT PRIMARY KEY,
```

```
     c  VARCHAR(100) NOT NULL)
ENGINE=MyISAM ROW_FORMAT=FIXED;

SELECT table_name, engine,row_format
FROM INFORMATION_SCHEMA.TABLES
WHERE table_name LIKE 'example_myisam_%';
+------------------------+--------+------------+
| table_name             | engine | row_format |
+------------------------+--------+------------+
| example_myisam_dynamic | MyISAM | Dynamic    |
| example_myisam_fixed   | MyISAM | Fixed      |
| example_myisam_fixed2  | MyISAM | Fixed      |
+------------------------+--------+------------+
```

You can see the difference in size when you load data into these tables. Using the standard Linux dictionary file generally located in /usr/share/dict/words you have the following table sizes as shown in Listing 3-5.

LISTING 3-5: load-myisam.sql

```
LOAD DATA INFILE '/usr/share/dict/words' INTO TABLE example_myisam_dynamic(c);
LOAD DATA INFILE '/usr/share/dict/words' INTO TABLE example_myisam_fixed(c);
LOAD DATA INFILE '/usr/share/dict/words' INTO TABLE example_myisam_fixed2(c);
SELECT table_name,table_rows,row_format,
       data_length/1024 AS data,index_length/1024 AS indx
FROM   INFORMATION_SCHEMA.TABLES
WHERE  table_name LIKE 'example_myisam_%';
+------------------------+------------+------------+------------+-------------+
| table_name             | table_rows | row_format | data       | indx        |
+------------------------+------------+------------+------------+-------------+
| example_myisam_dynamic |     234936 | Dynamic    |  4842.6484 |   2359.0000 |
| example_myisam_fixed   |     234936 | Fixed      | 24090.1172 |   2356.0000 |
| example_myisam_fixed2  |     234936 | Fixed      | 24319.5469 |   2356.0000 |
+------------------------+------------+------------+------------+-------------+
```

MyISAM provides a third row format called Compressed; however, there is no mysql client or SQL command to specify this format. This is created with the myisampack command. This command works directly on the .MYD data file, and should be executed only when the database is not in use.

```
$ myisampack data/test/example_myisam_fixed2.MYI

Compressing data/test/example_myisam_fixed2.MYD: (234936 records)
- Calculating statistics
- Compressing file
90.62%
Remember to run myisamchk -rq on compressed tables
myisamchk -rq data/test/example_myisam_fixed.MYI
- check record delete-chain
- recovering (with sort) MyISAM-table 'data/test/example_myisam_fixed.MYI'
Data records: 234936
- Fixing index 1
```

The key advantage of a compressed table is a reduction in disk footprint as now shown by reviewing the size of the table:

```
SELECT table_name,table_rows,row_format,
       data_length/1024 AS data,index_length/1024 AS indx
FROM   INFORMATION_SCHEMA.TABLES
WHERE  table_name LIKE 'example_myisam_%';
+-----------------------+------------+------------+------------+------------+
| table_name            | table_rows | row_format | data       | indx       |
+-----------------------+------------+------------+------------+------------+
| example_myisam_dynamic|     234936 | Dynamic    |  4842.6484 |  2359.0000 |
| example_myisam_fixed  |     234936 | Fixed      | 24090.1172 |  2356.0000 |
| example_myisam_fixed2 |     234936 | Compressed |  2280.2529 |  2356.0000 |
+-----------------------+------------+------------+------------+------------+
```

The difference with a compressed table is that you cannot insert any data. For example:

```
INSERT INTO example_myisam_fixed VALUES(NULL,'x');
Query OK, 1 row affected (0.00 sec)

INSERT INTO example_myisam_fixed2 VALUES(NULL,'x');
ERROR 1036 (HY000): Table 'example_myisam_fixed2' is read only
```

The current version for MyISAM data since MySQL 5.x has been Version 10. It is possible when upgrading MySQL from 4.x, that the internal structure of a MyISAM table is not upgraded to the current version. In this case you should always perform an ALTER statement to upgrade the version. The following code shows the difference in MySQL versions:

```
SELECT VERSION();
+-----------------+
| VERSION()       |
+-----------------+
| 4.1.22-standard |
+-----------------+

SHOW TABLE STATUS LIKE 'user'\G
*************************** 1. row ***************************
           Name: user
         Engine: MyISAM
        Version: 9
     Row_format: Dynamic
           Rows: 4
 ...

SELECT VERSION();
+-----------------+
| VERSION()       |
+-----------------+
| 5.1.31-1ubuntu2 |
+-----------------+

SHOW TABLE STATUS LIKE 'user'\G
*************************** 1. row ***************************
           Name: user
```

```
    Engine: MyISAM
   Version: 10
Row_format: Dynamic
      Rows: 6
...
```

When to Use MyISAM

MyISAM can be an ideal engine in a high read environment, or in a high write environment, but is not suited for a read/write environment. The key problem is that DML statements cause table-level locking. When this occurs all pending reads are blocked until the DML statement is completed.

You can see this in operation by running a benchmark that executes a large number of repeating SELECT statements. When reviewing the SHOW PROCESSLIST you will not see a state of Locked. When you introduce a single UPDATE, for example, that takes time to execute, you will see all future SELECT statements also displayed as Locked.

Perhaps the greatest problem with MyISAM is its lack of data integrity during a MySQL instance crash. MyISAM achieves its high volume write throughput in a number of ways. One way is the lack of transactions, and therefore the lack of overhead to provide consistency during rollback. The second is the lack of disk synchronization of index data during DML statements. In the example of an INSERT statement, the data is written and synced on disk, but the index data is not. It is held in the key_buffer and written to disk, but not synced.

In the event of a server crash, the index file may be inconsistent, and may require recovery via the REPAIR TABLE command. There are several problems here. The first is that you generally do not know the extent of corruption until the table and index is accessed. Although there is a CHECK TABLE command, this is only an indicator, and can provide a false positive. The second is that recovery time is dependent on your database size. As your database grows, the time for possible recovery also increases. This lack of reproducibility in time can cause great problems in planning and support of a timely recovery. The future replacement to MyISAM is the Maria storage engine, which provides the benefits of MyISAM and includes full crash recovery.

Though many installations move to using transactional tables for all data, it is not possible to eliminate MyISAM because this is used internally by MySQL in the mysql meta schema.

InnoDB

While the MyISAM storage engine is the default and widely used due to lack of knowledge of understanding the different storage engines, the InnoDB storage engine is the most popular engine used by more established MySQL users and organizations. The primary reason is full transactional support.

Key Features

➤   Transactional

➤   Fully ACID compliant

➤   Supports MVCC (Multi Version Concurrency Control) and four isolation levels

➤   Row level locking

➤ Supports foreign keys

➤ Supported by a commercial entity Innobase as the primary product

➤ Primary key is a clustered index

Limitations

➤ Does not support full text indexes

➤ Table level locking on DDL statements

➤ Owned by company with other commercial interests and competing products

➤ Not as open as other open source offerings in the development roadmap

➤ Generally 2x–3x greater disk space requirements to `MyISAM`

Important Parameters

➤ **`innodb_buffer_pool_size`**: Defines the amount of system memory allocated to `InnoDB` internal data storage.

➤ **`innodb_log_file_size`**: Defines the amount of disk storage assigned for the `InnoDB` transaction logs. The total disk size is `innodb_log_file_size` times `innodb_log_files_in_group`.

➤ **`innodb_flush_log_at_trx_commit`**: Defines how `InnoDB` should flush the transaction logs to disk. A change in this variable is used to increase performance; however, this decreases durability.

➤ **`innodb_thread_concurrency`**: Defines the number of internal threads the `InnoDB` kernel can use to manage transaction concurrency.

➤ **`innodb_flush_method`**: Determines which system calls and options are used to flush data and log transactions.

Of all the storage engines `InnoDB` *has the greatest number of parameters. For a full list of parameters go to* `http://dev.mysql.com/doc/refman/5.1/en/innodb-parameters.html`. `InnoDB` *also has the most information on monitoring output via the* `SHOW ENGINE INNODB STATUS` *and* `SHOW GLOBAL STATUS LIKE 'innodb%'` *commands.*

Understanding InnoDB Table Usage

By default an `Innodb` table is represented as two separate files in the file system located in the defined data directory for the MySQL instance. These files are:

➤ **`table.frm`**: This is the table format definition file.

➤ **`ibdata1`**: This is the default `InnoDB` tablespace for all tables.

In addition, `InnoDB` generally has two transaction log files that are critical for operation:

➤ `ib_logfile0`

➤ `ib_logfile1`

You can change the names and locations of the default names for `InnoDB` tablespace and log files via various configuration options.

Differences from MyISAM

As a developer you should be aware of specific differences between `MyISAM` and `InnoDB`. As mentioned, the primary reason to use `InnoDB` is transactional support. With this support comes a number of other features — a significant one is that of row-level locking. `MyISAM`, though very fast, suffers from table-level locking in a high write and read environment. This can be overcome by simply changing tables to use `InnoDB`.

However, impacts to altering the storage engine can affect both functionality and performance of your MySQL databases. A few important considerations for developers are:

➤ Increase in disk footprint

➤ Impact on disk storage due to Primary key type

➤ Performance of `COUNT(*)`

➤ No support for `FULLTEXT` indexes

➤ Differences in SQL Query Execution Plan (QEP)

The first is disk footprint. `InnoDB` generally uses two to three times more disk space. Although the sample table is very basic, you can see an increase in disk space (see Listing 3-6).

LISTING 3-6: innodb-example.sql

Available for download on Wrox.com

```
CREATE TABLE example_innodb(
    id INT UNSIGNED NOT NULL AUTO_INCREMENT PRIMARY KEY,
    c  VARCHAR(100) NOT NULL)
ENGINE=InnoDB;
LOAD DATA INFILE '/usr/share/dict/words' INTO TABLE example_innodb(c);
SELECT table_name,table_rows,row_format,
        data_length/1024 AS data,index_length/1024 AS indx
FROM   INFORMATION_SCHEMA.TABLES
WHERE  table_name LIKE 'example_myisam_%';
+------------------------+------------+------------+------------+-------------+
| table_name             | table_rows | row_format | data       | indx        |
+------------------------+------------+------------+------------+-------------+
| example_myisam_dynamic |     234936 | Dynamic    |  4842.6484 |   2359.0000 |
| example_innodb         |     240903 | Compact    |  8720.0000 |      0.0000 |
+------------------------+------------+------------+------------+-------------+
```

The primary cause for this is the use of a clustered primary key index that stores all data in the table in primary key order. This provides significant benefits for primary key ordered searching; however this impacts disk footprint. This is important to understand because `InnoDB` disk pages that are 16K are read and stored into the `innodb_buffer_pool` also as 16K pages. Inefficient disk storage with unused portions of these pages leads to less effective memory usage, and ultimately an impact in overall performance.

When data is inserted into an `InnoDB` table in primary key order, for example an `AUTO_INCREMENT` column, `InnoDB` will use 15/16th of the data page. When data is not inserted in primary key order, for example a natural key, by default `InnoDB` will use only a 50 percent fill factor of data pages. These figures are not tunable.

> *While* `MyISAM` *provides exact counts of the number of rows in given tables in the MySQL meta data,* `InnoDB` *row counts are approximate as shown in the preceding example. Care should be taken because in some circumstances these names can be drastically inaccurate. For an example, see* `http://ronaldbradford.com/blog/mysql_information_schema-table_rows-out-by-a-factor-of-100x-2009-09-09/`.

`InnoDB` also stores information in secondary indexes differently from `MyISAM`. Within the btree structure of the secondary index, `InnoDB` stores the value you are indexing, and also stores the value of the primary key. In `MyISAM` the index stores the value you are indexing and a pointer to the row of data that includes the value of the primary key. This is very significant when you have tables with large-width primary keys and your table has a lot of secondary indexes. An example is using a 40 byte, 3-column primary key column and having 19 indexes. By introducing a short 4-byte primary key, the index disk footprint was reduced by 75 percent of the original size.

Generally when using `InnoDB`, it is best to keep your primary key as short as possible. Listing 3-7 only has a small number of indexes, but gives you an indication.

LISTING 3-7: wide-innodb.sql

```sql
CREATE TABLE wide_myisam (
  word VARCHAR(100) NOT NULL,
  reverse_word VARCHAR(100) NOT NULL,
  soundex_word VARCHAR(100) NOT NULL,
  contains_a  ENUM('Y','N') NOT NULL DEFAULT 'N',
  md5 CHAR(32) NOT NULL,
PRIMARY KEY(word),
INDEX (soundex_word),
UNIQUE INDEX (md5),
INDEX (reverse_word(10))
) ENGINE=MyISAM DEFAULT CHARSET latin1 COLLATE latin1_general_cs;
INSERT INTO wide_myisam (word,reverse_word,soundex_word,contains_a,md5)
SELECT DISTINCT c,REVERSE(c),SOUNDEX(c),IF(INSTR(c,'a')>0,'Y','N'),MD5(c)
FROM example_innodb;

CREATE TABLE wide_innodb (
```

```
    word VARCHAR(100) NOT NULL,
    reverse_word VARCHAR(100) NOT NULL,
    soundex_word VARCHAR(100) NOT NULL,
    contains_a  ENUM('Y','N') NOT NULL DEFAULT 'N',
    md5 CHAR(32) NOT NULL,
PRIMARY KEY(word),
INDEX (soundex_word),
UNIQUE INDEX (md5),
INDEX (reverse_word(10))
) ENGINE=InnoDB DEFAULT CHARSET latin1 COLLATE latin1_general_cs;
INSERT INTO wide_innodb (word,reverse_word,soundex_word,contains_a,md5)
SELECT DISTINCT c,REVERSE(c),SOUNDEX(c),IF(INSTR(c,'a')>0,'Y','N'),MD5(c)
FROM example_innodb;

SELECT table_name,table_rows,row_format,
       data_length/1024 AS data,index_length/1024 AS indx
FROM    INFORMATION_SCHEMA.TABLES
WHERE   table_name LIKE 'wide_%';
+-------------+------------+------------+------------+------------+
| table_name  | table_rows | row_format | data       | indx       |
+-------------+------------+------------+------------+------------+
| wide_innodb |     224025 | Compact    | 23104.0000 | 39536.0000 |
| wide_myisam |     234936 | Dynamic    | 15086.1836 | 20962.0000 |
+-------------+------------+------------+------------+------------+
```

You see from this example that the total disk footprint of the InnoDB table is an increase of 70 percent over MyISAM; however, the index portion is 100 percent larger. When you introduce an AUTO_INCREMENT primary key as shown in Listing 3-8 you see a reduction in disk footprint of the data portion by 10 percent. You also see a 5 percent reduction in index space, but you have indeed added an additional index to simulate the primary key.

LISTING 3-8: wide-innodb-with-pk.sql

```
CREATE TABLE wide_innodb_with_pk (
    id INT UNSIGNED NOT NULL AUTO_INCREMENT,
    word VARCHAR(100) NOT NULL,
    reverse_word VARCHAR(100) NOT NULL,
    soundex_word VARCHAR(100) NOT NULL,
    contains_a  ENUM('Y','N') NOT NULL DEFAULT 'N',
    md5 CHAR(32) NOT NULL,
PRIMARY KEY(id),
UNIQUE INDEX(word),
INDEX (soundex_word),
UNIQUE INDEX (md5),
INDEX (reverse_word(10))
) ENGINE=InnoDB DEFAULT CHARSET latin1 COLLATE latin1_general_cs;


INSERT INTO wide_innodb_with_pk (word,reverse_word,soundex_word,contains_a,md5)
SELECT DISTINCT c,REVERSE(c),SOUNDEX(c),IF(INSTR(c,'a')>0,'Y','N'),MD5(c)
FROM example_innodb;
SELECT table_name,table_rows,row_format,
```

```
            data_length/1024 AS data, index_length/1024 AS indx
FROM     INFORMATION_SCHEMA.TABLES
WHERE    table_name LIKE 'wide_%';
```

```
+---------------------+------------+------------+------------+------------+
| table_name          | table_rows | row_format | data       | indx       |
+---------------------+------------+------------+------------+------------+
| wide_innodb         |     243525 | Compact    | 23104.0000 | 39536.0000 |
| wide_innodb_with_pk |     244771 | Compact    | 21040.0000 | 39040.0000 |
| wide_myisam         |     234936 | Dynamic    | 15086.1836 | 20962.0000 |
+---------------------+------------+------------+------------+------------
```

As you start to add additional indexes you get to see a greater difference. Using the MyISAM index data as a control test, the InnoDB table with the same structure is 100 percent larger, whereas the InnoDB table with the AUTO_INCREMENT primary key is only 80 percent larger. Although these tables are small, you can see the impact of a single column change.

```
+---------------------+------------+------------+------------+------------+
| table_name          | table_rows | row_format | data       | indx       |
+---------------------+------------+------------+------------+------------+
| wide_innodb         |     239154 | Compact    | 21056.0000 | 67408.0000 |
| wide_innodb_with_pk |     235054 | Compact    | 22064.0000 | 59488.0000 |
| wide_myisam         |     234936 | Dynamic    | 16003.9023 | 32535.0000 |
+---------------------+------------+------------+------------+------------+
```

Applications that use SELECT COUNT(*) FROM TABLE when using MyISAM will find an instant response, whereas for InnoDB this must be calculated by reading the data. For large tables this can cause a high performance impact as disk I/O, and flushing of data from the internal buffer pool affects other online operations significantly. Using an index to retrieve a portion of rows to perform a COUNT(*) is the necessary alteration to overcome a full table scan for your application.

In smaller MySQL environments you can find the use of the FULLTEXT index for text searching. This type of index is only supported in MyISAM. In this situation is it generally the approach to duplicate the columns in a second table that remains a MyISAM table. This generally gives you all the features of InnoDB, as well as the FULLTEXT feature of MyISAM. There are data integrity, performance, and disaster recovery impacts with this approach. Care should always be taken with important design considerations to realize the total impact for your entire system.

Optimizing SQL Using InnoDB

The final point for discussion about InnoDB is that of SQL optimizations. Internally MySQL parses a SQL query and then determines via a cost-based optimizer the best means of satisfying the query in the quickest time. The optimizer uses information about table indexes and the statistics of column distribution to determine the best execution path. MySQL by default uses only one index per table in an SQL query (with a few minor exceptions). When joining multiple tables, especially intersection tables, only one index is used. When converting a table from MyISAM to InnoDB, you cannot assume the same indexes will be used when your query is executed. It is important that you review the Query Execution Plan (QEP) via the EXPLAIN syntax. Two differences that affect how data is stored and retrieved have already been discussed. With InnoDB data is now in primary key order, and this provides for sequential reading of data when using a primary key. The second point is that the value of the primary key is stored in a secondary index, allowing for this value to be used in some situations as if it were a second indexed column of the index.

As with any changes in your application it is important that you test these changes under realistic production conditions. Converting tables from MyISAM to InnoDB while changing application functionality can result in worse performance when the MySQL environment is not tuned appropriately, or particular situations including those discussed are not understood and considered as impacts.

Memory

The Memory storage engine, also known historically as the Heap storage engine, is an in-memory only table that does not provide data persistence. The Memory storage engine is actually used internally by the mysql kernel when a temporary table is required.

Key Features

➤   Very fast, in memory

➤   Non-transactional

➤   Supports the hash index by default

➤   Btree indexes also supported

➤   Ideal for primary key lookups

Limitations

➤   Does not support transactions

➤   Table level locking on DML and DDL statements

➤   Data not persistent

➤   Does not support TEXT/BLOB data types

➤   Fixed row width

➤   No ability to limit the total amount of memory for all Memory tables

Important Parameters

➤   **max_heap_table_size**: Defines the maximum size of a single Memory table.

➤   **tmp_table_size**: Defines the maximum size of the table when used for internally temporary tables.

➤   **init_file**: Defines a SQL file of commands that are executed when the MySQL instance is started. Used as a means to seed Memory tables.

Example Table Usage

The syntax for creating a Memory table (as shown in Listing 3-9) is identical to previous examples.

LISTING 3-9: memory-example.sql

```
CREATE TABLE example_memory(
    id INT UNSIGNED NOT NULL AUTO_INCREMENT PRIMARY KEY,
    c  VARCHAR(100) NOT NULL)
ENGINE=Memory;
```

Memory tables are confined to a maximum table size as defined by the `max_heap_table_size` system variable. Listing 3-10 demonstrates the table full error message, and corrects the maximum size, based on the size of the comparison `Fixed MyISAM` table size to show the data in a `Memory` table.

LISTING 3-10: memory-load.sql

```
LOAD DATA INFILE '/usr/share/dict/words' INTO TABLE example_memory (c);
ERROR 1114 (HY000): The table 'example_memory' is full

SELECT table_name,table_rows,row_format,
       data_length/1024 AS data,index_length/1024 AS indx
FROM   INFORMATION_SCHEMA.TABLES
WHERE  table_name LIKE 'example_memory%';
+----------------+------------+------------+------------+-----------+
| table_name     | table_rows | row_format | data       | indx      |
+----------------+------------+------------+------------+-----------+
| example_memory |     144595 | Fixed      | 15310.2539 | 1134.4219 |
+----------------+------------+------------+------------+-----------+

SHOW GLOBAL VARIABLES LIKE 'max_heap_table_size';
+---------------------+----------+
| Variable_name       | Value    |
+---------------------+----------+
| max_heap_table_size | 16777216 |
+---------------------+----------+

SET SESSION max_heap_table_size = 256*1024*1024;
TRUNCATE TABLE example_memory
LOAD DATA INFILE '/tmp/words' INTO TABLE example_memory (c);
Query OK, 234936 rows affected (0.37 sec)

SELECT table_name,table_rows,row_format,
       data_length/1024 AS data,index_length/1024 AS indx
FROM   INFORMATION_SCHEMA.TABLES
WHERE  table_name LIKE 'example_memory%';
+----------------+------------+------------+------------+-----------+
| table_name     | table_rows | row_format | data       | indx      |
+----------------+------------+------------+------------+-----------+
| example_memory |     234936 | Fixed      | 24927.4258 | 1897.1172 |
+----------------+------------+------------+------------+-----------+
```

When using large memory tables, a consideration is table-level locking. While adding an index is generally considered a method for performance tuning SQL queries, with memory tables you need to factor the size of the memory table, the cost of maintaining the index, and the type of index. For example, take a typical session table. While the purpose is to insert and update content, it is necessary to implement a purging process of old or stale sessions. It is important to consider two limitations of the Memory table: table-level locking and the index type. Listing 3-11 is an example session table.

LISTING 3-11: memory-session.sql

```
CREATE TABLE example_memory_session(
   user_id   INT UNSIGNED NOT NULL,
   session   VARCHAR(1000) NOT NULL,
   created   TIMESTAMP NOT NULL DEFAULT CURRENT_TIMESTAMP,
   updated   TIMESTAMP NOT NULL,
PRIMARY KEY(user_id))
ENGINE=Memory;
```

The SQL of your application would include statements to create and modify session information for example:

```
INSERT INTO example_memory_session (user_id,session,created,updated)
                          VALUES  (?, ?, NOW(), NOW());
UPDATE example_memory_session
SET    session=?, updated = NOW()
WHERE user_id =?
```

You would remove old session information with a DELETE statement such as:

```
DELETE from example_memory_session WHERE updated < NOW() - INTERVAL ? HOUR;
```

Listing 3-12 simulates existing sessions by using a stored procedure to create data for a 24 hour period.

LISTING 3-12: load-session.sql

```
/* Based on
   http://datacharmer.blogspot.com/2006/06/filling-test-tables-quickly.html
*/

delimiter $$

drop procedure if exists make_dates $$
CREATE PROCEDURE make_dates( max_recs int)
begin
  declare updated datetime;
  declare rand_min int;
  declare numrecs int default 1;

  truncate table example_memory_session;
  while numrecs < max_recs
  do
    select round(rand() * 1440) INTO rand_min;
    set updated = date_format( now() -
                  interval rand_min minute, '%Y-%m-%d %H:%i:00');
    insert into example_memory_session (user_id, session, updated)
```

```
                                        values (numrecs, REPEAT('A',5), updated);
      set numrecs = numrecs + 1;
    end while;
    select count(*) from example_memory_session;
  end $$

  delimiter ;
```

You can run this on a table to create 1,000,000 records. You need about 1 GB of RAM to simulate this deleting process.

```
SET SESSION max_heap_table_size = 1024*1024*1024;
call make_dates (1000000);
DELETE from example_memory_session WHERE updated < NOW() - INTERVAL 10 HOUR;
Query OK, 587795 rows affected (2.08 sec)
```

Note that during this time of approximately two seconds, the table is locked, and no INSERT or UPDATE statements can be performed. This is unusable in most production environments with any reasonable number of concurrent users. The obvious choice is to add an index and test:

```
ALTER TABLE example_memory_session ADD INDEX (updated);
call make_dates (1000000);
DELETE from example_memory_session WHERE updated < NOW() - INTERVAL 10 HOUR;
Query OK, 585065 rows affected (29.29 sec)
```

This was an unexpected result. With an index, you generally see an improvement in performance; however, the DELETE now takes 10 times as long. Let's review the Query Execution Plan (QEP) to identify a possible cause.

```
EXPLAIN SELECT * from example_memory_session
WHERE updated < NOW() - INTERVAL 10 HOUR\G
*************************** 1. row ***************************
           id: 1
  select_type: SIMPLE
        table: example_memory_session
         type: ALL
possible_keys: updated
          key: NULL
      key_len: NULL
          ref: NULL
         rows: 999999
        Extra: Using where


SHOW CREATE TABLE example_memory_session\G
*************************** 1. row ***************************
       Table: example_memory_session
Create Table: CREATE TABLE `example_memory_session` (
  `user_id` int(10) unsigned NOT NULL,
  `session` varchar(1000) NOT NULL,
  `created` timestamp NOT NULL DEFAULT CURRENT_TIMESTAMP,
  `updated` timestamp NOT NULL DEFAULT '0000-00-00 00:00:00',
```

```
  PRIMARY KEY (`user_id`),
  KEY `updated` (`updated`)
) ENGINE=MEMORY DEFAULT CHARSET=latin1
```

As you can see, the EXPLAIN shows that a possible index exists, but the QEP reports is not being used. It is possible that the index is actually being used, with this index being the table default hash index type and not a btree index. With the Memory engine it is possible to specify a different index type. For example:

```
TRUNCATE TABLE example_memory_session;
ALTER TABLE example_memory_session DROP INDEX updated,
ADD INDEX (updated) USING BTREE;
call make_dates (1000000);

EXPLAIN SELECT * FROM example_memory_session
WHERE updated < NOW() - INTERVAL 10 HOUR\G
*************************** 1. row ***************************
           id: 1
  select_type: SIMPLE
        table: example_memory_session
         type: range
possible_keys: updated
          key: updated
      key_len: 4
          ref: NULL
         rows: 612792
        Extra: Using where

DELETE from example_memory_session WHERE updated < NOW() - INTERVAL 10 HOUR;
Query OK, 583834 rows affected (2.33 sec)
SHOW CREATE TABLE example_memory_session\G
*************************** 1. row ***************************
       Table: example_memory_session
Create Table: CREATE TABLE `example_memory_session` (
  `user_id` int(10) unsigned NOT NULL,
  `session` varchar(1000) NOT NULL,
  `created` timestamp NOT NULL DEFAULT CURRENT_TIMESTAMP,
  `updated` timestamp NOT NULL DEFAULT '0000-00-00 00:00:00',
  PRIMARY KEY (`user_id`),
  KEY `updated` (`updated`) USING BTREE
) ENGINE=MEMORY DEFAULT CHARSET=latin1
```

As you can see, while the index is used there is no improvement in time. Though this exercise shows the potential impact of the default heap index, in design you would never implement this functionality due to limitations of table level locking in this particular engine. The correct way to implement this solution is to change the actual DELETE query to be more efficient. Because there is no requirement to delete all the data in one statement, deleting small chunks achieves the same result, and causes locking of 5–10 ms.

```
DELETE FROM example_memory_session
WHERE updated < NOW() - INTERVAL 10 HOUR
LIMIT 1000;
```

Blackhole

The `Blackhole` storage engine represents the same general characteristics of its celestial namesake. Information is accepted via DML statements; however, this information cannot be retrieved because it is never actually stored.

Key Features

➤ Very fast

➤ No disk space requirements

➤ Ideal for benchmarking

Limitations

➤ Does not support transactions

➤ Does not store data

Important Parameters

➤ N/A

Uses for Blackhole

While it may seem that this table is impractical in a production MySQL system it does serve specific benefits in isolated cases. Two example reasons for using `Blackhole` are for security and for replication performance.

When important information is stored in the MySQL table outside of a firewall environment, for example, credit card details on a public website, the use of `Blackhole` combined with MySQL replication can ensure this data is never actually stored in the external database which is accessible for possible attack.

When `Blackhole` is used in a MySQL replication topology, this can speed up performance.

You can also use `Blackhole` for selective tables on a master or slave servers to preserve the structure of the database schema and DML statements; however, the data is never stored.

Listing 3-13 shows how you can INSERT, UPDATE, and SELECT from a `Blackhole` table; however, the results are not as expected with a regular table:

Available for download on Wrox.com

LISTING 3-13: blackhole-example.sql

```
CREATE TABLE example_blackhole(
    id INT UNSIGNED NOT NULL AUTO_INCREMENT PRIMARY KEY,
    c  VARCHAR(100) NOT NULL)
ENGINE=blackhole;

INSERT INTO example_blackhole VALUES (1,'a'), (2,'b'), (3,'c');
```

```
Query OK, 3 rows affected (0.00 sec)

UPDATE example_blackhole SET c = 'x' WHERE id = 1;
Query OK, 0 rows affected (0.00 sec)

SELECT * FROM example_blackhole;
Empty set (0.00 sec)
```

Archive

The `Archive` storage engine was specifically designed for the storage of large amounts of sequential write once only data, generally logging or auditing information.

Key Features

- ➤ Very fast, ideal for logging data

- ➤ High compression factor

- ➤ Row level locking

Limitations

- ➤ Non-transactional.

- ➤ `INSERT` only. Does not support `UPDATE` or `DELETE`.

- ➤ Does not support indexes.

Important Parameters

- ➤ N/A

Understanding Archive Tables Usages

An `Archive` table is represented as three or four separate files in the file system located in the defined data directory for the MySQL instance. These files are:

- ➤ **table.frm**: This is the table format definition file.

- ➤ **table.ARZ**: This is the `Archive` table data file.

- ➤ **table.ARM**: This is the `Archive` table meta data.

- ➤ **table.ARN**: This is a temporary file that is present during a table optimization process.

When comparing the size of `Archive` to the `MyISAM` compressed table, you see a future improvement in disk storage without the requirement of manual commands to produce the compressed format. You can create the `Archive` table by repeating the syntax as detailed in previous examples.

```
SELECT table_name,table_rows,row_format,
       data_length/1024 AS data,index_length/1024 AS indx
FROM   INFORMATION_SCHEMA.TABLES
WHERE  table_name LIKE 'example_%';
```

```
+------------------------+------------+------------+------------+------------+
| table_name             | table_rows | row_format | data       | indx       |
+------------------------+------------+------------+------------+------------+
| example_myisam_dynamic |     234936 | Dynamic    |  4842.6484 |  2359.0000 |
| example_myisam_fixed   |     234936 | Fixed      | 24090.1172 |  2356.0000 |
| example_myisam_fixed2  |     234936 | Compressed |  2280.2529 |  2356.0000 |
| example_archive        |     234936 | Compressed |  1588.9619 |     0.0000 |
+------------------------+------------+------------+------------+------------+
```

The only operations that are permitted with an `Archive` table are `INSERT` and `SELECT`. No other DDL is permitted. An `Archive` table is also only permitted a primary key, and no additional indexes are permitted. The following are example error messages when attempting these operations:

```
update  example_archive set id=1 where id=2;
ERROR 1031 (HY000): Table storage engine for 'example_archive'
doesn't have this option
truncate table example_archive;
ERROR 1031 (HY000): Table storage engine for 'example_archive'
doesn't have this option
alter table example_archive add index (c);
ERROR 1069 (42000): Too many keys specified; max 1 key allowed
```

Merge

The `Merge` storage engine is effectively a view over `MyISAM` tables. This engine was originally designed to overcome operating system limitations when file systems could not support individual files greater than 2G.

With `Merge` you can select data from multiple identical defined tables. You can then update and delete data appropriately. Inserts occur on the last specified table in the merge definition. While you can perform DML and `SELECT` statements on the `Merge` table, you can also perform these on the underlying `MyISAM` tables. Primary key and unique key constraints are also on a per-table basis, not on the `Merge` table.

To understand the properties and parameters of `Merge`, refer to `MyISAM`. Though this may appear to be similar to partitioning, there is no intelligence with `Merge`. Queries are executed against underlying tables serially.

`Merge` can be successfully used when you want to manage manual partitioning and improved locking strategy with `MyISAM`.

Be careful when using `myisam-recover=FORCE,BACKUP` with `Merge`. There have been many reported problems in this area.

A `Merge` table is represented by the individual files for each underlying `MyISAM` table and two additional tables in the file system located in the defined data directory for the MySQL instance. These files are:

➤ **table.frm**: This is the `Merge` table format definition file.

➤ **table.MRG**: This is the `Merge` table meta data of underlying tables.

Listing 3-14 shows how you create a `Merge` table and how data can be inserted and retrieved directly or with the underlying tables:

LISTING 3-14: merge-example.sql

```
CREATE TABLE example_merge1 (
id INT UNSIGNED NOT NULL AUTO_INCREMENT PRIMARY KEY,
c  VARCHAR(100) NOT NULL)
ENGINE=MyISAM;
CREATE TABLE example_merge2 (
id INT UNSIGNED NOT NULL AUTO_INCREMENT PRIMARY KEY,
c  VARCHAR(100) NOT NULL)
ENGINE=MyISAM;
CREATE TABLE example_merge3 (
id INT UNSIGNED NOT NULL AUTO_INCREMENT PRIMARY KEY,
c  VARCHAR(100) NOT NULL)
ENGINE=MyISAM;

CREATE TABLE example_merge_all (
id INT UNSIGNED NOT NULL AUTO_INCREMENT PRIMARY KEY,
c  VARCHAR(100) NOT NULL)
ENGINE=MERGE
UNION=(example_merge1,example_merge2,example_merge3)
INSERT_METHOD=LAST;

INSERT INTO example_merge_all (id, c) VALUES (NULL,'a');
SELECT * FROM example_merge_all;
+----+---+
| id | c |
+----+---+
|  1 | a |
+----+---+
1 row in set (0.00 sec)

SELECT * FROM example_merge1;
Empty set (0.00 sec)

SELECT * FROM example_merge2;
Empty set (0.00 sec)

SELECT * FROM example_merge3;
+----+---+
| id | c |
+----+---+
|  1 | a |
+----+---+
1 row in set (0.00 sec)

INSERT INTO example_merge1 (id, c) VALUES (NULL, 'b');
SELECT * FROM example_merge_all;
+----+---+
| id | c |
+----+---+
|  1 | b |
|  1 | a |
+----+---+
2 rows in set (0.00 sec)
```

CSV

The CSV (Comma Separated Value) storage engine allows the management of an underlying CSV file via SQL statements. In MySQL 5.1, the general query log and the slow query log are actually implemented as the CSV engine.

Key Features

➤ Plain text data format

➤ Interchangeable data with other programs

➤ Fast import time via file copy

Limitations

➤ Table level locking

➤ Non-transactional

➤ Does not support indexes

Important Parameters

➤ N/A

Understanding CSV Table Usage

An CSV table is represented as three separate files in the file system located in the defined data directory for the MySQL instance. These files are:

➤ **table.frm**: This is the table format definition file.

➤ **table.CSV**: This is the table data file.

➤ **table.CSM**: This is the CSV table meta data.

Federated

The Federated storage engine is a storage engine that, instead of accessing data from a local file or tablespace, accesses data from a remote MySQL table through the MySQL client API. It builds SQL statements internally, based on what the query was against the Federated table, and runs those statements on the remote MySQL table.

If the query against the Federated table is a write statement such as INSERT or UPDATE, the Federated storage engine builds a query, deriving the column names and values from internal data structures that are dependent on the fields and values of the original query. Then it executes the SQL to perform that write operation on the remote table, reporting back to the storage engine the number of rows affected.

If it's a read operation, it constructs a SELECT statement also built using internal data structures for column names, as well as WHERE clauses for ranges and indexes. It then executes that statement after which the Federated storage engine retrieves the result set from the remote table and iterates over that result. It then converts the results into the same internal format that all other storage engines use and then returns the data to the user.

A DELETE statement is similar to a SELECT statement in how the column names are built into the constructed SQL statement, as well as in building the WHERE clause. The main difference is that the operation is DELETE FROM versus SELECT, resulting in the rows specified in the SQL statement being deleted and the count of the rows affected being returned to the storage engine, which in turn decrements its total row count.

Characteristics of the Federated Storage Engine

The Federated storage engine was developed as a standard by IBM and others defining Federated functionality. The standards for Federated are as follows:

➤ **Transparency:** The remote data sources and details thereof are not necessarily known by the user, such as how the data is stored, what the underlying schema is, and what dialect of SQL is used to retrieve information from that data source.

➤ **High degree of function:** To be able to have, as much as possible, the same functionality that is had with regular tables.

➤ **Extensibility and openness:** To adhere to a standard as defined in the ANSI SQL/MED (Management of External Data) extension to the SQL standard.

➤ **Autonomy of data sources:** Not affecting the remote data source, not interfering with its normal operation. This also means that the Federated storage engine cannot modify the definition of the remote data source, as in the case of statements such as ALTER and DROP TABLE not being sent to the remote data source.

➤ **Optimized performance:** Utilizing the optimizer to create the most efficient statements to run on the remote data source. Also, the long-term goal is to have a means of delegating operations to the local server and remote server according to which is best suited for each operation.

Of course, not all of these guiding principles have been achieved, but these are certainly goals for development of the Federated storage engine that provide a roadmap of the long-term direction of Federated development.

Some of the basic characteristics of the Federated storage engine are outlined in Table 3-1.

TABLE 3-1: Federated Characteristics

CHARACTERISTIC	DESCRIPTION
Column Requirements	When creating a Federated table, the table must have the same named columns as the remote table, and no more columns than the remote table. The remote table can have more columns than the Federated table.

continues

TABLE 3-1 *(continued)*

CHARACTERISTIC	DESCRIPTION
Queries and Results	A query on a Federated table internally produces an entire result set from a table on a remote server, and as such, if that table contains a lot of data, all of that data will be retrieved. One way to deal with huge result sets is to define an index on a column of the Federated table, even if that column is not indexed on the remote table, and try to use any means to limit the result set. However, note that `LIMIT` *does not* affect the size of the result set from the remote table.
Remote Table	The remote table must be in existence prior to creating the Federated table that references it.
Index Support	The Federated storage engine supports indexes insofar as the column that is defined as an index is specified in a `WHERE` clause in the SQL query the table generates, and that the column it specifies is an index on the remote table. This means that you could have a Federated table with an index on a column that is not an index on the remote table, which is not a problem, and in fact can be used to reduce result set size.
Referencing Another Federated Table	The manual states a Federated table can reference a Federated table. This is a bad idea. Don't do it.
Transactions	Transactions aren't supported in Federated, but are support with FederatedX if using a transactional engine (InnoDB, MariaDB, Falcon, and so on) as the remote data source.
What Federated Supports	Federated supports `SELECT`, `INSERT`, `UPDATE`, and `DELETE`. However, `ALTER TABLE` cannot be used to change the remote table's definition (this would violate the very definition of a Federated table), but it can be used to modify the local Federated table's definition.
Using `DROP TABLE`	This only drops the local Federated table.

It's worthwhile to mention that although the Federated storage engine may not support some features such as transactions as well as other enhancements, there is a fork of Federated called FederatedX, which is a more active development branch of Federated initiated by the authors of Federated: Patrick Galbraith and Antony Curtis.

Creating a Federated Table

As with other storage engines, creating a Federated table involves setting `ENGINE=FEDERATED`. Also necessary with Federated is specifying a connection string of either a connection URL or a server name (the next subsection covers more about Federated servers):

```
CONNECTION=scheme://user:password@host/schema/table
CONNECTION=server
CONNECTION=server/tablename.
```

The following shows the creation of a non-Federated table on a remote data source, and then the creation of a Federated table.

The remote server is 192.168.1.118, and the schema is *remote*:

```
mysql> CREATE TABLE `t1` (
    ->   `id` int(3) NOT NULL auto_increment,
    ->   `name` varchar(32) NOT NULL default '',
    ->   PRIMARY KEY  (`id`)
    -> );

mysql> INSERT INTO t1 (name) VALUES ('first'), ('second'), ('hello world');
```

Then on a local server, 192.168.1.100, in a schema named *federated*:

```
mysql> CREATE TABLE `t1` (
    ->   `id` int(3) NOT NULL auto_increment,
    ->   `name` varchar(32) NOT NULL default '',
    ->   PRIMARY KEY  (`id`)
    -> ) ENGINE=FEDERATED
    -> CONNECTION='mysql://feduser:feduser@192.168.1.118/remote/t1';
Query OK, 0 rows affected (0.07 sec)

mysql> SELECT * FROM t1;
+----+-------------+
| id | name        |
+----+-------------+
|  1 | first       |
|  2 | second      |
|  3 | hello world |
+----+-------------+

mysql> INSERT INTO t1 (name) VALUES ('hello federated');

mysql> SELECT * FROM t1;
+----+-----------------+
| id | name            |
+----+-----------------+
|  1 | first           |
|  2 | second          |
|  3 | hello world     |
|  4 | hello federated |
+----+-----------------+
```

Then back on the remote server:

```
mysql> SELECT * FROM t1;
+----+-----------------+
| id | name            |
+----+-----------------+
|  1 | first           |
|  2 | second          |
|  3 | hello world     |
|  4 | hello federated |
+----+-----------------+
```

This means there has been a successful Federated table creation.

Federated Servers

As you've seen in the preceding example, a URL-like string was specified to give the necessary information for the Federated table in order to connect to the remote data source. In cases where there is a large number of Federated tables, changing these tables' connection information can be cumbersome and requires altering all of the tables with a modified connection string. For instance, if you needed to change what server 1000 Federated tables connect to, you would have to alter each one of those tables to have a new server in its connection string.

To devise a better solution, in MySQL 5.1, the idea of a *Federated Server* was developed. This concept was part of the SQL/MED specification. It essentially lets you create a named database object called a SERVER that is associated with various connection meta-data information. The other half of this functionality is that the Federated storage engine can merely specify the server name (as well as table if it is desired to name the table differently than the Federated table). This means you can change the connection information of the table that one or more Federated tables use to connect to their remote data source with a single SQL statement against the SERVER. So, in the 1000-table scenario, not a single table would have to be changed!

The syntax for a Federated Server is straightforward:

```
CREATE SERVER
server_name
FOREIGN DATA WRAPPER wrapper_name
OPTIONS (option [, option] ...)
```

In this example, to use a Federated server, you would create it as:

```
mysql> CREATE SERVER
    -> 'servera' FOREIGN DATA WRAPPER 'mysql'
    -> OPTIONS
    -> (HOST '192.168.1.118',
    ->  DATABASE 'remote',
    ->  USER 'feduser',
    ->  PASSWORD 'feduser',
    ->  PORT 3306,
    ->  SOCKET '',
    ->  OWNER 'root' );
```

Then, to use this server with the previously created table, you would have to drop the table first (this is the Federated standard method; the engine does not support ALTER on the remote table) and then re-create it, using the server name that was just created instead of a URL connection string:

```
mysql> DROP TABLE t1 ;
Query OK, 0 rows affected, 1 warning (0.00 sec)

mysql> CREATE TABLE `t1` (
    ->  `id` int(3) NOT NULL AUTO_INCREMENT,
    ->  `name` varchar(32) NOT NULL DEFAULT '',
    ->  PRIMARY KEY (`id`)
    -> ) ENGINE=FEDERATED DEFAULT CHARSET=latin1 CONNECTION='servera';

mysql> SELECT * FROM t1;
```

```
+----+----------------+
| id | name           |
+----+----------------+
|  1 | first          |
|  2 | second         |
|  3 | hello world    |
|  4 | hello federated|
+----+----------------+
```

A table name could have been specified in this example and would be separated from the server name with a forward slash ' / '.

```
CONNECTION= 'servera/t1'
```

This would be useful if the remote table name and Federated table name differed.

Federated under the Hood

To gain a little insight to how Federated works, you can observe several things. First, as mentioned before, Federated accesses its data not from a local file, but from a remote data source through the MySQL client library. This means there will only be one file created for a Federated table, the .frm file, which is the table definition file. For Federated, this file merely contains the connection information for the Federated table:

```
ishvara:/home/mysql/var/federated # ls
db.opt  t1.frm
```

The other revealing thing to look at is the SQL log, if it is turned on, on the remote server. On the server with the Federated table, you issue:

```
mysql> SELECT * FROM t1;
```

The query log on the remote server shows:

```
080823 11:17:56          181 Connect      feduser@arjuna on remote

        181 Query        SET NAMES latin1

        181 Query        SHOW TABLE STATUS LIKE 't1'

        181 Query        SELECT `id`, `name` FROM `t1`
```

As you can see:

➤ The first command the server with the Federated table sends is SET NAMES <character set>. This is to ensure that the character set of the Federated table is set on the remote server.

➤ The second command sent is SHOW TABLE STATUS. This command obtains information on the remote table, which Federated then uses to set values for the local Federated table, such as the number of records in the table.

➤ Finally, the Federated storage engine sends the query to obtain the data that was specified in the original query. The difference between the original query on the Federated table and the query that Federated constructs to be run against the remote table is that Federated specifies each column. It does this internally by looping over each field (column) in a data structure representing the structure of the table and appending each to the complete statement.

If data is inserted into the Federated table, such as with this query:

```
mysql> INSERT INTO t1 (name) VALUES ('one more value');
```

then the statement as found in the log on the remote server is:

```
080823 11:29:06  181 Query  INSERT INTO `t1` (`id`, `name`)
VALUES  (0, 'one more value')
```

Just as with the SELECT statement, the INSERT statement is built by the Federated storage engine, additionally appending into the VALUES half of the INSERT statement the values being inserted.

Viewing the SQL log on a remote server that a Federated table utilizes can be a very useful means of seeing how the Federated storage engine works, as well as a good debugging tool.

OTHER MYSQL SUPPLIED ENGINES

Official MySQL binaries that can be found at http://www.mysql.com include two further engines that have been developed internally by the MySQL team. These are the Falcon storage engine and the Maria storage engine.

 Neither of these engines is in the current Generally Available (GA) products, or the most current Alpha version of MySQL.

Falcon

Falcon is a purchased technology from Netfrastructure in 1996. That was incorporated as a storage engine and was designed to be a possible replacement to InnoDB as the default transactional storage engine. This was due to the purchase of Innobase, the creators of InnoDB by Oracle Corporation, a competitor of the MySQL product.

Unfortunately this engine has never lived up to the published hype. A key feature of the now defunct MySQL 6.0 product, Falcon is not included in the current alpha version of MySQL 5.4. With a change in policy of future products from feature-based releases to time-based and feature-complete requirements, there is no schedule on when Falcon will be available and production ready. In addition, the original architect of Falcon is no longer a member of the development team or working actively on the product.

Key Features

- Transactional
- Supports MVCC (Multi Version Concurrency Control)
- Designed for machines with lots of RAM
- Dynamic data compression
- Page and record caches
- Flexible page size for tablespace
- Additional meta data information in the `INFORMATION_SCHEMA`

Limitations

- Not a GA product
- No roadmap for implementation

Important Parameters

- `falcon_page_cache_size`: This defines the amount of memory used for caching data.
- `falcon_io_threads`: This defines the number of background threads for performing disk writes.
- `falcon_page_size`: This defines the size of the data pages for tablespaces.
- `falcon_checkpoint_schedule`: This defines the frequency of checkpoints that synchronize in memory and disk information. The specification is a crontab format string.

 There is no current product listed on the MySQL web site to download the `Falcon` *storage engine. You need to look at the product archives to find MySQL 6.0.11 which is available at* `http://downloads.mysql.com/archives.php?p=mysql-6.0&v=6.0.11`.

Falcon Table Usage

By default, `Falcon` tables are represented within a common tablespace. You can also define named tablespaces that can store specific tables. These are located in the data directory for the MySQL instance. The related files are:

- `falcon_user.fts`: This is the default tablespace.
- `falcon_temporary.fts`: This is used for temporary tables.
- `falcon_master.fl1` and `falcon_master.fl2`: These are the transaction log files.

Falcon has a large number of system parameters (currently 29) that you can view using SHOW GLOBAL VARIABLES LIKE 'falcon%'. Though there is no output from the commands used by other engines such as SHOW GLOBAL STATUS LIKE 'falcon%' and SHOW ENGINE FALCON STATUS. All diagnostic information is available via Falcon specific INFORMATION_SCHEMA tables. The current list is:

➤ FALCON_RECORD_CACHE_SUMMARY

➤ FALCON_SYSTEM_MEMORY_DETAIL

➤ FALCON_TABLESPACE_IO

➤ FALCON_SYSTEM_MEMORY_SUMMARY

➤ FALCON_VERSION

➤ FALCON_TRANSACTION_SUMMARY

➤ FALCON_SERIAL_LOG_INFO

➤ FALCON_SYNCOBJECTS

➤ FALCON_TRANSACTIONS

➤ FALCON_RECORD_CACHE_DETAIL

The following example shows detailed information about database reads and writes to the individual tablespaces:

```
SELECT * FROM INFORMATION_SCHEMA.FALCON_TABLESPACE_IO;
+------------------+-----------+---------+---------+------+-----------+-------+
| TABLESPACE       | PAGE_SIZE | BUFFERS | P_READS |WRITES| LOG_READS | FAKES |
+------------------+-----------+---------+---------+------+-----------+-------+
| FALCON_MASTER    |      4096 |    1024 |      88 |    0 |   1410947 |     2 |
| FALCON_TEMPORARY |      4096 |    1024 |       1 |    0 |         0 |     1 |
| FALCON_USER      |      4096 |    1024 |    4416 |    0 |   5140107 |  6617 |
+------------------+-----------+---------+---------+------+-----------+-------+
```

 You can find a more detailed description of the Falcon storage engine at http://dev.mysql.com/doc/falcon.

Maria

The Maria storage engine also has a unique history. Originally part of a supported MySQL 5.1 branch of the official product, Maria is now the storage engine of MariaDB, a new MySQL-compatible product created by the original MySQL founder, Michael "Monty" Widenius. Maria is designed as a replacement to MyISAM including new features such as automatic crash recovery, foreign keys, and in the future, transactional support. An easy way to think of MariaDB is to consider the relationship with CentOS and Red Hat. This includes all the features of the original product and the closest compatibility but also value added features that are user friendly and hopefully may become features of the original product in the future.

Key Features

➤ Crash save

➤ Higher insert concurrency

➤ Improved code quality

➤ Transactional (in 2.x versions) supporting ACID compliance, MVCC, and row-level locking

While you can download a historical version of Maria from the MySQL official web site in the 6.0.11 archive version as used with the `Falcon` engine, all current development is included in MariaDB and is available from `http://mariadb.com`.

PLUGGABLE ENGINES

Although MySQL created the pluggable storage engine architecture (PSEA) in 5.1 to enable third parties to provide products that integrate with MySQL, most engines have failed to leverage the fully pluggable architecture as detailed in the following section. Those that are pluggable at present include `InnoDB` (the plugin version), `PBXT`, and `XtraDB`.

InnoDB Plugin

The pluggable storage engine architecture has enabled Innobase, the creators of the built-in `InnoDB` storage engine, to release new features independently of the limited official MySQL product release cycle. Some of these features are significant improvements to the built-in version. The most recent point releases of MySQL 5.1, starting with MySQL 5.1.38 (01 September 2009), now include both the built-in and plugin versions of `InnoDB`.

Key Features (in Addition to Those Listed in `InnoDB`) Include:

➤ Improved performance in locking and large core systems

➤ Dynamic control of additional variables

➤ Fast index creation

➤ Data compression

➤ New row format

➤ `INFORMATION_SCHEMA` tables

Important Parameters

➤ **`ignore-builtin-innodb`**: In order to use the plugin version, you must disable the built in version.

➤ **`plugin-load`**: This defines the list of plugins which includes the storage engine and `INFORMATION_SCHEMA` tables.

➤ **innodb_file_format:** To use new DYNAMIC and COMPRESSED formats, you need to set this parameter to Barracuda.

➤ **innodb_file_per_table:** In order to use the new file formats you must also specify this parameter which changes the storage of tables from a common tablespace to per table tablespaces.

You can find the MySQL Reference Manual at http://dev.mysql.com/doc/refman/5.1/en/innodb.html *for introduction and configuration information necessary with your* my.cnf *configuration file. More information is also available at* http://innodb.com/products/innodb_plugin.

With the introduction of the new Barracuda file format it is possible to specify additional arguments on the CREATE TABLE statement to specify the ROW_FORMAT and the KEY_BLOCK_SIZE. However, if you fail to set the correct parameters as listed in the important parameters, the table is created but with warnings, and you may not get what you expect. For an example see the following Listing 3-15.

LISTING 3-15: innodb-plugin-example.sql

Available for
download on
Wrox.com

```
CREATE TABLE example_innodb_dynamic (
  id INT UNSIGNED NOT NULL AUTO_INCREMENT PRIMARY KEY,
  c VARCHAR(100) NOT NULL)
ENGINE=InnoDB ROW_FORMAT=DYNAMIC;
SHOW WARNINGS;
+---------+------+-----------------------------------------------------------+
| Level   | Code | Message                                                   |
+---------+------+-----------------------------------------------------------+
| Warning | 1478 | InnoDB: ROW_FORMAT=DYNAMIC requires innodb_file_per_table.|
| Warning | 1478 | InnoDB: assuming ROW_FORMAT=COMPACT.                      |
+---------+------+-----------------------------------------------------------
```

The InnoDB *Plugin versions 1.0.4 and 1.05 that are included with MySQL are still considered beta quality.*

PBXT

The Primebase Transaction engine (PBXT) was the first truly pluggable engine and leverages underlying internal MyISAM data structure to achieve a greater compatibility with MySQL.

Key features

➤ Transactional

➤ ACID compliant

➤ Row level locking

➤ Truly pluggable

➤ Short auto recovery

➤ Logged based design aligns well with SSD technology.

Limitations

➤ Almost solely developed by one individual

➤ Long development lifecycle

➤ Not yet GA

Important Parameters

➤ `pbxt_index_cache_size`: The amount of memory assigned for index caching.

➤ `pbxt_record_cache_size`: The amount of memory assigned for caching the table record data.

➤ `pbxt_log_cache_size`: The amount of memory assigned for the transaction log data.

➤ `pbxt_checkpoint_frequency`: The time for a checkpoint of the data written to the transaction log file. This affects the performance of MySQL during a disaster recovery.

➤ `pbxt_data_log_threshold`: The size of an internal data log file. This affects the maximum amount of data possible in the data tablespace.

You can find more information about the PBXT storage engine at `http://primebase.org`.

XtraDB

The Percona `XtraDB` storage engine is a drop-in and backward-compatible `InnoDB` storage engine. This engine includes all the listed features of `InnoDB` but includes specific modifications to provide additional instrumentation, better memory management, and performance and scalability improvements for large core and highly concurrent work environments.

See `http://www.percona.com/docs/wiki/percona-xtradb:start` *for more information.*

ENGINES AS STANDALONE PRODUCTS

Though MySQL created the pluggable storage engine architecture (PSEA) as discussed in the previous section, many service providers have been unable to integrate with MySQL. The most common problem is requiring changes in the internal MySQL optimizer. Because of the current MySQL architecture and development life cycle this is unfortunately unlikely to be provided.

One solution is in the form of Drizzle, an original fork of MySQL. While Drizzle has many features, one key feature was to ensure that core components of an RDBMS product are indeed fully pluggable. A number of the engines discussed in this section are better supported with the Drizzle product. For more information see `http://drizzle.org`.

Some providers, for example Tokutek, have provided patches for incorporation into MySQL to enable their respective engine to become fully pluggable. Unfortunately, feature changes and community patches with the MySQL product can have a long lead time for production implementation.

InfiniDB

`InfiniDB` is a data warehousing and data analytics product from Calpont (`http://calpont.com`) that integrates with MySQL but is not limited to some of the restrictions of other storage engine providers. `InifiniDB` leverages the essential components of MySQL including the communication protocol, user authentication, and query parsing, but bypasses other limitations to provide some true high concurrency, parallel processing, and multi-node capabilities. Internally, data is stored in a column-oriented architecture and requires far less tuning with no index requirements, and horizontal and vertical partitioning is provided automatically. This engine supports ACID-compliant transactions and MVCC (multi-version concurrency control).

The greatest promise with `InfiniDB` is the true capacity of parallel processing.

 `InfiniDB` *is available as an open source product at* `http://infinidb.org`.

TokuDB

Providing a clustered index for all indexes via the Fractal Tree™ technology, `TokuDB` aims to improve performance and scalability in given workloads by at least 10 times. The underlying storage engine transforms the way information is managed, and can turn random I/O from index scans into sequential I/O, thereby producing dramatic gains. In addition, the underlying disk footprint has shown to be less than `InnoDB` and `MyISAM`. Tokutek also provides the iiBench (Indexed Insertion Benchmark) as a better example of typical social media–related operations.

`TokuDB` is a commercial product from Tokutek that provides a free version for smaller databases (currently less than 50GB).

You can find full details at `http://tokutek.com.`

Infobright

Infobright is an engine designed for data warehousing and analytics. This is provided with a custom MySQL binary and includes open source and commercial versions.

An Infobright community version is available at `http://www.infobright.org` *and a commercial version is available at* `http://www.infobright.com.`

OTHER MYSQL OFFERINGS

Though understanding the approximately dozen described storage engines can be a complicated undertaking by software developers, there is significant opportunity for more flexibility and complexity in the MySQL ecosystem. It is important to realize that significant development is occurring in this technology space, and many of the listed products can operate and appear much like a MySQL official product.

Storage Engine Patch Products

Two primary products exist that provide the basic MySQL built-in storage engines as well as additional engines and patches for features and performance. These are the Percona performance builds and the Our Delta community builds.

Percona Performance Builds

The Percona builds for Version 5.0 include a number of performance patches developed by Percona and the MySQL community to greatly improve performance and instrumentation in high concurrency situations. Many of these patches have now been included in the `InnoDB` Plugin and the MySQL 5.4 alpha version. For those wishing to not upgrade to new MySQL versions but remain with Version 5.0, these builds can generally be a drop-in replacement to existing MySQL binaries.

You can find more details at `http://www.percona.com/mysql/.`

Our Delta

Our Delta is a community effort to provide enhanced builds of MySQL 5.0 and MariaDB 5.1 on the most popular platforms. As discussed, it is often difficult to get community patches or improvements into the mainline product managed by MySQL. Our Delta seeks to leverage the power of the open source license and provide modified versions that include many of the popular patches that provide many features such as greater performance, instrumentation, and reliability. Contributions come from companies including Google, Innobase, Facebook, Open Query, Percona, Primebase, Proven Scaling, and Sphinx.

 More information is available at `http://ourdelta.org`.

MySQL-Related Products

Two products of note that are not MySQL storage engine products or enhanced builds of the MySQL product are Drizzle and MariaDB. Both will play a significant role in the MySQL ecosystem.

Drizzle

Drizzle was originally a MySQL fork, but has now developed into an individual database product with many differences and fewer features than MySQL. Many of the storage engines discussed are included in Drizzle. Designed for large core servers and more distributed computing, it includes an improved pluggable architecture for all components, not just storage engines. While still under heavy development, benchmarks show that Drizzle outperforms MySQL 5.1 for large core systems.

 For more information see `http://drizzle.org`.

MariaDB

MariaDB is designed as a drop-in replacement for MySQL. While providing the greatest compatibility and matching the features of MySQL, there is a different development approach designed for more features, fewer bugs, and greater performance. Many of the original development team for the MySQL product now work on the MariaDB product. In addition to the default storage engines found in MySQL, MariaDB includes by default additional storage engines including `Maria`, `PBXT`, `XtraDB`, and `FederatedX`.

 For more information see `http://mariadb.com`.

Other Engines

These additional engines form the basis of different products, have been included as patches, or used by certain companies and provided to the community for possible future use. The following list is just a highlight and many not listed include storage engines for file system files, memcached, IBM DB2I, Sphinx full-text search, and AWS S3, for example.

NDB

This engine is actually an entire product originally purchased by MySQL and incorporated into the MySQL Cluster product. NDB includes a number of key features that distinguish it from a more traditional MySQL storage engine. The NDB engine provides transaction support and synchronous replication ensuring that all data nodes are consistent. It also provides a native C interface to directly with the data by passing the SQL interact if desired for three to five times performance improvement.

NDB has a number of strengths and weaknesses in comparison to the MySQL server product which this book covers. This does not make this a drop-in replacement for a MySQL replication topology. NDB is popular with the telecommunication and gaming industries that use primary key lookups, few joins, and require much high availability.

 More information is available at http://mysql.com/products/database/cluster/.

eBay Memory Engine

The eBay Memory engine extends the default Memory storage engine by providing variable-length record support. As discussed in the Memory section, one key use of this engine is for session management. One key disadvantage here is the fixed-width limitation. This engine enables a far greater amount of in-memory session data to be maintained, and could be ideal for large web sites that manage in-session information. This engine is also the default temporary table engine and Memory storage engine for the Drizzle product.

 You can find more information at http://code.google.com/p/mysql-heap-dynamic-rows/.

NitroEDB

The NitroEDB storage engine was developed by Nitro Security. The underlying database product was developed in relative isolation from traditional relational databases and included some amazing features, including insert performance at 50,000 statements per second and aggregated index queries on large data sets up to 1,000 times faster than existing storage engines. This engine also supported patented technologies in N-Tree management that extended traditional relational functionality.

For more information see `http://nitrosecurity.com/information/tech/EDB/`.

Solid

Solid is a transactional engine from Solid Tech that was acquired by IBM and effectively shelved. The current IBM solidDB product page does not include any references to the originally developed MySQL storage engine.

Integrated Hardware Engines

Available MySQL storage engines are not limited to just software. Two commercial providers include specialized hardware with their respective implementation of customized MySQL storage engines.

Kickfire

Kickfire is a column-oriented data store with additional specific hardware for compression and indexing. Due to the nature of requiring the specialized hardware it's not possible to evaluate or demonstrate this product.

 More information is available at `http://www.kickfire.com`.

Virident

Virident is a combination of custom improvements in memory management based on the `InnoDB` storage engine, as well as providing a dedicated memory hardware appliance.

 More information is available at `http://www.virident.com`.

Other Solutions

In addition to previously mentioned engines that also include hardware components, various storage engines can involve integration of MySQL with other products. We conclude this section on storage engines with one example.

Wafflegrid

Wafflegrid is actually a custom patch and extension to InnoDB where memached, a distributed in-memory infrastructure, is used as a level 2 cache for InnoDB. The concept is very simple, leveraging two existing technologies to boost performance in data access. The benefit of memcached as an LRU cache is the built-in distributed nature allowing a group of servers to act as secondary cache of the InnoDB buffer pool.

> *For more information see* http://wafflegrid.com/.

SUMMARY

With all the flexibility of MySQL storage engines comes great responsibility for a developer to ensure the best solution for the product you are developing.

It is very easy to have a mis-configured or poorly performing MySQL installation due to the lack of correct storage engine configuration or the specific limitations of storage engines. Knowing the relative strengths of the MySQL product, combined with the business requirements of the customer, allows you the opportunity to consider not just MySQL features, but various MySQL storage engines.

While MySQL provides an easy method to mix and match different storage engines for individual tables within a MySQL instance, care should be taken. The lack of transaction support when expected and the complexity of consistent backups are a common problem in a mixed engine instance.

You should first start with a decision of the default storage engine. This is generally a decision of a transactional storage engine or a non-transactional storage engine. This affects the development approach that is undertaken. Generally by default the options chosen are InnoDB or MyISAM, respectively. However, as discussed there are multiple variances of InnoDB at present, and Maria as a MyISAM replacement.

With the stability of newer engines you should strongly consider a dedicated engine when your requirements are for a specific purpose such as a data warehouse.

Improving Performance through Caching

➤ Using eAccelerator and APC for opcode and user caching

➤ Using memcached in PHP

➤ Using memcached in MySQL

➤ Methods for maintaining cache and database integrity

A PHP web application's ability to display information — data from a database — is one of its most crucial, core functions. The speed at which this data is retrieved from the database is made manifest to the end user as overall site performance. So, whichever way you can, you try to make your database calls as efficient as possible. This includes trying to get as much information as possible in as few queries as possible, yet ensuring your queries perform optimally.

However, as your web site or web application realizes increased traffic, your database's performance soon becomes a bottleneck and much of what is being continually displayed requires a huge number of queries against the database, causing your database to reach read capacity. This is where you want to employ caching to temporarily cache data that is repetitively needed to provide common data for your web application.

For instance, imagine a popular blog web site. This blog would contain a listing of blog entries composed of a title, the first paragraph of the blog entry, a link to the entire post body, a date, and even a summary of the comment count. Without caching, you would have to run a query against the database for every page display to obtain a listing of blog entries from at least a blog table. You might even possibly join this against the comment table to obtain an aggregate count of the comments for this blog entry or join against a user preferences table to obtain display, time zone, or ordering preferences for the given blog's user.

Yet, if the blog web site were to have a caching mechanism, you can run these data retrieval queries on a less frequent basis, caching the same data into a cache that would previously have been obtained from the database for each access. This provides much faster response time to the blog web site because you access the database less. It is now possible to display the blog entries using a simple key lookup from the cache instead of a complex query against a database.

A common problem with modern web applications is the *C10K problem* — which is how does your server handle ten thousand concurrent client connections. Two primary components that help solve the C10K problem are the use of asynchronous/non-blocking calls, and effective caching. This chapter focuses on the caching component.

This chapter explores PHP optimization through caching, including *opcode* caching (more on that later) but also user caching to store arbitrary key and value pairs for quick retrieval without increasing load on the database or other external date sources.

EACCELERATOR AND APC

PHP intermediate code caching (more commonly called bytecode or opcode caching) extensions take the code generated by the PHP compiler and store it in its compiled form. The result is that the PHP file no longer needs to be compiled on each execution. There are two popular opcode caching extensions: eAcellerator and APC.

Both store the compiled version of PHP scripts and both extensions also have the added ability of allowing for arbitrary values to be stored in the cache as well. There will be more on that second part later.

Both extensions use the system memory and the disk for caching. Memory caching provides much better performance over hard drive–based access. However, regardless of whether the file is in memory or on disk, the fact that the opcodes are stored and not the raw unprocessed PHP can increase the performance of an application many times over. Both extensions will try to use memory first and most compiled PHP files will fit nicely into memory without having to resort to the disk.

The bottom line is that it is always a good idea to have one of the opcode caching extensions installed. Not having one installed not only increases page load time by having to compile the PHP scripts on every execution, but also decreases the ability for a server to handle load as a result. Because compiling a PHP script inherently requires disk access as well as a significant amount of computation, a server with an opcode cache enabled will always be faster than the same server without any cache.

Installing and Configuring APC

Alternative PHP Cache (APC) was originally developed by Community Connect Inc. and was contributed to the PHP community in 2002. It was updated in 2005 by Yahoo! Inc. to support the then brand new PHP 5.1. It is completely open source under the PHP license and is community maintained.

APC is developed and deployed as a PECL extension and as such follows a standard method of installation and configuration. The entire extension can be installed in one line:

```
pecl install APC
```

Alternatively, you can download it from SVN and compile and install it manually. It may also be necessary to enable the extension in the `php.ini` file. Once the extension is installed, you can use several configuration variables to change its behavior. Some of the most common configurations are outlined in this section.

Setting `apc.stat` to 0 can turn off the file-stat operation for the opcode cache. Under normal operation APC checks to see if the PHP file has been modified before executing the cached version. If the file was modified, the cache is refreshed. Turning off the `file-stat` means that if a PHP file is cached, no hit is made to the file system at all. This option can improve performance but you should use it with care, because changes to PHP files are not be reflected until the cache is cleared or the server is restarted. This setting is ideal for production systems where files typically only change during the release of a new version, but it should be left as the default in development environments where the PHP changes often. In practice, however, file stat operations are very fast on most file systems so don't expect immense speed improvements by using this directive.

The directives `apc.ttl` and `apc.user_ttl` are used to specify the default time to live for cached opcode files and user data, respectively, in seconds. The default for both is 0, which means that the data will never be cleared. This means that it is possible for the cache to fill up with stale, rarely used data, which will block additional and potentially more relevant data from being stored. A time to live of zero may be desirable for opcode cache but it is often not ideal for user data. The meaning of user data is covered shortly.

Installing and Configuring eAccelerator

eAccelerator is another popular opcode caching extension. It is based on an open source project called *Turck MMCache* and still retains some of the original code. It is licensed under the GNU General Public License and like APC also makes the full source code available. However, it is maintained independently from the PHP community.

Installing and configuring eAccelerator on a Linux-based system with a compiler and build environment already set up is easy:

```
phpize
./configure --with-eaccelerator-shared-memory
make
make install
mkdir -p /var/cache/eaccelerator
chmod 0777 /var/cache/eaccelerator
```

The parameter passed to the configuration script is important for enabling user caching. If you do not want a user cache, you can exclude it. The next step is to configure eAccelerator, which you must do manually by adding a few lines to the `php.ini` file:

```
extension="eaccelerator.so"
eaccelerator.shm_size="16"
eaccelerator.cache_dir="/tmp/eaccelerator"
eaccelerator.enable="1"
eaccelerator.optimizer="1"
eaccelerator.check_mtime="1"
eaccelerator.debug="0"
eaccelerator.filter=""
```

```
eaccelerator.shm_max="0"
eaccelerator.shm_ttl="0"
eaccelerator.shm_prune_period="0"
eaccelerator.shm_only="0"
eaccelerator.compress="1"
eaccelerator.compress_level="9"
```

The `eaccelerator.cache_dir` directive must be the same as the directory created in the previous step. All directives that include the term "shm" refer to shared memory. By setting time to live values and a maximum size of the shared memory it is possible to prevent the cache from becoming overwhelmingly large.

eAccelerator also has a built-in opcode optimizer that attempts to make the compiled PHP scripts more efficient. The optimization step occurs only during the initial compilation so it is inexpensive and it is usually best to leave it on.

Like APC, eAccelerator does not automatically evict data from the cache unless a time to live is specified. This means that the cache can become full or too large to fit in shared memory (and therefore slower). You can use the `eaccelerator.shm_ttl` directive to configure a default time to live for all data in shared memory. Unlike APC there is no way to configure the value for just the user cache, so the time to live will also affect opcode caches.

User Cache

The user cache doesn't have anything to do with any application-level concept of a user, but is rather a cache that can be used to store whatever the application wants. APC has user cache as a basic feature whereas, as mentioned earlier, it needs to be enabled at compile time in newer versions of eAccelerator.

User cache can store arbitrary values using an application-defined key. It is up to the application to make sure that the key is unique. Also, when caching a value into the cache it is possible to set a time to live for just that key. Because both extensions do not expire, cached data by default makes it possible to exclude this value from the function call if the data never changes or include it if the data is expected to become stale or irrelevant.

It is the responsibility of the application developer to determine the optimal time to live. There is a definite trade-off between keeping data longer and incurring extra storage costs or evicting data and requiring additional calculation if the data needs to be re-accessed later. However, when properly tuned the cache can prevent excess hits to external resources — like the MySQL database — and dramatically improve application performance.

The two most common methods in either extension are the set and get/fetch operations. The two operations can be easily invoked. For APC:

```
apc_store( "key", $object, 3600 );
$stored_object = apc_fetch( "key" );
```

For eAccelerator:

```
eaccelerator_put( "key", serialize($object), 3600 );
$store_object = unserialize( eaccelerator_get( "key" ));
```

Both store methods have the same parameters in the same order: key, value, and then time to live. In each case the key is the word "key" (which is, incidentally, a very bad key name) and the time to live of one hour. The key difference is that eAccelerator does not automatically serialize the data. Forgetting to serialize an object when using eAccelerator causes a fatal error when the application tries to retrieve the data, making it difficult to debug errors.

In both cases it is not a bad idea to serialize objects. APC is known to have issues with some complex array structures, which can be solved by serializing. Also, in both cases, it is not necessary to serialize strings, Booleans, and numbers because those are already primitives.

The one thing that can never be stored in cache is a resource, which includes MySQL and file handles. Those have to be reopened on each execution.

The most common use of the user cache is to store content from a resource that is expensive to access, such as a database server, external HTTP server, or even the file system. It will always be faster to access the data from memory.

Checking the Cache Status

It is often desirable to check the status of the cache to determine if it is effective and if the system has the right amount of resources allocated for it. Both APC and eAccelerator have different methods for determining cache utilizations and provide different qualities of information.

In eAccelerator it is possible to display all the keys currently stored in the user cache using the function `eaccelerator_list_keys()`. The return value is an array of key information that looks something like this:

```
Array
(
    [0] => Array
        (
            [name] => key_name
            [ttl] => 1256555832
            [created] => 1256555787
            [size] => 23583
        )
)
```

Each item in the array is a different stored value. The output tells you the name of the key, the time when the key becomes stale, the time it was created, and the size in bytes. The value of `ttl` will be −1 if the key is stale and is ready to be garbage collected; however, the key will remain in memory until space is needed for additional storage.

Another useful function is `eaccelerator_info()`, which returns all the information available in `phpinfo()` about eAccelerator but also some additional data such as memory usage and how many scripts are cached:

```
Array
(
    [version] => 0.9.5.3
    [shm_type] => mmap_anon
```

```
        [sem_type] => spinlock
        [logo] => PHPE6F78DE9-13E4-4dee-8518-5FA2DACEA803
        [cache] => 1
        [optimizer] => 1
        [memorySize] => 33554396
        [memoryAvailable] => 5139408
        [memoryAllocated] => 28414988
        [cachedScripts] => 162
        [removedScripts] => 0
        [cachedKeys] => 1206
    )
```

The third eAccelerator function gets a list of all the scripts currently cached. The function `eaccelerator_cached_scripts()` returns an array:

```
    Array
    (
        [0] => Array
            (
                [file] => /path/to/web/root/index.php
                [mtime] => 1256557026
                [size] => 948
                [reloads] => 1
                [usecount] => 0
                [hits] => 100
            )
    )
```

The script information is the only data available that provides a little bit of usage information. For each script the application can determine how many times the script was accessed as well as how many times the script has changed and was reloaded from the hard drive. Aside from that information the application knows very little about cache usage.

The last function requires that the value of `eaccelerator.allowed_admin_path` is set in the `PHP.ini` file and that the script calling the function is in that path. The allowed admin path should be password protected to avoid unauthorized access. Other functions that are required to be in that path are functions that turn on and off caching as well as the function to clean up the cache. The directory is specified as an absolute path on the server and not a web URI/URL.

All the eAccelerator functions in this section can be used to create an admin control panel that can be helpful for monitoring and making runtime changes to eAccelerator. It would be useful to obtain a percentage of cache hits versus misses and other similar information, but that is not currently available. It is, however, available with APC.

APC provides a function called `apc_cache_info()` that returns various pieces of information about the cache. The information includes the number of hits to the cache as well as the number of misses, which is very helpful for determining the usefulness of the cache. It also determines the number of hits to each individual key. The returned results look something like this:

```
    Array
    (
        [num_slots] => 2000
```

```
[ttl] => 0
[num_hits] => 100
[num_misses] => 25
[start_time] => 1256555787
[cache_list] => Array
    (
        [0] => Array
            (
                [filename] => /path/to/web/root/index.php
                [device] => 29954
                [inode] => 1130511
                [type] => file
                [num_hits] => 10
                [mtime] => 1256555787
                [creation_time] => 1256555777
                [deletion_time] => 0
                [access_time] => 1256555900
                [ref_count] => 1
                [mem_size] => 23583
            )
    )
)
```

The information provided is very similar to that of eAccelerator. The `cache_list` array also contains values from the user cache. Another useful function in APC is `apc_sma_info()`, which returns information about the shared memory allocation. Specifically, it returns the number of segments of memory, how large a segment is, and a list of all blocks of memory:

```
Array
(
    [num_seg] => 1
    [seg_size] => 31457280
    [avail_mem] => 31448408
    [block_lists] => Array
        (
            [0] => Array
                (
                    [0] => Array
                        (
                            [size] => 31448408
                            [offset] => 8864
                        )

                )

        )
)
```

The only value that is typically useful from the shared memory allocation is the available memory. If all the application needs to do is gather some statistics, both `apc_sma_info()` and `apc_cache_info()` accept a `$limited` parameter that can be `true` to exclude the array of information (memory blocks and cached keys, respectively), which is not immediately useful for statistical purposes. In the case of `apc_cache_info()` it is actually the second parameter because the first is the type of cache to return information on. See the PHP manual for more information.

Like eAccelerator, you can use the APC functions to create an administrator control panel to view usage statistics as well as the removal of values stored in cache. However, because of the nature of both systems the status functions become less useful the more servers that the application has.

When to Use APC and eAccelerator

APC and eAccelerator are both very useful and very similar tools. Each yields similar performance and both provide the same functionality. APC is a more open project and may appeal to developers who want to hack the source code to provide custom functionality; which is easy because it is based on PECL. eAccelerator is more restrictive, but is also an active project and is open source so it can be modified as well.

It is up to the individual application team to determine which license is more appropriate and which system is easier to work with. An application should never be deployed to a production environment without one of these because they both increase performance dramatically.

Several other opcode caching solutions are available that provide the same functionality but are either less common or not open source. This book chooses to use open source software whenever possible, so proprietary closed source solutions are not included here.

Although the usefulness of the opcode caching is undeniable it is up to the application developer to decide when and where to apply user cache techniques in particular applications.

One case in which a local user cache should never be used is when the data changes frequently. In these cases it is extremely difficult (if not impossible, depending on the system architecture) to invalidate or change a cached value across multiple machines. The result is a very inefficient cache where some servers might display one version of the data while other servers display a completely different version.

Finally, the biggest disadvantage of a local user cache is that it produces many copies of the same data across multiple servers. Local user cache is not something you want to use if you have more than one web server. Though it may be the most efficient way to go for a single web server because it guarantees that the cache is always on the local machine, it is often necessary in complex applications to have a distributed cache to optimize resource allocation. That is where memcached comes into play.

MEMCACHED

Many of the caches that have been already discussed in this chapter have more to do with caching precompiled code for faster execution as well as optimization. The other type of caching that you want to take advantage of is caching data that your application normally obtains from a database — without having to access the database. This helps to relieve the load on your database so that every access to your site that requires data doesn't always have to obtain that data from the database, which on extremely busy sites can adversely affect your database's, and your site's, overall performance. Furthermore, having a cache that is distributed and shared allows you to *scale out* by using commodity hardware to provide distributed services such as cache. With the huge web sites that are now commonplace, scaling out, versus the traditional scaling up, is how organizations are now dealing with growth. Many great innovative solutions have been borne out of necessity, and one of those solutions that provides distributed caching is *memcached*.

What Is memcached?

Memcached is a high-performance, distributed memory object caching system. It is essentially a simple multi-threaded server that allocates memory to provide a key/value cache for applications to cache data to alleviate database load or reduce file system access. Applications utilize memcached through a client that communicates with memcached using either the ASCII or binary protocol. Memcached was created by Brad Fitzpatrick and his company Danga Interactive to reduce the load on the stressed database for their extremely busy web site, `Livejournal.com`. At the time, `Livejournal.com` had about 1 million users and 20 million dynamic page views per day. With the advent of memcached, their database load dropped to almost nothing. Since then, many other web sites have adopted the use of memcached: Facebook, Slashdot.org, Fotolog, and Digg, to name a few. These are all sites that are extremely busy, and in recent years, there are now thousands of web sites with the C10K problem — which is the need to serve 10,000 clients on your web site simultaneously. Application caching using memcached is a crucial component for solving this problem because the database is often the bottleneck for a web site. You, too, can take advantage of memcached for the benefit of your database and web site. This chapter introduces you to how to use memcached with your PHP web applications.

What memcached Does for You

Memcached allows you to take extra, unused memory and make it available to your applications that could use extra memory for caching. It also allows you to make better use of your memory in that it conglomerates disparate memcached servers into one memory pool. In traditional caching systems, memory would be used on each server separately, which was wasteful because the capacity of this type of cache was only a fraction of what it could be when you consider the sum total of memory across your server farm. Also, it was complex to keep the data stored in the cache consistent. Figure 4-1 illustrates traditional caching per server with what memcached gives you.

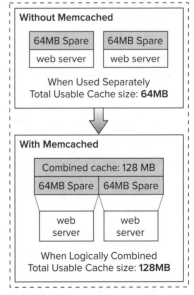

How Does memcached Work?

Memcached at its core utilizes a slab allocator, providing a dictionary, or hash lookup table where items are cached in memory, which is networked using a server built with libevent, a non-blocking networking library, for extremely fast performance. The important thing to realize is that data "stored" in memcached is not durable — meaning it's not really stored in

FIGURE 4-1

a traditional on-disk sense and is gone when the memcached server goes away by being either shut down or restarted.

For more info on Slab allocators see Jeff Bonwicks article http://www.ibm
.com/developerworks/linux/library/l-linux-slab-allocator/ *as well as*
Steve Yen's article about memcached's slab allocator at http://code.google
.com/p/memcached/wiki/MemcachedSlabAllocator.

Memcached has no failover or built-in replication, so it is up to the application using memcached to implement how data is managed and kept up to date. It should be noted that the memcached project is one that is constantly being improved upon by the diligent efforts of Alan Kasindorf, Dustin Sallings, Trond Norbye, and Turo Maesaka. You can always find out answers to questions or other information about memcached using the memcached user mailing list or IRC channel #memcached at Freenode.

Memcached is an *LRU* (*Least Recently Used*) cache, which means that the stored data that is the oldest and least accessed is evicted and replaced with newer items when memcached's memory capacity is reached. Also, memcached enables you to set an expiration value for the object being stored, meaning that you can provide an expiration time, in seconds, for an object you are storing to expire sometime in the future or not at all, at least until the LRU functionality results in the object being evicted. In terms of eviction precedence, memcached first replaces expired objects followed by objects that are the oldest and least recently used.

One thing to know about memcached is that it has a *contract* with the user that says "you are not completely guaranteed that an item will be in the cache or will obtain the desired item you are requesting, but you will never get what you *did not* ask for." This doesn't mean that memcached is unreliable and that you will get a ton of cache misses. It merely means that because it is an LRU cache, sometimes items could have either expired or been evicted, but you will certainly never get something you didn't ask for.

Memcached can run in any type of configuration: either on one or more servers, or even multiple instances on the same server. The memcached server itself is very simplistic; sometimes even the term *dumb server* is used. This isn't a negative connotation. It merely means that it has no concept of other memcached servers. All the functionality and intelligence for how items are set and retrieved and on which server they are found is implemented in the memcached client.

In terms of your application, whether you have one or a hundred memcached servers, that particular client connection to memcached acts as if it is connected to one single source of storage — a memcached cluster. This is the one of the greatest things about memcached! You can use cheap, commodity hardware to solve your caching requirements. Also, memcached is not CPU intensive. It simply uses memory.

Memcached, up until recently, did not require any authorization to connect. At the time of this writing, Dustin Sallings (one of the current developers of memcached) has implemented SASL support, and by the time you read this book memcached will be a well-tested and mature feature!

The mechanism that the client uses to treat multiple memcached servers as one is called *consistent hashing*. It's implemented in the client, which determines what server an object is stored to or retrieved from. Consistent hashing essentially computes a hashed value of the servers connected to and compares that to the hashed value of the key of the object for computing which memcached server to use.

Once the client knows which servers to request for a given item, it sends the requests in parallel to the appropriate servers. Each server then uses its hash key lookup table to retrieve the stored item and sends the results to the client. The client then aggregates the results together for the application to use.

Figure 4-2 shows the basic concept of how mem-cached works — your PHP application using a memcached library (which is discussed shortly) connects to one or more memcached servers in a server pool. How items are cached among these multiple servers is accomplished through the function of consistent hashing, allowing multiple servers to be treated as a single pool in the first place.

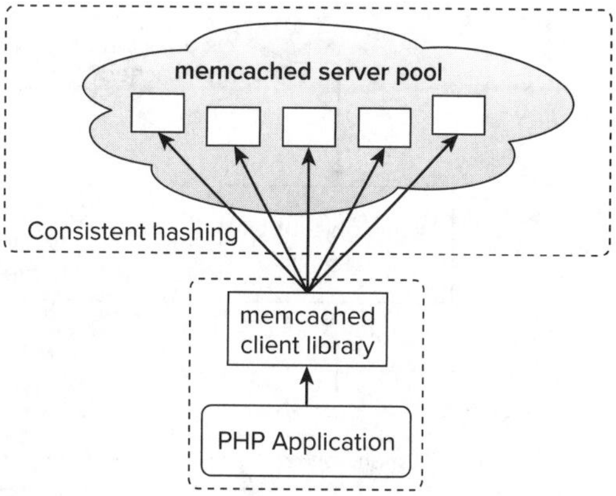

FIGURE 4-2

How to Use memcached

Traditionally, to store or retrieve data in your application, you would run SQL queries or stored procedure calls from your application to the database. With caching available, you can modify your applications to take advantage of the caching to first check the cache before accessing the database.

One example of caching for a web application is the web site Slashdot.org. As most geeks know, Slashdot has its stories, which are regularly posted and displayed on the front page or in sectional pages. Slashdot was originally designed prior to the existence a good caching solution. The front page was displayed dynamically, and required several SQL queries against the database were required to obtain information such as the story title, first paragraph, author's name, user display options, and other required data. These front page stories changed on an hourly basis at most, so this was definitely something that was a good candidate for caching.

The first attempt at caching for these front-page stories was accomplished using a global variable per Apache child process. This was better than nothing, but still not the most ideal solution. Along came memcached, which made it possible to cache this information using a database query that ran only as often needed to keep the cache up to date versus every front page access!

Types of Caching

You will employ three primary types of caching within your applications: *read-through* caching for reads, and *write-through* and *write-back* caching for writes:

➤   **Read-through caching:** When data is retrieved, the application checks the cache first to see if the retrieved data is already cached. If the data is in the cache, it just returns that data without having to query the database. If the data is not in the cache, the data is first obtained from the database, then stored in the cache, and finally returned to the user. The idea is for a read operation not only to obtain the requested data, but also to ensure the cache has the required data for subsequent reads. Figure 4-3 shows a diagram of how a read-through cache works.

➤   **Write-through caching:** When data is written to memcached, it is also written to the database, synchronously. Figure 4-4 shows how straightforward write-through caching is.

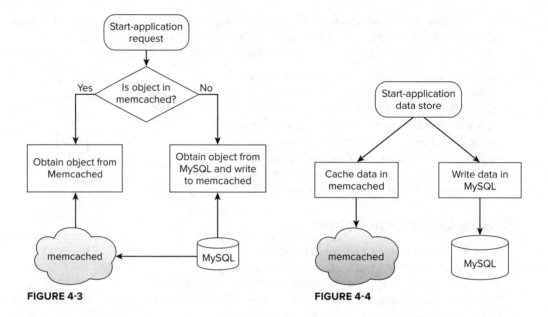

FIGURE 4-3

FIGURE 4-4

➤ **Write-back caching:** When data is written to memcached, some mechanism eventually writes the data to the database, asynchronously. This mechanism uses a separate process that needs to know what data items have been cached, and uses that information to read the stored data from memcached to the databases. For any process to know what items have been cached, you need something that at least stores the keys for stored items, which you can then use as a catalogue to know what to fetch from memcached and then store in the database. A *catalogue* table is suitable for this. It's simply for saving entries for each key of items that need to be processed from memcached to the database. The mechanisms that initiate this separate asynchronous process to store data into the database (or other persistent store) can be implemented in several ways, some of which are:

➤ **Using a job server such as Gearman.** When the data is written to memcached, the key of the item is stored in the catalogue table and a job is requested to process cached items using a Gearman client either from within the application or by a trigger on the catalogue table. Gearman then assigns the job to a worker that obtains the stored data from memcached and stores it in MySQL, and finally the entry for the processed item is removed from the catalogue table.

➤ **Using the catalogue table.** When the data is written to memcached, an entry is made into the catalogue table that a cron job would then run at a given frequency. This works much in the same way that the Gearman worker works except it operates on a batch of item keys and can run as frequently or infrequently as needed. This is known as lazy processing/caching because you can control how often data is retrieved from the cache and stored in the database.

Figure 4-5 shows write-back caching with three possible mechanisms, as just described, of getting data that is stored in memcached stored into MySQL.

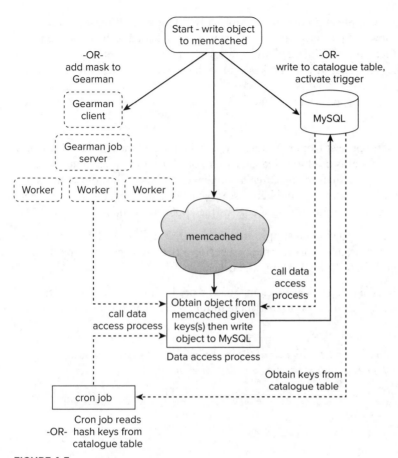

FIGURE 4-5

Another benefit of caching is that it gives you the flexibility to use all sorts of useful tricks. You can use the cache to perform "lazy" processing. For instance, imagine an application that processes RSS feeds and needs to both store the components of the feed into the database and provide a JSON cache of the feed for an AJAX client application to display.

One part of the application, run via a web request, requests an RSS feed from the Internet. It obtains the RSS feed content, which is an XML file. The application then parses this XML file into a DOM Perl object and converts the XML into JSON. The JSON is then stored in memcached, and becomes available for the application to serve it to the AJAX client. The XML DOM object is stored as a separate object in memcached and an entry is made in a queue table containing the key of the DOM object. By some mechanism, either a cron job or a trigger to a UDF on the queue table, yet another process (non-web) reads from the queue table, which obtains all keys stored in this queue table and retrieves the DOM objects stored in memcached with these key values. This process then loops through each DOM object, storing each feed item in the database. This process also deletes the entries in the queue table and deletes the processed DOM objects from memcached.

What all this means is that an application that would normally perform all of these actions in the web application layer can now be split into two processes by memcached: a web application, which mainly has to take care of fetching and caching, and a non-web application that can run asynchronously, separately from the web request, which takes care of the heavier database processing at whatever frequency is desired.

What Is Gearman?

Gearman is yet another useful project from the same people who created memcached: Danga, Brian Fitzpatrick, et al. It is a server that is used to dispatch, assign, or "farm out" jobs to machines that are better suited to run these tasks than the machine having made the call. This allows tasks to be run in parallel, allowing for load balancing and better scaling as well as being able to call functions that are not written in the same programming language as the application code.

Gearman consists of a server — called interestingly enough *gearmand* — and clients: caller clients, which make requests to the server, and workers that can perform the work requested by the clients. There are client APIs for PHP, Perl, Ruby, Python, and others.

You can use Gearman to handle things like processing items stored in memcached (write-through caching) as well as any processing you want to distribute to relieve the load on your main server.

 In Chapter 10 you will see just how useful Gearman is, with the demonstration of building a search engine application as a practical example of how you can use Gearman.

Caching Strategies

You can employ different types of caching strategies for different types of data, depending on how often that data changes and what type of data is being stored, as shown in Table 4-1:

TABLE 4-1: Caching Strategies

STRATEGY	DESCRIPTION
Deterministic cache	The caching described in the read-through cache example. The client application requests data. If the data is in memcached, it's simply returned. If it is not, the data is obtained from MySQL, written to memcached and then returned to the requester.
Non-deterministic cache	Data that you assume to always be in memcached. This is particularly useful for more static data. This also requires the promise that the data is always loaded into memcached, such as when a web server starts. Also, if possible, you should attempt to keep this cache on its own server if it has other types of stored objects that might cause the more static data to be replaced through the LRU mechanism.

STRATEGY	DESCRIPTION
Session or state cache	The cache that you use for storing data such as user session data. It is particularly useful for applications such as shopping carts.
Proactive caching	Similar to non-deterministic cache, this is where data is automatically updated in cache on a database write. You could do this using triggers and the Memcached Functions for MySQL, which are covered in Chapter 5.
File system or page caching	Caching templates or HTML code that comprises the design of your web site. This allows you to avoid using the file system to obtain your site content.
Partial page caching	Where page components are stored. Allows you to avoid using expensive queries that provide calculations, such as comment or story popularity, to display a page every time. Instead, you can build these components on a regular basis and then store them in memcached. When the page displays, it just obtains these pre-built components from memcached and displays them!
Cache replication	Functionality built into your application that writes data to multiple memcached servers for each item stored. This ensures that you have redundancy.

INSTALLING MEMCACHED

Installing memcached is very simple. You can either use a package installer for most Linux distributions or compile the source. There is only one prerequisite package that memcached requires — libevent. *Libevent* is an API that memcached uses to scale any number of open connections. You can also install this on most Linux distributions with package management or by source.

CentOS

To install memcached on a CentOS Linux server, follow these steps:

1. Start out by running

```
[root@testbox ~]# yum search memcached
```

This produces various results. The two most important are (this is on a 64-bit CPU; on 32-bit it may be i386):

```
memcached.x86_64: High Performance, Distributed Memory Object Cache
memcached-selinux.x86_64: SELinux policy module supporting memcached
```

The SELinux package is to ensure that memcached has the correct firewall settings to be allowed to be run. Memcached runs by default on port 11211. You could just as easily set the firewall to allow 11211 through.

2. Next you run the install:

```
[root@testbox ~]# yum install memcached.x86_64
. . . .
Dependencies Resolved

===============================================================================
 Package                 Arch        Version         Repository        Size
===============================================================================
Installing:
 memcached               x86_64      1.2.5-2.el5     epel              59 k
Installing for dependencies:
 libevent                x86_64      1.1a-3.2.1      base              21 k

Transaction Summary
===============================================================================
Install      2 Package(s)
Update       0 Package(s)
Remove       0 Package(s)

Total download size: 80 k
Is this ok [y/N]:
```

As you can see, libevent is automatically included as a dependency, so there is no need to specifically install it.

3. Select "y" to complete the installation. The installer will also set up the init scripts that start memcached when the operating system is booted.

Ubuntu

With Ubuntu, use `apt-cache` search:

```
$ apt-cache search memcached
libcache-memcached-perl--Cache::Memcached--client library for memcached
libmemcache-dev--development headers for libmemcache C client API
libmemcache0--C client API for memcached memory object caching system
memcached--A high-performance memory object caching system
```

All of these packages are ones that you might as well install. The *libmemcached* packages are for the high-performance client library Libmemcached, which is explained later in this chapter. Use `apt-get install` to install these packages:

```
$ apt-get install memcached libmemcache-dev
libmemcache0
Reading package lists.. Done
Building dependency tree
Reading state information.. Done
The following extra packages will be installed:
  libevent1
```

```
The following NEW packages will be installed:
  libevent1 libmemcache-dev libmemcache0
  memcached
0 upgraded, 6 newly installed, 0 to remove and 96 not upgraded.
Need to get 227kB/278kB of archives.
After unpacking 946kB of additional disk space will be used.
Do you want to continue [Y/n]? Y
```

As with yum, `apt-get` ensures libevent is installed, taking care of any dependencies.

OpenSolaris

With OpenSolaris, you can install from the package manager GUI, or from the command line:

```
$ pfexec pkg install SUNWmemcached
DOWNLOAD                              PKGS     FILES    XFER (MB)
Completed                             1/1      11/11    0.1/0.1

PHASE                                 ACTIONS
Install Phase                         43/43
```

Installing Memcached from Source

You can also install memcached by source. This may be your preferred option especially if you want the latest and greatest release. You can find the web page for memcached at `Danga.com`: `http://www.danga.com/memcached/`. From there you will find a link to the latest source, or repository in either git or subversion. If you are not using a packaged version of libevent, you'll need to obtain that too — from `http://monkey.org/~provos/libevent/`.

Now, follow these steps:

1. Download libevent:

```
$ wget http://monkey.org/~provos/libevent-1.4.10-stable.tar.gz
```

2. Compile and install libevent:

```
$ tar xvzf libevent-1.4.8-stable.tar.gz
```

```
$ cd libevent-1.4.8-stable
```

```
$ ./configure
```

```
$ make
```

```
$ make install
```

3. Download memcached:

```
$ wget http://memcached.googlecode.com/files/memcached-1.4.4.tar.gz
```

Or use `git`:

```
$ git clone git://github.com/memcached/memcached.git
```

4. Compile and install memcached:

```
$ tar xvzf memcached-1.4.4.tar.gz

$ cd memcached-1.4.4

$ ./configure

$ make

$ sudo make install
```

STARTING MEMCACHED

Depending on where memcached is installed, you will need to start it from that location. You can start memcached by hand. To see all options available to memcached, use the -h switch:

```
$ /usr/local/bin/memcached -h
memcached 1.4.4
-p <num>      TCP port number to listen on (default: 11211)
-U <num>      UDP port number to listen on (default: 11211, 0 is off)
-s <file>     UNIX socket path to listen on (disables network support)
-a <mask>     access mask for UNIX socket, in octal (default: 0700)
-l <ip_addr>  interface to listen on (default: INADDR_ANY, all addresses)
-d            run as a daemon
-r            maximize core file limit
-u <username> assume identity of <username> (only when run as root)
-m <num>      max memory to use for items in megabytes (default: 64 MB)
-M            return error on memory exhausted (rather than removing items)
-c <num>      max simultaneous connections (default: 1024)
-k            lock down all paged memory.  Note that there is a
              limit on how much memory you may lock.  Trying to
              allocate more than that would fail, so be sure you
              set the limit correctly for the user you started
              the daemon with (not for -u <username> user;
              under sh this is done with 'ulimit -S -l NUM_KB').
-v            verbose (print errors/warnings while in event loop)
-vv           very verbose (also print client commands/responses)
-vvv          extremely verbose (also print internal state transitions)
-h            print this help and exit
-i            print memcached and libevent license
-P <file>     save PID in <file>, only used with -d option
-f <factor>   chunk size growth factor (default: 1.25)
-n <bytes>    minimum space allocated for key+value+flags (default: 48)
-L            Try to use large memory pages (if available). Increasing
              the memory page size could reduce the number of TLB misses
              and improve the performance. In order to get large pages
              from the OS, memcached will allocate the total item-cache
              in one large chunk.
-D <char>     Use <char> as the delimiter between key prefixes and IDs.
              This is used for per-prefix stats reporting. The default is
```

```
                    ":" (colon). If this option is specified, stats collection
                    is turned on automatically; if not, then it may be turned on
                    by sending the "stats detail on" command to the server.
-t <num>            number of threads to use (default: 4)
-R                  Maximum number of requests per event, limits the number of
                    requests process for a given connection to prevent
                    starvation (default: 20)
-C                  Disable use of CAS
-b                  Set the backlog queue limit (default: 1024)
-B                  Binding protocol--one of ascii, binary, or auto (default)
-I                  Override the size of each slab page. Adjusts max item size
                    (default: 1mb, min: 1k, max: 128m)
-S                  Turn on Sasl authentication
```

The most common options you will use are –u and –m. The first option, –u, specifies the user, defaults to the current user, and won't let you run memcached as root, so if you start memcached as root, you will have to specify a non-root user. The second option, –m, is the size in megabytes of the block of memory that will be slated for memcached. The default is 64 megabytes.

> *You cannot (nor would you want to) run memcached as the root user. If you do, memcached will not start and will inform you that you have to use the –u flag.*

If you are logged in as yourself, and just want to run memcached with defaults, you can certainly just start it, backgrounded:

```
$ /usr/local/bin/memcached &
```

Or with the daemonize flag:

```
$ /usr/local/bin/memcached -d
```

If you want to run memcached in super-mega-uber verbose mode to a log file:

```
$ /usr/local/bin/memcached –u username -vv >>/tmp/memcached.log 2>&1 &
```

The –vv flag causes memcached to print out any request to the server. You can see exactly what memcached is doing if you run it with –vv. This can be very useful for debugging your application to ensure that it is using memcached and to see the items being set or retrieved.

Startup Scripts

Alternatively, you can use startup scripts that come with memcached if you are running a UNIX variant that uses SYSV startup scripts. You can find them in the *scripts* directory of the source package. Some of these scripts are a bit dated and you will most likely have to edit them for the particular setup of your system. This requires system privileges, such as root (or using sudo):

```
$ ls
memcached-init  memcached.sysv  memcached-tool  start-memcached
```

Debian-Based Startup Scripts

`memcached-init` relies on `start-memcached`, which you also need to edit and place in a directory specified in `memcached-init`. Once you have `memcached-init` edited, copy it as `/etc/init.d/memcached`. Make sure to set the correct permissions:

```
# chmod 755 /etc/init.d/memcached
```

Then set up the run-level permissions for this script (linked to their appropriate run-levels) to ensure that memcached automatically starts up at system boot:

```
# update-rc.d memcached-init defaults
 Adding system startup for /etc/init.d/memcached-init ..
   /etc/rc0.d/K20memcached-init -> ./init.d/memcached-init
   /etc/rc1.d/K20memcached-init -> ./init.d/memcached-init
   /etc/rc6.d/K20memcached-init -> ./init.d/memcached-init
   /etc/rc2.d/S20memcached-init -> ./init.d/memcached-init
   /etc/rc3.d/S20memcached-init -> ./init.d/memcached-init
   /etc/rc4.d/S20memcached-init -> ./init.d/memcached-init
   /etc/rc5.d/S20memcached-init -> ./init.d/memcached-init
```

Redhat-Based Startup Scripts

You must edit `scripts/memcached.sysv`. You will need to run these steps as root or using `sudo`. You must ensure that the correct paths, port, and the user that memcached runs as are used:

```
PORT=11211
USER=nobody
MAXCONN=1024
CACHESIZE=64
OPTIONS=""
```

One other change you might have to make to ensure the path to memcached is known to the startup script is to add the variable `prog_path`, right after `prog`:

```
prog="memcached"
prog_path="/usr/local/bin/memcached"
```

Then you would change:

```
daemon memcached -d -p $PORT -u $USER  -m $CACHESIZE -c $MAXCONN. . .
```

to:

```
daemon $prog_path -d -p $PORT -u $USER  -m $CACHESIZE -c $MAXCONN. . .
```

Once the script is ready, it can be copied as `/etc/init.d/memcached`. To set up the script to be started upon system reset, first add it:

```
[root@host]# chkconfig --add memcached
```

Verify that it will still need to have its levels set up:

```
[root@host]# chkconfig --list memcached
memcached              0:off   1:off   2:off   3:off   4:off   5:off   6:off
```

Set memcached to run in the proper levels (2, 3, 4, 5):

```
[root@host]# chkconfig --level 2345 memcached on
```

Then verify that the changes were made:

```
0:off   1:off   2:on   3:on   4:on   5:on   6:off
```

OpenSolaris

Memcached is registered as a service in SMF and you must use `svccfg` if you want to start memcached with specific options. This is documented in memcached (1M).

To start memcached simply run the following command:

```
$ svcadm enable memcached
```

To check the status of memcached, run the following command:

```
$ svcs memcached
STATE           STIME    FMRI
online          Dec_09   svc:/application/servers/buildbot:memcached
```

To stop memcached simply run the following command:

```
$ svcadm disable memcached
```

Testing Your memcached Installation

You can verify that you have installed memcached successfully as well as gain a simple understanding of how easy it is to run memcached. You have been shown that you can use startup scripts to automatically have memcached start up along with the operating system as well as have an easy start/stop control over the server. Sometimes you may want to debug your application to determine if it is correctly caching. In this case, you can start up memcached by hand (not with the init script — and make sure to shut down memcached with the init script before doing the following steps). The command-line option to run memcached to be verbose about what the server is doing is the –v flag, to which you append more "v"s to make memcached print more verbose messages. The –vvv is the flag that gives you all the details of what memcached is doing, including the internal function calls it is making. The next example uses only –vv because all you want to see is memcached setting and fetching values; two "v"s are sufficient for this level of detail:

```
mybox:~ username$ /usr/local/bin/memcached -vv
```

This is running memcached with the –vv flag, non-backgrounded, so leave the terminal you started it in open. In another terminal, telnet the memcached server at port 11211 (the default memcached port) to see if your server is running and that you can run a few commands:

```
mybox:~ username$ telnet localhost 11211
Trying::1..
Connected to localhost.
Escape character is '^]'.
version
VERSION 1.4.4
```

```
set t1 0 0 4
test
STORED
get t1
VALUE t1 0 4
test
END
delete t1
DELETED
get t1
END
```

Though this chapter hasn't covered the various memcached operations yet, you can easily under-stand what is being done here. As mentioned in the introduction, memcached has both an ASCII and a binary client protocol. The preceding example uses the ASCII protocol (which a human can type into a telnet session), which is a very simple protocol that is described at http://github.com/memcached/memcached/blob/master/doc/protocol.txt.

This process has the following steps:

1. The version command is run, which produces as response of 1.4.4 the version of this spe-cific memcached server running locally.

2. The set command is run, along with the key name "t1", flags, expiration value, and the length of the data you intend to cache in memcached for this key. The response of STORED verifies that t1 was stored.

3. The get command is run, specifying only the key, which results in the value for this item being fetched.

4. A delete command deletes the item using the key "t1" with a response of DELETED verifying the item was deleted, which a subsequent get of "t1" shows to not be available anymore.

Back in the terminal, you had started memcached with the –vv flag, you can see the server doing its job:

```
<32 version
>32 VERSION 1.4.4
<32 set t1 0 0 4
>32 STORED
<32 get t1
>32 sending key t1
>32 END
<32 delete t1
>32 DELETED
<32 get t1
>32 END
```

Which indeed it is!

You can also use this if you are troubleshooting caching issues in your application — such as deter-mining if items are being cached on a given server or whether your application is using the cache to obtain data first before attempting to obtain data from the database.

memcached Clients

To use memcached, as with any server, you also need a client to interact with the server. As already mentioned, the client is where all the functionality is implemented for making memcached instances work as one single unit, or pool of cache through consistent hashing. The clients you will want to be familiar with as a PHP developer are:

➤ **libmemcached:** This is a fast and efficient C library originally written by Brian Aker, now actively maintained by Brian Aker, Trond Nordbye, and several other developers that many different interpreted languages such as PHP, Perl, Python, and Ruby wrap around.

➤ **PECL/memcached:** This is a newer PHP PECL memcached client, interfaced to libmemcached.

➤ **PECL/memcache:** This is the original PHP memcached client (note the "e" versus "ed" at the end), implemented in pure PHP, not wrapped around any C library.

➤ **PHP libmemcached:** This client is a wrapper of libmemcached.

So, what client do you use? Well, the most recent, actively developed and feature-rich client is PECL/memcached. PECL/memcached, because it uses libmemcached, has more features than PECL/memcache:

➤ Optional use of the new memcached binary protocol

➤ Supports CAS operations

➤ Supports delayed `get`

➤ Supports `get`/`set` to a specific server

➤ Can store numeric values natively versus converting them to string values

➤ Allows you to set timeout as well as other options (behaviors) in the client

➤ Supports append and prepend operations

PECL/memcache does have one feature that PECL/memcached does not: Automatic key fixup for invalid keys. PECL/memcached will return a false for invalid keys.

LIBMEMCACHED

Libmemcached is a faster memcached client library written in C that both the PECL/Memcached (the PHP client, discussed in the next section) and the Memcached Functions for MySQL (discussed in the next chapter) are built on top of. It is a faster, more efficient, thread-safe, full-featured C library that has a significant performance gain over existing client libraries. Not only that, but you also have much more control over how the client functions because you can set the client behavior (`memcached_behavior_set()`) with numerous behavior settings such as hashing algorithm or controlling whether the client is blocking or non-blocking, providing CAS (Check and Set) support, and sorting server host sorting, and so on.

This section gives you some familiarity with libmemcached because it is now the de facto client library on top of which so many other interpreted languages, including PHP, are built. Also, libmemcached has a number of useful client tools that can help you to work with memcached directly rather than having to write a utility in an interpreted language.

Libmemcached Features

Some of the design notes for memcached are that libmemcached has:

> ➤ Synchronous and Asynchronous support.

> ➤ A high degree of control in setting how the client itself behaves.

> ➤ The ability to fetch and store data by a master key which means you can group values or objects to a specific server.

> ➤ TCP and Unix Socket protocols.

> ➤ A half dozen or so different hash algorithms.

> ➤ Implemented new CAS, replace, and append operators.

> ➤ Extensive documentation. Man pages cover, in detail, the entire API.

> ➤ Implemented both modulo and consistent hashing solutions, having to do with how data is partitioned among servers within the cluster.

Libmemcache Utility Programs

Libmemcached also includes several command-line tools, shown in Table 4-2, that allow you to debug your memcached cluster as well as gauge its performance:

TABLE 4-2: Command-Line Tools

COMMAND	DESCRIPTION
memcat	Copies the value of a key to standard output
memflush	Flushes the contents of your servers
memrm	Removes a key(s) from the server
memcp	Copies files to a memached server
memstat	Dumps the stats of your servers to standard output
memslap	Generates testing loads on a memcached cluster

Also of particular interest to readers of this book, libmemcached provides several client interfaces/libraries to other languages such as Ruby, Python, Perl, and for this book, PHP.

Installing libmemcached

You can install libmemcached via the OS vendor's specific install utilities such as yum or apt-get; however, because libmemcached is a new project and changes often, it's preferable to compile libmemcached from source or use the latest RPM from the libmemcached project page if you're using a Linux distribution that utilizes RPM. The project page for libmemached is found at `http://tangent.org/552/libmemcached.html`.

The following shows the code for installing via RPM, Ubuntu/Debian and source:

➤ RPM (Redhat, Suse, Fedora, Centos):

```
wget http://download.tangent.org/libmemcached-0.34-1.x86_64.rpm
rpm -ihv libmemcached-0.34-1.x86_64.rpm
```

➤ Ubuntu/Debian:

```
$ sudo apt-cache search libmemcached
libmemcached-dbg - Debug Symbols for libmemcached
libmemcached-dev - Development files for libmemcached
libmemcached-tools - Commandline tools for talking to memcached via libmemcached
libmemcached2 - A C and C++ client library to the memcached server
sudo apt-get install libmemcached2
```

➤ Source:

```
tar xvzf libmemcached-0.35.tar.gz
./configure
make
sudo make install
```

At this point, libmemcached will be installed. You can write programs that utilize the libmemcached library (including the PHP driver PECL/memcached, discussed in the section "PECL/Memcached") as well as use the utility programs.

LIBMEMCACHED UTILITY PROGRAMS

As mentioned before, libmemcached includes useful utility programs that provide various functionalities for testing your memcached cluster. These utilities are simple to use and all specify a list of servers included with the `servers` option.

memcat

This utility displays the output of one or more cached values in memcached by key value. For example, two values were stored using the code:

```
$memc = new Memcached();

$servers array(
            array('localhost', 11211),
```

```
                         array('localhost', 22122) );

    $memc->set('somekey', "This is a value in memcached");
    $memc->set('anotherkey', 123456789);
```

You can view these stored values by using memcat:

```
$ memcat -servers=localhost:22122,localhost:11211 somekey anotherkey
This is a value in memcached
123456789
```

This code is a convenient means to quickly check what you have stored for a certain value without writing any code. Now, if you have stored a PHP object or other data structure — something other than a simple scalar, the object will probably not display correctly because it is stored serialized in memcached. You can also use the following code to figure out what value is cached on what server:

```
$ memcat --servers=localhost:11211 somekey anotherkey
123456789

$ memcat --servers=localhost:22122 somekey anotherkey
This is a value in memcached
```

As you can see, in both cases, both keys were used and only one value was fetched. In the first case, you see how the value for *anotherkey* is obtained from the memcached server running on port 11211. In the second case, the value for *somekey* is obtained from the memcached server running on port 22122.

memflush

This utility does what the name implies — cleans house. It flushes all servers listed in the argument to --servers. The following code shows the usage and result after using memflush (or lack thereof).

```
$ memflush --servers=127.0.0.1:22122,127.0.0.1:11211

$ memcat --servers=localhost:22122,localhost:11211 somekey anotherkey

$
```

memcp

This is a really nifty utility that allows you to copy a file to memcached. The file is keyed with the name of the file sans directory path

```
$ cat /etc/redhat-release
CentOS release 5.2 (Final)

$ memcp --servers=localhost:11211 /etc/redhat-release
$ memcat --servers=localhost:11211 redhat-release
CentOS release 5.2 (Final)
```

memstat

This utility lists the status of one or more memcached servers — just like the PECL/Memcached method `stats()`.

```
$ memstat --servers=localhost:11211
Listing 1 Server

Server: localhost (11211)
 pid: 3055
 uptime: 1367933
 time: 1229221949
 version: 1.2.6
 pointer_size: 64
 rusage_user: 2.904558
 rusage_system: 2.159671
 curr_items: 3
 total_items: 18
 bytes: 323
 curr_connections: 2
 total_connections: 80
 connection_structures: 3
 cmd_get: 103
 cmd_set: 18
 get_hits: 78
 get_misses: 25
 evictions: 0
 bytes_read: 323
 bytes_written: 323
 limit_maxbytes: 67108864
 threads: 1
```

memrm

This utility removes a value from memcached:

```
$ memrm --servers=localhost:11211 redhat-release

$ memcat --servers=localhost:11211 redhat-release

$
```

memslap

This utility is a load generation simulation and benchmark tool for memcached servers. The options it takes can be displayed with `--help`

```
$ memslap --help
memslap v1.0

Generates a load against a memcached cluster of servers.

Current options. A '=' means the option takes a value.

 --concurrency=
```

```
    Number of users to simulate with load.
     --debug
    Provide output only useful for debugging.
     --execute-number=
    Number of times to execute the given test.
     --flag
    Provide flag information for storage operation.
     --flush
    Flush servers before running tests.
     --help
    Diplay this message and then exit.
     --initial-load=
    Number of key pairs to load before executing tests.
     --non-blocking
    Set TCP up to use non-blocking IO.
     --servers=
    List which servers you wish to connect to.
     --tcp-nodelay
    Set TCP socket up to use nodelay.
     --test=
    Test to run (currently "get" or "set").
     --verbose
    Give more details on the progression of the application.
     --version
    Display the version of the application and then exit.
     --binary
    forgot to document this function :)
```

An example of running memslap with a concurrency of 100 and 10 test runs is:

```
$ memslap --servers=localhost:22122,localhost:11211 --concurrency=500
  --execute-number=20 --verbose

Threads connecting to servers 500
Took 1.020 seconds to load data
```

As you can see, this is quite faster than such a test would be against a database server!

memerror

This prints the canonical error message for a given memcached server error code. The example that follows uses an error code of 13.

```
memerror 13

CONNECTION DATA DOES NOT EXIST
```

PECL/MEMCACHED

For client access to memcached, PECL/memcached provides numerous methods of the `Memcached` class to access a pool of memcached servers. The first thing in understanding how to use memcached using a client such as PECL/memcached is to know the basic operations that you perform on memcached to either retrieve from memcached or cache an item in memcached.

You can run the code snippets presented in this section with the programs that the author included with the source code.

You have already seen some simple `set`, `get`, and `delete` operations. These of course are the core operations involved in any key/value stored, but there is more to memcached than this. Being that memcached is a key/value store, you will use a key for all data operations. The operations available are shown in Table 4-3:

TABLE 4-3: Available PECL/memcached Operations

OPERATION	DESCRIPTION
Set	Caches an item in memcached using the key specified, whether it is already in memcached or not. In addition to a key for the item, an expiration time, in seconds, means you can determine how long you want this item to remain in cache (for all "set" operations). As mentioned, memcached is an LRU cache, and normally items expire that are least recently used and have the longest time value. This expiration value essentially makes it so the item is marked as expired and the space becomes available for use by memcached.
Add	Caches an item in memcached, but only if it doesn't already exist for the key specified. You can also provide an expiration time, in seconds, for how long you want this item to remain in cache.
Replace	Replaces an item in memcached only if it exists for the key specified, replacing the value of the existing item for that key. An expiration value in seconds can also be set.
CAS	Stands for check and set. Only cache an item if no one else has updated the item since you last fetched it.
Append	Appends the supplied value to the end of the existing value for the given item specified by key.
Prepend	Prepends the supplied value to the beginning of the existing value for the given item specified by key.
Get	Obtains an item from memcached for the given key.
Delete	Deletes an item from memcached for a given key.
Increment	Increments the value (numeric) of an item for the key specified. You can use this as a sequence.
Decrement	Decrements the value (numeric) of an item for the key specified. You can use this as a "reverse" sequence.

continues

TABLE 4-3 *(continued)*

OPERATION	DESCRIPTION
Stats	Obtains the statistics for the memcached server. This returns a list of various statistic names and values for each memcached server in the pool of servers specified in the connection.
Flush_all	Flushes all items from the pool of memcached servers specified in the connection.
Version	Reports the version of memcached.

Now that you've seen the essential operations with memcached, next you learn how to use PECL/memcached to perform these operations and effectively implement caching.

Connecting, Instantiation

To begin using memcached, you must connect to one or more memcached servers. Before you connect to a memcached server pool, you will instantiate a Memcached instance. The usage of the constructor is:

```
Memcached::__construct([string $persistent_id]);
```

The constructor returns a handle to the connection pool that you use for all subsequent method calls. The $persistent_id value is optional and represents a unique ID you assign this connection and makes it so the instance persists between requests. If you do not use a $persistent_id value, the instance is destroyed at the end of the request. An example of this would be:

```
$memc = new Memcached('mymemc');
```

Another step you can perform when connecting to memcached is to set some client options, or behaviors, for the duration of the connection:

```
public bool Memcached::setOption(int $options, mixed $value);
```

The behaviors include utilizing different distribution and hashing algorithms, determining the type of serializer to use for serializing and de-serializing objects, determining timeout values, using the binary protocol (or not), as well as many other options. Please refer to the documentation on the full list of options you can set. The setOption() method returns a true or false for success or failure.

Next, you need to set which servers comprise the memcached pool you are connecting to. For this, the Memcached method addServer() or addServers() is used:

```
public bool Memcached::addServer(
                        string $host,
                        int $port
                        [, int $weight ] )

public bool Memcached::addServers( array $servers )
```

addServer() takes a single $host, $port, and optional $weight, whereas addServers() takes an array of servers where each array member is an array of a host, port, and optional weight. What is the weight value? This value places a value of precedence of a given server for determining which server among all specified in the pool in which to cache an item. This affects the distribution of how items are stored as a whole.

The following is an example of how a connection is initiated:

```php
<?php

# setting id 'mymemc'
$memc = new Memcached('mymemc');

# prefix every item key with "myapp:"
$memc->setOption(Memcached::OPT_PREFIX_KEY, "myapp:");

# set server distribution to consistent hashing
$memc->setOption(Memcached::OPT_DISTRIBUTION, Memcached::DISTRIBUTION_CONSISTENT);

# two servers
$servers = array (
  array ('192.168.1.126', 11211),
  array ('127.0.0.1', 11211)
  );

# now add the servers
$memc->addServers($servers);

$memc->addServer('192.168.1.133', 11211);


?>
```

As shown, first a Memcached object is instantiated. Next two options are set: Memcached::OPT_PREFIX_KEY and Memcached::OPT_DISTRIBUTION.

➤ OPT_PREFIX_KEY: Causes the key of the stored item to be prefixed with the value specified, in this case with myapp:. This allows you to give a namespace to your keys so what you are caching can be per application, all without having to explicitly set the prefix value.

➤ OPT_DISTRIBUTION: Specifies the type of server distribution algorithm that determines which server sets or fetches an item to or from. In this example, consistent hashing is used. Again, to see all options, please refer to the documentation (http://us3.php.net/manual/en/memcached.constants.php).

Next, you define an array with two members, two arrays, each a server IP address and port, and then add it to the Memcached connection handle using addServers(). A third single server is added using addServer(). Note that you generally want to define all your servers prior to fetching or setting any of your items in memcached, otherwise changing the list of servers changes the distribution of how items are stored and could result in cache misses.

Setting Client Behavior

PECL/memcached has client behavior functions that allow you to set and retrieve numerous settings, which determine how the client behaves such as distribution, network timeouts, serializer, automatic prefixing of keys, the hashing algorithm used. You set these behaviors, or options, prior to connection. You can find the numerous options you have at your disposal can at the PHP site http://us2.php.net/manual/en/memcached.constants.php.

The following example shows how you can both set and retrieve some of the client options. In this case, the default distribution is printed (which is DISTRIBUTION_MODULA) and then is changed to DISTRIBUTION_CONSISTENT. Then the serializer is changed to use JSON for encoding. The server array is stored and then retrieved.

```
$memc = new Memcached();

// find out the current distribution type
$distribution = $memc->getOption(Memcached::OPT_DISTRIBUTION);

// since the value is numeric, set to a text value
$distribution = $distribution == Memcached::DISTRIBUTION_CONSISTENT ?
                                 "CONSISTENT, KETAMA": "MODULA";

echo "The distribution is currently: $distribution\n";

$memc->setOption(Memcached::OPT_DISTRIBUTION, Memcached::DISTRIBUTION_CONSISTENT);

$distribution = $memc->getOption(Memcached::OPT_DISTRIBUTION);
$distribution = $distribution == Memcached::DISTRIBUTION_CONSISTENT ?
                                 "CONSISTENT, KETAMA": "MODULA";

echo "The distribution is now set to: $distribution\n";

// a very cool feature is setting the serializer to JSON
$memc->setOption(Memcached::OPT_SERIALIZER, MEMCACHED_SERIALIZER_JSON);

# two servers in the pool
$servers = array (
    array ('192.168.1.106', 11211),
    array ('127.0.0.1', 11211)
);

# now add the servers
$memc->addServers($servers);
$memc->addServer('192.168.1.125', 11211);

// set a value
if ($memc->set('t1', $servers)) {
  // if true, success setting
  echo "t1 was set.\n";
}
else {
  // if false, failed to set
  echo "failed to set t1\n";
```

```
    }

    // now fetch t1
    $t1= $memc->get('t1');

    $result_code= $memc->getResultCode;
    if ($result_code == Memcached::RES_SUCCESS) {
      print_r($t1);
    }
    elseif ($result_code == Memcached::RES_NOTFOUND) {
      print "t1 not found\n";
    }
```

Code snippet `memc_behaviors.php`

Just to see how changing the serializer to use JSON works, telnet port 11211 of the memcached server where t1 was cached and you will see that it is in fact serialized using JSON! This can be very useful if you are storing data that could simply be fetched and displayed through JavaScript in your application. It also makes it possible to share data with other components or applications that might be written in other languages.

```
get t1
VALUE t1 4 95
a:2:
{i:0;a:2:{i:0;s:13:"192.168.1.106";i:1;i:11211;}
 i:1;a:2:{i:0;s:9:"127.0.0.1";i:1;i:11211;}}
END
```

Putting and Retrieving Data

Now that you have a memcached client connection, the next thing to demonstrate is how to cache and retrieve that data to/from memcached. When caching items in memcached, the value can be a string, a number, or a serialized PHP variable or object. Regarding objects, PECL/memcached automatically handles serialization — if you cache a PHP object, for instance an array. The Memcached class methods for doing this are:

➤ add: The method add() adds a given item keyed by $key with the value of $value, with the optional integer $expiration (seconds). The method addByKey() has as its first value the $server_key variable. This is an arbitrary string value you use throughout your code that causes items to be cached on a specific server as opposed to using a distribution algorithm. It should be noted that you cannot specify the particular server — the server chosen for the server key is a function of consistent hashing. This method can be useful if you want to ensure particular items are on one server. An optional numeric expiration time (in seconds) can be specified by $expiration. Upon success, true will be returned, and upon failure false will be returned. Failures of the add operation includes either a server error or attempting to add an item for a key that already exists.

```
    public bool Memcached::add(
                        string $key,
                        mixed $value
```

```
                                     [, int $expiration   ] )

       public bool Memcached::addByKey(
                                  string $server_key,
                                  string $key,
                                  mixed $value
                                  [, int $expiration   ] )
```

➤ **set:** The method set() sets, regardless of whether it already exists, a given item keyed by $key with the value of $value, with the optional expiration time in seconds. The method setByKey() will set a given item, regardless of whether it exists, to a specific server specified by the arbitrary string value $server_key.

```
       public bool Memcached::set(
                                  string $key,
                                  mixed $value [, int $expiration   ] )

       public bool Memcached::setByKey(
                                  string $server_key,
                                  string $key,
                                  mixed $value
                                  [, int $expiration   ] )
```

➤ **replace:** The method replace() replaces the value of an existing item with the value of $value keyed by $key. You can specify an optional numeric expiration time (in seconds). The method replaceByKey() takes as its first argument an arbitrary string value you specify within your application to ensure items are stored on a specific server. The method returns true upon success, and false upon failure. Possible failures of the replace operation could be either a server error or attempting to replace a non-existing item.

```
       public bool Memcached::replace(
                                  string $key, mixed $value
                                  [, int $expiration ] )

       public bool Memcached::replaceByKey(
                                  string $server_key,
                                  string $key,
                                  mixed $value
                                  [, int $expiration   ] )
```

➤ **get:** The methods get() and getByKey() fetch an item from memcached for a given key. As you can already assume, getByKey() lets you specify a server key as the first argument. Also, just as the set* methods automatically serialize PHP objects, likewise get methods de-serialize PHP objects.

```
       public mixed Memcached::get(
                                  string $key
                                  [, callback $cache_cb
                                  [, double &$cas_token   ]] )

       public mixed Memcached::getByKey(
                                  string $server_key,
                                  string $key
```

```
                        [, callback $cache_cb
                        [, double &$cas_token  ]] )
```

The arguments for `get()` are first the key of the item, the string value `$key`. The next argument, which is optional, is a *read-through caching callback*, which is a function that you specify that obtains the item data being requested should it not exist in memcached. The last argument is an optional reference variable for obtaining the CAS token value of the item to be used for CAS operations. For `getByKey()`, as with the other `*ByKey` methods, the first argument is the string `$server_key` value, followed by the same order and number of arguments as `get()`.

The following are some simple examples of how to use these methods. Assume for these examples that the previously shown connection has already been made. The first example is a simple `set` and `get`:

```php
// set a value
if ($memc->set('t1', 'some value')) {
  // if true, success setting
  echo "t1 was set.\n";
}
else {
  // if false, failed to set
  echo "failed to set t1\n";
}

// now fetch t1
$t1= $memc->get('t1');
// Obtain the result code
$result_code= $memc->getResultCode;
if ($result_code == Memcached::RES_SUCCESS) {
  print "t1 is $t1\n";
}
elseif ($result_code == Memcached::RES_NOTFOUND) {
  print "t1 not found\n";
}
```

Code snippet memc.php

As you can see, this example is painfully simple. You have a key and a value. You set the value using the key and then you can retrieve it using the key. This is memcached! Of course there is more than just `get` and `set`. The next example shows you that you can add and replace, depending on whether the item already is in memcached.

```php
// if $val exists, then it can be replaced
if ($val = $memc->get('t2')) {
  // if successful replace, then print so
  if ($memc->replace('t2', 'replaced value')) {
    echo "replaced t2's value\n";
  }
  else {
    // otherwise, print that replace failed
    echo "failed to replace t2's value\n";
  }
}
// if the value didn't exist, then add it
else {
```

```php
  // success
  if ($memc->add('t2', 'added value')) {
    echo "added t2's value\n";
  }
  // failure
  else {
    echo "failed to add t2's value\n";
  }
}
```

Code snippet memc.php

In this example, what is shown is that if a value exists using a `get`, it is replaced. Otherwise, add the value. There are times when you may prefer to use `replace()` or `add()`, but you most likely will just use `set()` for simplicity.

The next snippet shows how expiration works:

```php
  // set expiration to 6 seconds
  if ($memc->set('t3', 'this will expire in 6 seconds', 6)) {
    $i = 0;
    // loop until the value has expired, using print statements to demonstrate
    while(1) {
      if ($val = $memc->get('t3')) {
        echo "\$val (t3) still exists after $i seconds.\n";
        sleep(1);
        $i++;
      }
      else {
        echo "\$val (t3) has expired after $i seconds.\n";
        break;
      }
    }
  }
}
```

The output of this shows that expirations work as advertised:

```
$val (t3) still exists after 0 seconds.
$val (t3) still exists after 1 seconds.
$val (t3) still exists after 2 seconds.
$val (t3) still exists after 3 seconds.
$val (t3) still exists after 4 seconds.
$val (t3) still exists after 5 seconds.
$val (t3) has expired after 6 seconds.
```

Setting an expiration value is useful when you want to refresh the cached items in your data more often. For such functionality, you can add a check for the existence of a value that has expired, which if not present (expired) would force a re-caching of the value.

Append and Prepend

Two other data modification operations are append and prepend. These are useful operations particularly for string data — you wouldn't want to perform these operations against serialized objects!

For example, if you have some components of your site's design or even a block of HTML you've already cached and you want to concatenate data to the beginning or end of them, these methods are what you use to do so.

You can use the methods `append()` and `appendByKey()` to concatenate a value to the end of the value of an existing item, and use `prepend()` and `prependByKey()` to concatenate a value to the beginning of a value of an existing item:

```
public bool Memcached::append(string $key, string $value);

public bool Memcached::appendByKey(string $server_key, string $key, string $value);

public bool Memcached::prepend(string $key, string $value);

public bool Memcached::prependByKey(string $server_key,
                                    string $key, string $value);
```

One demonstration of how you might use something like this is in some sort of application that posts a listing of RSS items for a blog application as seen in the following code.

```
// turn compression off
$memc->setOption(Memcached::OPT_COMPRESSION, false);
$memc->set('rss_entries', $entries);
$entries = '';
$header = "<rss version='2.0'>\n  <channel>\n";
$footer = "  <channel>\n</rss>\n";

// get a new rss entry
$entry = getNewRssEntry();

// prepend to the beginning of the entries
if ($memc->prepend('rss_entries', $entry)) {
  echo "prepended\n";
}
else {
  echo "not prepended.\n";
}

// get the entries
$entries = $memc->get('rss_entries');

// display the entries, should have the new entry at the beginning
displayRss($header . $entries . $footer);
```

Code snippet pend.php

In this example, there is already a cached block containing existing entries. The function `getNewRssEntry()` obtains the latest entry content with some regularity, and that new entry prepends to the beginning of the existing entries. The newly modified entries then wraps with a header and footer and displays using `displayRss()`.

Delete

Obviously, you may want to also delete items in memcached. The `delete()` and `deleteByKey()` methods perform this operation. `delete()` has as its first argument the string value, `$key`, of the item you want to delete. `deleteByKey()` has as its first argument the server key `$server_key`, followed by `$key` and `$time`.

```
public bool Memcached::delete( string $key  )

public bool Memcached::deleteByKey(
                              string $server_key,
                              string $key
                              )
```

A simple example is:

```
memc->delete('t1');
```

Increment and Decrement

Increment and decrement operations enable you to have a sequence or global counter — not only one that increments, but also decrements — using memcached. Unlike a database, you don't have to concern yourself with what database server you connect to nor have any replication complexity with an auto-increment value if you are using a dual-master setup. Also, you can explicitly specify how much you wish to increment or decrement your sequence. However, the one issue is that memcached is not a durable store. The methods `increment()` and `decrement()` provide the increment and decrement operations:

```
public int Memcached::increment(
                          string $key
                          [, int $offset ] )

public int Memcached::incrementByKey(
                              string $server_key,
                              string $key
                              [, int $offset ] )

public int Memcached::decrement(
                          string $key
                          [, int $offset ] )

public int Memcached::decrementByKey(
                              string $server_key,
                              string $key
                              [, int $offset ] )
```

These methods not only change the value of the integer but also return the incremented or decremented values. An example of usage is:

```
if ($memc->set('counter', 1)) {
  echo $memc->increment('counter') . "\n";
  echo $memc->increment('counter', 10) . "\n";
```

```
        echo $memc->decrement('counter') . "\n";
        echo $memc->decrement('counter', 5) . "\n";
    }
```

This simple example shows both increment and decrement, as well as specifying and omitting the value to increment by. The output of this code snippet is:

```
2
12
11
6
```

As you can imagine, you could make use of this functionality in a number of ways, depending on what functionality your application requires.

Multi-get

You can also retrieve multiple items simultaneously using the getMulti() and getMultiByKey() methods, which take advantage of the memcached client protocol that enables you to specify multiple keys for a get. You most certainly want to use a multi-get if you need to obtain several values at once because you can obtain more items per request, hence fewer network round-trips. More bang for the buck!

```
public mixed Memcached::getMulti(
                            array $keys
                            [, array &$cas_tokens
                            [, integer $flags  ]] )

public mixed Memcached::getMultiByKey(
                            string $server_key,
                            array $keys
                            [, array &$cas_tokens
                            [, integer $flags  ]] )
```

getMulti() has as its first argument an array of strings — the keys for items you are requesting. The next optional argument is an array reference to CAS token values (double) that correspond to each item being requested. This array contains the CAS token values following the call to getMulti(). The last argument is an optional integer value for the particular flags you want to use for this getMulti() call. For instance, you can set a flag to specify that you want the order of items being returned to be the same order as the item keys you specified, as shown in the following example:

```
// set a value
for ($i = 1; $i <= 5; $i++) {
  $key = "t$i";
  if ($memc->set($key, "$i: some value")) {
    // if true, success setting
    echo "t$i was set.\n";
  }
  else {
    // if false, failed to set
```

```
            echo "failed to set t$i\n";
    }
}

$null_val = null;
$t_array = $memc->getMulti( array ('t5','t3','t1'),
                            $null_val,
                            Memcached::GET_PRESERVE_ORDER);

print_r($t_array);
```

Code snippet mget.php

In this example, five items are set starting from t1 through t5. Then there is a subsequent call to
getMulti(), but only specifying three of the items and in reverse order. The output of print_r()
shows that using the flag Memcached::GET_PRESERVE_ORDER resulted in the items being returned in
the order requested, assigned to the array $t_array as this snippet of the output shows:

```
Array
(
    [t5] => 5: some value
    [t3] => 3: some value
    [t1] => 1: some value
)
```

Multi-set

The memcached client protocol doesn't have the ability to allow multiple set-type of operations;
however, PECL/memcached provides functionality to provide multi-set with the Memcached class's
methods setMulti() and setMultiByKey(). Essentially, you set multiple items using an associative array — the keys corresponding with the key for the single item and value the value of the item.
There is an optional array that you can supply that provides an array of expiration times corresponding with each item being set.

```
public bool Memcached::setMulti(
                        array $items
                        [, int $expiration  ] )

public bool Memcached::setMultiByKey(
                        string $server_key,
                        array $items
                        [, int $expiration  ] )
```

The following code snippet is a very simple example showing you how you use setMulti() with
a modification of the previous example for getMulti(). You can get items using getMulti() to
obtain an array of the items you want or you can get them separately as the loop shows.

```
$items = array ();
// build up the associative array
for ($i = 1; $i <= 5; $i++) {
    $items["t$i"] = "$i: some value";
}

// multi-set each item of the array
```

```php
$memc->setMulti($items);

// You can perform a multi-get
$null_val = null;
$t_array = $memc->getMulti( array ('t5','t3','t1'),
                            $null_val,
                            Memcached::GET_PRESERVE_ORDER);

// just as before, you have an array of the keys you requested
print_r($t_array);

// or get each item individually
for ($i = 1; $i <= 5; $i++) {
  $val = $memc->get("t$i");
  print "$val\n";
}
```

Code snippet mset.php

Cache Locality Using byKey Methods and Multi get/set

In some cases, you may prefer behavior that allows you to cache related data on one server. Doing this along with multi-get methods reduces the number of network round-trips. This is what the various *byKey methods are for. These methods are useful for partitioning your cache per server and for sending any items you cache to a specific server — specified by the server key — rather than having the client automatically caching an item on whatever server the distribution algorithm determines it should use. These methods do not let you determine on *which* server items are stored, but they do guarantee that only one server is used for the given server key.

The following code drives home how cache partitioning works along with your useful -vv command-line argument (your memcached debug tool) when you run memcached (using a different terminal window for each server):

```php
// arbitrary list of server keys, can be any name you chose
$server_keys = array('serverA', 'serverB', 'serverC');
// loop through for each server key
foreach ($server_keys as $server_key) {
  // loop through, assigning
  $items = array();
  for ($i = 0; $i < 4; $i++) {
    // use a random string for the key
    $key = "$server_key:" . rand_str(8);
    $items[$key] = "value for $key";
  }
  $key_list[$server_key] = $items;
  $memc->setMultiByKey($server_key, $items);

}
```

Code snippet by_key_mget.php

The previous example uses three different server keys that are defined in an array, which is then iterated over and which sets four items for each server. The key for each item contains the server key, which allows you view, along with the verbose output of each server, where each was stored. In addition, a multi-dimensional array keeps track of what keys and to what server key items are set. You can use this to fetch these items later.

```
<32 new auto-negotiating client connection
32: Client using the ascii protocol
<32 set myapp:serverC:xrfKYehz 0 0 26
>32 STORED
<32 set myapp:serverC:TbSY42SI 0 0 26
>32 STORED
<32 set myapp:serverC:oaXHEWkO 0 0 26
>32 STORED
<32 set myapp:serverC:gwOi3xxp 0 0 26
>32 STORED
<32 quit
<32 connection closed.
```

So, as shown, localhost was the server used for serverC. Next, in a terminal window to another server, 192.168.1.126, you will see:

```
<6 server listening
<7 send buffer was 124928, now 268435456
<7 server listening (udp)
```

Interesting, nothing happened there. Curious and curiouser! What about the terminal window for 192.168.1.133?

```
<10 new auto-negotiating client connection
10: Client using the ascii protocol
<10 set myapp:serverA:tUzhFpjr 0 0 26
>10 STORED
<10 set myapp:serverA:0tzhCQhG 0 0 26
>10 STORED
<10 set myapp:serverA:zwNNAqhu 0 0 26
>10 STORED
<10 set myapp:serverA:0eLt123j 0 0 26
>10 STORED
<10 set myapp:serverB:LsHRXr0X 0 0 26
>10 STORED
<10 set myapp:serverB:ay5dFcj5 0 0 26
>10 STORED
<10 set myapp:serverB:OwHOdo9c 0 0 26
>10 STORED
<10 set myapp:serverB:JKM0CFjO 0 0 26
>10 STORED
<10 quit
<10 connection closed.
```

Aha! So, the client used 192.168.1.133 for both serverA and serverB. In summary, the servers used for each server key were:

➤ **serverA:** 192.168.1.133

➤ **serverB:** 192.168.1.133

➤ **serverC:** localhost

This demonstrates that by using the *ByKey methods, a specific server will be used for caching items for a given server key, but again, not *which* server. You have no control over that. The next code snippet shows fetching of these items — with a multi-get, something you want to do as often as possible — using the getMultiByKey() method and the array for keeping track of which keys map to which server in the previous example:

```
foreach ($server_keys as $server_key) {
   // loop through for each server key, multi-get all items
   $items = array();
   $keys = array_keys($key_list[$server_key]);
   $items = $memc->getMultiByKey($server_key, $keys);
   var_dump($items);
}
```

If you look at the terminal windows for each memcached server, you will see a similar verification stating which server keys are being mapped to which server.

getDelayed

You also have the ability to call a get without waiting for the data (non-blocking, asynchronous get). This works so that a request for items is made and immediately returned without waiting for the data. The data can be later fetched when needed, much in the same way that a database query calls a prepare, executes it, and then fetches the data result. For PECL/memcached, this functionality is implemented with the methods getDelayed() and getDelayedByKey() in conjunction with the fetch() or fetchAll() methods to later retrieve the data.

```
public bool Memcached::getDelayed(
                            array $keys
                            [, bool $with_cas
                            [, callback $value_cb]] )

public bool Memcached::getDelayedByKey(
                              $server_key,
                              array $keys
                              [, bool $with_cas
                              [, callback $value_cb ]] )
```

The arguments to getDelayed() are first $keys, an array of keys for requested items, followed by an optional Boolean flag, $with_cas, that toggles whether the CAS tokens for the items being requested should be returned. The last argument is an optional callback function that you can specify and that handles each item returned in the result set when it's fetched. As with all ByKey* methods, getDelayedByKey() has as its first argument the string server key. Both getDelayed() and getDelayedByKey() return true or false, which correspond to success and failure, respectively.

An example of usage is:

```
if ($memc->getDelayed(array ('t1','t2','t3'), true)) {
   echo "mget successful.\n";
   $result = array();

   while ($result = $memc->fetch()) {
     echo "key: " . $result["key"] .
        " value: '" . $result["value"] .
```

```
            "' cas: " . $result["cas"] . "\n";
    }
  }
  elseif ($memc->getResultCode() == Memcached::RES_NOTSTORED) {
    echo "error: NOT STORED\n";
  }
```

Code snippet getdelayed.php

You can alternatively use a callback for processing each item returned as shown in the following example, which modifies the previous example:

```
$memc->getDelayed(array ('t1','t2','t3'), true, 'print_item');

if ($memc->getResultCode() == Memcached::RES_NOTSTORED) {
  echo "error: NOT STORED\n";
}
else {
  echo "mget successfull.\n";
}

function print_item($memc, $item) {
  echo "key: " . $item["key"] .
      " value: '" . $item["value"] .
      "' cas: " . $item["cas"] . "\n";
}
```

As you can see, this negates the need for explicitly fetching and processing all retrieved items — the callback function does it all for you.

CAS

If you want to add some atomicity to your application with regards to get and set, you use *CAS*, which stands for *check and swap*. CAS is a set operation that works so that your attempt to set an item only succeeds if the item was not updated since you last fetched it. If some other client modified the item since you last fetched it, your attempt at modification fails. Also, for any CAS operation to succeed, you must have the correct CAS token value for that item or the attempt to modify the item will fail. You obtain this CAS token value using a get operation:

```
public bool Memcached::cas(
                        double $cas_token,
                        string $key,
                        mixed $value
                        [, int $expiration  ] )

public bool Memcached::casByKey(
                        double $cas_token,
                        string $key,
                        mixed $value
                        [, int $expiration  ] )
```

The first argument is $cas_token, which is a double value for the stored item that you can obtain in a previous get. The remaining arguments are the same as the set() and setByKey() methods. And of course casByKey() has as its first argument the server key. Just like set(), cas() also returns a Boolean true if successful, false if failure.

The following simple example shows how CAS works. In this example, assume that there are two Memcached instances, each a client connected to the same memcached pool of servers. The reason for two clients is to give an example that distills down to the most basic concept of why you would want to use CAS.

```php
// set a value
if ($memc->set('t1', 'initially set value')) {
  // if true, success setting
  echo "t1 initially set.\n";
}
else {
  // if false, failed to set
  echo "failed to set t1\n";
}

// now fetch t1
if ($t1= $memc->get('t1', null, $cas)) {
  print "t1 value is '$t1'\n";
}
elseif ($memc->getResultCode() == Memcached::NOT_FOUND) {
  print "t1 not found\n";
}
echo "cas value $cas\n";

// did anyone else change it since?
sleep(2);
if ($memc->cas($cas, 't1', 'a new value using cas')) {
  echo "t1 set with cas\n";
}
else {
  echo "t1 not set with cas\n";
}
// now fetch t1 again
if ($t1= $memc->get('t1', null, $cas)) {
  echo "t1 value is '$t1'\n";
}
elseif ($memc->getResultCode() == Memcached::NOT_FOUND) {
  echo "t1 not found\n";
}
echo "cas value $cas\n";

sleep(2);
// another client, t2 is setting
echo "memc2 is setting t1\n";
$memc2->set('t1', 'memc2 changed me');
sleep(2);
// did anyone else change it since?
sleep(2);

// this should not succeed
if ($memc->cas($cas, 't1', 'check if cas can set')) {
  echo "t1 set with cas\n";
```

```
    }
    else {
      echo "t1 not set with cas\n";
    }
```

Code snippet cas.php

This example shows how CAS succeeds if another client hasn't modified the item since you last fetched it and then how CAS fails if another client ($memc2) did modify it in between the last fetch. The sleep() calls are for accentuating the central point of the example when running the program. The following output verifies that the second client, $memc2, having modified t1 since it was last fetched by $memc, causes the second cas() call to fail:

```
t1 initially set.
t1 value is 'initially set value'
cas value 14
t1 set with cas
t1 value is 'a new value using cas'
cas value 15
memc2 is setting t1
t1 not set with cas
```

Also note in this output that the CAS token increments each time there is a successful CAS operation.

Statistics

You may, in fact, want to write internal utility applications to monitor memcached and provide information about how your memcached server pool is functioning. This includes information such as how much memory is being used, how many items have been stored, how many cache hits and misses there have been, and so on. The method for this information is getStats():

```
public array Memcached::getStats( void  )
```

The following code if run with the previous connection the pool of three memcached servers:

```
$stats_ar = $memc->getStats();

print_r($stats_ar);
```

Code snippet memc_stats.php

produces the output showing three servers' stats:

```
Array
(
    [192.168.1.106:11211] => Array
        (
            [pid] => 45035
            [uptime] => 75925
            [threads] => 4
            [time] => 1256400151
            [pointer_size] => 32
            [rusage_user_seconds] => 0
```

```
            [rusage_user_microseconds] => 729726
            [rusage_system_seconds] => 1
            [rusage_system_microseconds] => 519083
            [curr_items] => 0
            [total_items] => 0
            [limit_maxbytes] => 67108864
            [curr_connections] => 10
            [total_connections] => 12
            [connection_structures] => 11
            [bytes] => 0
            [cmd_get] => 0
            [cmd_set] => 0
            [get_hits] => 0
            [get_misses] => 0
            [evictions] => 0
            [bytes_read] => 20
            [bytes_written] => 745
            [version] => 1.4.1_25_g2c7bfeb
    )

[127.0.0.1:11211] => Array
    (
            [pid] => 743
            [uptime] => 75921
            [threads] => 1
            [time] => 1256400151
            [pointer_size] => 64
            [rusage_user_seconds] => 0
            [rusage_user_microseconds] => 70000
            [rusage_system_seconds] => 0
            [rusage_system_microseconds] => 10000
            [curr_items] => 2
            [total_items] => 9
            [limit_maxbytes] => 67108864
            [curr_connections] => 2
            [total_connections] => 13
            [connection_structures] => 3
            [bytes] => 329
            [cmd_get] => 10
            [cmd_set] => 9
            [get_hits] => 10
            [get_misses] => 0
            [evictions] => 0
            [bytes_read] => 956
            [bytes_written] => 1491
            [version] => 1.2.6
    )

[192.168.1.125:11211] => Array
    (
            [pid] => 11596
            [uptime] => 75889
            [threads] => 2
            [time] => 1256399615
```

```
        [pointer_size] => 32
        [rusage_user_seconds] => 0
        [rusage_user_microseconds] => 8000
        [rusage_system_seconds] => 0
        [rusage_system_microseconds] => 12000zzzzzzzzz


        [curr_items] => 1
        [total_items] => 5
        [limit_maxbytes] => 67108864
        [curr_connections] => 4
        [total_connections] => 10
        [connection_structures] => 5
        [bytes] => 66
        [cmd_get] => 5
        [cmd_set] => 5
        [get_hits] => 4
        [get_misses] => 1
        [evictions] => 0
        [bytes_read] => 260
        [bytes_written] => 733
        [version] => 1.2.8
    )


)
```

For information on what each statistic means, please consult the memcached project web site at http://memcached.org.

Server List

One other useful informational method is the getServers() method, which returns a list of servers as an array that the server pool is composed of — just like the server list shown previously, used in creating a connection:

```
public array Memcached::getServerList  ( void  )
```

This simple snippet shows how this works:

```
$server_ar = $memc->getServerList();
print_r($server_ar);
```

Error Handling

Throughout these examples, you have seen various ways of dealing with errors. In some cases, for instance, a set operation is performed as the conditional to an if-else block. If true, the value was set; if false, something failed. This is one way of dealing with an error of a set. For get, you sometimes use the simple check that a value was fetched to conditionally determine if there was an error. However, as shown in some examples, you might want to know what the specific error was or use a condition of a specific error in an `if-else` block. To retrieve the specific error of something that failed, you can use the following methods:

```
public string Memcached::getResultMessage(void)
public int Memcached::getResultCode(void)
```

The first method, `getResultMessage()`, returns a string message from the particular operation that was performed. The method `getResultCode()` returns a numeric code from the server. You can find the result codes and what they mean at `http://us2.php.net/manual/en/memcached.constants.php`. The following example shows how you can use these two methods:

```
// set a value
if ($memc->set('t1', 'initially set value')) {
  echo "success setting\n";
}
elseif ($memc->getResultCode() == Memcached::RES_NOTSTORED) {
  echo "'t1' was not set\n";
}

echo "return message from set operation was: " . $memc->getResultMessage() . "\n";

$t1= $memc->get('t1', null, $cas);
echo "return message from get operation was: " . $memc->getResultMessage() . "\n";

if ($memc->add('t1', 'added value should not work')) {
  echo "success adding\n";
}
elseif ($memc->getResultCode() == Memcached::RES_NOTSTORED) {
  echo "'t1' was not added\n";
}
echo "return message from get operation was: " . $memc->getResultMessage() . "\n";

$memc->delete('t1');
$t1= $memc->get('t1', null, $cas);
echo "return message from get operation was: " . $memc->getResultMessage() . "\n";
```

Code snippet `result.php`

The output of this code gives you:

```
success setting
return message from set operation was: SUCCESS
return message from get operation was: SUCCESS
't1' was not added
return message from add operation was: NOT STORED
return message from get operation was: NOT FOUND
```

Interestingly, if you were to shut down your memcached servers within the pool (just for testing — don't do this in a production environment!) all calls to `getResultMessage()` would return:

```
return message from set operation was: SYSTEM ERROR
return message from get operation was: SYSTEM ERROR
return message from add operation was: SYSTEM ERROR
return message from get operation was: SYSTEM ERROR
```

PRACTICAL CACHING

Now that you have seen the numerous operations available with PECL/memcached, it would be useful to see how to modify a simple database-driven class to utilize caching. The first thing to think about is what data you want to cache. How much must this cached data match what is in the database or other durable store? Is it data that can be lazily cached or copied from a cache to a durable store, or does it have to be read without the chance of a cache miss or written so that whenever any data is written to the database it is also cached? These are the questions that will determine how you build a caching layer into your application — and the nature and functionality requirements of your application are probably what will in large part provide the answers to those questions.

Another thing to consider is what sort of value you want to use for the keys of items that are cached. The most important thing is that it makes sense — keep it simple! One way to categorize or organize your keys is to use a namespace of sorts. In this example, the key will be composed of the name of the database table as the first part of the key, separated by a colon, and then the unique id of the item being stored — in this example, the user id.

The following example is very simple and a standard type of read-through and write-through cache example. It consists of a `User` object. This is an object that you instantiate. If upon instantiation, you provide a user id, the user data is retrieved using that id from the database and then each `User` class attribute is set with the retrieved data which are accessible with `get` and `set` methods of the class. What is needed is a caching layer. This will be implemented in several places:

> *You can run the code snippets presented in this section with the programs that the author included with the source code.*

➤ Check cache when the user data is retrieved. If the data is in the cache, set the user attributes with the data retrieved from cache. There is no need to check the database, so you can proceed. If the data is not in the cache, retrieve it from the database and then cache the data retrieved.

> *You don't want to cache a database raw result set. You do want to cache the data in some sort of ready-to-use form. In this example, an associative array is used.*

➤ Write to cache whenever you either insert into or update the database.

➤ Delete from cache if the user is deleted from the database.

In the following examples, the code where caching logic was added are in bold for clarity. The first method is of course the constructor. The constructor takes two arguments — either the user id (`$uid`) or the username. Originally, the class had only a connection to the database established accessible with the private class member `$dbh`. As shown in bold, to add caching, a connection handle (the member $memc) to memcached is created. This is the connection the various methods will use for caching.

```php
Require "globals.php";

class User {

  static $userAttribs = array(
    'uid',
    'username',
    'firstname',
    'lastname',
    'password',
    'email',
    'address',
    'city',
    'state',
    'age',
    'zip',
  );

  private $dbh, $memc;

  private $uid, $username, $firstname, $lastname, $password, $email,
    $address, $city, $state, $age;

  private $_user_loaded;

  public function __construct( $uid = 0, $username = '' ) {

    $this->uid = intval($uid);
    $this->username = $username;

    // database connection
    $this->dbh = new mysqli($MYSQL_HOST, $MYSQL_USER, $MYSQL_PASS, $SCHEMA);

    // handle error connecting
    if (mysqli_connect_errno() != 0) {
      printf("Can't connect to MySQL Server. Errorcode: %s\n",
             mysqli_connect_error());
      exit;
    }

    if (!$this->dbh) {
      printf("Can't connect to MySQL Server. Errorcode: %s\n",
             mysqli_connect_error());
      exit;
    }

    // memcached server pool connection
    $serverlist = $MEMCACHED_SERVER_LIST;

    // set the memc private member
    $this->memc = new Memcached();
```

```
    $this->memc->AddServers($serverlist);

    // this loads the user data for the instantiated class to be able to use
    $this->load();
    }
```

Code snippet User.php *and* user_client.php

The load() method is called from the constructor so that instantiation with a given user id or username will result in the instantiated User object's having various user attributes (private attributes, listed in the static array $userAttribs) set with the data for the given user, accessible with get and set methods (not shown in this example). The changes to load() are to simply add a condition that checks if the user data was found in memcached, and if so, the method returns without needing to access the database. If the data is not found in memcached, it must be retrieved from the database and then cached in memcached. This is a read-through cache.

```
public function load() {
    // if the user data has been loaded, no need to do so again
    if ( $this->_user_loaded ) {
      return true;
    }

    // get the UID from the database
    if (!$this->uid) {
      $this->uid = $this->uidFromName($this->username);
    }
    // still no UID, this is a new user
    if (!$this->uid) {
      $this->loadNewUser( $this->username);
    }

    // if user is in cache
    if ( ! $this->getFromCache()) {
      // if user wasn't in DB, return false
      if (! $this->getFromDB()) {
        // if not in database nor memcached, return false, no such user exists
        return false;
      }
      // if user was in DB, read-through cache
      else {
        $this->setToCache();
        return true;
      }
    }
    return true;
  }
```

The save() method handles both inserts of new users and updates to existing users. The caching implemented here is a very simple write-through cache as accomplished with the method setToCache():

```
public function save() {
    if ($this->uid) {
      $this->update();
    }
```

```
    else {
      $this->insert();
    }
    // write to cache, regardless (write-through)
    $this->setToCache();
  }
```

Because so little code is required for the database deletion, it's just as simple to add the delete-
FromCache() method call to this database method.

```
    /*
     * delete existing user object from the database
     */
    function delete () {

      $this->load();

      $delete = 'DELETE FROM users WHERE uid = ?';

      $sth = $this->dbh->prepare($delete);
      $sth->bind_param('i', $this->uid);

      $sth->execute();

      $rows = $sth->affected_rows;

      $sth->close();

      // delete from cache
      $this->deleteFromCache();

      return $rows ? true: false;
    }
```

Next the caching methods are shown. The method getFromCache() simply retrieves the serialized
array from memcached for the given key $key, then loops through each attribute, setting the class
attributes to the values from the retrieved array:

```
    private function getFromCache() {
        $key = "user:$this->uid";
        $user = $this->memc->get($key);
        if ($user) {
          // set object attribs from $user fetched
          foreach (self::$userAttribs as $attrib) {
            print "$attrib $user[$attrib]\n";
            $this->$attrib = $user[$attrib];
          }
          $this->_user_loaded  = true;
          return true;
        }
        else {
          return false;
        }
    }
```

The method `setToCache()` performs a similar looping through each attribute as `getToCache()` except the values of the array that is serialized are set to the values of the class attributes, then the array is stored serialized using the key specified by `$key`:

```php
private function setToCache() {
    $key = "user:$this->uid";
    $user = array();
    // set $user array with each attrib for object
    foreach (self::$userAttribs as $attrib) {
        $user[$attrib] = $this->$attrib;
    }

    // use return value of set
    return ($this->memc->set($key, $user));

}
```

The method `deleteFromCache()` is an extremely simple method that deletes the item for the given key `$key` from memcached:

```php
private function deleteFromCache() {
    $key = "user:$this->uid";
    // use return value of set
    return ($this->memc->delete($key));
}
```

Now, a simple program to verify this class works. Also, if you run `memcached -vvv`, as well as tail your MySQL query log, you can see that the data is being written and retrieved from both memcached and MySQL appropriately:

```php
<?php

require "User.php";

// instantiate with uid 12345
$user = new User(12345);

print "age: " . $user->getAge() . "\n";
print "email: " . $user->getEmail() . "\n";
print "current address: " . $user->getAddress() . "\n";
print "city: " . $user->getCity() . "\n";
print "state: " . $user->getState() . "\n";
print "zip: " . $user->getZip() . "\n";

// change email address
$user->setEmail("patg@northscale.com");

// why not shave off a decade or so?!
$user->setAge(30);

// move to Portsmouth, NH
$user->setCity("Portsmouth");
$user->setAddress("33 Concord St.");
```

```
$user->setZip("03801");

// write data
$user->save();

// verify it was saved!
print "age: " . $user->getAge() . "\n";
print "email: " . $user->getEmail() . "\n";
print "current address: " . $user->getAddress() . "\n";
print "city: " . $user->getCity() . "\n";
print "state: " . $user->getState() . "\n";
print "zip: " . $user->getZip() . "\n";

?>
```

The output shows the data was in fact updated:

```
age: 41
email: patg@northscale.com
current address: 38 Granite St.
city: Cheshire
state: NH
zip: 03320
age: 30
email: patg@northscale.com
current address: 33 Concord St.
city: Portsmouth
state: NH
zip: 03801
```

If you were to write a program that simply accesses data for the user (no updates), you would see that the database isn't being touched once the user is initially loaded.

memcached Proxy: moxi

As you've seen, in your application code you have deal with setting up which servers the pool comprises. You may want to abstract this information in your application, or better yet, you could use a proxy. There just happens to be a memcached proxy called moxi. Developed by Steve Yen of NorthScale, the idea was to develop a proxy that used the same client protocol as memcached that could handle connecting to servers in a given pool, allowing the application using the proxy to not have to maintain any sort of server list — just connecting to one connection. Also, the proxy was developed to provide a better way to add and remove memached server nodes. Other features moxi provides include:

➤ Front cache. Hot keys are cached and are handled by moxi without having to fetch data from the actual memcached server nodes for "hot" keys.

➤ Get de-duplication. This means that if several client connections to moxi are requesting the same keys, those requests are consolidated into a single request to reduce network requests.

➤ Authenticated connections to memcached server nodes.

➤ Aggregation of statistics.

Moxi is built using the memcached codebase, so it closely follows the development of memcached. To obtain memcached, access `http://labs.northscale.com/moxi` for both documentation and download instructions.

As an example, moxi is run with a pool of three server instances shown in the previous sessions:

```
./moxi -z 22122=localhost:11211,192.168.1.118:11211,192.168.1.125:11211
```

This means that moxi is running on port 22122 and is proxying to the pool of three servers shown on port 11211. The connections to moxi from your application are considered *upstream*, whereas the connections from moxi to the pool of memcached servers are considered *downstream*. In your PHP code, you no longer need to set up the server list. You only have to connect to one server — in this case, localhost on port 22122:

```
$memc = new Memcached('moxicon');
$memc->addServer('localhost, 22122');
```

… if you want to see a trace of what moxi is doing, what items it is caching, and what is occurring with downstream and upstream connections.

> *One thing to keep in mind with using moxi is that if you have logic in your application that uses the* byKey *methods that you use to ensure items are stored on a particular server, they will not work as advertised because the key distribution is not handled by moxi.*

Other "memcapable" Key-Value Stores

The term *memcapable* was coined by Matt Ingenthron. It simply means a given key-value store has support for the memcached client protocol. Trond Norbye wrote a tool with the namesake `memcapable`, which is included with libmemcached. Although the term itself has come to mean that there is support for both binary and ASCII memcached protocols, this tool was originally developed to be run against a particular key-value store to first check if the server supports the memcached binary protocol.

Some memcapable key/value stores worth mentioning are:

➤ **Tokyo Tyrant:** A network server for the key-value database library Tokyo Cabinet storing backend (`http://1978th.net/tokyotyrant/`).

➤ **MemcacheDB:** Distributed key-value database using Berkeley DB as a storing backend (`http://memcachedb.org/`).

➤ **Lightcloud:** Distributed and persistent key-value database built on top of Tokyo Tyrant (`http://opensource.plurk.com/LightCloud/`).

Tokyo Tyrant is discussed in a bit more detail in the following section.

Tokyo Tyrant

Tokyo Tyrant is the network interface (database server) on top of the engine Tokyo Cabinet, a database library. Both these projects are written by Mikio Hirabayashi and development of both is supported by the popular Japanese web site `Mixi.com` (`http://mixi.com`) since they extensively use both projects. Tokyo Tyrant has its own networking protocol as well as an HTTP and memcached protocol interface, that latter of which you can utilize the same way you would for memcached itself.

Tokyo Cabinet is a high-concurrency database library. It is a key-value store and works much like DBM or Berkeley DB. Interestingly, it supports several APIs for storage:

➤ In-memory extensible string, array list, map of hash table, and map of ordered tree

➤ On-disk file hash, B+tree, fixed-length array, and table database

The library itself has bindings for a number of languages including PHP. Note — these bindings are not the network API that Tokyo Tyrant provides.

Tokyo Tyrant is the server your application code will talk to using a memcached client such as PECL/memcached. Some of its features include:

➤ Memcached client protocol

➤ Hot backups and update log

➤ Asynchronous replication

You can use Tokyo Tyrant the same way you use memcached for caching data. The memcached client you use will interact with any Tokyo Tyrant server as if it were a memcached server except it runs on a different port (default 1978). The difference between Tokyo Tyrant and memcached is that Tokyo Tyrant uses Tokyo Cabinet for storing data that provides you with a number of storage mechanism choices either in-memory or on-disk, which can give you a caching layer that is also durable. Note, though, that memory is faster than disk, so if you use an on-disk storage, you gain durability but lose in speed — all depending on what you require for your application. Another feature, as already listed, is that Tokyo Tyrant supports asynchronous replication. This can make for an interesting setup in the case where you have two servers that run in a dual master setup. Using Tokyo Tyrant through the memcached protocol uses consistent hashing to distribute items you cache between the two servers, yet replication would ensure that both servers have all keys. Again, this might be a useful setup for you depending on your application's needs. In fact, you could use any mixture of memcached and Tokyo Tyrant for your application and even use moxi as a proxy to any one of them. The memcached client protocol is the key to being able to work with either!

You can obtain both Tokyo Cabinet and Tokyo Tyrant from `http://1978th.net/` (along with some other interesting projects).

To run Tokyo Tyrant, you can either use the server directly or edit the utility script that needs to be copied to your `/etc/init.d` directory. Table 4-4 show how to run the server on the command line and how the options specified determine what storage mechanism it uses:

TABLE 4-4: Running Tokyo Tyrant on the Command Line

COMMAND	STORAGE MECHANISM
`ttserver "*"`	In-memory hash
`ttserver "+"`	In-memory tree
`ttserver /var/ttserver/casket.tch`	On-disk hash
`ttserver /var/ttserver/casket.tcb`	On-disk b-tree
`ttserver /var/ttserver/casket.tct`	On-disk fixed-length

As you can see, the argument given to the Tokyo Tyrant server, `ttserver`, determines what storage mechanism it uses through Tokyo Cabinet. The file-based storage mechanisms specify the data file that is used and the file extension determines what type of file-based storage mechanism is used, as indicated. You want to ensure that the path you provide is writable by Tokyo Tyrant.

An interesting example involves using moxi as a proxy to two Tokyo Tyrant servers. First moxi is started — this time specifying port 1978 for the downstream:

```
host$ /usr/local/bin/moxi -z
22122=localhost:1978,192.168.1.118:11211,192.168.1.125:1978
```

And Tokyo Tyrant started on two servers:

```
otherhost$ ttserver ~/ttserver/casket.tch
```

You will run your PHP script against moxi, on port 22122, just as you did before with memcached as the downstream servers!

Some aspects of the memcached protocol that are not supported with Tokyo Tyrant are:

➤   Prepend and append.

➤   Expirations don't work out of the box when on-disk stores are used.

Another point of interest in this example is that moxi is incredibly useful for easily switching out whatever backend you want to use for caching or even durable storage — without having to change anything in your application!

SUMMARY

Using caching can vastly improve the performance of an application. Opcode caching is used to store PHP documents in their compiled form, allowing for significant performance increases during code execution. User cache stores arbitrary values in a native format that is easy for the application to use. Two types of user cache were discussed in this chapter: local and distributed. eAccelerator and APC (Alternative PHP Cache) provide opcode caching and the application should always have one of them installed. Both extensions are much faster than compiling the PHP script on the fly and/or hitting the database; however, they only provide local user caching for arbitrary data.

Memcached is a high-performance, distributed memory object caching system that enables you to cache data that you would otherwise have to obtain from the database. This can benefit your application in many ways, such as relieving the load on the database, reducing application calls to the database, and providing faster data access because obtaining data from memcached is extremely fast — faster than obtaining it from the database. Unlike local solutions, memcached also provides redundancy and has the benefits of pooled resources and the ability to invalidate and change values across all machines that use the cache.

This chapter showed you everything you could possibly want to know about using caching in PHP. First, the local data and opcode caching systems were discussed. Then the basic concept of memcached was explained: how memcached is a simple memory server that allocates a block of memory for storing data, which is accessible with key values. Also, how memcached can run on multiple servers making it so you can utilize less-powerful machines (than database or web server machines) that have ample memory and have all machines work collectively as a cluster.

This chapter also explained read-through, write-through, and write-back cache and some simple demonstrations of each.

5

memcached and MySQL

WHAT'S IN THIS CHAPTER?

> ➤ Obtaining, installing, and configuring the Memcached Functions for MySQL

> ➤ Syntax and usage examples for various user-defined functions included with Memcached Functions for MySQL

> ➤ Constructing database statements that obtain data from both memcached and MySQL

> ➤ Using triggers to automatically cache data in memcached

In Chapter 4, the PHP client library PECL/memcached that PHP applications use to interface with memcached server pools is implemented at the application layer. What about memcached and MySQL? Is there any sort of interoperability between the two given that they are so commonly used together? It would be great if there was some sort of "glue" between the two, perhaps not even requiring you to have your interaction to each implemented in your PHP application code.

In the open-sourced world, if there is a need, then there is probably a solution to that need! This is why the Memcached Functions for MySQL — aka Memcached UDFs — were written.

This chapter shows you how to take advantage of the Memcached Functions for MySQL, a suite of user-defined functions that make it possible to cache and retrieve cached data at the database layer — from within MySQL.

THE MEMCACHED FUNCTIONS FOR MYSQL

As you will see in Chapter 7, MySQL has an API for writing *user defined functions,* otherwise known as UDFs. That chapter shows an example of a UDF that has a file stat on a directory containing a schema's data files to calculate how much disk space a given schema uses. Because the UDF API is so flexible, it's possible to write many different user-defined functions to do a number of things. With the advent of libmemcached, it became obvious that you could take advantage of this API, along with the UDF API, to create functions that interact with memcached through libmemcached. This could provide all the functionality that you would normally implement with an external language, at the application layer, and this gives you the ability to interact directly with memcached at the database level.

Developed and maintained by the author of this chapter, the Memcached Functions for MySQL are a suite of functions available to use with MySQL that provide you the ability to interact with memcached from MySQL. These functions perform most of the operations shown in Chapter 4, just like PECL/memcached, because these functions are also built using libmemcached.

Because you can use these functions from within MySQL, you have at your disposal the power of an SQL engine in order to initiate caching or data retrieval using the result sets from query. You can combine the fetching of data from one or more tables with the fetching of data from memcached and apply any SQL operations on that result set, such as LIMIT, sorting, and other conditional operations.

Some other aspects of these functions are that they:

➤ Are written in C using libmemcached and the Memcached Functions for MySQL API

➤ Provide get, set, CAS, append, prepend, increment, decrement, delete, replace, add, flush, stats, client behavior setting and retrieval functions, as well as other functionality

➤ Can be used to store procedures and triggers

➤ Allow you to interact with memcached and MySQL independent of the language in which the application is written, or for languages that don't have clients for memcached

➤ Are open source

HOW THE MEMCACHED FUNCTIONS FOR MYSQL WORK

These user-defined functions are built with the libmemcached client library for various operations with a memcached server pool. When a particular UDF is called — say, when the user types memc_get('mykey') — the UDF processes the arguments, ensuring the proper number of arguments have been passed — in this case one argument, the key mykey — for the value that you desire to be retrieved. The UDF then passes this argument to the appropriate libmemcached API call, in this case memcached_mget(), memcached_fetch_result() and memcached_result_value(). So, what these UDFs provide are convenient functions that have the advantage of using the fast, lightweight libmemcached library, hiding the implementation details of the libmemcached calls, much in the same way that the PECL/memcached Memcached class does for PHP.

Figure 5-1 illustrates how these UDFs give the user the ability to access data from MySQL and memcached, and how simple they are implemented using API functions of libmemcached. Although memcached client support isn't an issue with PHP, these UDFs make it possible to interact with memcached using any client that can talk to MySQL and solves the problem of an application that has no client support for memcached.

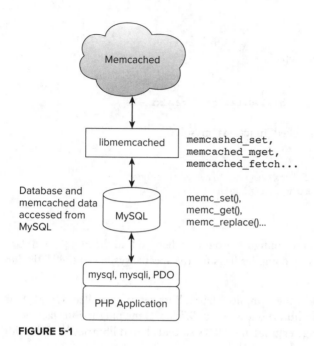

FIGURE 5-1

INSTALLING THE MEMCACHED FUNCTIONS FOR MYSQL

The MySQL plugin interface allows you to easily load UDFs. All that is involved is compiling, installing, and then running the SQL command to load the UDF shared library.

> *To obtain the source for the Memcached Functions for MySQL go to:* `https://launchpad.net/memcached-udfs`. *This page provides links to the source code either as a source archive file or as a Bazaar revision control system through Launchpad repository where you can obtain the latest source.*

Prerequisites

The prerequisites for building, installing, and actually using the memcached functions for MySQL are:

- ➤ A MySQL or MariaDB database server
- ➤ libmemcached installed (Chapter 4)
- ➤ One or more memcached servers
- ➤ A compiler

Configure the Source

To configure the source, follow these simple steps:

1. Untar/gzip the source package:

```
gzcat memcached_functionVs_mysql-1.0.tar.gz | tar xf -
```

2. Enter the project directory: **cd memcached_functions_mysql**

3. Run the configure script:

```
./configure --with-mysql=/usr/local/mysql/bin/mysql_config
--libdir=/usr/local/mysql/lib/mysql/plugin/
```

The two arguments are as follows:

➤ **--with-mysql**: This argument tells the configure program where to find the mysql_config program, which provides the necessary compiler flags for the specific system so the UDFs can be built properly.

➤ **--libdir**: This is the directory where the compiled shared libraries are installed. On MySQL 5.0, this is the directory where other libraries are found. With 5.1, the plug-in interface was changed for programs such as storage engines and UDFs so that shared libraries would reside in a directory one level deeper within the normal library directory, called plugin.

Additionally, you may want to add an entry on your operating system so you can load the shared library. Some operating systems might need this set because, by default, they don't load dynamic libraries in directories that are in their library path. For example, if you must add an entry for /usr/local/mysql/lib/mysql/plugin, you would add a mysql.conf file in /etc/ld.so.conf.d that might look like this:

```
/usr/local/mysql/lib/mysql
/usr/local/mysql/lib/mysql/plugin
/usr/lib64/mysql/
```

You would then run ldconfig to create the necessary links and cache to the most recent shared libraries found in the directories you specified in /etc/ld.so.conf.d/mysql.conf:

```
sudo ldconfig
```

Build the Source

The next thing you do is compile the source:

```
make
sudo make install
```

When you install the built source, the dynamic library created from the compilation are installed to the directory specified in the directory you used in the --libdir argument.

Install the UDF

Now that the dynamic library is installed, you can load the various UDFs. The source package comes with several goodies and you can install using one of two methods:

➤   An SQL script that you can either run or cut and paste

➤   A Perl utility

Using SQL Script Install

The SQL script, `install_functions.sql`, contains the SQL statements to install the UDFs and can be found in the `sql` directory of the source distribution. It contains statements for each function, just as shown in the following code for `memc_get`:

```
CREATE FUNCTION memc_get RETURNS STRING SONAME "libmemcached_functions_mysql.
so";
```

You can simply run this script by loading with the mysql client, which you will need to run as the root user because creating functions in mysql requires this privilege level:

```
mysql --user root --password < sql/install_functions.sql
```

Using the Perl Install Utility

Another alternative is to use the utility `install.pl` to install the UDFs. This utility can be run interactively or non-interactively. To see the available options for this program, run the program with the following options:

```
./utils/install.pl -h
```

To run this utility, you must specify a user and password and the user must be one that has system privileges. With only the `--user` and `--password` arguments, the program runs interactively:

```
./utils/install.pl -u root -p s3krit
function memc_cas_by_key doesn't exist. Create? [Y|n]
Y
Running: CREATE FUNCTION memc_cas_by_key
RETURNS INT SONAME 'libmemcached_functions_mysql.so'
function memc_cas doesn't exist. Create? [Y|n]
Y
Running: CREATE FUNCTION memc_cas
RETURNS INT SONAME 'libmemcached_functions_mysql.so'
function memc_servers_set doesn't exist. Create? [Y|n]
```

If you supply the argument `-s` or `--silent`, the utility runs without interaction:

```
./utils/install.pl -u root -p s3krit -s
```

Checking Installation

After installing the functions, you can check the `func` table in the `mysql` system schema to verify that the UDFs were installed. You should see the following code:

```
ysql> select * from mysql.func where name like 'memc%';
+----------------------------+-----+------------------------------------+----------+
| name                       | ret | dl                                 | type     |
+----------------------------+-----+------------------------------------+----------+
| memc_set                   |   2 | libmemcached_functions_mysql.so    | function |
| memc_stat_get_keys         |   0 | libmemcached_functions_mysql.so    | function |
| memc_stats                 |   0 | libmemcached_functions_mysql.so    | function |
| memc_set_by_key            |   2 | libmemcached_functions_mysql.so    | function |
| memc_delete_by_key         |   2 | libmemcached_functions_mysql.so    | function |
| memc_cas_by_key            |   2 | libmemcached_functions_mysql.so    | function |
| memc_stat_get_value        |   0 | libmemcached_functions_mysql.so    | function |
| memc_delete                |   2 | libmemcached_functions_mysql.so    | function |
| memc_get_by_key            |   0 | libmemcached_functions_mysql.so    | function |
| memc_get                   |   0 | libmemcached_functions_mysql.so    | function |
| memc_append                |   2 | libmemcached_functions_mysql.so    | function |
| memc_append_by_key         |   2 | libmemcached_functions_mysql.so    | function |
| memc_prepend               |   2 | libmemcached_functions_mysql.so    | function |
| memc_prepend_by_key        |   2 | libmemcached_functions_mysql.so    | function |
| memc_increment             |   2 | libmemcached_functions_mysql.so    | function |
| memc_decrement             |   2 | libmemcached_functions_mysql.so    | function |
| memc_replace               |   2 | libmemcached_functions_mysql.so    | function |
| memc_replace_by_key        |   2 | libmemcached_functions_mysql.so    | function |
| memc_servers_behavior_get  |   0 | libmemcached_functions_mysql.so    | function |
| memc_servers_behavior_set  |   2 | libmemcached_functions_mysql.so    | function |
| memc_list_behaviors        |   0 | libmemcached_functions_mysql.so    | function |
| memc_behavior_get          |   0 | libmemcached_functions_mysql.so    | function |
| memc_behavior_set          |   2 | libmemcached_functions_mysql.so    | function |
| memc_servers_set           |   2 | libmemcached_functions_mysql.so    | function |
| memc_list_distribution_types |  0 | libmemcached_functions_mysql.so    | function |
| memc_udf_version           |   0 | libmemcached_functions_mysql.so    | function |
| memc_cas                   |   2 | libmemcached_functions_mysql.so    | function |
| memc_list_hash_types       |   0 | libmemcached_functions_mysql.so    | function |
| memc_add                   |   2 | libmemcached_functions_mysql.so    | function |
| memc_add_by_key            |   2 | libmemcached_functions_mysql.so    | function |
| memc_libmemcached_version  |   0 | libmemcached_functions_mysql.so    | function |
| memc_server_count          |   2 | libmemcached_functions_mysql.so    | function |
+----------------------------+-----+------------------------------------+----------+
```

The output above shows the numerous UDFs that were installed, verifying a successful installation. Actual usage of the functions will verify that these UDFs work.

USING THE MEMCACHED FUNCTIONS FOR MYSQL

The Memcached Functions for MySQL use libmemcached, and each function mirrors the API functions of libmemached. As you recall from Chapter 3, the way to call a UDF is to use either a SELECT statement:

```
mysql> select memc_get('abc');
```

```
+----------------+
| memc_get('abc') |
+----------------+
| this is a test |
+----------------+
```

...or a SET statement, assigning the variable to a user-defined variable:

```
mysql> set @test = memc_get('abc');

mysql> select @test;
+----------------+
| @test          |
+----------------+
| this is a test |
+----------------+
```

Depending on which memcached UDFs you run, some may return a value retrieved from memcached or set a value in memcached (retrieving a true/false of success/failure).

> To obtain the source for the Memcached Functions for MySQL go to: https://
> launchpad.net/memcached-udfs. This page provides links to the source code
> either as a source archive file or as a Bazaar revision control system through
> Launchpad repository where you can obtain the latest source.

Establishing a Connection to the memcached Server

When using these UDFs, you must first establish a connection to the memcached server pool you intend to utilize for caching. Just as with the PECL/memcached Memcached class's connection method, you have a UDF method for initiating a connection.

memc_servers_set

memc_servers_set makes a connection to the memcached server pool being used.

```
memc_servers_set('server1:port, server2:port, serverN:port ...');
```

You supply a list of servers with their port numbers — as many as you like — delimited by comma. Upon success, 1 is returned; –1 is returned upon a failure.

```
mysql> SELECT memc_servers_set('127.0.0.1:11211, 127.0.0.1:22122');
+------------------------------------------------------+
| memc_servers_set('127.0.0.1:11211, 127.0.0.1:22122') |
+------------------------------------------------------+
|                                                    0 |
+------------------------------------------------------+
```

Once a connection is established, you can use all the other functions to store and retrieve values.

memc_server_count

The function `memc_server_count()` takes no arguments and returns the number of memcached servers that are connected to.

```
memc_server_count();
```

If for instance, two servers were connected to as in the preceding example of `memc_servers_set()`, `memc_server_count()` will show:

```
mysql> select memc_server_count();
+---------------------+
| memc_server_count() |
+---------------------+
|                   2 |
+---------------------+
```

Data Setting Functions

Just as with libmemcached, the Memcached Functions for MySQL allows you to cache values in memcached servers. These functions all return true upon success and false upon failure, so you can also use SQL statements to test their return values, such you would do in a stored procedure.

memc_set

The function `memc_set()` allows you to store a value in memcached. It takes two required arguments — the key for what's being stored, and a value. The stored value can be either a string or a numeric value. If it's a string, you must place the string in quotes; if it's numeric, you don't need quotes. `memc_set()` can also take an optional third numeric expiration argument of the expiration time in seconds. `memc_set()` returns a zero upon success or a non-zero value upon failure. The syntax for `memc_set()` is:

```
memc_set('key', value, expiration);
memc_set('key', value);
```

The example that follows shows a value of `'xyz'` being stored with the key `'foo'` for five seconds:

```
mysql> select memc_set('foo', 'xyz', 5);
+---------------------------+
| memc_set('foo', 'xyz', 5) |
+---------------------------+
|                         1 |
+---------------------------+
```

Also shown is a successful `set()` results in a return value of `1` (true).

If you run the following four statements on the same line (so they run all at once), you can see the effect of putting an expiration value on something stored in memcached. You'll also see the use of `memc_get()`, which is explained in detail later.

```
mysql> select memc_set('foo', 'xyz', 5); select memc_get('foo'); select sleep (6);
    -> select memc_get ('foo');
```

```
+--------------------------+
| memc_set('foo', 'xyz', 5) |
+--------------------------+
|                        0 |
+--------------------------+
1 row in set (0.01 sec)

+----------------+
| memc_get('foo') |
+----------------+
| xyz            |
+----------------+
1 row in set (0.00 sec)

+-----------+
| sleep (6) |
+-----------+
|         0 |
+-----------+
1 row in set (6.01 sec)

+------------------+
| memc_get ('foo') |
+------------------+
| NULL             |
+------------------+
1 row in set (0.01 sec)
```

As you see, after six seconds, foo is expired to the bit-bucket in the sky.

The following code, of course, sets foo to the value of xyz without an expiration.

```
mysql> select memc_set('foo', 'xyz');
+-----------------------+
| memc_set('foo', 'xyz') |
+-----------------------+
|                     1 |
+-----------------------+
```

memc_set_by_key

The function memc_set_by_key() works the same way as memc_set() except the first argument is a master server key, which allows you to group stored values by server. The rest of the arguments are the same as memc_set, except they shifted by one. The second argument is the key for the object being stored. The third argument is the value being stored and the optional fourth value is a numeric expiration in seconds.

The syntax for memc_set_by_key() is:

```
memc_set_by_key('master key', 'key', value);
memc_set_by_key('master key', 'key', value, expiration);
```

The example that follows shows how you store a value using a server key:

```
mysql> select memc_set_by_key('A', 'key1', 'test');
+--------------------------------------+
| memc_set_by_key('A', 'key1', 'test') |
+--------------------------------------+
|                                    1 |
+--------------------------------------+
```

memc_add

The function `memc_add()` takes two required arguments: a string key and a value. The value can be either numeric or a string that is cached in memcached and that is specified by *key* if this isn't already set. This function also has a third, optional, numeric argument for the number of seconds that the value is stored before it expires. `memc_set()` returns a zero upon success or a non-zero value upon failure.

The function `memc_add_by_key()` works the same as `memc_add()` except it has as its first argument a master server key that allows you to group stored values by server. The arguments following the master key argument are the same as for `memc_add()` — just shifted in order.

The syntax of `memc_add()` and `memc_add_by_key()` is:

```
memc_add('key', value);
memc_add('key', value, expiration);
memc_add_by_key('master key', 'key', value);
memc_add_by_key('master key', 'key', value, expiration);
```

The example that follows shows a value being added that, as yet, doesn't exist:

```
mysql> select memc_set('key1', 333);
+----------------------+
| memc_set('key1', 333) |
+----------------------+
|                    1 |
+----------------------+
```

memc_replace

The function `memc_replace` takes two required arguments: a string key and a value, either numeric or string, that replaces the existing value of the *key* already stored. `memc_replaced` returns a zero upon success or a non-zero value upon failure.

The function `memc_replace_by_key()` works the same as `memc_replace()` except it has as its first argument a master server key which allows you to group stored values by server. The arguments following the master key argument are the same as for `memc_replace()` — just shifted in order.

The syntax for `memc_replace()` and `memc_replace_by_key()` is:

```
memc_replace('key', value);
memc_replace('key', value, expiration);
memc_replace_by_key('master key', 'key', value);
memc_replace_by_key('master key', 'key', value, expiration);
```

The example that follows shows the retrieval of a previously stored value that is then replaced:

```
mysql> select memc_get('key2');
+------------------+
| memc_get('key2') |
+------------------+
| before value     |
+------------------+

mysql> select memc_replace('key2', 'replaced value');
+----------------------------------------+
| memc_replace('key2', 'replaced value') |
+----------------------------------------+
|                                      0 |
+----------------------------------------+
mysql> select memc_get('key2');
+------------------+
| memc_get('key2') |
+------------------+
| replaced value   |
+------------------+
```

The next example shows how to replace a value that doesn't exist and returns an error code of 14:

```
mysql> select memc_replace('doesntexist', 'abcdefg');
+----------------------------------------+
| memc_replace('doesntexist', 'abcdefg') |
+----------------------------------------+
|                                     14 |
+----------------------------------------+
```

memc_cas

If you recall from Chapter 4, CAS stands for *check and set*. The Memcached Functions for MySQL also have CAS UDFs. The function memc_cas() sets a value if the cas value is the same as the cas value on the server itself.

The syntax for memc_cas() and memc_cas_by_key() is:

```
memc_cas('key', value, cas);
memc_cas('key', value, cas, expiration);
memc_cas_by_key('master_key', 'key', value, cas, expiration);
```

This functionality is still experimental and you have to enable it by setting the behavior MEMCACHED_BEHAVIOR_SUPPORT_CAS.

```
mysql> select memc_servers_behavior_set('MEMCACHED_BEHAVIOR_SUPPORT_CAS', 1);
+----------------------------------------------------------------+
| memc_servers_behavior_set('MEMCACHED_BEHAVIOR_SUPPORT_CAS', 1) |
+----------------------------------------------------------------+
|                                                              0 |
+----------------------------------------------------------------+
```

memc_prepend

The function `memc_prepend()` prepends *value* to the beginning of an existing stored value, stored by `key`. The value being prepended can be either numeric or a string *if* the value already stored is a string. You *cannot* prepend anything to an *existing* stored numeric value or it results in that value being set to NULL. The expiration argument is optional and sets the expiration time in seconds.

The function `memc_prepend_by_key()` works the same as `memc_prepend` except the first argument is a master server key to which the value is prepended, all other values working the same.

The syntax for `memc_prepend()` and `memc_prepend_by_key()` is:

```
memc_prepend('key', value);
memc_prepend('key', value, expiration);
memc_prepend_by_key('master key', 'key', value);
memc_prepend_by_key('master key', 'key', value, 'expiration');
```

The example that follows shows a value initially set to ' this is some text' but that has 'this will be prepended.. ' prepended to it using `memc_prepend()`:

```
mysql> select memc_set('abc', ' this is some text');
+--------------------------------------+
| memc_set('abc', ' this is some text') |
+--------------------------------------+
|                                    1 |
+--------------------------------------+

mysql> select memc_get('abc');
+-------------------+
| memc_get('abc')   |
+-------------------+
|  this is some text |
+-------------------+

mysql> select memc_prepend('abc', 'hither... ');
+----------------------------------+
| memc_prepend('abc', 'hither... ') |
+----------------------------------+
|                                1 |
+----------------------------------+

mysql> select memc_get('abc');
+----------------------------+
| memc_get('abc')            |
+----------------------------+
| hither...  this is some text |
+----------------------------+
```

memc_append

The function `memc_append()` appends the argument *value* to the existing value stored as *key*. The value being appended can be either numeric or a string *if* the value already stored is a string. You *cannot* append anything to an existing stored numeric value or it will result in that value being set to NULL. The argument *expiration* is optional and specifies the expiration time in number of seconds.

The function memc_append_by_key() works the same as memc_append() except the first argument is a master key that the value was stored as.

The syntax for memc_append() and memc_append_by_key() is:

```
memc_append('key', value);
memc_append('key', value, expiration);
memc_append_by_key('master key', 'key', value):
memc_append_by_key('master key', 'key', value, expiration);
```

An example showing what memc_append() does is shown in the following code. First an existing value has text appended to it, and a subsequent memc_get() retrieves the value, verifying that it had the text appended by memc_append()

```
mysql> select memc_append('abc', ' ...tither');
+---------------------------------+
| memc_append('abc', ' ...tither') |
+---------------------------------+
|                               1 |
+---------------------------------+

mysql> select memc_get('abc');
+-------------------------------------+
| memc_get('abc')                     |
+-------------------------------------+
| hither... this is some text ...tither |
+-------------------------------------+
```

memc_delete

The function memc_delete() deletes the value stored as *key* from memcached. The return value is zero if the value is deleted and non-zero value if not.

Just as with any of the other *_by_key() functions, memc_delete_by_key() works the same as memc_delete() except it has the master key representing the server where the object is stored as its first argument.

The syntax for memc_delete() and memc_delete_by_key() is:

```
memc_delete('key');

memc_delete_by_key('master key', 'key');


mysql> select memc_delete('foo');
+----------------------+
| memc_delete('foo', 15) |
+----------------------+
|                    1 |
+----------------------+
```

Data Fetching Functions

The Memcached Functions for MySQL, of course, are the means to fetch data. These return the actual stored value, one value per function call. Currently, there aren't any functions to fetch multiple values at once because the UDF interface only allows for one row to be returned.

memc_get

As you have seen in the setting functions examples, `memc_get()` fetches a value stored in memcached. Additionally, `memc_get_by_key()` has as its first argument the server key, which would be whatever the server key was when caching the item.

The syntax for `memc_get()` and `memc_get_by_key()` is:

```
memc_get('key');
memc_get_by_key('master_key', 'key');
```

The example that follows shows how `memc_get()` is used:

```
mysql> select memc_get('abc');
+---------------------------+
| memc_get('abc')           |
+---------------------------+
| A value that was stored... |
+---------------------------+


mysql> set @a = memc_get('abc');

mysql> select @a;
+---------------------------+
| @a                        |
+---------------------------+
| A value that was stored... |
+---------------------------+
```

Increment and Decrement

Occasionally, you might want a centralized counter or sequence, without having to use a database table or sequence. You can accomplish this using the memcached increment or decrement (if you want an *anti* counter!) operation. The thing to remember is that that data is not durable.

memc_increment

The function `memc_increment()` increments an integer value stored in memcached by `key`. The `value` argument is optional and is the number by which the stored value is incremented. If the value is not supplied, the value of 1 is the default assumed. The incremented value is returned upon a successful increment of the value. If you use an invalid value to increment, `memc_increment()` ignores the increment operation and returns the existing value.

The syntax for `memc_increment()` is:

```
memc_increment('key');
memc_increment('key', value);
```

The example that follows shows how to use `memc_increment()` to increment a value by 1, the default increment value. The first calls `memc_increment()` without an increment value (defaulting to 1) and then with an increment value of 12.

```
mysql> select memc_set('counter', 1);
+-----------------------+
| memc_set('counter', 1) |
+-----------------------+
|                     1 |
+-----------------------+

mysql> select memc_get('counter');
+--------------------+
| memc_get('counter') |
+--------------------+
| 1                  |
+--------------------+

mysql> select memc_increment('counter');
+-------------------------+
| memc_increment('counter') |
+-------------------------+
|                       2 |
+-------------------------+

mysql> select memc_increment('counter', 10);
+-----------------------------+
| memc_increment('counter', 10) |
+-----------------------------+
|                          12 |
+-----------------------------+
```

memc_decrement

The function `memc_decrement()` decrements an integer value stored in memcached, stored as the first argument *key*. The optional *value* argument is the amount to decrease by, defaulting to 1 if not supplied. You cannot decrement a value below zero. The return value of `memc_decrement()` is the decremented value.

The syntax of `memc_decrement()` is:

```
memc_decrement('key');
memc_decrement('key', value);
```

The examples that follow show how to use `memc_decrement()` to decrement a cached value by 1 (the default), by not supplying a decrement value, and then decrementing the value by 20 by supplying an explicit decrement value of 20.

```
mysql> select memc_decrement('counter');
```

```
+---------------------------+
| memc_decrement('counter') |
+---------------------------+
|                        21 |
+---------------------------+

mysql> select memc_decrement('counter',20);
+------------------------------+
| memc_decrement('counter',20) |
+------------------------------+
|                            1 |
+------------------------------+
```

Behavioral Functions

As you saw in Chapter 4 when you used PECL/memcached, libmemcached gives you a lot of control over the behavior of the client and since these UDFs are building on top of libmemcached, they also provide this same versatility.

memc_list_behaviors

The function `memc_list_behaviors()` displays a list of all the available behavior types that are available for setting the client to.

The syntax for `memc_list_behaviors()` is:

```
memc_list_behaviors()
```

The example that follows shows the output of `memc_list_behaviors()`:

```
mysql> select memc_list_behaviors()\G
*************************** 1. row ***************************
memc_list_behaviors():
MEMCACHED SERVER BEHAVIORS
MEMCACHED_BEHAVIOR_SUPPORT_CAS
MEMCACHED_BEHAVIOR_NO_BLOCK
MEMCACHED_BEHAVIOR_TCP_NODELAY
MEMCACHED_BEHAVIOR_HASH
MEMCACHED_BEHAVIOR_CACHE_LOOKUPS
MEMCACHED_BEHAVIOR_SOCKET_SEND_SIZE
MEMCACHED_BEHAVIOR_SOCKET_RECV_SIZE
MEMCACHED_BEHAVIOR_BUFFER_REQUESTS
MEMCACHED_BEHAVIOR_KETAMA
MEMCACHED_BEHAVIOR_POLL_TIMEOUT
MEMCACHED_BEHAVIOR_RETRY_TIMEOUT
MEMCACHED_BEHAVIOR_DISTRIBUTION
MEMCACHED_BEHAVIOR_BUFFER_REQUESTS
MEMCACHED_BEHAVIOR_USER_DATA
MEMCACHED_BEHAVIOR_SORT_HOSTS
MEMCACHED_BEHAVIOR_VERIFY_KEY
MEMCACHED_BEHAVIOR_CONNECT_TIMEOUT
MEMCACHED_BEHAVIOR_KETAMA_WEIGHTED
MEMCACHED_BEHAVIOR_KETAMA_HASH
MEMCACHED_BEHAVIOR_BINARY_PROTOCOL
```

```
MEMCACHED_BEHAVIOR_SND_TIMEOUT
MEMCACHED_BEHAVIOR_RCV_TIMEOUT
MEMCACHED_BEHAVIOR_SERVER_FAILURE_LIMIT
MEMCACHED_BEHAVIOR_IO_MSG_WATERMARK
MEMCACHED_BEHAVIOR_IO_BYTES_WATERMARK
```

memc_behavior_get

The function `memc_behavior_get()` retrieves the current value of any of the behaviors that you set in libmemcached, either numeric or a named value. If the value returned is one of the object distribution or hash algorithm behaviors, `memc_behaviors_get()` is versatile enough to convert the numeric behavioral value to the named canonical.

The function `memc_servers_behavior_get()` is the same function as `memc_behavior_get()` and exists for historical purposes.

You must call the function `memc_servers_set()` to connect to one or more memcached servers prior to calling `memc_behavior_get()`. In the example that follows, you can see that `memcached_behavior_get` obtains a named hash algorithm, a binary true or false value, and an integer value — all of which depend on the an already established connection to memcached.

The syntax of `memc_behavior_get()` and `memc_servers_behavior_get()` is:

```
memc_behavior_get('<behavior name>');
memc_servers_behavior_get('<behavior name>');
```

An example of using `memc_behavior_get()` to obtain the values of several behaviors is as follows:

```
mysql> select memc_behavior_get;('MEMCACHED_BEHAVIOR_HASH');
+------------------------------------------------------+
| memc_servers_behavior_get('MEMCACHED_BEHAVIOR_HASH') |
+------------------------------------------------------+
| MEMCACHED_HASH_DEFAULT                                |
+------------------------------------------------------+

mysql> select memc_behavior_get('MEMCACHED_BEHAVIOR_SUPPORT_CAS');
+-------------------------------------------------------------+
| memc_servers_behavior_get('MEMCACHED_BEHAVIOR_SUPPORT_CAS') |
+-------------------------------------------------------------+
| 1                                                           |
+-------------------------------------------------------------+

mysql> select memc_behavior_get('MEMCACHED_BEHAVIOR_POLL_TIMEOUT');
+--------------------------------------------------------------+
| memc_servers_behavior_get('MEMCACHED_BEHAVIOR_POLL_TIMEOUT') |
+--------------------------------------------------------------+
| 1000                                                         |
+--------------------------------------------------------------+
```

memc_behavior_set

The function `memc_behavior_set()` allows you to set any one of the behaviors that libmemcached lets you modify, as shown in `memc_behaviors_list()`. Some behaviors are boolean 1 or 0, numeric, as well as canonical constant values that are internally converted to their actual numeric values. The numeric values can either be quoted or not, but the canonical values must be quoted.

You must call `memc_servers_set()` to connect to one or more memcached servers prior to setting a client behavior.

The syntax of `memc_behavior_set()` is:

```
memc_behavior_set('<behavior name>', value);
memc_servers_behavior_set('<behavior name>', value)
```

The following example shows the setting of a numeric as well as canonical hash type value and then retrieving those behaviors to verify that they were indeed set:

```
mysql> select memc_behavior_set('MEMCACHED_BEHAVIOR_POLL_TIMEOUT', 2000);
+------------------------------------------------------------+
| memc_behavior_set('MEMCACHED_BEHAVIOR_POLL_TIMEOUT', 2000) |
+------------------------------------------------------------+
|                                                          0 |
+------------------------------------------------------------+

mysql> select memc_behavior_set('MEMCACHED_BEHAVIOR_HASH', 'MEMCACHED_HASH_MD5');
+-------------------------------------------------------------------+
| memc_behavior_set('MEMCACHED_BEHAVIOR_HASH', 'MEMCACHED_HASH_MD5') |
+-------------------------------------------------------------------+
|                                                                 0 |
+-------------------------------------------------------------------+

mysql> select memc_behavior_get('MEMCACHED_BEHAVIOR_POLL_TIMEOUT');
+------------------------------------------------------+
| memc_behavior_get('MEMCACHED_BEHAVIOR_POLL_TIMEOUT') |
+------------------------------------------------------+
| 2000                                                 |
+------------------------------------------------------+

mysql> select memc_behavior_get('MEMCACHED_BEHAVIOR_HASH');
+----------------------------------------------+
| memc_behavior_get('MEMCACHED_BEHAVIOR_HASH') |
+----------------------------------------------+
| MEMCACHED_HASH_MD5                           |
+----------------------------------------------+
```

> *Before tuning the client behavior, it would be prudent to read the documentation for libmemcached because changing values can lead to a non-working setup. Manual pages are great for this. Just type:*
>
> ```
> man memcached_behavior_set
> ```
> *or*
> ```
> man memcached_behavior_get
> ```

memc_list_hash_types

The function `memc_list_hash_types()` lists the canonical hash value types that can be assigned using `memc_behavior_set()` or are returned from using `memc_behavior_get()` for the behavior types `MEMCACHED_BEHAVIOR_HASH` or `MEMCACHED_BEHAVIOR_KETAMA_HASH`.

The syntax for `memc_list_hash_types()` is as follows:

```
memc_list_hash_types();
```

The code that follows shows an example of the output of `memc_list_hash_types()`:

```
mysql> select memc_list_hash_types()\G
*************************** 1. row ***************************
memc_list_hash_types():
MEMCACHED_HASH_DEFAULT
MEMCACHED_HASH_MD5
MEMCACHED_HASH_CRC
MEMCACHED_HASH_FNV1_64
MEMCACHED_HASH_FNV1A_64
MEMCACHED_HASH_FNV1_32
MEMCACHED_HASH_FNV1A_32
MEMCACHED_HASH_JENKINS
MEMCACHED_HASH_HSIEH
```

To read more about these hash types, read the libmemcached manual page on behaviors by typing:

```
man memcached_behavior_set
```

memc_list_distribution_types

The function `memc_list_distribution_types()` lists the canonical distribution types for values among servers that can be assigned using `memc_behavior_set()` or are returned using `memc_behavior_get()` for the behavior type `MEMCACHED_BEHAVIOR_DISTRIBUTION`.

The syntax for `memc_list_distribution_types()` is:

```
memc_list_distribution_types()
```

The code that follows shows an example of the output of running `memc_list_distribution_types()`:

```
mysql> select memc_list_distribution_types()\G
*************************** 1. row ***************************
memc_list_distribution_types():
MEMACHED_DISTRIBUTION_MODULA
MEMCACHED_DISTRIBUTION_CONSISTENT
MEMCACHED_DISTRIBUTION_KETAMA
```

Statistical Functions

You can also obtain statistics about each memcached server with the various statistical functions. This can be extremely useful in obtaining information such as usage statistics, server version, process id, uptime, and many other details. This type of information could be used in managing connections to memcached as well as if you were building an application that keeps and displays statistics on your overall system.

memc_stats

The function `memc_stat()` will return a list of the various statistics from one or more memcached servers specified in the single argument for servers, which is in the same format you would provide to the function `memc_server_add()`.

The syntax for `memc_stats()` is as follows:

```
memc_stats();
```

To which it will use the existing specified server pool, or specific servers can be specified:

```
memc_stats('server1:port, server2:port, ...');
```

The output of `memc_stats()`, shown in the code that follows, is of two servers — one a memcached server and one a Tokyo Tyrant server:

```
mysql> select memc_stats('127.0.0.1:11211,127.0.0.1:1978')\G
*************************** 1. row ***************************
memc_stats('127.0.0.1:11211,127.0.0.1:1978'): Listing 2 Server

Server: 127.0.0.1 (11211)
        pid: 23408
        uptime: 6072
        time: 1257307515
        version: 1.4.2
        pointer_size: 32
        rusage_user: 0.64484
        rusage_system: 0.131676
        curr_items: 2
        total_items: 7
        bytes: 122
        curr_connections: 13
        total_connections: 24
        connection_structures: 14
        cmd_get: 21
        cmd_set: 14
        get_hits: 21
        get_misses: 1
        evictions: 0
        bytes_read: 122
        bytes_written: 122
        limit_maxbytes: 67108864
        threads: 4

Server: 127.0.0.1 (1978)
        pid: 14551
        uptime: 52356
        time: 1257307515
```

```
version: 1.1.34
pointer_size: 0
rusage_user: 32.216153
rusage_system: 45.921686
curr_items: 7
total_items: 0
bytes: 529216
curr_connections: 0
total_connections: 0
connection_structures: 0
cmd_get: 0
cmd_set: 0
get_hits: 0
get_misses: 0
evictions: 0
bytes_read: 529216
bytes_written: 529216
limit_maxbytes: 0
threads: 0
```

memc_stat_get_value

The function `memc_stat_get_value()` can be used to retrieve a particular statistic from a memcached server. The first argument is a comma separated list of one or more servers, the second argument the statistic name.

The syntax for `memc_stat_get_value()` is as follows:

```
memc_stat_get_value('server1:port, server2:port, ...', 'stat name');
```

The code that follows shows how this can be quite handy to retrieve the a statistic such as the memcached server version.

```
mysql> select memc_stat_get_value('127.0.0.1:11211', 'version');
+--------------------------------------------------+
| memc_stat_get_value('127.0.0.1:11211', 'version') |
+--------------------------------------------------+
| 1.4.2                                            |
+--------------------------------------------------+
```

memc_stat_get_keys

The function `memc_stat_get_keys()` takes no arguments and returns statistic keys available to be used with the function `memc_stat_get_value()`. The syntax is:

```
memc_stat_get_keys()
```

Version Functions

Also available are version functions provided version information for both the UDF package itself as well as the library that the Memcached Functions for MySQL were built against.

memc_libmemcached_version

The function `memc_libmemcached_version()` takes no arguments and returns the version of lib-memcached library that the Memcached Functions for MySQL were linked against.

The syntax for `memc_libmemcached_version()` is as follows:

```
memc_libmemcached_version()
```

The code that follows shows the output of `libmemcached_version()`:

```
mysql> select memc_libmemcached_version();
+----------------------------+
| memc_libmemcached_version() |
+----------------------------+
| 0.33                       |
+----------------------------+
```

memc_udf_version

The function `memc_udf_version()` takes no arguments and returns the version of the Memcached Functions for MySQL that are being used.

The syntax for `memc_udf_version()` is:

```
memc_udf_version()
```

The output of `memc_udf_version()` is shown in the following code:

```
mysql> select memc_udf_version();
+--------------------+
| memc_udf_version() |
+--------------------+
| 1.0                |
+--------------------+
```

Fun with Triggers (and UDFs)

You can get really creative with the use of triggers and the Memcached Functions for MySQL. As you recall, triggers provide a means to have a given action take place upon a change to a row in a table — insert, update and delete, either before or after the change is made. With memcached, you could hide a lot of the details of caching from the application code, at least the part of caching where data is written to the database and you want to ensure that the data in memcached mirrors the changes made to the database.

The Source Distribution Directory

In the distribution directory containing the source code to the Memcached Functions for MySQL, there is a file in the `sql/` directory called, interestingly enough, `trigger_fun.sql`. This file contains some practical examples of how you can employ triggers to use these UDFs to do things such as work as a sequence, as well as store data in memcached whenever there is a change to a row in a table.

1. The first thing this file creates is a simple table called *urls* that contains two columns: an *id* which is the primary key, and *url* which is a string in which URL values are stored.

```
drop table if exists urls;
create table urls (
  id int(3) not null,
  url varchar(64) not null default '',
  primary key (id)
  );
```

2. It then sets up the connection to memcached:

```
select memc_servers_set('localhost:11211');
```

And a simple sequence object that will start at 0:

```
select memc_set('urls:sequence', 0);
```

3. Then the insert triggers is created:

```
DELIMITER |

DROP TRIGGER IF EXISTS url_mem_insert |
CREATE TRIGGER url_mem_insert
BEFORE INSERT ON urls
FOR EACH ROW BEGIN
    SET NEW.id = memc_increment('urls:sequence');
    SET @mm = memc_set(concat('urls:',NEW.id), NEW.url);
END |
```

The trigger url_mem_insert does two things upon (before) the insert of a row to *urls*:

➤ Increments the counter object urls:sequence by one.

➤ Sets the URL value keyed by concatenating the string urls: with the new id value, which was just incremented and then calls memc_set(). The SQL statement SET must be used because you cannot call SELECT from within a trigger.

For instance, the first record inserted will increment urls:sequence to 1, which the value of id will assume, hence the key created will be urls:1, then whatever *url* value is being inserted into *urls* will also be inserted into memcached as urls:1.

4. Next, an update trigger :

```
DROP TRIGGER IF EXISTS url_mem_update |
CREATE TRIGGER url_mem_update
BEFORE UPDATE ON urls
FOR EACH ROW BEGIN
    SET @mm = memc_replace(concat('urls:',OLD.id), NEW.url);
END |
```

The trigger `url_memc_update` is executed any time a record in *urls* is updated. It uses the same scheme to create a memcached key by concatenating *urls*: with the id of the record being updated. For example, the first record initially has the value of `http://www.foo.com`, which, if updated with the URL value of `http://www.fee.com`, in the updated trigger, results in the call of `memc_replace('urls:1', 'http://www.fee.com')`; replaces the URL value in memcached as well. The syntax SET is used because you cannot call SELECT from within a trigger.

5. Then finally, a delete trigger:

```
DROP TRIGGER IF EXISTS url_mem_delete |
CREATE TRIGGER url_mem_delete
BEFORE DELETE ON urls
FOR EACH ROW BEGIN
    SET @mm = memc_delete(concat('urls:',OLD.id));
END |
```

Trigger Execution

The trigger `url_mem_delete` is executed on the deletion of any row in *urls*. It also uses the scheme to build a memcached key that the other two triggers use. For example, upon the deletion of a record that contains `http://www.fee.com`, which has the id value of 1, the UDF `memc_delete('urls:1')` is called.

`trigger_fun.sql`, which comes with the source distribution, also has some use case SQL statements to show the triggers in action.

1. First, the data is inserted:

```
insert into urls (url) values ('http://google.com');
insert into urls (url) values ('http://lycos.com/');
insert into urls (url) values ('http://tripod.com/');
insert into urls (url) values ('http://microsoft.com/');
insert into urls (url) values ('http://slashdot.org');
insert into urls (url) values ('http://mysql.com');
insert into urls (url) values ('http://northscale.com/');
insert into urls (url) values ('http://memcached.org/');
```

2. An SQL statement to verify that the data exists in the table is issued:

```
select * from urls;
```

Yet another handy SQL statement verifies each value that you expect to be stored as a result of the previous inserts statements. You can use `memc_get()` within a query to return several results to select the *id* from *urls* for all URLs in the *urls* table. This constructs a key that can fetch the items cached in memcached.

```
select id, memc_get(concat('urls:', id)) from urls;
```

One of the records is updated and immediately the key for this record is selected from the table as well as fetched from memcached. It should have the updated value — the same value as the select statement following the update:

```
update urls set url= 'http://mysql.com/sun' where url = 'http://mysql.com';
select url from urls where url = 'http://mysql.com/sun';
select memc_get('urls:6');
```

The same type of test is performed, except this time deleting a record:

```
delete from urls where url = 'http://microsoft.com/';
select * from urls where url = 'http://microsoft.com/';
select memc_get('urls:4');
```

Now you can run `trigger_fun.sql` by command line to verify that these triggers work as advertised:

```
mysql --user root --password test < trigger_fun.sql

memc_servers_set('localhost:11211')
1
memc_set('urls:sequence', 0)
1
```

This is the output of selecting all records from the *urls* table after inserting the six records:

```
Id      url
1       http://google.com
2       http://lycos.com
3       http://tripod.com
4       http://microsoft.com
5       http://slashdot.org
6       http://mysql.com
7       http://northscale.com
8       http://memcached.com
```

The following is the output of fetching the items from memcached using the aggregate query of the *id* column of the *urls* table to call `memc_get()` for each key. You'll see that all the values were in fact stored via the trigger and exactly match the output of the previous query against the *urls* table:

```
Id      memc_get(concat('urls:', id))
1       http://google.com
2       http://lycos.com
3       http://tripod.com
4       http://microsoft.com
5       http://slashdot.org
6       http://mysql.com
7       http://northscale.com
8       http://memcached.com
```

The following code is the output after the update statement in `trigger_fun.sql`:

```
update urls set url= 'http://mysql.com/sun' where url = 'http://mysql.com';
```

Then the *urls* table is queried with the query:

```
select url from urls where url = 'http://mysql.com/sun';
url     http://mysql.com/sun
```

Then the query is run:

```
select memc_get('urls:6');
```

Resulting in the output:

```
memc_get('urls:6')    http://mysql.com/sun
```

...verifying that the URL `http://mysql.com` was updated to `http://mysql.com/sun` both in the *urls* table and memcached!

Then finally, the record is deleted. Of course, the select from *urls* for the url `http://microsoft.com` yields nothing, but for memcached NULL is returned (correct).

```
memc_get('urls:4')
NULL
```

So, you can see all the triggers work as advertised!

Using triggers can hide all of these details from the application. Values are automatically cached upon writing to the database. This is very convenient and powerful in that it offers an integration of durable data store as well as a method of organizing the keys for the cached items (MySQL) and lightweight, fast caching (memcached)!

 You don't want to use insert or update triggers that automatically set values in memcached when you work with tables that have huge data sets that frequently update; you could end up calling set() *or* replace() *when it's not needed. This is because a trigger doesn't check whether the item in memcached should be set or replaced in the first place; a trigger runs regardless of whether an item in memcached needs to be updated. It's reasonable to use the insert or update triggers on more "static" (tables that don't change often) or small tables that don't have huge data sets. You can definitely use delete triggers on any size table.*

Read-Through Caching with Simple Select Statements

One last part of this chapter is to show how you can use these UDFs to cache data in a single select.

As you saw in Chapter 6, a user would be fetched from the database and memcached in separate SQL statements. You can combine obtaining data and caching in one step.

For example, you can cache a single user, in this case the user with the username of *capttofu*.

```
mysql> SELECT uid, username, email, firstname, surname,
    -> memc_set(concat('users:uid:',username), uid),
    -> memc_set(concat('users:username:',uid), username),
    -> memc_set(concat('users:email:', username), email),
    -> memc_set(concat('users:firstname:', username), firstname),
    -> memc_set(concat('users:surname:', username), surname)
    -> from users where uid = 1\G
*************************** 1. row ***************************
                                                      uid: 1
                                                 username: capttofu
                                                    email: capttofu@capttofu.org
                                                firstname: Patrick
                                                  surname: Galbraith
              memc_set(concat('users:uid:',username), uid): 0
         memc_set(concat('users:username:',uid), username): 0
```

```
            memc_set(concat('users:email:', username), email): 0
    memc_set(concat('users:firstname:', username), firstname): 0
      memc_set(concat('users:surname:', username), surname): 0
```

In this example, the key used is `tablename:column:unique_identifier`. Also, because both *uid* and *username* are unique, you can create a key using both, particularly storing, so you can look up each based off the other. For example, if you cache `user:uid:capttofu` to have the value of `1` and `user:username:1` to have the value of `capttofu`, you can look either up given either key.

To see that these values were stored, you can select them all out on one line:

```
mysql> select memc_get('users:uid:capttofu') as uid,
    -> memc_get('users:username:1') as username,
    -> memc_get('users:email:capttofu') as email,
    -> memc_get('users:firstname:capttofu') as firstname,
    -> memc_get('users:surname:capttofu') as surname;
+-----+----------+----------------------+-----------+-----------+
| uid | username | email                | firstname | surname   |
+-----+----------+----------------------+-----------+-----------+
| 1   | capttofu | capttofu@capttofu.org | Patrick  | Galbraith |
+-----+----------+----------------------+-----------+-----------+
```

…which is how you can cache without using serialization. You just have to keep your keys in order!

Also, you can use the Power of the SELECT™ to cache multiple records in one fell swoop!

If you recall, some things such as geographical data like states can be pre-cached at the beginning of a program's execution, and the UserApp example did this very thing. This can be done with one simple SQL statement as follows:

```
mysql> select state_abbr, state_name,
    -> memc_set(concat('states:state_abbr:',state_name), state_abbr),
    -> memc_set(concat('states:state_name:', state_abbr), state_name),
    -> memc_set(concat('states:state_flower:',state_abbr), state_flower)
    -> from states\G
*************************** 1. row ***************************
                                                  state_abbr: AL
                                                  state_name: Alabama
     memc_set(concat('states:state_abbr:',state_name), state_abbr): 0
    memc_set(concat('states:state_name:', state_abbr), state_name): 0
 memc_set(concat('states:state_flower:',state_abbr), state_flower): 0
*************************** 2. row ***************************
                                                  state_abbr: AK
                                                  state_name: Alaska
     memc_set(concat('states:state_abbr:',state_name), state_abbr): 0
    memc_set(concat('states:state_name:', state_abbr), state_name): 0
 memc_set(concat('states:state_flower:',state_abbr), state_flower): 0
*************************** 3. row ***************************
                                                  state_abbr: AR
                                                  state_name: Arkansas
     memc_set(concat('states:state_abbr:',state_name), state_abbr): 0
    memc_set(concat('states:state_name:', state_abbr), state_name): 0
 memc_set(concat('states:state_flower:',state_abbr), state_flower): 0
    ...
```

```
...
*************************** 49. row ***************************
                                               state_abbr: WI
                                               state_name: Wisconsin
     memc_set(concat('states:state_abbr:',state_name), state_abbr): 0
    memc_set(concat('states:state_name:', state_abbr), state_name): 0
memc_set(concat('states:state_flower:',state_abbr), state_flower): 0
*************************** 50. row ***************************
                                               state_abbr: WY
                                               state_name: Wyoming
     memc_set(concat('states:state_abbr:',state_name), state_abbr): 0
    memc_set(concat('states:state_name:', state_abbr), state_name): 0
memc_set(concat('states:state_flower:',state_abbr), state_flower): 0
*************************** 51. row ***************************
                                               state_abbr: DC
                                          state_name: District of Columbia
     memc_set(concat('states:state_abbr:',state_name), state_abbr): 8
    memc_set(concat('states:state_name:', state_abbr), state_name): 0
memc_set(concat('states:state_flower:',state_abbr), state_flower): 0
```

This query caches all the states for the columns specified in `memc_set` using concatenation to create the key, just like the previous example, except with this there are 51 records in the result set, all of which are now cached!

To select the data from memcached using the results of a query against the `states` table, run the following:

```
mysql> select memc_get(concat('states:state_abbr:',state_name)) as state_abbr,
memc_get(concat('states:state_name:',state_abbr)) as state_name,
memc_get(concat('states:state_flower:',state_abbr)) from states limit 20;
```

state_abbr	state_name	memc_get(concat('states:state_flower:',state_abbr))
AL	Alabama	Camellia
AK	Alaska	Forget Me Not
AR	Arkansas	Apple Blossom
AZ	Arizona	Saguaro Cactus Blossom
CA	California	California Poppy
CO	Colorado	Rocky Mountain Columbine
CT	Connecticut	Mountain Laurel
DE	Delaware	Peach Blossom
FL	Florida	Orange Blossom
GA	Georgia	Cherokee Rose
HI	Hawaii	Pua Aloalo
ID	Idaho	Syringa - Mock Orange
IA	Iowa	Wild Prairie Rose
IN	Indiana	Peony
IL	Illinois	Purple Violet
KS	Kansas	Sunflower
KY	Kentucky	Goldenrod
LA	Louisiana	Magnolia
ME	Maine	White Pine Cone and Tassel
MD	Maryland	Black-Eyed Susan

Fantastic! You now have a multiple-key data fetch from memcached. The table *states* essentially provides the list of keys. Notice also that any SQL statement condition can be used, in this case a LIMIT clause.

OK, so you think this chapter is done and you can go to sleep (if you aren't already!)? Well, there's one more trick to show you!

Updates

Consider a simple table `foo` which has only one column, `a`, which is an `int` (not important other than for showing this example). To use the `memc_replace()` with an UPDATE statement to update both a table and memcached, follow these steps:

1. Insert four values into this table and then set a value in memcached using a key that maps to the table:

```
mysql> INSERT INTO foo VALUES (1), (2), (3), (4);
Query OK, 4 rows affected (0.00 sec)
Records: 4  Duplicates: 0  Warnings: 0

mysql> SELECT memc_set('foo:3', 3);
+----------------------+
| memc_set('foo:3', 3) |
+----------------------+
|                    0 |
+----------------------+
```

2. Fetch the value to verify it was set:

```
mysql> SELECT memc_get('foo:3');
+-------------------+
| memc_get('foo:3') |
+-------------------+
| 3                 |
+-------------------+
```

3. Now update the table *and* memcached! Notice here that the call to `memc_replace()` returns a true, so that is included in the WHERE clause with the AND conjunction.

```
mysql> UPDATE foo SET a = 33 WHERE a = 3 AND memc_replace('foo:3', 33);
Query OK, 1 row affected (0.00 sec)
Rows matched: 1  Changed: 1  Warnings: 0
```

4. Verify it was replaced:

```
mysql> SELECT memc_get('foo:3');
+-------------------+
| memc_get('foo:3') |
+-------------------+
| 33                |
+-------------------+
```

Which it was!

The trick, here, is that you can use a conjunction in an update statement — so long as the condition evaluates to true. If you recall, `memc_set()`, and `memc_replace()` return false, a zero, upon successful data store. So, in order for the condition to be evaluated as true and therefore make the update statement occur, you would negate the return value of `memc_replace()`.

SUMMARY

Interacting with memcached at the database layer can provide you a whole range of benefits that you might not otherwise have if your interactions were limited to only being in the application layer. Because MySQL is a relational database management system, you can leverage the database's relational and management capabilities along with the power of fast caching that memcached provides to tie the durable data store of the database with the caching layer of memcached using the Memcached Functions for MySQL. This moves some of the complexity that would otherwise be found in your PHP application code to a lower level.

This chapter introduced you to the Memcached Functions for MySQL, showing you how to obtain, install, and configure these functions to use from within MySQL. As shown in Chapter 4 with PECL/memcached, the various functions provide the operations that memcached affords. Next, you saw examples of using triggers to automatically cache, replace/update, and delete values from memcached based on actions performed against a database table. Having read this chapter, you should now have an idea of how to take advantage of the power these user-defined functions can provide you!

6

Advanced MySQL

WHAT'S IN THIS CHAPTER?

- ➤ Understanding the usage and flexibility of views

- ➤ Encapsulating business logic within stored procedures and functions

- ➤ Extending statement DDL operations with triggers

- ➤ Enhancing data consistency with transactions

- ➤ Understanding and using MySQL Replication to extend your database usage

- ➤ Scheduling one-time or recurring database events

After mastering MySQL tables and columns and the various SQL commands for data management in your application, this chapter looks at key advanced features of MySQL that can enhance your application programming features and functionality.

Throughout this chapter, you create a number of different objects; some examples may specifically reference the database schema. You can ensure all examples work with the following new schema:

```
DROP SCHEMA IF EXISTS chapter6;
CREATE SCHEMA chapter6;
USE chapter6;
```

VIEWS

A view in MySQL is a server definition that enables a simpler representation of underlying tables and columns. This can lead to an easier understanding of a complex data model, and ultimately easier coding practices. Views were first available in MySQL 5.0. A view may be of benefit when you integrate data from an existing legacy system. For example, perhaps you extract data from a mainframe and use the same table structure in your MySQL database, but its structure is cryptic at best:

```
CREATE TABLE  tbl1453 (
    i_id  INT UNSIGNED NOT NULL,
    s_nm VARCHAR(100) NOT NULL,
    s_txt1  VARCHAR(50) NULL,
    s_txt2  VARCHAR(50) NULL,
    d_c  DATE NOT NULL,
    d_m DATE NOT NULL,
    stat  CHAR(1) NOT NULL
) ENGINE=InnoDB DEFAULT CHARSET=latin1;

INSERT INTO tbl1453(i_id, s_nm, s_txt1, s_txt2, d_c, d_m, stat) VALUES
(1,'Acme Corp',NULL,NULL,'2001-10-04','2008-07-01','A'),
(2,'Example Co.',NULL,NULL,'2002-02-02','2002-02-02','A'),
(3,'Defunct Inc',NULL,NULL,'2005-01-01','2005-12-31','I');
```

You can create a view to easily describe the active customers based on knowledge determined from the data:

```
CREATE VIEW  active_customers AS
SELECT i_id AS id, s_nm AS name,
     d_c AS date_created, d_m AS date_modified
FROM tbl1453
WHERE stat = 'A';


mysql> SELECT * FROM active_customers;
+----+-------------+--------------+---------------+
| id | name        | date_created | date_modified |
+----+-------------+--------------+---------------+
|  1 | Acme Corp   | 2001-10-04   | 2008-07-01    |
|  2 | Example Co. | 2002-02-02   | 2002-02-02    |
+----+-------------+--------------+---------------+
```

This view provides a clear level of human readability.

A second benefit is that it provides a simplified and human readable representation for end user reporting by joining multiple tables together that are in defined in a normalized form. Chapter 1 provides a complex SQL statement that gives details of countries where the flags include the colors of Red, White, and Blue. This could be simplified to a view, and to the end user all the normalization and joins to additional tables are removed:

```
CREATE VIEW RWB_flags AS
SELECT f1.country, c.population,
       IFNULL(ci.city,'Not Recorded') AS city, s.abbr, s.state
FROM    flags f1
INNER JOIN flags f2 ON f1.country = f2.country
INNER JOIN flags f3 ON f1.country = f3.country
INNER JOIN countries c ON f1.country = c.country
LEFT JOIN cities ci ON f1.country = ci.country
       AND ci.is_country_capital = 'yes'
```

```
LEFT JOIN states s  ON f1.country = s.country
      AND ci.state = s.state
WHERE f1.color = 'Red'
AND   f2.color = 'White'
AND   f3.color = 'Blue';


SELECT * FROM RWB_flags;
+-----------+------------+----------------+------+-------+
| country   | population | city           | abbr | state |
+-----------+------------+----------------+------+-------+
| Australia |  21888000  | Not Recorded   | NULL | NULL  |
| USA       | 307222000  | Washington DC  | NULL | NULL  |
+-----------+------------+----------------+------+-------+
```

Another benefit of views is the ability to grant different permissions to access your data. You may, for example, have a table that contains sensitive data in several columns. Creating a view that excludes these columns can give access to some data to users without the need to make expensive schema changes to the tables. An example is provided in the following section.

Access Permissions

The correct use and management of views requires a more in-depth knowledge of the underlying MySQL security model. The ability to create views requires a greater privilege than normally provided to create tables. For example, a normal application DBA account should have only the following privileges:

```
$ mysql -uroot -p

CREATE USER expert@localhost IDENTIFIED BY 'wroxbooks';
GRANT SELECT,INSERT,UPDATE,DELETE,CREATE  ON chapter6.* TO expert@localhost;
```

Though it is possible to create the data as shown earlier, an attempt to create the view would result in the following error:

```
$ mysql -uexpert -pwroxbooks chapter6

CREATE VIEW  active_customers AS
SELECT i_id AS id, s_nm AS name, d_c AS date_created, d_m AS date_modified
FROM tbl1453 WHERE stat = `A';

ERROR 1142 (42000): CREATE VIEW command denied to user
  'expert'@'localhost' for table 'active_customers'
```

You require the CREATE VIEW privilege in addition to the general CREATE privilege used to create table objects. The following code creates a different user to show the interaction:

```
$ mysql -uroot -p

CREATE USER expert_admin@localhost IDENTIFIED BY 'wroxadmin';

GRANT SELECT,INSERT,UPDATE,DELETE,CREATE,CREATE VIEW  ON chapter6.* TO
```

```
      expert_admin@localhost;

$ mysql -uexpert_admin -pwroxadmin chapter6

CREATE VIEW  active_customers AS
SELECT i_id AS id, s_nm AS name, d_c AS date_created, d_m AS date_modified
FROM tbl1453 WHERE stat = `A';
```

An attempt to create a view on tables where the user does not have permissions also results in an error. For example, this new user has permissions to create views only in a specific schema. If you attempt to access data to which you do not have permission, you'll get the following error:

```
mysql> CREATE VIEW system_users AS SELECT host,user,password FROM mysql.user;
ERROR 1142 (42000): ANY command denied to user 'expert_admin'@'localhost'
for table 'user
```

If, for example, you created this view with a user that had sufficient permissions such as the MySQL root user, other users will, by default, get the ability to view the information:

```
$ mysql -uroot -p chapter6

CREATE VIEW system_users AS SELECT host,user,password FROM mysql.user;
```

The user that previously did not have permission to view the data when creating the view now has read permissions to a subset of data:

```
$ mysql -uexpert_admin -pwroxadmin chapter6

mysql> SELECT * FROM system_users;
+--------------------+----------------+------------------------------------+
| host               | user           | password                           |
+--------------------+----------------+------------------------------------+
| localhost          | root           | *FDAF706717E70DB8DDAD0C5214B13770E1 |
| localhost          | drizzle        | *F86E8EF33D51597CCF3D822F3E78FE6715 |
| localhost          | monitor        | *80B4B538AB825D18DA6292E50F4D916C0E |
| localhost          | expert         | *FDAF706717E70DB8DDAD0C5214B13770E1 |
| localhost          | expert_admin   | *FDAF706717E70DB8DDAD0C5214B13770E1 |
+--------------------+----------------+------------------------------------+
```

 The password values in this example have been truncated for display purposes.

The reason here is that by default, the permissions to use the view are that of the DEFINER of the view. You can also change this for a view definition, so that you must have permissions to also see the underlying data, for example. You can do this by adding the SQL SECURITY INVOKER clause to the CREATE VIEW statement, as shown in the code that follows.

```
$ mysql -uroot -p chapter6

DROP VIEW IF EXISTS system_users;
CREATE
SQL SECURITY INVOKER
```

```
VIEW system_users AS SELECT host,user,password FROM mysql.user;


$ mysql -uexpert_admin -pwroxadmin chapter6
mysql> SELECT * FROM system_users;

ERROR 1356 (HY000): View 'chapter6.system_users' references invalid table(s)
or column(s) or function(s) or definer/invoker of view lack rights to use them
```

You also require greater permissions to view the syntax of a view definition:

```
$ mysql -uexpert_admin -pwroxadmin chapter6

mysql> SHOW CREATE VIEW system_users;

ERROR 1142 (42000): SHOW VIEW command denied to user 'expert_admin'@'localhost'
  for table 'system_users'
$ mysql -uroot -p chapter6

SHOW CREATE VIEW system_users\G
*************************** 1. row ***************************
                View: system_users
         Create View: CREATE ALGORITHM=UNDEFINED DEFINER=`root`@`localhost` SQL
SECURITY DEFINER VIEW `chapter2`.`system_users` AS select `mysql`.`user`.`Host`
 AS `host`,`mysql`.`user`.`User` AS `user`,`mysql`.`user`.`Password` AS
 `password` from `mysql`.`user`
character_set_client: latin1
collation_connection: latin1_swedish_ci
```

Additional Information about Views

The following additional points are relevant to the experienced developer in understanding the limitations of view functionality:

➤ **A view name must be unique with the table namespace.** It is not possible to have a view that is the same name as a table for a given schema.

➤ **It is possible in MySQL to update a view in some circumstances.** The primary requirement is that there exists a one-to-one relationship between a given row in the table and a corresponding row.

➤ **Views are commonly used in data warehousing solutions.** MySQL does not generally perform well with views on top of other views. It may be necessary to rewrite views when possible that include other views for more optimized performance.

➤ **A number of caveats exist for using views.** The most significant points are that you cannot use temporary tables in views and a FROM clause table cannot be a derived table.

➤ **MySQL does not have the concept of a materialized view.** You can create the illusion of a materialized view by using MySQL replication and stopping the process at defined times; however, this is only possible for the entire MySQL instance, not individual views.

STORED PROCEDURES AND FUNCTIONS

MySQL provides stored procedures and stored functions to encapsulate business functionality at the database level. MySQL refers to procedures and functions as *routines*. Some clear advantages for using stored routines include:

➤ They historically have been used to *ensure* important business decisions are at the database level, and that any application that accesses the data does so via stored procedure. This can be important when client applications support multiple programming languages.

➤ They have the ability to reduce the network roundtrip when several commands can occur at the same time. An example may be when data for a given record is stored in two tables in a one-to-one relationship.

➤ It is possible to provide a different level of security access to data, with access to data only via stored procedures.

General Attributes

With the exception of stored functions returning a MySQL data type, the following attributes apply to both stored procedures and stored functions:

➤ The routine can accept a fixed number of parameters.

➤ The routine has a number of characteristics defining its usage and nature.

➤ The routine has a block of executable MySQL code.

Parameters

Parameters include a parameter type (IN, OUT, INOUT), a name, and a data type. When no parameter type is specified, the IN type is the default. The name and data type are required. Stored routines can be defined without parameters. Listing 6-1 shows a few parameter examples.

LISTING 6-1: sp-param.sql

```
DELIMITER //
DROP PROCEDURE IF EXISTS sample_no_param//
CREATE PROCEDURE sample_no_param()
BEGIN
  SELECT 1 + 1;
END//

DROP PROCEDURE IF EXISTS sample_2_param//
CREATE PROCEDURE sample_2_param(param1 INT, param2 INT)
BEGIN
  SELECT param1 + param2;
END//

CREATE PROCEDURE sample_out(OUT o_param INT)
```

```
BEGIN
  SELECT 1 + 1 INTO o_param;
END//

CREATE FUNCTION sample_func(param1 INT)
RETURNS INT
BEGIN
  RETURN 1 + param1;
END//

DELIMITER;
```

The following output shows the execution and resources of these routines with various parameter declarations.

```
mysql> CALL sample_no_param();
+-------+
| 1 + 1 |
+-------+
|     2 |
+-------+

mysql> CALL sample_2_param(2,3);
+-----------------+
| param1 + param2 |
+-----------------+
|               5 |
+-----------------+

mysql> CALL sample_out(@param_out);
mysql> SELECT @param_out;
+------------+
| @param_out |
+------------+
|          2 |
+------------+

mysql> SELECT sample_func(2);
+----------------+
| sample_func(2) |
+----------------+
|              3 |
+----------------+
```

 MySQL stored routines do not support parameters that are sets or arrays as data types. It is also not possible for a stored routine to accept a variable number of parameters, and overloading parameters is also not supported.

Characteristics

Following the parameters specification you can specify characteristics about the data used by the routine. These characteristics are presently only information and are not enforced:

➤ **LANGUAGE SQL:** Defines the language that may be used. The only valid value is SQL.

➤ **[NOT] DETERMINISTIC:** Defines whether the routine, generally a function, returns the same value for the given parameters every time. By default a routine is defined as NOT DETERMINISTIC.

➤ **NO SQL:** Indicates that the routine does not contain any SQL statements.

➤ **CONTAINS SQL:** The default characteristic of the SQL options.

➤ **READS SQL DATA:** indicates that the routine reads data only and does not modify any data.

➤ **MODIFIES SQL DATA:** Indicates that the routine reads and modifies data.

Stored Routine Logic

A stored routine may contain an individual SQL statement, or it can include multiple SQL statements when enclosed with a BEGIN.END statement block.

The key areas within a statement block are:

➤ Variables

➤ Cursors

➤ Handlers and conditions

➤ Flow control

➤ Return (stored functions only)

Variables

For local variables within a stored routine you need to first define these variables within a DECLARE statement. Variables can be assigned a default value, assigned a value with SET command, or with the INTO syntax in a SELECT statement:

LISTING 6-2: sp-variables.sql

```
DELIMITER //
DROP FUNCTION IF EXISTS variable_example//
CREATE FUNCTION variable_example (seed INT)
RETURNS INT
BEGIN
  DECLARE example_int   INT;
  DECLARE example_result   INT;

  SET example_int:= 1;
```

```
    SELECT example_int + seed INTO example_result;

    RETURN example_result;
END//

DELIMITER;

SELECT variable_example(5);
+--------------------+
| variable_example(5) |
+--------------------+
|                   6 |
+--------------------+
```

Cursors

A MySQL cursor is a read-only, forward-only looping SELECT query. Cursors must be specified by the DECLARE clause after variable declarations. Data is retrieved in cursors via the OPEN, FETCH, and CLOSE commands. Listing 6-3 is the basic construct for a cursor.

Available for download on Wrox.com

LISTING 6-3: sp-cursor.sql

```
DELIMITER //
DROP FUNCTION IF EXISTS cursor_example//
CREATE PROCEDURE cursor_example ()
BEGIN
  DECLARE l_user VARCHAR(50);
  DECLARE done BOOLEAN DEFAULT FALSE;
  DECLARE cur1 CURSOR FOR SELECT user FROM mysql.user;
  DECLARE CONTINUE HANDLER FOR NOT FOUND
    SET done = TRUE;

  OPEN cur1;

  lab:
  LOOP
    FETCH cur1 INTO l_user;
    IF (done) THEN
      LEAVE lab;
    END IF;
  END LOOP;
END//

DELIMITER;
```

Handlers and Conditions

As demonstrated in the previous cursor code you can declare a HANDLER for logic control based on given MySQL error codes. The MySQL Reference Manual defines the syntax of the HANDLER and CONDITION clauses as:

```
DECLARE condition_name CONDITION FOR condition_value

condition_value:
```

```
      SQLSTATE [VALUE] sqlstate_value
    | mysql_error_code

    DECLARE handler_type HANDLER FOR condition_value[,.] sp_statement

    handler_type:
      CONTINUE
    | EXIT
    | UNDO

    condition_value:
      SQLSTATE [VALUE] sqlstate_value
    | condition_name
    | SQLWARNING
    | NOT FOUND
    | SQLEXCEPTION
    | mysql_error_code
```

Flow Control

MySQL provides a number of constructs for managing program flow. Most are familiar to software developers.

➤   IF . THEN . ELSEIF THEN . ELSE . END IF

➤   CASE . WHEN . THEN . ELSE . END CASE

➤   LOOP . END LOOP

➤   REPEAT . UNTIL . END REPEAT

➤   WHILE . DO . END WHILE

➤   LEAVE

➤   ITERATE (similar to a loop continue)

It is worth noting that the most obvious omission is a FOR loop.

Using Stored Routines Privileges and Meta Data

To implement stored routines you need to provide additional user privileges for the creation and management of routines, and for users to execute routines. For your DBA user, the CREATE ROUTINE and ALTER ROUTINE privileges are necessary to manage objects. For your read/write and read-only users, the EXECUTE privilege is required.

MySQL provides information about routines in the mysql.proc and mysql.procs_priv tables. Information is also available in the INFORMATION_SCHEMA.ROUTINES table. A number of SHOW commands exist to provide various information:

➤   SHOW PROCEDURE STATUS

➤   SHOW FUNCTION STATUS

➤   `SHOW CREATE PROCEDURE`

➤   `SHOW CREATE FUNCTION`

The following commands are extensions that are only available for MySQL server installations with debugging support enabled.

➤   `SHOW PROCEDURE CODE`

➤   `SHOW FUNCTION CODE`

The MySQL `INFORMATION_SCHEMA` does not include a cross-reference between routines and tables used.

Extending Stored Routines

Although some limitations have been listed, the MySQL Stored Routines Library at `http://mysql-sr-lib.sourceforge.net/` can provide some working solutions for features you may find with other stored database languages, such as:

➤   Globals

➤   Arrays

➤   Named parameters

➤   "for each" loops

➤   Syntax helpers

➤   Testing

Stored Routine Disadvantages

Stored routines are not precompiled for optimized operation. A stored procedure is received and re-parsed on a per-connection basis. When used by a language such as PHP, the overhead does not lead to the potential speed improvement that you can obtain using stored procedures in other RDBMS products.

Stored routines are not automatically marked as invalid due to a schema change. This requires the first re-execution of the stored procedure to fail to determine invalid syntax. Unfortunately it can be difficult to test this in a production environment without affecting production data.

The greatest missing functionality of stored routines is the lack of a SQL standard `SIGNAL` syntax. This is similar to other RDBMS products' `RAISE` syntax that provide the developer the opportunity to manage exceptions for both database and application logic with stored routines.

User Defined Functions

MySQL provides a third means for including business functionality within the database. This is a **user defined function** (UDF) that is written and compiled C code. These functions use a very restricted set of return values but can provide an interface to existing external code.

The memcached functions are good examples of user defined functions. Check out `https://launchpad.net/memcached-udfs`.

TRIGGERS

Triggers, as the name suggests, perform an action based on a certain DML statement being triggered or executed. MySQL triggers can be defined at six different integration points:

➤   BEFORE INSERT

➤   AFTER INSERT

➤   BEFORE UPDATE

➤   AFTER UPDATE

➤   BEFORE DELETE

➤   AFTER DELETE

This functionality is in line with more traditional relational databases. You will notice there are no triggers for REPLACE. This is discussed in more detail later. MySQL does not provide triggers on other events, such as system startup or shutdown, or ALTER commands. For example, MySQL triggers have a number of limitations:

➤   Only one trigger can be specified for each of the previously defined six points. Other databases, for example, enable you to specify multiple triggers, such as two AFTER INSERT triggers for the same table.

➤   Triggers are possible FOR EACH ROW only; there is no per-statement level functionality.

➤   There is no instead of trigger syntax.

➤   There is no when clause restriction.

The following examples show the use of triggers to produce an audit trail of changes to data for a given table. Listing 6-4 shows the prerequisite tables for the following examples.

LISTING 6-4: trigger-tables.sql

```
USE chapter6;
DROP TABLE IF EXISTS trigger_test;
CREATE TABLE trigger_test (
id   INT UNSIGNED NOT NULL AUTO_INCREMENT,
val  VARCHAR(10) NOT NULL,
PRIMARY KEY(id)
) ENGINE=InnoDB DEFAULT CHARSET latin1;

DROP TABLE IF EXISTS logger;
CREATE TABLE logger (
action       ENUM ('Insert','Update','Delete') NOT NULL,
occurred     TIMESTAMP NOT NULL DEFAULT CURRENT_TIMESTAMP,
id           INT UNSIGNED NOT NULL
) ENGINE=InnoDB DEFAULT CHARSET latin1;
```

No Triggers

By default, no information is logged based on an INSERT statement when no triggers are defined:

```
INSERT INTO trigger_test (id,val) VALUES (NULL, 'a');
SELECT * FROM logger;

Empty set (0.01 sec)
```

Trigger Syntax

The syntax of the trigger is quite straightforward. It consists of four components:

```
1: CREATE TRIGGER <trigger_name>
2: BEFORE|AFTER INSERT|UPDATE|DELETE ON <table>
3: FOR EACH ROW
4: <sql statement(s)>
```

➤ **CREATE TRIGGER <trigger_name>:** Defines the name of the trigger.

➤ **BEFORE|AFTER INSERT|UPDATE|DELETE ON <table>:** Defines which table the trigger is associated with and when this trigger is executed.

➤ **FOR EACH ROW:** Is a required syntax that states the trigger fires for each row of the executed query. There is no companion syntax for triggers to fire for the statement only.

➤ **<sql statement(s)>:** Specifies the statements to be executed.

Insert Triggers

Listing 6-5 demonstrates the BEFORE|AFTER INSERT syntax.

LISTING 6-5: insert-triggers.sql

Available for
download on
Wrox.com

```
DELIMITER $$
DROP TRIGGER IF EXISTS trigger_test_bri$$
CREATE TRIGGER trigger_test_bri
BEFORE INSERT ON trigger_test
FOR EACH ROW
  INSERT INTO logger(action,occurred,id) VALUES('Insert',NOW(),NEW.id);
$$
DROP TRIGGER IF EXISTS trigger_test_ari$$
CREATE TRIGGER trigger_test_ari
AFTER INSERT ON trigger_test
FOR EACH ROW
  INSERT INTO logger(action,occurred,id) VALUES('Insert',NOW(),NEW.id);
$$
DELIMITER;
```

What is introduced with the TRIGGER syntax is the NEW and OLD context. These represent the values of the row of data before and after the statement being executed.

As an example, insert a new row into the example table:

```
INSERT INTO trigger_test (id,val) VALUES (NULL, 'b');
SELECT * FROM trigger_test;
+----+-----+
| id | val |
+----+-----+
|  1 | a   |
|  2 | b   |
+----+-----+

SELECT * FROM logger;
+--------+---------------------+----+
| action | occurred            | id |
+--------+---------------------+----+
| Insert | 2009-09-20 23:41:01 |  0 |
| Insert | 2009-09-20 23:41:01 |  2 |
+--------+---------------------+----+
```

You will see there are two rows in the logger table to reflect the before and after insert triggers firing. The AUTO_INCREMENT value for id is not yet defined before the INSERT statement has occurred, and the value is defined after the INSERT statement.

Update Triggers

Now try adding BEFORE|AFTER UPDATE triggers and test the UPDATE syntax as shown in Listing 6-6:

Available for download on Wrox.com

LISTING 6-6: update-triggers.sql

```
DELIMITER $$
DROP TRIGGER IF EXISTS trigger_test_bru$$
CREATE TRIGGER trigger_test_bru
BEFORE UPDATE ON trigger_test
FOR EACH ROW
   INSERT INTO logger(action,occurred,id) VALUES('Update',NOW(),OLD.id);
$$
DROP TRIGGER IF EXISTS trigger_test_aru$$
CREATE TRIGGER trigger_test_aru
AFTER UPDATE ON trigger_test
FOR EACH ROW
   INSERT INTO logger(action,occurred,id) VALUES('Update',NOW(),NEW.id);
$$
DELIMITER;
```

For this example, you update multiple existing rows to show the use of the FOR EACH ROW syntax:

```
INSERT INTO trigger_test (id,val) VALUES (NULL, 'b');
UPDATE trigger_test SET id = id + 10 WHERE val = 'b';

SELECT * FROM trigger_test;
+----+-----+
| id | val |
```

```
+----+-----+
|  1 | a   |
| 12 | b   |
| 13 | b   |
+----+-----+

SELECT * FROM logger;
+--------+---------------------+----+
| action | occurred            | id |
+--------+---------------------+----+
| Insert | 2009-09-20 23:41:01 |  0 |
| Insert | 2009-09-20 23:41:01 |  2 |
| Insert | 2009-09-20 23:42:49 |  0 |
| Insert | 2009-09-20 23:42:49 |  3 |
| Update | 2009-09-20 23:42:49 |  2 |
| Update | 2009-09-20 23:42:49 | 12 |
| Update | 2009-09-20 23:42:49 |  3 |
| Update | 2009-09-20 23:42:49 | 13 |
+--------+---------------------+----+
```

In this example, you see the change in value before and after the actual UPDATE statement. You can also see that the triggers operate on all rows that are affected.

Delete Triggers

Listing 6-7 completes the remaining valid triggers for BEFORE | AFTER DELETE.

Available for
download on
Wrox.com

LISTING 6-7: delete-triggers.sql

```
DELIMITER $$
DROP TRIGGER IF EXISTS trigger_test_brd$$
CREATE TRIGGER trigger_test_brd
BEFORE DELETE ON trigger_test
FOR EACH ROW
  INSERT INTO logger(action,occurred,id) VALUES('Delete',NOW(),OLD.id);
$$
DROP TRIGGER IF EXISTS trigger_test_ard$$
CREATE TRIGGER trigger_test_ard
AFTER DELETE ON trigger_test
FOR EACH ROW
  INSERT INTO logger(action,occurred,id) VALUES('Delete',NOW(),OLD.id);
$$
DELIMITER;
```

You will now see the deletion of rows:

```
DELETE FROM trigger_test WHERE id > 10;

SELECT * FROM trigger_test;
+----+-----+
| id | val |
+----+-----+
```

```
| 1 | a  |
+----+-----+

SELECT * FROM logger;
+--------+---------------------+----+
| action | occurred            | id |
+--------+---------------------+----+
| Insert | 2009-09-20 23:41:01 |  0 |
| Insert | 2009-09-20 23:41:01 |  2 |
| Insert | 2009-09-20 23:42:49 |  0 |
| Insert | 2009-09-20 23:42:49 |  3 |
| Update | 2009-09-20 23:42:49 |  2 |
| Update | 2009-09-20 23:42:49 | 12 |
| Update | 2009-09-20 23:42:49 |  3 |
| Update | 2009-09-20 23:42:49 | 13 |
| Delete | 2009-09-20 23:43:50 | 12 |
| Delete | 2009-09-20 23:43:50 | 12 |
| Delete | 2009-09-20 23:43:50 | 13 |
| Delete | 2009-09-20 23:43:50 | 13 |
+--------+---------------------+----+
```

You are unable to use the NEW context for a DELETE trigger. An attempt will result in the following error:

```
ERROR 1363 (HY000): There is no NEW row in on DELETE trigger
```

You are unable to create multiple triggers of the same type on the same table. An attempt will result in the following error:

```
ERROR 1235 (42000): This version of MySQL doesn't yet support 'multiple
   triggers with the same action time and event for one table'
```

 The DELETE *trigger will not occur for other DML that removes data such as* TRUNCATE TABLE *or* DROP TABLE.

Replace Triggers

MySQL provides an additional DDL command to the normal CRUD functions: REPLACE. Unlike its name, which implies an update to the current row and, if it doesn't exist, the creation of a new row, a REPLACE command is executed as a DELETE command and an INSERT command. This can introduce unexpected behavior, especially when combined with foreign keys and triggers.

```
TRUNCATE TABLE trigger_test;
TRUNCATE TABLE logger;
INSERT INTO trigger_test (id,val) VALUES (100, 'insert');
REPLACE INTO trigger_test (id, val) VALUES (100,'replace');
Query OK, 2 rows affected (0.00 sec)
REPLACE INTO trigger_test (id, val) VALUES (101,'replace');
Query OK, 1 row affected (0.00 sec)

mysql> SELECT * FROM logger;
```

```
+--------+---------------------+-----+
| action | occurred            | id  |
+--------+---------------------+-----+
| Insert | 2009-10-17 14:07:06 | 100 |
| Insert | 2009-10-17 14:07:06 | 100 |

| Insert | 2009-10-17 14:13:02 | 100 |
| Delete | 2009-10-17 14:13:02 | 100 |
| Delete | 2009-10-17 14:13:02 | 100 |
| Insert | 2009-10-17 14:13:02 | 100 |

| Insert | 2009-10-17 14:13:08 | 101 |
| Insert | 2009-10-17 14:13:08 | 101 |
+--------+---------------------+-----+
```

You can distinguish the three different statements in the logger table by the occurred timestamp.

Trigger Permissions

If you have SUPER privileges you can specify a user as the definer of the trigger. By default when a trigger is executed, the permissions of the current user are used for underlying tables. You can change this to enable a specific user to perform the operations. Use this with caution, because you may introduce a situation where data is correctly inserted or updated, but the trigger fails due to permission errors. The syntax occurs after the CREATE keyword:

```
CREATE [ DEFINER <user> | CURRENT_USER  ]
TRIGGER <trigger_name>
```

Although MySQL triggers were introduced in 5.0, no new features or function-ality have been introduced since 5.0.15 production was announced as gener-ally available (GA) on 19 October 2005. The next major release, 5.1, did not provide any additional functionality and there is also no new functionality in the current 5.4 alpha version. Though this feature was implemented to provide compatibility with major features and more popular commercial RDBMS prod-ucts, the depth of functionality is very limiting and you should factor in this consideration if you choose to use triggers.

TRANSACTIONS

MySQL provides a unique feature to other traditional relational databases because it supports both a transactional and a non-transactional state. Though you can operate a transactional RDBMS in an auto-commit mode simulating no transactions, you incur the overhead of the management that exists to support transactions. In MySQL and by default, there is a true non-transactional mode and this can provide significant performance improvements; however, this also requires the developer to manage any database errors in consistency.

Many terms are relevant to transactions; however, ACID is the key difference between a transactional mode and a non-transactional mode. ACID is defined as:

➤ Atomicity

➤ Consistency

➤ Isolation

➤ Durability

In MySQL it is important to realize that managing transactions is the responsibility of the storage engine. These are discussed in detail in Chapter 3. For the purposes of these examples, the InnoDB storage engine will be referenced; this engine is the only included transactional storage engine in the current MySQL 5.1 production version.

Atomicity

In simple terms **atomicity** is all or nothing. That means that all statements within a transaction are successful or are not successful.

Non-transactional Tables

To show the difference, Listing 6-8 demonstrates that atomicity is not possible with non-transactional tables. The following MyISAM tables are used in this example.

LISTING 6-8: non-trans-tables.sql

```
DROP TABLE IF EXISTS non_trans_parent;
CREATE TABLE non_trans_parent (
    id   INT UNSIGNED NOT NULL AUTO_INCREMENT,
    val  VARCHAR(10) NOT NULL,
PRIMARY KEY (id),
UNIQUE KEY (val)
) ENGINE=MyISAM DEFAULT CHARSET latin1;

DROP TABLE IF EXISTS non_trans_child;
CREATE TABLE non_trans_child (
    id        INT UNSIGNED NOT NULL AUTO_INCREMENT,
    parent_id INT UNSIGNED NOT NULL,
    created   TIMESTAMP NOT NULL,
PRIMARY KEY (id),
INDEX (parent_id)
) ENGINE=MyISAM DEFAULT CHARSET latin1;
```

To test things out, perform a sample transaction that inserts records into these two tables:

```
START TRANSACTION;
INSERT INTO non_trans_parent(val) VALUES('a');
```

```
         INSERT INTO non_trans_child(parent_id,created) VALUES(LAST_INSERT_ID(),NOW());

         INSERT INTO non_trans_parent (val) VALUES('a');
         ERROR 1062 (23000): Duplicate entry 'a' for key 'val'
         ROLLBACK;
         Query OK, 0 rows affected, 1 warning (0.00 sec)

mysql> SHOW WARNINGS;
+---------+------+------------------------------------------------------------------
| Level   | Code | Message
+---------+------+------------------------------------------------------------------
| Warning | 1196 | Some non-transactional changed tables couldn't be rolled back
+---------+------+------------------------------------------------------------------

SELECT * FROM non_trans_parent;
+----+-----+
| id | val |
+----+-----+
|  1 | a   |
+----+-----+

SELECT * FROM non_trans_child;
+----+-----------+---------------------+
| id | parent_id | created             |
+----+-----------+---------------------+
|  1 |         1 | 2009-09-21 23:44:25 |
+----+-----------+---------------------+
```

As you can see, data that you would have expected to not exist from the transaction is present.

Transactional Tables

Repeat these SQL statements using the transactional storage engine InnoDB; you will observe the difference between transactional and non-transactional processing. The following tables, shown in Listing 6-9, are used in this example.

Available for
download on
Wrox.com

LISTING 6-9: trans-tables.sql

```
DROP TABLE IF EXISTS trans_parent;
CREATE TABLE trans_parent (
  id   INT UNSIGNED NOT NULL AUTO_INCREMENT,
  val  VARCHAR(10) NOT NULL,
PRIMARY KEY (id),
UNIQUE KEY (val)
) ENGINE=InnoDB DEFAULT CHARSET latin1;

DROP TABLE IF EXISTS trans_child;
CREATE TABLE trans_child (
  id         INT UNSIGNED NOT NULL AUTO_INCREMENT,
  parent_id INT UNSIGNED NOT NULL,
  created    TIMESTAMP NOT NULL,
PRIMARY KEY (id),
INDEX (parent_id)
) ENGINE=InnoDB DEFAULT CHARSET latin1;
```

Perform a sample transaction that inserts records into these two tables:

```
START TRANSACTION;
INSERT INTO trans_parent (val) VALUES('a');
INSERT INTO trans_child (parent_id,created) VALUES(LAST_INSERT_ID(),NOW());

INSERT INTO trans_parent (val) VALUES('a');
ERROR 1062 (23000): Duplicate entry 'a' for key 'val'
ROLLBACK;
Query OK, 0 rows affected (0.01 sec)

SELECT * FROM trans_parent;
Empty set (0.00 sec)

SELECT * FROM trans_child;
Empty set (0.00 sec)
```

As you can see, no data has been recorded as part of the failing transaction.

Consistency

Consistency ensures that the integrity of the entire database data remains consistent as the result of a given transaction. The following is an example where the data is consistent based on the defined referential integrity rules:

```
START TRANSACTION;
INSERT INTO trans_parent(val) VALUES('a');
INSERT INTO trans_child(parent_id,created) VALUES(999,NOW());
COMMIT;

SELECT * FROM trans_parent;
+----+-----+
| id | val |
+----+-----+
|  3 | a   |
+----+-----+

mysql> SELECT * FROM trans_child;
+----+-----------+---------------------+
| id | parent_id | created             |
+----+-----------+---------------------+
|  2 |       999 | 2009-09-21 23:53:02 |
+----+-----------+---------------------+
```

In this example, you obviously created a child record with an invalid and non-existing `parent_id`; however, you have not defined any constraints to enforce this consistency. So, in Listing 6-10, create the tables with these additional constraints.

LISTING 6-10: trans-table-fk.sql

Available for
download on
Wrox.com

```
TRUNCATE TABLE trans_parent;
DROP TABLE IF EXISTS trans_child;
CREATE TABLE trans_child (
```

```
   id        INT UNSIGNED NOT NULL AUTO_INCREMENT,
   parent_id INT UNSIGNED NOT NULL,
   created   TIMESTAMP NOT NULL,
PRIMARY KEY (id),
INDEX (parent_id),
FOREIGN KEY (parent_id) REFERENCES trans_parent(id)
) ENGINE=InnoDB DEFAULT CHARSET latin1;
```

Repeat the sample transaction that inserts records into these two tables:

```
START TRANSACTION;
INSERT INTO trans_parent(val) VALUES('a');
INSERT INTO trans_child(parent_id,created) VALUES(999,NOW());

ERROR 1452 (23000): Cannot add or update a child row: a foreign key constraint
 fails (`chapter6`.`trans_child`, CONSTRAINT `trans_child_ibfk_1` FOREIGN KEY
 (`parent_id`) REFERENCES `trans_parent` (`id`))
ROLLBACK;
```

In this example, the data that was previously successfully added now fails. This integrity requires valid data to be entered. For example:

```
START TRANSACTION;
INSERT INTO trans_parent(val) VALUES('a');
INSERT INTO trans_child(parent_id,created) VALUES(LAST_INSERT_ID(),NOW());
COMMIT;
```

This transaction added a parent record and a child record. Now try to break this integrity:

```
START TRANSACTION;
DELETE FROM trans_parent;
ERROR 1451 (23000): Cannot delete or update a parent row: a foreign key
constraint fails (`chapter6`.`trans_child`, CONSTRAINT `trans_child_ibfk_1`
 FOREIGN KEY (`parent_id`) REFERENCES `trans_parent` (`id`))
ROLLBACK;
```

As you can see, an attempt to delete the parent record, when a child record exists, results in an error. You can address this by providing a cascading constraint:

```
ALTER TABLE trans_child
DROP FOREIGN KEY trans_child_ibfk_1,
ADD FOREIGN KEY (parent_id) REFERENCES trans_parent(id) ON DELETE CASCADE;

START TRANSACTION;
DELETE FROM trans_parent;
COMMIT;

SELECT * FROM trans_parent;
Empty set (0.00 sec)
SELECT * FROM trans_child;
Empty set (0.00 sec)
```

The deletion of the parent data, with a foreign key constraint to cascade the delete, also deletes the child records.

Isolation

MySQL provides four different isolation levels to support multiversion concurrency control (MVCC). These are all used by InnoDB. If you are unfamiliar with the isolation concept, you can think of this as the amount of data that has been saved in separate concurrent transactions, which is available in the current transaction.

The default transaction isolation level is REPEATABLE-READ. This means that during a transaction the values retrieved in a SELECT will remain consistent for all repeating SELECT statements during the transaction irrespective of other committed statements.

The isolation level READ-COMMITTED enables SELECT statements to see committed data that has occurred in other transactions during the execution of the current transaction.

> *It is often the misconception of Oracle Database administrators to change the default isolation level from* REPEATABLE-READ *to* READ-COMMITTED. *In Oracle, the default transaction level is* READ-COMMITTED; *however, though the name is used in MySQL, its underlying functional specification is indeed different.*

The modification of the isolation level has an impact on MySQL replication. This is discussed in detail in the following section. The best advice is to not modify the isolation level value from the default of REPEATABLE_READ.

You only need one table to demonstrate the various options as shown in Listing 6-11.

LISTING 6-11: isolation-table.sql

```
DROP TABLE IF EXISTS transaction_test;
CREATE TABLE transaction_test(
    id   INT UNSIGNED NOT NULL AUTO_INCREMENT,
    val  VARCHAR(20) NOT NULL,
    created TIMESTAMP NOT NULL DEFAULT CURRENT_TIMESTAMP,
PRIMARY KEY(id)
) ENGINE=InnoDB DEFAULT CHARSET latin1;
```

Start with some initial seeded data for reference within the transaction:

```
INSERT INTO transaction_test(val) VALUES ('a'),('b'),('c');
```

Repeatable Read

To perform these tests you will need two open mysql client sessions. These commands will be run in parallel.

In the first session, run the following commands:

```
SELECT @@global.tx_isolation, @@session.tx_isolation;
START TRANSACTION;
```

```
SELECT * FROM transaction_test;
SELECT SLEEP(20);
INSERT INTO transaction_test(val) VALUES (@@session.tx_isolation);
SELECT * FROM transaction_test;
COMMIT;
```

In the second session, you need to execute these commands immediately while the first session is running (i.e. during the SLEEP() portion of this example):

```
START TRANSACTION;
INSERT INTO transaction_test(val) VALUES ('x'),('y'),('z');
SELECT * FROM transaction_test;
+----+----------------+---------------------+
| id | val            | created             |
+----+----------------+---------------------+
|  1 | a              | 2009-09-21 00:19:43 |
|  2 | b              | 2009-09-21 00:19:43 |
|  3 | c              | 2009-09-21 00:19:43 |
|  4 | x              | 2009-09-21 00:21:00 |
|  5 | y              | 2009-09-21 00:21:00 |
|  6 | z              | 2009-09-21 00:21:00 |
+----+----------------+---------------------+
COMMIT;
```

As you can see, in the second session you added three additional rows and committed the data before the first session transaction completed. Look at the results of the first session commands now for comparison of the data visible in the table:

```
SELECT * FROM transaction_test;
+----+------+---------------------+
| id | val  | created             |
+----+------+---------------------+
|  1 | a    | 2009-09-21 00:19:43 |
|  2 | b    | 2009-09-21 00:19:43 |
|  3 | c    | 2009-09-21 00:19:43 |
+----+------+---------------------+
3 rows in set (0.00 sec)

SELECT SLEEP(20);
INSERT INTO transaction_test(val) VALUES (@@session.tx_isolation);

mysql> SELECT * FROM transaction_test;
+----+----------------+---------------------+
| id | val            | created             |
+----+----------------+---------------------+
|  1 | a              | 2009-09-21 00:19:43 |
|  2 | b              | 2009-09-21 00:19:43 |
|  3 | c              | 2009-09-21 00:19:43 |
|  7 | REPEATABLE-READ | 2009-09-21 00:21:01 |
+----+----------------+---------------------+
4 rows in set (0.00 sec)
```

The first transaction did not see the results of the second completed transaction. After the COMMIT has been executed in the first session, you can see the complete results by running the following query:

```
mysql> SELECT * FROM transaction_test;
+----+----------------+---------------------+
| id | val            | created             |
+----+----------------+---------------------+
|  1 | a              | 2009-09-21 00:19:43 |
|  2 | b              | 2009-09-21 00:19:43 |
|  3 | c              | 2009-09-21 00:19:43 |
|  4 | x              | 2009-09-21 00:21:00 |
|  5 | y              | 2009-09-21 00:21:00 |
|  6 | z              | 2009-09-21 00:21:00 |
|  7 | REPEATABLE-READ | 2009-09-21 00:21:01 |
+----+----------------+---------------------+
```

Read Committed

You can rerun the same SQL statements with the transaction isolation level set to READ-COMMITTED. First reset your seed data:

```
TRUNCATE TABLE transaction_test;
INSERT INTO transaction_test(val) VALUES ('a'),('b'),('c');
```

In session 1, re-run the following SQL:

```
SET @@session.tx_isolation = 'READ-COMMITTED';
SELECT @@global.tx_isolation, @@session.tx_isolation;
START TRANSACTION;
SELECT * FROM transaction_test;
SELECT SLEEP(20);
INSERT INTO transaction_test(val) VALUES (@@session.tx_isolation);
SELECT * FROM transaction_test;
COMMIT;
```

In session 2, re-run the following SQL:

```
START TRANSACTION;
INSERT INTO transaction_test(val) VALUES ('x'),('y'),('z');
SELECT * FROM transaction_test;
COMMIT;
```

If we now look at the actual output of the SQL statements in session 1, we will see a difference between this output and that of the REPEATABLE-READ example.

```
SET @@session.tx_isolation = 'READ-COMMITTED';
SELECT @@global.tx_isolation, @@session.tx_isolation;
+-----------------------+-----------------------+
| @@global.tx_isolation | @@session.tx_isolation |
+-----------------------+-----------------------+
| REPEATABLE-READ       | READ-COMMITTED        |
+-----------------------+-----------------------+

START TRANSACTION;
SELECT * FROM transaction_test;
```

```
+----+-----+---------------------+
| id | val | created             |
+----+-----+---------------------+
|  1 | a   | 2009-09-21 00:27:35 |
|  2 | b   | 2009-09-21 00:27:35 |
|  3 | c   | 2009-09-21 00:27:35 |
+----+-----+---------------------+

SELECT SLEEP(20);

mysql> SELECT * FROM transaction_test;
+----+----------------+---------------------+
| id | val            | created             |
+----+----------------+---------------------+
|  1 | a              | 2009-09-21 00:27:35 |
|  2 | b              | 2009-09-21 00:27:35 |
|  3 | c              | 2009-09-21 00:27:35 |
|  4 | x              | 2009-09-21 00:26:44 |
|  5 | y              | 2009-09-21 00:26:44 |
|  6 | z              | 2009-09-21 00:26:44 |
|  7 | READ-COMMITTED | 2009-09-21 00:26:54 |
+----+----------------+---------------------+

COMMIT;
```

As you can see, the results of the data within the transaction changed during the transaction to reflect a committed transaction.

Though this is just a demonstration, it is possible that your application would never experience the need to select the same information more than once during a transaction.

In closing, REPEATABLE-READ is the most widely used and tested isolation level as it is the default value and should be used in preference to READ-COMMITTED.

Read Uncommitted

As the name suggests, READ-UNCOMMITTED shows dirty data, that is, data that is not committed. This section won't demonstrate the full output here; however, if you run the SQL statements from the previous section and exclude the COMMIT of the second session, you will observe the characteristics of the identical output as provided in the READ-COMMITTED example. You could then, for example, perform a ROLLBACK, yet the first transaction would still have recorded these now three phantom rows of values for x, y and z.

In session 1:

```
SET @@session.tx_isolation = 'READ-UNCOMMITTED';
```

The following code shows the last portion of session 1:

```
SELECT * FROM transaction_test;
+----+----------------+---------------------+
| id | val            | created             |
+----+----------------+---------------------+
|  1 | a              | 2009-10-17 16:12:33 |
|  2 | b              | 2009-10-17 16:12:33 |
```

```
|  3 | c                |  2009-10-17 16:12:33 |
|  4 | x                |  2009-10-17 16:12:49 |
|  5 | y                |  2009-10-17 16:12:49 |
|  6 | z                |  2009-10-17 16:12:49 |
|  7 | READ-UNCOMMITTED |  2009-10-17 16:13:02 |
+----+------------------+----------------------+
```

The following code shows the last portion of session 2 with ROLLBACK:

```
SELECT * FROM transaction_test;
+----+-----+----------------------+
| id | val | created              |
+----+-----+----------------------+
|  1 | a   | 2009-10-17 16:12:33  |
|  2 | b   | 2009-10-17 16:12:33  |
|  3 | c   | 2009-10-17 16:12:33  |
|  4 | x   | 2009-10-17 16:12:49  |
|  5 | y   | 2009-10-17 16:12:49  |
|  6 | z   | 2009-10-17 16:12:49  |
+----+-----+----------------------+
6 rows in set (0.00 sec)

# Wait for first session to complete.
ROLLBACK;

SELECT * FROM transaction_test;
+----+------------------+----------------------+
| id | val              | created              |
+----+------------------+----------------------+
|  1 | a                | 2009-10-17 16:12:33  |
|  2 | b                | 2009-10-17 16:12:33  |
|  3 | c                | 2009-10-17 16:12:33  |
|  7 | READ-UNCOMMITTED | 2009-10-17 16:13:02  |
+----+------------------+----------------------+
```

Serializable

The final isolation level is SERIALIZABLE. In this situation, tables are effectively locked in shared mode, which forces transactions to block other transactions. If you were to repeat the REPEATABLE_ READ test as previously shown, you would see an identical final output for the first session. The impact, however, would be a delay of the INSERT in the second session, which is blocked until the first transaction completes, and you then in turn see the row from the first session:

```
SET @@session.tx_isolation = 'SERIALIZABLE';
```

The following code shows the end of first session:

```
SELECT * FROM transaction_test;
+----+--------------+----------------------+
| id | val          | created              |
+----+--------------+----------------------+
|  1 | a            | 2009-10-17 16:15:34  |
|  2 | b            | 2009-10-17 16:15:34  |
|  3 | c            | 2009-10-17 16:15:34  |
|  7 | SERIALIZABLE | 2009-10-17 16:16:06  |
+----+--------------+----------------------+
```

```
4 rows in set (0.00 sec)

COMMIT;
```

The following code shows the end of second session:

```
INSERT INTO transaction_test(val) VALUES ('x'),('y'),('z');
Query OK, 3 rows affected (14.02 sec)

mysql> SELECT * FROM transaction_test;
+----+--------------+---------------------+
| id | val          | created             |
+----+--------------+---------------------+
|  1 | a            | 2009-10-17 16:15:34 |
|  2 | b            | 2009-10-17 16:15:34 |
|  3 | c            | 2009-10-17 16:15:34 |
|  4 | x            | 2009-10-17 16:15:52 |
|  5 | y            | 2009-10-17 16:15:52 |
|  6 | z            | 2009-10-17 16:15:52 |
|  7 | SERIALIZABLE | 2009-10-17 16:16:06 |
+----+--------------+---------------------+
7 rows in set (0.00 sec)

COMMIT;
```

It is interesting to note the order of the AUTO_INCREMENT column. The order as shown is the order as the actual statement was initiated. Because this value is managed as a separate internal global value held against the table, it was obtained in an internal exclusive mutex at the time of execution. It acts independently of the isolation level, contrary to the SERIALIZABLE mode of the actual SQL data that did not release the second session lock until after the INSERT completion of the locking transaction.

Isolation Levels and Replication

Be aware that MySQL replication does not work by default with an isolation level other than REPEATABLE-READ (the default isolation level). You will receive an error similar to the following:

```
mysql> INSERT INTO transaction_test(val) VALUES (@@session.tx_isolation);
ERROR 1598 (HY000): Binary logging not possible. Message: Transaction level
 'READ-COMMITTED' in InnoDB is not safe for binlog mode 'STATEMENT'
```

To use any other isolation level in MySQL 5.1, it is necessary to change MySQL replication to row-based replication, not statement-based replication. The impact of row based replication can be significant on overall database performance.

Durability

It is more complicated to easily demonstrate and confirm a working example of durability. You start, first, with the principle of database durability. When an acknowledgment of a successfully completed transaction is returned to the client, InnoDB guarantees the data is consistent, even though the data on disk at the time of the operation is not. This is due to the InnoDB logs (redo logs), which have serially recorded the completed transactions. InnoDB does not write the updated data to disk immediately; this is performed by a background worker thread within the InnoDB storage engine. This is a key difference between the non-transactional MyISAM engine and the transactional InnoDB engine.

In one session you run the following stored procedure to dump data into an InnoDB table (Listing 6-12):

LISTING 6-12: trans-tables.sql

```
use chapter6
drop table if exists durability_test;
create table durability_test (id int unsigned not null auto_increment primary
key, c1 varchar(2000) not null) engine = innodb default charset latin1;

delimiter $$

drop procedure if exists fill_durability $$
create procedure fill_durability()
deterministic
begin
  declare counter int default 0;
  truncate table durability_test;
  while TRUE
  do
    start transaction;
    set counter:= 0;
    while counter < 10
    do
      insert into durability_test(c1) values (repeat ('Expert PHP and MySQL',100));
      set counter:= counter + 1;
    end while;
    commit;
  end while;
end $$
delimiter;

call fill_durability();
```

After a period of time in a separate session, you collect the output of SHOW ENGINE INNODB STATUS, and then execute a kill on the mysqld process, both via the command line to minimize the delay between commands. What you collect is the following information about the InnoDB logs from the output:

```
---
LOG
---
Log flushed up to    0 856873708
Last checkpoint at   0 851353156
```

This information is the position the log files were flushed to, and the position of the last checkpoint where the data on disk reflects the committed transactions in the log file.

When you attempt to restart MySQL, the system automatically detects any inconsistency and performs an automatic crash recovery, which performs a serialized roll forward of all SQL commands between the reported two log positions. For this durability test, it's impossible to prove the state of the database because you cannot inspect those transactions in the log file or the state of the database before these transactions are applied; therefore you cannot confirm the ultimate results. The following is the MySQL error log output of a crash recovery to produce durability:

```
091017 17:14:13 mysqld_safe Starting mysqld daemon with databases from
InnoDB: Log scan progressed past the checkpoint lsn 0 851353156
091017 17:14:13  InnoDB: Database was not shut down normally!
InnoDB: Starting crash recovery.
InnoDB: Reading tablespace information from the .ibd files.
InnoDB: Restoring possible half-written data pages from the doublewrite
InnoDB: buffer.
091017 17:14:13  InnoDB: Starting an apply batch of log records to the database.
InnoDB: Progress in percents: 3 4 5 6 7 8 9 10 11 12 13 14 15 16 17 18 19 20 21
 22 23 24 25 26 27 28 29 30 31 32 33 34 35 36 37 38 39 40 41 42 43 44 45 46 47
 48 49 50 51 52 53 54 55 56 57 58 59 60 61 62 63 64 65 66 67 68 69 70 71 72 73
 74 75 76 77 78 79 80 81 82 83 84 85 86 87 88 89 90 91 92 93 94 95 96 97 98 99
InnoDB: Apply batch completed
InnoDB: Doing recovery: scanned up to log sequence number 0 856595968
InnoDB: Doing recovery: scanned up to log sequence number 0 856873708
091017 17:14:14  InnoDB: Starting an apply batch of log records to the database.
InnoDB: Progress in percents: 0 1 2 3 4 5 6 7 8 9 10 11 12 13 14 15 16 17 18 19
 20 21 22 23 24 25 26 27 28 29 30 31 32 33 34 35 36 37 38 39 40 41 42 43 44 45
 46 47 48 49 50 51 52 53 54 55 56 57 58 59 60 61 62 63 64 65 66 67 68 69 70 71
 72 73 74 75 76 77 78 79 80 81 82 83 84 85 86 87 88 89 90 91 92 93 94 95 96 97
 98 99
InnoDB: Apply batch completed
InnoDB: Last MySQL binlog file position 0 33100, file name ./binary-log.000003
091017 17:14:15  InnoDB: Started; log sequence number 0 856873708
091017 17:14:15 [Note] Event Scheduler: Loaded 1 event
091017 17:14:15 [Note] /Users/mysql/alpha/bin/mysqld: ready for connections.
Version: '5.1.39' socket: '/tmp/mysql.sock' port: 3306 MySQL Community Server (GPL)
```

The greatest impact of durability on a database is performance; though the data is not written to disk in InnoDB at the time of the transaction, this is performed in a background thread that flushes dirty pages from the buffer pool to disk. The innodb logs are written in a doublewrite fashion and by default are flushed to disk per transaction. In a high-volume system, the limitation is the speed of writing data to disk.

You can alter the InnoDB durability for performance by setting the `innodb_flush_log_at_trx_commit` variable to a value of 0 or 2, where the default value is 1. The three values produce different results in durability and they are listed here in most to least durable:

➤   When set to 1 (the default), Innodb writes to disk and flushes to disk every log transaction. This is the slowest but most durable.

➤   When set to 2, Innodb writes to disk all log transactions as they occur, and flushes this data approximately per one second.

➤   When set to 0, Innodb writes to disk all log transaction that have occurred in approximately the last one second, and then flushes these to disk.

The end result is that by breaking true durability, performance is increased significantly, and in a Web 2.0 world, it is generally acceptable that in the event of a crash, the loss of up to one second of data is acceptable. With the addition of battery-backed write cache disk controllers it is possible that no data loss occurs when using a value of 2.

Implied Commit

Wrapping a series of commands with START TRANSACTION and COMMIT block does not imply that ACID compliance is always enforced. Some commands create an implied COMMIT including CREATE, ALTER, and DROP commands and therefore can break the understanding of a transaction that is using these commands.

 Refer to the MySQL reference manual at http://dev.mysql.com/doc/refman/ 5.1/en/implicit-commit.html *for a full list of statements that implicitly end a MySQL transaction.*

REPLICATION

MySQL replication is a means to produce copies/replicas of your MySQL data on different servers regardless of their physical location. MySQL replication is a one-way asynchronous process that involves a primary server, known as a master, and one or more slave servers, configured to connect to the master. It is possible to create more complex relationships, with slaves acting as masters for additional slaves, for example.

Replication can operate over a LAN or WAN; the process of the slave pulling from the master enables slaves to be not always connected. This provides for an eventually consistent view of your data.

MySQL replication is a key component to the success of MySQL within the LAMP stack and for Web 2.0 social media websites such as Facebook, YouTube, and Twitter. Used effectively, replication can provide great scalability options, and combined with other products and design principles can ensure an infrastructure that can support scalability in an automated and near seamless approach.

MySQL replication provides features that can be used for many different purposes.

Replication Purposes

You can use MySQL replication to create various MySQL topologies that you can then use for many different purposes. The more popular options include:

- ➤ Read scalability
- ➤ Primary backup server
- ➤ Failover server
- ➤ Geo redundancy
- ➤ Data warehouse
- ➤ Benchmarking
- ➤ Software upgrades

Some of the more unique approaches include using MySQL replication as a means to share different workloads across multiple servers while supporting the same data, but different storage engines and index configurations to better suit the read work load. You can use replication as a proxy of database security leveraging the BLACKHOLE storage engine, for example to accept data on a public site; however, the data is never stored.

Replication Setup

MySQL replication is relatively easy to configure. It is even possible to run a MySQL master and slave replication configuration on a single server. To demonstrate MySQL replication, you should first consider the normal situation of using two servers. After installing a new instance of MySQL on each individual server as you would normally do, you need to make the following configuration changes on each server in order to have a working MySQL replication environment.

Master Configuration

On the master MySQL server, which this example codenames Alpha, you need to make the following minimum changes to the my.cnf file:

```
[mysqld]
log-bin=binary-log
server-id=1
```

When you have made these changes you need to restart the MySQL daemon process:

➤ To use replication you must enable binary logging with the log-bin parameter. Binary logging serves multiple purposes in a MySQL environment. For MySQL replication it provides a stream of DDL and DML statements that can be reapplied to the replication slaves. This option optionally accepts a filename prefix and a directory. By default, the binary logs are stored in the MySQL data directory.

➤ The second parameter listed is server-id. This is required to be a unique number within the MySQL topology and is used to identify the source location of a given SQL statement.

The enabled binary log information can be confirmed with the following SQL command:

```
SHOW MASTER STATUS;
+-------------------+----------+--------------+------------------+
| File              | Position | Binlog_Do_DB | Binlog_Ignore_DB |
+-------------------+----------+--------------+------------------+
| binary-log.000001 |    106   |              |                  |
+-------------------+----------+--------------+------------------+
```

This information is necessary to configure the replication slaves. You can also obtain this information with the following command, which actually provides the correct SQL syntax of the command needed to execute on the slave:

```
$ mysqldump -uroot -p --master-data tmp
CHANGE MASTER TO MASTER_LOG_FILE='binary-log.000001', MASTER_LOG_POS=106;
mysqldump: Got error: 1049: Unknown database 'tmp' when selecting the database
```

There is no way to retrieve the master data information without specifying a database. If you specify an invalid database, you get an error message that you can ignore. You require one more step on the master server, and this is to create an appropriate user for any MySQL slaves to pull changes from the master. You perform this after retrieving the binary log position because you want this command to be replicated:

```
CREATE USER repl@'192.168.%' IDENTIFIED BY 'repl2009';
GRANT REPLICATION SLAVE ON *.* TO repl@'192.168.%';
```

You use an IP range for host authentication. See the section on "Hardening Your MySQL Server" in Chapter 14, which discusses in detail the use and best practices of these specified permissions.

Slave Configuration

To configure the slave server, which is codenamed Beta, you need to make the following `my.cnf` changes and restart the MySQL server as you performed on the master:

```
[mysqld]
server-id=2
read_only=TRUE
```

➤ **The first parameter is `server-id`.** This is required to be a unique number within the MySQL topology and identifies the source location of a given SQL statement.

➤ **The second parameter is `read_only`.** This states that the server cannot receive DDL or DML statements. This is an important consideration in a MySQL topology because MySQL lacks any tools to support collision detection. It is possible — but highly discouraged — to create a Master/Master MySQL topology where both servers can receive writes at the same time. To achieve this, you must design your application with specific replication configuration, specific database architecture design, and also use recoverable SQL syntax.

The following SQL configures your running server as a slave. Note, the CHANGE MASTER commands include the username and password specified on the master, and the log file name and position are retrieved from the previous commands executed on the master.

```
SHOW SLAVE STATUS;
CHANGE MASTER TO
MASTER_HOST='192.168.100.1',
MASTER_USER='repl',
MASTER_PASSWORD='repl2009';

CHANGE MASTER TO
MASTER_LOG_FILE='binary-log.000001',
MASTER_LOG_POS=106;
```

Slave Operation

You now have a correctly configured slave. The final step is to start the slave and confirm operation:

```
SLAVE START;

SHOW SLAVE STATUS\G
*************************** 1. row ***************************
               Slave_IO_State: Waiting for master to send event
                  Master_Host: 192.168.100.1
                  Master_User: repl
                  Master_Port: 3306
                Connect_Retry: 60
              Master_Log_File: binary-log.000001
          Read_Master_Log_Pos: 327
               Relay_Log_File: macmarvin-relay-bin.000002
                Relay_Log_Pos: 473
        Relay_Master_Log_File: binary-log.000001
             Slave_IO_Running: Yes
            Slave_SQL_Running: Yes
              Replicate_Do_DB:
          Replicate_Ignore_DB:
           Replicate_Do_Table:
       Replicate_Ignore_Table:
      Replicate_Wild_Do_Table:
  Replicate_Wild_Ignore_Table:
                   Last_Errno: 0
                   Last_Error:
                 Skip_Counter: 0
          Exec_Master_Log_Pos: 327
              Relay_Log_Space: 632
              Until_Condition: None
               Until_Log_File:
                Until_Log_Pos: 0
            Master_SSL_Allowed: No
            Master_SSL_CA_File:
            Master_SSL_CA_Path:
               Master_SSL_Cert:
             Master_SSL_Cipher:
                Master_SSL_Key:
        Seconds_Behind_Master: 0
Master_SSL_Verify_Server_Cert: No
                Last_IO_Errno: 0
                Last_IO_Error:
               Last_SQL_Errno: 0
               Last_SQL_Error:
```

If you can confirm that Slave_IO_Running and Slave_SQL_Running are Yes, you have a running Master/Slave MySQL topology.

Testing MySQL Replication

The following examples use the code names `alpha` and `beta` for simplicity to ensure confirmation on which server the MySQL commands are performed. The best way to test this is to have two separate sessions open. The first step is to better identify your mysql client sessions.

➤ The following code tests on `alpha`:

```
mysql> PROMPT alpha>;
alpha>
```

➤ The following code test on `beta`:

```
mysql> PROMPT beta>;
beta>
```

Create a new schema and table in your tests by following these steps:

1. First confirm nothing exists on the slave:

```
beta>    SHOW SCHEMAS;
+--------------------+
| Database           |
+--------------------+
| information_schema |
| mysql              |
| test               |
+--------------------+
```

2. Create the schema and table on the master and confirm this:

```
alpha>   CREATE SCHEMA chapter6;
alpha>   USE chapter6;
alpha>   CREATE TABLE replication_test(id INT UNSIGNED NOT NULL
         AUTO_INCREMENT PRIMARY KEY) ENGINE=INNODB DEFAULT CHARSET latin1;

beta>    SHOW SCHEMAS;
+--------------------+
| Database           |
+--------------------+
| information_schema |
| chapter6           |
| mysql              |
| test               |
+--------------------+
```

3. Verify the table exists on the client by retrieving the contents of the table:

```
beta>    SELECT * FROM chapter6.replication_test;
Empty set (0.00 sec)
```

4. Add some data on the master and confirm this is replicated:

```
alpha>   INSERT INTO chapter6.replication_test(id) VALUES (1),(2),(3);
alpha>   SELECT * FROM chapter6.replication_test;
```

```
+----+
| id |
+----+
| 1 |
| 2 |
| 3 |
+----+
```

5. Confirm the same data exists on the slave:

```
beta>   SELECT * FROM chapter6.replication_test;
+----+
| id |
+----+
| 1 |
| 2 |
| 3 |
+----+
```

If you attempt to add information to the slave, and not the master, you receive an error because of your initial MySQL configuration:

```
beta>   INSERT INTO chapter6.replication_test(id) VALUES (4);
ERROR 1290 (HY000): The MySQL server is running with the --read-only option
so it cannot execute this statement
```

> *A user with* SUPER *privileges overrides the* read_only *security. Never run an*
> *application user with* SUPER *privileges. More information on user security can*
> *be found in Chapter 14 in the section "Hardening your MySQL Server".*

How Does MySQL Replication Work?

This section breaks down the moving parts of MySQL replication step by step, using some more internal commands and operating system files to see the flow of how SQL is executed and replicated. For this, you stop the slave process to ensure you can see the SQL before execution:

```
beta>   SLAVE STOP;
```

Master Analysis

To perform master analysis, follow these steps:

1. Add some new data to the master for your test:

```
alpha>  SHOW MASTER STATUS;
+-------------------+----------+--------------+------------------+
| File              | Position | Binlog_Do_DB | Binlog_Ignore_DB |
+-------------------+----------+--------------+------------------+
| binary-log.000001 |     828  |              |                  |
+-------------------+----------+--------------+------------------+

alpha>  INSERT INTO chapter6.replication_test(id) VALUES(10);
```

```
alpha>  SHOW MASTER STATUS;
+-------------------+----------+-------------+------------------+
| File              | Position | Binlog_Do_DB | Binlog_Ignore_DB |
+-------------------+----------+-------------+------------------+
| binary-log.000001 |    1046  |             |                  |
+-------------------+----------+-------------+------------------+
```

2. The details in the SHOW MASTER STATUS commands actually reflect the filename and character pointer position in this file. You did not specify the location of these binary logs with the log-bin command, so you will find them in the MySQL data directory. This may vary depending on how you installed MySQL:

```
alpha$ ls -l /var/log/mysql/binary-log.000001
-rw-rw--- 1 rbradfor  staff  1046 Oct  4 00:08 binary-log.000001
```

3. Use the name of the file as shown in the preceding SHOW MASTER STATUS command. The position is actually a byte count of the listed binary file.

4. To show how the binary logs work, you rotate these files. By default MySQL rotates the files based on a given size; however, you can also rotate them manually:

```
alpha>  FLUSH LOGS;
alpha>  SHOW MASTER STATUS;
+-------------------+----------+-------------+------------------+
| File              | Position | Binlog_Do_DB | Binlog_Ignore_DB |
+-------------------+----------+-------------+------------------+
| binary-log.000002 |     106  |             |                  |
+-------------------+----------+-------------+------------------+


alpha$  ls -l /var/log/mysql/binary-log*
-rw-rw--- 1 rbradfor  staff  1090 Oct  4 00:11 binary-log.000001
-rw-rw--- 1 rbradfor  staff   106 Oct  4 00:11 binary-log.000002
-rw-rw--- 1 rbradfor  staff    40 Oct  4 00:11 binary-log.index
```

As you can see, the master status shows a new filename, and this is confirmed on the filesystem.

Binary Log File Analysis

You can actually interrogate these files with the mysqlbinlog command. For example, you can look at the log from the position of the binary log before you ran your test INSERT statement:

```
alpha$ mysqlbinlog --start-position=828 /var/log/mysql/binary-log.000001
```

This command produces a lot of verbose information. Some lines have been removed for simplicity and due to space constraints.

```
# at 828
#091004  0:08:21 server id 1  end_log_pos 900  Query  thread_id=8  exec_time=0
    error_code=0
.
# at 900
#091004  0:08:21 server id 1  end_log_pos 1019 Query  thread_id=8  exec_time=0
    error_code=0
use chapter6/*!*/;
```

```
SET TIMESTAMP=1254629301/*!*/;
INSERT INTO chapter6.replication_test(id) VALUES(10)
/*!*/;
# at 1019
#091004  0:08:21 server id 1  end_log_pos 1046 Xid = 47
COMMIT/*!*/;
# at 1046
#091004  0:11:51 server id 1  end_log_pos 1090 Rotate to binary-log.000002  pos: 4
DELIMITER;
# End of log file
ROLLBACK /* added by mysqlbinlog */;
/*!50003 SET COMPLETION_TYPE=@OLD_COMPLETION_TYPE*/;
```

As you can see, the command you executed is in the replication stream.

The `mysqlbinlog` command has many arguments; for consideration of display output you restricted what was displayed here with one option. Refer to `mysqlbinlog --help` or the MySQL Reference Manual for additional information on this command.

Now that you understand how information is held on the master, turn your attention to the slave for the second part of MySQL replication.

Slave Analysis

First, look at the current slave status. The following code is a summarized view:

```
beta>   SHOW SLAVE STATUS\G
*************************** 1. row ***************************
              Master_Log_File: binary-log.000001
          Read_Master_Log_Pos: 828
               Relay_Log_File: relay-bin.000002
                Relay_Log_Pos: 974
        Relay_Master_Log_File: binary-log.000001
             Slave_IO_Running: No
            Slave_SQL_Running: No
          Exec_Master_Log_Pos: 828
               Relay_Log_Space: 1133
        Seconds_Behind_Master: NULL
```

Note that the master log position is the position before you started. The slave replication process is actually two threads. These perform two very different functions:

➤ **The IO thread:** Responsible for reading new transactions from the master, and writing these to the relay log file that is on the slave server.

➤ **The SQL thread;** Responsible for replaying the SQL statements that are held in the relay log.

For the purpose of this test, you can look at each thread individually. First, start just the IO thread:

```
beta> START SLAVE IO_THREAD;
beta> SHOW SLAVE STATUS\G
*************************** 1. row ***************************
              Master_Log_File: binary-log.000002
          Read_Master_Log_Pos: 106
               Relay_Log_File: relay-bin.000002
                Relay_Log_Pos: 974
```

```
              Relay_Master_Log_File: binary-log.000001
                  Slave_IO_Running: Yes
                 Slave_SQL_Running: No
                Exec_Master_Log_Pos: 828
             Seconds_Behind_Master: NULL
```

The slave now records the current position of the MySQL Master. Look at the data in the table:

```
beta> SELECT * FROM chapter6.replication_test;
+----+
| id |
+----+
|  1 |
|  2 |
|  3 |
+----+
```

As you can see, the row does not exist. This is because you have not started the SQL thread that will execute all SQL statements in the relay log:

```
beta> START SLAVE SQL_THREAD;
Query OK, 0 rows affected (0.00 sec)

beta> SHOW SLAVE STATUS\G
*************************** 1. row ***************************
               Slave_IO_State: Waiting for master to send event
                  Master_Host: 192.168.100.3
                  Master_User: repl
                  Master_Port: 3306
              Master_Log_File: binary-log.000002
          Read_Master_Log_Pos: 106
               Relay_Log_File: relay-bin.000005
                Relay_Log_Pos: 252
        Relay_Master_Log_File: binary-log.000002
             Slave_IO_Running: Yes
            Slave_SQL_Running: Yes
          Exec_Master_Log_Pos: 106
              Relay_Log_Space: 455
        Seconds_Behind_Master: 0
```

Now look for your data:

```
beta> SELECT * FROM chapter6.replication_test;
+----+
| id |
+----+
|  1 |
|  2 |
|  3 |
| 10 |
+----+
```

This section did not look into the detail of the relay logs on the filesystem; however, they operate the same way as the binary log files. You can confirm them on the filesystem, and use the `mysqlbinlog` command to review the contents.

Testing MySQL Replication

There is a very easy way to demonstrate MySQL replication and watch it in operation: On the slave, you monitor MySQL replication dynamically with the `watch` command.

```
beta$ watch -n 1--differences 'mysql -e "SHOW SLAVE STATUS\G"'
```

 This is a Linux/UNIX-specific command.

On the master, create and run the following stored procedure as shown in Listing 6-13, which inserts a 2 factorial number of rows for each iteration. Carefully monitor the `watch` command and you will see various counters in action by a change in values and highlighting:

LISTING 6-13: numbers-sp.sql

Available for download on Wrox.com

```
use chapter6
drop table if exists numbers;
create table numbers (id int unsigned not null primary key);

delimiter $$

drop procedure if exists fill_numbers $$
create procedure fill_numbers(in p_max int)
deterministic
begin
  declare counter int default 1;
  truncate table numbers;
  insert into numbers values (1);
  while counter < p_max
  do
      insert into numbers (id)
          select id + counter
          from numbers;
      select count(*) into counter from numbers;
      select counter;
  end while;
end $$

delimiter;

call fill_numbers(2000000);
```

As the number of rows inserted increase and are then replicated you will observe the change in binary log position, relay log position, and also the reported seconds behind the master the slave presently is. You also see the slave catch up, and report an eventually consistent state. Refer to http://ronaldbradford.com/blog/verifying-mysql-replication-in-action-2009-06-28/ for additional information.

Important Configuration Options

The following are a number of additional replication configuration options you should be aware of. It is not possible to detail all the options and provide full details of the benefits of options. This could be a topic for an entire chapter or section of a book. Hopefully, the information provided in Table 6-1 will give you a greater understanding of the possible options and encourage you to read further to better understand all the options.

TABLE 6-1: Additional Replication Configuration Options

OPTION	DESCRIPTION
skip-slave-start	By default, a MySQL slave automatically starts when MySQL starts; that is, effectively running START SLAVE automatically. If you want to perform this manually, use this option.
log-slave-updates	If you want to run binary logging on your MySQL slave as well as on the master, you should also enable this option to ensure any commands executed directly on the slave are also logged. This is important when the slave is used in a fail-over situation.
sync_binlog	This is an important command to ensure consistency of data between servers during a server crash.
innodb_support_xa	This is an important command to ensure consistency and synchronization between the InnoDB redo log files and the binary log file in the event of a server crash.
max_binlog_size	This option defines the maximum size of the binary log before it is rolled to a new file.
expire_logs_days	This option defines the number of days the binary logs are kept. Logs are automatically deleted by MySQL after this number of days.
binlog_cache_size	This option defines how much data can be cached during a transaction before the information is written to the binary log file.
auto_increment_increment	This option enables you to change the amount an auto-increment number increases. Combined with auto_increment_offset this can be used to insert data across multiple servers to avoid potential collision.
replication-format	New in 5.1. The current default value is STATEMENT which reflects the only option in 5.0. Other options include MIXED and ROW format. Until 5.1.29 the default option was MIXED. Changing the transaction_isolation level from the system defaults requires the use of the ROW format.

Important Replication Commands

As you have seen, a number of commands such as SHOW MASTER STATUS, SHOW SLAVE STATUS, and START SLAVE are used to monitor MySQL replication. The following additional commands are also important:

➤ **FLUSH LOGS:** Performs a manual rotation of the underlying binary and relay log files.

➤ **SHOW MASTER LOGS:** Shows a list of binary log files that are presently available to the MySQL server.

➤ **PURGE MASTER LOGS:** Deletes binary logs. By default the expire_logs_days variable can be used to perform this operation automatically.

Do not delete old binary log files manually. This will cause an inconsistency with MySQL, and though MySQL may appear to be operating normally, any operations such as database recovery that rely on a consistency of meta information and filesystem information will fail.

Also, never let your binary log filesystem fill up on your master. This will ruin your entire MySQL replication topology, including your master and all your slaves. Your backup infrastructure may also be useless if you use a slave for your backup approach as this slave will now be corrupt.

Breaking Replication

Although this chapter has shown MySQL replication in normal operation, it is important you know how to identify and handle any possible errors. You can easily simulate an error situation by following these steps:

1. Break the read-only characteristics of the MySQL slave:

```
beta>    SET GLOBAL read_only=FALSE;
beta>    SELECT * FROM chapter6.replication_test WHERE id > 100;
Empty set (0.02 sec)

beta>    INSERT INTO chapter6.replication_test VALUES (101);
beta>    SELECT * FROM chapter6.replication_test WHERE id > 100;
+-----+
| id  |
+-----+
| 101 |
+-----+
```

2. On the master, insert the same data that now already exists on the slave:

```
alpha>   SELECT * FROM chapter6.replication_test WHERE id > 100;
Empty set (0.02 sec)

alpha>   INSERT INTO chapter6.replication_test VALUES (101);
alpha>   SELECT * FROM chapter6.replication_test WHERE id > 100;
```

```
+-----+
| id  |
+-----+
| 101 |
+-----+
```

3. On the slave, review the status of replication:

```
beta>   SHOW SLAVE STATUS\G
*************************** 1. row ***************************
               Slave_IO_State: Waiting for master to send event
              Master_Log_File: binary-log.000003
          Read_Master_Log_Pos: 306
               Relay_Log_File: relay-bin.000013
                Relay_Log_Pos: 252
        Relay_Master_Log_File: binary-log.000003
             Slave_IO_Running: Yes
            Slave_SQL_Running: No
                   Last_Errno: 1062
                   Last_Error: Error 'Duplicate entry '101' for key
'PRIMARY'' on query. Default database: ''.
Query: 'INSERT INTO chapter6.replication_test VALUES (101)'
                 Skip_Counter: 0
           Exec_Master_Log_Pos: 106
```

4. You now see an error in replication, but the cause is known, and you now have a possible inconsistency in the data. You know the cause because this is a simulated test, but in a production environment, this is not obvious and appropriate verification of underlying data on the master and slave is necessary:

```
beta>   SET GLOBAL SQL_SLAVE_SKIP_COUNTER=1;
beta>   SLAVE START SQL_THREAD;
beta>   SHOW SLAVE STATUS\G
```

You should now see a running MySQL slave as was previously demonstrated.

If you follow these two rules, you eliminate user-introduced errors and the most likely causes of replication failure:

➤ Always run your MySQL slaves in read-only mode.

➤ Never use a user with SUPER privileges to run DDL or DML statements.

Using Replication Selectively

It is also possible to run commands that are not replicated. For example, you can selectively disable replication on a per-command basis:

```
alpha>   SET SESSION SQL_LOG_BIN=FALSE;
alpha>   INSERT INTO chapter6.replication_test VALUES (201);
alpha>   SET SESSION SQL_LOG_BIN=TRUE;
```

```
alpha>   INSERT INTO chapter6.replication_test VALUES (202);
alpha>   SELECT * FROM chapter6.replication_test WHERE id > 200;
+-----+
| id  |
+-----+
| 201 |
| 202 |
+-----+
```

As you will observe, not all data inserted was applied to the slave:

```
beta>    SELECT * FROM chapter6.replication_test WHERE id > 200;
+-----+
| id  |
+-----+
| 202 |
+-----+
```

 You should never use these commands lightly. MySQL does not provide any means to ensure your database is consistent. By selectively disabling MySQL, you introduce inconsistency and MySQL does not provide any tools to identify or correct it. Check out the Maatkit toolkit for options to perform this.

You can also configure MySQL on the master or the slave to selectively log or process binary log events. The following various options provides various ways of selecting certain operation. We are not going to discuss these options in detail. Refer to the MySQL Reference Manual for detailed instructions at `http://dev.mysql.com/doc/refman/5.1/en/replication-options.html`.

➤   `replicate-do-db`

➤   `replicate-do-table`

➤   `replicate-ignore-db`

➤   `replicate-ignore-table`

➤   `replicate-wild-do-table`

➤   `replicate-wild-ignore-table`

The Issues with MySQL Replication

Two primary issues exist with MySQL replication, predominantly due to the asynchronous nature of the process. These are:

➤   **Lag:** A direct result of the asynchronous nature of MySQL replication. It is important that you monitor replication lag in your topology because generally the purpose of a MySQL slave is for an online processing such as read scalability or for MySQL backups.

➤   **Consistency:** There is no guarantee the slave data is consistent with the master. In previous examples, two instances were shown that can produce an inconsistent data set.

Several patches are now available to improve consistency and as a side result improve lag. The first patch provided in the Google MySQL Patches `http://code.google.com/p/google-mysql-tools/` gives a level of semi-synchronous replication. Additional ports of MySQL including the Percona performance builds now include similar patches.

The possibility of inconsistency is often not considered, especially when a MySQL slave is your primary backup process. MySQL does not provide an ability to ensure consistency via a table checksum, for example. The popular Maatkit toolkit available at `http://maatkit.org` has a very good tool for performing table checksums.

> *Although not discussed in this book, there is a MySQL product that provides synchronous replication to overcome these two points. MySQL Cluster can operate similar to MySQL replication; however, it is actually a different product. Though it may appear to operate like MySQL via an SQL interface, it has different features as well as relative strengths and limitations. Refer to the official MySQL product page for additional information at* `http://www.mysql.com/products/database/cluster/`.

The Benefits of MySQL Replication

It is important to recognize the strengths of MySQL and maximize these while minimizing the weaknesses. Though some issues were listed first, the benefits of MySQL can easily outweigh the limitations. MySQL replication is successfully used in many major websites today. Combined with other products, such as memcached, and principles, such as sharding, the combination can provide a powerful and scalable solution.

> *The MySQL Sandbox (*`http://mysqlsandbox.net/`*), originally created by MySQL community member Giuseppe Maxia, is an invaluable tool in learning about MySQL replication. With this tool you can create and deploy various types of different MySQL replication topologies in seconds in a totally isolated environment for testing.*

EVENTS

Events are a new feature of MySQL 5.1. Events enable the scheduling of one-off or recurring work within the MySQL database, similar to the process of scheduling on Linux systems using cron. To demonstrate events, create a test table that you will use as verification (Listing 6-14):

LISTING 6-14: event-table.sql

Available for download on Wrox.com

```
DROP TABLE IF EXISTS event_test;
CREATE TABLE event_test(
    id      INT UNSIGNED NOT NULL AUTO_INCREMENT,
```

```
created  TIMESTAMP NOT NULL DEFAULT CURRENT_TIMESTAMP,
action   VARCHAR(10) NOT NULL,
val      VARCHAR(10) NOT NULL,
PRIMARY KEY (id)
) ENGINE=InnoDB DEFAULT CHARSET latin1;
```

Creating Events

To create your first event, follow these steps:

1. Create an event that runs every minute (Listing 6-15):

LISTING 6-15: every-min-event.sql

```
CREATE EVENT e_minute
ON SCHEDULE EVERY 1 MINUTE
COMMENT 'Perform event every minute'
DO
  INSERT INTO event_test (action,val)
  VALUES ('Minute',DATE_FORMAT(NOW(),'%i%s'));
```

2. Confirm that nothing has happened as yet:

```
SELECT * FROM event_test;
Empty set (0.00 sec)

SELECT NOW();
+---------------------+
| NOW()               |
+---------------------+
| 2009-10-17 14:52:23 |
+---------------------+
```

3. Create an event that runs just once (Listing 6-16):

LISTING 6-16: once-off-event.sql

```
CREATE EVENT e_nextminute
ON SCHEDULE AT CURRENT_TIMESTAMP + INTERVAL 1 MINUTE
COMMENT 'Perform event just once'
DO
  INSERT INTO event_test (action,val)
  VALUES ('1 Minute',DATE_FORMAT(NOW(),'%i%s'));
```

4. You can view the scheduling information of events with the SHOW EVENTS command:

```
mysql> SHOW EVENTS\G
*************************** 1. row ***************************
                  Db: chapter6
                Name: e_minute
             Definer: rbradfor@localhost
           Time zone: SYSTEM
```

```
                Type: RECURRING
          Execute at: NULL
      Interval value: 1
      Interval field: MINUTE
              Starts: 2009-10-17 14:51:42
                Ends: NULL
              Status: ENABLED
          Originator: 0
  character_set_client: latin1
collation_connection: latin1_swedish_ci
  Database Collation: latin1_swedish_ci
*************************** 2. row ***************************
                  Db: chapter6
                Name: e_nextminute
             Definer: rbradfor@localhost
           Time zone: SYSTEM
                Type: ONE TIME
          Execute at: 2009-10-17 15:00:07
      Interval value: NULL
      Interval field: NULL
              Starts: NULL
                Ends: NULL
              Status: ENABLED
          Originator: 0
  character_set_client: latin1
collation_connection: latin1_swedish_ci
  Database Collation: latin1_swedish_ci
2 rows in set (0.00 sec)
```

5. Now that a few minutes have passed, look at the data that has been inserted:

```
SELECT * FROM event_test;
Empty set (0.00 sec)
```

There is no information in the table. The output in SHOW EVENTS does not indicate any problems. A review of the MySQL error log does not provide any errors. The problem is that the event scheduler is not enabled by default. When the author first tested events in version 5.1.6, this was not required. The MySQL reference manual confirms that the default behavior of events has changed in different versions.

Never assume the default value of a given MySQL configuration variable. Default values can change between versions, and there are numerous occurrences of these. It is important to read the documentation carefully, and ensure you read the version that is consistent with the specific point release of the MySQL product and also the various MySQL connectors.

Enabling the Events Scheduler

Armed with this new knowledge, you can, indeed, confirm that the scheduler is defined by default as not running:

1.   Enable this:

```
SHOW GLOBAL VARIABLES LIKE 'event_scheduler';
+-----------------+-------+
| Variable_name   | Value |
+-----------------+-------+
| event_scheduler | OFF   |
+-----------------+-------+
SET GLOBAL event_scheduler = TRUE;
```

2.   Let the scheduler run for a few minutes to see the output you first expected:

```
mysql> SELECT * FROM event_test;
+----+---------------------+----------+------+
| id | created             | action   | val  |
+----+---------------------+----------+------+
|  1 | 2009-10-17 15:08:36 | 1 Minute | 0836 |
|  2 | 2009-10-17 15:08:42 | Minute   | 0842 |
|  3 | 2009-10-17 15:09:42 | Minute   | 0942 |
|  4 | 2009-10-17 15:10:42 | Minute   | 1042 |
+----+---------------------+----------+------+
```

3.   If you review the schedule of events, you'll find now that only one is defined:

```
mysql> SHOW EVENTS\G
*************************** 1. row ***************************
                  Db: chapter6
                Name: e_minute
             Definer: root@localhost
           Time zone: SYSTEM
                Type: RECURRING
          Execute at: NULL
      Interval value: 1
      Interval field: MINUTE
              Starts: 2009-10-17 14:51:42
                Ends: NULL
              Status: ENABLED
          Originator: 1
character_set_client: latin1
collation_connection: latin1_swedish_ci
  Database Collation: latin1_swedish_ci
```

Altering Events

By default an event is automatically dropped when it is completed. You can override this behavior with the ON COMPLETION PRESERVE syntax when defining the event. For an existing recurring event you have the option to disable or drop the event to stop operation:

```
ALTER EVENT e_minute DISABLE;
mysql> SHOW EVENTS\G
```

```
*************************** 1. row ***************************
               Db: chapter6
             Name: e_minute
          Definer: root@localhost
        Time zone: SYSTEM
             Type: RECURRING
       Execute at: NULL
   Interval value: 1
   Interval field: MINUTE
           Starts: 2009-10-17 14:51:42
             Ends: NULL
           Status: DISABLED
       Originator: 1
character_set_client: latin1
collation_connection: latin1_swedish_ci
Database Collation: latin1_swedish_ci
```

You can also re-enable events. You can then observe the data to show a gap of data to correspond with the time the event was disabled:

```
ALTER EVENT e_minute ENABLE;
SELECT SLEEP(60);
SELECT * FROM event_test;
+----+---------------------+----------+------+
| id | created             | action   | val  |
+----+---------------------+----------+------+
|  1 | 2009-10-17 15:08:36 | 1 Minute | 0836 |
|  2 | 2009-10-17 15:08:42 | Minute   | 0842 |
|  3 | 2009-10-17 15:09:42 | Minute   | 0942 |
|  4 | 2009-10-17 15:10:42 | Minute   | 1042 |
|  5 | 2009-10-17 15:11:42 | Minute   | 1142 |
|  6 | 2009-10-17 15:12:42 | Minute   | 1242 |
|  7 | 2009-10-17 15:13:42 | Minute   | 1342 |
|  8 | 2009-10-17 15:18:42 | Minute   | 1842 |
+----+---------------------+----------+------+
```

As you can see, the every minute event did not run for five minutes.

To conclude the life cycle, you can remove events like other database objects with the DROP syntax:

```
DROP event e_minute;
SHOW EVENTS\G
Empty set (0.00 sec)
```

Event Privileges

In order to have permission to create or modify events you need an additional privilege: the EVENT permission. You can use the standard GRANT and REVOKE commands to grant this privilege to users for specific database schemas or all schemas. For example:

```
GRANT EVENT ON chapter6.* TO wrox@localhost;
REVOKE EVENT on chapter6.* FROM wrox@localhost;
```

Event Meta Data

MySQL event information is available from two sources: the INFORMATION_SCHEMA and the mysql meta schema. For example:

```
mysql> select * from mysql.event\G
*************************** 1. row ***************************
               db: chapter6
             name: e_minute
             body: INSERT INTO event_test (action,val)
                   VALUES ('Minute',DATE_FORMAT(NOW(),'%i%s'))
          definer: root@localhost
       execute_at: NULL
   interval_value: 1
   interval_field: MINUTE
          created: 2009-10-17 14:51:42
         modified: 2009-10-17 14:51:42
    last_executed: 2009-10-17 19:12:42
           starts: 2009-10-17 18:51:42
             ends: NULL
           status: ENABLED
    on_completion: DROP
         sql_mode:
          comment: Perform event every minute
       originator: 1
        time_zone: SYSTEM
character_set_client: latin1
collation_connection: latin1_swedish_ci
     db_collation: latin1_swedish_ci
        body_utf8: INSERT INTO event_test (action,val)
                   VALUES ('Minute',DATE_FORMAT(NOW(),'%i%s'))


mysql> SELECT * FROM INFORMATION_SCHEMA.EVENTS\G
*************************** 1. row ***************************
      EVENT_CATALOG: NULL
       EVENT_SCHEMA: chapter6
         EVENT_NAME: e_minute
            DEFINER: root@localhost
          TIME_ZONE: SYSTEM
         EVENT_BODY: SQL
   EVENT_DEFINITION: INSERT INTO event_test (action,val)
                     VALUES ('Minute',DATE_FORMAT(NOW(),'%i%s'))
         EVENT_TYPE: RECURRING
         EXECUTE_AT: NULL
     INTERVAL_VALUE: 1
     INTERVAL_FIELD: MINUTE
           SQL_MODE:
             STARTS: 2009-10-17 15:23:59
               ENDS: NULL
             STATUS: ENABLED
      ON_COMPLETION: NOT PRESERVE
            CREATED: 2009-10-17 15:23:59
        LAST_ALTERED: 2009-10-17 15:23:59
```

```
        LAST_EXECUTED: 2009-10-17 15:23:59
        EVENT_COMMENT: Perform event every minute
           ORIGINATOR: 1
   CHARACTER_SET_CLIENT: latin1
COLLATION_CONNECTION: latin1_swedish_ci
   DATABASE_COLLATION: latin1_swedish_ci
```

SUMMARY

This chapter covered a number of SQL advanced features you will find in other relational database products and a number of MySQL specific advanced features that you can use in your software development practices to enrich the functionality of your products.

The use of transactions is a key component of normal application development and users who only know MySQL may not utilize this important business feature. The added benefits of ACID capabilities, referential constraints, MVCC, and automatic crash recovery are key considerations for a MySQL application provided by transactions. By default, applications should be written with transactions in mind. The use of stored procedures, stored functions, and triggers provides an alternative means of providing business logic at a layer closer to the database and agnostic to front-end development technologies. Views in MySQL can provide a layer of abstraction and simplification to the application layer, as well as provide a different means of read security to underlying information.

Finally, MySQL replication gives a means to extend operations against your data by providing additional copies of your data. Used for many purposes including backups, read scalability and database maintenance, MySQL replication is an essential advanced feature for the PHP and MySQL expert.

7

Extending MySQL with User-Defined Functions

WHAT'S IN THIS CHAPTER?

➤ An introduction the MySQL UDF application programming interface (API)

➤ The complete steps for designing, implementing, testing, and debugging a UDF

➤ An introduction to using the gnu debugger, gdb

Have you ever been assigned a project that required some functionality from MySQL that wasn't included or where writing a stored procedure or function didn't quite implement the functionality you needed? Perhaps you have a custom library or C-program that you want to access from within MySQL, one you could use in the database calls that your application makes and which makes use of any performance advantages your library offers?

MySQL, being the flexible system that it is, offers you a way to extend the server and create your own functions — different than stored procedures or functions — which perform like standard built-in functions that come included with MySQL. MySQL provides an API for writing *user-defined functions*, otherwise known as *UDFs*, which are functions written in C or C++ that can do whatever the user needs them to do, limited only by imagination in terms of functionality. Though this book is for PHP programmers, extending MySQL by writing your UDF in either C or C++ using the UDF API is pretty straightforward and the results are extremely useful. Any experienced PHP developer with a mind for programming should be able to easily grasp how to implement a UDF — and in the process gain a deeper understanding for some internals of MySQL as well as get a C or C++ refresher!

This chapter demonstrates how to implement a functional, useful UDF. You may be saying to yourself while reading this: "Hey, I thought this was supposed to be a PHP book!" However, any true geek hacker wants to learn something new, and this chapter shows you how you can use a UDF from PHP code. So, you might want to crack open a book or perform a search online for a refresher on some basic C/C++ concepts, but you won't need to be a C or C++ guru to do this. An advantage to this is you can always add another bullet-point to your resume after making an attempt to write a UDF!

INTRODUCTION TO UDFS

As mentioned already, a UDF is a user-defined function, and this book uses the acronym UDF from here on. A UDF is a means for you to extend MySQL by writing a function — different than a stored function — that runs within the MySQL server instead of being stored as a program. It can be written in C or C++ as opposed to SQL, in which stored functions are written. The UDF source code is compiled into a shared library and loaded within MySQL, which then makes it usable.

A UDF runs within the confines of the MySQL server and has to adhere to some basic constructs, which this chapter discusses. Also, it should be noted that a UDF's execution cannot be controlled by database user privileges as stored functions and procedures can. Being a function, like any other function (stored or built-in), a UDF can return only a single value, either a string or numeric value, and is also executed the same way as other functions. UDFs enable Web developers who are familiar with C and C++ and the UDF API to implement many kinds of database functionality.

UDFs can be particularly useful in combination with a C-library such as the libmemcached, or a C client library such as libgearman. For instance, the Memcached Functions for MySQL (`https://launchpad.net/memcached-udfs`) make it possible to both store and retrieve values, as well as various other functions that the libmemcached C-library provides in interacting with the memcached server. Likewise, the Gearman User Defined Functions for MySQL provide many of the operations the libgearman C client library provides for interacting with the Gearman job server (`https://launchpad.net/gearman-mysql-udf`). Basically, if you have a well-defined client API with some standard functions you would like to have available to MySQL, writing a UDF gives you the ability to call the client functions within MySQL.

Additionally, numerous open source UDFs are available. One useful site is `http://www.mysqludf.org/`, which has a number of UDFs that you can use for your database application environment as well as to learn more about UDF programming.

The first thing that you need to develop a UDF is to determine what you want it to do. What functionality do you want to have access to from within MySQL? It could be something as simple as a conversion function — for instance, you have a useful C program you've written before that converts metric to standard, or something more complex that initiates some external process when run.

For instance, before Eric Day rewrote the Gearman job server and client library in C, I (Patrick Galbraith) required functionality similar to what Gearman provides, which is to have a means to call external programs from within MySQL. To do this, I wrote a UDF that took as an argument an ID of a column of a queuing table, which in turn was written to a socket that a simple server read. It retrieved the row of that ID and then ran external Perl processes with that ID as a program argument. This program argument used a trigger that activated upon a record being inserted into a queuing table, which called the UDF, which in turn resulted in a Perl process handling the ID of the row just inserted. This made it possible to implement an event-driven model of acting on the queue with Perl programs, as opposed to a constantly polling cron Perl script. The benefit of this scheme was that the process ran only when there was an insert to the queuing table. When the web site was slow and experiencing little activity, the Perl script was not being called unnecessarily. This is just one example of how a UDF extended the functionality of MySQL.

DEVELOPING A UDF

If you have experience writing C or C++ programs, you can write a UDF. You should become familiar with the UDF API, and a great way to get started is studying the UDF examples in the MySQL source code that implements five different functions.

EXPERT ADVICE

You can find five UDF examples in the MySQL source code within the directory and file `sql/udf_example.c`.

UDF Development Requirements

If you have a great idea for a UDF that you want to implement, just use these examples as a template and start from there. Things to know about writing a UDF include:

➤ It must be run on an operating system that supports dynamic loading of libraries.

➤ You will need a compiler to build your UDF. Most UNIX variants include either a compiler that is installed by default with the operating system or you that one can easily install even after UDF installation.

➤ You will also want a debugger installed on your operating system. This can help immensely during the debugging process. You can have a perfect compile, but run time can be a whole other matter! The gdb debugger on UNIX systems is one such debugger; for Windows, the Microsoft debugger is also a useful tool.

➤ The UDF must be written in C or C++.

➤ Functions return and accept a string, an integer, and real values.

➤ You can use simple, single-row and multiple-row aggregate UDFs.

➤ All functions must be thread-safe. This means that you cannot use global or static variables that are changed.

➤ You can have MySQL coerce arguments to a specific type. For instance, you may want to always use a string as an argument, when internally the function expects an integer. You can force the function to accept a string, but internally convert it to an integer (using the C function `atoi()`).

➤ A standard functionality in the API allows for checking the type of argument. For example, you can check that the argument is a number as well as check the number of arguments.

➤ A UDF can return three types of values:

   ➤ **STRING_RESULT**: Any string value

   ➤ **INT_RESULT**: Integer value

   ➤ **REAL_RESULT**: Float or double value

UDF Required Functions

To create a UDF, some standard, basic C functions must be implemented. These are functions, written in C, that correspond to the name of the function as they are called in SQL. For the sake of conversation, let's assume the function name is `feet_to_meters()`. The three basic functions (the first of which, `feet_to_meters()`, is mandatory; the last two are optional) that would be implemented are:

➤ **feet_to_meters()**: This is the main function where all the real work happens. Whatever output or action your function performs — calculations, connections to sockets, conversions, and so on — you implement it here. For instance, if you had C code in a simple program that you wrote to convert the standard foot into the metric equivalent, this is where the bulk of your code would go.

➤ **feet_to_meters_init()**: This is the first function called, and is a setup function. This is where basic structures are initialized as well as checking argument counts. For instance, in `feet_to_meters()`, you would have one argument, a numeric value in feet. This is where you would ensure that the function received one and only one argument and returned an error if not. Also, this is a good place to check whether the argument passed was a numeric or a string value. If the argument was a string value, you would obtain the numeric value from the string value. You can also coerce the argument type to a string (STRING_RESULT), integer (INT_RESULT), or real number (REAL_RESULT). Also, this is a good place to allocate anything that is used throughout the UDF that requires allocation.

➤ **feet_to_meters_deinit()**: This function is a cleanup function. This is where you would free anything you allocated in `feet_to_meters_init()` or `feet_to_meters()`.

A PRACTICAL UDF EXAMPLE

In the following example, try to envision that you have been given the task to write a database administrative PHP application that displays a listing of all schemas you have available in your MySQL instance; how many tables does each have? How much space does each of these schemas use? You can use the information schema to obtain the first two values:

```
mysql> select table_schema, count(*)
    -> as num_tables
    -> from information_schema.tables
    -> group by table_schema
    -> order by table_schema;
```

```
+--------------------+------------+
| table_schema       | num_tables |
+--------------------+------------+
| cacti              |         49 |
| drizzle_stats      |          6 |
| hipergate3         |        183 |
| information_schema |         17 |
| mediawiki          |         38 |
| mysql              |         17 |
| radius             |         93 |
| remote             |          1 |
| sugarcrm           |         98 |
| test               |          9 |
| wats               |         14 |
| webapps            |         17 |
| wordpress          |         10 |
+--------------------+------------+
```

But how would you obtain the actual space used on disk for each schema? Some ways of doing this provide an approximate value using the information schema, but this number is not exact and has more to do with the space used in terms of what's being used internally as seen by MySQL. How could you obtain the actual value of disk space used by a database schema (which is a directory location in MySQL's data directory) in the same way you would see with a command such as du? This is where a UDF can be employed.

UDF High-Level Design

The first thing you might want to do (at least to my way of thinking) is to come up with a simple C code snippet to obtain the value of a given directory. One family of standard C functions on UNIX for obtaining file information is the stat() family of functions. The manual page for fstat() gives information on what each of these functions provides and how they are used. Also, you will need functions and data types for working with directories and directory entries (the files and subdirectories contained within a directory). For this, you want to use the dirent.h system header file, which provides functions and data types for POSIX directory operations.

You will also want to gain an understanding of how MySQL stores data on disk. A schema in MySQL is organized as a directory within the data directory, known as the system variable datadir, which you can find out using the SQL statement:

```
mysql> show variables like 'datadir';
+---------------+----------------+
| Variable_name | Value          |
+---------------+----------------+
| datadir       | /var/lib/mysql/ |
+---------------+----------------+
```

In this MySQL instance, the value is /var/lib/mysql, which is most often the value of the datadir for installations of MySQL on various Linux platforms as configured by the operating system installation or package management tools. To see what is contained in these directories, simply view a given schema's directory within the data directory (you will need adequate permissions to view this directory). The following example views the directory for the schema *test*:

```
root@hanuman:/var/lib/mysql# ls -l test/
total 508
-rw-rw---- 1 mysql mysql  8586 2009-02-27 16:04 a1.frm
-rw-rw---- 1 mysql mysql    40 2009-02-27 16:12 a1.MYD
-rw-rw---- 1 mysql mysql  2048 2009-02-28 09:44 a1.MYI
-rw-rw---- 1 mysql mysql  8588 2009-07-14 10:28 a2.frm
-rw-rw---- 1 mysql mysql 98304 2009-07-14 10:28 a2.ibd
-rw-rw---- 1 mysql mysql  8602 2009-07-10 15:24 bench1.frm
-rw-rw---- 1 mysql mysql 98304 2009-07-10 15:24 bench1.ibd
-rw-rw---- 1 mysql mysql    65 2008-03-07 05:04 db.opt
-rw-rw---- 1 mysql mysql  8560 2009-01-26 17:20 schemalist.frm
-rw-rw---- 1 mysql mysql   184 2009-01-26 17:22 schemalist.MYD
-rw-rw---- 1 mysql mysql  1024 2009-01-29 18:16 schemalist.MYI
-rw-rw---- 1 mysql mysql  8556 2009-07-14 10:27 t3.frm
-rw-rw---- 1 mysql mysql 98304 2009-07-14 10:28 t3.ibd
-rw-rw---- 1 mysql mysql  8584 2008-08-15 07:12 test_table.frm
-rw-rw---- 1 mysql mysql     0 2008-08-15 07:12 test_table.MYD
-rw-rw---- 1 mysql mysql  1024 2008-08-15 07:12 test_table.MYI
-rw-rw---- 1 mysql mysql  8586 2009-07-14 10:19 users.frm
-rw-rw---- 1 mysql mysql 98304 2009-07-14 10:19 users.ibd
```

As you can see, there are two to three sets of files, each corresponding to a table name. This example contains several types of files:

➤ **.Files that end with** .frm. These are table definition files, describing the table's format. Every table in MySQL has a .frm file, regardless of the storage engine used.

➤ **Both .MYD and .MYI** files. These files are the table data and index files, respectively, for the MyISAM storage engine.

➤ **Files ending with** .ibd. These are tablespace files for the InnoDB storage engine — *if* the setting innodb_file_per_table is set to 1 (innodb_file_per_table = 1) in your my.cnf. This setting basically means that each table will have its own tablespace, containing both data and indexes. Having innodb_file_per_table set to 1 is a requirement for this UDF to properly give a summation of the byte count of all objects that comprise a schema. Otherwise, you would have a single InnoDB tablespace file for all tables in all schemas in your MySQL instance, and there would be no way to discern how many bytes a given schema uses.

You can see by using the following information schema that the tables listed correspond to the file types that you saw in the previous code:

```
mysql> SELECT TABLE_NAME, ENGINE FROM TABLES WHERE TABLE_SCHEMA='test';
+------------+--------+
| TABLE_NAME | ENGINE |
+------------+--------+
| a1         | MyISAM |
| a2         | InnoDB |
| bench1     | InnoDB |
| schemalist | MyISAM |
```

```
| t3          | InnoDB |
| test_table  | MyISAM |
| users       | InnoDB |
+-------------+--------+
```

Designing an Algorithm to Use for Your UDF

Now that you know what files you are examining, next you need to come up with a simple C program (if you don't already have one) that you can use for the bulk of the UDF C function. This program will be a good refresher in C as well and allow you to iron out the logic of your program. You can also deal with any bugs you encounter and isolate them within a small program more easily than from within the MySQL server.

This program is a very simple program: given a directory path, it calculates the size of the files, recursively within the directory.

Implementing the Program

The following code described here can be found within the code for Chapter 7, in particular the db_bytes sub-directory. The first file to be discussed is db_bytes/src/db_bytes.c.

To implement this program, follow these steps:

1. Include the necessary header files. The first header files are the standard files you might use in just about any C program:

```
#include <stdio.h>
#include <stdlib.h>
#include <string.h>
```

2. Use an integer value for adding up the byte counts of each file. To ensure you have a large enough numeric value, unsigned (you won't have a negative byte count!), you can use the type uint64_t, which requires including the stdint.h header file:

```
#include <stdint.h>
```

3. For printing out an error in the program, should the directory that you supply be unreadable — such as being nonexistent or not having the correct privileges — include the errno.h header file:

```
#include <errno.h>
```

4. For reading the directory to obtain the directory entries (files and directories), as well as be able to call fstat() on the directory entry, and have access to the primitive system data types, the following header files are also included:

```
#include <dirent.h>
#include <sys/stat.h>

#include <sys/types.h>
```

5. Determine the name of the function to do all the work of calculating the file sizes. For this example, the function is called db_bytes(). It takes one argument, a string, containing the value of the directory to be examined for total byte count. So you would then declare this function:

```
/* declare dir_byte_count */
uint64_t db_bytes(char *dir_str);
```

6. Next is the entry point to the program. This is C, so main() is the entry point. To make this program useful, you will want it to process a directory name, one string argument. You will also want main() to ensure the proper number of arguments, one, are passed, and if not, exit with an error.

```
/* main */
int main(int argc, char *argv[])
{
  uint64_t total;
  /* must have 1 argument (1st arg is prog name) */
  if (argc != 2)
  {
    printf("Error: you must supply a directory name!");
    exit(EXIT_FAILURE);
  }

/* pass the directory */
  total= dir_byte_count(argv[1]);
  /* print total */
  fprintf(stderr, "total size of %s in bytes: %lu\n", argv[1], total);

  exit(EXIT_SUCCESS);
}
```

7. Define the function dir_byte_count(). This function takes as a single argument a string, which contains the directory name and recursively adds up the file sizes.

```
uint64_t dir_byte_count(char *dir_str)
{
  /*
    the variable containing the sum of file sizes
  */
  uint64_t total= 0;

  /* for return values from functions */
  uint64_t retval;

  /*
    pointer to the directory, when opened
  */
  DIR *pdir;

  /*
    pointer to current directory entry
  */
```

```
struct dirent *pdirent;

/*
  stat structure for obtaining the status of the current directory
  entry
*/
struct stat fstats;
```

8. To read and obtain the size of each file, the directory must be opened. If the return value is NULL, that means there was a problem opening this directory. This could be due to any number of errors: the directory doesn't exist, permission restrictions, or the directory is a file, not a directory — this next block of code handles any of these errors and prints an informational message:

```
/* open the directory */
pdir= opendir(dir_str);

/*
  if the pointer is null, then there was a problem
  so return an error
*/
if (pdir == NULL) {
    printf("ERROR: %s %d: opendir(%s) failed (%s)\n",
            __FILE__, __LINE__, dir_str, strerror(errno));
    return 0;
}
```

9. Once the directory is successfully opened, read the first entry, which you use to start a while loop. In the while loop, you perform an lstat() on the entry to obtain its size and add that to the sum of the number of bytes, total. The last step in the loop is to read the next entry, which if not NULL, is a condition for the while loop to continue, and iterate over and sum the size for each entry in total, until all entries have been read:

```
/* read the directory */
pdirent= readdir(pdir);

/* iterate over each directory entry */
while (pdirent != NULL) {
  /* buffer for appending directory entries to */
  char dir_buff[500]= "";

  /* we do not care about reading . or . */
  if (! strcmp(pdirent->d_name, ".") || ! strcmp(pdirent->d_name, "."))
  {
    pdirent= readdir(pdir);
    continue;
  }

  /* copy the initial directory */
  strncpy(dir_buff, dir_str, strlen(dir_str));

  /* add delimiter */
```

```
          strncat(dir_buff, "/", 1);

          /* add the file or directory name */
          strncat(dir_buff, pdirent->d_name, pdirent->d_reclen);

          /* stat the entry--file or directory */
          retval= lstat(dir_buff, &fstats);

          /* directories have sizes too */
          total += fstats.st_size;

          /* if a file . */
          if (pdirent->d_type == DT_REG) {
            fprintf(stderr, "file: %s size: %d ", dir_buff, fstats.st_size, total);
            fprintf(stderr, "total %lu\n", total);
          }
          /* if a directory, then recurse */
          else if (pdirent->d_type == DT_DIR) {
            uint64_t tmp_total;
            fprintf(stderr, "dir: %s total so far: %lu\n", dir_buff, total);
            tmp_total= dir_byte_count(dir_buff);
            /* add total from subdirs */
            total += tmp_total;
            fprintf(stderr, "tmp_total %lu ", tmp_total);
            fprintf(stderr, "total %lu\n", total);
          }
          /* get next directory entry */
          pdirent= readdir(pdir);
        }
        /* close the directory */
        closedir(pdir);

        return (total);
      }
```

Now you have a program you can use to test if your idea works!

10. Compile this program:

```
gcc -o total_bytes_dir total_bytes_dir.c
```

11. Once compilation is complete, you can test the program. To make testing easy, you can create a test directory, and even include subdirectories. Copy a file into each subdirectory, as
in the following code listing, and you will see that the same file was copied into each subdirectory. The goal in testing is to verify that the program sums the file sizes, recursively. The
structure appears as this:

```
ls -latRF testdir/
total 72
drwxr-xr-x  93 pgalbraith  22256    3162 Jul 14 17:56 ./
drwxr-xr-x   4 pgalbraith  22256     136 Jul 14 09:40 subdir/
drwxr-xr-x   4 pgalbraith  22256     136 Jul 14 09:40 ./
```

```
-rw-r--r--  1 pgalbraith  22256  34813 Jul 14 09:21 wroxcode-0216.tar.gz

testdir/subdir:
total 72
drwxr-xr-x  3 pgalbraith  22256    102 Jul 14 09:40 subsubdir/
drwxr-xr-x  4 pgalbraith  22256    136 Jul 14 09:40 ./
-rw-r--r--  1 pgalbraith  22256  34813 Jul 14 09:40 wroxcode-0216.tar.gz
drwxr-xr-x  4 pgalbraith  22256    136 Jul 14 09:40 ./

testdir//subdir/subsubdir:
total 72
drwxr-xr-x  3 pgalbraith  22256    102 Jul 14 09:40 ./
-rw-r--r--  1 pgalbraith  22256  34813 Jul 14 09:40 wroxcode-0216.tar.gz
drwxr-xr-x  4 pgalbraith  22256    136 Jul 14 09:40 ./
```

12. Run the program:

```
./total_bytes_dir testdir/
dir: testdir//subdir total so far: 136
dir: testdir//subdir/subsubdir total so far: 102
file: testdir//subdir/subsubdir/wroxcode-0216.tar.gz size: 34813 total 34813
tmp_total 34813 total 34915
file: testdir//subdir/wroxcode-0216.tar.gz size: 34813 total 69728
tmp_total 69728 total 69864
file: testdir//wroxcode-0216.tar.gz size: 34813 total 104677
total size of testdir/ in bytes: 104677
```

Excellent! As you can see, the numbers add up correctly! Now you have most of the functionality you need for your UDF. Better yet, because MySQL schema directories don't contain subdirectories, you don't even need to worry about recursion.

Now that you have functioning code that you know works, the next thing to do is to create your UDF using this code.

Coding the UDF

The next question to ask yourself is: what should you call this UDF? If you call the function from within in an SQL statement, what should you name the function? For this example, the name that is chosen is db_bytes().

Project Directory Organization — Creating an Open Source Project

When writing a UDF, the first thing you probably want to do is create a directory to contain the source code. For this example, the directory is structured as an open source project, because after all, don't you want to be an open source hacker and share your work with the community? The source code for this UDF example is also available for download from the Wrox web site, which you can use as a template to create your own UDFs. In this example, a directory called db_bytes is created.

You can have it arranged so that there are subdirectories. Table 7-1 shows a list of these subdirectories.

TABLE 7-1: Subdirectories for an Open Source Project

SUBDIRECTORY	DESCRIPTION
`src/`	Contains any source files, both `.c` and `.h`.
`docs/`	Contains document files. For several projects, using Perl's POD documentation, which can be converted to main pages with a `Makefile`, is convenient for writing documentation and has a simple markup language.
`sql/`	Contains any SQL files needed for the UDFs to function, such as the `CREATE FUNCTION` statement to install the functions.
`tests/`	Contains tests. Usually this is a file containing a series of SQL statements that you run against the server and concatenate the output to a result file that you then use for subsequent tests for output comparison.
`utils/`	Can contain any extra utilities you use. This could include PHP command-line scripts that install the functions or showcase how to take advantage of the functions.
`config/`	Contains autoconf macros and automation scripts. Usually, if you have these files from another project and they work, you won't change the contents of this directory. If you have a spare weekend, this is a good place to examine to learn more about the auto-build tools if you like.

Then of course there's the top-Level directory, as shown in Table 7-2, which itself contains these subdirectories as well as the files:

TABLE 7-2: Top-Level Directory for an Open Source Project

DIRECTORY	DESCRIPTION
`AUTHORS:`	This is where you would list the developer of the project.
`COPYING`	This is the license file. Choose from a number of licenses such as BSD, GPL various versions, Artistic, and so on.
`ChangeLog`	Every time you make a formal release of your project, include in this file a header of your name, date, and version, under which there will be notes about what has changed with this release.
`INSTALL`	This file explains how to install the UDFs.
`README`	This file gives an explanation about the UDFs. This can be any information you want to provide. Also, this can be a top-level documentation that instructs the user where to find more detailed information within the repository (docs, `INSTALL`, and so on) as well as online sources.

DIRECTORY	DESCRIPTION
`configure/` `configure.ac`	Official releases contain `configure`, which is generated by autoconf based on `configure.ac`. You will not usually make `configure` part of the repository, instead leaving it to the user to run the autoconf generation script to create one.
`Makefile.am`	This is the template the autoconf uses to build `Makefile` when `configure` is run.

It's good to set up a basic package to contain source and header files, documentation, and auto-build files for making the build process easy:

```
radha:db_bytes patg$ ls
AUTHORS             Makefile.am     aclocal.m4    docs        utils
COPYING             Makefile.in     config        sql
ChangeLog           NEWS            configure     src
INSTALL             README          configure.ac  tests
```

Even if at first not everything is fully completed or fleshed out, it's a good practice to have this structure in place to facilitate the start of a good project.

Source Code Implementation

As already stated, the `src` directory contains source and header files. For this project, one header file, `common.h`, is created. It contains the data types, constants, and so on needed for the one or more UDF source files. This file can be included and makes it convenient for having all data types available defined. The following is what is included in `common.h`, which defines several UDF constants, particularly those that have to do with string lengths, especially the length of the result string, which will be allocated in the `init()` function:

```
#define VERSION_STRING "0.1\n"
#define VERSION_STRING_LENGTH 4

#define DIR_PATH_LENGTH 255

#define RESULT_LENGTH sizeof(char) * 16;
```

`db_bytes.c` is the next source file that is created. This is where you implement your UDF. It contains all the functions for this example. When creating other UDFs, they, too, can be included in this file, or a separate file, depending on what you prefer. If you create separate files for each UDF, you will have to make a modification to include these files to the autoconf configuration file (`Makefile.am`).

As mentioned before, three primary functions are defined for each UDF. For this example, the functions are named as follows:

➤ **db_bytes()**: This is the actual value function that performs the main operation of the UDF — and where you will work in the bulk of the functionality of the test program you wrote. It's also a good place to implement the check from the section "Implementing the Program" to ensure the directory name supplied (this will be the schema name supplied to the UDF) exists and can be accessed.

➤ **db_bytes_init()**: Used to check the number of arguments supplied and type, and if not correct, returns an error informing the user.

➤ **db_bytes_deinit()**: This normally would be used for freeing any data allocated in either db_bytes_init() or db_bytes().

To implement the UDF, follow these steps:

1. In this source file is the header file, which includes:

```
/*
  Copyright (C) 2009 Patrick Galbraith

  See COPYING file found with distribution for license.

*/

#include <mysql.h>
#include <string.h>

#include <stdio.h>
#include <stdlib.h>

#include <time.h>
#include <sys/types.h>
#include <sys/stat.h>
#include <errno.h>
#include <unistd.h>
#include <dirent.h>

#include "db_bytes.h"
```

2. Next the string containing MySQL's datadir value is declared. It is declared extern to expose the variable to the MySQL server, which will set this variable with the correct value.

```
/*
  this variable contains the directory path of datadir
  as read by MySQL, usually a relative path to the server
*/
extern char *mysql_data_home;
```

3. Before you implement any of the functions, declare them at the top of the file, before the definitions of the functions for the UDF:

```
/* function declaration */
/* init function */
my_bool db_bytes_init(UDF_INIT *initid,
                      UDF_ARGS *args,
                      char *message);

/* value function */
char *db_bytes(UDF_INIT *initid,
                      UDF_ARGS *args,
                      char *result, unsigned long *length,
```

```
                char *is_null,
                char *error);

/* de-init function */
void db_bytes_deinit(UDF_INIT *initid);
```

4. Next is the definition of `db_bytes_init()`. The implementation includes checking the argument count and whether the argument is a string. If either of those checks fails, an error is returned. Also, memory is allocated for the string that will contain the results. The arguments are described in the function comments at the beginning of the function. Of interest is the `UDF_INIT` pointer `*initid`. This is a useful pointer that is passed to all functions. It allows you to allocate memory or set values that all functions have access to, as has been done here for storing the string result of the sum of file sizes.

Because `*initid` is passed to all functions, you can use the memory you allocated in the init function in the value function, which you also have to free in the `deinit()` function.

An important thing to know here is that you might have the impulse to perform other types of checking in the `init()` *function. In this case, you may think it good to check whether the directory name is a directory that exists, or whether it is an empty string. Beware! This works fine for literal values you supply to the UDF; for instance, in the statement:*

```
SELECT some_function('some value');
```

the value "some value" is accessible and works without a problem.

However, if you make a call to the UDF within an SQL statement to provide the argument to the function such as using the name column of a SELECT *statement on the table* t1:

```
SELECT some_function(name) from t1;
```

the argument value will be NULL *(the debugger shows* 0x0*), which can cause your UDF to crash if you try utilize or depend on this value. This is by design and due to how the call to the UDF is parsed. Literal values are available because they are part of the statement. However, values that need to be transliterated, such as those that have yet to be read from a table (as is the case above with the value of the* name *column) are not yet accessible within the* init() *function. Therefore, any such check should be implemented in the value function.*

```
/*
  db_bytes_init

  Checks the number of arguments passed to the UDF and
  returns an error if not exactly one argument

  Also, memory is allocated for string result returned
  in value function db_bytes() which must be freed in
```

```
db_bytes_init()

ARGUMENTS:
        UDF_INIT *initid
          UDF_INIT pointer which can be used to make
          allocated memory available to the other functions

        UDF_ARG *args
          UDF_ARG pointer to the UDF arguments, which includes
          the argument lengths and types

        char *message
          String for setting errors

     RETURNS boolean value, 0 success, 1 failure
*/
my_bool db_bytes_init(UDF_INIT *initid,
                      UDF_ARGS *args,
                      char *message)
{
  char *total_bytes;

  /*
    check the number of arguments and if a string and if
    not only one, return an error
  */
  if (args->arg_count != 1 || args->arg_type[0] != STRING_RESULT)
  {
    /*
      copy a useful message to the char pointer *message
      this will be returned to the user
    */
    strncpy(message, " USAGE: db_bytes('<schema>').",
                  MYSQL_ERRMSG_SIZE);
    return 1;
  }

  /*
    allocated a character sequence (string) pointer
    this will be used for the results in the value
    function, db_bytes()
  */
  total_bytes = malloc(RESULT_LENGTH);

  /*
    coerce the single argument to a string
  */
  args->arg_type[0]= STRING_RESULT;

  /*
    initid can be used in _init to point to allocated memory
    for use in the value function. This must be freed in
    db_bytes_deinit()
```

```
*/
initid->ptr= (char *)total_bytes;

/*
  return of 0 is success
*/
return 0;
}
```

5. Next comes the heart of the program, the value function `db_bytes()`. This is where you will implement the functionality you already created with the test program earlier, of course within the UDF API confines. As with `db_bytes_init()`, copious commenting on how the function works is a good practice and it provides an explanation of how this code works.

> *The arguments are explained in the code comments.* `db_bytes()` *as* `db_bytes_init()`, *has as its first two arguments, the pointers* `*initid` *and* `*args`, *which are the same arguments and serve the same purpose in both functions. The argument* `*result` *is a string up to 255 bytes. Although it is unused in this example, you could use it to store the result. For this example, to demonstrate how the* `init()` *function can be used to allocate memory used by the value function, an allocated string is used instead. You'll see the compiler directive* `__attribute__ ((unused))` *that is used to avoid warnings for when this variable is not used in the body of the function.*

6. The next argument, `*length`, is a long pointer that you must use to set the length of the return value in your UDF, otherwise your UDF will not know what length the result is going to be and you could end up with the data being truncated. The last argument, `*error`, seems like it would be used for an error message, but is instead used to make it so the function returns a NULL on all calls of the current copy of the function.

```
/*
  db_bytes()

  This is the value function that given a schema name
  argument (string) it then obtains the number of bytes of
  all files in a MySQL schema subdirectory, then that
  value is stored in the return string and returned to the user

  ARGUMENTS:
          UDF_INT *initid
              UDF_INIT pointer which can be used to make
              allocated memory available to the other functions

          UDF_ARG *args
              UDF_ARG pointer to the UDF arguments, which includes
              the argument lengths and types

          *result
```

```
                    Unused, but could alternatively be used to store the result,
                    255 bytes long

                *length
                 Pointer, specifies the length of the return value

                *is_null
                  Set to true, denotes that the value being returned
                  is NULL


                *error
                   if set to 1 the function will not be
                   called anymore and mysqld will return NULL
                   for all calls to this copy of the function.

                RETURNS
                   string pointer containing the value returned by the UDF
*/
char *db_bytes(UDF_INIT *initid,
               UDF_ARGS *args,
               __attribute__ ((unused)) char *result,
               unsigned long *length,
                char *is_null,
                char *error)

    {
```

7. Next, the memory that was allocated in `db_bytes_init()` for the result string is pointed to via `initid->ptr`, which in turn points to this allocated memory. Other variables are then declared, which will be used per the comments in the code.

```
    /*
        set a char pointer to point to the memory allocated
        in db_bytes_init() for storing the result
    */
    char *total_bytes= (char *)initid->ptr;


    /* for return values from functions */
    int retval;
    /*
       the variable containing the sum of file sizes
    */
    uint64_t total_size= 0;

    /*
       for printing errors to which you then pass to stderr
    */
     char errstr[255];

    /*
      pointer to the directory, when opened
    */
    DIR *pdir;

    /*
```

```
    character sequence/array for appending directory path to
  */
  char schema_path[DIR_PATH_LENGTH]= "";

  /*
    pointer to current directory entry
  */
  struct dirent *pdirent;
/*
    stat structure for obtaining the status of the current directory
    entry
  */
  struct stat fstats;
```

Checking That the UDF Is Installed

Now, the UDF is checked by the following process:

1. The first check made is to see if the schema specified is *INFORMATION_SCHEMA* schema. The information schema is a schema containing materialized views and does not have an actual schema directory or database files, so for this there will never be any size, so NULL is returned. Note that you set is_null to 1, length to 0 (if you set them that way, they use pointer notation), and then set the returning NULL, of course cast as a char pointer.

```
  /*
    return a NULL if information_schema, but not an error
  */
  if (!strcasecmp("information_schema", args->args[0]))
  {
    /*
      setting is_null and returning NULL ensures a NULL is returned
      in MySQL
    */
    *is_null= 1;
    *length= 0;
    return (char *)NULL;
  }
```

2. The value in *mysql_data_home, the datadir value, is the first value appended to the character sequence/array schema_path, and then the other values are appended to build up the full schema path for the given schema:

```
  /*
    start off concatentating the datadir value set in mysql_data_home
  */
  strncat(schema_path, mysql_data_home,
                                   strlen(mysql_data_home));

  /* need to add a delimiter */
  strncat(schema_path, "/", 1);

  /* now add the schema name */
  strncat(schema_path, args->args[0], args->lengths[0]);
  strncat(schema_path, "/", 1);
```

3. A check is made to ensure that the schema name supplied results in a valid directory (or file) by a simple `lstat()` check. If there is an error reading `schema_path`, the return value is set to null, and an error is printed to `stderr` (MySQL error log). You have two ways to do this — the way shown here is to return null and log the error to the log. You could alternatively return the string value of the error, but that would prevent you from using a true/false check with something as the built-in function `isnull()`.

```
/* stat the schema_path value  */
  retval= lstat(schema_path, &fstats);
  /*
    if -1 is the return value, print an error to the error log
    and return null
  */
  if (retval == -1 || )
{
    sprintf(errstr, "ERROR with schema '%s': (%s)\n",
            args->args[0], strerror(errno));

fprintf(stderr, errstr, errstr);
    *length= 0;
    /* *length= strlen(errstr); */
    /* return tmp_errstr; */
    is_null= 1;
    return (char *)NULL;
  }
```

4. The directory is opened, and the value of `pdir` is checked to see if that directory was opened successfully. If not, an error is set with `sprintf()` of `errstr`, printed to `stderr` (MySQL error log) and `NULL` is returned.

```
/* open the directory */
  pdir= opendir(schema_path);
/*
    if the pointer is null, then there was a problem
    so return an error
  */
  if (pdir == NULL) {
    sprintf(errstr, "ERROR with schema '%s': (%s)\n",
            args->args[0], strerror(errno));
    *length= strlen(errstr);
    *is_null= 1;
    *error= 1;
    return (char *)NULL;
  }
```

5. The first directory entry is read. This gives the initial entry, something to check in the subsequent while loop, which will iterate as long as directory entries exist. This while loop basically consists of performing an `lstat()` on each entry to obtain the size of the entry. There is no concern whether the entry is a file or directory because both types have a size. Also, it should be noted that with a MySQL schema directory, there shouldn't be any subdirectories contained within — only files. The one check that is performed within the while loop is to check whether the directory entry has the name of ".." or ".." (the parent directory or current directory, respectively), either of which should be skipped. Each entry size is added to the overall total contained in `total_size`. No recursion is necessary because MySQL schema directories have no subdirectories.

6. At the end of the loop, the directory is finally closed:

```
/*
   read the first directory entry
*/
pdirent= readdir(pdir);

/*
   in a while loop, continue to read directory entries, summing of the
   directory entry sizes
*/
while (pdirent != NULL) {
  /* buffer for appending directory entries to */
  char path_buf[DIR_PATH_LENGTH] = "";

/* we do not care about reading . or .. */
  if (! strcmp(pdirent->d_name, ".") || ! strcmp(pdirent->d_name, ".."))
  {
    pdirent= readdir(pdir);
    continue;
  }

  /* start out concatenating the schema path */
  strncat(path_buf, schema_path, strlen(schema_path));

  /* add the entry - file or directory name */
  strncat(path_buf, pdirent->d_name, pdirent->d_reclen);

  /* stat the entry - file or directory */
  retval= lstat(path_buf, &fstats);

  /*
     directory entries have a size too, so add to total
  */
  total_size+= fstats.st_size;

  /* rinse, lather, repeat - read the next entry */
  pdirent= readdir(pdir);
}
/* all done now, so close the directory */
closedir(pdir);
```

7. Finally, the value of the summed file sizes in the schema directory, `total_size`, is printed to the string `total_bytes` using `sprintf()`, `*length` set with `strlen()`, and `total_bytes` is returned, resulting in the value being returned to the user of the UDF:

```
/*
    need to return a string, so use sprintf to convert the total_size
    to a string value contained in total_bytes
*/
sprintf(total_bytes, "%d", total_size);

/*
```

```
    length MUST be set for the UDF to properly return the value
    */
    *length= strlen(total_bytes);

    /* now return the string */
    return (total_bytes);
}
```

The purpose of db_bytes_deinit() is to free any remaining allocations or perform other "clean-ups" that were allocated during db_bytes_init() or db_bytes_get(). The only memory that was allocated in db_bytes_init() was for the string total_bytes, used in db_bytes(), and the address of which was pointed to by initid->ptr. Within db_bytes_init(), initid->ptr is referenced to a local char pointer *total_bytes pointer and then freed.

```
/* de-init function */
void db_bytes_deinit(UDF_INIT *initid)
{
  char *total_bytes= initid->ptr;

  /* free the allocated memory */
  free(total_bytes);

  return;
}
```

This completes the source code implementation of the db_bytes() UDF. Now it is time to build it!

Building the UDF

The UDF example shown here uses *autoconf*, which is a tool that builds the necessary makefiles needed for compilation. For autoconf to be able to properly set up everything that is needed for building your project, it requires the setup of some files you might want to become familiar with. To set things up, follow these steps:

1. The first file, Makefile.am, is the top-most autoconf file:

```
INCLUDES =
SUBDIRS = src docs
EXTRA_DIST = utils sql
```

You shouldn't have to modify this file. It just specifies that there are other subdirectories as well as files to include when you make a distribution (more about this later).

2. The next file is configure.ac. This is the autoconf file used to run the autoconf macros that set up the configure script as well as create the makefiles in all necessary directories. You need to specify the source file src/db_bytes.c in the AC_INIT() macro as well as the name of the UDF, *db_bytes*, and the version 0.1 in the AM_INIT_AUTOMAKE() macro. The rest you should never have to modify.

```
AC_INIT(src/db_bytes.c)
AC_CONFIG_AUX_DIR(config)
```

```
AM_CONFIG_HEADER(src/config.h)

AM_INIT_AUTOMAKE("db_bytes", 0.1 )

AC_PROG_CC
AC_PROG_LIBTOOL
LIBTOOL="$LIBTOOL --preserve-dup-deps"
AC_SUBST(LIBTOOL)dnl

sinclude(config/ac_mysql.m4)
MYSQL_CONFIG_TEST

AC_SUBST(MYSQL_CONFIG)
AC_SUBST(MYSQL_INC)
AC_SUBST(MYSQL_LIB)

AC_SUBST(DEPS_CFLAGS)
AC_SUBST(DEPS_LIBS)

AC_C_CONST
AC_TYPE_SIZE_T
AC_CHECK_HEADERS(limits.h syslimits.h)
AC_OUTPUT(Makefile src/Makefile docs/Makefile)
```

3. Then in the `src/` directory, add the `Makefile.am` file. This file is another that you modify to create your own UDF project. The file specifies the source file, any extra files such as header files, and sets any additional compile, linker and loader flags. You can clearly see what settings are specific to the project that you would have to change for your own project.

```
EXTRA_DIST = common.h
INCLUDES = -I$(top_builddir)/include $(MYSQL_INC) $(DEPS_CFLAGS)

lib_LTLIBRARIES = db_bytes.la
db_bytes_la_SOURCES = db_bytes.c
db_bytes_la_LDFLAGS = -module
db_bytes_la_LIBADD = $(DEPS_LIBS)
```

4. Now that the autoconf files are set up, you will soon execute the script, `bootstrap`, that runs autoconf to generate the configure script and other files needed for build configuration. First, observe before running this script:

```
patg@hanuman:~/db_bytes$ ls
AUTHORS   ChangeLog Makefile.am NEWS     config       docs   src    utils
COPYING   INSTALL   Makefile.in README   configure.ac sql    tests
patg@hanuman:~/db_bytes$ ls src/
Makefile.am  common.h  db_bytes.c
```

5. Then run the script:

```
patg@hanuman:~/db_bytes$ sh config/bootstrap
config/bootstrap: running `aclocal-1.9'
config/bootstrap: running `autoheader'
config/bootstrap: running `libtoolize --automake --copy --force'
config/bootstrap: running `automake-1.9 --add-missing --copy --force'
config/bootstrap: running `autoconf'
```

6. Afterward, observe the files that were generated:

```
patg@hanuman:~/db_bytes$ ls
AUTHORS  ChangeLog  Makefile.am  NEWS     aclocal.m4      config
     configure.ac
sql  tests COPYING  INSTALL   Makefile.in  README  autom4te.cache
   configure  docs          src  utils
patg@hanuman:~/db_bytes$ ls src/
Makefile.am  Makefile.in  common.h  config.h.in  db_bytes.c
```

7. The next thing you need to do is run the `configure` script:

```
./configure --with-mysql=/usr/bin/mysql_config --libdir=/usr/lib/mysql/lib
```

8. The argument `--with-mysql` provides automake the path to `mysql_config`, a script that comes with MySQL development packages (or from the source build) that provides compiler and linker flags needed to build programs with MySQL. The configuration argument `--libdir` is the value of the directory location where the shared library produced during compilation will be installed. This is the library directory from which MySQL can load the UDF's shared library. You may need to make sure this directory is in the `LD_LIBRARY_PATH`.

9. After running `configure`, now you can build the UDF:

```
patg@hanuman:~/db_bytes$ make
patg@hanuman:~/db_bytes$ sudo make install
```

Now you should be able to install the UDF!

Installing the UDF

Installing the UDF is quite simple. You just need to make sure the UDF plug-in shared library file is installed, which the `make install` command in the previous section should have automatically done for you.

You will need to run the following SQL statement using the root database user or a database user with privileges to the table *func* in the *mysql* system schema:

```
mysql> CREATE FUNCTION db_bytes RETURNS STRING SONAME "db_bytes.so";
```

This makes it so MySQL is able to call this function and know where to find the dynamic library file for this function so that it can be dynamically loaded.

If ever you need to see what functions are installed on MySQL, you can view the contents of the func table by running this query:

```
mysql> SELECT * FROM mysql.func;
+----------+-----+------------------------+----------+
| name     | ret | dl                     | type     |
+----------+-----+------------------------+----------+
| http_get |   0 | curl_functions_mysql.so | function |
+----------+-----+------------------------+----------+
```

As you can see, in this instance the query shows that only one function is installed, which the previous statement CREATE FUNCTION accomplished.

If you modify or add functionality to your UDF and you release a new version, you should compile the UDF and run `make install` to install the modified UDF. So long as the shared library file is named the same and the function is named the same, you don't have to perform the preceding `CREATE FUNCTION` statement. If you do change it, however, you will have to restart MySQL to ensure the changes are loaded.

Running Your New UDF

The next thing to do is to run the new UDF. The following four statements test that your UDF works by handling schemas (*test* and *mysql*) that have actual schema subdirectories: *information_schema*, which consists of materialized views and has no actual storage, and a bogus schema, *foo*, that doesn't even exist. All of these cases should work:

```
mysql> select db_bytes('test');
+------------------+
| db_bytes('test') |
+------------------+
| 476921           |
+------------------+

mysql> select db_bytes('mysql');
+-------------------+
| db_bytes('mysql') |
+-------------------+
| 780084            |
+-------------------+

mysql> select db_bytes('information_schema');
+--------------------------------+
| db_bytes('information_schema') |
+--------------------------------+
| NULL                           |
+--------------------------------+

mysql> select db_bytes('foo');
+-----------------+
| db_bytes('foo') |
+-----------------+
| NULL            |
+-----------------+
```

And to check your work:

```
root@hanuman:/var/lib/mysql# du -s -b test/ mysql/
481017 test/
784180 mysql/
```

Pretty close — there are some differences, probably in the way that du obtains file size versus how `lstat()` obtains it. Close enough to get a good byte count of how much space your schema uses. The next thing to check is that the erroneous schema name, *foo*, produced an error in the MySQL error log, and upon viewing the log:

```
ERROR with schema 'foo': (No such file or directory)
```

Excellent! Your hard work on this UDF has paid off.

As for the original requirement that you obtain a listing of schemas and the byte count use of each schema, you can now use your UDF to obtain this value. This is one of the most useful things about a UDF — being able to call the UDF within a SELECT statement, and using the result set of that statement as an argument to your UDF.

```
mysql> select table_schema,
    -> count(*) as num_tables,
    -> db_bytes(table_schema) as bytes
    -> from information_schema.tables
    -> group by table_schema
    -> order by table_schema;
+--------------------+------------+----------+
| table_schema       | num_tables | bytes    |
+--------------------+------------+----------+
| cacti              |         49 | 1089453  |
| drizzle_stats      |          6 | 642409   |
| hipergate3         |        183 | 2887849  |
| information_schema |         17 |          |
| mediawiki          |         38 | 5081212  |
| mysql              |         17 | 780084   |
| radius             |         93 | 1788965  |
| remote             |          1 | 10867    |
| sugarcrm           |         98 | 1800256  |
| test               |          9 | 476921   |
| wats               |         14 | 121859   |
| webapps            |         17 | 172266   |
| wordpress          |         10 | 576978   |
+--------------------+------------+----------+
```

Now you have a query with the result set that you want, which you can use with your application.

USING A UDF WITH PHP

Now that you have a working UDF to use for the task you were given, you need to utilize it from within your application. The following simple class shows how you can do so. This simple class performs the query in the previous example and additionally allows a variable to be passed for a specific schema name.

Connecting and Disconnecting to MySQL

The first two methods are both the constructor and destructors, which primarily deal with connecting and disconnecting to MySQL:

```
# this contains all the globals that this application will use
require('SchemasConf.php');

class Schemas
{
  # class member declarations
  private $mysqli;
  private $dbName;
```

```
        private $dbHost;
        private $dbUser;
        private $dbPass;
        private $_rows;
        private $_fields;
        private $_hash_result;

        #
        # constructor
        #
        public function __construct()
        {
          # obtain the connection information
          $this->dbHost= $GLOBALS['dbHost'];
          $this->dbUser= $GLOBALS['dbUser'];
          $this->dbPass= $GLOBALS['dbPass'];
          $this->dbName= $GLOBALS['dbName'];

          # connect to the database
          $this->mysqli= new mysqli($this->dbHost,
                                    $this->dbUser,
                                    $this->dbPass,
                                    $this->dbName);

          if ($this->mysqli->connect_error) {
            die('Connect Error (' . $mysqli->connect_errno . ') '
                . $mysqli->connect_error);
          }

        }

        #
        # destructor
        #
        public function __destruct()
        {
          $this->mysqli->close();
        }
```

Returning the Result Set Array

The next method listed is the get() method, which is the method that returns the result set array of the query utilizing db_bytes(). It utilizes the mysqli prepared statement API and takes an optional argument specifying a particular schema name if all you want to know is the information for a specific schema rather than all schemas.

As you can see, there's nothing particularly special about how you call the UDF in your query. If you were just calling db_bytes() alone as opposed to a query specifying a particular column as a result set to the UDF as shown in this example, you could also specify a placeholder in the function call:

```
        #
        # get()
        #
        # this function simply gets an array containing the result
```

```
  # set of the query that utilizes the db_bytes() UDF
  #
  # ARGUMENTS
  #  optional schema_name, used in the where clause of the query
  #
  # RETURNS
  #  array containing the result set of the query
  #
  public function get($schema_name = null)
  {
    # the main query
    $query= <<<EOQUERY
SELECT table_schema,
       count(*) AS num_tables,
       db_bytes(table_schema) AS bytes
FROM information_schema.tables
EOQUERY;

    # if schema_name set, append WHERE clause to query
    if (isset($schema_name)) {
      $query .= ' WHERE table_schema = ?';
    }
    # append GROUP BY and ORDER BY
    $query .= ' GROUP BY table_schema ORDER BY table_schema';

    # initialize the statement
    $stmt= $this->mysqli->stmt_init();

    # prepare the query
    if ($stmt->prepare($query)) {
      # bind the single placeholder if $schema_name set
      if (isset($schema_name)) {
        $stmt->bind_param("s", $schema_name);
      }
    }

    # execute the statement
    $stmt->execute();

    # obtain the fields to bind to
    $this->get_fields($stmt);

    # set an array to bind to for the result set
    call_user_func_array(array($stmt, 'bind_result'), $this->_fields);

    # fetch all the rows
    $this->fetchall_hash_result($stmt);

    # close the statement
    $stmt->close();

    return $this->_hash_result;
  }
```

The `get_fields()` private method obtains the field names of the query that was prepared in the private class member `_fields`. The main purpose of this is to create an associative array for binding the output parameters to for fetching the result set.

```
#
# get_fields()
#    a method to obtain field names, storing in class member
#    _fields
#
# ARGS
#    $stmt--prepared statement
#
private function get_fields(&$stmt) {
  $metadata= $stmt->result_metadata();
  while ($field = $metadata->fetch_field()) {
    $this->_fields[] = &$this->_row[$field->name];
  }
  $metadata->close();

}
```

The `fetchall_hash_result()` method is used to build an associative array containing the result of the query, stored in the class member `_hash_result`. This is the array that is inevitably returned to the program using the *Schemas* class when it calls `get()`.

```
#
# fetchall_hash_result()
#    a method to obtain the result of the executed prepared statement
#    storing the result as a hash/associative array the class member
#    _hash_result
#
# ARGS
#    $stmt--prepared statement
#
private function fetchall_hash_result(&$stmt) {
  call_user_func_array(array($stmt, 'bind_result'), $this->_fields);

  while ($stmt->fetch() ) {
    foreach($this->_row as $field => $val) {
      $tmp_ar[$field]= $val;
    }
    $this->_hash_result[] = $tmp_ar;
  }
}
}
```

Finally, the client program instantiates and utilizes this class, which simply instantiates a *Schemas* object and calls `$schemas->get()` to obtain an associative array containing the result set of the list of schemas:

```
require("Schemas.php");

$schemas= new Schemas();

$result= $schemas->get();
print_r($result);
```

And with this, you now have a means to satisfy your task requirement of printing out all schemas, the number of tables, and the size in bytes of each.

OTHER UDF SQL STATEMENTS

You've seen how to aggregate calls to a UDF, `get_bytes()`, by using an SQL statement to produce arguments to the UDF. There are other useful SQL statements that you can use with UDFs.

You can specify a UDF call as a means of supplying a value to be inserted in an `INSERT` statement:

```
mysql> INSERT INTO schema_sizes (schema_name, size)
    -> VALUES ('test', db_bytes('test'));
Query OK, 1 row affected (0.01 sec)

mysql> select * from schema_sizes;
+----+-------------+--------+
| id | schema_name | size   |
+----+-------------+--------+
|  1 | test        | 583855 |
+----+-------------+--------+
```

Another query performs as a useful update and sets a user-defined variable to the value being updated:

```
mysql> UPDATE schema_sizes SET size= @size:= db_bytes('test')
    -> WHERE schema_name='test';
Query OK, 0 rows affected (0.00 sec)
Rows matched: 1  Changed: 0  Warnings: 0

mysql> select @size;
+--------+
| @size  |
+--------+
| 583855 |
+--------+
```

In this example, an `UPDATE` statement simultaneously updates the size column of the *schema_sizes* table and sets the user-defined variables `@size` to the value to which the size column is updated. This is one way to both update and read a value, which can be extremely useful.

You can use UDFs in pretty much any SQL statement, so the only limit to what you can do is your imagination!

DEBUGGING A UDF

When you develop UDFs, you will most likely encounter bugs in your code. That is a given. The UDF API is fairly easy to use, but you will stumble upon some things that necessitate the use of a debugger to help you sort things out. This section is a brief aside on how to debug your UDF, and how to use a debugger with MySQL in general. In this demonstration, *gdb*, the GNU Debugger, is used.

Say, for instance, you are running your UDF, and you see the results:

```
mysql> select db_bytes(name) from sch;
ERROR 2013 (HY000): Lost connection to MySQL server during query
```

This is because the author added the following to `db_bytes_init()` to illustrate a point made earlier in this chapter:

```
/* test block for debugging */
  if (strcmp("test", args->args[0])) {
    fprintf(stderr, "matches: %s\n", args->args[0]);
  }
```

That point being that the value of `args->args[0]` is NULL if you use the UDF within a SELECT statement that provides the UDF with an argument of a column name. If you try to utilize `args->args[0]`, you will get a segfault. This provides a good reason to use the debugger, gdb.

Attaching gdb to an Already Running Process

You can either run MySQL from the debugger, or attach to an already running process. In this demonstration you attach gdb to a running process. To attach to the running MySQL process, you need to find out what its process ID is:

```
ps auxww|grep mysqld|grep -v mysqld_safe|grep -v grep
mysql    17629  0.4  4.1 1412436 164476 pts/4   Sl   22:48    0:03
/usr/sbin/mysqld
--basedir=/usr
--datadir=/var/lib/mysql
--user=mysql
--pid-file=/var/run/mysqld/mysqld.pid
--skip-external-locking
--port=3306
--socket=/var/run/mysqld/mysqld.sock
```

As you can see, the process ID (PID) is 17629. Follow these steps:

1. Because `mysqld` is running as the *mysql* user, you will need to run `gdb` as root:

```
sudo gdb /usr/sbin/mysqld 17629
```

2. You will see a lot of output showing you the various MySQL threads, and then end up at the prompt:

```
Reading symbols from /usr/lib/db_bytes.so.done.
Loaded symbols for /usr/lib/db_bytes.so
0x00007f267de42db2 in select () from /lib/libc.so.6
(gdb)
```

3. Tell the debugger to "continue" program execution by entering the command `continue`:

```
(gdb) continue
Continuing.
```

4. In another terminal, connected to MySQL, run the offending statement:

```
mysql> select db_bytes(name) from sch;
ERROR 2006 (HY000): MySQL server has gone away
```

5. Back in the terminal window of gdb:

```
Program received signal SIGSEGV, Segmentation fault.
[Switching to Thread 0x41891950 (LWP 17662)]
0x00007f2633820bbe in db_bytes_init (initid=0x53e4500, args=0x53e44c8,
    message=<value optimized out>) at db_bytes.c:91
91      if (strcmp("test", args->args[0])) {
(gdb)
```

6. A segmentation fault is shown! You already know that this block of code would cause grief, but gdb verifies this for you. You can also run a backtrace:

```
(gdb) backtrace
#0  0x00007f2633820bbe in db_bytes_init (initid=0x53e4500, args=0x53e44c8,
    message=<value optimized out>) at db_bytes.c:91
#1  0x0000000000566fba in udf_handler::fix_fields ()
#2  0x00000000005704fd in Item_udf_func::fix_fields ()
#3  0x0000000000609407 in setup_fields ()
#4  0x0000000000624a32 in JOIN::prepare ()
#5  0x0000000000632216 in mysql_select ()
#6  0x0000000000632603 in handle_select ()
#7  0x00000000005e2dd7 in mysql_execute_command ()
#8  0x00000000005e5beb in mysql_parse ()
#9  0x00000000005e6959 in dispatch_command ()
#10 0x00000000005e73d6 in do_command ()
#11 0x00000000005e7d7e in handle_one_connection ()
#12 0x00007f267ecc53f7 in start_thread () from /lib/libpthread.so.0
#13 0x00007f267de49b3d in clone () from /lib/libc.so.6
```

7. You can see clearly where the problem is — in frame zero, db_bytes_init. If you switch to frame zero with the command frame 0, you'll see the line of code that caused the segfault, and you can verify what caused the segfault by printing out args->args. The program segfaulted by trying to perform strcmp() on a NULL value:

```
(gdb) frame 0
#0  0x00007f1e29eb4bbe in db_bytes_init (initid=0x53e62c0, args=0x53e6288,
    message=<value optimized out>) at db_bytes.c:91
91      if (strcmp("test", args->args[0])) {
 (gdb) print *args->args
$2 = 0x0
```

Setting a BreakPoint and Stepping through Code

Now that you know which function is the problem, you can also set a breakpoint to db_bytes_init() and step through from that breakpoint until the offending line of code. To do so:

1. You will of course need to restart MySQL, which if you are using mysqld_safe, is done for you; however, you will have to look at the process list to find out the new process ID. Now set the breakpoint:

```
(gdb) break db_bytes_init
Breakpoint 1 at 0x7f424da2db40: file db_bytes.c, line 66.
```

```
(gdb) continue
Continuing.
```

2. In the other terminal, re-run the offending SQL statement:

```
mysql> select db_bytes(name) from sch;
ERROR 2006 (HY000): MySQL server has gone away
No connection. Trying to reconnect.
Connection id:    125
Current database: test
```

3. The command will hang there, because the debugger has stopped execution at the breakpoint you previously set, db_bytes_init(). Back in the debugger terminal window you will see:

```
[Switching to Thread 0x41cf6950 (LWP 18597)]

Breakpoint 1, db_bytes_init (initid=0x53f7610, args=0x53f75d8,
    message=0x53eb6ad "")
   at db_bytes.c:66
{
```

4. You will want to step through the execution of db_bytes_init() by entering the gdb command step (or alternatively just the letter s):

```
(gdb) step
if (args->arg_count != 1 || args->arg_type[0] !=
STRING_RESULT)
(gdb) step
66    {
(gdb) s
if (args->arg_count != 1 || args->arg_type[0] !=
STRING_RESULT)
(gdb) s
total_bytes = malloc(sizeof(char) * 12);
```

5. Next you step to the line containing the offending block of code. You can print out args->args to see what the value is, which in this case is NULL (0x0):

```
(gdb) s
91    if (strcmp("test", args->args[0])) {
(gdb) print *args->args
$1 = 0x0
```

6. The next step will result in a segfault:

```
(gdb) s

Program received signal SIGSEGV, Segmentation fault.
0x00007f424da2dbbe in db_bytes_init (initid=0x53f7610, args=0x53f75d8,
    message=<value optimized out>) at db_bytes.c:91
91    if (strcmp("test", args->args[0])) {
```

Dealing with Literal Values

So, now you know where the bug is. What if you had used a literal value for the argument to db_bytes()? Follow these steps:

1. In the MySQL client terminal window, the UDF is called with a literal value, 'test':

```
mysql> select db_bytes('test') from sch;
```

2. In the debugger terminal window the debugger will stop at the same breakpoint, db_bytes_init(). Though this time, you'll see args->args is actually set. If you continue the program execution, there is no segfault this time:

```
(gdb) continue
Continuing.
[Switching to Thread 0x41a1c950 (LWP 18907)]

Breakpoint 1, db_bytes_init (initid=0x53f75e0, args=0x53f75a8,
   message=0x53eb66d "")
     at db_bytes.c:66
66      {
 (gdb) s
73          if (args->arg_count != 1 || args->arg_type[0] != STRING_RESULT)
 (gdb) s
88          total_bytes = malloc(sizeof(char) * 12);
 (gdb) s
91          if (strcmp("test", args->args[0])) {
 (
(gdb) print *args->args
$1 = 0x53f7410 "test"
(gdb) continue
Continuing.
```

3. And the SQL statement successfully completes:

```
mysql> select db_bytes('test') from sch;
ERROR 2006 (HY000): MySQL server has gone away
No connection. Trying to reconnect.
Connection id:    125
Current database: test

+------------------+
| db_bytes('test') |
+------------------+
| 583855           |
+------------------+
1 row in set (38.32 sec)
```

Debugging Summary

As mentioned before, this is by design and how UDF calls are parsed, and using the debugger is a great way to demonstrate this as well as learn how UDFs work.

Now you have seen the basics of using a debugger with MySQL. This is just an introduction, but does give you a taste of what is involved in troubleshooting problems you encounter in writing UDFs.

You can also use the debugger as a way of analyzing how MySQL works. Pick a breakpoint in the code and step through. You can learn a lot by crawling through the program execution this way. There are also other ways of debugging MySQL. On UNIX systems, you can use DDD (a front-end for gdb) and Eclipse for more graphical debugging user interfaces. For Windows, the Microsoft debugger has a great visual interface and I have even seen UNIX developers sometimes use Windows for debugging certain problems just so they can use the Microsoft debugger!

SUMMARY

This chapter introduced you to using and developing MySQL user-defined functions, or UDFs. These allow you to extend the functionality of MySQL by creating your own functions that run within the MySQL server, which you can use through SQL statements your PHP application would make. User-defined functions are written in C or C++ and need to be compiled into a shared library, which you then install into MySQL. This chapter showed you the entire development process of a practical UDF example, db_bytes(), which simply sums the byte count of the files contained within a MySQL schema subdirectory. The chapter took you from conceptualization, project setup, coding of the necessary C functions for implementing a UDF, compilation and installation of the UDF, as well as using the UDF in an SQL statement that provided a listing of all schemas with their byte count on disk.

You also learned how to use db_bytes() from a PHP application, other useful SQL statements you can use a UDF with, and how to debug a UDF with the GNU Debugger, gdb.

8

Writing PHP Extensions

Sometimes pure PHP is not enough. Most commonly, this happens when speed is an issue or integration with a third-party non-PHP library is necessary. Writing extensions is also very useful for creating persistent resources.

This chapter builds a fully functional PHP extension that works with MySQLi Result objects and also performs various tasks relating to each type of data. It is intended for demonstration purposes only, but it works well and can be a good starting point for a custom extension.

This chapter assumes an intermediate understanding of the C language. Particular skill sets that are useful include pointers and memory allocation.

SETTING UP THE BUILD ENVIRONMENT

For many developers, one of the most frustrating parts about writing a PHP extension is simply that the extensions aren't written in PHP. Like MySQL UDFs, PHP extensions are also written in C. The C language doesn't have an automatic garbage collector, memory management, or any of the niceties of PHP so it can be much more difficult to work with. However, thanks to the Zend engine that powers PHP and the PHP engine itself, it maintains all the flexibility of PHP while adding the benefits of a lower-level language with direct access to files and memory.

PHP and the Zend engine are written in C. It is important to note the distinction between C and C++ because some developers who know C may find common tasks like file and memory access to be different. When compiling a PHP extension you have the option to include the header files for both Zend and PHP. The headers define many different functions and macros that can be used inside the extension. Documentation for many of them is difficult to find; this book covers the most common ones which almost all extensions need as well as some more advanced ones.

Before digging into setting up an extension it is important to first have the PHP sources on your machine. If you have compiled PHP from scratch you probably already do. If not, you can download them from the PHP web site. The more adventurous can download the current source from subversion, which is useful if you decide to release the extension publicly and want a head start developing and testing for the next version.

The PHP source directory has many folders. In most cases you only need to care about three of them:

➤ The `Zend` directory contains header and source files for the Zend engine (the core engine that powers PHP). A basic extension will allow you to access much of the functionality of PHP using just the standard PHP APIs; however, the Zend engine has tools for performing many of the more complex and lower-level tasks.

➤ The `main` directory is like the `Zend` directory, only for PHP-specific functionality. Here you will find headers that define access to all the PHP API functions. Notably, this is where the PHP stream wrappers (used for I/O) are defined. The PHP library contains a lot of functionality that may seem redundant; however, they are important because the PHP versions obey all of the security and configuration settings in the `php.ini` file.

➤ The third directory, and the one where you'll be spending most of your time, is the `ext` directory. The `ext` directory is where the source for all the PHP extensions — including the one that you write yourself — is stored.

Once the source is on your machine it is necessary to make sure that you have all the tools needed to build PHP. If you have built PHP in the past it shouldn't be a problem. On Linux/UNIX systems it is necessary to have gcc, flex, and bison installed. On Windows the configuration and compilation is more difficult. In general, however, an extension written in a Linux/UNIX environment is compatible with Windows, assuming best practices are adhered to. This book recommends doing your development on a UNIX/Linux environment if you plan on distributing your extension. Because most extensions are deployed to a Linux server, the rest of this chapter focuses only on Linux/UNIX.

CREATING AN EXTENSION WITH EXT_SKEL

It is entirely possible to create a PHP extension from scratch. However, to create an extension that is compliant with the *PHP Extension Community Library* (PECL) standards in addition to just functioning, it is a lot of work. Also, the first stages of writing a component are largely shared by most PHP extensions so it is unnecessary to create duplicate effort. The initial stages of development are:

➤ Creating the configuration and build files for both Windows and UNIX/Linux

➤ Creating the header and basic C files, which includes:

    ➤ Creating initialization and destruction functions

    ➤ Including the correct headers

    ➤ Creating functions for use by PHP info tools

➤ Creating test files

➤ Creating CSV ignore files to make sure files that shouldn't get into subversion don't

Fortunately, a tool exists to do all the tedious work for you. There are actually at least two tools. The second one is covered next. But first, the PHP source comes with a shell script called ext_skel, which as the name implies, generates the skeleton of a PECL-compliant PHP extension.

You have two ways to use ext_skel: with and without a function definitions file. The definitions file contains a name and optional prototype for all the functions you want to be callable from PHP. It also helps to develop good habits by forcing all the functionality of an extension to be designed and thought through ahead of time.

Creating and Compiling Skeleton Code

This section and the section later that uses a different prototyping method are only one that assumes that the functions are generated with the definition file. The rest of the chapter discusses extensions as if you were starting from the most basic configuration. The basic usage of ext_skel is like this:

```
cd ext
./ext_skel --extname=helloworld
```

Best practice is to use one word, all-lowercase, without any dashes or underscores as your extension name. After running the command you will have a new folder with the name of the extension as well as a few files. It also outputs some helpful instructions to the screen:

```
Creating directory helloworld
Creating basic files: config.m4 config.w32 .cvsignore helloworld.c
php_helloworld.h CREDITS EXPERIMENTAL tests/001.phpt helloworld.php [done].

To use your new extension, you will have to execute the following steps:
1.  $ cd ..
2.  $ vi ext/helloworld/config.m4
3.  $ ./buildconf
4.  $ ./configure --[with|enable]-helloworld
5.  $ make
6.  $ ./php -f ext/helloworld/helloworld.php
```

```
7.  $ vi ext/helloworld/helloworld.c
8.  $ make

Repeat steps 3-6 until you are satisfied with ext/util/config.m4 and
step 6 confirms that your module is compiled into PHP. Then, start
writing code and repeat the last two steps as often as necessary.
```

The preceding output highlights the module name to make it easier to read. Eight files are created. They are the bare minimum that you need for an extension:

➤ **config.m4:** A macro file that builds configuration files for UNIX/Linux. This file is not yet ready. You have to edit it first, but it's a start.

➤ **config.w32:** A very short configuration file for Windows.

➤ **.cvsignore:** Is for when you are using subversion as a version system (most PHP extensions as well as PHP itself do). This particular file tells subversion to ignore any compiled object files or intermediary files. After all, you won't typically store a compiled binary in revision control.

➤ **One C file and one header file:** They contain basic skeleton code, include the correct files, as well as define some example constants and functions.

➤ **CREDITS:** Where you should put the names of everyone who works on the extension. Convention is to put the extension name on the first line and the developers' names on the second line separated by commas.

➤ **EXPERIMENTAL:** Used to flag the extension as being a work in progress that may change. If you plan on releasing your extension as experimental you should edit this file to include a warning to the user. Otherwise, you should delete it before releasing your extension.

➤ **One PHP file:** The PHP file calls a basic function within your extension to verify that the extension is installed and working or can be loaded at run time. You can change this file all you want.

➤ **tests directory:** Created with a single test in it.

As mentioned earlier, the work isn't done yet. The most complicated part is to edit `config.m4`. The m4 file contains many macros that will be used later to build configurations. However, much of the file is commented out. For the purposes of this book, you won't worry about module dependencies (when the extension needs to access the library functions of a different extension). At a bare minimum it is necessary to add a configuration line, set an enable flag, and add the module code.

The file contains instructions on how to use it and most of the lines are commented out. They include methods for checking dependencies, among other things. The minimum working m4 file looks like this (replace `helloworld` with your extension name):

```
PHP_ARG_ENABLE(helloworld, whether to enable helloworld support,
 [ --enable-helloworld         Enable helloworld support])

if test "$PHP_HELLOWORLD" != "no"; then
  AC_DEFINE(HAVE_HELLOWORLD,1,[Whether helloworld is present])
  PHP_NEW_EXTENSION(helloworld, helloworld.c, $ext_shared)
fi
```

Modules that have library dependencies should be compiled using `with` instead of `enable`. The external library can then be specified in the configuration command line. The m4 file generates configure files. Specifically, the steps printed out by `ext_skel` are to create an extension that can then be compiled directly into PHP. The first step after editing the m4 file is to build the PHP configurations:

```
./buildconf --force
```

The command must be executed from within the root of the PHP source. The `--force` option is only needed if the source distribution you chose was a release package. Unless you are hacking the PHP source, it must be there. Supplying this option will regenerate the PHP configure file. Then run the PHP configuration file and recompile PHP. Remember to enable the new extension:

```
./configure --enable-helloworld
make
make install
```

The configuration process takes some time. Once it is done you shouldn't have any warnings or errors. If you do it is necessary to go back and edit the extension again. If all went well you should now have a completely working (although not very useful) extension. You can test it with the PHP script generated by `ext_skel`:

```
php ./ext/helloworld/helloworld.php
```

If the extension was successfully compiled and enabled, you should see a message like this:

```
Functions available in the test extension:
confirm_helloworld_compiled

Congratulations! You have successfully modified ext/helloworld/config.m4.
Module helloworld is now compiled into PHP.
```

At this point you are done with the configuration. But remember that this is your module and you can configure it any way that you want. For example, if you want it to always compile into PHP and have it explicitly disabled you can change the beginning part of your m4 file to look like this:

```
PHP_ARG_ENABLE(helloworld, whether to enable helloworld support,
[  --disable-helloworld          Enable helloworld support], yes)
```

The highlighted code changed since the previous version. The fourth parameter tells the configuration that the variable is "yes" by default and "no" is the configuration parameter if found.

It is also possible to install an extension as shared. A shared extension creates a library file that can then be enabled in the PHP configuration rather than being built into PHP statically. This is the method of extension writing that you will find with many of the PECL extensions. It requires very few additional steps. To compile the `helloworld` extension as shared, type this into the command line:

```
cd ext/helloworld
phpize
./configure
make
make install
```

The `phpize` program will take the m4 file and create a configure script for the shared version of the extension. In general it is not a good idea to check the `phpize` output into subversion, so keep that in mind. You may want to make a copy of the directory first (when using `phpize` you no longer have to compile from within the `ext` directory) or just make sure the generated files are in your svn-ignore list.

 A quick note on testing: to avoid headaches, make sure to recompile PHP without support for your extension before trying to use the shared version.

Once the extension is compiled it is necessary to edit `php.ini` to load the extension. If you are running a web server, now is the time to restart the server. However, extensions are often easier to test on the *Command Line Interface (CLI)*. Add this to your `php.ini` file:

```
extension=helloworld.so
```

If the extension did not install into the search path you may need to specify the full path to the extension instead.

Sometimes you may not want the extension to be compiled as shared. In those cases you can include a few lines of code in the m4 file to disable the build if the extension is compiled as shared:

```
if test "$ext_shared" = "yes"; then
  AC_MSG_ERROR(Cannot build helloworld as a shared module)
fi
```

Many options are available for configuration. Often a safe approach is to find another extension that does what you need it to and to use it as an example.

Using a Function Definitions File

To simplify the process of creating a module you can specify a list of functions to auto-generate inside of the module. The `ext_skel` script will not generate all the code for you but it can create all the basic functionality such as proper formatting and parameter parsing.

The file can have any name and includes exactly one function definition per line. In its simplest form, a line contains only one word (the function name). In the more complex form you can also specify a parameter list after the function name.

The parameter list is enclosed in parentheses and includes a data type for each parameter. The available data types are:

➤   array

➤   bool

➤   double

➤   float

➤   int

➤　resource

➤　string

The document also has the ability for optional parameters. For example, say that you wanted to create a function that prints "hello name" or returns the string instead of printing if the second parameter is true. The prototype may look like this:

```
mixed helloworld_say( string name [, bool return] )
```

By convention all PHP function names start with the extension name followed by an underscore. In the preceding example the return type is for documentation purposes. Its value doesn't make any difference when you generate the code. However, it is used when generating help files and comments.

The file can then be passed directly to ext_skel. In the next example the file is saved to protofile (no file extension):

```
./ext_skel --proto=protofile --stubs=output.c
```

The second parameter is optional; however, if it is not there an extension name must be specified like it was in previous examples. The `--stubs` option tells the script to create a new file that contains only the definitions for the new function. It separates the header entry, the entries to appear at the top of the file, and the function code, which you can then paste into an existing module. It is very useful if you want to add new functions to an existing module. However, once you are comfortable with the extension API it may be just as easy to write the function from scratch.

Generating Help Files

Another ability of ext_skel is to generate help XML. The PHP documentation uses an XML format for all of its documentation. The document can then be easily merged into PHP.net should the extension ever become official or on any site using phpdoc.

The documentation is only relevant if there is a function prototype file, so if you are not using the prototype you need to create the documentation from scratch. To create documentation it is only necessary to specify an `--xml` option:

```
./ext_skel --xml --proto=protofile
```

This example lets ext_skel determine the location (always an XML file named after the extension). However, it is possible to specify a location manually in the same manner as with stubs. Doing so can be particularly useful, like with stubs, when the module already exists. Keep in mind that when generating documentation either the stub file must be present or an extension name must be given.

After the code is generated, you are left with a partial documentation file. To complete it, you must remove all the warnings and fill in every description and paragraph area. However, some of the warnings should actually stay until your extension is no longer experimental.

It is perfectly all right to have some functions marked as experimental but not others. As a general rule, it is experimental if the function signature or the structure of the returned data is likely to change.

CREATING AN EXTENSION WITH CODEGEN_PECL

As mentioned earlier, there is more than one way to create a PECL extension skeleton automatically. The second one is CodeGen_PECL, which is actually a PEAR package. You can install it quite simply by typing:

```
pear install codegen_pecl
```

The package is a native PHP script that creates a skeleton for the application much like `ext_skel` does. The largest difference is that in addition to the `ext_skel` prototype format, CodeGen_PECL lets you specify the extension as an XML document. The XML format also allows for a more complete extension description than `ext_skel`'s flat function definition file, which means that CodeGen_PECL can generate more of the code for you.

Both systems have their pros and cons and it is up to the developer to decide which one to use. Here are a few of the features of CodeGen_PECL that are not provided by `ext_skel`:

➤ Defining constants

➤ Defining `php.ini` directives

➤ Defining per-thread global variables

➤ Defining resources

➤ Defining classes and methods

➤ Creating test cases

➤ Specifying dependencies

➤ Specifying a logo

➤ Creating a PECL/PEAR package XML file

➤ Creating more complete m4 and w32 configuration files

➤ Supporting multiple licenses

➤ Generating a Microsoft Visual Studio project file for Windows

In additional to all this, CodeGen_PECL typically produces code that is immediately ready to compile without any edits. However, it does take more work to create the XML document initially and `ext_skel` is still useful if you want to get up and running quickly and you don't have a good plan for exactly how your extension is going to work.

Creating the Basic XML File

You can name the XML file whatever you want; however, the name of your extension is a safe bet to keep things organized. The first step is to create the basic format and specify attribution and "about" information for the extension. This is actually backwards from the way many developers would normally do it. This chapter covers manually specifying the information last, because it is typically more important that the code works than that the license is decided, logo created, and so on. However, when using CodeGen_PECL it is easy to specify these things at this stage and once your extension is created changes must be done manually.

The minimal XML for the extension looks like this:

```
<?xml version="1.0" ?>
<!DOCTYPE extension SYSTEM "../extension.dtd">
<extension name="helloworld" version="0.1.0">
 <summary>A Hello World extension</summary>
 <description>
  This is a sample "Hello World" extension using
  PeclCode_Gen for the book Expert PHP and MySQL.
 </description>
</extension>
```

The XML header is fairly standard. The highlighted parts are the ones that you want to change to match your own extension. At this point it is possible to generate your extension:

```
pecl-gen helloworld.xml
```

 If you've already created a helloworld *extension via* ext_skel *you need to either delete it, overwrite it, or change the name of this extension.*

The XML file is optional. If you don't use the XML specification you need to specify the `--ext-name` and you'll end up with an extension that doesn't do anything useful, but it is still good starting point.

CodeGen_PECL also supports much of the functionality supported by `ext_skel`. For example, you can use the `--proto` option to specify an `ext_skel` style function prototype file. Also, `--xml` will create XML documentation in much the same way.

There are some additional tags that most extensions need. Include ones specifying information about the version and the team members. You can specify the maintainers of the extension with this code:

```
...
  <maintainers>
    <maintainer>
      <user>pecl_user_name</user>
      <name>Andrew Curioso</name>
      <email>andrew@andrewcurioso.com</email>
      <role>lead</role>
    </maintainer>
  </maintainers>
...
```

You can have any number of maintainers. The information is used to create the CREDITS file as well as the package files. An alternative role for additional maintainers is `developer`. Another important tag is the license:

```
<license>PHP</license>
```

The license is used to generate a LICENSE file as well as put the license at the top of each source file. Because the generator needs to know the details of the license it is limited in the types of licenses it supports. The basic types are:

➤ PHP

➤ BSD

➤ LGPL

If you specify any other type it is treated as an unknown license. All PHP extensions should have a predetermined license, and in order for the extension to be listed in the PECL directory it must have a license that is compatible with the PHP license. The common choice is to use the PHP license itself. Using GPL is not allowed (although LGPL is) because GPL is not compatible. Be sure to read the license well before adopting it and ask for help if you are not sure. Licenses are very difficult to change after you release your extension in any form and old released code is often subject to the old license.

The final thing that you probably want to include in your XML file is the current version information:

```
...
  <release>
    <version>0.1</version>
    <date>2009-12-12</date>
    <state>alpha</state>
    <notes>
     Taking a run at extension writing.
    </notes>
  </release>
...
```

Valid states for the release are stable, beta, alpha, devel, and snapshot. Once the extension is past the first version and onto version two you have a couple options. There can only be one <release> tag in the main extension; however, you can use a <changelog> tag to include multiple releases. The two approaches are to regenerate the extension when a new release comes out and merge the code, or just edit the package.xml and package2.xml files directly.

Defining Functions

CodeGen_PECL has two different types of functions that can be defined. One is a public function (the same as in ext_skel) and the other is an internal function, which you can use in the extension and Zend engine which isn't visible in PHP.

Defining a Public Function

Public functions are usable from within PHP. You can define them in ext_skel and CodeGen_ PECL using the prototype file format (see the section "Using a Function Definitions File") or in the XML. You use the XML tag <function> for all function definitions. If you can't think of all the functions that you want to add to your extension, don't worry, you can always add more functions directly to the C code later.

The function tag must have, at a minimum, a name and role. The role is always `public` for functions that can be called from PHP. The function must also contain a prototype and optionally it can include code directly in the XML file. For example:

```
<function name="helloworld_say" role="public">
  <proto>void helloworld_say( string name [, bool return] )</proto>
  <summary>Say hello to someone</summary>
  <description>Prints a hello message or returns a string.</description>
  <code>
  <[CDATA[
    /* C code goes here */
  ]]>
  </code>
</function>
```

The two attributes as well as the `<proto>` tag are required. Prototypes follow the same format as the function prototype file in the `ext_skel` format. All the possible data types are the same and it follows the same format for optional parameters.

The code is completely optional. One thing to remember is that if you specify any code at all you will lose the warning message output that says, "This function is not yet implemented." Also, because it is an XML document, standard XML practices should be applied, including enclosing the code in a CDATA block to avoid having to escape special characters.

The description and summary document the function. Both are optional. The summary is a short description and it appears in the actual code files. The description, on the other hand, can be longer and appears in the generated documentation.

 The documentation that CodeGen_PECL generated is different than the documentation generated by `ext_skel`*. CodeGen_PECL uses DocBook XML format, which can easily be integrated into PHP documentation.* `ext_skel`*, on the other, hand uses phpdoc format.*

Defining Internal Functions

There are few differences between generating an internal function and a public one. The main differences are that an internal function has the `internal` role and internal functions do not use prototypes. The reason is that internal functions are predefined. They are called at various points during the extension life cycle and have set function signatures.

The basic internal functions are MINIT, MSHUTDOWN, RINIT, and RSHUTDOWN. There is a fifth function but it is generated almost entirely automatically when using CodeGen_PECL. All five are discussed in more detail later in this chapter. To specify one of the internal functions just create a `<function>` tag with the name attribute set to one of those functions.

Defining Constants, INI Directives, and Globals

You have three basic ways to create values that are accessible by both PHP and your C extension. They are constant, INI directives, and globals. They are all defined in the XML using similar patterns, but each serves its own unique purpose.

Defining Constants

Constants are unchangeable values that can be referenced in PHP. By convention they are always capitalized and they are often passed to functions that expect a finite set of values. You have probably set a constant at one point or another using:

```
<?php
define('CONSTANT_NAME', "value");
?>
```

You can define them in PHP extensions as well. In CodeGen_PECL it is just one XML tag per constant. Constants can be strings, floating-point numbers, and integers. They must all be enclosed in a `<constants>` tag:

```
<constants>
  <constant name="MAX_BYTE" type="int" value="255">
    The maximum value of a byte.
  </constant>
  <constant name="GRAVITY_MPS2" type="float" define="yes" value="9.81">
    The value of gravity in m/s^2
  </constant>
  <constant name="BOOK_NAME" type="string" value="Expert PHP and MySQL">
   The name of this book.
  </constant>
</constants>
```

The text inside the tags is used only for documentation. The second constant also has a `#define` directive placed into the header file to make the constant available within the C code.

Defining INI Directives and Globals

Sometimes a constant is not enough. It is often necessary to have a configuration value that has a reasonable default but can be overridden on individual servers. For that, there are INI directives.

The INI directives fall under one of three types:

➤ *system* directives may be set in the `php.ini` file and cannot be changed once the server is started.

➤ *perdir* or per-directory directives can be set on a directory basis via an `.htaccess` file provided that they are allowed by the Apache configuration.

➤ *user* directives can be changed by the PHP code.

If no type is specified it is assumed that the value can be changed from anywhere. In most cases, the default is acceptable. The format for the parameters is almost identical as with constant:

```
<globals>
  <phpini name="greeting" type="string" access="perdir" value="hello">
    The way to greet someone.
  </phpini>
</globals>
```

The `define` attribute wouldn't make any sense in the context of INI directives and the `access` attribute is optional. The value of `access` can be any of the three values discussed earlier.

The full directive name in configuration files is the name of the extension and the directive name separated by a dot, so the previous example would be `helloworld.greeting`.

Globals and INI directives are similar and defined in much the same way. One difference is that globals can be complex C types. So, for example, to specify a string you should use `char *` and not `string` as you would with constants or INI directives.

The reason is that globals are actual PHP variables that can be accessed and changed at run time. As such it is more important to worry about things like thread safety and other lower-level concepts. Globals are covered in more detail later in the chapter. For now it is only important to know that they are defined in the XML like this:

```
<globals>
  <global name="foo" type="char *" />
  <phpini name="greeting" type="string" access="perdir" value="hello">
    The way to greet someone.
  </phpini>
</globals>
```

It is possible to specify text inside the global definition; however, it doesn't affect documentation in some versions of CodeGen_PECL. The previous example leaves in the INI directive from earlier to show that they can be defined together. It also uses a data-type of `char *` for the global. Even though the global tag can have a value attribute it does not have one here. The reason is that it is recommended to do the initiation for the complex types manually. Later sections go into more detail.

Defining Objects, Methods, and Properties

One of the largest benefits of the CodeGen_PECL package is that it supports PHP5-style object definitions. If you have a choice, all new extensions should be object-oriented. Later sections in the chapter do go into detail on how to define objects from scratch; however, you can save a lot of time by having the package do all the tedious heavy lifting so that you can concentrate on implementation.

The only thing that a class requires is a name; however, that makes for a very boring class. Classes in PHP extensions have most of the same abilities as classes in PHP itself.

Defining Methods

The method definition format is much the same as the function definitions in earlier sections. Even the tag name stays the same. The big difference is that they can now have three new attributes.

The `access` attribute defines the function as either `public`, `private`, or `protected`, and you can set `procedural` to `yes` to indicate that the method can also be called in the procedural format. For example, say a class called `foo` has a method `bar`. It can then be called using both of these two formats:

```
$fooInstance->bar();
foo_bar( $fooInstance );
```

See the class MySQLi for an example of a class that has both procedural and object-oriented implementations.

The attributes `abstract` and `final` define a method that doesn't have a definition and a method that cannot be overridden in descendant classes. Just like in PHP it doesn't make any sense to have both of those attributes on the same method.

Defining Properties

Properties are defined using the aptly named `<property>` tag. Property tags have type and value attributes similar to INI directives and constants. However, properties have the additional type of NULL. If you don't specify a value it will default to NULL.

Variables types in PHP can change at any time and cannot be relied on to stay at the default type. The exception is if the property is private and thus cannot be edited from other scopes or by descendant classes.

Properties, just like methods, have an access type of `public`, `private`, or `protected`. They also have an additional `static` attribute. If the property is marked as static it is shared among all instances of the class.

An Example Class

All the properties and methods must be written inside of a `<class>` tag. The tag itself has a few familiar attributes. The first is that if you define any abstract methods you will also want to define the entire class as abstract by using `abstract="yes"`.

In addition, classes in extensions can inherit from other classes using the `extends` attribute. If you choose to inherit the class from a class defined in another extension it is important that you include that extension as a dependency. Dependencies are not covered in detail here. What is more common is to inherit a class from within your own extension. PHP handles all the issues of polymorphism and type hinting.

So if an abstract class called `first` has an abstract protected method `bar`, a concrete method `foo`, and the property `count`, it would look something like this:

```
<class name="first" abstract="yes">
  <function name="foo" abstract="yes" access="protected">
   <proto>int foo()</proto>
  </function>
```

```
<function name="bar">
 <proto>void bar()</proto>
</function>

<property name="count" type="int" visibility="protected" value="0" />
</class>
```

Now if you wanted to create a class that extends `first` and implements the function `foo`:

```
<class name="second" extends="first">
  <function name="foo" abstract="yes" access="protected">
   <proto>int foo()</proto>
  </function>
</class>
```

Interfaces

Classes can also inherit interfaces. *Interfaces*, as you probably recall, are definitions that describe the functions that a class needs to implement but does not implement any of the functionality itself. Because they do not provide functionality, a class can implement any number of interfaces, provided, of course, that the class also implements all the functionality of each.

As you may have guessed, interfaces can be both defined and used inside of a PHP extension. Interfaces are essentially stripped down versions of classes. An interface can extend another interface and has a name, but that is about it. Also, method definitions are less detailed: prototype and name only. Remember that methods inside interfaces are always static and public:

```
<interface name="interface2" extends="interface1">
  <function name="foo">
   <proto>int foo()</proto>
  </function>
</class>
```

To implement an interface in a class you just need to add a new tag to your class definition:

```
<class name="interfacetest">
  <implements interface="interface1" />
  <implements interface="interface2" />
</class>
```

The rest of the chapter focuses on implementing the actual module, but it also goes over all the topics covered earlier in more detail. From this point forward it is assumes that you are starting from a bare-minimum module. However, in practical cases you will probably want to use one of the tools already covered in this chapter.

VARIABLES IN PHP EXTENSIONS

Variables in PHP are loosely typed. They can change type at any time and can be evaluated in multiple contexts. For that reason, they need a special variable type. That is where the `zval` comes into play.

You need to be aware of a few structures, although you will rarely interact directly with them. Most of the actual interaction is done through macros. The `zval` structure contains all the information that the application needs (see Listing 8-1):

```
struct _zval_struct {
  zvalue_value value;
  zend_uint refcount__gc;
  zend_uchar type;
  zend_uchar is_ref__gc;
};
```

The __gc values are for the garbage collector. The first (`refcount__gc`) stores the number of references to a variable. When the reference count hits zero the garbage collector frees up the memory. The second (`is_ref__gc`) is either a 1 or a 0. The type can be one of these values:

➤ `IS_NULL` (0)

➤ `IS_LONG` (1)

➤ `IS_DOUBLE` (2)

➤ `IS_BOOL` (3)

➤ `IS_ARRAY` (4)

➤ `IS_OBJECT` (5)

➤ `IS_STRING` (6)

➤ `IS_RESOURCE` (7)

➤ `IS_CONSTANT` (8)

➤ `IS_CONSTANT_ARRAY` (9)

The data types are defined in the same header as the structures. The value of the type has an impact on the values inside of the struct. The actual values are stored in a different struct:

```
typedef union _zvalue_value{
  long lval;
  double dval;
  struct{
    char *val;
    int len;
  } str;
  HashTable*ht;
  zend_object_value obj;
} zvalue_value
```

Managing these values can be extremely complicated. The two main complicating factors are that variables can change type at any time and that the garbage collector needs to keep track of each of them. For that reason the Zend engine defines many macros for setting the values, returning the values, and retrieving them.

Setting and Testing zvals

Zend also includes macros for referencing, dereferencing, and getting the reference counts for variables. However, you will not use those very often in basic extensions.

Most of the more common macros are in `zend_API.h`. For example, to assign a value to a zval you can use one of these macros:

➤ `ZVAL_RESOURCE(z, 1)` will set the zval to a resource defined by the value of `1`.

➤ `ZVAL_BOOL(z, b)` expects a `1` or `0` as a Boolean value.

➤ `ZVAL_NULL(z)`

➤ `ZVAL_LONG(z, 1)` expects a long (integer).

➤ `ZVAL_DOUBLE(z, d)` expects a double (decimal value).

➤ `ZVAL_STRING(z, s, dup)` expects a character pointer (`char *`) as well as a `0` or `1` to indicate whether to duplicate the string or reference the original string. Usually you will want to duplicate.

➤ `ZVAL_STRINGL(z, s, 1, dup)` is the same as the previous macro only you can specify the length of the string. The result is that it is binary safe (can include null characters).

➤ `ZVAL_ZVAL(z, zv, dup, dtor)` expects a zval, a `1` or `0` indicating whether to duplicate the zval or reference it, and a destructor for the zval.

Each macro accepts the zval to set as the first parameter. If you studied the data structures from earlier it may not surprise you that the `ZVAL_BOOL` macro expands to be this:

```
Z_TYPE_P(z) = IS_BOOL;
Z_LVAL_P(z) = ((b) != 0);
```

`LVAL` might be a strange term depending on your background. In this case it references the storage space for long values (Booleans are stored internally as integers). The `_P` indicates that the value being acted on is a pointer. It is very common in Zend to see double pointers. In those cases you will see `_PP` at the end. Many macros that have one will also have the other, so you can see that the macros listed earlier for setting values expect to be passed a pointer to a zval (`zval *`).

Some useful shorthand macros include `ZVAL_FALSE`, `ZVAL_TRUE`, and `ZVAL_EMPTY_STRING`. Each does what you would expect them to.

Because it is so easy for a variable to change type in PHP it is necessary to have a way to test the type stored in a value. The `Z_TYPE_P` that was seen earlier in the expanded `ZVAL_BOOL` macro can also be used to read the type. To test to see if a value is a double, you can do:

```
if ( Z_LVAL_P(z) == IS_DOUBLE ) ...
```

Because the garbage collector in PHP/Zend is so important, it is necessary to pay special attention to variable allocation. It can get particularly messy when you deal with strings and values passed to functions. You have a few ways to allocate a new zval. The most direct is with the `ALLOC_ZVAL` macro.

However, in practice it is best to use a higher-level macro instead. To allocate a new integer you can do this:

```
zval *my_int;
MAKE_STD_ZVAL(my_int);
ZVAL_LONG(my_int, 3.14);
```

You may want to allocate a new zval for a few reasons. One of the more common reasons is to pass it to another function. Incidentally, it is not very common to allocate zvals to return directly from a function. For that, there are other macros, which are covered in the next sections.

Reading and Comparing zvals

Once you have a zval it is likely that you want to retrieve the value back out of it. For that there are yet more macros:

> *Now is a good time to reiterate that you can do everything the macros are doing by writing out the code the long way, but it is always better to use the macros. They optimize to the same thing during compilation and using the macros ensures that if Zend or PHP change in the future your code will still work.*

➤ `z_LVAL` returns the integer part of zval.

➤ `z_BVAL` returns a `zend_bool`.

➤ `z_DVAL` returns the double value.

➤ `z_STRVAL` and `z_STRLEN` return a char pointer and the length of the string stored at the pointer, respectively.

➤ `z_RESVAL` returns a resource id.

Several other macros exist as well and these are covered in the sections on objects, hash tables, and arrays. For now, the basic ones are listed here. In most cases you'll work with a pointer to a zval so you want to use the _P version of each.

In PHP it is easy to get accustomed to the automatic conversions of different values between strings and numbers. It is important to note that the preceding macros do not change the content at all. For example, if the zval is not already a string, the `z_STRVAL` macro won't have the desired result. For that you use conversion functions. They are:

➤ `convert_to_string`

➤ `convert_to_long`

➤ `convert_to_double`

➤ `convert_to_long_base` (same as `convert_to_long` only it takes the base as a second parameter. For example, 16 for hexadecimal.)

➤ `convert_to_null`

➤   `convert_to_boolean`

➤   `convert_to_array`

➤   `convert_to_object`

None of the functions return a value; instead they change the original zval. Also, some of the values are not compatible with each other but in general it is safe to convert between strings and numbers and back again. If you are not sure if a string is numeric it is easy to test. Given a value z that you already know is a string:

```
if ( is_numeric_string( Z_STRVAL_P(z), Z_STRLEN_P(z), NULL, NULL, 1 ) == 0 )
   ...
```

The preceding code behaves exactly like the PHP `is_numeric()` function. In fact the actual PHP function uses that same function. The third and fourth parameters can pass in zvals that store the already converted string. The first is for integers and the second is for doubles. You can tell which one by checking the return value of the function. It is either 0 for "not numeric" or IS_LONG or IS_DOUBLE. The last parameter is set to 1 to mimic PHP's behavior of evaluating to true if the prefix is numeric even if the entire string is not. If the last parameter is 0, it is less forgiving and the whole string must be numeric.

You can also convert directly to long or double using the function `string_to_long` or `string_to_double`. Both take the string as the first parameter and the length as the second, so if you want to work directly with a zval, it is better to use the macros mentioned earlier.

One useful test is to see if a zval evaluates to true by using `zval_is_true`. Additional testing functions compare the zval regardless of type. Here are some Zend functions with their PHP equivalent above them in the comments:

```
// if ( $op1 === $op2 ) ...
if ( is_identical_function( result, op1, op2 ) == SUCCESS &&
     Z_LVAL_P(result) == 1 ) ...

// if ( $op1 == $op2 ) ...
if ( is_equal_function( result, op1, op2 ) == SUCCESS &&
     Z_LVAL_P(result) == 1 ) ...

// if ( $op1 < $op2 ) ...
if ( is_smaller_function( result, op1, op2 ) == SUCCESS &&
     Z_LVAL_P(result) == 1 ) ...

// if ( $op1 <= $op2 ) ...
if ( is_smaller_or_equal_function( result, op1, op2 ) == SUCCESS &&
     Z_LVAL_P(result) == 1 ) ...

// if ( $op1 > $op2 ) ...
if ( is_larger_function( result, op1, op2 ) == SUCCESS &&
     Z_LVAL_P(result) == 1 ) ...

// if ( $op1 >= $op2 ) ...
if ( is_larger_or_equal_function( result, op1, op2 ) == SUCCESS &&
     Z_LVAL_P(result) == 1 ) ...
```

The functions `is_not_equal_function` and `is_not_identical_function` are also valid and may be useful to create cleaner code. However, they are not strictly necessary. In fact, almost all the functions in the list are just wrappers around the function `compare_function`, which return 0 if the values are equal, -1 if the first operator is smaller than the second, and 1 if the second is smaller. The two exceptions are the checks for identical values because the comparison function doesn't check for type.

 All the comparison functions expect zval pointers for each parameter.

Two other useful comparison functions are `string_compare_function` and `numeric_compare_function`. Both convert the value to either a string or number before making the comparison.

Dealing with Strings as zvals

The Zend engine also provides numerous operations for dealing with strings. First, one of the most common comments about getting started with PHP extension writing is to not use `sprintf`. You should use `spprintf` or `vsprintf` instead, which is correct because both functions have better ways of managing memory and preventing buffer overflow than the standard `sprintf` does. The second function even accepts an array for the replacement list.

However, numerous other functions also exist for modifying strings from within an extension, many of which provide the underlying implementation for standard PHP functions.

Manipulating and Comparing Strings

Anything you can do in PHP with a string you can also do in a PHP extension. The most common actions are concatenating strings and converting to upper- and lowercase.

You have two ways to do a string concatenation on zvals in PHP extensions. The first is useful if you already know that both values are strings. The second is useful if you don't know the type of either of the values. They are:

```
zval result;
add_string_to_string( &result, str1, str2 );
concat_function( &result, str1, str2 );
```

Both `str1` and `str2` must be zval pointers. The result can also be a pointer to a zval that is being passed as one of the other parameters. For example, if in either of these functions you were to change `&result` to `str1` you would end up with `str1` changed to have the second string appended to it.

You may also find yourself needing to convert strings to lowercase. For that, you can use three functions which all perform different tasks. All three act on strings and not zvals. However, because a zval string is stored in memory as a `char *` it is also possible to modify it directly. So if you want to convert the contents of the string portion of a zval to lowercase you can use:

```
zend_str_tolower( Z_STRVAL_P(z), Z_STRLEN_P(z) );
```

On the other hand, if you have an existing buffer already allocated or you want to create a duplicate string you can use one of these:

```
zend_str_tolower_copy( dest, Z_STRVAL_P(z), Z_STRLEN_P(z) );
dest = zend_str_tolower_copy( Z_STRVAL_P(z), Z_STRLEN_P(z) );
```

The main difference between the two is that the first expects the buffer (destination) to already be created and returns a pointer back to the destination. The second creates a new buffer for you and returns a pointer to that. In the latter case the buffer is created using `emalloc` (which is covered in more detail a little later).

For any of the previous three functions you can, of course, pass an actual `char *` value rather than reference a zval.

The functions to convert to lowercase are mainly used for case-sensitive comparisons. There aren't any functions in the Zend engine to convert to uppercase. This is mainly because the transformation to a consistent case is usually used for case-insensitive comparison. In that case it doesn't matter whether you do upper- or lowercase, you only need one. However, looking at the code for the previous functions you may find that creating such a function would not be difficult. In addition, the standard PHP extension — which has an exposed API — does have a function to convert to uppercase.

If you are converting to lowercase for the sole purpose of comparing a string it may be easier to just use the string comparison function directly. The next two function calls are functionally identical:

```
result = zend_binary_zval_strcasecmp( str1, str2 );
result = zend_binary_strcasecmp( Z_STRVAL_P(str1), Z_STRLEN_P(str1),
                                 Z_STRVAL_P(str2), Z_STRLEN_P(str2) );
```

The word *binary* indicates that the function uses the given length to determine the end of the string as opposed to using a `null` byte to terminate. Removing the word `case` from the preceding functions results in a case-sensitive comparison. Also, adding the literal n after the literal `str` in any of the functions (with or without case sensitivity) adds a final parameter that takes the maximum length to check for comparison. These are both valid:

```
// Case sensitive comparison
zend_binary_zval_strncmp( str1, str2 );
// Check only the first n characters where n is a zval
zend_binary_zval_strncasecmp( str1, str2, n );
```

String management is one of the more common tasks in a PHP extension. However, sometimes values are not in a string format to begin with. In those cases it is necessary to do a conversion.

Converting to Strings

When converting a zval to a string you have two basic choices. The first is to use the `convert_to_string` method from before. The other is to use `zend_make_printable_zval`. Both produce very similar results. This is what the two functions look like:

```
zval copy;
int use_copy;
zend_make_printable_zval(z, &copy, &use_copy);

convert_to_string(z);
```

The first difference is that one makes a copy of the zval and the other — `convert_to_string` — requires that you make a copy manually or risk destroying the original zval. The second difference is how they handle objects. The Zend function attempts to do a conversion whereas the basic conversion function just returns the literal string "Object" instead. The latter also throws warnings if you try to convert an array, resource, or object because it can, after all, destroy data.

Advanced Memory Management

Another thing to worry about is allocating and freeing additional memory. If each function was guaranteed to execute undisrupted, it would not be much of a problem. Just make sure to free all the memory that you allocate by the time the function exits. The problem is that PHP has a concept of fatal errors and also contains two very interesting functions: `die()` and `exit()`. All three things can immediately terminate (bail out) a script causing your function to exit without freeing any of the memory.

To solve this problem and others, Zend has its own memory manager. The memory manager (ZendMM) keeps track of all the allocated memory and makes sure to free it when bailing or when the script finishes executing, but in order for it to work you'll need to use the ZendMM allocation functions. The ZendMM functions have the same name as their C counterparts only with a letter "e" prepended to them, so `malloc()` becomes `emalloc()`.

The result is that not only can Zend keep track of the memory but it can also enforce the memory allocation limits imposed by the PHP configuration. Be aware of double freeing of memory, though. That is the main cause of the dreaded "segmentation fault" error.

Zend also provides a series of macros for persistent allocation. The persistent allocation basically calls the standard memory allocation functions if the value should be persistent or calls the ZendMM functions if it shouldn't. Just don't forget to free the persistent variables before the extension exits or you will end up with memory leaks. Table 8-1 shows a full list of the memory allocation functions:

TABLE 8-1: Memory Allocation Functions

STANDARD C	ZEND STANDARD	ZEND PERSISTENT
malloc	emalloc	pemalloc
calloc	ecalloc	pecalloc
realloc	erealloc	perealloc
strdup	estrdup	pestrdup
free	efree	pefree

In each case the persistent version takes one extra parameter: a 1 or 0 indicating if the value is persistent. The persistent macros are particularly useful if you are not sure at design time whether the value should be persistent.

There isn't any guarantee that the next execution of the script will happen on the same thread as the first, so it is not a good idea to rely on persistent values to always be there.

It is important to free all the memory that you use once you are done with it. The exception is if it is registered with the Zend engine or returned from a function. The two main functions that you need to know about are `zval_dtor` and `FREE_ZVAL`. They should always be called in that order.

The `FREE_ZVAL` macro frees the memory used by the zval itself, but it won't free the actual data in memory used for complex variables. That includes objects, arrays, string, and resources. For that you need to use `zval_dtor` (destructor). Both take a pointer to a zval as a sole parameter.

It is also good practice to call `zval_dtor` prior to setting a zval to something completely different. That way the existing data is freed before the new data is put in. The function completely ignores Booleans, longs, doubles, and of course nulls because none explicitly allocate blocks of memory.

You could guess that if there is a destructor there is a constructor; and you would be half right. Previous sections showed how to allocate and assign to a zval, which will take care of all the hard work for you. However, there is something called a *copy constructor* that creates a new zval that is a copy of the original. For example, a developer could do this:

```
zval *foo;
MAKE_STD_ZVAL(foo);
*foo = *bar;
```

He could, but it would be incorrect to make a reference to another zval, and doing so has the potential to create havoc with the garbage collector. This is especially true if the zval bar contains an object, array, resource, or strings. The copy constructor rectifies the situation:

```
zval_copy_ctor(foo);
```

Note that the new value of `foo` is not a reference to `bar` but rather an exact copy of all the data. Changes to a string (or any other data type) in one do not change the string in the other.

At this point, you know much of what there is to know about memory management and variables within the Zend engine and PHP. The two largest things that haven't come up yet are arrays and objects. Those were intentionally left out but they are covered very soon.

USING FUNCTIONS IN EXTENSIONS

The first part of this chapter explained how to add functions to an extension the easy way, through `ext_skel` and CodeGen_PECL. Now that you have an understanding of variables in Zend, this section covers defining functions manually.

Basic Definitions

Defining a function is actually quite easy. This is thanks to a number of Zend and PHP macros that make it so that you don't have to worry about naming conventions, data types, or thread safety parameters. The engine takes care of all that for you.

There are three steps to defining a function. They can be done in any order so the starting place might as well be the function body itself. Once you open up the extension's main C file (the name of your extension ".c") you'll see all the generated code from whichever script you chose to generate your extension. Function implementations usually go at the end but before the editor definitions (the part that tells text editors like Vim how to behave).

The function always starts with a comment. The comment should always be two lines or more. The first line is function prototype and the rest consist of a brief description of what the function does. The prototype should look familiar because it is the same one used by both CodeGen_PECL and `ext_skel`:

```
/* {{{ proto string helloworld_say( string name [, bool return] )
   Say hello to a person */
```

Ignore the three opening brackets for now. The next step is to define the function signature. This is one of the parts that can be uncomfortable for people who have to know everything that is going on because it is done via a macro instead of traditional function definitions. A PHP function definition looks like this:

```
PHP_FUNCTION(helloworld_say)
{
...
}
```

Note that this style of definition is only for functions that should be available to PHP scripts. Other functions are used differently and are covered soon. The definition ultimately expands to:

```
void zif_helloworld_say( int ht, zval *return_value, zval **return_value_ptr,
                         zval *this_ptr, int return_value_used TSRMLS_DC )
```

A prefix is added to the function to avoid name conflicts. Fortunately for everyone, Zend and PHP abstract such definitions to avoid human error and increase productivity. However, it won't hurt to go over some of the parameters and what they do:

➤ The first parameter stores the number of parameters passed to the function from the user (via PHP). It can be retrieved by using `ZEND_NUM_ARGS()`.

➤ The second and third are the return value and a pointer to the return value for returning references (not recommended). At this point the return value is already initialized to `IS_NULL`. There is more on return values in the coming sections.

➤ The `this_ptr` parameter is, as the name implies, the PHP variable that holds the value of the current object. It is exactly the same as if you were to use `$this` inside of a PHP script. The macro `getThis()` takes care of retrieving it for you.

➤ The final integer is a flag indicating whether or not the return value is being used by the calling function. If the return value isn't being assigned to anything in PHP, this will be 0, which could save some processing time.

➤ The final macro at the end is used for thread safety. It will be touched on again when defining internal functions and yet again later in the chapter.

For now, there is only one step left and the function body is defined. Close it with this after the final bracket: `/* }}} */`.

The brackets at the beginning and end help to do code folding and unfolding in editors like vim and emacs. Even if you don't use code folding yourself it is still a good idea to include them for the benefit of other people who might be editing your code. Even if you will be the only one using your extension, you might be using code folding in the future.

The final two pieces are to add an entry to the functions table and add a prototype to the headers. Adding the prototype to the header is easy. There is already a macro to expand function definitions so there is just one simple line to add to the header:

```
PHP_FUNCTION(function_name);
```

The semicolon at the end is important because the macro is used both for prototypes in the header and complete function definitions in the extension's C code.

Assuming that you used one of the generator scripts, you already have a function table. For the helloworld module it would be called `helloworld_functions`. If `helloworld_say` is the only function in the extension, the table entry will look like this:

```
const zend_function_entry andrew_functions[] = {
        PHP_FE(helloworld_say, NULL)
        {NULL, NULL, NULL}  /* Must be the last line in helloworld_functions[] */
};
```

The macro `PHP_FE` is for a function entry. The preceding one expands to this:

```
{ "helloworld_say", "zif_helloworld_say", NULL,
  (zend_uint) (sizeof(NULL)/sizeof(struct _zend_arg_info)-1), 0 },
```

You may recall the "zif_" value as a prefix added by the `PHP_FUNCTION` macro. That is because the `PHP_FE` macro actually uses other macros internally to do its job. One such macro is `ZEND_FN`, which adds the prefix.

The second parameter to the `PHP_FE` macro is the `arg_info` structure. This is covered in the section "Defining Argument Information."

Using Arguments

The previous section went over all the parameters to PHP function calls. However, they can all be safely forgotten for most extensions. The first step with any function is to parse the parameters into usable values. For that there is a helper function.

The function `zend_parase_parameters` takes arguments specifying the number of parameters to expect, the signature of the parameters, and pointers, and in turn stores all of them for easy retrieval. Additionally, it has the ability to validate the parameters against data types. If the user calls it with an invalid number of arguments or an argument of an incompatible type it will issue a warning and return `FAILURE`.

The function looks like this:

```
char *name;
int name_len;

if (zend_parse_parameters(ZEND_NUM_ARGS() TSRMLS_CC, "s",
                          &name, &name_len) == FAILURE) {
   RETURN_NULL();
}
```

You saw the ZEND_NUM_ARGS macro earlier. The second argument (actually, the third, but there will be more on that later) is for the parameters. There is one character per parameter and it indicates the type. For example, the preceding function accepts a string. If it were to accept two strings it would look like "ss" instead.

The valid values are:

➤   Array (a) as zval **

➤   Boolean (b) as zend_bool *

➤   Double (d) as zval **

➤   Long (l) as zval **

➤   Object (o) as zval **

➤   Object of a specific class (O) as zval ** and zend_class_entry *

➤   String (s) as char ** and int *

➤   Zval (z) as zval **

➤   Zval reference (Z) as zval ***

Additionally, a few other options are available. It is easy to make arguments optional simply by specifying a pipe. Everything after the pipe is optional. Now would be a good time to demonstrate how to accept the arguments for the helloworld_say function that you have seen so many times in this chapter:

```
char *name;
int name_len;
zend_bool do_return;

if (zend_parse_parameters(ZEND_NUM_ARGS() TSRMLS_CC, "s|b",
    &name, &name_len, &do_return) == FAILURE) {
  ...
}
```

Return values from functions are covered later. You may have noticed that there are three remaining parameters. They are used to store the values passed into the function. Strings take two variables (to deal with binary data) while most others only take one.

All parameters are passed as pointers to the original zval. The Zend engine does not make copies (or references) unless you explicitly ask it to. As a result, changes made to the zval *will* change the original in PHP. In order to perform calculations on the value without affecting the outside data it is necessary to make a copy.

Separation is the process of taking one zval and creating a new one that is initially a reference to the first; however, it will dereference and create a new value if you try to write to it. In PHP 5 it can be done implicitly by flagging the argument for separation. To flag a value for separation you can put a slash (/) after it.

So what happens when you pass a value that isn't a string to a function that only accepts "s" as a type of value? There are two possible outcomes. If the value can be safely converted to a string without data loss, then PHP will do it. That includes longs, doubles, and Booleans. If it can't be converted without losing any data (object, arrays, and resources), PHP will print a warning and the parameter parsing function will return `FAILURE`.

Alternatively, it is possible to accept a zval instead and convert to a string. Say that you have a function `foo()` that expected a string. You could do something like this:

```
zval *my_str;

if (zend_parse_parameters(ZEND_NUM_ARGS() TSRMLS_CC, "z", &my_str) == FAILURE) {
  RETURN_NULL();
}
convert_to_string( my_str );
```

There are a few problems with this code. The first is that `convert_to_string` issues a warning if you pass an array — or anything else that can't be converted to a string without data loss — to the function. The second is that, because all values are passed to the extension as a pointer to the original variable in PHP, the code will change the value of the variable in PHP. Take this code, for example:

```
<?php
$bar = array( 1, 2, 3 );
helloworld_foo($bar);
echo '$bar IS '.(is_array($bar) ? '' : 'NOT ').'an array.';
?>
```

Using the parameter parsing code from before, this code will print $bar IS NOT an array. At that point $bar is equal to the string literal Array instead of the original actual array.

That is where separation comes in. There are two ways to do separation of parameters in PHP5. They both work fine; one is just newer and a little bit less code. The following pieces of code are functionally identical. One way is:

```
zval **my_str;
if (zend_parse_parameters(ZEND_NUM_ARGS() TSRMLS_CC, "Z", &my_str) == FAILURE) {
  RETURN_NULL();
}
SEPARATE_ZVAL_IF_NOT_REF(my_str);
```

Another way is:

```
zval *my_str;
if (zend_parse_parameters(ZEND_NUM_ARGS() TSRMLS_CC, "z/", &my_str) == FAILURE) {
  RETURN_NULL();
}
```

The biggest difference is that one requires that the zval be a double pointer and the other method requires a single pointer. Both options separate the value only if it is not a reference, which means that if the user does this:

```
$foo = "world";
helloworld_say( &$world );
```

it will not get separated. The end result is that any changes you make to the zval inside of the function still affect the original variable in memory. This is a problem that affects a good number of

extensions and even some built-in functionality. The way to avoid that is by using the SEPARATE_
ZVAL macro instead of its conditional equivalent.

Defining Argument Information

The arg_info is the second argument to the PHP_FE macro. It provides information about the arguments for a function, which in turn can be used with the PHP inspection APIs and is new in PHP 5.
As a result, ext_skel does not use it (as of PHP 5.3) but CodeGen_PECL does. So, if you were to
add arguments you would define the argument list in the header file:

```
#if (PHP_MAJOR_VERSION >= 5)
ZEND_BEGIN_ARG_INFO_EX(helloworld_say_arg_info, ZEND_SEND_BY_VAL,
                       ZEND_RETURN_VALUE, 1)
  ZEND_ARG_INFO(0, name)
  ZEND_ARG_INFO(0, return)
ZEND_END_ARG_INFO()
#else /* PHP 4.x */
#define helloworld_say_arg_info NULL
#endif
```

The arguments for the highlighted macro are, in order:

➤   The first argument is the name of the variable to store the information in. Do not define the
    variable ahead of time because the macro does it for you.

➤   The second flag indicates how the user should pass the additional arguments in a variable
    argument function. The most common and recommended value is ZEND_SEND_BY_VAL. You
    also have ZEND_SEND_BY_REF and ZEND_SEND_BY_PREFER_REF; however, they are rarely
    used and usually the sending by value is the right flag.

➤   The third is whether the return value is by value or reference. Just like the argument list there
    is a way to return by reference but it is not used very often. If you are returning by reference,
    odds are that you really want to create a new resource type.

➤   The final argument is the number of required arguments. In the preceding example there are
    two arguments, but only one is required.

After the argument information is started it is time to define individual arguments using ZEND_ARG_
INFO. The macro is fairly self-explanatory. The first is a 1 or 0 depending on whether the argument
should be passed by reference. The second is the name of the argument. The argument names should
not be quoted (the macro does that for you).

Documentation systems and some extensions rely on being able to inspect functions, so a valid argument list is very helpful. Once the list is complete it can be passed to the PHP_FE macro as the second
argument.

Returning Values

Once you have your function set up and your parameters are being passed, returning a value back
to PHP is the easy part. The return set of functions is analogous to the zval assignment macros. As a
general rule, if you can assign to a zval with a macro you can return a value with a similar macro.

PHP return values are handled by changing the zval referenced by the `return_value` argument passed to the function (see the previous section on defining functions). So what you are doing when you return a double, for instance, is really this:

```
ZVAL_DOUBLE(return_value, 1.34);
return;
```

What you put in your code instead is:

```
RETURN_DOUBLE(1.34);
```

So, if you need to do calculations it is sometimes more efficient to edit the return value directly rather than do all the calculations in a temporary variable. That is particularly true when it comes to arrays and hash tables, which are covered a little further on.

As you may expect, the value return functions are:

➤ `RETURN_RESOURCE(l)`

➤ `RETURN_BOOL(b)`

➤ `RETURN_NULL()`

➤ `RETURN_LONG(l)`

➤ `RETURN_DOUBLE(d)`

➤ `RETURN_STRING(s, dup)`

➤ `RETURN_STRINGL(s, l, dup)`

➤ `RETURN_ZVAL(z, dup, dtor)`

➤ `RETURN_TRUE()`

➤ `RETURN_FALSE()`

That is all there is to returning values from a function in Zend.

Built-In Functions

An extension can optionally implement five built-in functions. They are called at various points during the extension's life cycle:

➤ `MINIT` is called when the extension (module) is initialized. The module is initialized once per thread so this is a good place to do things like register globals and INI entries, which are covered later in the chapter.

➤ `MSHUTDOWN` cleans up anything that was created during module initializations. This is where INI entries and globals are cleaned up.

➤ `RINIT` is called when a request is initialized. Use this to set up any request variables.

➤ `RSHUTDOWN` should clean up any request variables so that the next request starts with a clean slate.

➤ Finally, `MINFO` is called to print out information about a module.

None of these can be defined using the standard methods of defining functions. Instead, each one of them has its own macro to create the function names and signatures. They are:

```
PHP_MINIT_FUNCTION( extname ) ...
PHP_SHUTDOWN_FUNCTION( extname ) ...
PHP_RINIT_FUNCTION( extname ) ...
PHP_RSHUTDOWN_FUNCTION( extname ) ...
PHP_MINIT_FUNCTION( extname ) ...
```

Like normal functions, a prototype must also be put into the header. Also, the functions must be referenced in the function entry structure (inside of the C file). If you used a script to generate the extension, this is all taken care of for you.

What you might want to do with the auto-generated files is get rid of functions that you don't use. The first step is to remove the items from the function entry structure by putting NULL in their place. After that, it is safe to remove the function prototype and implementation.

One final note on the built-in functions is that they should always return either the SUCCESS or FAILURE constant. Not doing so could result in undesirable effects.

Creating and Consuming PHP API Functions

PHP API functions are special types of functions that are usable by other modules. In general, if there is functionally that you think other extensions may benefit from, it is generally a good idea to make an API version of it.

Consuming PHP APIs

In addition to producing API endpoints it is often a good idea to consume other extension APIs rather than try to reinvent the wheel (no matter how easy that may seem).

Numerous extensions come with PHP. You can use APIs from any of the ones that provide them. The catch is that if PHP is compiled without the extension enabled, you are out of luck. Some extensions are more ubiquitous than others. This book references MySQL constantly and an extension later in the chapter actually uses MySQLi objects. However, MySQLi is not enabled in the default configuration.

The most common extension to hook into is the aptly named "standard" extension, which is located in a subdirectory of that name within the ext directory. Most modules already depend on it because it defines the API functions for use with MINFO. The standard extension includes exported API functionality for:

➤ Math

➤ Strings

➤ MD5

➤ Base64

➤ Dynamic extension loading

➤ Image mime-type detection

➤ Shell execution

➤ HTML escaping

➤ Random number generation

➤ File operations

➤ Serialization

➤ Headers and cookies

➤ SHA1

➤ URL parsing and encoding

➤ And, of course, PHP info functionality

It's important to know that any function within PHP can be called from any extension. After all, an extension should be able to do anything a PHP script can do. However, if there is an API function available and it is acceptable to have a dependency on that extension, you should use the API instead. The API will always be faster and more efficient.

Not all extensions have API calls available. Some interesting ones that do are:

➤ JavaScript Object Notation

➤ DOM

➤ XML

➤ Reflection

➤ Session

➤ MySQL Native Driver

In addition, the core PHP code also exports many functions for use by extension. This chapter uses many of them. The most common ones are streams, networking, output buffering/control, and file operations.

To consume an API, it is only necessary to include the headers and start calling functions. Because there is not much by way of documentation for many of the API functions a very useful grep is:

```
grep -r PHPAPI /path/to/extension/*.h
```

From that you can see that the prototype for explode looks like this:

```
PHPAPI php_explode(zval *delim, zval *str, zval *return_value, long limit);
```

Not all API functions take zvals. Because they don't have to be called from PHP, they can take regular data types like char * as well. Now that the prototype is known it can be called from within an extension. First, include the header file at the top of the C files that need to access the API:

```
#include "ext/standard/php_string.h"
```

Once that is done it can be easily used within a function:

```
PHP_FUNCTION(andrew_explode_on_pipe) {
        zval *my_str, *delim;

        if ( zend_parse_parameters( ZEND_NUM_ARGS() TSRMLS_CC,
```

```
        "z", &my_str) == FAILURE ) {
            RETURN_NULL();
    }

    MAKE_STD_ZVAL(delim);
    ZVAL_STRING(delim,"|",0);

    array_init( return_value );
    php_explode(delim, my_str, return_value, 100 );
}
```

This is one of the cases where setting the `return_value` variable directly is useful. The code also initializes an array. Arrays are covered later in this chapter.

DEALING WITH DEPENDENCIES

Specifying dependencies for your application is important. In this case, the application is dependent on the standard extension. However, in other cases it may be dependent on others. Later in this chapter you see an extension that depends on MySQLi to work.

You can specify dependencies with CodeGen_PECL by listing them in your XML document like this:

```
<deps>
   <extension name="standard"/>
   <extension name="mysqli" type="OPTIONAL"/>
   <extension name="foo"    type="CONFLICTS"/>
</deps>
```

The preceding XML indicates a requirement for the standard library, an optional dependency on MySQLi, and a conflict with a fictional foo library. You can use conflicts when the extension exposes an API method that is known to also be in another library.

The code in the C source files looks a lot like the function tables:

```
/* {{{ cross-extension dependencies */

#if ZEND_EXTENSION_API_NO >= 220050617
static zend_module_dep helloworld3_deps[] = {
        ZEND_MOD_REQUIRED("standard")
        ZEND_MOD_OPTIONAL("mysqli")
        ZEND_MOD_CONFLICTS("foo")
        {NULL, NULL, NULL, 0}
};
#endif
/* }}} */
```

You also need to make entries into the package XML documents if you want to distribute your extension. In addition, you need to change the module entry structure to support dependencies. The structure needs to have a `STANDARD_MODULE_HEADER_EX` type, which brings with it two additional fields. The second new field is the module's dependencies array.

Providing an API

If you think your extension would be useful for other extensions, a good next step is to make functions available via an API. Providing functions for the API is much easier than creating PHP visible functions (or even the helper functions that are covered next) because they are just traditional C functions. All you need to do is put PHPAPI in front of it.

One benefit of API functions is that they can return a value. However, doing things the PHP way — by providing the return value via an argument as a pointer — is also possible. That is the way the explode function from the previous section worked.

The other clear benefit is that the arguments can be of any type. See the prototype for php_explode in the previous section for an example.

You must also put the prototype (complete with PHPAPI in front) in the header. That is the only way that other modules can reference it. Also, in addition to functions, you can specify structures as being exported by the API.

More Notes and Creating Helper Functions

Helper and PHP API functions are almost the same thing. The difference is that API functions are exported for other extensions to see and helper functions are declared as static instead.

Helper functions are intended for use within your extension only. As such, they do not need to be defined in the header. C compilers will parse your source from top to bottom, though, so best practice is to put all the helper functions at the top of the C file or at least define the prototype at the top.

You should know a few tricks for helper and API functions. The first is that it is easy to pass all the parameters from a PHP function straight through to a helper function. It is particularly useful if you want to implement shared functionality across multiple PHP accessible functions.

The trim behavior for the standard string library works in this way. The PHP accessible function takes all its calling data and passes it through to a helper function along with a flag indicating what type of trim to perform. Passing through is necessary if you want to use built-in macros to parse arguments and return values. The second function, callable from PHP, passes the arguments to the first helper function:

```
static void do_something_helper( INTERNAL_FUNCTION_PARAMETERS, int flags )
{
... parse parameters, set return value, etc. here ...
}

PHP_FUNCTION(do_something)
{
   do_something_helper(INTERNAL_FUNCTION_PARAMETERS_PASSTHRU, 3);
}
```

To get an idea of what exactly is passing through, refer back to the "Basic Definitions" section. It is the exact same set of variables that are passed to functions when you define them with the PHP_ FUNCTION macro.

That includes TSRMLS. It is used for thread-safe access to global variables and must be included if you want access to the global variable pool.

However, it is possible to pass TSRMLS manually using some built-in definitions. You have already done this in previous sections while parsing arguments. Following are four definitions to keep in mind:

➤ **TSRMLS_D** is used within function definitions.

➤ **TSRMLS_DC** is used within function definitions when there aren't any other parameters.

➤ **TSRMLS_C** is for function calls.

➤ **TSRMLS_CC**, the counterpart to TSRMLS_C is for function calls when there aren't any other parameters.

The big difference is that two of them — the ones that end in DC and CC — each start with a comma intended to separate them from the parameter in front. The section on global variables has much more information on the TSRMLS family of definitions.

INPUT/OUTPUT

This chapter already covered input and output via function parameters and return values. This section covers input and output from other sources. Specifically, standard output, errors and warnings, and files and network connections the PHP way.

Standard Out

Up until now the chapter has focused on two methods of providing feedback to PHP. The first was through parameters passed by reference and the second was return values. Another method of providing feedback is through standard output.

Numerous functions are available for standard output. The one that you'll likely use the most often is php_printf, which behaves similarly to its PHP counterpart. For example:

```
php_printf("The value of some_zval is: %s", Z_STRVAR_P(some_zval));
```

The php_printf function takes all the same values as its PHP and C counterparts. Alternatively, when variable substitution isn't necessary you can use this instead:

```
php_write( Z_STRVAL_P(some_zval), Z_STRLEN_P(some_zval) );
```

With those two functions it is possible to write anything to the standard output stream. But sometimes it is necessary to have more structured data in order to debug and see the current values of variables. Such data can be difficult to format. Zend has some functions for those times:

➤ zend_print_zval takes a zval as the first parameter and an indentation amount (long) as the second. It outputs a flat representation of the zval and prints text descriptions for complex types that can't be displayed elegantly.

➤ zend_print_zval_r prints the zval recursively. Its output is identical to print_r in PHP.

Files and Streams

Input and output should always be handled through PHP functions. One of the main reasons for that is because PHP imposes limits on what type of streams the script can open. The restrictions can easily be circumvented by a C script, which can introduce security issues.

The other big reason is that PHP has stream wrappers. Stream wrappers are what allow PHP to transparently open a range of stream types from the file system to HTTP and FTP.

Basic Streams

All the PHP stream functions follow the pattern `php_stream_`. File I/O is probably one of the more common tasks. A simple function that writes a zval to a file identified by a user-supplied filename looks like this:

```
char *filename;
int filename_len;
php_stream *stream;
zval *val;

if (zend_parse_parameters(ZEND_NUM_ARGS() TSRMLS_CC, "sz/", &filename,
    &filename_len, &val ) == FAILURE) {
  RETURN_FALSE;
}

stream = php_stream_open_wrapper_ex(filename, "w+",
            ENFORCE_SAFE_MODE | REPORT_ERRORS, NULL, NULL );

if ( stream ) {
  convert_to_string(val);
  php_stream_write(stream, Z_STRVAL_P(val), Z_STRLEN_P(val));

  php_stream_close(stream);
}
```

It is very important to do validation on the stream before performing any operations on it, particularly when closing the stream (which will cause a segmentation fault trying to free a file that isn't open).

The flags are highlighted in the preceding code sample. You can use flags to disable security features or enable additional checking of the file. Some of the available flags are listed in Table 8-2:

TABLE 8-2: FLAGS IN BASIC STREAMS

FLAG	DESCRIPTION
IGNORE_PATH	Evaluates to 0 indicating that the search paths should not be used. This flag is meaningless if combined with other flags; it just makes the intention of the operation clearer.

continues

TABLE 8-2 *(continued)*

FLAG	DESCRIPTION
USE_PATH	Indicates that the include search path should be used if the file cannot be found in the relative path.
IGNORE_URL	Ignores any paths that are URLs.
ENFORCE_SAFE_MODE	Tells the engine whether or not to check against safe mode restrictions.
REPORT_ERRORS	Indicates that stream errors should be reported in the error logs. Warnings are still sent to the standard output.
STREAM_MUST_SEEK	Indicates that seeking is a requirement for the stream but writing to the stream is not.
STREAM_WILL_CAST	Should be used if the stream is going to be cast to a FILE* or socket. It turns off buffering so if you don't plan on casting the stream, omitting the flag actually means better performance.
STREAM_OPEN_FOR_INCLUDE	Used by require and include calls. It is unlikely that this is needed in many extensions.
STREAM_USE_URL	Uses only URLs. Attempting to open anything that isn't a URL results in an error.
STREAM_ONLY_GET_HEADERS	Causes the stream to only return headers. It is only relevant for wrappers that have headers such as HTTP.
STREAM_DISABLE_OPEN_BASEDIR	Ignores restrictions on the base directory (PHP scripts are normally not allowed to open files that aren't under the base directory).
STREAM_OPEN_PERSISTENT	Creates or opens a persistent file stream.
STREAM_DISABLE_URL_ PROTECTION	Ignores any PHP configurations that may disable opening of URLs via streams.
STREAM_ASSUME_REALPATH	Indicates that the path given to open the file is indeed real and does not try to calculate a real path or check the search paths.

The stream API implements the C Standard I/O library as well as many other functions to help make development easier. Streams can also act on directories. All the basic stream functions are listed in Table 8-3.

TABLE 8-3: Streams Functions

CREATING STREAMS	COPYING (CONTINUED)
php_stream_open_wrapper	php_stream_copy_tostream_ex
php_stream_open_wrapper_ex	**WRAPPERS**
php_stream_from_persistent_id	php_register_url_sream_wrapper
STREAM OPERATIONS	php_unregister_url_stream_wrapper
php_stream_close	php_register_url_stream_wrapper_volatile
php_stream_read	php_unregister_url_stream_wrapper_volatile
php_stream_get_line	php_stream_locate_url_wrapper
php_stream_get_record	php_stream_wrapper_log_error
php_stream_write	**DIRECTORIES**
php_stream_seek	php_stream_mkdir
php_stream_tell	php_stream_rmdir
php_stream_rewind	php_stream_opendir
php_stream_eof	php_stream_readdir
php_stream_getc	php_stream_scandir
php_stream_putc	**CONTEXT FUNCTIONS**
php_stream_flush	php_stream_context_set
php_stream_puts	php_stream_context_free
php_stream_stat	php_stream_context_alloc
php_stream_set_options	php_stream_context_get_option
php_stream_free	php_stream_context_set_option
COPYING	php_stream_context_get_link
php_stream_copy_to_mem	php_stream_context_set_link
php_stream_copy_to_stream	php_stream_context_del_link

Using Context

In addition the stream API also has some functions to make reading structured data a lot easier. A large portion of that functionality deals with contexts. *Contexts* allow specific information to be passed to wrappers.

One use of contexts is to provide additional data for the HTTP stream wrapper. The next example specifies a user agent for a HTTP request using a context:

```
char *filename, *mode, *agent;
int filename_len, mode_len;
php_stream *stream;
php_stream_context *context = NULL;

if (zend_parse_parameters(ZEND_NUM_ARGS() TSRMLS_CC, "s",
    &filename, &filename_len, &mode, &mode_len ) == FAILURE) {
  RETURN_FALSE;
}

MAKE_STD_ZVAL(mode);
ZVAL_STRING(mode,"r",0);

MAKE_STD_ZVAL(agent);
ZVAL_STRING(agent,"Expert PHP and MySQL book",0);

context = php_stream_context_alloc();
php_stream_context_set_option(context, "http", "user_agent", agent);

stream = php_stream_open_wrapper_ex(filename, mode,
          ENFORCE_SAFE_MODE | REPORT_ERRORS, NULL, context);

if ( stream ) {
  ...

  php_stream_close(stream);
  php_stream_context_free(context);
}
```

Different types of wrappers have different context options. The HTTP wrapper includes options for setting headers, proxy, timeout, post data, and maximum number of redirects.

Wrappers also sometimes return data in addition to the main stream. The information for HTTP, for instance, includes all the headers sent by the server. Because wrapper data often uses hash tables it is covered in the "Arrays and Hash Tables" section.

Networking

Networking across platforms can be difficult. Fortunately, PHP already has a strong set of libraries for TCP/IP communication. Combined with the stream API, a PHP extension can satisfy all its networking needs. The network APIs are used by the HTTP and FTP stream wrappers.

Building a Client

PHP is capable of being both a client and a server. Being a client is much more common. The first step in building a client is to create the socket. After that it is possible to get a stream from the socket.

This section builds a very simple client that connects first to a port, then dumps a string and listens for a response. It prints the response and then disconnects.

Before starting, be sure that `php_network.h` is included in the extension.

If you are using a Linux or UNIX system you can install the tcplisten *application and use that as a way to debug your client.*

Connecting to a server returns a php_socket_t structure:

```
socklen_t size;
php_socket_t socket;
struct timeval tv;

tv.tv_sec = 10;
tv.tv_usec = 0;

socket = php_network_connect_socket_to_host("localhost", 7777, SOCK_STREAM,
                            0, &tv, NULL, NULL, NULL, 0 TSRMLS_CC);
if (socket == -1) {
    /* could not connect */
}
```

The preceding example is hard coded, for simplicity, to connect to port 7777 on localhost. The values can, of course, be variable. Once connected, it is time to get the stream from the socket. After that, you can read and write as you would with a normal stream.

```
php_stream *stream;
stream = php_stream_sock_open_from_socket(socket, 0);
php_stream_write("Ping\n");
php_printf("Pong: %s", php_stream_get_line(stream, NULL, 0, NULL));
```

And, of course, it is necessary to close the stream and free the socket at the end of the script:

```
php_stream_close(stream);
closesocket(socket);
```

Building a Server

PHP is most often seen acting as a daemon on a local host. It is very rare to see PHP acting as a server in either a web server or an Apache environment. It is also uncommon to see PHP acting as a server for outside connections from the cloud. However, both are definitely possible.

The first step is always to bind to a socket. After that, depending on the mode, it might be useful to set the socket to non-blocking. PHP allows the socket to accept multiple connections. Each connection has its own socket and its own stream. The simple server in this section just accepts one connection and could be used as a basic server for the client from the previous section.

The code to open the socket is straightforward:

```
php_socket_t server;

server = php_network_bind_socket_to_local_addr("127.0.0.1", 7777,
            SOCK_STREAM, NULL, &error
            TSRMLS_CC);
listen(server, 5);
```

After that it is necessary to listen for a new connection. This is a blocking socket so it just waits until a connection arrives and does everything in sequence. A non-blocking socket would create a loop that simultaneously looks for new connections and reads data from existing connections.

```
socket = php_network_accept_incoming(server,
            NULL, NULL, NULL, NULL, &tv, NULL,
            &error  TSRMLS_CC);

if (socket == -1) {
  closesocket(server);
  RETURN_NULL();
}

stream = php_stream_sock_open_from_socket(socket, 0);
php_stream_write(stream, "Ping\n", 5);

char *pong;
int pong_len = spprintf(&pong, 0, "Pong: %s",
                php_stream_get_line(stream, NULL, 0, NULL));
php_stream_write(stream, pong, pong_len);
efree(pong);
```

Note that you can get a lot more information about the client that is connecting to your server by passing additional parameters to the `php_network_accept_incomming` function. For simplicity, the preceding script uses all `NULL`.

Closing the sockets and freeing the streams work the same way as before. Just remember that you may have more than one socket and many streams open at a time so be sure to close them all.

Errors and Warnings

All errors and warnings in PHP are output via the same function. The engine then decides how to display the error and log it. You can log an error and display it to the standard output or web page in one of the following ways:

```
php_error(E_WARNING, "Method %s not yet implemented.", method_name);
php_error_docref(NULL TSRMLS_CC, E_ERROR, "Could not connect to server %s:%i.",
                server_name, port_name);
```

The second and fourth arguments — the format strings bolded in the preceding example — are the same as with `printf` so you can do replacements into it.

The second function also automatically takes care of putting the current function information in the error if you pass the first argument as `NULL`. It also highlights HTML when appropriate. Because of the added features, the second is preferable in just about all cases. One notable exception is during initialization and shutdown when there isn't any active function or page.

Possible values for types of errors are:

➤   E_ERROR

➤   E_WARNING

➤   E_NOTICE

➤ E_PARSE

➤ E_CORE_ERROR

➤ E_CORE_WARNING

➤ E_USER_ERROR

➤ E_USER_WARNING

➤ E_USER_NOTICE

➤ E_STRICT

➤ E_RECOVERABLE_ERROR

➤ E_DEPRECATED

➤ E_USER_DEPRECATED

The first three in the list are by far the most common from within extensions. It is also possible (although not common or recommended) to output directly to the error log. That is done via the php_error_log function:

```
php_error_log(0, "Message", NULL, NULL TSRMLS_CC);
```

The error log function is identical to its PHP counterpart. It does not output anything to the screen and does not contain any file or line information. The function also accepts all the same additional parameters that allows for the error to be sent via email or output to a different log file.

The preceding example uses 0 to output to the error logs. Other possible options for the first parameter are:

➤ **A value of 1:** Send via email. Use the third parameter as an email address string and the fourth parameter as optional mail headers.

➤ **A value of 2:** Send via TCP/IP. The third parameter is a host:port pair.

➤ **A value of 3:** Save to the file specified by the third parameter.

ARRAYS AND HASH TABLES

This chapter already covered Boolean, long, double, and string data types. Two big things that were missing were arrays and hash tables. First, as you may have guessed, the two are the same. Arrays are numerically indexed and pure hash tables act like associative arrays and can be referenced by keys.

Even though both are extremely similar and they share the same data types, they each have their own set of useful functions to create, read, and modify them. Arrays are a tiny bit less complicated so they are covered first.

Building and Accessing Arrays

Many functions are available for building an array. The first thing that is needed in all cases is to get a handle to the array. There are two possible situations. One is that a zval already exists and it is necessary to get the hash table object, and the other is that a new hash table should be created. Creating a new array/hash table in a zval looks like this:

```
zval *new_array;
array_init( new_array );
```

Accessing an existing hash table like the one just created based on a zval looks like this:

```
HashTable *hash;
hash = Z_ARRVAL_P( new_array );
```

This is the first time you're seeing the `HashTable` data type in this book. The array is being initialized inside of the zval and then being retrieved and pointed to by the hash table. Once the hash table is retrieved or created, new values can then be added or deleted. There are three basic situations with arrays. They are:

➤ Adding at a specific index

➤ Using a specific key

➤ Adding to the next available index

The three functions are very similar:

```
add_assoc_double( new_array, "key_name", 3.14 );
add_index_double( new_array, 3 /* add at index 3 */, 3.14 );
add_next_index_double( new_array, 3.14 );
```

This code shows the double version of each of the functions. In addition to strings there are also functions for all the other data types. The data types have already been mentioned several times in this chapter, but just for review, they are:

➤ `bool`

➤ `double`

➤ `long`

➤ `null`

➤ `resource`

➤ `string` and `string1` (takes a length)

➤ `zval`

Additionally, each associative array function also has an extended version that takes an extra parameter after the key for the length, thus allowing for binary safe keys. By now it should be clear that whenever a function takes string length it is always passed as an integer immediately after the string.

All the functions that add a value to an array — with the exception of a zval directly — create a new zval. It would be inefficient to add a value and then immediately try to fetch it. For the situations where it is necessary to reference the created zval later there is another set of functions:

```
zval *new_item;
add_get_next_index_double( new_array, 3.14, new_item);
```

The `add_get_*` functions exist for every type of indexing and every type of data except zval, where it wouldn't make any sense. Extended versions also exist that allow string lengths to be specified for associative array keys.

The downloadable code for this book has some additional examples for using arrays.

Accessing and Modifying Hash Tables

As mentioned earlier, all arrays are hash tables, so by definition all the functions that work on hash tables will also work on arrays. In fact, all of the functions from the previous section were just easy-to-use wrappers around hash tables. However, it is often useful to access the hash table directly.

Hash tables have additional benefits such as the ability check if a key exists, and apply functions to the entire hash at one time. However, perhaps the most useful feature is simulating a `foreach` loop. After reviewing iterators in Chapter 2 this should be fairly familiar code:

```
HashTable *hash = ...
zval **data;

for ( zend_hash_internal_pointer_reset_ex(hash, &pointer);
      zend_hash_get_current_data_ex(hash, (void **) &data, &pointer ) == SUCCESS;
      zend_hash_move_forward_ex(hash, &pointer) ) {

  /* the zval data is filled with the current hash value */

}
```

Note the double pointer for the data variable. Be sure when accessing it to use the `_PP` macros and not the ones ending in simply `_P`. You can also get the number of elements in the hash by using `zend_hash_num_elements( hash )`.

It is not necessary to loop through the hash table to perform common operations such as looking up the value associated with a key and checking if a key exists. Finding elements in a hash table if you know the key is fairly simple:

```
zend_hash_find( hash, key, strlen(key), (void **)&data );
```

`data` is a double pointer to a zval just like before. Finding it if you know the index is similar:

```
zend_hash_index_find( hash, 3 /* index of 3 */, (void **)&data );
```

Finally, the code that checks if a key exists looks like this:

```
int exists;
exists = zend_hash_exists( hash, key, strlen(key) );
exists = zend_hash_index_exists( hash, 3 /* index of 3 */ );
```

Hash tables are used all over PHP. They are the core concepts used for everything from global values to the return values from many API functions, so it is very important to understand everything about them.

OBJECTS AND INTERFACES

The first part of the chapter explained how to define classes using the CodeGen_PECL utility. This section explains how to create classes and interfaces from scratch.

Perhaps as important, this section reviews how to inspect a class, modify it at run time, and access its properties and methods. By the end of this section you should be able to create an extension that can access data directly from an object passed into a function.

Creating a Class

Classes are created in much the same way as basic extensions and functions. They contain their own methods table and have their own set of macros; however, most of them should seem familiar.

Class Definition, Inheritance, and Namespaces

At a minimum there needs to be a class entry pointer, a methods table, and initialization code. It is best practice to put all the initialization in a function to call from the MINIT function but it is also possible to put all the code in MINIT directly, as illustrated in the following steps:

1. Define the class entry pointer in the C file:

   ```
   static zend_class_entry *helloworld_ce_ptr = NULL;
   ```

   The class entry is a structure that stores information about the class in order to be used by the engine when initializing instances and accessing the object. It includes several hash tables for methods and properties as well as special pointers especially for magic methods.

2. The next step is to define the methods table, which bears a not-coincidental resemblance to the extension function table. The methods table must be there even if it is empty. An empty methods table looks like this:

   ```
   static zend_function_entry helloworld_methods[] = {
     { NULL, NULL, NULL }
   }
   ```

3. The class entry pointer was defined but it is empty right now. A simple initialization function can be created and then called from MINIT. This is a very simple class but classes will only get larger from here so it is always a good idea to separate out the functionality.

   ```
   zend_class_entry ce;
   INIT_CLASS_ENTRY(ce, "helloworld", helloworld_method);
   helloworld_ce_ptr = zend_register_internal_class( &ce );
   ```

The code is straightforward and simply registers the class so that Zend knows it exists and can instantiate it. In the process it stores the pointer to the new class entry. Note that the returned class entry is not the same in memory as the original passed into it.

There is also an extended version of the macro for binary strings that takes the length of the class name as an argument after the class name. Ultimately all the macros end up expanding to the same one:

```
INIT_OVERLOADED_CLASS_ENTRY_EX(class_container, class_name,
  class_name_len, functions, handle_fcall, handle_propget, handle_propset,
  handle_propunset, handle_propisset)
```

There is also a macro `INIT_OVERLOADED_CLASS_ENTRY` (without the `_EX`) that takes all the parameters of its extended version except `handle_propunset` and `handle_propisset`. It also doesn't expect a length for the class name.

 If you wanted to have your class inside of a namespace there are three macros for that. Each macro is identical to its default namespace counterpart except that it takes the namespace as the second argument:

```
INIT_NS_CLASS_ENTRY
INIT_OVERLOADED_NS_CLASS_ENTRY
INIT_OVERLOADED_NS_CLASS_ENTRY_EX
```

The handlers at the end of the overloaded macros are expecting to be defined with `PHP_FUNCTION`. However, you can always define a `PHP_FUNCTION` and not put it in the function table. If you don't put it in the function table for your extension (remember: `PHP_FE`) it won't be callable from within PHP.

As you may have guessed, they correspond to the `__call`, `__get`, `__set`, `__unset`, and `__isset` methods. All magic methods have dedicated pointers in the `zend_class_entry` structure; however they can still be easily defined by creating a method of that name just as you would in PHP.

Inheriting from another class is as simple as using `register_internal_class_ex` instead of its non-extended counterpart:

```
zend_register_internal_class_ex( &ce, NULL, "parent_class_name" );
```

The second parameter is the parent class entry and the third is the name of the parent class. You should only use one or the other. The class does not need to be in the same extension as the child class; however, if the parent class is specified as a string and it is not found, you will end up with a null class entry.

It is also possible to define a class as abstract:

```
helloworld_ce_ptrn->ce_flags |= ZEND_ADD_EXPLICIT_ABSTRACT;
```

Remember to make changes to the class entry pointer after the class is registered. Changing the local structure before registering it won't have an effect.

Using Methods

Defining a method works much the same way as defining a function except the macro `PHP_METHOD` should be used instead of `PHP_FUNCTION` (don't forget to also put it in the header). The `PHP_METHOD` macro also takes two arguments instead of one. The first is the class name and the second is the method name.

Also, `PHP_FE` becomes `PHP_ME` and must be put in the class function table instead of the global function table. The `PHP_ME` macro takes `visibility` as its final argument. The possible values for `visibility` are:

➤ `ZEND_ACC_PUBLIC`

➤ `ZEND_ADD_PROTECTED`

➤ `ZEND_ACC_PRIVATE`

You can also use a binary or operation to combine either of the three with ZEND_ACC_STATIC to make the method statically accessible. As with many things when writing extensions, it doesn't make much sense to have a statically callable private method but public and protected are more useful. Just like in PHP, a static method can be called either truly static or as if it were a real method. Even so, it should only access other static properties and methods (never use "this").

The method implementation is just like a function implementation except you will probably want to get the value of $this at the top every time it is called, especially because the value should be passed in for argument parsing:

```
PHP_METHOD(helloworld, method_name)
{
  zend_class_entry * _this_ce;
  zval * _this_zval = NULL;


  if (zend_parse_method_parameters(ZEND_NUM_ARGS() TSRMLS_CC, getThis(),
      "O", &_this_zval, helloworld_ce_ptr) == FAILURE) {
    RETURN_NULL;
  }

  _this_ce = Z_OBJCE_P(_this_zval);

  ...
}
```

The value of the current object is always passed as a zval to the first parameter. After parsing the parameters it is often desirable to get the class entry structure from the object as well. At first glance it looks redundant. Although it doesn't happen during typical use for most extensions, when you deal with inheritance and polymorphism it is possible for the values of _this_zval to be different than getThis() and _this_ce to be different than hello_ce_pointer.

At this point it may be natural to assume that the if method always takes the object as the first argument it can then also be called procedurally like with MySQLi:

```
mysqli_query( $mysqli_obj, "SELECT * FROM example" );
```

Close, but not quite there. It must be added to the extension method table as an alias in addition to the entry in the methods table of the class:

```
PHP_MALIAS(parent, true, foo, NULL, ZEND_ACC_PUBLIC)
```

The main difference between the previous macro and the PHP_ME macro is that it accepts an alias name that is different than the method name as the third argument. It is important to define the function and its implementation using the alias and not the method name. Also, in PHP the class name is automatically prepended to the alias.

It is possible to make a method abstract. Because abstract methods don't have an implementation it is necessary to define them in the function table a little differently. To do that it is necessary to dive a little bit deeper into the macros. Both PHP_FE and PHP_ME eventually expand out to reveal that they are shortcuts for the function ZEND_FENTRY. To define an abstract method, the function entry table ends up looking something like this:

```
ZEND_ACC_ABSTRACT(method_name, NULL, NULL, ZEND_ACC_PUBLIC )
```

For the previous code, consider:

➤ The first argument is the method name but it is the second argument that references the actual function implementation or, because there isn't any implementation, a value of NULL instead. The second parameter is automatically derived from the method name when using PHP_ME or from the function name when using PHP_FUNCTION.

➤ The second argument is the new one. It is always NULL for abstract methods.

➤ The third argument is the argument info array, which is NULL because the sample method here doesn't have any arguments.

In all likelihood at some point it will be necessary to call a method of a class. There is a section on that later.

Using Properties

Declaring a property should be done when the class is initialized (either in the MINIT function or in a helper function like it was suggested in the previous section).

The declaration takes the class entry, the property name, the length of the string, the default value, and the visibility:

```
zend_declare_property_string(helloworld_ce_ptr, "bar", 3,
            "default value", ZEND_ACC_PUBLIC TSRMLS_DC);
```

By now the meaning of the TSRMLS_DC constant should be clear. The preceding declaration is for a string. Like in other parts of the API there are corresponding functions for the other data types. However, it is possible for properties to change type (temporarily) at run time.

Setting and getting properties is similar to the way it is done with arrays. Setting a property to a double is done with:

```
zend_update_property_double( _this_ce, _this_zval, property_name,
                         strlen(property_name), 1 TSRMLS_CC)
```

Getting properties returns a zval so it will most likely be wrapped around something like Z_VALSTR_P. The second to last parameter indicates whether a warning should be thrown if the property doesn't exist (1 for silent and 0 for verbose):

```
Z_LVAL_P(zend_read_property(_this_ce, _this_zval, property_name,
                         strlen(property_name), 1 TSRMLS_CC))
```

Depending on how you generated your class there may be predefined macros in the header that wrap common property getting functionality. Check the header to see if they exist for your extension. If not, it is useful to define some helpful macros because it can get tedious manually passing all the parameters.

Of course, properties can be declared as static using ZEND_ACC_STATIC just like with methods. The read and write functions for properties have static variants that don't require an object zval to be passed to them.

Using Class Constants

Classes can also have class-specific constants. As mentioned in Chapter 1, class constants are always public and static. They are defined during class initialization:

```
zval *tmps;

tmp = (zval *) malloc(sizeof(zval));
INIT_PZVAL(tmp);
ZVAL_LONG(tmp, 255);
zend_symtable_update(&(helloworld_ce_ptr->constants_table), "MY_PI",
                     8, (void *) &tmp, sizeof(zval *), NULL);
```

The code directly references the symbol table for constants. Incidentally, symbol tables are also used for a variety of other things including storing the variables that are available in the global PHP scope. They are implemented behind the scenes using hash tables and can, in fact, be referenced just like a normal hash table.

The symbol table expects a zval so one must be initialized prior to being inserted into the table. This is one of the cases where malloc is appropriate to use instead of emalloc because the latter will incorrectly get cleaned up by the garbage collector between requests.

Although there isn't anything preventing it, it is not a good idea to change the constants after initialization.

You have two ways to use the constant in your application:

➤   The simplest is to just define it via the preprocessor and reference it in the code, which will work fine because the constants should never change.

➤   Another approach would be to use zend_symtable_find:

```
zend_symtable_find( &(helloworld_ce_ptr->constants_table), key,
                    strlen(key), (void **)&data );
```

The function behaves the same way as zend_hash_find which has special macros to handle numeric symbol keys.

Creating an Interface

Interfaces are almost identical to classes in how they are defined. The difference lies in how they are registered and how methods are defined. Also, as you probably know from PHP, an interface cannot have properties. In addition, all interface methods are public and do not have implementations.

Follow these basic steps:

1.   Define the interface as you normally would for a class, except replace the call to zend_register_internal_class to:

```
helloworld_ce = zend_register_internal_interface(&ce, TSRMLS_CC);
```

2. Interfaces can also extend other interfaces. The code to extend the class sheds some insight into the inner workings of object-oriented programming in PHP. First attempt to find the class entry for the interface that is being extended and then, if it is found, extend it:

```
if (SUCCESS == zend_hash_find(CG(class_table), "interface_to_extend",
    8, (void **)&parent_ce)) {
  if (parent_ce) {
    zend_do_inheritance(new_interface_ce_ptr, *parent_ce TSRMLS_CC);
  }
}
```

3. Interface methods are abstract so defining one is very similar to defining an abstract method in a traditional class. Enter it into the method table but don't implement it:

```
ZEND_FENTRY(interfaceMethod, NULL, NULL,
            ZEND_ACC_ABSTRACT | ZEND_ACC_INTERFACE | ZEND_ACC_PUBLIC)
```

4. Implement the interface in a class. It is actually two steps; the second is to implement all the methods in the interface — which by now should be clear — but first the class must be specified as an implementation of the interface:

```
zend_class_entry **tmp;
if (SUCCESS == zend_hash_find(CG(class_table), "interface_name",
    8, (void **)&tmp)) {
  zend_class_implements(hellworld_ce_ptr TSRMLS_CC, 1, *tmp);
}
```

It is possible to implement more than one interface at once. The second to last parameter is the number of interfaces being implemented. The function itself is variable length.

As you may have guessed from the code, the interface does not need to be in the same extension as the class. It will try to locate the interface at run time. Not having an interface affects polymorphism but it does not affect any of the other functionality of the class, so if the interface is not found it is acceptable to ignore it or issue a warning. However, it is still important to remember to indicate dependencies.

Interacting with Objects

All the classes are immediately available in PHP. Often it is useful, though, to access the class from within a PHP extension. For the rest of the extension writing process, everything that can be done in PHP can also be done in the extension.

Identifying Objects

Objects are identified by class entries. If the object is local to the extension, there is a readily available pointer to the class entry. For objects of external or unknown types, ways exist to retrieve the class entry:

```
zval *my_obj;
zend_class_entry *ce;
...
ce = zend_get_class_entry(my_obj TSRMLS_CC);

/* or */
ce = Z_OBJCE_P(my_obj);
```

It is also possible to retrieve the class entry given only a class name:

```
zend_class_entry **ce;
ce = zend_lookup_class( class_name, strlen(class_name), &ce );
```

Once you have one or two class entries there is a lot you can do. One of the most useful things to do is to identify and check for relationships between classes. The class entry and the zval can both be used to retrieve the class name for string comparison or whatever else it may be needed for:

```
char *class_name;
chat *class_name_len;
zend_get_object_class_name( my_obj, &class_name, &class_name_len );

class_name = emalloc( class_entry->name_len*sizeof(char *) );
memcpy( class_name, class_entry->name, class_entry->name_len );
```

The first few lines of code get the class name given a zval, and the second few get the class name given a class entry object. However, it is not a good idea to do testing on the class name directly. After all, polymorphism comes into play. To properly check you can use `instanceof` instead:

```
zend_bool is_instance = instanceof_function( class_entry_1, class_entry_2 );
```

It is necessary to test classes ahead of time in some cases to emulate type-hinting behavior and throw a warning if the object is not appropriate for a specific situation.

Calling Methods

Calling methods on objects doesn't actually require a class entry. Instead it only requires a zval for the class. There are two main functions for calling methods — one is for methods with zero parameters and the other is for methods with one or more parameters:

```
zend_call_method_with_0_params( &my_obj, NULL, NULL, "method_name", &return_val);
```

There are also macros for one, two, and three parameters. The return value is stored in the last parameter (which is a zval pointer). The second parameter is for a class entry, which is used for static methods, and the third is for a function proxy if you are using one.

Using all the tools from this chapter it is easy to accept a `mysqli_result` object and loop through all the rows:

```
zval *result, *row;
...

zend_call_method_with_0_params( &result, NULL, NULL, "fetch_assoc", &row);

while ( Z_TYPE_P( row ) != IS_NULL ) {
  HashTable *realRow = Z_ARRVAL_P(row);

  /* do something with the row */

  zval_dtor( row );
  zend_call_method_with_0_params( &result, NULL, NULL, "fetch_assoc", &row);
}
```

CONSTANTS, INI DIRECTIVES, AND GLOBALS

Even though the code generators make it look easy, quite a few steps are required for defining constants, INI directives, and globals. The following sections go into a little bit more detail about each as well as demonstrate how to create them from scratch.

The previous sections also left out a very important part: how to access the values from within an extension. This section covers that as well.

Constants

Constants are the simplest to deal with. Typically, because a constant doesn't change, it is good practice to define the constant in the header. Preprocessor definitions in C, of course, look like this:

```
#define MY_PI 3.14
```

The next step is to register the constants. After everything in this chapter, something is finally going to go into the module initialization function. In the `MINIT` call add this code:

```
REGISTER_DOUBLE_CONSTANT( "MY_PI", 3.14, CONST_PERSISTENT | CONST_CS );
```

The third argument consists of the flags for creating the constant. Most of the time the flags are identical to the previous example. The flags indicate that the constant is persistent and case sensitive. If you were to have a non-persistent constant you want to register it in the request initialization function instead.

It is also possible to register a constant within a PHP namespace. The macros are almost the same as before, only the name is slightly different and the first argument is now the namespace:

```
REGISTER_NS_DOUBLE_CONSTANT( "namespace_name", "MY_PI", 3.14,
                    CONST_PERSISTENT | CONST_CS );
```

Finally, it is sometimes desirable to load the constant into a zval at run time. You have two ways to do this. The first is if you happened to define the constant using a C preprocessor directive you can allocate a new standard zval and populate it. The other option is to tell Zend to fetch it:

```
zval *my_const;
zend_get_constant( constant_name, strlen(constant_name), my_const );
```

That is all there is to constants. It is not necessary to free the constants when the extension exits. Constants are actually stored in a global hash table, and the garbage collector will take care of freeing all the constants for you.

Globals and INI Directives

Globals and INI directives both have the same root methods of defining and accessing them. The major difference is that INI directives must be registered with PHP and can easily be overridden and accessed by the PHP scripts.

Defining Globals and INI Directives

Each is stored in a structure that must be defined in the header of the extension using special macros. When using extension generating scripts the structure is probably already there. The ext_skel script puts some dummy values in and CodeGen_PECL puts in and registers whatever values you specified in the XML file. The ext_skel structure looks like this:

```
ZEND_BEGIN_MODULE_GLOBALS(andrew)
   long  global_value;
   char *global_string;
ZEND_END_MODULE_GLOBALS(andrew)
```

What the code is actually doing isn't creating a structure in memory but rather a type of structure that can be used to store the globals. That is very important later in the section.

They are always accessible from anywhere within your extension and they stick around for the lifetime of your extension. If PHP is compiled with thread safety, the globals should also be thread-specific.

If any of the variables also happen to be INI entries, it is necessary to register them as such somewhere in the C file:

```
#ifndef ZEND_ENGINE_2
#define OnUpdateLong OnUpdateInt
#endif

PHP_INI_BEGIN()
   STD_PHP_INI_ENTRY("helloworld.greeting", "default greeting", PHP_INI_PERDIR,
      OnUpdateString, greeting, zend_helloworld_globals, helloworld_globals)
PHP_INI_END()

/* in MINIT */
REGISTER_INI_ENTRIES();
```

After all the globals are defined and the INI entries are registered it is time to initialize everything. The initialization takes place in the module initialization function (MINIT). It is typical to also create helper functions to initialize and free the globals:

```
ZEND_INIT_MODULE_GLOBALS(helloworld, php_helloworld_init_globals,
                         php_helloworld_shutdown_globals);
REGISTER_INI_ENTRIES();
```

If you don't have one or both of the helper functions you can simply pass NULL to the macro instead.

There isn't any need to explicitly free the global values (although if there is any memory allocated for the globals it should be freed in the shutdown_globals function). However, INI directives require an additional step to deregister them:

```
UNREGISTER_INI_ENTRIES();
```

Globals do stick around for the entire time that the extension is loaded. As a result, if PHP is running attached to a web server, changing a global in one request causes subsequent requests on that thread to have the same value. However, you can easily change the default behavior.

As mentioned earlier in the chapter, `RINIT` is a function that is called at the beginning of every request. To create a global that is reset at the beginning of the request it is necessary to set them in that function.

Accessing Globals

Of course, having all these globals around is useless if they can't be accessed. Globals can't be accessed from PHP unless you write a wrapper function or register them as an INI entry.

Although it is possible to access the globals directly, the name of the global structure is obscured by macros and also, there are various threading issues to consider. Usually, accessing the globals is also done through macros. The standard code to access the globals looks like this (assuming that the extension name is `helloworld`):

```
TSRMG(helloworld_globals_id, zend_helloworld_globals *, global_name)
```

The actual meaning of the macros will make more sense soon. Remember that the globals are C data types, not zvals, so if you wanted to return a global you would do something like this:

```
RETURN_LONG( HELLOWORLD_G(my_global_long) );
```

...or if you want to write a value, simply:

```
HELLOWORLD_G(my_global_long) = 1234;
```

Globals are the only thread-safe way (without reinventing some wheels that Zend already made) to store values.

True Globals and Thread Safety

The entire chapter up to this point has been brushing off some important concepts and then saving them for right now. The Zend engine handles all the thread safety in the application using an abstraction layer called the *Thread Safe Resource Management (TSRM)* layer. You've already seen it several times in this chapter, the most recent being at the end of the previous section.

It is all part of a package called *Zend Thread Safety (ZTS)*. Of course, a good portion of servers are not compiled with thread safety, so sometimes it is necessary to write two versions of code. That is why there are so many macros dealing with thread safety. Revisiting previous macro definitions will show `#ifdef ZTS` as a way of conditionally compiling depending on whether thread safety is enabled.

In actuality, if Zend is compiled thread safe, the global structures are initialized once per thread and the `TSRMG` macro takes care of retrieving pointers to the value. The macro does, however, rely on the variable `tsrm_ls` being defined. For that, it is necessary to recall the beginning of the chapter when defining functions.

Hopefully, when you defined functions, it was clear that in one way or another one of the TSRMLS values is passed to a function. Return to the section "Helper Functions" for some notes on how they are used. Their only purpose is to pass global variable storage from one function call to another. Forgetting to pass this value to a function causes the macro to retrieve the globals to break.

If for whatever reason tsrm_ls wasn't sent into a function it is possible to fetch it explicitly using the TSRMLS_FETCH macro, which evaluates to:

```
void ***tsrm_ls = (void ***) ts_resource_ex(0, NULL);
```

Of course, on occasion it is desirable to have a global that is available in all threads. For that, there are static global variables. You won't typically define static global variables (sometimes referred to as *True Global Resources*) in the header. Instead they are usually defined near the top of the C file:

```
static int hello_world_true_global = 0;
```

Simple globals are fairly problem free; however, as soon as a global gets more complex it runs into problems. It is important to take proper care when using static global variables. The proper approach is to designate a *critical section* using a mutex to lock a block of code.

Locking memory can become tricky, particularly because different operating systems have different methods of doing it. Fortunately, Zend provides a convenient way of doing it with tsrm_mutex lock:

```
# ifdef ZTS
tsrm_mutex_lock( example_mutex );
# endif

/* Access to shared resources goes here */

# ifdef ZTS
tsrm_mutex_unlock( example_mutex );
# endif
```

And don't forget to define a static global variable for your mutex somewhere near the top of your C file:

```
# ifdef ZTS
static MUTEX_T example_mutex = null;
# endif
```

You must also allocate your mutex (normally in the MINIT function) and free it when the extension is done with it (normally in MSHUTDOWN):

```
# ifdef ZTS
example_mutex = tsrm_mutex_alloc();
# endif
...

# ifdef ZTS
tsrm_mutex_free( example_mutex );
# endif
```

The mutex locking can only be done if ZTS is enabled so there is a little extra code to do the checking. Locking manually — in the Zend engine, at least — is typically only needed for very specialized tasks, many of which involve database servers. So before manually locking to access global static variables ask, "Can this be done with Zend global variables instead?"

DESCRIBING AN EXTENSION

The easiest to overlook, but still important aspect of writing a PHP extension is implementing the info function. You may recall from the CodeGen_PECL section and the section on adding functions that there is one internal function that hasn't been mentioned yet: MINFO.

The info function's job is to output information about an extension. The function does this by using built-in functions designed specifically for that purpose in addition to the standard output functionality. The biggest reason for the wrappers is that there are two possible places that the output from the MINFO function can go:

➤ Via a call to `<?php phpinfo() ?>`

➤ On the command line with `php --info`

The built-in functions simplify the process of outputting to both types of media (terminal and HTML).

Without implementing the function, users of the extension cannot quickly verify if the extension is installed or find out how it is configured. If the extension is part of a software distribution you also miss an important branding opportunity.

If you plan on distributing your extension at all it is important to provide information about it.

Printing a Description

Although not all extensions do, they can print blocks of text in the PHP information output. Typical information to display includes copyright information, credits, and descriptions of the extension.

The basic `php_printf` functionality works as expected even in a MINFO function. However, PHP also provides ways to specify boxes around content. The CodeGen_PECL script generates a block for you with information about the extension maintainers and basic version information; however, adding new boxes manually is easy. They all follow the same basic format:

```
php_info_print_box_start(0);
php_printf("<p>Content goes here…</p>");
...
php_info_print_box_end();
```

The first and only parameter passed to `php_info_print_box_start` is for the box type flag (different boxes have different background colors). A value of zero produces a normal box with the same background color as a table cell and a value of 1 produces a header box with the header background color. It is rare to see a 1 in this parameter.

Building a Table

Tables with extension information are one of the particularly helpful uses of the information page. Because the tables are printed differently in HTML and on the command line it is necessary to use wrapper functions instead. The two flavors of output look like this:

```
Extname Support => enabled
Extname Version => 0.1
```

...and, in the HTML format using `phpinfo()`, this:

```
<table border="0" cellpadding="3" width="600">
  <tr class="h"><th>Extname support</th><th>enabled</th></tr>
  <tr><td class="e">Extname Version </td><td class="v">0.1 </td></tr>
</table><br />
```

By convention the first line is always an indicator as to whether or not the extension is enabled and it is always a header (`<th>` instead of `<td>`) row.

The rest of the rows are great for information about the module, such as what features are compiled into it and which versions of third-party libraries it is linked against. The first step is to start the table and then print each row. Once you are done, you can close the table in much the same way that it was opened:

```
php_info_print_table_start();
php_info_print_table_header(2, "Extname Enabled", "enabled");
php_info_print_table_row(2, "Extname Version", "0.1");
php_info_print_table_end();
```

The first parameter is the number of columns to expect. The tables can be any number of columns, but it is a good idea to stick with the same number throughout. The typical value is two (for a key/value pair).

INI directives are slightly different. They have three columns instead: one for the label, one for the master value of the INI directive, and one for the local value. Fortunately, it is very easy to print the table for all of the INI directives:

```
DISPLAY_INI_ENTRIES();
```

That's all there is to it. Be sure to take a look at the example extension for more information.

Specifying a Logo

It is not very common to specify a logo with a PHP extension. That may be because a lot of extensions are small-time projects and don't have their own logo or it may be because logos are very tedious to implement manually.

The easiest way to create the logo code is by using a script like CodeGen_PECL; however, it is not the only way. The source code that comes with this chapter has a simple script that generates the encoded image data when given a filename.

The image needs to be stored in memory as binary data. The easiest way to specify that in C is to convert the image to a comma-separated byte-array, which is then assigned to a variable.

The logo is then registered with a *GUID* (Globally Unique Identifier). When handling a request for an information page, PHP looks for a ?=GUID. When PHP encounters one it returns the image directly instead of the requested file. You can use this same technique to display the PHP and Zend logos on the info pages so each GUID must be unique at least to that degree.

Once all the pieces are there, you can follow these five steps to get the logo to display:

1. Include the appropriate header files.

2. Store the image data in a variable.

3. Register the logo.

4. Make sure that the MINFO function prints out an image tag.

5. Unregister the logo.

Because the logo code is not in one of the standard extension headers it must be included with #include "php_logos.h". The header file includes a few basic functions. The first needs to be put in the extension's MINIT code:

```
php_register_info_logo("FULL_GUID_FOR_LOGO", "", my_logo, 1234);
```

Regarding this code:

➤ The first parameter is the GUID. Either make one up or use a GUID generator script (the second option is better). It will be used in a couple places so it may be a good idea to define a constant.

➤ The second is the mime type. In this case the code is forcing the browser to auto-detect it.

➤ The third and fourth parameters are the actual image data followed by the size of the data. These two are the most difficult pieces of information to get. Before getting past this step the size needs to be correct and my_logo needs to be defined somewhere and initialized with the image information. The next step is to make sure that the MINFO function prints the data:

```
php_printf("<img src=\"");
if ( SG(request_info).request_uri )
  php_printf("%s", SG(request_info).request_uri );
php_printf("?=%s", "FULL_GUID_FOR_LOGO");
php_printf("\" style=\"float: right; border: 0;\" alt=\"Hello World Logo\"");
```

When the module is shut down you must unregister the logo:

```
php_unregister_info_logo("FULL_GUID_FOR_LOGO");
```

Your extension should now have a logo floating off to the right when the PHP info page is loaded.

SUMMARY

There is so much to writing PHP extensions and this chapter has only scratched the surface. Some of the things not covered in this book include exception handling, variable argument functions, callback functions, closures, and debugging. However, this chapter should put you well on your way to developing great PHP extensions.

The beginning of the chapter focused on scripts used to generate extensions. It is strongly recommended that you use one. CodeGen_PECL is by far the more robust of the two; however, any good code generator is useful for creating directory layouts and file structures that conform to the PECL community standards.

Here are a few tips:

➤ **Generated code is great but take it with a grain of salt.** Always understand what the code is doing and if something seems out of place, don't hesitate to fix it.

➤ **Watch memory usage.** Make sure to free any variables that you allocate, but don't double free any variables or free variables that you didn't personally allocate. Doing that is almost guaranteed to cause a segmentation fault.

➤ **Don't hesitate to explore the PHP and Zend source code.** It is full of useful comments and the bundled extensions have many examples of how to use certain functions.

The PECL web site is a great place to find notes on coding standards and PECL specifications. It also has notes on documentation as well, so it is a good place to go once you're up on your feet and you want to learn more.

The main PHP source directory also has numerous text documents on everything from configuration to coding standards. When you feel ready, the PECL mailing list is a good place to discuss your project or patches and the IRC chat room is fairly active.

Full-Text Searching

WHAT'S IN THIS CHAPTER?

➤ Understanding and using MySQL FULLTEXT indexes

➤ Installing, configuring, and using the more efficient Sphinx Full-Text Search Index for full-text searching

➤ Developing PHP applications that use Sphinx

Searching text is one of the most common functions of a web site and a must-have for RDBMSs. Sometimes, developers will search text in the database using the LIKE operator, but this is very inefficient, especially if there is a large data set involved. This is where full-text search engines become a necessity.

This book covers two means of supporting full-text search functionality using MySQL: FULLTEXT indexes, which are part of the functionality of MySQL, and the Sphinx Full-Text Search Engine, an open-source project that is designed to work well with MySQL.

MYSQL FULLTEXT INDEXES

MySQL supports FULLTEXT indexes (which are pretty much b-tree indexes at least in terms of behavior) that are created against columns containing text. These indexes are built by indexing words found in the text fields using a pointer to the word in the actual location where it exists, thus eliminating stop words such as *the*, *and*, and so on. For a complete list of default stop words see http://dev.mysql.com/doc/refman/5.1/en/fulltext-stopwords.html.

When the index is used in a search, the search term is matched against the index. The location is known because the index provides a pointer to the text where the term is physically located.

Creating a `FULLTEXT` index is as easy as creating a regular index. You can specify it when you create a table or when you use an existing table:

```
mysql> CREATE TABLE books_text (
    -> book_id int(8) NOT NULL DEFAULT 0,
    -> title varchar(64) DEFAULT '',
    -> content text,
    -> PRIMARY KEY (book_id),
    -> FULLTEXT INDEX title (title),
    -> FULLTEXT INDEX content (content)) ENGINE=MyISAM;
```

 `FULLTEXT` *indexes are only supported with tables created using either the MyISAM or Maria storage engines.*

Or, alternatively:

```
mysql> CREATE FULLTEXT INDEX title ON books_text (title);
 mysql> CREATE FULLTEXT INDEX content ON books_text (content);
```

Once these indexes are created, they are ready for use.

To use `FULLTEXT` indexes, you utilize the `FULLTEXT` search function `MATCH() ... AGAINST`. Its syntax usage is:

```
MATCH (col1,col2,...) AGAINST (expr  [search_modifier])

search_modifier:
  {
       IN BOOLEAN MODE
     | IN NATURAL LANGUAGE MODE
     | IN NATURAL LANGUAGE MODE WITH QUERY EXPANSION
     | WITH QUERY EXPANSION
  }
```

The search modifier values are as follows:

➤ **BOOLEAN MODE:** Uses a search string that has its own syntax containing the terms to be searched for. This syntax allows word weighting, negation, and/or, and so on, omitting stop words.

➤ **NATURAL LANGUAGE MODE:** Uses a string as is, without special syntax, and searches for the specified string. Words that are present in more than 50 percent of the rows are not matched.

➤ **NATURAL LANGUAGE MODE WITH QUERY EXPANSION:** Basically the same as NATURAL LANGUAGE MODE except the results from the search of the initial search terms aren't returned to the user, but are added to the original search terms, which are then searched again. These results are then returned to the user. This is also known as *bling query expansion*. An example of this is if the initial search term was *database* and returned results with MySQL and Oracle, which then were searched to return results containing database, Oracle, or MySQL.

Using MySQL FULLTEXT Indexes

MySQL provides a sample database that you can load into any schema on your instance of MySQL. It's called *sakila*, and you can find it on MySQL's developer web site at `http://dev.mysql.com/doc/sakila/en/sakila.html`.

This database contains a table, complete with data, called `films_text`, which has FULLTEXT indexes used for demonstration of FULLTEXT indexes in this book.

The best way to see how to use FULLTEXT is to provide several examples of wacky films as illustrated in the next two sections.

Natural Language Mode

An example of Natural Language mode is as follows:

```
mysql> SELECT film_id, title FROM film_text
    -> WHERE MATCH(title,description)
    -> AGAINST('Frisbee' IN NATURAL LANGUAGE MODE) LIMIT 5;
+---------+---------------+
| film_id | title         |
+---------+---------------+
|     308 | FERRIS MOTHER |
|     326 | FLYING HOOK   |
|     585 | MOB DUFFEL    |
|     714 | RANDOM GO     |
|     210 | DARKO DORADO  |
+---------+---------------+
```

Boolean Mode

The following example matched term must have *technical* and *writer*:

```
mysql> SELECT film_id, title, description FROM film_text
    -> WHERE MATCH(title,description)
    -> AGAINST('technical +writer' IN BOOLEAN MODE) LIMIT 5\G
*************************** 1. row ***************************
    film_id: 19
      title: AMADEUS HOLY
description: A Emotional Display of a Pioneer And a Technical
Writer who must Battle a Man in A Balloon
*************************** 2. row ***************************
    film_id: 43
      title: ATLANTIS CAUSE
description: A Thrilling Yarn of a Feminist And a Hunter
who must Fight a Technical Writer in A Shark Tank
*************************** 3. row ***************************
    film_id: 44
      title: ATTACKS HATE
description: A Fast-Paced Panorama of a Technical Writer
And a Mad Scientist
who must Find a Feminist in An Abandoned Mine Shaft
*************************** 4. row ***************************
    film_id: 67
```

```
         title: BERETS AGENT
   description: A Taut Saga of a Crocodile And a Boy who
must Overcome a Technical
Writer in Ancient China
*************************** 5. row ***************************
       film_id: 86
         title: BOOGIE AMELIE
   description: A Lacklusture Character Study of a Husband
And a Sumo Wrestler who must Succumb a Technical Writer
in The Gulf of Mexico
```

The following example uses the Boolean mode where the title or description must contain the term *technical* but not *writer*:

```
mysql> SELECT film_id, title, description FROM film_text
    -> WHERE MATCH(title,description)
->    -> AGAINST('technical -writer' IN BOOLEAN MODE) LIMIT 5\G
Empty set (0.00 sec)
```

In this Boolean mode, the title or description must contain the exact phrase "Fight a Pastry Chef":

```
mysql> SELECT film_id, title, description FROM film_text
    -> WHERE MATCH(title,description)
    -> AGAINST('"Fight a Pastry Chef"' IN BOOLEAN MODE) LIMIT 5\G
*************************** 1. row ***************************
       film_id: 11
         title: ALAMO VIDEOTAPE
   description: A Boring Epistle of a Butler And a Cat who must Fight a Pastry Chef
in A MySQL Convention
```

MySQL FULLTEXT Index Issues

You should be aware of the various issues you might encounter when using FULLTEXT indexes. These primarily have to do with performance. FULLTEXT indexes are very easy to use, and are part of MySQL functionality, but they can also affect a table's performance.

➤ FULLTEXT indexes minimum word length (ft_min_word_len) limit is 3. This can be frustrating if you wish to index on smaller words.

➤ Searching FULLTEXT indexes is limited to only the columns that you pre-grouped with an index.

➤ FULLTEXT query language is limited when compared to more recent fulltext indexing solutions

➤ FULLTEXT indexes can be used only with tables created using the MyISAM storage engine. This is fine if you are using mostly MyISAM or if you have no problem with multiple storage engine types for your database. However, if you want to use InnoDB as the sole storage engine for all tables in a schema or an entire database, a FULLTEXT index prevents you from doing so on the table or tables on which you want to have that index.

For some implementations, the very table that contains text you want to search is large and you might actually want the benefits that InnoDB provides, particularly with regard to recovery time in case of a crash. Repairing MyISAM tables can take a long time on large tables that are corrupt: phones will ring and bosses will be unhappy while you have the table out of use during table repair! Given this, you are faced with using FULLTEXT indexes but not InnoDB, or vice versa for the table containing the text. This can be a limitation particularly if you need to use InnoDB because it is a transactional table type.

➤ FULLTEXT indexes are updatable indexes. When a new record is inserted, updated, or deleted from a table that is using FULLTEXT, the index must be modified each time. This can slow down performance of queries against this table — especially the larger the table gets — both in terms of the time it takes to update the index and the fact that the table is locked for each modification, thus preventing other modifications from occurring.

➤ FULLTEXT indexes also do not work well with ideographic languages (such as Chinese, Japanese, Korean, and so on). Because these languages do not have word delimiters it's impossible to determine where words begin and end.

A BETTER SOLUTION: THE SPHINX FULL-TEXT SEARCH ENGINE

Sphinx (an acronym for *SQL Phrase Index*) is a full-text search engine, distributed under GPL version 2, developed by Andrew Aksyonoff. It closely integrates with MySQL, Drizzle, PostgreSQL, MS SQL, Oracle, Firebird and any other database that supports ODBC.

Sphinx is a standalone search engine that provides fast, efficient, and relevant searching. For its data sources, it uses SQL databases (MySQL, Drizzle, PostgreSQL, or even any RDBMS that has an ODBC interface) or XML pipe (reading in XML streams and creating indexes based off the content). Table 9-1 lists the several utilities and programs that come with it:

TABLE 9-1: Sphinx Utilities and Programs

UTILITY OR PROGRAM	DESCRIPTION
Indexer	The program that builds indexes using a data source such as MySQL.
Search	A command-line utility program that searches an index directly. You use this for testing searches and general index functionality.
Searchd	The daemon that provides the search functionality for Sphinx clients, handling inputs or search requests, searching indexes, and returning results of searches. This daemon is what makes *distributed indexes* possible, which are explained in more detail later.

continues

TABLE 9-1 *(continued)*

UTILITY OR PROGRAM	DESCRIPTION
SphinxQL	The combination of searchd now having support for the MySQL binary networking support as well as a small sub-set of SQL
Sphinxapi	A set of searchd client API libraries for use with various scripting languages (PHP, Perl, Python, Ruby).
Spelldump	A command-line tool to extract the items from an ispell or MySpell (Open Office) format dictionary for index customization.
Indextool	A command-line utility for dumping information pertaining to an index as well as being able to check index consistency.

Sphinx has its own Sphinx API, which has bindings for various programming languages such as PHP, Perl, Python, Java, and Ruby. Also, the Sphinx distribution contains the Sphinx Storage Engine, which can be used internally with MySQL to provide even further integration with MySQL.

Unlike MySQL FULLTEXT indexes, the steps to retrieve data from the database after using the Sphinx full-text index are a somewhat manual process. The index is separate from MySQL, being served out with a network server, searchd, versus being a component of MySQL. The basic idea has been that with Sphinx, you perform a search against an index that returns one or more IDs of the relevant documents, which corresponds to a record in the database. In previous versions of Sphinx, it would be this list of IDs that you'd use to retrieve the actual string data from the database. You would also be able to retrieve numeric columns from Sphinx. However, with the current release of Sphinx and later, you can retrieve strings from Sphinx. In some cases, you can eliminate the need to touch the database.

Another difference in overall functionality between Sphinx and MySQL FULLTEXT indexes is that Sphinx indexes are separate indexes from MySQL, generated by an indexer program rather than being internal MySQL indexes, which are automatically created and updated upon the execution of data-modification statements (insert, update, delete). Not being an internal component to MySQL might sound like a negative, but this actually works out as a positive; it allows the decoupling of a fast database such as MySQL from full-text index generation or updates, which with FULLTEXT indexes results in poor write performance. Sphinx also allows you to decouple the database sharding from full-text index sharding. With Sphinx, the database can execute data-modification statements on a database table without the overhead of having to generate an index, hence better write performance. This all makes full-text indexing much easier than before!

Sphinx Configuration and Installation

Installing Sphinx is a very straightforward task.

In this book, just as a MySQL installation requires the setup of a mysql user and group, the Sphinx installation described here utilizes a sphinx user and group. This is not a requirement but a preference by the author and a way of organizing Sphinx into its own user-space.

The steps are as follows:

1. Logged in as the root user or using sudo, create a sphinx user and group on the host:

```
root# groupadd sphinx

root# useradd -d /usr/local/sphinx -g sphinx -s /bin/bash -m sphinx
```

2. Download the latest Sphinx source code from the Sphinx web site (http://sphinxsearch .com/downloads.html) and untar/gzip the downloaded file to the directory of choice for building software:

```
shell> wget http://www.sphinxsearch.com/downloads/sphinx-0.9.9.tar.gz
shell> tar xvzf sphinx-0.9.9.tar.gz
```

3. Change into the newly created sphinx-version directory and run the configure script, specifying the install prefix as the home directory of the sphinx user; enabling the option --enable-id64 allows Sphinx indexes to work with 64-bit document IDs (BIGINT UNSIGNED) in your data source.

```
shell> cd sphinx-0.9.9
shell>./configure --prefix=/usr/local/sphinx --enable-id-64
```

4. Compile and install Sphinx:

```
radha:sphinx-0.9.9 patg$ make
```

And if there are no errors during compile, run this:

```
radha:sphinx-0.9.9 patg$ sudo make install
radha:sphinx-0.9.9 patg$ sudo chown -R sphinx /usr/local/sphinx
```

5. Set up the sphinx.conf configuration file. This requires that you sudo to the *sphinx* user, which places you in the *sphinx* user's home directory, /usr/local/sphinx, where Sphinx was installed. In the *sphinx* user's home directory, there is a subdirectory etc/, containing several configuration files. A copy of the file sphinx.conf.dist is used as a starting point so copy sphinx.conf.dist to sphinx.conf:

```
radha: $ sudo su - sphinx

radha:sphinx sphinx$ ls etc
example.sql           sphinx-min.conf.dist   sphinx.conf.dist
radha:sphinx sphinx$ cp etc/sphinx.conf.dist etc/sphinx.conf
```

With the editor of choice, edit etc/sphinx.conf. This requires some explaining of the sphinx.conf configuration file.

Sphinx.conf Settings

The sphinx configuration file comprises several sections, which the following sections discuss. This configuration file can be found in the code for this chapter as sphinx.conf.

Sphinx Data Sources

The Sphinx configuration file, `sphinx.conf`, contains various data sources. These sources are defined as:

```
source src1 {
    sql_host    = localhost
    sql_user    = test
    sql_pass    =
    sql_db      = test
    sql_port    = 9312
    sql_query   = select id, content FROM foo_text;

    ... numerous other parameters, options ...

}
```

Data sources have an inheritance scheme. For instance, in this example, `src1` is defined and has its own options. You can have an inherited data source from `src1`, shown as:

```
source src1_delta : src1 {
    ... inherits options/parameters from parent unless otherwise specified ...

    sql_query = select id, content FROM foo_text WHERE id > (SELECT MAX(id) FROM
            index_counter WHERE index_name = 'src1');

}
```

The derived data source inherits all the parameters and options of its parent, unless otherwise overridden. In this example, the entire SQL query was overridden, now additionally specifying the range.

 The `delta` *index is explained in further detail later in the section "Delta Indexes."*

Sphinx Indexes

The Sphinx configuration file can contain various indexes. The actual Sphinx indexes (files) are stored locally on the file system (in `/var/data` of the Sphinx installation directory). Just as with data sources, indexes can also have inheritance. An example of an index section is:

```
index main_idx {
    ... numerous parameters, options ...
    source      = src1
    path        = /usr/local/sphinx/var/data/main_idx

}

index main_idx_stemmed : main_idx {
   ...(inherits everything from parent) ...
```

```
   morphology              = stem_en
}

index main_idx_delta : main_idx {
   source = src1_delta
}
```

In this example, three indexes are defined, two inheriting from `main_idx`. One, `main_idx_stemmed`, only overrides the morphology value, causing the index to include word stemming. The other, `main_idx_delta`, only overrides the data source, using `src1_delta` for the source that it is built from.

One of the best features of Sphinx is a *distributed index*. A distributed index is a distributed (think clustered) index that includes one or more actual indexes, either locally or residing on any number of remote Sphinx servers. `searchd` is the daemon that makes networked index querying possible and makes it so you treat this distributed index as a single, logical, index. Figure 9-1 shows the concept of a distributed index.

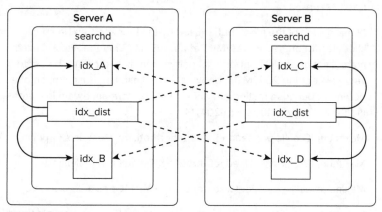

FIGURE 9-1

In Figure 9-1, each of the two servers has two indexes — `idx_A`, `idx_B` on ServerA and `idx_C` and `idx_D` on ServerB. Also, each server has its own `idx_delta` distributed index. For instance, ServerA has defined `idx_dist`, which includes its local indexes `idx_A` and `idx_B` which are on ServerA and as well as the remote indexes `idx_C` and `idx_D` on ServerB. This enables you to search all six indexes on each server from one index! This is a great way to have multiple, smaller, easier-to-manage indexes and still be able to search all of them as one index.

The following is an example of how to define a distributed index:

```
index idx_dist {
   type  = distributed
   agent = ServerA:9312:idx_A
   agent = ServerA:9312:idx_B
   agent = ServerB:9312:idx_C
   agent = ServerB:9312:idx_D
}
```

Indexer Options

The next section in the `sphinx.conf` is the indexer program, named interestingly enough `indexer`. The `indexer`, as mentioned before, is the program that connects to the data source and then builds the index as specified in `sphinx.conf`. Its section appears as follows:

```
indexer {
    # maximum IO calls per second (for I/O throttling)
    # optional, default is 0 (unlimited)
    # max_iops                 = 40
    max_iosize = <according to your machine, in bytes>
}
```

The options for the `indexer` section are shown in Table 9-2.

TABLE 9-2: Indexer Options

OPTION	DESCRIPTION
`mem_limit`	Memory limit of the index buffer used by the indexer. Can be specified in kilobytes (K) or megabytes (M). Default is 32M (32 megabytes). Caveat: mem_limit does NOT support 1 Gigabyte syntax and cannot be set to a value exceeding 2047M (megabytes). This limitation is isn't much of a detriment because testing has shown little performance gain in increasing the value from 1024M to 2047M.
`max_iops`	Maximum IO calls per second. Used for throttling. Default is 0 (unlimited).
`max_iosize`	Maximum IO call size. Used for throttling. Default is 0 (unlimited).
`max_xmlpipe2_field`	Maximum `xmlpipe2` field size (for using XML Pipe as a data source).
`write_buffer`	Maximum size of the write buffers. These are buffers that are allocated in addition to the `mem_limit` setting.

searchd Options

searchd is the daemon that provides distributed indexing. `searchd` accepts search terms, searches indexes — either locally or remotely through other `searchd` instances — and returns the results of those searches, which in turn obtain the actual document content from the data source (the database):

```
searchd {
    listen = 192.168.1.100:9312
    log    = /usr/local/sphinx/var/log/searchd.log
    ... plus numerous other options/parameters ...
}
```

`searchd` options are shown in Table 9-3.

TABLE 9-3: searchd Options

OPTION	DESCRIPTION
listen	The hostname, port or hostname:port or unix socket path that the searchd daemon runs on.
log	The searchd daemon log. Default is searchd.log.
query_log	This log lists all search queries. Default empty, no query logging.
read_timeout	Client read timeout, in seconds. Default is 5 seconds.
max_children	Maximum number of children that will be spawned. Default is 0, unlimited.
max_matches	The maximum number of matches, per-index, kept in RAM. This is per-query. Despite this limit, if you have two million matches and the value is set to 1K matches, searchd still processes all the two million matches and tracks the 1000 best matches at every given moment, but never keeps two million matches in RAM at once. The point here is that max_matches is not a detrimental setting. It only limits RAM use for those matches.
seamless_rotate	Whether or not to pre-open indexes upon index pickup. As of version 0.9.9, new indexes can be picked up on the fly, without restarting searchd.
preopen-indexes	Whether to pre-open all index files, or open them per each query. Optional, default is 0 (do not pre-open).
unlink_old	Whether or not to unlink old indexes upon index rotation.
attr_flush_period	Timeout for flushing attribute updates to disk in seconds.
ondisk_dict_default	Whether is not to use an on-disk dictionary. Default is 0, meaning the setting is off, hence pre-caching dictionaries in RAM.
mva_updates_pool	Size of shared pool for attribute updates, if set at all. This disables attribute flushes.
max_packet_size	Maximum packet size for both query packets from clients and responses from agents. The default is 8MB.
crash_log_path	If set, this specifies the log that records queries that crash.
max_filters	Maximum number of filters. The default is 256.
max_filter_values	Maximum number of values per filter. The default is 4096.
listen_backlog	Length of socket listen queue. The default is 5.

continues

TABLE 9-3 *(continued)*

OPTION	DESCRIPTION
read_buffer	Read-buffer size, per-keyword. The default is 256K.
read_unhinted	Un-hinted read size used when reading hits. The default is 32K.

Data Sources

A data source is what tells Sphinx where to obtain content from to build an index with the indexer. An index can have multiple data sources. As mentioned, Sphinx has a number of data source types — both database and XML pipe. For this example, using MySQL as a data source is the focus of discussion.

For a database source, an SQL query obtains the content from the database, which the indexer then uses to build the index. An index can have multiple *fields* from which it creates full-text indexes. You can also define attributes, which are named values that are associated with each document (in terms of a database, think *column* about the attribute, think *row* about the document) and are used to sort, group, or filter a search. Attributes cannot themselves be searched because they are not indexed. An example of a good use of attributes is in the case where you have a table containing web pages and you indexed the fields `content` and `title`. That table might also have a `category`, `date`, or URL that you would want to sort or filter on — these are the attributes and `content` and `title` represent the full-text indexed fields.

The SQL query you define in your data source can also make use of the special variables `$start` and `$stop`. These values are set by Sphinx using the option `sql_range_query`. If set, the option obtains the minimum and maximum values of a table. The idea of the range query is to obtain the result set containing the min and max values you wanted indexed from the result set. You do this by querying the table in batches, or increments instead of querying the whole table. You specify the number of records per batch using `sql_range_step`. The main reason for query in batches is that querying an entire table can mean a huge result set and can therefore be a resource hog on the database. This is vital for Postgres, which returns the entire result set to the client side first, then returns rows to the application.

You have a number of options to define a data source, as shown in Table 9-4. In addition, the default `sphinx.conf` that comes with Sphinx gives examples of how you can set each option.

TABLE 9-4: Data Source Options

OPTION	DESCRIPTION
type	The type of data source. The types of data sources used are mysql, drizzle, pgsql, mssql, xmlpipe, xmlpipe2, and odbc.
sql_host	The database host that Sphinx connects to.
sql_user	The database user that Sphinx connects as; in the example, this is connecting as the webuser.

OPTION	DESCRIPTION
sql_pass	This is the MySQL password.
sql_db	The schema/database that Sphinx will connect to.
sql_port	The MySQL port; default is 9312.
sql_sock	The MySQL socket file.
sql_query	The database query that the indexer uses to build the index. The table used for this data source is *film_text* as shown in the previous section on FULLTEXT indexes. The primary key (or a unique index) *must* be the first column specified. This is because the index has to have a unique identifier for each "document" (meaning row for the database query). Also, you obviously need your text searches to have the same primary key ID as the row from the database, which you use to retrieve data from the database after a Sphinx index search. After the first primary key column, other columns can follow.
sql_query_info	The query the utility `search` uses for obtaining the data from the database, using the document IDs from the index after searching the index.
mysql_connect_flags	Different connection flags to pass upon connecting to MySQL. For instance, 32 would be to enable compression. Default is 0.
mysql_ssl_cert	Path to the SSL certificate file for connecting to MySQL over SSL.
mysql_ssl_key	Path to the SSL key file for connecting to MySQL over SSL.
mysql_ssl_ca	Path to the SSL certificate authority file for connecting to MySQL over SSL.
mssql_winauth	Use logged-on user credentials to connect to the database if set to 1, when using MS SQL Server.
mssql_unicode	Use Unicode, if set to 1, when using MS SQL Server.
odbc_dsn	Data source name, if using ODBC.
sql_query_pre	The query that is run prior to the primary SQL query.
sql_query_range	The query used to obtain the minimum and maximum ID values of the table, which utilizes minimum and maximum value boundaries if the indexer is using a ranged query
sql_range_step	The number of records per interval when you use a ranged query.

continues

TABLE 9-4 *(continued)*

OPTION	DESCRIPTION
`sql_ranged_throttle`	If set, this option creates a delay between ranged queries, in milliseconds.
`sql_attr_uint`	Name of an unsigned integer column or columns that exist in the result set from the `sql_query` to index on. Also allows for bit size (foo:8) of the attribute.
`sql_attr_bool`	Name(s) of a Boolean column to index. Formally, to store as an attribute because attributes are not (yet) indexed.
`sql_attr_bigint`	Name(s) of bigint column to index.
`sql_attr_timestamp`	Name(s) of timestamp column to index.
`sql_attr_str2ordinal`	Name(s) of string column to index.
`sql_attr_float`	Floating-point column to index.

`sql_attr_multi`	Multi-valued attribute (MVA) attribute declaration. Syntax is `ATTR-TYPE ATTR-NAME 'from' SOURCE-TYPE [;QUERY] [;RANGE-QUERY]`
	
	An example would be:
	
	    `uint tag from query; SELECT id, tag FROM tags`
	
	or ranged:
	
	    `uint tag from ranged-query; \`
	       `SELECT id, tag FROM tags WHERE id>=$start`
	    `AND id<=$end; \`
	       `SELECT MIN(id), MAX(id) FROM tags`

`sql_query_post`	Query run after the main data gathering query. Can be used for a task such as cleanup. Can have multiple queries specified.
`sql_query_post_index`	Query to run after the index is generated. This is especially useful for updating the sphinx counter table. Can have multiple queries specified.
`sql_query_killlist`	Fetches document IDs for the kill-list. The kill-list suppresses matches from preceding indexes in the current query. The default for this option is off.
`unpack_zlib`	Columns to unpack on the index side when indexing multi-value, using zlib compression.
`unpack_mysqlcompress`	Columns to unpack on the index side when indexing multi-value, using mysql compression.

OPTION	DESCRIPTION
unpack_mysqlcompress_maxsize	Maximum unpack length when using MySQL compression.
xmlpipe_command	Path to command that is used to pipe an XML file to the indexer.
xmlpipe_field	Specifies unique fields to be indexed when using XML pipe.
xmlpipe_attr_xxx	Specifies attributes to be indexed when you use XML pipe (same types as `sql_xx` counterparts).
xmlpipe_fixup_utf8	Performs UTF-8 validation and filter out invalid codes. Default is 0 (off).

Defining the *sakila_main* Data Source

To set up a data source using Sphinx with the `sakila` schema, as shown in the previous section using `FULLTEXT` indexes, start by defining the main data source:

```
source sakila_main
{
    sql_host       = localhost
    sql_user       = webuser
    sql_pass       = mypass
    sql_db         = sakila
    sql_port       = 9312  # optional, default is 9312
    sql_sock       = /tmp/mysql.sock
    sql_query      = SELECT film_id, title, description FROM film_text
    sql_query_info = SELECT * FROM film_text WHERE film_id=$id
}
```

Defining the Indexes

Next, the main index is defined, `film_main`. The index is a data structure stored in a file on disk that is the result of building an index. Available `index` options are shown in Table 9-5:

TABLE 9-5: Index Options

OPTION	DESCRIPTION
source	Name of the data source, as specified in the source section.
path	Path to the index file. Indexes are stored in the base sphinx directory under `var/data`.
docinfo	Document attribute values storage method. Values are `extern`, `inline`, and `none`.
mlock	Determines whether to use memory locking for cached data.

continues

TABLE 9-5 *(continued)*

OPTION	DESCRIPTION
morphology	Type of built-in preprocessors such as `stem_en`, `stem_ru`, `soundex`, `libstemmer_german`, and so on. The default is `none`.
min_word_len	Minimum length of words to index. For instance, MySQL's FULLTEXT min word length is 3, but Sphinx allows 1 (default, index everything).
min_stemming_len	The minimum word length at which to enable stemming. Default is 1, meaning stem everything.
stopwords	Stop words files list.
wordforms	`wordforms` file, in `"mapfrom > mapto"` plain text format.
exceptions	Plain text, case-sensitive, space-insensitive, case-sensitive in map-from part one `"AT&T => TATT"` entry per line. Being able to use several tokens is a nice side effect.
charset_type	The `charset` encoding type.
ignore_chars	The ignored characters list.
min_prefix_len	Minimum length of prefix length to index. The default for this option is 0.
min_infix_len	Minimum word infix length to index. The default is 0.
overshort_step	This is the position on overshoot (words less than `min_word_len`). Allowed values are 0 and 1 with the default being 1.
stopword_step	The position increment on stop word. Values are 1 and 0 with the default being 1.
prefix_fields	The fields to prefix.
infix_fields	The fields to infix.
index_exact_words	Determines whether to index original keywords along with stemmed versions. This enables the use of the `=exactform` operator to work.
enable_star	This enables star syntax when you search prefix/infix indexes.
ngram_len	The n-gram length to index.
ngram_chars	The n-gram characters list for CJK indexing. The default is empty.
phrase_boundary	The phrase boundary characters list. The default is empty.
phrase_boundary_step	The phrase boundary word position increment.

OPTION	DESCRIPTION
`html_strip`	Determines whether HTML is stripped out from documents being indexed. The default is 0 (don't strip).
`html_remove_elements`	Determines what HTML elements to remove.
`preopen`	Determines whether pre-open index files open upon restarting searchd.
`ondisk_dict`	Determines whether to keep dictionary (.spi) on disk, or cache it in RAM. This is optional with the default being 0 (RAM only).
`inplace_enable`	Determines whether in-place inversion is enabled (uses 2x less disk, but at a cost of 5–10% indexing speed). This is optional with the default being 0 (use separate temporary files), indexer-only.

Defining the film_main and Its Inherited Indexes

To define the indexes, follow these steps:

1. If you're figuring the `sphinx.conf` for several indexes, you define the first index `film_text`, which is an index of the `film_text` table. Because `film_text` has a default character set of UTF-8, you should set the value for `charset_type` to `utf-8`:

```
index film_main
{
    source        = sakila_main
    path          = /usr/local/sphinx/var/data/film_main
    charset_type  = utf-8
}
```

2. Also, a stemmed index is shown. This index inherits from `film_main` and only overrides the *morphology* option to be an English stemmed index:

```
index film_main_stemmed : film_main
{
        path =
        /usr/local/sphinx/var/data/film_main_stemmed
        morphology = stem_en
}
```

3. A distributed index `film_dist` is defined, using only the local `film_main` index, but as an agent (through `searchd`). This doesn't really show you the full benefit of distributed indexes because it is only used on a single agent. However, the section "Starting Sphinx" discusses distributed indexes.

```
index film_dist
{
        type  = distributed
        agent = localhost:9312:film_main
}
```

Specifying the Indexer Options

The option for the `indexer`, `mem_limit`, is set to 32 megabytes for this installation. This is the maximum amount of memory that the indexer is allowed to use.

```
indexer
{
        mem_limit = 32M
}
```

Specifying the searchd Options

`searchd` options are also defined:

➤ `address`: 127.0.0.1, localhost address will be used.

➤ `port`: searchd port 9312 (default port for `searchd`).

➤ `searchd_log`: The log that shows requests to the local instance of `searchd`.

➤ `query_log`: Shows what queries were run against indexes.

➤ `max_children`: The maximum number of search processes that can run.

➤ `pid_file`: The pid file used by `searchd`.

➤ `max_matches`: The maximum number of matches returned (1000).

➤ `seamless_rotate`: Set this to 1. This means `searchd` can be restarted without any effect on applications using `searchd`.

```
searchd
{
        listen          = 127.0.0.1
        port            = 9312
        log             = /usr/local/sphinx/var/log/searchd.log
        query_log       = /usr/local/sphinx/var/log/query.log
        read_timeout    = 5
        max_children    = 30
        pid_file        = /usr/local/sphinx/var/log/searchd.pid
        max_matches     = 1000
        seamless_rotate = 1


}
```

Starting Sphinx

Now that the `sphinx.conf` is set up, and you have a running Sphinx system, you will need to run the indexer and start the search daemon, `searchd`.

Running the Indexer

At this point, you have not yet run the indexer. When you do so, the indexer runs the queries you specified for your data sources and then builds the local indexes you specified. Because they are distributed indexes, the distributed indexes are not and cannot be built by the indexer.

To run the indexer for the first time from within the main Sphinx directory (*sphinx* user home directory in this example, `/usr/local/sphinx`) use the following code:

```
./bin/indexer --all
Sphinx 0.9.9-id64-release (r2117)
Copyright (c) 2001-2009, Andrew Aksyonoff

using config file '/usr/local/sphinx/etc/sphinx.conf'...
indexing index 'film_main'...
collected 1000 docs, 0.1 MB
sorted 0.0 Mhits, 100.0% done
total 1000 docs, 108056 bytes
total 0.046 sec, 2339583 bytes/sec, 21651.58 docs/sec
indexing index 'film_main_stemmed'...
collected 1000 docs, 0.1 MB
sorted 0.0 Mhits, 100.0% done
total 1000 docs, 108056 bytes
total 0.039 sec, 2746162 bytes/sec, 25414.25 docs/sec
distributed index 'film_dist' can not be directly indexed; skipping.
total 2 reads, 0.000 sec, 111.3 kb/call avg, 0.1 msec/call avg
total 10 writes, 0.000 sec, 55.6 kb/call avg, 0.0 msec/call avg
```

The line "`distributed index 'film_dist' can not be directly indexed`" simply means the specified distributed index, `film_dist`, cannot be indexed as a local file.

Starting the Search Daemon

To perform queries against your indexes and utilize distributed indexes, you need to have the search daemon, `searchd`, running.

To start `searchd`:

```
./bin/searchd
Sphinx 0.9.9-id64-release (r2117)
Copyright (c) 2001-2009, Andrew Aksyonoff

using config file '/usr/local/sphinx/etc/sphinx.conf'...
listening on all interfaces, port=9312
```

You do not have to explicitly run `searchd` backgrounded because it automatically runs as a daemon in the background.

Now the indexes are ready to be searched! Test searches (only against local indexes) can be performed using the `search` utility. You can also use SphinxAPI (through PHP) or SphinxQL (more about this in the section "Searching Sphinx") to test.

Searching Sphinx

Sphinx has its own query language, similar to MySQL FULLTEXT indexes but it also offers options for searching text.

Search Modes

Sphinx has different search modes, which are specified in the program and which you can set using the Sphinx API. The search modes are shown in Table 9-6:

TABLE 9-6: Sphinx Search Modes

SEARCH MODE	DESCRIPTION
SPH_MATCH_ALL	Matches all query words. This mode is used by default.
SPH_MATCH_ANY	Matches any of the query words.
SPH_MATCH_PHRASE	Matches query as a phrase, requiring perfect match.
SPH_MATCH_BOOLEAN	Matches query as a Boolean expression.
SPH_MATCH_EXTENDED	An alias for SPH_MATCH_EXTENDED2.
SPH_MATCH_EXTENDED2	Matches the query using the second version of extended matching mode (as of version 0.9.9). Matches query as an expression in the Sphinx internal query language.
SPH_MATCH_FULLSCAN	Matches the query forcibly using the *full scan* mode which means all the indexed documents are considered as matching. Such queries still apply filters, sorting, and group by, but do not perform any full-text searching.

Sort Modes

Sphinx also allows you to see different sort modes. These modes set what type of sorting mechanism Sphinx uses when it sorts search results.

TABLE 9-7: Sphinx Sort Modes

SORT MODE	DESCRIPTION
SPH_SORT_RELEVANCE	Sorts by relevance in descending order with best matches first.
SPH_SORT_ATTR_DESC	Sorts by an attribute in descending order with biggest attribute values first.
SPH_SORT_ATTR_ASC	Sorts by attribute in ascending order, smallest attribute values first.
SPH_SORT_TIME_SEGMENTS	Sorts by time segments — last hour, day, week, etc — in descending order, and then by relevance in descending order.
SPH_SORT_EXTENDED	Sorts by SQL-like combination of columns in ascending or descending order. This one is "king" according to Andrew, the creator of Sphinx, allowing you do anything the legacy sort modes allow.
SPH_SORT_EXPR	Sorts by arithmetic expression.

Boolean Query Syntax

The Boolean query syntax is as follows:

➤ AND: Both terms must be found, anywhere in the source. It can be specified either with a space (implicit AND), or an ampersand (&). For example, both the terms *technical* and *writer*.

```
technical writer
technical & writer
```

➤ OR: One or both terms. Either *technical* or *writer*, or both.

```
technical | writer
```

➤ NOT: (the hyphen) Negation of the term. In this example, the term would have to have *technical*, but not *writer*.

```
technical -writer
```

➤ Grouping, so you can have multiple terms specified: In this example you would specify both *technical* and *writer* or *database* and *administrator*.

```
(technical  writer) | (database administrator)
```

Extended Query Syntax

Boolean query syntax allows you to have proximity searching as well as specify fields to search against.

➤ **AND:** Searches for *technical* and *writer* against only the `title` column.

```
@title technical writer
```

➤ **Explicit AND:** This searches `title` for *technical* and *writer* and searches for *bhagavad* against the `description` field:

```
@title technical writer & @description bhagavad
```

➤ **Field position limit modifier:** Specifies searching the first 30 characters of the `description` column for the term `monty`.

```
@description[30] monty
```

➤ **Multiple field search operator:** The following would search for term `andrew` within the description and title columns both.

```
@(title,description) andrew
```

➤ **All field search operator:** In this example, the term `Andrew` would be searched for in all columns.

```
@* andrew
```

➤ **EXACT phrase:** Only the exact phrase within the quotes would return a result.

```
"technical writer"
```

➤ **Proximity:** Allows for no more than five words in between the two terms. This means that the phrase *technical writer* and the phrase *technical expertise, database administration, novel writer* would both be found.

```
"technical writer"~5
```

➤ **Strict order operator:** This will only match words in the exact order. This example would only match *patram push toyam phalam* in the exact order.

```
patram << pushpam << toyam << phalam
```

➤ **Exact form modifier:** This makes it so that there will only be a match if the form of the term is exactly as specified. In the snippet below, The order of any match would require that *Sphinx*, *fulltext*, and *index* be in that exact order.

```
=Sphinx is a =fulltext =index
```

➤ **Field-start and field-end modifier:** The first example would match anything in the hello world field, but not Patrick says hello field. The second example would search "*Andrews FielD*" or even "*Andrews?!! Field!!*" but not the field "*Andrews football field*"

```
^hello
^Andrews field$
```

The Search Utility

Whether or not your index is working, the utility search is a useful tool for debugging — specifically if you are trying to determine if there's a problem with Sphinx and how you've generated an index, or if there's a problem with your application. It bypasses your application as well as searchd to search the index directly.

> The search *utility does not work with distributed indexes because it searches the index at a file-level versus performing the search through* searchd. *Other ways to test your indexes include using a PHP program (which uses the SphinxAPI) or SphinxQL.*

search has the following options:

```
./bin/search
Sphinx 0.9.9-id64-release (r2117)
Copyright (c) 2001-2009, Andrew Aksyonoff

Usage: search [OPTIONS] <word1 [word2 [word3 [...]]]>

Options are:
-c, --config <file> use given config file instead of defaults
-i, --index <index> search given index only (default: all indexes)
-a, --any           match any query word (default: match all words)
-b, --boolean       match in boolean mode
```

```
-p, --phrase           match exact phrase
-e, --extended         match in extended mode
-f, --filter <attr> <v>   only match if attribute attr value is v
-s, --sortby <CLAUSE>     sort matches by 'CLAUSE' in sort_extended mode
-S, --sortexpr <EXPR>     sort matches by 'EXPR' DESC in sort_expr mode
-o, --offset <offset>     print matches starting from this offset (default: 0)
-l, --limit <count> print this many matches (default: 20)
-q, --noinfo           don't print document info from SQL database
-g, --group <attr>   group by attribute named attr
-gs,--groupsort <expr>     sort groups by <expr>
--sort=date            sort by date, descending
--rsort=date           sort by date, ascending
--sort=ts              sort by time segments
--stdin                read query from stdin
```

```
This program (CLI search) is for testing and debugging purposes only;
it is NOT intended for production use.
```

For instance, to search for the terms *technical* and *writer*, limiting your results to only three, `search` is run with the following options:

```
    ./bin/search -i film_main -e 'technical writer' -l 3
Sphinx 0.9.9-id64-release (r2117)
Copyright (c) 2001-2009, Andrew Aksyonoff

using config file '/usr/local/sphinx/etc/sphinx.conf'...
index 'film_main': query 'technical writer ':
returned 76 matches of 76 total in 0.007 sec

displaying matches:
1. document=19, weight=2582
      film_id=19
      title=AMADEUS HOLY
      description=A Emotional Display of a Pioneer And a Technical Writer who must
      Battle a Man in A Baloon
2. document=43, weight=2582
      film_id=43
      title=ATLANTIS CAUSE
      description=A Thrilling Yarn of a Feminist And a Hunter who must Fight a
      Technical Writer in A Shark Tank
3. document=44, weight=2582
      film_id=44
      title=ATTACKS HATE
      description=A Fast-Paced Panorama of a Technical Writer And
    a Mad Scientist who must Find a Feminist in An
    Abandoned Mine Shaft

words:
1. 'technical': 76 documents, 76 hits
2. 'writer': 76 documents, 76 hits
```

As you can see, Sphinx not only finds results, but also gives you information about the search, such as the weight of what was found, as well as a summary of all results found.

Or, say you want to search only the title column for the exact phrase *attacks hate*, with no limit on the results:

```
./bin/search -i film_main -e '@title("attacks hate")'
Sphinx 0.9.9-id64-release (r2117)
Copyright (c) 2001-2009, Andrew Aksyonoff

using config file '/usr/local/sphinx/etc/sphinx.conf'...
index 'film_main': query '@title("attacks hate") ':
returned 1 matches of 1 total in 0.001 sec

displaying matches:
1. document=44, weight=2697
        film_id=44
        title=ATTACKS HATE
        description=A Fast-Paced Panorama of a Technical Writer And a
        Mad Scientist who must Find a Feminist in An Abandoned
        Mine Shaft

words:
1. 'attacks': 3 documents, 3 hits
2. 'hate': 2 documents, 2 hits
```

The search utility handles taking the results from a search (the `film_id` values) and retrieving the results from `film_text` using the query that was specified in `sphinx.conf` by the parameter `sql_query_info`, which is located in the `sakila_main` data source section.

SphinxQL

Just when you thought there couldn't possibly be any more features to Sphinx, think again! As of version 0.9.9, the `searchd` daemon had added to it the MySQL binary network protocol. This makes it possible to use the MySQL client API to talk to Sphinx! This means you can use the MySQL client, `mysql`, as well as any PHP MySQL client API to talk to Sphinx! In addition, Sphinx has a tiny subset of SQL dubbed *SphinxQL*. This allows you to not only connect to `searchd` with any MySQL client, but also run SQL-like queries against Sphinx!

In the following example, the query that searches for the words *Small Business* in proximity of one and not with the word *Big* is performed, and it returns one record.

```
sphinx@hanuman:~$ mysql -h 127.0.0.1 -P 9312
Welcome to the MySQL monitor.  Commands end with ; or \g.
Your MySQL connection id is 1
Server version: 0.9.9-rc2 (r1785)

Type 'help;' or '\h' for help. Type '\c' to clear the buffer.

mysql> select * from url where match('@content "Small -Big business"~2') ;
+------+--------+
| id   | weight |
+------+--------+
|  487 |   1466 |
+------+--------+
1 row in set (0.01 sec)
```

The *id* column is the ID value you use to retrieve the actual content from MySQL and the `weight` column is how Sphinx weights the document relevancy.

To use SphinxQL, all you need to add to your `sphinx.conf` is another `listen` option line (shown here after the original Sphinx `listen` option)

```
listen                  = localhost:9312
listen                  = localhost:9306:mysql41
```

This means that `searchd` answers on both ports 9306 and 9312, though 9312 is the only port you can connect to searchd using a MySQL client.

One Last Step to Using Sphinx

You can perform one more step to use full-text searching as shown in the following code:

```
mysql> ALTER TABLE film_text DROP INDEX idx_title_description;

mysql> ALTER TABLE film_text ENGINE=InnoDB;
```

You can now use InnoDB if you want! Because Sphinx is an external index to MySQL, there is no longer the need for the FULLTEXT index that was created on `film_text`, so the MyISAM-only restriction no longer applies. You can use whatever storage engine you like with Sphinx. The only requirement is that Sphinx can select data out of that table, as defined in the data sources section of `sphinx.conf`.

Delta Indexes

As previously mentioned, Sphinx provides the functionality of distributed indexes. This makes it possible for you to spread indexes across a cluster of machines. For instance, you could have millions of records of textual data. With Sphinx, you can arrange it so the entire range of data is spread out over this cluster of machines.

Figure 9-2 is another illustration of distributed indexes, but the purpose of this example is to show, for the sake of conversation, a simple arrangement of three servers, each running four `searchd` daemons and each serving an index containing 250,000 records. The numbers listed represent the ID values of the documents (database row IDs) that each index comprises. With distributed indexes, an entire range from record 1 through record 2,999,999 is serviced from a distributed index.

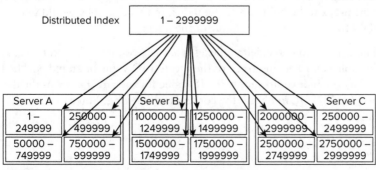

FIGURE 9-2

What about new data that is incrementally added on a regular basis? Sphinx indexes are not automatically updated as FULLTEXT indexes (which is one of the reasons FULLTEXT indexes are slow and Sphinx indexes are so fast). How do you have some means to provide an updating functionality? The answer to this question is using a *delta index*.

 The realtime index backend is another means to update functionality and it will be available by the time this book is printed.

A delta index is basically a smaller index that you regenerate more often. Sphinx indexes can be generated very fast. However, you wouldn't want to regenerate your entire data set on a regular basis. The solution to this is to more regularly regenerate a relatively small index that is composed of the most recent records that have been inserted into the database. Because a distributed index can be treated as a logical index, the user (the application) of Sphinx has no idea that there is a smaller underlying index being regenerated. Also, another feature is that the indexer program has the ability to transparently restart searchd after completing the index regeneration.

Figure 9-3 shows just how a delta index works.

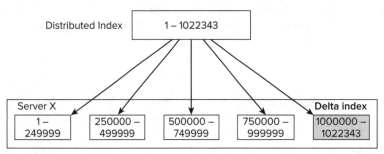

FIGURE 9-3

Figure 9-3 shows that you have an arbitrary server with four primary indexes that are not regularly regenerated and the delta index, which is generated for every given number of new records inserted into the source table — as you recall, defined as a source the sphinx.conf. Each index would have a common parent source, inheriting everything about the parent index except in the sql_query that selects the specific range for the index to be built. The delta index, in this example, would select everything from ID of 1000000 to the maximum ID value of the table.

The other component of the machinery to make delta indexes work is a counter table, in this case called sphinx_counter. This table is for keeping track of the greatest ID value of an index. The ID values from this table are used by the indexer to supply the ID value for the sql_query in the data source of the index when querying MySQL to obtain the content for indexing. You can also use timestamp columns to do this.

```
CREATE TABLE sphinx_counter (
    id int(11) NOT NULL,
    max_id int(11) NOT NULL,
```

```
    index_name varchar(32) NOT NULL,
    PRIMARY KEY  (id),
    KEY index_name (index_name)
) ENGINE=InnoDB
```

The indexer uses the positional information in the table `sphinx_counter` to obtain the maximum and minimum IDs to determine what records are included in the indexes. The indexer uses this to determine what data should be selected when indexing.

An example of a delta index and how you use the `sphinx_counter` table is if you have your main `url` index that contains all records having an ID value less than the value of column `max_id` in the table `sphinx_counter`. The delta index, `url_delta`, will contain records having their ID value starting from the value of the column `sphinx_counter.max_id` and no upward limit.

Where the main index ends and the delta index starts is only set when the main index is re-indexed. The delta index grows over time, and at some point, you merge the two them. The break point is set to the maximum of the main index, which now contains what was previously in the delta, and the delta is rebuilt with a starting point equal to the maximum of the newly merged index.

Each index has exactly one entry in this table and the position data is updated during indexing.

An example showing the positional data of a running setup is:

```
mysql> select * from sphinx_counter;
+----+--------+-----------+---------------------+
| id | max_id | index_name| last_updated        |
+----+--------+-----------+---------------------+
|  1 |   1133 | url       | 2009-03-02 11:05:30 |
|  2 |   1181 | url_delta | 2009-03-02 11:12:12 |
+----+--------+-----------+---------------------+
```

For example, the main index, `url`, contains records with the `url.id` value of 0 through 1133, and the delta index, `url_delta`, contains records with the `url.id` value of 1134 through 1181.

The entry in the `sphinx_counter` counter table for the delta index is not necessary, but an added informational benefit to show you the state of what records your indexes represent. The single entry for the main index is sufficient to delineate the extents of the main and the delta indexes for indexing.

To set up Sphinx to utilize a delta index, you would define the data sources that will be used:

1. The first source, `url`, is set to use the MySQL server running on localhost on port 9312. The `sql_query_pre` option defines the query that is run prior to the main document fetching query. In this case, the `sphinx_counter` table is updated with the `max(id)` value from the `url` table, moving the positional information up to represent the index that is about to be regenerated.

2. The `sql_query` option specifies the main query that will run. The primary key or other unique identifier must always be the first column specified in this query. In this instance, it is the id column of the `url` table. This makes it so when you perform a search against Sphinx, you will obtain one or more values of the primary key id, which you will subsequently use to retrieve the actual data from MySQL, making for a fast lookup.

About this query: it performs a join of url with url_content to obtain the actual content from the blob table as well as the other columns specified after the primary key value. These columns create a full-text index and are therefore searchable. Sphinx has a very flexible query language, allowing you to specify on which columns to search. Also, this query uses a WHERE clause to select records less than or equal to the value in the sphinx_counter table for the main index. This is the mechanism that applies an extent to the data being gathered.

3. The option `sql_query_info` provides a query to the search command-line program, which is good for running test queries against your index. Do note that this does not search against Sphinx through the Sphinx search daemon, `searchd` — it searches on the index itself, so it does not work with distributed indexes.

```
source url
        {
                type                    = mysql
                sql_host                = localhost
                sql_user                = narada
                sql_pass                = n@r@d@
                sql_db                  = narada
                sql_port                = 9312
                sql_query_pre           = UPDATE sphinx_counter SET max_id=
                                          (SELECT MAX(id) FROM url)
                                          WHERE index_name = 'url'
                sql_query               = SELECT id, content FROM url_content
                                          WHERE id <= (SELECT max_id
                                          FROM sphinx_counter
                                          WHERE index_name = 'url')
                sql_query_info          = SELECT * FROM url_content WHERE id=$id
        }
```

4. The source for the delta index, *url_delta*, is defined. The notation url_delta : url means that *url_delta* will inherit every option from the data source URLs, unless otherwise overridden. In this case, the options `sql_query_pre` and `sql_query` are overridden to specify a different range than is used with the *url* data source. For the *url_delta* data source, all records greater than the *max_id* value for the data source *url* are specified:

```
source url_delta : url
{
        sql_query_pre           = UPDATE sphinx_counter SET max_id=
                                  (SELECT MAX(id) FROM url)
                                  WHERE index_name = 'url_delta'
        sql_query               = SELECT id, content FROM url_content
                                  WHERE id > (SELECT max_id
                                      FROM sphinx_counter
                                      WHERE index_name = 'url')
}
```

5. The indexes are defined. The options shown here are the most important. The option `source` defines the data source that is used to build this index, in this case the source `url` is used. The option `path` specifies the path and base name of the actual index files. Other index options are omitted for the sake of brevity.

```
index url
{
        source                  = url
        path                    = /usr/local/sphinx/var/data/url
        ...
}
```

6. The delta index, `url_delta`, inherits everything from the index `url`, except path and source, which it overrides. Because the source for `url_delta` is also called `url_delta`, this is the data source that has a different range than `url`, hence `url_delta` is a smaller index composed of a smaller range, the topmost records, of the database table `url`.

```
index url_delta : url
{
        source                  = url_delta
        path                    = /usr/local/sphinx/var/data/url_delta
}
```

7. Next, the distributed index `dist_url` is defined. This is the glue that makes the delta index and main index work together as one index. Queries run against this distributed index without the user ever knowing that the index is made up of parts.

```
index dist_url
{
        type                    = distributed
        agent                   = localhost:3312:url
        agent                   = localhost:3312:url_delta
        agent_connect_timeout   = 1000
        agent_query_timeout     = 3000
}
```

8. The final piece in making delta indexes work is that the indexer has another feature — index merging. This is the feature that you use at a given interval in which you merge the delta index into the main index or indexes. For the sake of having fast index regeneration of the delta index, you cannot allow your delta index to grow too large.

The indexer configuration is simple enough, and the option `mem_limit` specifies how much memory is used for the indexer, when it runs, to generate indexes.

```
indexer
{
        # memory limit, in bytes, kilobytes (16384K) or megabytes (256M)
        # optional, default is 32M, max is 2047M, recommended is 256M to
        # 1024M
        mem_limit                       = 32M



}
```

9. The searchd daemon is configured in the following section. The listen option specifies which port or socket the daemon binds to. In this case, none are specified, so all interfaces are used. The log option specifies the log for the searchd daemon — this log will log the status of the searchd daemon. The query_log option specifies a log used to log search queries run against searchd.

The other options set timeout values, max number of children to run, a pid file, maximum number of matches returned, and whether the searchd daemon can be restarted seamlessly after running the indexer.

Also listed is the option seamless_rotate. As mentioned, this feature makes it possible to have the delta index generated without users of the index noticing. When you run the indexer, searchd is seamlessly restarted once the indexer completes (kill HUP).

```
searchd
{
        log                      = /usr/local/sphinx/var/log/searchd.log
        query_log                = /usr/local/sphinx/var/log/query.log
        read_timeout             = 5
        client_timeout           = 300
        max_children             = 30
        pid_file                 = /usr/local/sphinx/var/log/searchd.pid
        max_matches              = 1000
        seamless_rotate          = 1
        preopen_indexes          = 0
        unlink_old               = 1
        mva_updates_pool         = 1M
        max_packet_size          = 8M
        max_filters              = 256
        max_filter_values        = 4096

}
```

Merging Indexes

As mentioned already, you would have a primary index that you merge with a delta index on a particular frequency. In order to do this, you run the indexer program with the main and delta index names, as shown in the following code example:

```
sphinx@hanuman:~$ ./bin/indexer --merge url url_delta --rotate
Sphinx 0.9.9-rc2 (r1785)
Copyright (c) 2001-2009, Andrew Aksyonoff

using config file '/usr/local/sphinx/etc/sphinx.conf'...
FATAL: no merge source index 'url_detla'
sphinx@hanuman:~$ ./bin/indexer --merge url url_delta --rotate
Sphinx 0.9.9-rc2 (r1785)
Copyright (c) 2001-2009, Andrew Aksyonoff

using config file '/usr/local/sphinx/etc/sphinx.conf'...
merged 63.4 Kwords
merged in 0.424 sec
total 457 reads, 0.010 sec, 32.6 kb/call avg, 0.0 msec/call avg
total 60 writes, 0.051 sec, 246.2 kb/call avg, 0.8 msec/call avg
rotating indices: succesfully sent SIGHUP to searchd (pid=9238).
```

The --rotate argument simply means that searchd is restarted seamlessly after the index is finished being merged.

DEVELOPING APPLICATIONS THAT USE SPHINX

In applications you write yourself, you have to implement the same type of functionality that the search utility gives you, except you'll use the Sphinx client API, whereas the search utility performs the search on an index at a file-level. To use Sphinx, your application will perform a search against Sphinx on whatever index you specify, obtaining the unique document or record IDs of the results found in your search, and then you query MySQL against the table of the data source with those IDs to obtain the results from the database. With these results, you can generate *excerpts*. As part of the Sphinx API, Sphinx includes the means for generating excerpts — which are text with the original search terms enclosed in HTML tags, such as bold, emphasis, and so on (<b> .. </b>), to highlight the original search terms.

Sphinx and PHP

The Sphinx source distribution comes with an API for PHP and is a pure PHP implementation for the SphinxAPI. You can find the main PHP API file in the api directory in the top-level source directory as the file sphinxapi.php. Ensure this file is copied to a location where you put common PHP library files. In this example, /usr/lib/php5 is used (Ubuntu). To begin using Sphinx with PHP, a simple program, sphinx_ch09.php, is written that uses the *sakila* database and a distributed index called *film_dist* which is the full-text index of the *sakila* table *film*.

Like so many client APIs, the first thing you need to do is to instantiate a client object and then connect to a server or servers

```
require('/usr/lib/php5/sphinxapi.php');

# mysql options
$dbhost = '192.168.1.106';
$dbuser = 'sakila';
$dbpass = 's@k1la';
$dbschema = 'sakila';

# connect to mysql
$dbh = new mysqli($dbhost, $dbuser, $dbpass, $dbschema);

# sphinx host and port
$host = '192.168.1.106';
$port = 9312;
# instantiate a SphinxClient object
$sphinx= new SphinxClient();
# connect to the server
$sphinx->SetServer($host, $port);
# set match mode
$sphinx->SetMatchMode(SPH_MATCH_EXTENDED2);
# set the sort mode
$sphinx->SetSortMode(SPH_SORT_ASC);

# the index to perform searches against
```

```
$search_index = 'film_dist';
# the index to build excerpts against. Cannot be a distributed index
$excerpt_index = 'film_main';
# the search term for this example
$search_term = 'Ancient India';
# the search query
$search_query = "@description $search_term";

# perform the search
$search_results = $sphinx->Query($search_query, $search_index);
```

The result set of the search, `$search_results`, is a multi-dimensional array chock full of data for the returned result. It contains the standard members shown in Table 9-8:

TABLE 9-8: $search_results Standard Members

MEMBER	DESCRIPTION
error	A string containing an error message, if any.
warning	A string containing a warning message, if any.
Status	The numeric status code returned from the search.
Fields	An array containing the string names of each field in the index.
Attrs	An array of string attributes returned from the result set.
Matches	The member of the result set that fetches the data from the database. `matches` is a multi-dimensional array containing numeric key values pointing to arrays. The value of the key is the document ID (the id value it was indexed by) for each matched document. Each document id key value points to an array containing the members with `weight` being the numeric weight of the match and `attrs` containing the attributes for the match.
words	A multi-dimensional array containing string key values, each being a word in the search query. Each of these keys points to a two-member array. The array for each word contains two members: `docs`, a numeric value for the total number of documents the word was found in, and `matches`, the total number of matches found for that word, regardless of how many documents it was found in.

Next you want to obtain the actual document content for each match. As mentioned, the result set member, `matches`, contains what you need to do this. The query in this example returned one result set. To see what `matches` gives you, the following codes shows `matches` from the result set `$search_result` that would be found in the search above:

```
var_dump($search_result['matches']);
```

Produces:

```
array(20) {
  [8]=>
  array(2) {
```

```
        ["weight"]=>
        string(4) "2583"
        ["attrs"]=>
        array(0) {
        }
    }
    [29]=>
    array(2) {
        ["weight"]=>
        string(4) "2583"
        ["attrs"]=>
        array(0) {
        }
    }
}
```

...and many more matches...

The key value for the single array is 8 and is the ID value of the document corresponding to the primary key of the *film* table, *film_id*. You would then need to build a query obtaining the document having a film_id of 8:

```
# base query, then use explode to build the IN list for film_id values
$query= 'SELECT film_id, title, description from film WHERE film_id IN ('
        . implode(",", array_keys($search_results["matches"])) . ')';

$db_results= $dbh->query($query);
```

At this point, you need to start constructing two arrays: one you pass to build excerpts which is called $docs, and another array, called $results, combines the excerpts with the original data in order for when you print the results.

```
$results = array();
$docs = array();

# push each row into the $results array to maintain order
while ($row = $db_results->fetch_array())
{
    array_push($results, array('film_id'     => $row["film_id"],
                               'title'       => $row["title"],
                               'description' => $row["description"]) );

    array_push($docs, $row["description"]);

}
```

Now that $docs has all the descriptions for each match, you can obtain excerpts. An excerpt essentially takes the original text that the index was built against and makes a smaller, printable paragraph, which highlights the search term. There are a number of options you can set to pass to the excerpt building method, BuildExcerpts(). Here these are set in the $options array.

```
# Note: excerpt index used for building indexes must be an on-disk index
# non-distributed index
$options = array('before_match'  => '<b>',
                 'after_match'   => '</b>',
                 'around'        => 3,
```

```
                    'single_passage'   => 0,
                    'chunk_separator'  => '...',
                    'limit'            => 180);

    # obtain the excerpts. Notice passing $docs
    $excerpts = $sphinx->BuildExcerpts($docs,
                                       $excerpt_index,
                                       $search_word,
                                       $options);
```

The options passed to `BuildExcerpts()` in this example are:

TABLE 9-9: Options Passed to BuildExcerpts()

OPTION	DESCRIPTION
before_match	The opening HTML tag to insert before the search term.
after_match	The closing HTML tag to insert after the search term.
around	The number of words to pick around each matching keywords (search term) block. Default is 5.
single_passage	Determines whether to extract single best passage only. Boolean, default is false.
chunk_separator	A string to insert between snippet chunks (passages). Default is " ... ".
limit	Maximum snippet size. Default is 256.

There are more options to you can use. For more information, please refer to the Sphinx manual section 6.7.1, at the URL `http://www.sphinxsearch.com/docs/manual-0.9.9.html#sources`.

Now that you have excerpts, and because the order of `$excerpts` is the same as `$results`, you can now print the results!

```
for ($x= 0; $x < count($results); $x++) {
  print "<p>" . $results[$x]["title"] . "</p>\n";
  print "<p>" . $excerpts[$x] . "</p>\n";
}
```

The output appears as:

```
<p>Moose vs. Monkey</p>
<p>A Epic Tale of a Moose And a Girl who must Confront a Monkey in
 <b>Ancient</b> <b>India</b></p>
<p>ANTITRUST TOMATOES</p>
<p>A Fateful Yarn of a Womanizer And a Feminist who must Succumb a Database
    Administrator in <b>Ancient</b> <b>India</b></p>
<p>BIRDCAGE CASPER</p>
<p>A Fast-Paced Saga of a Frisbee And a Astronaut who must Overcome a Feminist
```

```
      in <b>Ancient</b> <b>India</b></p>
<p>CALIFORNIA BIRDS</p>
<p>A Thrilling Yarn of a Database Administrator And a Robot who must Battle a
    Database Administrator in <b>Ancient</b> <b>India</b></p>
```

...and more results...

This is very simple, plain HTML, but imagine — you could design as elaborate and aesthetically pleasing a results page for a search engine website as you like. The important thing is that you have the data, as well as the excerpts having the search terms within bold tags. The rest is icing on the cake and is up to you!

Now you have been introduced to using PHP with Sphinx so you can add search functionality to your PHP applications. This was a simple PHP program intended to introduce you to using Sphinx and PHP. Chapter 10 has a more complete PHP application example using Sphinx.

For more information about the complete Sphinx PHP API, please consult the Sphinx manual, Sphinx API reference at `http://www.sphinxsearch.com/docs/manual-0.9.9.html#api-reference`.

SUMMARY

This chapter introduced you to full-text search options available as a PHP programmer using MySQL. Using the `sakila` database for search data, you were first introduced to MySQL FULLTEXT indexes, which were the traditional way you would have implemented search functionality in your PHP applications. Next, you were introduced, using the same `sakila` database, to the Sphinx full-text search engine that offers a huge number of improvements over MySQL FULLTEXT indexes, some of these benefits being that you can use any table type in MySQL with Sphinx as well as the benefit of using distributed indexes.

You were shown how to obtain, compile, configure and use Sphinx, particularly how to set up a distributed index, delta index and a counter table for managing how the delta index is merged with the main index. You saw how there are a number of ways to access Sphinx: SphinxQL, SphinxAPI (with PHP), as well as the search utility. Finally, you were walked through writing a simple PHP program that uses both Sphinx and MySQL that can be the core of a search application written in PHP.

10

Multi-tasking in PHP and MySQL

WHAT'S IN THIS CHAPTER?

➤ Efficiently multi-tasking in PHP

➤ Using Gearman to multi-task and farm out work

➤ Seeing an application put Gearman and various other components
   discussed in this book together to build a search application

How many times have you developed a web application that has some functionality which requires running an external program or even forking a separate process? This is not something you generally like to do from your web application because you want to make it run as fast and efficiently as possible, yet you want to provide a lot of functionality for end users. Thus the problem arises of how to get a fast but full-featured application that can process as much as possible.

GEARMAN

Many years ago (in the Internet time line) a web site, livejournal.com, was facing a similar dilemma. Users were uploading so many pictures to the web site that had to be processed into their respective accounts. This included resizing functionality such as creating thumbnails or reducing the raw image size to something more appropriate for the web site to display. These pictures mostly consisted of kittens — millions of pictures of kittens — overloading the web application that is Livejournal. Then the creative mind of Brad Fitzpatrick formulated a great idea to deal with this overload: have a server that spawns processes that do things such as processing pictures of kittens, outside of the web server application. Thus came the advent of Gearman.

WHAT IS GEARMAN?

Gearman comprises a client component, one or more job servers that assign jobs requested by clients, and worker programs that register themselves for work and then carry out those job requests. It provides a distributed application framework. Gearman is used to farm out work to other machines in a distributed fashion, dispatching function calls to machines that are better suited to do work, to do work in parallel, to load balance many function calls, or to call functions between languages (as described on the project site). Gearman is multi-threaded and is known to be able to carry out 50 thousand jobs per-second. Hence, Gearman is the solution to splitting some functionality from your web application and handling it separately. Gearman is the ultimate tool for making this a reality. As Joe Stump from Digg put it:

> *"The way I like to think of Gearman is as a massively distributed, massively fault-tolerant fork mechanism."*

Some of the well-known sites using the C version of Gearman are:

➤ Digg: 45+ servers, 400 thousand jobs a day

➤ Yahoo: 120+ servers, 12 million jobs a day

➤ Livejournal, SixApart, DealNews, `Xing.com`, and others

Gearman was originally written in Perl, but the job servers and client API were recently rewritten in C by Eric Day because he wanted better performance. The process gearmand is the actual job server — it receives requests for jobs and then assigns them. The job server also keeps track of what workers are available and which ones have been tasked with jobs. It then handles the results from a worker, passing them back to the client that requested the job.

The basic Gearman setup consists of a client, a worker, and gearmand, the job server. The client creates a job request to send to the job server. The job server delegates the job to an appropriate worker and returns a response to the client when assigned. Workers, when started, register themselves for a particular kind of job, and when the job server receives a request for that type of job, it assigns the appropriate worker to it. Workers can do anything that you want them to do — fetch documents off the Web, cache data in memcached, stop and restart other servers — just about anything that you can code. A worker is somewhat a server and somewhat a client. The worker runs in a continual loop interestingly called `work()`, but has to connect to the job server to register itself and to await assignment to a job.

A worker can be run either synchronously or asynchronously, depending on what task you need done. For instance, think about the many web applications that you use to do something such as upload an image or leave a message. Often, you don't need this task done immediately and in fact the web site will often have its application present a message that states "this thing you need done will happen eventually." This concept is known as *eventual consistency* — which means that something will indeed happen, just not right away, and the ability to run Gearman workers asynchronously facilitates eventual consistency in your application.

If you think about it, many things in life are eventually consistent. For example, when you deposit money into your bank account at night by dropping a payment into the drop box, you get a receipt that you did this (a reply that the job was assigned!), but that deposited money doesn't immediately go into your account, though the act of depositing the money has been initiated and you have some record for it. You accept this behavior because the money will eventually make its way into your account. You have a contract there that says "yes, we will get this money from the drop box to fund your account." The same applies for checks eventually clearing and the actual monetary funds transferring from the payer's to the payee's bank account. So, too, you have a variety of particular, everyday actions on a dynamic web site where this eventually consistent behavior is considered satisfactory. Consider when you post a comment on your Facebook account. Sometimes your comment won't immediately show up. Having your comment show up immediately is not a life or death situation so this behavior is sufficient.

Another application where Gearman is well suited is for *map/reduce* operations, a model of distributed computing over a large number of computers, or cluster, introduced by Google (see `http://labs.google.com/papers/mapreduce.html`). The idea is to take the large data set and break it up into smaller pieces and distribute each to worker nodes that process those pieces — this is the "map" stage. The "reduce" stage is to conglomerate the fractional results of the map stage and into one consistent result — think federation. As you can imagine, because Gearman enables you to farm out jobs to workers, it is well-suited for map/reduce.

 Although this book is about PHP, Gearman clients and workers can be written in other languages and for a number of environments and databases. There are language bindings and database bindings for PHP/C, Perl/C, MySQL (through UDFs), PostgreSQL, Java, JMS, Python/C, Twisted Python, OCaml, and many others.

A web environment utilizing Gearman is shown in Figure 10-1.

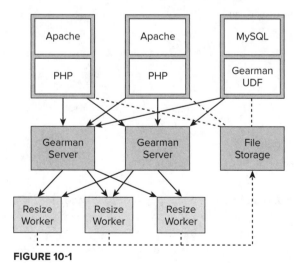

FIGURE 10-1

Figure 10-1 shows the type of setup you might use for image resizing. Traditionally, the image resizing would have been implemented completely within the web application. The user would upload an image, and within the HTTP request to serve the page, the PHP code would have to run the image conversion — perhaps even using imagemagick — to perform the resizing. The page load would not be completed until the image resizing was completed. Now, with Gearman, the PHP web application can request image resizing by way of a Gearman client to the Gearman job server, gearmand, which would in turn tell a resize worker to perform the resizing operation. Now, the web application can return immediately with a message stating that the image is being processed and results will soon be provided, making the web application lighter weight than the traditional design. This changes the whole concept of how web applications can be written into distributed applications that work in concert instead of a single heavy-duty web application! With this in mind, you now have an application that has no single point of failure and offers a tremendous amount of flexibility.

Installing and Running Gearman

Installing the latest version of Gearman is a very straightforward task. You can obtain the latest source on `http://www.gearman.org/doku.php?id=download` or visit `https://launchpad.net/gearmand`. These sites include links to every component you would need to run Gearman, the job server itself, and the Gearman MySQL UDFs.

gearmand Job Server Install

To install the Gearman job server, follow these steps:

1. Download the latest source distribution for gearmand into a directory where you usually compile source code such as `/usr/local/src` (you can also use the bazaar revision control system for the repository `lp:gearmand`). The first thing is to unpack the source distribution:

    ```
    tar xvzf gearmand-1.0.tar.gz
    ```

2. Enter the gearmand source distribution directory:

    ```
    cd gearmand-1.0
    ./configure
    ```

3. Now build and install gearmand:

    ```
    make
    make install
    ```

At this point, gearmand is installed and ready to use.

PECL/Gearman

To install PECL/Gearman, consult the project page at `http://pecl.php.net/package/gearman`. The steps are essentially:

```
cd gearman-0.6.0/
 phpize
./configure
make
 sudo make install
```

Then make sure to specify loading the shared library, `gearman.so`, in `/etc/php5/conf.d/gearman.ini` (This is how it is done for Ubuntu. Other Linux distrubtions or UNIX variants might possibly have a different setup.) with:

```
extension="gearman.so"
```

Depending on OS, this may already be done for you. Another option is to add this line to your `php.ini`. Refer to your OS manual.

Gearman MySQL UDF Install

Also available for use with Gearman are the Gearman MySQL user-defined functions, or UDFs. In addition to the new C-based Gearman, Eric Day also wrote these UDFs. These UDFs offer even more power when you use Gearman than with just using external programs. The UDFs are themselves client programs and run internally within the MySQL server. With these UDFs, you can add jobs to the Gearman job server just as you do regular client programs, but from within MySQL rather than using an external program or from within your application code. This may sound confusing at first — running a client within a server. However, if you recall from earlier chapters, both the example Curl UDF `http_get()` and the memcached UDFs are also clients.

The Gearman MySQL UDFs enable you to request jobs of the Gearman job server from within MySQL. This means you can have triggers on tables so that when an UPDATE, DELETE, or INSERT occurs, a job can also be added. Think of the power this gives you!

To begin installation of the Gearman MySQL UDFs, follow these steps:

1. Download the latest UDF source, which you can find on Launchpad at `https://launchpad.net/gearman-mysql-udf`, into the same directory where you downloaded the Gearman job server source code and untar/gzip the distribution file:

```
wget http://launchpad.net/gearman-mysql-udf/trunk/0.4/+download/gearman-mysql-udf-
0.4.tar.gz
tar xvzf gearman-mysql-udf-0.4.tar.gz
```

2. Enter the Gearman MySQL UDF source directory:

```
cd gearman-mysql-udf-0.4
```

3. Configure the package for compiling. The path you use depends on what distribution of MySQL you have, source or binary, and so on. You need to locate the path where `mysql_config` exists. You will probably have to install whatever MySQL development or community development package (`yum search mysql`, `apt-cache search mysql`, `yast`, and so on) is required.

On an Ubuntu system, it would be:

```
./configure --with-mysql=/usr/bin/mysql_config --libdir=/usr/lib/mysql/lib
```

`--with-mysql` is the argument that tells the configuration program where to find `mysql_config`. `--libdir` is where the shared UDF libraries will be installed and this will have to be a directory that MySQL can load the libraries from. You may have to add or edit `/etc/ld.so.conf.d/mysql.conf` to make sure that the path is listed, and then run `ldconfig`.

4. Next, build and install the UDF source code:

```
make
make install
```

5. To load the UDFs, you need to do so from within MySQL:

```
CREATE FUNCTION gman_do RETURNS STRING SONAME "libgearman_mysql_udf.so";
CREATE FUNCTION gman_do_low RETURNS STRING SONAME "libgearman_mysql_udf.so";
CREATE FUNCTION gman_do_high RETURNS STRING SONAME "libgearman_mysql_udf.so";
CREATE FUNCTION gman_do_background RETURNS STRING SONAME "libgearman_mysql_udf.
so";
CREATE FUNCTION gman_do_low_background RETURNS STRING SONAME "libgearman_mysql_
udf.so";
CREATE FUNCTION gman_do_high_background RETURNS STRING SONAME "libgearman_mysql_
udf.so";
CREATE AGGREGATE FUNCTION gman_sum RETURNS INTEGER SONAME "libgearman_mysql_udf.
so";
CREATE FUNCTION gman_servers_set RETURNS STRING SONAME "libgearman_mysql_udf.so";
```

At this point, the Gearman MySQL UDFs are installed.

Running the Gearman Job Server

Running gearmand, the Gearman job server, is the next thing you do to use it.

To start gearmand:

1. Run (whatever path it is installed in):

```
/usr/local/bin/gearmand -d
```

This tells gearmand to run detached in the background.

2. Now, run a worker. gearmand includes both some sample worker and client programs in the examples/ directory of the source directory. To really do something, you need to run a worker program. For testing out the gearmand (as well as both the workers and client to get a concept of how Gearman as a whole works), use two windows to see what exactly it does. In one window, start up the reverse worker. Do not background it by using &:

```
./reverse_worker
```

3. Run a client program. With the Gearman job server, you have two ways of requesting a job:

➤ Attached/callback, which will wait until the job that the server has delegated is completed and returns a return value of that worker.

➤ Detached/backgrounded, which lets the process run at its own volition, not waiting for a return value of the worker.

For this example, the callback/attached client will run.

4. In another window, run the reverse_client_cb program:

```
./reverse_client_cb "This is a test"

Created: H:hanuman:929
```

```
Created: H:hanuman:930
Created: H:hanuman:931
Created: H:hanuman:932
Created: H:hanuman:933
Created: H:hanuman:934
Created: H:hanuman:935
Created: H:hanuman:936
Created: H:hanuman:937
Created: H:hanuman:938
Completed: H:hanuman:929 tset a si sihT
Completed: H:hanuman:930 tset a si sihT
Completed: H:hanuman:931 tset a si sihT
Completed: H:hanuman:932 tset a si sihT
Completed: H:hanuman:933 tset a si sihT
Completed: H:hanuman:934 tset a si sihT
Completed: H:hanuman:935 tset a si sihT
Completed: H:hanuman:936 tset a si sihT
Completed: H:hanuman:937 tset a si sihT
Completed: H:hanuman:938 tset a si sihT
```

If you look in the window there the worker is running:

```
Job=H:hanuman:929 Workload=This is a test Result=tset a si sihT
Job=H:hanuman:930 Workload=This is a test Result=tset a si sihT
Job=H:hanuman:931 Workload=This is a test Result=tset a si sihT
Job=H:hanuman:932 Workload=This is a test Result=tset a si sihT
Job=H:hanuman:933 Workload=This is a test Result=tset a si sihT
Job=H:hanuman:934 Workload=This is a test Result=tset a si sihT
Job=H:hanuman:935 Workload=This is a test Result=tset a si sihT
Job=H:hanuman:936 Workload=This is a test Result=tset a si sihT
Job=H:hanuman:937 Workload=This is a test Result=tset a si sihT
Job=H:hanuman:938 Workload=This is a test Result=tset a si sihT
```

As you can see, the client requests a job from the job server, gearmand, to the *reverse worker*, which was dispatched via job server to the workers, which in turn reversed the text and returned the result of that reversal.

Using the Gearman MySQL UDFs

Another way to make job requests to the Gearman job server is to use the Gearman MySQL UDFs. The UDFs that are offered are discussed in detail in the following sections.

gman_severs_set()

This UDF, which you *must* call before calling any other of the Gearman MySQL UDFs, sets the server pool that will be used for any UDF call within the client session. It takes as its first argument one or more comma-separated servers, port optional — it will default to port 4730. The second argument can be used to set a particular server to run a specific job!

```
gman_servers_set("<server list>", "<optional: job>")
```

An example of a single server is:

```
SELECT gman_servers_set("192.168.1.33:7004")
```

Here's an example of assigning 192.168.1.33 to run the reverse worker:

```
SELECT gman_servers_set("192.168.1.33:4730", "reverse");
```

Here's an example of assigning two servers to run the indexer worker:

```
SELECT gman_servers_set("192.168.1.88:4730,192.168.1.99:7004", "indexer");
```

Once your servers are set up, you can then request jobs from your UDF queries using the Gearman MySQL UDFs.

gman_do()

These UDFs send job requests to the Gearman job server, gearmand:

```
gman_do("<function name>", "<input value>")
gman_do_low("<function name>", "<input value>")
gman_do_high("<function name>", "<input value>")
gman_do_background("<function name>", "<input value>")
gman_do_low_background("<function name>", "<input value>")
gman_do_high_background("<function name>", "<input value>")
<job name> should be <function name>
```

gman_do() runs a normal job, waiting for the job to finish before returning a result. If there is one, gman_do_low|high() is a low/high priority job that waits as well, and gman_do_background() and gman_do_background_low|high() run the job in the background (asynchronous) at a normal, low, or high priority, returning only the host and job number (job handle) that you can later query for the results.

If you want a job request to be made through a Gearman MySQL UDF using a trigger, you need to call gman_do_background(). *Otherwise, the* INSERT *statement for the data being inserted into the table will not complete until the job is done.*

gman_sum()

This is an aggregate function used to run jobs in parallel. It is much faster than using sum(gman_do(...)) because it runs the jobs simultaneously.

```
SELECT gman_sum("wc", Host) AS test FROM mysql.user;
```

Usage Examples

Here are some examples of using the Gearman UDFs to submit a jobs to the Gearman job server to assign work to the reverse worker you already started:

```
mysql> select gman_servers_set('127.0.0.1');
+------------------------------+
| gman_servers_set('127.0.0.1') |
+------------------------------+
| NULL                         |
+------------------------------+

mysql> select gman_do('reverse', 'This is a test');
+-------------------------------------+
| gman_do('reverse', 'This is a test') |
+-------------------------------------+
| tset a si sihT                      |
+-------------------------------------+

mysql> select gman_do_background('reverse', 'This is a test');
+-------------------------------------------------+
| gman_do_background('reverse', 'This is a test') |
+-------------------------------------------------+
| H:hanuman:940                                   |
+-------------------------------------------------+

mysql> set @a = gman_do_background('reverse', "XYZ");

mysql> select @a;
+---------------+
| @a            |
+---------------+
| H:hanuman:945 |
+---------------+

mysql> set @a = gman_do('reverse', "XYZ");

mysql> select @a;
+------+
| @a   |
+------+
| ZYX  |
+------+
```

As you can see from the output of `gman_do_background()`, it returns the name of the host and job number.

PHP and Gearman

Using Gearman with PHP certainly makes for an ideal combination and is easy to use. You have a Gearman client, which is usually in your application and is the code that sends jobs to the Gearman job server. You also have the worker component, which uses the PHP Gearman worker library to register itself as handling a named job and then specifies the function name for the job.

Writing Gearman-enabled PHP applications is amazingly simple, as shown in the following short example.

First, a client, `client.php`:

```
<?

$client= new GearmanClient();
$client->addServer('127.0.0.1');
for ($i = 0; $i <= 360; $i++) {
  print "sine $i: " . $client->do("sine", $i) . "\n";
}

?>
```

In this client example, a `GearmanClient` object is instantiated. Next, the Gearman client API `addServer()` method is called to add a server to be used for the client connection. Multiple servers could be added if desired. An empty argument would be the localhost, and here for clarity it was explicitly specified. A loop is initiated starting from 0 through 360 (degrees) and the Gearman client API method is called for each iteration.

Next is the worker, `worker.php`. A GearmanWorker object is instantiated, and just like the client, `addServer()` adds a server. Next, the worker adds a function — registers a function to be used for work — to handle a job request for the "sine" job, and the "my_sine_function" function does the work. The `while` loop runs the Gearman server API method `work()` until the worker is shut down or killed. The function, `my_sine_function()`, was the name of the function specified to handle the "sine" job, and contains the implementation that passes the value from the Gearman server API method `workload()`, which is the argument passed from the client when the client sent the job to the job server. As you recall, for this test, it will be values from 0 to 360.

```
<?php

$worker= new GearmanWorker();
$worker->addServer('127.0.0.1');
$worker->addFunction("sine", "my_sine_function");
while ($worker->work());

function my_sine_function($job)
{
  return sin(deg2rad($job->workload()));
}

?>
```

To illustrate just how this works, Figure 10-2 shows the relation of the client, job server, and worker.

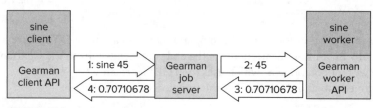

FIGURE 10-2

The first step, the sine client sends a job `'sine'` to the Gearman job server with the value of 45. Next, the Gearman job server sends the value of 45 using the Gearman client API call (using PECL/Gearman) `do()`, which the sine worker reads from the Gearman worker API call `workload()`. The `my_sine_function()` returns the value of 0.70710678... to the Gearman job server, which the Gearman job server then returns to the sine client via the Gearman client API.

The first thing you need to make sure is that gearmand is running. Next, the worker is run in one terminal:

```
patg@hanuman:~/wrox$ php worker.php
```

The client is run in another terminal:

```
patg@hanuman:~/wrox$ php client.php
sine 0: 0
sine 1: 0.0174524064373
...
sine 29: 0.484809620246
sine 30: 0.5
sine 31: 0.51503807491
...
sine 44: 0.694658370459
sine 45: 0.707106781187
sine 46: 0.719339800339
...
sine 89: 0.999847695156
sine 90: 1
sine 91: 0.999847695156
...
sine 209: -0.484809620246
sine 210: -0.5
sine 211: -0.51503807491
...
sine 269: -0.999847695156
sine 270: -1
sine 271: -0.999847695156
sine 359: -0.0174524064373
```

And it works!

You can also use this from a UDF:

```
mysql> select gman_do('sine',45);
+-------------------+
| gman_do('sine',45) |
+-------------------+
| 0.707106781187    |
+-------------------+

mysql> select gman_do('sine',90);
+-------------------+
| gman_do('sine',90) |
+-------------------+
| 1                 |
```

```
            +--------------------+
mysql> select gman_do('sine',361);
            +--------------------+
| gman_do('sine',361) |
            +--------------------+
| 0.0174524064373     |
            +--------------------+
```

And that also works.

So, by now you should probably understand just how simple using Gearman is. Also, you can see that with the Gearman client and worker API in conjunction with the Gearman job server, scheduling, management, and network communication are dealt with so you can focus on developing your application. Now you can probably imagine just how many ways you might use it — the possibilities are endless!

NARADA: A SEARCH ENGINE APPLICATION

Your curiosity should be sparked by what you just have read about regarding Gearman. Now you will really see Gearman, along with MySQL, memcached, memached Functions for MySQL, Sphinx, Apache, and PHP in action!

Search engines are applications most likely to have a lot of moving parts and functionality, which are required to dispense information and make for a good example of a distributed application. In a previous book by the author of this chapter, this idea was demonstrated in Perl. After the book was published, Eric Day worked with the author to make this idea into an actual project, named Narada, after the name of the divine sage from the Vedic tradition (India) who travels the universe playing a Tambura and visiting distant worlds ("Lokas" in Sanskrit). This seemed to be a good name for the search application because it needs to fetch remote content, sort of "traveling the universe," in a sense.

Eric Day also convinced the author that it would be a fun to write this application in PHP to match the Perl version as a good exercise in how Gearman really is language independent. This was in response to the need to feature Narada at Java One which required that Narada needed to be re-implemented in Java for the conference using the new Drizzle RDBMS as the data store. Sun wanted to use Narada to demonstrate how it can be run in their cloud computing platform (`http://www.sun.com/solutions/cloudcomputing/index.jsp`). Out of that, Narada was reimplemented on both PHP and Java, although you could use any one of the parts interchangeably regardless of what language it was implemented in.

Narada has a quite few moving parts — a bit like a Rube Goldberg contraption — but in a good way! Narada is an excellent application to demonstrate just how useful all these new technologies — particularly Gearman, Sphinx, and memcached — can be when used together to develop a distributed application. Narada is still a bit of a prototype, and is subject to change or better ideas that people want to contribute. The main point in this demonstration is to show you how using Gearman allows you to spread out processing to various jobs and across various servers, thus alleviating the work that a web application has to perform.

Obtaining Narada

The best way to obtain the source code for Narada is to visit `https://launchpad.net/narada`, where you can obtain the source file or simply use the bazaar revision control system to check out the source. From whatever directory within your document root you can run PHP in, type the following:

```
bzr clone lp:narada
```

The code structure is basically four top-level directories — `php`, `perl`, `sphinx`, and `sql`. The `php` directory contains all the source code you need to set up PHP-based Narada and you can copy this to any directory in your document root for your web server. The `sphinx` directory contains the `sphinx.conf` file, which you'll copy to wherever you keep your `sphinx.conf` (`/usr/local/sphinx/etc`). The `sql` directory contains the schema file, `narada.sql`, for creating the tables used by Narada regardless of whether it is the PHP-based or Perl-based Narada. Make sure to create a database/schema for Narada and grant permissions to whatever user you choose and then run this schema file to create the tables.

Narada Components

This application has two major parts:

➤ A data gathering system for data retrieval, storage, and creating full-text indexes

➤ A search engine user application

Narada consists of the components listed in Table 10-1.

TABLE 10-1: Narada Components

COMPONENT	DESCRIPTION
Gearman	`gearmand` running, along with workers and clients.
Narada.php	Implements the Narada class, which contains the methods the index page and the various workers use.
NaradaConf.php	This is the global variables configuration file. This provides global settings used by the various workers.
index.php	Displays the search page, allowing you to enter a URL to be fetched as well as a search term for searching the content that has been indexed by Sphinx.
NaradaFetch.php	Given a URL, this retrieves the page at that URL and parses through the document at that URL, calling the insert worker (`NaradaInsert.php`) for any URLs found. Also, the indexer worker NaradaIndex is called and checks if the Sphinx index should be regenerated. Finally, the fetched content is stored in MySQL.

continues

TABLE 10-1 *(continued)*

COMPONENT	DESCRIPTION
NaradaInsert.php	This worker is first called either by the fetch worker (NaradaFetch.php) or when a URL is inserted via the index page, index.php.
NaradaIndex.php	When requested, this worker checks the value of a frequency counter, corresponding to the number of web pages that have been stored, and if the frequency counter exceeds the number you specify in NaradaConf.php, it calls the Sphinx indexer program to re-index the Sphinx index for the table containing the retrieved web pages.
NaradaSearch.php	This worker is called by the index page, index.php, with search terms. It then obtains the search results from Sphinx and obtains the content from the cache (if cached) or MySQL and returns the results to the index page as a JSON object.
NaradaIndexTimer.php	Depending on the global setting from NaradaConf.php, this worker simply requests the indexer worker NaradaIndex.php if the amount of time specified has been exceeded. This is to ensure the index is regenerated at some given interval.
MySQL	Three tables: meta-data table, blob/text table, and a sphinx counter table.
A meta-data table url	For storing information about the web page such as its URL, unique id, date, and so on.
A blob/text table url_content	Has a 1:1 relation to the meta-data table that stores the actual content and title of the web page for the particular URL in a TEXT column.
Sphinx full-text index	Built from the blob/text table containing the web pages.
memcached	For caching searches so subsequent searches use memcached to obtain the content versus retrieving the content from the database. The more popular a search term, the more likely it will be cached!

The flow of how content is fetched from a web page, parsed, stored, and then indexed is as follows:

1. A user enters a URL value into the URL entry field on the index page and the URL value is stored in the url table. The index page calls the Narada class's insert() method which in turn requests that the URL be stored by the insert, NaradaInsert.php, through the Gearman client API.

2. The insert worker, NaradaInsert.php, checks the validity of the URL specified, then calls the Narada method store(), which in turn inserts the URL into the url table and returns the insert_id (value of the auto_increment id column returned from insert). This is the ID of the URL. If an ID is returned, the insert worker then calls the Narada method fetch(), which in turn results in a request to Gearman for a fetch of that URL, provided by the fetch worker, NaradaFetch.php.

3. The fetch worker, `NaradaFetch.php`, fetches the web page of the URL specified and then proceeds to parse any URLs in the content of the page. For any URLs found, it requests the URL to be inserted using the Narada method `insert()`, which in turn results in the insert worker inserting the URL and calling a fetch on that URL — so you can quickly see that both the insert worker and the fetch worker feed on themselves and continue crawling and parsing web pages without relent! The last thing, after requesting an insert of any URLs found, is to request that the indexer be run by calling the Narada method `index()`, which in turn requests the index worker, `NaradaIndex.php`, through gearmand.

4. The index worker, `NaradaIndex.php`, runs the Sphinx indexer if the count for indexing has reached the value determined by the global variable `$GLOBALS['NaradaIndexFrequency']`.

5. The index timer is not a worker but a program that runs in perpetuity, sleeps for the duration of the value of the global `$GLOBALS['NaradaIndexTimer']`, and then requests the indexer to be run. This ensures that the indexer is run even when there is low activity and no event-driven indexing resulting from documents being fetched.

The search functionality can be described as follows:

1. The user enters a search term on the main index page, `index.php`, which results in a request of the search worker through the Narada method `search()`. This is a synchronous method that returns the search results as JSON, which `index.php` de-serializes into a PHP search results object.

2. The search worker performs a search against the Sphinx index by calling the Narada method `searchIndex()` for the search term and then obtains the content for the document IDs (ids to the `url_content` table) from either memcached, if already cached, or MySQL. The results are then cached for subsequent searches for that term by calling the Narada method `getContent()`. The results are then returned as JSON to the caller, `index.php` in this case.

Database Tables for the Search Engine Application

When building a search engine, the first thing to think about is how the data is stored. For this application, as shown in Table 10-1, there will be four database tables which are as follows:

```
CREATE TABLE url (
    id int NOT NULL auto_increment,
    url_md5 varbinary(32) NOT NULL,
    url varchar(255) NOT NULL,
    created date default NULL,
    last_updated timestamp NOT NULL default CURRENT_TIMESTAMP on
                                    update CURRENT_TIMESTAMP,
    PRIMARY KEY  (id),
    UNIQUE KEY url_md5_idx (url_md5)
) ENGINE=InnoDB ;
```

The `url` table will store the meta-data information for a web page retrieved. This includes column such as the URL of the page itself, `url`, the unique MD5 value of the URL `url_md5`, last updated, `last_updated`, and the created date, `created`, but not the actual web page content. It's good practice to keep your BLOB or text data in a separate table so that any queries for meta-data type values don't have to be retrieved from a table containing TEXT or BLOBs; combining tables would make these queries perform slower and would require more memory.

```
CREATE TABLE url_content (
    id int NOT NULL,
    title varchar(255) NOT NULL default '',
    content blob NOT NULL,
    PRIMARY KEY  (id)
) ENGINE=InnoDB;
```

The `url_content` table stores the title and the actual web page contents. It also has a primary key `id`, which is a direct relation to the `url` table `id` column:

```
create table urls_queue (
    url_md5 char(32) NOT NULL default '',
    url   varchar(128) NOT NULL default '',
    last_updated timestamp,
    primary key url_md5 (url_md5)
) ENGINE=InnoDB;
```

The `sphinx_counter` table is for keeping track of what the greatest ID value of an index is. The ID (`id`) values from this table are used by the indexer to supply the ID value for the SQL query when querying MySQL to obtain the content for indexing.

```
CREATE TABLE sphinx_counter (
    id int NOT NULL,
    max_id int NOT NULL,
    index_name varchar(32) NOT NULL,
    PRIMARY KEY  (id),
    KEY index_name (index_name)
) ENGINE=InnoDB
```

Sphinx Setup

To index web pages stored in MySQL using the Sphinx full-text index, Sphinx also has to be set up. This example uses a simple Sphinx setup with a single distributed index, which has two sphinx agents: one for the main index, `url`, and one for the delta index, `url_delta`.

You have two indexes — one main large index and a smaller delta index — for good reason: you don't want to re-index a continually growing large data set too often in its entirety and have changes, or deltas, added to it. Because Sphinx has distributed index functionality, you can treat these two indexes as if they are a single index, and you only need to update the smaller delta index. Then at some interval, you merge the delta index into the main index.

The first thing to review is the MySQL table that will contain the positions of both the main and delta indexes. The indexer uses this positional information in the `sphinx_counter` table to obtain the limits or extents of what records the indexes has. The indexer uses this to determine what data should be selected when indexing.

The main `url` index will contain all records having an id value less than the value of column `max_id` in the table `sphinx_counter`. The delete index, `url_delta`, will contain records having their `id` value starting from the value of the column `sphinx_counter.max_id` and no upward limit.

Where the main index ends and the delta index starts is set only when the main index is re-indexed. The delta index grows over time, and at some point, you merge the two them. The break point is set to the maximum of the main index, which now contains what was previously in the delta, and the delta is rebuilt with a starting point equal to the maximum of the newly merged index.

Each index has exactly one entry in this table and the position data is updated during indexing.

An example showing the positional data of a running setup is:

```
mysql> select * from sphinx_counter;
+----+--------+-----------+---------------------+
| id | max_id | index_name| last_updated        |
+----+--------+-----------+---------------------+
|  1 |   1133 | url       | 2009-03-02 11:05:30 |
|  2 |   1181 | url_delta | 2009-03-02 11:12:12 |
+----+--------+-----------+---------------------+
```

To use this to explain the topic further, the main index, `url`, will contain records with the `url.id` value of 0 through 1133, and the delta index, `url_delta`, will contain records with the `url.id` value of 1134 through 1181.

The entry in the `sphinx_counter` counter table for the delta index is not really necessary, but is an added informational benefit to show you the state of what record range (of IDs) your indexes are searchable for. The single entry for the main index is sufficient to delineate the extents of the main and the delta indexes for indexing.

To set up Sphinx for Narada, follow these steps:

1. **Define the data sources to use.** The first source, `url`, is set to use the MySQL server running on localhost on port 3306. The `sql_query_pre` directive defines the query that is run prior to the main document fetching query. In this case, the `sphinx_counter` table is updated with the `max(id)` value from the `url` table, moving the positional information up to represent the index that is about to be regenerated.

2. **The `sql_query` directive specifies the main query that will run.** The primary key or other unique identifier must always be the first column specified in this query. In this instance, it is the id column of the `url` table. This makes it so when you perform a search against Sphinx, you obtain one or more values of the primary key id that you will subsequently use to retrieve the actual data from MySQL, making for a fast lookup.

 The query specified with the directive `sql_query` *performs a join of* `url` *with* `url_content` *to obtain the actual content from the blob table as well as the other columns specified after the primary key value. These columns create a full-text index and are therefore searchable. Sphinx has a very flexible language, allowing you to specify which columns to search on. Also, this query uses a* WHERE *clause to select records less than or equal to the value in the* `sphinx_counter` *table for the main index. This is the mechanism that applies an extent to the data being gathered.*

3. The directive **sql_query_info** provides a query to the search command-line program. This is good for running test queries against your index. Note that search does not search against Sphinx through the Sphinx search daemon, `searchd` — it searches on the index itself, so it does not work with distributed indexes.

    ```
    source url
    {
            type                    = mysql
            sql_host                = localhost
            sql_user                = narada
            sql_pass                = n@r@d@
            sql_db                  = narada
            sql_port                = 3306
            sql_query_pre           = UPDATE sphinx_counter SET max_id=
                                      (SELECT MAX(id) FROM url) WHERE index_name =
    'url'
            sql_query               = SELECT id, content FROM url_content WHERE id <=
                                      (SELECT max_id FROM sphinx_counter WHERE index_
    name = 'url')
            sql_query_info          = SELECT * FROM url_content WHERE id=$id
    }
    ```

4. **The source for the delta index, url_delta, is defined.** The notation `url_delta : url` means that `url_delta` inherits every option/directive from the data source `url`, unless otherwise overridden. In this case, the directives `sql_query_pre` and `sql_query` are overridden to specify a different range than is used with the `url` data source. For the `url_delta` data source, all records greater than the `max_id` value for the data source `url` are specified.

    ```
    source url_delta : url
    {
            sql_query_pre           = UPDATE sphinx_counter SET max_id=
                                      (SELECT MAX(id) FROM url) WHERE index_name =
    'url_delta'
            sql_query               = SELECT id, content FROM url_content WHERE id >
                                      (SELECT max_id FROM sphinx_counter WHERE index_
    name = 'url')
    }
    ```

5. **The indexes are defined.** The directives shown here are the most important. The directive source defines the data source that is used to build this index; in this case the source `url` is used. The directive path specifies the path and base name of the actual index files. `docinfo` just specifies the storage mode. `min_word_len` specifies the minimum size of a word that is indexed. The value of 1 specifies all words. It's important to point out that MySQL full-text indexes have a limit of three, so this is yet another improvement over MySQL full-text indexes.

    ```
    index url
    {
            source                  = url
            path                    = /usr/local/sphinx/var/data/url
            docinfo                 = extern
            mlock                   = 0
    ```

```
        morphology                = none
        min_word_len              = 1
        charset_type              = sbcs
}
```

6. The delta index, **url_delta**, inherits everything from the index **url**, except path and source, which it overrides. Because the source for url_delta is url_delta, this is the data source that has a different range than url, hence url_delta is a smaller index composed of a smaller range — the topmost records — of the database table *url*.

```
index url_delta : url
{
        source                    = url_delta
        path                      = /usr/local/sphinx/var/data/url_delta
}
```

7. The distributed index **dist_url** is defined. This is the glue that makes the delta index and main index work together as one index. Queries run against this distributed index. As far a searching an index is concerned, the has no way of knowing that the index is composed of partial, distributed indexes.

```
index dist_url
{
        type                      = distributed
        agent                     = localhost:3312:url
        agent                     = localhost:3312:url_delta
        agent_connect_timeout     = 1000
        agent_query_timeout       = 3000
}
```

8. The indexer is configured. The directive mem_limit specifies how much memory is used for the indexer, when it runs, to generate indexes.

```
indexer
{
        # memory limit, in bytes, kilobytes (16384K) or megabytes (256M)
        # optional, default is 32M, max is 2047M, recommended is 256M to 1024M
        mem_limit                 = 32M


}
```

9. The **searchd** daemon is configured. The listen directive specifies which port or socket the daemon will bind to. In this case none are specified, so all interfaces are used. The log directive specifies the log for the searchd daemon. This log incrementally logs the status of the searchd daemon. The query_log directive specifies a log that records search queries run against searchd.

The other directives set timeout values, max number of children to run, a pid file, maximum number of matches returned, and whether the searchd daemon can be restarted seamlessly after running the indexer.

Also listed is the directive `seamless_rotate`. When you run the indexer, `searchd` is seamlessly restarted once the indexer completes.

```
searchd
{
        log                     = /usr/local/sphinx/var/log/searchd.log
        query_log               = /usr/local/sphinx/var/log/query.log
        read_timeout            = 5
        client_timeout          = 300
        max_children            = 30
        pid_file                = /usr/local/sphinx/var/log/searchd.pid
        max_matches             = 1000
        seamless_rotate         = 1
        preopen_indexes         = 0
        unlink_old              = 1
        mva_updates_pool        = 1M
        max_packet_size         = 8M
        max_filters             = 256
        max_filter_values       = 4096
}
```

The Narada Configuration File

Various global variables work as settings that both the Narada class and the various workers use — such as the database connection parameters, memcached server settings, Sphinx server settings, and so on. `NaradaConf.php` is the file where you can control the overall behavior of the Narada application by adjusting the settings to your own needs. This file is nicely littered with ample comments to explain what each setting is for!

```php
<?php
# Narada Search Engine in PHP
# Copyright (C) 2009 Eric Day, Patrick Galbraith
# All rights reserved.
#
# Use and distribution licensed under the BSD license.  See
# the COPYING file in this directory for full text.

# This is the list of Gearman job servers to use. The format is:
# 'SERVER[:PORT][,SERVER[:PORT]]...'
# For example: '10.0.0.1,10.0.0.2:7003'
$NaradaGearmanServers= '127.0.0.1';

# DB connection options.
$NaradaDBHost= '127.0.0.1';
$NaradaDBPort= 3306;
$NaradaDBUser= 'narada';
$NaradaDBPass= 'n@r@d@';
$NaradaDBType = 'mysqli';
$NaradaDB= 'narada';

$NaradaMemcachedPort= '11211';
$NaradaMemcachedHost= '127.0.0.1';
```

```
# Available options: DRIZZLE_CON_MYSQL
$NaradaDBOptions= 0;
# Whether to enable debugging.
$NaradaDebug= true;

#
# Insert Worker Configuration.
#

# Name of the function the insert worker will register.
$NaradaInsertFunctionName= 'NaradaInsert';

#
# Fetch Worker Configuration.
#

# Name of the function the fetch worker will register.
$NaradaFetchFunctionName= 'NaradaFetch';

# Whether to crawl (search and insert) other URLs when fetching pages.
$NaradaFetchCrawl= true;

# Whether to limit crawling to URLs local to the original URL or not.
$NaradaFetchLocalURLs= true;

#
# Index Worker Configuration.
#
# Name of the function the index worker will register.
$NaradaIndexFunctionName= 'NaradaIndex';

# How often the index should run, per number of documents.
$NaradaIndexFrequency= 10;

# Command to execute when the indexer needs to run.
$NaradaIndexCommand= '/usr/local/sphinx/bin/indexer --rotate --all';

# How often the index timer should send a message to make sure unindexed
# documents eventually get indexed.
$NaradaIndexTimer= 60;

#
# Sphinx Configuration
#

# Path to the Sphinx PHP API. This needs to be included before the other Sphinx
# configuration in case API constants are used.
require('/usr/lib/php5/sphinxapi.php');

# Name of the function the search worker will register.
$NaradaSearchFunctionName= 'NaradaSearch';

# Name of the index to search
```

```
$NaradaSearchIndex= 'dist_url';

# Name of the non-distributed excerpt index (for creating excerpts)
$NaradaExcerptIndex= 'url';

# Name of the Sphinx host
$NaradaSearchHost= 'localhost';

# Name of the Sphinx host
$NaradaSearchPort= 3312;

# Sphinx search mode
$NaradaSearchMode= SPH_MATCH_EXTENDED2;

?>
```

The Narada Class

The next PHP code component of Narada is the Narada class. This class implements the bulk of the functionality needed for Narada, containing many of the methods that the various PHP Gearman workers — which are shown in the next section — will use.

First and foremost is the class definition:

```php
<?php
# Narada Search Engine in PHP
# Copyright (C) 2009 Eric Day, Patrick Galbraith
# All rights reserved.
#
# Use and distribution licensed under the BSD license.  See
# the COPYING file in this directory for full text.

# This is a helper/base class for all Narada components to use. It encapsulates
# common configuration and initialization of things like Gearman clients and
# workers.

require('NaradaConf.php');

#if ($GLOBALS['NaradaDebug'])
#  error_reporting(E_ALL | E_NOTICE | E_STRICT);

class Narada
{
  private $gearmanServers;
  private $gearmanClient;
  private $dbh;
  private $dbhCon;
  private $sphinx;
  private $sphinxIndex;
  private $sphinxHost;
  private $sphinxPort;
```

```
   private $sphinxMatchMode;
protected $functionName;
  protected $fetchFunctionName;
  protected $searchFunctionName;
  protected $insertFunctionName;
  protected $indexFunctionName;
```

The first method is the constructor, which performs the following:

➤ Obtains the Gearman job server list, parsing and initializing the list

➤ Sets the value of class variables for worker names

➤ Sets the class variables for Sphinx index, excerpt index, host, port, and search mode

➤ Connects to the memcached server pool

➤ Connects to MySQL

```
    public function __construct()
      {
        $servers= explode(',', $GLOBALS['NaradaGearmanServers']);
        foreach ($servers as $server)
          $this->gearmanServers[]= explode(':', $server);

        $this->gearmanClient= new GearmanClient();

        foreach ($this->gearmanServers as $server)
          $this->gearmanClient->addServer($server[0], $server[1]);

        $this->fetchFunctionName= $GLOBALS['NaradaFetchFunctionName'];
        $this->searchFunctionName= $GLOBALS['NaradaSearchFunctionName'];
        $this->insertFunctionName= $GLOBALS['NaradaInsertFunctionName'];
        $this->indexFunctionName= $GLOBALS['NaradaIndexFunctionName'];

        $this->sphinx= NULL;
        $this->sphinxIndex= $GLOBALS['NaradaSearchIndex'];
        $this->sphinxExcerptIndex= $GLOBALS['NaradaExcerptIndex'];
        $this->sphinxHost= $GLOBALS['NaradaSearchHost'];
        $this->sphinxPort= $GLOBALS['NaradaSearchPort'];
        $this->sphinxMatchMode= $GLOBALS['NaradaSearchMode'];

        $this->memc= new Memcached();
        $this->memc->addServer($GLOBALS['NaradaMemcachedHost'],
                               $GLOBALS['NaradaMemcachedPort']);

        $this->dbh= new mysqli($GLOBALS['NaradaDBHost'],
$GLOBALS['NaradaDBUser'],
                               $GLOBALS['NaradaDBPass'],
                               $GLOBALS['NaradaDB']);
        if ($GLOBALS['NaradaDBType'] == 'mysqli')
          $this->dbhCon= $this->dbh;
      }
```

For the previous code, note the following:

➤ The debug() method simply prints the messages that were passed to it if
$GLOBALS['NaradaDebug'] is set. This method is useful for printing out various messages
or var_dump() of PHP arrays when you are debugging Narada, should you want to extend it
and submit the code to the project!

```
public function debug($msg)
    {
      if ($GLOBALS['NaradaDebug'])
        print "$msg\n";
    }
```

➤ The insert() method performs an insert by way of requesting an insert job (backgrounded)
from the Gearman job server using the gearman client API method, doBackground().

```
public function insert($url)
    {
      $this->gearmanClient->doBackground($this->insertFunctionName, $url);
    }
```

➤ The search() method performs a search by way of the search worker, which it requests of the
Gearman job server. It returns the results of the search (non-backgrounded worker) using the
gearman client method do().

```
public function search($query)
    {
      return $this->gearmanClient->do($this->searchFunctionName, $query);
    }
```

➤ The fetch() method requests the retrieval of the content of a page for a given URL by way
of the fetch worker requested of gearmand as a background job.

```
protected function fetch($url)
    {
      $this->gearmanClient->doBackground($this>fetchFunctionName, $url);
    }
```

➤ The index() method requests that the Sphinx indexes are re-indexed by way of the index
worker requested of gearmand as a background worker.

```
public function index()
    {
      $this->gearmanClient->doBackground($this->indexFunctionName, NULL);
    }
```

➤ The store() method, which is called by the insert worker, inserts the specified URL. This
URL comes either from the initial submission on the index page of a URL or from a URL
parsed by the fetch worker.

It's important to note that the `store()` *method returns the insert id, which is the primary key value that is used for the subsequent insertion of the page content and title fetched from the page of the URL into the* `url_content` *table, maintaining the 1:1 relation between the* `url` *and* `url_content` *tables.*

```
protected function store($url)
  {
    $query= "INSERT INTO url (url_md5, url, created, last_updated)
"
        . "VALUES ('" . md5($url) . "','"
        . $this->dbh->real_escape_string($url) .
        "', now(), now())";

    $result= @$this->dbhCon->query($query);
    if ($result)
    {
      $id= $this->dbhCon->insert_id;
      return $id;
    }


    return 0;
  }
```

➤ The `storeContent()` method is called by the fetch worker after the page content and title are retrieved and parsed for a given URL. Note the useful application of the `INSERT INTO...ON DUPLICATE KEY UPDATE` statement — explained more in Chapter 18 — which essentially means if the record exists for a given record, update it instead; otherwise insert it.

```
protected function storeContent($id, $title, $content)
  {
    $query= "INSERT INTO url_content (id, title, content) VALUES ($id " .
        "','" . $this->dbh->real_escape_string($title) .
        "','" . $this->dbh->real_escape_string($content) . "') " .
        "ON DUPLICATE KEY UPDATE content='" .
        $this->dbh->real_escape_string($content) . "'";

    $this->dbhCon->query($query);
  }
```

➤ The `get()` method is called by the fetch worker to obtain the URL, which is obtained using the workload that happens to be the id value for the given URL.

```
protected function get($id)
  {
    $result= $this->dbhCon->query("SELECT url FROM url WHERE id=$id");
    if (!$result)
```

```
        return NULL;

    $row= $result->fetch_array();
    return $row[0];
}
```

➤ The `getContent()` method obtains the content for the document ids (the id values for records specified in the query of the *url* and *url_content* tables). The array `$search_results` contains the data from a Sphinx search, which includes the id values for the records found (`$search_results['matches']`). Next, a loop attempts to first try to obtain the content from memcached for each ID (id), and if found eliminates the id from the list, which is inevitably passed to the database query to obtain the content from the *url_content* table. Whatever id values remain are specified in the IN list using `implode()`. The result from the query is returned and if there is a result, each row of the result set is fetched and pushed into the `$results` array with any results retrieved from memcached. The content, found as `$row[5]` from the fetched row, is pushed into the `$docs` array. This `$docs` array is passed to the Sphinx PHP API method `BuildExcerpts()`, which creates excerpts for the term specified, using `<em>` to highlight the term in the excerpt. The `$results` array, which contains everything about the search results except the excerpt for each document, is then looped through and the excerpt for that result is added. Also within the loop, the document is cached in memcached.

➤ `$results` is returned to the calling program, the search worker in this case, which the search worker encodes the results as JSON and the index page displays the results.

```
    protected function getContent($search_results, $search_term)
    {
        if (!is_array($search_results["matches"]))
          return NULL;

        $docs= array ();
        $results= array();
        $to_cache = array();
        $cached = array();

        foreach (array_keys($search_results["matches"]) as $match) {
          $doc_key = "docs:" . $match;

          $cached = array();
          $cached = $this->memc->get($doc_key);

          # if there is a match, then we're happy and can use it
          if ($doc) {
            array_push($results, $cached);

            # since we have it already, take it out of list that
            # will be passed to DB
            unset($search_results["matches"][$match]);
          }
        }
        $query= 'SELECT id, url, created, last_updated, title, content ' .
                'FROM url JOIN url_content USING (id) ' .
                'WHERE id IN (' .
```

```
                    implode(",", array_keys($search_results["matches"])) . ')';

          $result= $this->dbhCon->query($query);

          if (result) {
            # Changed from earlier - push into array because we need to maintain
            # order, especially if we use Sphinx ordering/grouping
            while($row= $result->fetch_array())
            {
              array_push($results, array('id'                => $row[0],
                                  'url'               => $row[1],
                                  'url_created'       => $row[2],
                                  'url_last_updated'  => $row[3],
                                  'url_title'         => $row[4]));

              array_push($docs, $row[5]);

            }
          }
          # Note: excerpt index must be actual, not distributed index
          $options= array('before_match'     => '<em>',
                          'after_match'      => '</em>',
                          'around'           => 3,
                          'single_passage'   => 0,
                          'chunk_separator'  => '...',
                          'limit'            => 180);

          $excerpts= $this->sphinx->BuildExcerpts($docs, $this->sphinxExcerptIndex,
                                             $search_term, $options);

          for ($x= 0; $x < count($results); $x++) {
            $results[$x]["url_excerpt"] = $excerpts[$x];
            $doc_key= "docs:" . $results[$x]["id"];

            $this->memc->set($doc_key, $results[$x]);
          }

          return $results;
        }
```

➤ The searchIndex() method is used to pass a search query to Sphinx and retrieve the results from that search. This method is called by the search worker. The results from searchIndex() are what getContent() uses to obtain document content for the search results.

```
        protected function searchIndex($query)
        {
          if ($this->sphinx == NULL)
          {
            $this->sphinx= new SphinxClient();
            $this->sphinx->SetServer($this->sphinxHost, $this->sphinxPort);
            $this->sphinx->SetMatchMode($this->sphinxMatchMode);
          }

          return $this->sphinx->Query($query, $this->sphinxIndex);
        }
```

➤ The method `verify()` verifies if a URL is properly formed. If the URL value doesn't contain the scheme (`http://`) it adds it to the beginning of the URL.

```
protected function verify($url)
  {
    if (strstr($url, "://"))
    {
      if (substr($url, 0, 7) != "http://"
        && substr($url, 0, 8) != "https://")
        return NULL;
    }
    else
      $url= "http://$url";

    if (substr_count($url, "/") == 2)
      $url= "$url/";

    return $url;
  }
```

➤ The `runWorker()` method is the core of the work loop for each PHP worker. It sets which Gearman job servers and callback functions are used and then starts the `work()` loop where the worker awaits assignment to a job by the gearman job server.

```
# Derived worker classes should set functionName, define a callback member
  # function, and then call this.
  public function runWorker()
  {
    $worker= new GearmanWorker();

    foreach ($this->gearmanServers as $server)
      $worker->addServer($server[0], $server[1]);

    $worker->addFunction($this->functionName, "NaradaWorkerCallback", $this);

    while ($worker->work());
  }
};
```

➤ The `NaradaWorkerCallback()` method is a generic method of sorts. It is passed as the callback method in the previously listed method `runWorker()`. Where this method differs in implementation is how the worker implements the `callback()` function. The worker calls `runWorker()`, which sets `NaradaWorkerCallback()` as the callback function. When the callback function is called, it in turn calls the `callback()` method, using the implementation details the worker has specified.

```
# Callback function for Gearman worker interface.
  function NaradaWorkerCallback($job, &$narada)
  {
    return $narada->callback($job);
  }

  ?>
```

Now that the details of the Narada class have been explained, you'll be able to see how each worker is implemented and what Narada methods each worker uses.

Gearman Workers

This application utilizes four workers that take care of various parts of the data retrieval, caching, storage, and indexing of web pages. The following subsections discuss each one.

Insert Worker

The insert worker is the worker that starts the web page fetch process. The insert worker is called by either the index page, `index.php`, or the fetch worker. The initial insertion of a URL results in the insert worker inserting the URL in the database and then calling the fetch worker, which in turn calls the insert worker for any URLs obtained in the web page content — hence implementing web-crawling functionality for Narada.

As with all the workers, the insert worker is implemented as a subclass of Narada. The first method defined is the `__construct()` method, which sets the function name of the worker. This function name is the job name registered with the gearman job server. The next method is the `callback()` method. If you recall in the review of the Narada class's details, the `NaradaWorkerCallback()` method was the callback method specified in the Gearman worker method `addFunction()`. `NaradaWorkerCallback()` then called `callback()`, which is what is implemented in each worker. As you will see, the bulk of each workers' functionality will be implemented in the `callback()` method. For the insert worker, this involves taking the URL value and inserting it into the database via the call to the method `insert()`. If the insert is successful, it returns the ID value of the URL, and uses that id to call the fetch worker to fetch that URL.

The worker is initiated by instantiating a `NaradaInsert` object and then calling the method `runWorker()`, which runs the actual worker, as you saw in the Narada class explanation in the previous section.

```php
require('Narada.php');
class NaradaInsert extends Narada
{
  public function __construct()
  {
    parent::__construct();
    $this->functionName= $this->insertFunctionName;
  }

  public function callback($job)
  {
    $url= $job->workload();

    $this->debug("Insert URL: $url");

    $url= $this->verify($url);
    if (!$url)
    {
      $this->debug("Not a valid URL");
      return "Invalid URL";
```

```
    }

    # Store the URL in the database, if it is unique, trigger the fetch.
    if (($id= $this->store($url)))
      $this->fetch($id);
    return $id;
  }
}


# Now, actually run the index worker.
$insert= new NaradaInsert();
$insert->runWorker();
```

Fetch Worker

The fetch worker, implemented as `NaradaFetch.php`, accesses the URL specified, parsing through the requested remote document for other URLs. It calls the `insert()` method resulting in the insert worker being requested, which inevitably results in the fetch worker being requested — essentially a self-sustaining web page crawl. The fetch worker then stores the content of the web page and the parsed title for the URL requested.

The implementation of the fetch worker follows this process:

➤   The implementation of the fetch worker begins as a derived class definition, inheriting from the Narada class. The two private class variables are `$crawl` and `$local`. The worker uses the variable `$crawl` to determine whether to iterate through the web page, parsing for URLs within the page content. The variable `$local` determines whether or not to parse and process URLs parsed in the web page content that are of the same domain of the URL requested. You can use the variable to contain the crawling behavior to that particular domain. If set to `1` (true), only "local" URLs are processed.

```
require('Narada.php');

class NaradaFetch extends Narada
{
  private $crawl;
  private $local;

  public function __construct()
  {
    parent::__construct();
    $this->functionName= $this->fetchFunctionName;
    $this->crawl= $GLOBALS['NaradaFetchCrawl'];
    $this->local= $GLOBALS['NaradaFetchLocalURLs'];
  }
```

➤   The next method is the `callback()` method. If you recall in the review of the Narada class's details, the `NaradaWorkerCallback()` method was the callback method specified in the Gearman worker method `addFunction()`. `NaradaWorkerCallback()` then called `callback()`, which is what is implemented in each worker. For the fetch worker, the callback method performs the bulk of the work. It fetches the web page content using the class `DomDocument`'s `loadHTMLFile()` and uses `DomXpath()` to organize the web page content into a DOM structure and the `query()` method to obtain all the HREF nodes. Depending on how you set $crawl, the fetcher worker parses URLs from HREF nodes. It ignores anchor and mailto URLs. If a URL is found that is remote, it verifies the validity of that URL and if validated, adds that URL to the $new_url_list array.

➤ Next, the members of $new_url_list are reduced to unique URLs, then $new_url_list is iterated over for each URL it contains. The URL is checked to determine if it is within the same domain of the URL of the requested web page, and if so, the Narada insert() method is called resulting in the insert worker inserting that URL. Otherwise, the URL is not of the same domain and if the class variable $this->local is set, the URL is skipped. If $this->local is not set, the Narada insert() method is called for that URL.

➤ The title is then obtained from the title DOM node and the page content and title are stored in the database using the method storeContent(). Finally, a job is sent to the job server for the index worker through the call to the method index().

```php
public function callback($job)
{
  $url= $this->get($job->workload());

  list($protocol, $domain, $path, $file)= $this->split($url);

  $this->debug("Protocol: $protocol");
  $this->debug("Domain: $domain");
  $this->debug("Path: $path");
  $this->debug("File: $file");

  # Fetch document.
  $doc = new DomDocument();
  @$doc->loadHTMLFile($url);

  if ($this->crawl)
  {
    # Extract the URLs from document object.
    $xpath = new DomXpath($doc);
    $res = $xpath->query("//a/@href");
    $new_url_list= array();
    foreach($res as $href)
    {
      if (strstr($href->nodeValue, "mailto:"))
        continue;
      else if (strstr($href->nodeValue, "://"))
        $new_url= $href->nodeValue;
      else if (substr($href->nodeValue, 0, 1) == "#")
        continue;
      else if (substr($href->nodeValue, 0, 1) == "/")
        $new_url= $domain . $href->nodeValue;
      else
        $new_url= $domain . $path . $href->nodeValue;

      # Remove local references.
      if (strstr($new_url, "#"))
        $new_url= substr($new_url, 0, -strlen(strstr($new_url, "#")));

      $new_url= $this->verify($new_url);
      if ($new_url)
```

```
            $new_url_list[]= $new_url;
    }

        # Remove duplicate URLs.
        $url_list= array_unique($new_url_list);

        # Filter URL list into local and remote URLs.
        foreach ($url_list as $new_url)
        {
          if (strstr($new_url, $domain))
          {
            $this->debug("Local URL: $new_url");
            $this->insert($new_url);
          }
          else
          {
            if ($this->local)
              $this->debug("Skipping Remote URL: $new_url");
            else
            {
              $this->insert($new_url);
              $this->debug("Remote URL: $new_url");
            }
          }
        }
    }

    $nodes= $doc->getElementsByTagName('title');
    $title= '';
    foreach ($nodes as $node)
      $title .= $node->nodeValue;

    $this->debug("Title: $title");

    # Store the document in the database.
    $this->storeContent($job->workload(), $title, $doc->textContent);

    # Send a request to the indexer.
    $this->index();
  }
```

➤ The `split()` method is a helper function to parse the various components of a URL used in the `callback()` method:

```
private function split($url)
{
  $path= strstr(substr($url, 8), "/");
  $protocol= substr($url, 0, -(strlen(strstr($url, "://")) - 3));
  $domain= substr($url, strlen($protocol), -strlen($path));
  $file= substr(strrchr($path, "/"), 1);
  if (strlen($file) > 0)
```

```
            $path= substr($path, 0, -strlen($file));

          return array($protocol, $domain, $path, $file);
        }
     }
```

➤   The fetch worker is finally run by instantiating a `NaradaFetch` object and calling
    `runWorker()`:

```
    # Now, actually run the fetch worker.
    $fetch= new NaradaFetch();
    $fetch->runWorker();
```

Search Worker

The search worker, `NaradaSearch.php`, is called by the index page, `index.php`, which calls the
`search()` method with the search term specified in the form input field of the index page. The
search worker is implemented as the NaradaSearch class, derived from the Narada class.

The first method is the `__construct()` method, which simply sets the `functionName` class variable
that corresponds to the job name NaradaSearch (set in `NaradaConf.php`) that the worker registers
itself with the gearman job server as.

The `callback()` method implements the main functionality of the worker. The value of the search
query, `$query`, is obtained from the gearman worker API method `workload()`, and is then passed
to the call of the method `searchIndex()`. This method was defined in the previous section covering
the Narada class, which performs the search against Sphinx. Upon a search, Sphinx returns a result
object, `$results`, which contains the document IDs (these correspond to the *id* column of the *url*
and *url_content* tables). `$results` is then passed to the method `getContent()`, which obtains
from either memcached (if cached already from a previous search) or the database the excerpts and
titles for each page specified by the IDs in the search results.

The worker is run by instantiating a NaradaSearch object and then calling the `runWorker()`
method, which results in the `work()` loop being entered.

```php
require('Narada.php');

class NaradaSearch extends Narada
{

  public function __construct()
  {
    parent::__construct();
    $this->functionName= $this->searchFunctionName;
  }

  public function callback($job)
  {
    $query= $job->workload();
```

```
      $results= $this->searchIndex($query);

      if ($results == false)
        return;
      else
      {
        $this->debug($results['total'] . " Documents matched '$query'");

        $content= $this->getContent($results, $query);

        $this->debug($content);

        return json_encode($content);
      }
    }
  }
}


# Now, actually run the fetch worker.
$search= new NaradaSearch();
$search->runWorker();
```

Index Worker

The index worker, `NaradaIndex.php`, is an extremely simple worker. It is implemented as the NaradaIndex class, derived from the Narada class. The index worker's purpose in life is to rebuild the Sphinx index *urls* (built from the query of a join of the *urls* and *urls_content* tables). There are three private class variables: $command, $frequency, and $count:

➤ $command is the Sphinx indexer command (path and command flags).

➤ $frequency is how many times the index worker will be called before it actually runs the Sphinx indexer. Because indexing is not something you want to run excessively, you would want to adjust this variable to something commensurate for the amount of traffic your web site experiences.

➤ The construct method sets the private class variables with the values set in `NaradaConf.php` with the corresponding $GLOBALS and resets the private $count variable to 0.

```
      require('Narada.php');

      class NaradaIndex extends Narada
      {
        private $command;
        private $frequency;
        private $count;

        public function __construct()
        {
          parent::__construct();
          $this->functionName= $this->indexFunctionName;
          $this->command= $GLOBALS['NaradaIndexCommand'];
```

```
      $this->frequency= $GLOBALS['NaradaIndexFrequency'];
      $this->count= 0;
    }

  public function callback($job)
  {
      $this->count++;

      $this->debug("Index Count: $this->count");

      if ($this->count == $this->frequency)
      {
        $this->debug("Running Index");
        system($this->command);
        $this->count= 0;
      }
    }
  }

  # Now, actually run the index worker.
  $index= new NaradaIndex();
  $index->runWorker();
```

Index Page

The index page, index.php, is the front-end entry point to Narada. This is where you either enter
a term to search the documents that you have indexed, or enter a URL to initiate the web page
retrieval through the insert and fetch workers. The index page is a gearman client in that it instantiates a Narada object, which creates a connection to the gearman job server and will call either the
insert() method if a URL is entered and submitted from the URL field or search() if a search
term is entered and submitted in the search query field. With any web page, there is the HTML content of the page:

```
<html>
 <head>
  <title>Narada Search Engine, PHP Edition</title>
  <link type="text/css" href="search.css" rel="stylesheet">
 </head>
 <body>
  <div id="header">
   <h1 id="resume-title">Narada Search</h1>
   <p id="description">Narada Search</p>
  </div>
  <div id="content">
   <div id="main">
    <div id="main2">
     <form action="<?php print $_SERVER[PHP_SELF]; ?>"
            method="GET" name="searchform" />
      <fieldset>
       <label>Search:</label>
```

```
        <input type="text" name="q" size="30" />
        <input type="submit" name="s" value="Search">
        <br />
        <br />
        <label>Submit URL:</label>
        <input type="text" name="u" size="30" />
        <input type="submit" name="s" value="Submit" />
      </fieldset>
    </form>
```

Next is the PHP code for the index page. First a check is made to see if the form parameters u or q are supplied, and if so, a Narada object is instantiated.

```
if ($_GET['u'] || $_GET['q'])
{
  require('Narada.php');
  $narada= new Narada();
}
```

If u does not contain an empty string, obviously the user specified a URL to be inserted. With this URL value, the insert() method is called, making a job request to the Gearman job server for an insert job, handled by the insert worker, inevitably resulting in the fetch worker being called.

```
if ($_GET['u'] != '')
{
  $narada->insert($_GET['u']);
  print "<b>Indexing URL: " . $_GET['u'] . "</b></center><br />\n";
}
```

If q is set, the user is searching for a search term, which is then passed to the method search(). This results in a search request to the gearman job server, which the search worker is tasked with. The search worker is not a backgrounded worker like the other workers because the results of the search are required synchronously. These results are returned as a JSON object and immediately decoded (de-serialized) into a PHP variable, $result. This result variable is an array of various parameters such as id, title, excerpt, and the URL, which are then printed out. A message stating there were no results is displayed if there weren't any results.

```
if ($_GET['q'] != '')
{
  $result= json_decode($narada->search($_GET['q']), true);
  if ($result)
  {
    $x= 1;
    foreach ($result as $entry)
    {
      print '<div class="post" id="' . $entry['id'] . '">';
      print ' <h3 class="post-title">';
      print '   <a href="' . $entry['url'] . '" alt="'. $entry['url'] . '" target="_
new">' . $entry['url_title'];
```

```
        print ' </h3>';
        print ' <div class="post-body">' . $entry['url_excerpt'] . '</div>';
        print ' <h2 class="date-header">Last updated: ' . $entry['url_last_updated'] . "</
h2>";
        print '</div>';
$x++;
      }
    }
    else
      print "<center><b>No documents found!</b></center><br />\n";
    }

    ?>
      </div>
     </div>
    </body>
  </html>
```

The Narada index page, upon submitting the URL `http://news.google.com`, will appear as shown in Figure 10-3.

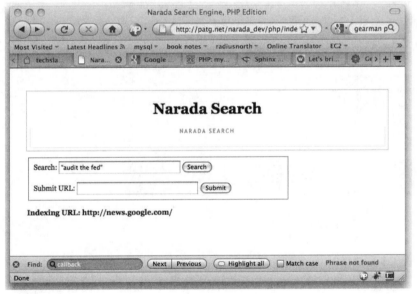

FIGURE 10-3

Next, the index page is shown after searching for the term "audit the fed" (with quotes). You can see the various results listed in Figure 10-4.

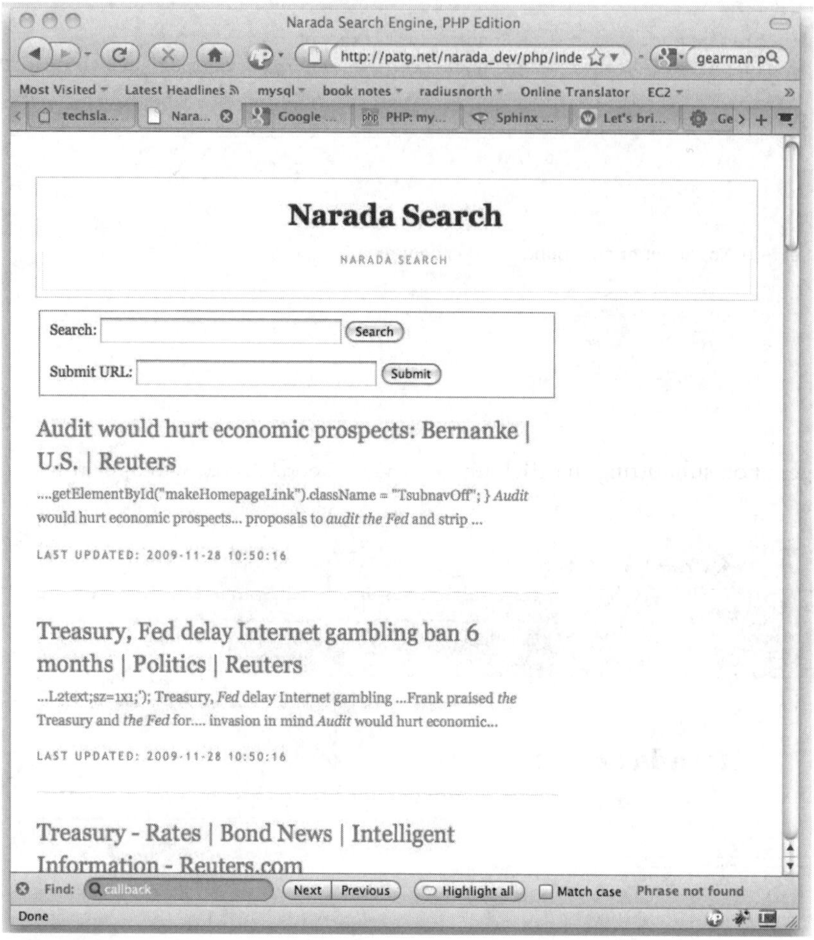

FIGURE 10-4

One Other Tidbit of Code

There is one more piece of code to cover: a simple process that is run — and it runs in a loop — called `NaradaIndexTimer.php`. This is not a worker but is a Gearman client by way of instantiating a Narada object. All this script does is run the Sphinx indexer by requesting an indexer job to the Gearman job server using the method `index()`. The interval for this script to call `index()` is determined by the global variable `$GLOBALS['NaradaIndexTimer']` in `NaradaConf.php`. This script essentially guarantees that the Sphinx index *url* is regenerated at some regularity.

```
require('Narada.php');

$narada= new Narada();

while (1)
```

```
{
    sleep($GLOBALS['NaradaIndexTimer']);
    $narada->index();
}
```

The Big Picture

Figure 10-05 gives a good idea of how all the pieces of Narada fit together. As you can see, everything previously explained is listed in this figure to give you a overall conception of how Narada works.

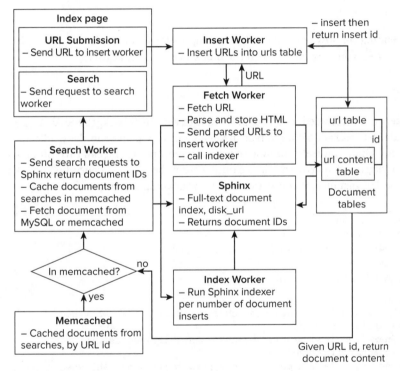

FIGURE 10-5

Running Narada

For the Gearman job server, gearmand, to assign jobs to specific workers, you need to run these workers. As stated before, these workers register themselves as being available for specifically named jobs when the Gearman job server, when receiving a request for a job by a client, assigns them to do the particular jobs. You can run these jobs either backgrounded (asynchronous) or not (synchronous), depending on whether you are testing them — once you know they are working properly, you would probably want to run them backgrounded. In the case of Narada, all the workers except the search worker are backgrounded because the results of the search worker are needed.

To run Narada, you need to run the following:

➤ A web server that can execute PHP

➤ Sphinx daemon `searchd`

➤ The Gearman job server, `gearmand`

➤ memcached

The workers are quite simple to run. For instance, for the insert workers, simply run:

```
php NaradaInsert.php
```

For the index worker, depending on how you have Sphinx set up — for instance, if you have Sphinx run as the sphinx system user — you may have to run the index worker as that user:

```
sudo su - sphinx
php NaradaIndex.php
```

You can also run the workers backgrounded, and probably want to run them backgrounded. To get a feel for how to run Narada, set `$NaradaDebug` to true in `NaradaConf.php` and run the workers without backgrounding them. Once you feel your system is working properly, you can turn off debugging and run the workers backgrounded. You should see output from the workers depending on what searches you are performing. For instance, if you search a term, you would see output such as:

```
php NaradaSearch.php
7 Documents matched 'ron paul'
282 Documents matched 'obama'
728 Documents matched '\"russia train\"'
```

For the insert worker, you would see:

```
php NaradaInsert.php
Insert URL: http://news.google.com/news/search?pz=1&cf=all&ned=us&hl=en&q=
    author%3A%22Amos+Harel%22&scoring=n
Insert URL: http://news.google.com/news/search?pz=1&cf=all&ned=us&hl=en&q=
    author%3A%22Avi+Issacharoff%22&scoring=n
Insert URL: http://news.google.com/news/search?pz=1&cf=all&ned=us&hl=en&q=
    author%3A%22Chaim+Levinson%22&scoring=n
Insert URL: http://news.google.com/news/search?pz=1&cf=all&ned=us&hl=en&q=author%3A
    %22Barak+Ravid%22&scoring=n
Insert URL: http://news.google.com/news/search?pz=1&cf=all&ned=us&hl=en&q=author%3A
    %22Jack+Khoury%22&scoring=n
id from store() 255166
FETCH: 255166
Insert URL: http://news.google.com/news/
Insert URL: http://news.google.com/news/search?pz=1&cf=all&ned=us&hl=en&q=
    author%3A%22Amos+Harel%22&cf=all&scoring=n&start=10
id from store() 255167
FETCH: 255167
Insert URL: http://news.google.com/news/search?pz=1&cf=all&ned=us&hl=en&q=
    author%3A%22Amos+Harel%22&cf=all&scoring=n&start=20
id from store() 255168
FETCH: 255168
```

For the fetch worker, you would see:

```
php NaradaFetch.php
Local URL: http://news.google.com/news/search?pz=1&cf=all&ned=us&hl=en&q=
    author%3A%22Avi+Issacharoff%22&cf=all
Local URL: http://news.google.com/news/search?pz=1&cf=all&ned=us&hl=en&q=
    author%3A%22Avi+Issacharoff%22&cf=all&scoring=d
Local URL: http://news.google.com/news/search?pz=1&cf=all&ned=us&hl=en&q=
    author%3A%22Avi+Issacharoff%22&cf=all&scoring=n&nolr=1
Local URL: http://news.google.com/news/search?pz=1&ned=us&hl=en&q=
    author%3A%22Avi+Issacharoff%22
Skipping Remote URL: http://www.haaretz.com/hasen/spages/1131613.html
Local URL: http://news.google.com/news/search?pz=1&cf=all&ned=us&hl=en&q=
    author%3A%22Amos+Harel%22&scoring=n
Local URL: http://news.google.com/news/search?pz=1&cf=all&ned=us&hl=en&q=
    author%3A%22Avi+Issacharoff%22&scoring=n
Skipping Remote URL: http://www.haaretz.com/hasen/spages/1131322.html
Skipping Remote URL: http://www.haaretz.com/hasen/spages/1131318.html
```

Once you have these workers all running, you can add URLs and search to your heart's content! You probably want to run more than one of each worker, too. The Gearman job server will use whatever is available. The more workers there are to handle jobs, the more work that can be done.

To-Do List for Narada

As stated, Narada is an open source project, using the BSD license. You are welcome and even encouraged to modify the code as much as you like. If you have some features, bug fixes, enhancements, or other modifications you would like to contribute the project, you are more than welcome to contribute and gain some fame and appreciation! Or you can make as many changes as you like for your own internal use for either yourself or the company you work for. Narada is a proof-of-concept project to show you the power of using MySQL/Drizzle, memcached, Gearman, and Sphinx together, and there are many other things you can do:

➤ The PHP fetch worker could clean up what it parses better. There are many non-alphanumeric characters showing up in the result set. The Perl version of the fetch worker does numerous regexes on the page content as opposed to using a DOM parsing method, as well as strips out all the HTML and non-alphanumeric characters. The DOM concept that the PHP version of the worker uses is certainly a cleaner way to do it, so perhaps some of the regex-fu from the Perl worker could be migrated to the PHP worker.

➤ The PHP fetch worker could have more intelligence to remove non-pertinent parts of the page and only obtain the actual core of the article that is contained in the page. For instance, many of the web sites have a navigation sidebar that lists the the titles of the site's news stories. This causes the page to be indexed with a lot of non-pertinent information.

➤ The index page could use pagination of results. The Perl version has a pagination method that could easily be converted to PHP to do this.

➤ It would be useful to have some means to control how deep the document crawl recursion goes. Right now, it is boundless, a bit like Vger from the first Star Trek movie! This could be done with some sort of global counter — perhaps using a memcached variable and the increment operation.

Those are just some ideas that would be interesting to develop for the PHP version. As with any project, there is never an end to code evolution!

Other Job Server Systems

Other systems similar to Gearman are worth mentioning as well. These systems are similar in that they provide the means to implement distributed computing.

➤ **Beanstalk:** This is a simple, fast workqueue system, much like Gearman. The server, beanstalkd, is C-based. There are clients for the various languages including PHP. The official website is `http://kr.github.com/beanstalkd/`.

➤ **Hadoop:** This is an Apache project written primarily in Java but can be used with PHP as well. Hadoop includes various components such as:

  ➤ **HBase:** A distributed database that supports structured data storage for large data sets.

  ➤ **HDFS:** A distributed file system.

  ➤ **MapReduce:** A software framework for distributed processing of large data sets on compute clusters.

  ➤ **ZooKeeper:** A high-performance coordination service for distributed applications.

SUMMARY

In this chapter, you learned about multi-tasking with PHP applications. You saw how you could use Gearman to handle functionality that was traditionally found in the web application. You can now implement these externally from your web application and thus achieve better performance while still supporting a lot of functionality in your application. The Narada application demonstrated the concept of a distributed application using Gearman as well as various other components that have been discussed in this book.

11

Rewrite Rules

WHAT'S IN THIS CHAPTER?

➤ Basic rewrite rules, taking into account the regular expressions reviewed in Chapter 1

➤ Conditional rules to display or deny access to content depending on the available data

➤ Logging rewrite events and optimizing rules and conditions

➤ Using built-in rewrite maps where a one-to-one data relationship can be used as a basis for altering URLs

➤ Building a custom rewrite map using PHP

A strong understanding of rewriting web URLs is vitally important for almost any web application. This chapter is one of the only chapters in this book that deals with concepts that are Apache web server–specific. Compatible modules do exist for other web servers; however, they are beyond the scope of this book.

The sections in the chapter include not only a traditional overview of mod_rewrite but also cover extending the rewrite capabilities using PHP and MySQL.

Rewrite rules are one of the final pieces of the PHP and MySQL puzzle and can be found in almost every major application that uses PHP. Rewrite rules serve two major purposes:

➤ Hiding the underlying functionality of PHP and thus exposing less of the site internals

➤ Creating clean and readable URLs that are easier to remember and aid in search engine optimization

It is important to use all available tools to have a coherent, easy to navigate, and easy to maintain application. A firm grasp of mod_rewrite is a welcome addition to any toolbox. The perfect application is one where a user can become an expert without ever knowing a thing about the workings of the underlying system.

USING REWRITE RULES

Rewrite rules must be defined in either the Apache configuration files or, if override is enabled, in an .htaccess file in the path of the URL that is being rewritten. Numerous tutorials are available on the Internet to set up rewrite rules and you are probably already somewhat familiar with them by now. Debugging rewrite rules can be difficult. When you have trouble getting a rule to work, it is often beneficial to simplify the rule and then rebuild it until it is fully functional and has the desired effect.

Understanding the Purpose and Structure of Rewrite Rules

Rewrite rules are most often used for masking otherwise complex URLs to improve search engine optimization as well as making the URL easier to read. Search engines often look for keywords in the URL of the document to help determine its relevance. In contrast, the query string part of the URL is often ignored when the search engine is determining relevancy. Consider these two URLs:

```
http://example.com/view.php?nodeid=123
http://example.com/2009/9/using-rewrite-rules/
```

The second URL is much easier to read and also contains keywords that a search engine can pick up. It has the added benefit of not exposing PHP to the client. By not directly exposing PHP, the URL hides one potential point of entry for would-be attackers. However, that approach is useless if view.php is still exposed directly by the web server and thus it provides only an illusion of security. The following three lines of code can be placed in the .htaccess file to allow the reader to access nodes through the friendly name but not directly through the view script:

```
RewriteEngine On
RewriteRule ^([0-9]{4})/([0-9]{0,2})/([^/]+)/$  /view.php?y=$1&m=$2&t=$4 [S]
RewriteRule ^view\.php   - [F]
```

This example is typical of rewrite rules. Each line is called a **directive**. The first directive turns on the rewrite engine. The second directive matches the pattern to the URL (see Chapter 1 on regular expressions) and, if the pattern matches, it rewrites the URL to the view script. The third line detects if the URL is the view script and forces a 403 (Forbidden) response if the URL matches the PHP file.

When you use a per-directory rule, the URL will always have the base path removed prior to evaluating the rules, then added back in when the engine completes. For example, if the URL for the file being requested is http://www .example.com/states/ma/ *and the rules exist for the directory* states, *the string being evaluated is* ma/ *and the rest of the path is added back in once processing is complete.*

This behavior is important because it acts as a kind of sandbox. The application does not need to know the full context of the URL to perform matching.

The base path can be changed using the RewriteBase *directive. For example, if* RewriteBase *is* /, *the new evaluated string becomes* states/ma/ *instead.*

Rules behave differently on a per-server configuration basis. If the rule is global to the entire server, the entire URL (including the http://*) is used for evaluation of the patterns.*

There are exceptions where the original path will not be prepended to the resulting URL:

➤ *If the replacement string starts with* http:// *or* https://*, it is treated as a redirect and executed immediately.*

➤ *If the replacement starts with a slash (like in the previous example), it is treated as relative to the site root, not the current director.*

Understanding and Controlling Rewrite Rule Flow

Rewrite directives are always executed in the order they are defined. For this reason, order does matter. In addition, flags can be defined at the end of a rule to manipulate Apache, and most flags are only read if the rule matches. The two flags used in the previous example are S and F.

The F flag is used to force a 403 (Forbidden) HTTP response. The first directive matches valid node viewing URLs and rewrites the URL to view.php. All subsequent rules will use this new URL to match against instead of the original. As a result, the third directive executes and a 403 response is generated. To prevent this, the S flag is used to skip the next directive if the pattern matches. In total there are 15 flags, as listed in Table 11-1.

TABLE 11-1: Rewrite Flags

FLAG	SHORTHAND	USAGE
redirect	R	The rule is a redirect. The status code is 302 (Found) and the second most common code is 301 (Moved Permanently), which can be specified by [R=301].
forbidden	F	Immediately returns a 403 (Forbidden) response and stops processing.

continues

TABLE 11-1 *(continued)*

FLAG	SHORTHAND	USAGE
gone	G	Returns a 410 (Gone) response. Used to indicate that a file no longer exists.
proxy	P	Indicates that the request is a proxy request and that the substitution is a valid URL. After this rule is encountered no further rules are processed.
last	L	If the rule matches use `last` to indicate that no subsequent rules should be processed.
next	N	Restarts the rewrite process from the first rule with substitute URL. This can easily create an infinite loop if you're not careful.
chain	C	Chains the current rule to the next. If the current rule is not matched, the chain will be broken and the engine will skip to the end of the chain. Any number of sequential rules can be chained.
type	T	Forces a particular mime type. For example: `[T=application/xml]`.
nosubreq	NS	Skips the rule if the current request is an internal sub-request and not a direct HTTP request by the client.
nocase	NC	Indicates that the condition is case-insensitive.
qsappend	QSA	Appends the query string to the end of the new URL. More on this later.
noescape	NE	Does not escape the output of the replacement. This is most often used when the replacement URL is already escaped. Without this flag characters such as % and $ are replaced with their hex code equivalents.
passthrough	PT	Passes the new URL to the next Apache module. This allows multiple modules that do URL translation or matching to work together. For example: mod_rewrite and mod_alias. This should be used when rewriting a URI to something that is known to be an alias.
skip	S	Skips the next rule if the current rule matches. Multiple rules can also be skipped by specifying a number. For example: `[S=2]`.

FLAG	SHORTHAND	USAGE
env	E	Sets an environmental variable, which can then be read by PHP. `[E=foo:bar]` will set the variable `foo` to the value `bar`. This is the only flag where it makes sense to have multiple occurrences in a single rule. It is also the only one where regular expression back-references can be used.

It is possible to have multiple flags for a single rewrite rule. For example, if you use both `last` and `qsappend`, the flag would look like this:

```
[L,QSA]
```

The `qsappend` flag (Query String Append — seen in the previous example using shorthand notation) is exceptionally common in web applications. It allows the entire query string to be passed through to the destination URL. This allows for rewritten URLs to also accept query parameters. Consider the difference in evaluating the URL `/search/images?q=hello%20world` between these two rules:

```
RewriteRule search/([a-z]+) /search.php?type=$1
RewriteRule search/([0-9]+) /search.php?type=$1 [QSA]
```

In the first rule the value of q will be lost in the rewriting process. In the second rule it will be appended to the query string. The second rule is much more useful. However, by appending the query string, the application suddenly allows itself to be handed arbitrary input so all input must be validated by the PHP as it would in any normal script.

Conditional Rules

Rewrite rules can be made conditional by using the `RewriteCond` directive. It takes two parameters: the first is the value to match and the second is either a pattern to match against or a conditional flag. The conditionals allow for checks against variables that are otherwise impossible to do with rewrite rules. There are 36 basic variables and four distinct categories as shown in Table 11-2.

TABLE 11-2: Rewrite Conditional Rules

HTTP HEADERS	CONNECTION AND REQUEST
HTTP_USER_AGENT	REMOTE_ADDR
HTTP_REFERER	REMOTE_HOST
HTTP_COOKIE	REMOTE_USER
HTTP_FORWARDED	REMOTE_IDENT
HTTP_HOST	REQUEST_METHOD
HTTP_PROXY_CONNECTION	SCRIPT_FILENAME
HTTP_ACCEPT	PATH_INFO
	QUERY_STRING
	AUTH_TYPE

continues

TABLE 11-2 *(continued)*

INTERNAL	TIME AND DATE
DOCUMENT_ROOT	TIME_YEAR
SERVER_ADMIN	TIME_MON
SERVER_NAME	TIME_DAY
SERVER_ADDR	TIME_HOUR
SERVER_PORT	TIME_MIN
SERVER_PROTOCOL	TIME_SEC
SERVER_SOFTWARE	TIME_WDAY
API_VERSION	TIME
THE_REQUEST	
REQUEST_URI	
REQUEST_FILENAME	
IS_SUBREQ	

Many of the variables have a PHP equivalent and should look familiar. They can be used for a variety of tasks such as redirecting the client based on user agent, time of day, accepted content types, or IP address. For example, to allow access to the admin area of a web site only from the local intranet:

```
RewriteCond %{REMOTE_ADDR}  !^192\.168\.1\.[0-9]+$
RewriteRule admin/ - [F]
```

The exclamation point at the beginning of the regular expression is specific to rewrite conditions and is used to negate the expression, so the preceding example reads: "if the remote address does not match the pattern and the URI matched the directory admin then return a forbidden message." In general it is best to use Apache-level IP security using the mod_access module. However, a more practical example is to redirect mobile phones to the mobile version of the web site:

```
RewriteCond %{HTTP_USER_AGENT} ^(Android|BlackBerry) [OR]
RewriteCond %{HTTP_USER_AGENT} ^(Motorolla|Nokia|Samsung|SonyEricson) [OR]
RewriteCond %{HTTP_USER_AGENT} iP(hone|od)
RewriteRule (.*) http://m.example.com/$1 [R=301]
```

The [OR] flag at the end of a rewrite condition indicates that if the condition does not match it should continue to find a match using the next condition. If a match is found, the engine skips to either the first rewrite condition that is not preceded by another rewrite condition with an OR flag or the first rewrite rule. Without the flag the engine assumes that all rewrite conditions preceding a rule must match in order for the rule to be evaluated.

You can use several more complex variables in addition to the simple variables listed in Table 11-1. Two of the most useful are %{ENV:name} to access an environmental variable and %{HTTP:header_name} to access an arbitrary HTTP header.

Rewrite maps, another form of pattern replacement in rewrite rules, can be used as ways to look up data that is based on input found in the URL or a constant. Rewrite maps are small programs that take a single input value and return exactly one value. They are covered in depth later in the chapter.

When using back-references in rewrite conditions, %n (where n is the index of the capture group) should be used instead of the $n that is used in rewrite rules. This has the benefit of values captured in a rewrite condition also being able to be referenced in the subsequent rules using a consistent syntax.

Besides testing for a pattern the rewrite condition can also check for other properties such as if a file exists, if it is a directory, if it is a symbolic link, and if it is an empty file. One common use is to cache thumbnail versions of an image and generate them if they do not exist:

```
RewriteCond %{REQUEST_FILENAME} !-f
RewriteCond %{REQUEST_FILENAME} -([0-9]+)x([0-9]+)\.(jpe?g|gif|png)$ [NC]
RewriteRule ^(.*)-(.+)x(.+)\.(.{3,4})$ /thumb.php?file=$1.$4&width=$2&height=$3
```

The first directive matches if the file does not exist (because of the exclamation point). The second directive matches if the filename ends in a dash followed by dimensions and an image file extension. The following filename matches the pattern:

```
example-256x128.jpg
```

The value 256 is then passed to the thumbnail generation script as the new width of the thumbnail and 128 is passed as the height. The second regular expression is less specific because at that point the string is already known to match the first expression. In this example, the PHP should never blindly create the thumbnail but instead ensure that the client has permission to create new thumbnails. Otherwise a malicious user can very quickly and easily fill the server storage with thumbnails.

You can perform six tests to check a specific file or path, as described in Table 11-3.

TABLE 11-3: Tests to Check File or Path

CONDITIONAL	USAGE
-d	Assumes the test string is a path name and the condition passes only if the path evaluates to a directory.
-f	Used in the previous example. Assumes the test string is a path and the condition passes if the path evaluates to a regular file.
-s	Same as -f only it also checks to see if the file size is greater than zero. Empty files do not pass the check (unless it is negated).
-l	Assumes the test string is a path and the condition passes if the string evaluates to a symbolic link.
-F	Same as -f, only validity is checked via an internal sub-request and tests against server access control. See the nosubreq flag for rewrite rules.
-U	Uses an internal sub-request to test if a URL is accessible.

In addition to the previous conditional tests and regular expressions, the test string is also evaluated relative to other strings. Equality can be checked via =, >, and <. As mentioned earlier, any of the conditionals in this section can be negated using an exclamation point.

Logging and Optimization

Logging is useful for debugging rewrite requests; however, it is known to slow down the server dramatically. It is a good exercise, when first starting with advanced rewrite rules, to enable logging and watch the output. Logs can also be used to find inefficiencies in the rewrite rules. Turning on logging consists of two steps; first choose the location of the log file and then choose the log level:

```
RewriteLog "/usr/local/var/apache/logs/rewrite.log"
RewriteLogLevel 9
```

A log level of nine logs everything done by the rewrite engine. The log file can only be specified per server and per virtual host. It is impossible to specify a different path to log rewrite events in a specific directory as well as to change the log level on a per-directory basis. Logging comes with significant overhead so it's recommended that you turn off logging in production environments to improve performance.

Other optimizations include using the [L] flag whenever possible in a rewrite rule when you know that no additional rules will match. skip is also useful when you know that if a rule matches, then a set number of subsequent rules are guaranteed to also not match.

> *The important thing to remember is that rewrite rules are executed on every single HTTP request so even a small inefficiency can have a large impact on busy servers. That does not mean that rewrite rules should not be used — to the contrary they are the best way to optimize a web site for search engines and to provide user-friendly URLs. However, care must be taken to not abuse them.*

Also, if there is a better tool for the job than mod_rewrite: use it instead. Although it is possible to do IP address–based restrictions via mod_rewrite, it is almost always better to use the Apache module mod_access.

REWRITE MAPS

Rewrite maps are small programs that can be referenced in rewrite rules and conditions and return a calculated result. The next couple of sections cover built-in mapping functionality and the final section demonstrates how to write a custom map with PHP and MySQL. You can also write maps in C++ or any other programming language; however, only PHP is covered in this part of the book.

A map is referenced in a similar way that variable substitutions were used in previous sections. Rewrite maps are always called using the following syntax:

```
${ map_name: key }
```

You can use several built-in internal rewrite maps to manipulate text and can use four types of maps for custom-defined mappings. This chapter covers all the internal maps and shows how to define three of the custom maps.

You can have any number of maps in a server configuration. You cannot define them on a per-directory basis; however, it is perfectly acceptable to set up a design policy where some rules are intended for use only in certain directories or hosts.

Built-in Maps

You can use several built in maps to transform text. In most cases it is better to postpone text transformation until the PHP script. However, it is sometimes desirable to do it in Apache before the PHP is processed; for example, when you evaluate a rewrite condition. Although the maps are built in, it is still necessary to define them inside your application:

```
RewriteMap toupper int:tolower
```

The same syntax is used to define maps later in the chapter. In this case int is the map type. It does not indicate an integer. What it does indicate is that the map in use is an *internal* map. Then to translate all image filenames to lowercase it becomes simple:

```
RewriteRule ^.*\.(jpe?g|png|gif) ${tolower:$0} [NC]
```

Predictably, there is also a touppercase internal map. The remaining two internal maps are escape and unescape. Escaping encodes special characters using their hex codes, and unescape converts the hex codes back to characters. They are tied in with the noescape flag for the RewriteRule directive.

Random and Text Lookups

Often, an application has a set of key/value pairs that you should use for writing a URL. For small sets of data it is often practical to use a txt rewrite map. Text maps expect a file that contains key/value pairs where the key and value are separated by white space and you can comment on them using a hash character. An example data set may map directories that have moved to their new location at a different domain:

```
documentation    docs.example.com
faqs             docs.example.com/faqs
api              api.example.com
```

The map must then be defined and accessed:

```
RewriteMap moved txt:/maps/moved.txt
RewriteRule ^(.*)/(.*)$ http://${moved:$1}/$2 [R=301,QSA]
```

Remember, the map declaration must be in the server configuration and the RewriteRule should be in a per-directory configuration (probably the root directory of the old site). For larger data sets, it becomes necessary to store the file in DMB format. The DMB format allows for quicker lookup of key/value pairs. Although this book does not cover the DMB format, in one of the next sections, you use PHP in conjunction with rewrite maps to look up data from a MySQL database.

Another type of basic map is rnd, which chooses a random value based on a key input. You often see this type of map as an inexpensive form of load balancing. For example:

```
video       01|02|03|04|05
images      06|07
audio       08
downloads   09|10|11
```

The corresponding map definition and usage looks like this:

```
RewriteMap media rnd:/maps/media.txt
RewriteRule ^media/(.*)$ http://www${media:$1}.example.com/$2 [R,QSA]
```

Text and random rewrite maps are useful for small to medium amounts of data that do not change often. However, it is often useful to rewrite URLs based on large or dynamic data sets. The example in the next section is a simple but fully functional shortened URL application.

Using PHP and MySQL

Shortened URL applications are common to create addresses that take up less space. They are particularly useful with microblogging applications and text messages that put a limit on the length of the message. In this next application, the URL will look like "/123" where 123 is the encoded index to a MySQL table. A simple PHP script is provided in the code examples to output a shortened version of a URL based on a command-line input.

First, you start with a short-URL class that encodes, decodes, and writes URLs to the database. The class uses the singleton pattern from Chapter 1, as shown in Listing 11-1.

LISTING 11-1: UrlShortener.class.php

```php
<?php

class UrlShortener {
  private $characterMap;
  private $base;
  const OFFSET = 512;

  public function __construct() {
    $this->characterMap = array(
      'q', 'w', 'r', 't', 'y', 'p', 's', 'd',
      'f', 'g', 'h', 'j', 'k', 'L', 'm', 'n',
      '3', '2', '1', 'z', 'x', 'c', 'v', 'b',
      '4', '5', '9', '6', '8', '7'
    );
    $this->base = sizeof($this->characterMap);
  }

  public static function getInstance() {
    static $instance = null;
    if ( $instance === null ) {
      $instance = new UrlShortener();
    }
```

```php
      return $instance;
  }

  public function shorten( $conn, $url ) {
    $escapedUrl = mysql_escape_string($url);

    $res = mysql_query(
      "SELECT `id` FROM urls WHERE `url` LIKE '$escapedUrl'",
      $conn
    );

    $row = mysql_fetch_row($res);
    mysql_free_result( $res );

    if ( $row )
      return $this->encode( $row[0]+self::OFFSET );

    $res = mysql_query(
      "INSERT INTO `urls` (`url`) VALUES('$escapedUrl')",
      $conn
    );
    return $this->encode( mysql_insert_id($conn)+self::OFFSET );
  }

  public function encode( $value ) {
    $value += 512;
    if ( $value < $this->base )
      return $this->characterMap[ $value ];
    else
      return $this->encode( floor($value/$this->base) ).
             $this->characterMap[ $value % $this->base ];
  }

  public function decode( $value ) {
    $decodeMap = array_flip( $this->characterMap );
    $parts = array_reverse( str_split( $value ) );

    $index = 0;
    $i = 0;
    foreach ( $parts as $char ) {
      $index += $decodeMap[$char] * pow( $this->base, $i++ );
    }
    return $index-512;
  }

  public function expand( $conn, $index ) {
    $id = $this->decode( $index )-self::OFFSET;
    $res = mysql_query("SELECT `url` FROM `urls` WHERE `id` = $id", $conn);
    $value = ( ($row = mysql_fetch_row( $res )) ? $row[0]: null );
    mysql_free_result( $res );
    return $value;
  }
};

?>
```

This class is a fully functional URL shortener. It contains a method to insert new URLs into the system as well as a method for retrieving them. To prevent the URLs from being predictable, they are encoded using a custom numbering system. Adding to the array in the constructor can easily expand the character set used for encoding. The only rule is that a character cannot appear in the array twice (doing so would introduce ambiguity when decoding). The offset 512 is also added to the base index to prevent the first few URLs from being too short.

> *The MySQL table for the short URLs is only two fields: the URL field, which can be a* VARCHAR *or* TEXT; *and the id field, which is an auto-incrementing integer. You can find the complete SQL file to re-create the database in the code listings under* UrlShortener.sql. *There is also a test data file available.*

The next step is to write the actual mapping program. External rewrite maps are of the type prg. The new file will be very short because the UrlShortener class does most of the heavy lifting. The completed rewrite map looks like Listing 11-2.

LISTING 11-2: ShortUrlMap.php

```php
#!/usr/local/bin/php
<?php

include( "UrlShortener.class.php" );
$shortener = UrlShortener::getInstance();

set_time_limit(0);

$stdin = fopen("php://stdin","r");
while ( true ) {
  $index = trim(fgets($stdin));
  return $shortener->expand( getDb(), $index)."\n";
}

function getDb() {
  static $db = null;

  if ( $db == null || !mysql_ping($db) ) {
    $db = mysql_connect('localhost','user','password',true);
    mysql_select_db('shorturl');
  }

  return $db;
}
?>
```

*The first line of the script is a **shebang**. It tells UNIX- and Linux-based systems where to find the executable used to run the file. This should be the path to PHP on your system. It is usually* `/usr/local/bin/php` *or* `/usr/bin/php`. *The file must then be made executable by typing* `chmod +x ShortUrlMap.php` *on the command line. It is also good practice to make the script owned by the same user as the web server.*

On Windows-based systems, you must remove the shebang and modify the rewrite map directive to include the full path to the PHP executable. The directive can be enclosed in quotes to allow for spaces.

Because the `ShortUrlMap.php` *script uses standard input, you can also use it as a command-line tool to test URLs by simply running the script on the command line, typing the encoded part of the short URL, and then pressing Enter.*

For more examples of command-line applications, see Chapter 15.

Rewrite maps are loaded into memory when the server starts or when new instances are needed. A single instance of the script serves up many rewrite responses, and the script loops indefinitely. A line feed terminates each request, and the output is expected to be a single line feed terminated string per request. There are a few things to be considered when writing maps:

➤ **PHP has a timeout for scripts.** The timeout must be turned off via the `set_time_limit()` function.

➤ **Each instance of the script will tie up exactly one connection to the database.** If the map is not often used, it may be a good idea to close the connection after each use.

➤ **MySQL has a timeout for connections.** For this reason the database handle is returned from a function that checks for a valid database connection and creates a new one if the connection is not valid. This saves hours of frustration when the map suddenly stops working after eight hours (the default timeout).

The map will never be executed if it is not defined in the server configuration. The definition for an external map looks very much like the definition for any other map:

```
RewriteMap shorturl prg:/maps/ShorturlMap.php
RewriteRule ^(.+)$ http://${shorturl:$1} [R=301]
```

The map, although functional, is missing some key elements. For example, it is inefficient to hit the MySQL database for every single request. This is especially true when considering the nature of real-time social networks, where a URL is likely to get most of its traffic in the first few hours after it is posted online. Performance could be greatly improved just by adding a simple local expiring cache. For tips on caching to improve performance, refer to Chapter 4.

SUMMARY

The use of the rewrite engine is limited by the creativity of the developer. However, as with many technologies, there can be too much of a good thing. The general best practices for deciding what method to use to process URLs are:

➤ Use `RewriteRule` to clean up a URL if a PHP script takes several logical parameters via the query string such as date, page number, and resource id.

➤ Use `RewriteRule` to deny access to a file if the mod_access module is not sufficient.

➤ Use `RewriteCondition` if the application is already using rewrite rules but some rules should only be executed if a certain condition has been met, such as if a file exists.

➤ Use a `txt` `RewriteMap` if there is a small and infrequently changing data set that has a one-to-one relationship between what is passed in the URL and what should be in the final rewritten URL.

➤ Use a `rnd` `RewriteMap` to provide inexpensive software-based load balancing or to cycle through content (for example, an advertising system).

➤ Use a custom PHP `RewriteMap` when working with large data sets that change frequently and are also frequently accessed, or when some calculations are needed.

➤ Use an actual PHP script and skip mod_rewrite altogether if determining the type of content requires significant calculation, or the content is accessed so infrequently that keeping one or more custom `RewriteMaps` loaded into memory is not justifiable.

Remember that data passed to a PHP script, even if it is through a rewrite rule, should not be trusted. Make sure to sanitize all data that may come either directly or indirectly from user input.

The next chapter covers user authentication using PHP and MySQL.

12

User Authentication

PHP is particularly well suited for user authentication, and where PHP is used for authentication you will usually find a MySQL database behind it. It doesn't take long for an application to grow to the point where it needs an authentication system, which will most likely include:

- ➤ User login and logout
- ➤ User roles (administrator, guest, and so on)
- ➤ User management

Similarly, it often isn't long before built-in Apache or IIS authentication becomes insufficient. In many cases, the authentication system is one of the first scripts that a PHP programmer attempts to write. Expert PHP programmers recognize that security — especially when it comes to sensitive user information — is paramount, and if the developer is not careful, it is easy to leave an application open to attacks such as session theft and replay attacks.

This chapter covers techniques and best practices for storing user account information, authenticating users, and maintaining sessions.

The chapter finishes off with a brief overview of Access Control List (ACL).

Two topics that are not covered in this chapter are OpenID and OAuth. Both are methods for authenticating users with third-party login credentials. Each method warrants discussion and is appropriate to use in many if not most applications. However, neither system is discussed in-depth in this book. For more information visit the OpenID foundation website at `http://www.openid.net/` *or the OAuth website at* `http://www.oauth.net`.

The start of any good authentication system is a strong database. The examples in this chapter build a database schema that can be used to store user information and then build three different authentication systems on top of it.

DESIGNING THE DATABASE

User authentication is one of the most used subsystems of an application. Because HTTP — the most common mechanism for accessing PHP scripts — does not maintain state it is necessary to re-evaluate user credentials on every page load. As a consequence, a database must not only be secure, but also sufficiently optimized.

This section first defines the database table and then goes piece-by-piece over every column in the table and defines the reasoning behind each. Listing 12-1 shows the create statement for the table:

LISTING 12-1: users.sql

Available for download on Wrox.com

```
CREATE TABLE `users` (
  `uid` INT AUTO_INCREMENT PRIMARY KEY,
  `username` VARCHAR(32) UNIQUE,
  `email` VARCHAR(128) UNIQUE,
  `password` VARCHAR(32),
  `created` DATETIME,
  `lastlogin` DATETIME
);
```

The uid field (User ID) is used to store a unique key for the user. The username is also a unique field; however, it is desirable to use the auto-increment field for the primary key. One of the main reasons for doing so is to decouple the real user information from the key. Using an auto-increment number means that customer service can change the username of a user without having to worry about maintaining the referential integrity of the data. Using numeric keys can also result in a less storage- and processor-intensive system.

The username is what the user actually types into the application in order to sign in. The length of a username is quite arbitrary and depends on the developer's discretion. The username must be unique so it is flagged as such in the database. An added benefit of making the value into a unique key is that unique keys are indexed, which improves lookup speed. The same is true for the next field, which is `email`. Email does not necessarily have to be unique, but requiring uniqueness solves a few problems:

➤ **It prevents an amateur attacker from easily signing up for many accounts.** However, that is only relative to the least sophisticated attacker. A more involved attack would include setting up a mail server and creating an arbitrary number of mailboxes.

➤ **Users often have accounts at many different services.** Requiring a unique email means that users can be warned when they accidentally try to sign up for another account. The warning message may be something along the lines of "An account already exists with this email. Did you forget your username or password?" If users forget their password and username, they can be very quickly queried on the indexed email field.

The final piece of required information is the password. Although it is not uncommon to store the password directly, this book does not recommend doing that. If it is absolutely necessary to store the original password, it should never be stored in unencrypted plain text.

The best practice is to store the password, at a bare minimum, as a salted MD5 hash. Many systems use just a simple MD5 hash, which maintains most of the effectiveness. The MD5 algorithm is a so-called one-way hash because it is designed to return a unique value (hash) for almost any input and that value cannot be decoded and returned back to the original. The hash is not, however, unique. Collisions are extremely rare but they do exist. The probability of someone accidentally entering another password that evaluates to the same hash or an attacker finding a password that evaluates to the same hash are both very low. Also, an attacker would have to know which username that password works for.

To add some additional security the application can use a different kind of hash such as SHA-1 in place of MD5.

Several methods currently exist to *decrypt* an MD5. The most popular method is called *rainbow tables*. Rainbow tables are lookup tables that allow someone to easily find a value that is not likely the same as the original password but evaluates to the same hash. That new string can then be used in place of the user's password to log in to websites without actually knowing the real password.

The worst-case scenario is if the user database is compromised and if the passwords gathered from the database are used to gain access to sensitive data in the user account or to other sites where the user is also registered (people tend to use the same password on multiple sites). Storing the MD5 hash instead of the actual password goes a long way. However, if the attacker simply finds another string that evaluates to the same hash, he can still log in much the same way. To emphasize the dangers, consider the following scenario:

➤ An ecommerce website's database is compromised and the user table is exposed.

➤ The passwords are stored as MD5 hashes but the attacker finds another string — using a rainbow table — that evaluates to the same hash.

➤ The attacker then logs in to the system as the user.

➤ PHP, seeing this login as a legitimate user, decrypts the user's credit card information and allows items to be purchased by the attacker.

The solution is to add a salt to the end of the password before sending it to the database. The salt is a string—usually private—that is known to the application. The new value in the database is actually the MD5 of the password concatenated the salt. Even if the attacker has both the salt and the MD5 hash, it is extremely unlikely that he will find another string that equates to the MD5 hash when concatenated with the salt. You can use the same salt throughout the application. Another alternative is to use the username as the salt so that it is unique for each user yet still easy to calculate without multiple hits to the database.

The final two fields in the table are nice to have but are not necessary from a purely technical standpoint. When running reports it becomes important to graph user activity. The most common of those activities are when the user signs in or signs up for new account. You can obtain a wealth of information using just these two values, such as:

➤ How many users signed up but never returned to the site for a second visit

➤ How many users have actively used the site for more than a month

➤ How many users haven't signed into the site in over a month

➤ How many of the active users have been members for more than a year

Depending on the application it may be desirable to store even more information, such as how many times the user has logged in as well as demographic information such as real name, birthday, and location.

HTTP-BASED AUTHENTICATION

The HTTP standard provides two methods of authentication: *basic* and *digest*. Both methods have commonality regarding both behavior and implementation.

In each method, a dialog box displays and prompts the user for the username and password. The web browser controls the dialog box and the PHP script has very little influence over what is displayed in the box. The one aspect that the script can control is the *realm*, which is a hint in the dialog box that tells the user what she is logging in to and is also used internally by the browser/client to differentiate between logins on the same host. This method is different than the HTML form-based methods used in many PHP applications in that it takes the user out of the normal flow of the application in order to request authentication.

Both methods of authentication are supported by Apache and Microsoft IIS natively without the need to use PHP. However, using the native methods has its disadvantages:

➤ *Logout and session management is left up to the client so it can be unreliable at times and may behave differently from client to client.*

➤ *Extra server extensions are often required to integrate with user tables on databases such as MySQL.*

➤ *Application level features such as Access Control Lists (covered later) are lost.*

Both methods use the HTTP 401 response to prompt the user for login information. The code 401 is the "Unauthorized" response. It is possible to send just that code without a directive instructing the client what authentication method to use, in which case the client displays the body of the response. Alternatively, a `WWW-Authenticate` header can be sent, which tells the client which of the two authentication schemes to use.

Basic Authentication

Basic Authentication has been available since the early days of HTTP. The standard defines a method for specifying login credentials as part of the URL as well as part of the HTTP headers.

Typically the username and password are only passed via the URL when a user clicks a link or bookmark, or when doing very simple HTTP fetch scripts. Passing information via a URL looks like this:

```
http://username:password@example.com/
```

It is important to note that this practice is so insecure that Internet Explorer, and perhaps other browsers, completely disabled its use, for two primary reasons, both revolving around the fact that the URL is often logged:

➤ **The username and password show up clearly in the web server logs.** Even if you trust your server administrators completely or you administer the logs yourself it is not a good idea to have user passwords lying around in plain text.

➤ **The URL also shows up in the client browser history**. Anyone can then easily return to the site that requires authentication. This one is particularly a problem on public computers.

The URL-based method should be avoided, even when using SSL, for those reasons. However, even when the password is not passed via the URL it is not secure. When password is passed through the HTTP Authorization request header it is sent as a base64-encoded string. Base64 is just another way of representing binary data using only ASCII characters; it is similar to hexadecimal (base16). In this case it is used primarily as a way of obscuring the data and ensuring proper handling if the password or username contain binary characters. It only gives the illusion of added security, because it can be easily decoded. But it is still better than having the username and password in the URL.

To force authentication, it is necessary to send the HTTP 401 response as well as the type of authentication. This section creates a basic authentication class so each part is presented as a member method. The following method forces the client to authenticate:

```
public function forceAuthentication() {
    header('WWW-Authenticate: Basic realm="'.$this->realm.'"');
    header('HTTP/1.0 401 Unauthorized');
    die( $this->unauthorizedNotice );
}
```

The method sends along the authentication type as well as the realm. The realm primarily displays a friendly name to the user but, as mentioned earlier, it does have other users. The message, referenced in the preceding code by the variable $unauthorizedNotice, displays when the user clicks Cancel in the authentication dialog box. Because at that point the user is not authenticated, it is desirable to end the execution of the script. The specification does not limit the number of username and password requests, so a complete application may also track the number of invalid password attempts and display the notice when the limit is reached. To display the message without a prompt for the password, just send the status header without the authentication header.

> *It is best practice to never send a 200 (Found) header when a user is not authorized to view a page. Instead, send the 401 (Unauthorized) header. The same practice applies to data that cannot be found (404) and application errors (500 range).*

Another method in the class can read in the server variables and validate them. The two variables available are PHP_AUTH_USER and PHP_AUTH_PW and both can be found in the $_SERVER global array:

```
public function requireAuthentication() {
    if ( array_key_exists('PHP_AUTH_USER', $_SERVER) &&
         array_key_exists('PHP_AUTH_PW', $_SERVER) ) {

        session_start();

        $saltedPassword = md5($_SERVER['PHP_AUTH_PW'].'-'.$this->salt);

        if ( $_SERVER['PHP_AUTH_USER'] != $_SESSION['user'] ||
             $saltedPassword != $_SESSION['password'] ) {

            $conn = mysql_connect( self::$db_host,
                                   self::$db_user,
                                   self::$db_password );
            mysql_select_db( self::$database, $conn );

            $query = "SELECT * FROM `users` WHERE `username`='%s' AND ".
                     "`password`='%s'";
            $query = sprinf($query, mysql_escape_string($_SERVER['PHP_AUTH_USER']),
                            $saltedPassword );

            $user = mysql_fetch_assoc( mysql_query($query) );
            mysql_close($conn);

            if ( $user ) {
                $_SESSION['user'] = $_SERVER['PHP_AUTH_USER'];
                $_SESSION['password'] = $saltedPassword;
            } else {
                $this->forceAuthentication();
            }

        }

    } else {
        $this->forceAuthentication();
    }
}
```

You've probably used sessions in the past. They are server-side data storage mechanisms that are linked to a particular client. They are usually keyed off of a cookie but sometimes a value passed in through the query string is used instead. In this case a session is used to store the logged in user and a hash of the password.

The method of storing sessions is customizable, as you will see later in the chapter.

The preceding example doesn't have any error checking. This is so you can easily read it to see what is going on. A production application should be more robust and have error checking in place.

The session in the preceding method stores the information for the authenticated user. It is not used to directly determine whether the user is logged in because the client will send the authentication header with every request. Instead, using the session is a more efficient method than triggering a database hit for each page view. If the username and password match the session, there is no need to check the database. The session can also be used to store other regularly referenced calculated information that may be expensive to retrieve later.

When using the Microsoft ISS web server, the PHP_AUTH variables are not set in older versions of PHP. This sample authentication code does not account for that because it is assumed that the application uses PHP 5 or higher. In the case of older versions, the HTTP_AUTHORIZATION server variable contains the full contents of the header (including the authentication type). The PHP reference manual contains an easy way to parse this data:

```
list($user, $pw) = explode(':',
    base64_decode(substr($_SERVER['HTTP_AUTHORIZATION'], 6)));
```

The completed class contains configuration variables for the database as well as the authentication realm. Remember, basic authentication should be done over SSL if there is any sensitive information on the website. Any unencrypted page can be used as a potential vector for attack because the authentication data is sent with each request.

An alternative authentication method — one that does not send the password in plain text — is digest authentication.

Digest Authentication

Digest authentication, unlike basic authentication, relies on creating a single-direction hash of various data using a shared secret key. The secret key is the user's password. This method makes it possible to authenticate the user without ever sending the password across the network.

The hash involves creating a long string based on data that both the client and the server know and then using that string to create an MD5 hash along with the password. The server is not required to store any of the public variables. They are, instead, passed along with each request. Several pieces of data are used to create the hash:

> ➤ **realm:** The same as with basic authentication. It is simply a string to display to the user and a way for the client to differentiate between multiple authentication areas. In digest authentication it is also used as part of the hash.

➤ **domain:** This directive is a value that is not used in the creation of the hash but allows you to use the same authentication across multiple domains. It is a space-separated list of domains that acts as a hint to the client. It is not a required value.

➤ **nonce:** Also known as "number used once." You use this directive to prevent replay attacks. A replay attack is when software on the user's computer or a malicious machine on the network records the user authentication information. That information is then later "replayed" to gain access to the application as the user. Ensuring that the same nonce is not used for multiple requests solves that problem. Nonce values are used in many forms of authentication including OpenID (a method for validating access to a website using credentials from a different site). In its strictest form, a nonce should become invalid (or stale) after a single use. It is also common to invalidate the nonce after a certain period of time.

The digest authentication specification does not require that the nonce actually be a number. It can, for example, be an encoded string that specifies values, such as when the nonce was created, which can later be decoded to determine if the nonce is stale. It is also possible to have a non-expiring nonce. However, that approach is not recommended because it provides absolutely no protection against replay attacks. The example in this section uses a nonce that expires after 120 seconds. More complicated methods of generating the nonce exist that won't be covered here.

➤ **opaque:** A string that should be passed unaltered back to the server. It can validate that the realm being accessed is the same realm for which the hash was generated; however, it is easily spoofed because it is not used to generate the hash.

➤ **stale:** The application can also pass a *stale* directive (set to TRUE) to the client indicating that the nonce was valid at one point but is no longer valid. The server should check that the hash is valid for the set nonce before sending this request. If the hash is not valid, the application should not indicate it is stale because when encountering a stale response message, the client has the option to simply regenerate the hash with the new nonce. Indicating that a nonce is stale when the username or password is wrong will cause confusion.

➤ **algorithm:** This does not need to be specified because it defaults to "MD5" (which is what the next example uses).

➤ **qop:** A quoted string that specifies the "quality of protection." It is optional but should be specified for backwards compatibility with previous digest specifications. The two common values are auth and auth-int (this book uses the former).

You can find more details about the directives and the hash calculations in RFC2617 (HTTP Authentication) and RFC2069 (Digest Access Authentication).

The headers for digest authentication are very similar to those of basic authentication. However, in digest authentication it is necessary to specify the directives that were listed earlier in this section. The only part of the response header that changes is `WWW-Authenticate`:

```
header('WWW-Authenticate: Digest realm="'.$this->realm.
        '",qop="auth",nonce="'.uniqid().'",opaque="'.md5($this->realm).
        '"'.($stale ? ',stale="TRUE"'));
```

A argument called `$stale` can now be passed to the `requireAuthentication()` call. Remember, `stale` is used to tell the client that the authentication is correct but is too old to use anymore. The client will likely respond by regenerating a hash using the same password without prompting the user for a password a second time.

To verify the sent password, it is necessary to use the shared secret to generate the same string that the client creates. If the strings do not match, the shared secret (the password) is wrong. This section covers the MD5 algorithm, which is the simplest to implement. The RFC specifies how to calculate the three parts: A1, A2, and the final result. Parts A1 and A2 are hashes of various directives concatenated together. The final string is both A1 and A2 concatenated with the nonce and hashed.

The PHP documentation provides a very useful helper function to parse the string returned from the client:

```
private function parseDigest($txt)
{
    // protect against missing data
    $needed_parts = array('nonce'=>1, 'nc'=>1, 'cnonce'=>1, 'qop'=>1,
                          'username'=>1, 'uri'=>1, 'response'=>1);
    $data = array();
    $keys = implode('|', array_keys($needed_parts));

    preg_match_all('@(' . $keys . ')=(?:([\'"])([^\2]+?)\2|([^\s,]+))@',
                   $txt, $matches, PREG_SET_ORDER);

    foreach ($matches as $m) {
        $data[$m[1]] = $m[3] ? $m[3] : $m[4];
        unset($needed_parts[$m[1]]);
    }

    return $needed_parts ? false : $data;
}
```

This book usually uses / to wrap regular expressions. However, it is also possible to use @ as in the preceding example, or any other character.

The code fetches all the parts of the string. If the array `$needed_parts` is not empty, some of the information required by the RFC was missing. Using that utility function (which was derived from an example at `http://us2.php.net/manual/en/features.http-auth.php`) it is then possible to generate the various parts:

```
public function requireAuthentication() {
    if ( !($directives = $this->parseDigest($_SERVER['PHP_AUTH_DIGEST'])) )
```

```
        $this->forceAuthentication();

   if ( $this->getValidDigest($directives) != $directives['response'] )
     $this->forceAuthentication();
}

private function getValidDigest( $directives ) {

   $conn = mysql_connect( self::$db_host,
                          self::$db_user,
                          self::$db_password );
   mysql_select_db( self::$database, $conn );

   $query = "SELECT * FROM `users` WHERE `username`='%s';"
   $query = sprinf($query, mysql_escape_string($directives['user']));
   $user = mysql_fetch_assoc( mysql_query($query) );
   mysql_close($conn);
   if ( !$user ) return false;

   $A1 = md5($directives['username'] . ':' .
              $this->realm . ':' . $user['password']);
   $A2 = md5($_SERVER['REQUEST_METHOD'].':'.$directives['uri']);
   $validDigest = md5($A1.':'.$directives['nonce'].':'.
                      $directives['nc'].':'.$directives['cnonce'].':'.
                      $directives['qop'].':'.$A2);
   return $validDigest;
}
```

The preceding example requires that the password used to calculate $A1$ *be plain text. This is just to make it easier to follow and should not be done in production applications. As mentioned earlier, it is not a good practice to store passwords in the database that way. Possible alternatives to storing the password in plain text are to store the entire value of* $A1$ *in the database (which will not change so long as the realm does not change) or to encrypt the password data using a bidirectional algorithm.*

The most common method of authentication in PHP applications is to actually create an authentication system from scratch. Although the built-in HTTP authentication methods are useful, they are not very customizable or flexible and they do have security issues associated with them. For instance, the login dialog box cannot be styled to meet the look and feel of the rest of the application, and both authentication methods are susceptible to man-in-the-middle attacks.

PURE PHP AUTHENTICATION

Pure PHP authentication takes a different approach than the standard HTTP methods that you have seen so far in this chapter. Instead of using standard HTTP headers, a pure PHP system typically displays a username and password form embedded within other content. Then, once the user authenticates, a cookie is dropped that maintains the user session. You can also implement other methods, such as OAuth and OpenID, in PHP; however, they do not prompt for a username and password but rather initiate a handshake between the application and an authentication server.

Without taking proper precautions it is easy to create an application where a malicious person can hijack a user's session. The two most common ways that this happens are as follows:

➤ The malicious user steals the user's cookies by sniffing traffic on the network or via an XSS attack (which is covered in Chapter 14). The malicious user then mirrors the cookies on his machine in order to appear to be the legitimate user.

➤ The malicious user sniffs the traffic on the network and sees the username and password transmitted in plain text in a cookie and uses that information to log in as the user.

The first scenario is actually a form of replay attack and would require client fingerprinting or a nonce to prevent. The second scenario is much easier to prevent, and most of the focus of this section will be given to it. There are two methods for preventing the username and password from being stolen. The first is to use server-side sessions to store user information. The second is to store all the credential information about the user in an encrypted cookie.

Using PHP Sessions

PHP sessions are a way to store information regarding the user on the server so that it does not all need to be passed through on every request via cookies. Instead, only a session ID is stored in a cookie, which then retrieves the complete session. Sessions in PHP are created and maintained via the session API, which consists of many functions, the most common being session_start(). After the session is initialized the session data is stored in the $_SESSION global array. Changes made to the array are reflected in the session.

 Sessions do not need to use cookies. The session ID can also be passed via GET and POST variables. The behavior of session ID passing can be controlled in the PHP configuration.

The default session handling stores session data on disk. It is possible to overwrite the session handling to use a different storage mechanism. The example in this section writes a class that stores session data in a MySQL database. The table for this new database looks like this:

```
CREATE TABLE `session` (
 `sessionid` VARCHAR(128),
 `uid` INT,
 `data` MEDIUMBLOB,
 `timestamp` INT,
 `ip` VARCHAR(15),
 PRIMARY KEY ( `sessionid` ),
 KEY ( `timestamp`, `sessionid` )
)
```

The last field before the keys is added for a little extra security to prevent session theft. When the session is opened the script checks that the IP matches the IP of the client and throws an exception if it does not. That way the session cookie becomes worthless if someone attempts to hijack it. Unfortunately, that is only true if the attacker is not on the same network and therefore does not have the same external IP address as the user. However, it does provide a finer grain of security.

The timestamp field is used later to expire old sessions. There will be more on it later in this section.

To use custom session handlers, you must first register them before the session starts. A good practice is to have a `session.php` file that is always included in the first line of the script.

The method that registers new session I/O handlers is `session_set_save_handler()`. The method takes six parameters, all of which are callback functions. Simple code to register the event handlers looks like this:

```
session_set_save_handler( 'custom_session_open', 'custom_session_close',
                          'custom_session_read', 'custom_session_write',
                          'custom_session_destroy', 'custom_session_gc' );
```

The first callback function is `open`, which in this example creates a connection to MySQL. The `open` function has two parameters. The first parameter is the path where the session should be saved. In the simple MySQL-based example this is just ignored. The path is the directory where the script is allowed to write session information. The filename typically consists of the session name with a prefix and extension. The session name is the second parameter and is used as the primary key of the table.

The second function, the `close` function, is called when the script is done reading and writing to the session and no longer plans to use it. It is important to note that sessions are locking. The same session cannot be read from or written to by more than one script at once. Sometimes it is useful to close the session ahead of time using `session_write_close()`. This method is discussed later in greater detail while reviewing the `CustomSession` class.

The `read` and `write` functions are complementary. The session data is stored as a string. The content of the string is not consequential under normal usage so the `read` function just returns a string unaltered from storage and the `write` function writes it to storage without altering or processing. In this example the `open` function is the equivalent of a MySQL SELECT and the `write` function is the INSERT / UPDATE query.

The `destroy` function is used only when the session is manually destroyed with `session_destroy()`. Destroying a session only removes all data associated with it. It does not invalidate the session ID or cookies. In the authentication system later in this chapter it will be necessary to unset the session cookies as well.

Old sessions need to be periodically purged from the system. That is the job of the garbage collection. Note that it is not the same one you saw in Chapter 8. It is executed periodically just to clean up old sessions. The probability of the collector being executed is a function of the `php.ini` variables: `session.gc_maxlifetime`, `session.gc_probability`, and `session.gc_divisor`. When the garbage collector is executed it takes the maximum lifetime of a session and is expected to delete all sessions that have exceeded that lifetime. The default is 24 minutes (or 1440 seconds).

If the timeout is not a key then deleting old sessions could be a costly operation, especially when you have millions of sessions. However, making the value a key has its own issues as well, mainly that all keys must be unique. The table design in this chapter uses a compound key with both the timestamp and the session ID to avoid collisions in situations where multiple users log in at the same second.

Chapter 3 covers callback functions in detail. This session class uses callback functions to reference session handling methods in a singleton session class. The basic session class looks like that in Listing 12-2:

LISTING 12-2: CustomSession.class.php

```php
<?php
class CustomSession {
  private static $db_host = "localhost";
  private static $db_user = "sessions";
  private static $db_password = "password";
  private static $database = "sessions";

  private $conn;

  public static function getInstance() {
    static $instance = null;
    if ( $instance == null ) {
      $instance = new CustomSession();
    }
    return $instance;
  }

  public function __construct() {
    session_set_save_handler(
      array($this,"open"), array($this,"close"),
      array($this,"read"), array($this,"write"),
      array($this,"destroy"), array($this,"gc") );
  }

  public function __destruct() {
    session_write_close();
  }

  public function open( $path, $id ) {
    $this->conn = mysql_connect( CustomSession::$db_host,
                                 CustomSession::$db_user,
                                 CustomSession::$db_password );
    mysql_select_db( CustomSession::$database, $this->conn );
  }

  public function close() {
    mysql_close($this->conn);
```

```php
    }

    public function read( $id ) {
      $escaped_id = mysql_escape_string( $id );
      $res = $this->query("SELECT * FROM `session` WHERE `sessionid`='$escaped_id'");
      if ( $row = mysql_fetch_assoc( $res ) ) {
        $this->query("UPDATE `session` ".
                     "SET `timestamp` = UTC_TIMESTAMP() ".
                     "WHERE `sessionid`='$escaped_id'");
        return $row['data'];
      }
      return "";
    }

    public function write( $id, $data ) {
      $query = "REPLACE  INTO `session` ".
               "(`sessionid`, `data`, `ip`, `timestamp`) ".
               "VALUES ('%s', '%s', '%s', UNIX_TIMESTAMP(UTC_TIMESTAMP()))";
      $this->query(
        sprintf( $query, mysql_escape_string($id),
                         mysql_escape_string($data),
                         $_SERVER["REMOTE_ADDR"] ) );
    }

    public function destroy( $id ) {
      $escaped_id = mysql_escape_string( $id );
      $res = $this->query( "DELETE FROM `session` WHERE `id`='$escaped_id'" );
      return ( mysql_affected_rows($res) == 1 );
    }

    public function gc( $lifetime ) {
      $this->query( "DELETE FROM `session` WHERE ".
        "UNIX_TIMESTAMP(UTC_TIMESTAMP())-`timestamp` > $lifetime"
      );
    }

    public function query( $query ) {
      $res = mysql_query($query, $this->conn);
      return $res;
    }

  };
?>
```

There are several important things to note in the previous code. The least obvious is that sessions are stored as serialized strings. Recall from Chapter 1 that serialized strings might contain binary characters even if the data itself is not binary. Also, the session data itself can be binary. It is very important, for this reason, to never use non-binary safe functions on the session data string. This is also the reason why the data type for the session data is a blob. Using a blob means you cannot query efficiently on the session data (which this class does not do anyway) but it gains you efficient storage of binary data.

As of PHP 5.0.5, the session is automatically written and closed after the objects are already garbage collected. This causes problems when using an object as a session handler like the preceding class does. To fix the problem, the class destructor calls `session_write_close()`, which causes the writing and closing to happen immediately. Although it is not a factor in this class, the same problem also affects exception throwing because once all the objects are cleaned up it is impossible to create new ones (which is necessary for exception handling).

The database design from earlier leaves room for storing the user ID with the session. By storing the user ID with the session, the application can determine what users are currently active. Because sessions expire it is safe to assume that any user with a row in the session table has recently viewed a page on the site. That, however, would require that the session class have knowledge of the contents of the session. That behavior is acceptable in most applications, but it is not ideal if the session class can be used in a generic case.

Sessions do expire. Therefore they should not be used to store data that cannot be later reconstructed. A session alone is not enough to determine the logged-in state of the user. It can contain information such as calculated and cached data. For example, it would be undesirable for the users of an ecommerce site to lose their shopping cart if they leave their computer unattended for 1440 seconds. One or more additional cookies can pass along user login credentials and other information (such as the shopping cart).

Building Secure Cookies

User login credentials should never be stored in an application using plain text, which an attacker can easily read or duplicate. The login cookie acts like a key that opens up all the functionality of a web page as well as accesses potentially sensitive user data. This section lays out a system that you can use to create hack- and hijack-resistant cookies. To accomplish that, the cookie must store some basic information:

➤ User ID

➤ Last known IP address of the user

➤ A timestamp

The first field is self-explanatory. It is needed in order to tell which user is logged in. The second two fields are there to add a little bit of extra security.

The last known IP address is used to compare to the IP address currently making the request to the server. It can also be used to compare to the IP address field in the session table. If the IP address in the cookie does not match the IP address of the remote client, it is possible that the cookie was hijacked. It is also possible that the user is simply using a laptop and walking between rooms with different WiFi access points.

The timestamp is the date and time that the cookie was created. This serves dual purposes. The first is to determine how long the user has been logged in. An extremely long login time may mean that the user has left the computer unattended. In that regard, the timestamp acts like a time-based nonce. The second use of the timestamp is to ensure that the cookie generated on login is never the same exact cookie twice. For example, if the user logs in once at noon and again at 3:00, the cookie will be different both times. This simple technique makes it more difficult for attackers to see patterns in the cookies and, when combined with expiration times, can close the window of opportunity for replay attacks.

Three levels of trust can be represented using this cookie design:

➤ **The most trusted:** IP address matches and timestamp is recent.

➤ **The second most trusted:** IP address matches but the timestamp is old. The user may have left the computer unattended.

➤ **The least trusted:** The IP address doesn't match.

It is up to the application designer to determine what level of trust is needed for specific pieces of data. For example, if all the page does is greet the currently logged-in user, it is not necessary to have a high level of trust. If the application displays sensitive data or allows the user to make a purchase, it becomes necessary to restrict access to only the most trusted sessions.

The user should not be automatically logged out in any of the preceding cases. Instead, the correct approach is to prompt the user for the password again. If the user enters the correct password, the timestamp and IP are reset. This is the case when, for example, a user visits a store online and decides to view her order history after spending some time shopping. The user may be prompted for a password again because the timestamp is old; adding items to a cart may not require high trust but viewing order history does.

None of the information is useful for security if it can easily be read or written to. To solve that problem it becomes necessary to encrypt the cookie. Fortunately, PHP provides many methods of encryption. The code to set an encrypted cookie may look like this:

```
$cookieData = serialize( $user );
$iv_size = mcrypt_get_iv_size(MCRYPT_RIJNDAEL_256, MCRYPT_MODE_CBC);
srand();
$iv = mcrypt_create_iv($iv_size, MCRYPT_RAND);
$encryptedData = mcrypt_encrypt(MCRYPT_RIJNDAEL_256, $secret,
                                $cookieData, MCRYPT_MODE_CBC, $iv);
setcookie( 'user', base64_encode($encryptedData).':'.$iv );
```

The code to decrypt the cookie is very similar:

```
list($encryptedData,$iv) = explode(':', $_COOKIE['user']);
$rawData = mycrypt_decrypt( MCRYPT_RIJNDAEL_256, $secret,
                            base64_decode($encryptedData),
                            MCRYPT_MODE_CBC, $iv );
$user = unserialize( $rawData );
```

The secret is something that only the application knows. In extremely secure environments it may be useful to have a dynamic secret based on which user is currently logged in. For that, an application can use a system where the cookie data is actually three parts: a key, the initialization vector ($iv), and the data. The key appends to the secret key to generate a new hybrid key and can be anything from a user ID all the way to a random string.

As a final level of security it is useful to validate the user ID with the session data. This approach requires that the user ID is actually set inside of the session. If the two do not match, something is seriously wrong (most likely tampering) and both the session and the login cookie should be destroyed. If there isn't any session, it can be assumed that the session expired, in which case it may be prudent to prompt for the password again before recalculating all the session data.

> *From a usability standpoint: Good software is not just functional and secure. It is also easy to use.*
>
> *Because the cookie contains the user ID number (uid) it is possible to determine the user login name. When re-prompting for a password after the session becomes stale, the login name should be auto-populated with that value.*

The end result is a cookie that cannot be spoofed by someone who is not within the same network and cannot be easily decrypted to gain information about the user. It also provides multiple levels of trust for accessing user data.

It might also be useful to store the username in this cookie to make displaying a login box even easier as well as free of database lookups. The final piece is to create a user class that accesses the authenticated user.

ACCESS CONTROL LISTS

Access Control Lists (ACL) are vital once an application reaches any level of complexity. They allow fine-grained control over who can perform what actions in the system. Anyone who has used a Content Management System has probably used ACLs.

There are two levels of permissions in most ACL systems:

➤ **Group Level:** A users can belong to one or more of groups and each group has its own sets of permissions. Groups can be anything but some common groups are anonymous, members, premium subscribers, moderators, and administrators.

➤ **User Level:** User level permissions always override group level permissions. For example, in a normal case only moderators and administrators can edit blog posts but you can give "Bob" permission to edit blog posts directly.

Most ACLs act as a white list. If the permission exists anywhere for the user then the user can do it. Otherwise, he can't. Knowing that, consider these four tables:

```
CREATE TABLE `groups` (
  id INT AUTO_INCREMENT PRIMARY KEY,
  name VARCHAR(128)
```

```
);

CREATE TABLE `group_users` (
  `user_id` INT,
  `group_id` INT,
  KEY ( `user_id`, `group_id` ),
  KEY ( `group_id` )
);

CREATE TABLE `group_permissions` (
  `group_id` INT,
  `permission` VARCHAR(50),
  KEY ( `group_id`, `permission` ),
  KEY ( `permission` )
);

CREATE TABLE `user_permissions` (
  `user_id` INT,
  `permission` VARCHAR(50),
  KEY ( `user_id`, `permission` ),
  KEY ( `permission` )
);
```

You can select all the permissions for a specific user by using a union of the two permission tables. The query looks like this (replace USER_ID with the ID of the user either using code or by hand):

```
( SELECT `permission` FROM `group_permissions`
  WHERE `group_id` IN (
    SELECT group_id FROM group_users WHERE user_id=USER_ID
  ))
UNION
( SELECT permission FROM user_permissions WHERE user_id=USER_ID )
```

The end result is a list of strings. Traditionally, permissions are stored a strings; however, it is entirely possible to add another level of normalization and have a table of possible permissions that has a numeric index. So granting a user permission to post a blog entry looks like this in SQL:

```
INSERT INTO `user_permissions` (`user_id`, `permission`)
  VALUES (USER_ID, "blog/add");
```

> *The design in this section is the bare minimum ACL. In a complete web based system you should also cache the ACL so that it is not necessary to hit the database on every request. Just don't forget to invalidate the cache when the user permissions change. Refer back to Chapter 4 for more information on caching.*
>
> *It is possible to customize the lists to meet your needs. This ACL is a white list but you may want a black list in your application to ban a user from performing some actions.*

SUMMARY

This chapter covered all the pieces needed for end-to-end implementation of PHP authentication allowing for basic HTTP-based authentication, digest authentication, and pure PHP-based authentication. The method used in a given application depends largely on the project requirements and it is possible to mix and match between PHP and either of the two HTTP methods.

Digest authentication is the only of the three methods covered in this chapter that does not send the password in plain text. However, it does require the password to be stored in the database, which can cause security problems if the application is not designed correctly. A properly designed digest-based system either stores the entire result of the A1 hash in the database instead of the password or encrypts the password using a bi-directional algorithm.

The other two methods should almost always be used over SSL. The few exceptions are when the user account does not contain any sensitive information, the application is a rapid prototype not being released to the public yet, it is an example application for a book, or it is on a corporate intranet. The last point is only partially true because an attacker can also come from inside. In practice, thousands of applications in use today do not take the proper steps to protect the users' passwords.

Chapter 14 covers security in more depth and details how to protect your MySQL server from attack.

13

Understanding the INFORMATION_SCHEMA

WHAT'S IN THIS CHAPTER?

➤ What tables exist in the INFORMATION_SCHEMA

➤ How to retrieve information on your schemas and tables

➤ How to list core MySQL metadata used for database objects

➤ How to retrieve instrumentation on a running MySQL instance

➤ What extensions to INFORMATION_SCHEMA exist

The ANSI Standard SQL (e.g, SQL:2003 and SQL:2008) defines the support for a level of database metadata using the concept of INFORMATION_SCHEMA. MySQL starting with version 5.0 has implemented the INFORMATION_SCHEMA, often referred to as I_S, to provide a level of SQL access to information previously found in the popular but not SQL standard SHOW commands. The metadata is a form of data dictionary that provides the user access to various information including database objects such as TABLES, COLUMNS, and VIEWS; schema metadata such as CHARACTER_SETS; and internal MySQL operations including GLOBAL_STATUS, GLOBAL_VARIABLES, and PROCESSLIST.

This chapter steps through the INFORMATION_SCHEMA tables from versions 5.0, 5.1, and the 5.4 alpha release. It also gives an example of the INFORMATION_SCHEMA extensions possible using the InnoDB Plugin 1.0.4 and greater, which is available separately and now included in MySQL starting with version 5.1.38.

USING THE INFORMATION_SCHEMA

The SHOW command can be used to retrieve information from the INFORMATION_SCHEMA tables. As you can see, this 5.1 schema contains a number of tables, which are discussed in detail in this chapter:

```
SHOW TABLES FROM INFORMATION_SCHEMA;
+---------------------------------------+
| Tables_in_INFORMATION_SCHEMA          |
+---------------------------------------+
| CHARACTER_SETS                        |
| COLLATIONS                            |
| COLLATION_CHARACTER_SET_APPLICABILITY |
| COLUMNS                               |
| COLUMN_PRIVILEGES                     |
| ENGINES                               |
| EVENTS                                |
| FILES                                 |
| GLOBAL_STATUS                         |
| GLOBAL_VARIABLES                      |
| KEY_COLUMN_USAGE                      |
| PARTITIONS                            |
| PLUGINS                               |
| PROCESSLIST                           |
| PROFILING                             |
| REFERENTIAL_CONSTRAINTS               |
| ROUTINES                              |
| SCHEMATA                              |
| SCHEMA_PRIVILEGES                     |
| SESSION_STATUS                        |
| SESSION_VARIABLES                     |
| STATISTICS                            |
| TABLES                                |
| TABLE_CONSTRAINTS                     |
| TABLE_PRIVILEGES                      |
| TRIGGERS                              |
| USER_PRIVILEGES                       |
| VIEWS                                 |
+---------------------------------------+
```

 One missing feature of the INFORMATION_SCHEMA *is the lack of sufficient permission restrictions necessary to limit viewing of the data. Though* SELECT *is the only operation possible, you can, for example, view the code of stored procedures and functions. If a user has* USAGE *permissions to connect to the MySQL instance, he or she has permissions to retrieve data from the* INFORMATION_SCHEMA *with exception for the* TRIGGERS *table.*

Unless otherwise stated, the listed INFORMATION_SCHEMA tables in this chapter are available in version 5.0. Tables that you will not find in 5.0 include ENGINES, EVENTS, FILES, GLOBAL_STATUS, PLUGINS, PROCESSLIST, REFERENTIAL_CONSTRAINTS, SESSION_STATUS, SESSION_VARIABLES.

For simplification we will be using the commonly accepted abbreviation I_S for INFORMATION_SCHEMA.

TABLE OBJECTS TABLES

We identify the following I_S tables as table objects tables as they hold valuable information on database table objects. These are outlined in Table 13-1.

TABLE 13-1: I_S Tables That Hold Database Table Object Information

OBJECT	DESCRIPTION
SCHEMATA	Shows the details of all schemas (also called databases) within the given MySQL instance.
TABLES	Shows the details of all tables that exist in the instance schemas.
COLUMNS	Shows the details of all columns for all tables.
PARTITIONS (5.4)	Shows the details of table partitions.
TABLE_CONSTRAINTS	Describes the tables that have constraints.
KEY_COLUMN_USAGE	Describes which table columns have any constraints and includes details for PRIMARY KEY, UNIQUE KEY, and FOREIGN KEY constraints.
REFERENTIAL_CONSTRAINTS (5.1)	Used in conjunction with KEY_COLUMN_USAGE and provides additional constraint information for foreign keys.
STATISTICS	Shows details on the columns in table indexes including cardinality. These details are used by the MySQL optimizer for determining the best indexes to use for queries.

Listing 13-1 shows a popular query to list all schemas including data and index size and number of tables:

Available for download on Wrox.com

LISTING 13-1: schemas.sql

```
SELECT table_schema,
       SUM(data_length+index_length)/1024/1024 AS total_mb,
       SUM(data_length)/1024/1024 AS data_mb,
       SUM(index_length)/1024/1024 AS index_mb,
       COUNT(*) AS tables
FROM   information_schema.tables
GROUP BY table_schema
ORDER BY 2 DESC;

+----------------------+-----------+-----------+----------+--------+
| table_schema         | total_mb  | data_mb   | index_mb | tables |
+----------------------+-----------+-----------+----------+--------+
| xxxxxxx_xxx_xxxx_xx1 | 45314.477 | 38458.889 | 6855.587 |   2359 |
| xxxxxxx_xxx_xxxx_xx2 | 28758.386 | 24461.270 | 4297.116 |    275 |
```

```
| xxxxxxx_xxx_xxxx_xx3 | 28732.414 | 24464.203 | 4268.211 |  368 |
| xxxxxxx_xxx_xxxx_xx4 | 24586.482 | 20941.441 | 3645.041 |  302 |
| xxxxxxx_xxx_xxxx_xx5 |  3128.635 |  2664.547 |  464.087 |   48 |
| xxxxxxx_xxx_xxxx_xx6 |  2865.366 |  2440.443 |  424.922 |  265 |
| xxxxxxx_xxx_xxxx_xx7 |  1635.165 |  1388.688 |  246.477 | 2034 |
| xxxxxxx_xxx_xxxx_xx8 |  1442.157 |  1231.418 |  210.739 |   17 |
+----------------------+-----------+-----------+----------+------+
```

Listing 13-2 shows the top five tables for the current schema by table size:

LISTING 13-2: tables.sql

```sql
SELECT table_schema,table_name,engine, table_rows, avg_row_length,
       (data_length+index_length)/1024/1024 as total_mb,
       (data_length)/1024/1024 as data_mb,
       (index_length)/1024/1024 as index_mb
FROM   information_schema.tables
WHERE  table_schema=DATABASE()
ORDER  BY 7 DESC
LIMIT  5;
```

```
+------------+--------+--------+--------+----------+----------+----------+
| table_name | engine | rows   | avg_row| total_mb | data_mb  | index_mb |
+------------+--------+--------+--------+----------+----------+----------+
| xxxxxxx    | InnoDB | 778523 |    314 | 658.3906 | 533.8437 | 124.5468 |
| xxxxxxxxx  | InnoDB | 553266 |    846 | 472.2500 | 446.7500 |  25.5000 |
| xxxxxxx    | InnoDB | 435892 |    884 | 392.2500 | 367.8125 |  24.4375 |
| xxxxxxxxx  | InnoDB | 106547 |     65 | 133.2656 |  68.5937 |  64.6718 |
| xxxxxxxxxx | InnoDB |  58281 |    531 |  30.3437 |  29.5156 |   0.8281 |
+------------+--------+--------+--------+----------+----------+----------+
```

For the previous code, output has been reformatted for display purposes.

The INFORMATION_SCHEMA appears like normal tables when using SELECT statements; however, these tables are internally generated metadata. These tables do not perform like normal tables. It is also not possible to index data to improve performance for example. Queries that operate on these I_S tables can be very expensive.

For InnoDB tables, the table_rows *and subsequent* avg_row_length *calculation is approximate and can vary wildly. The data and index sizes are considered accurate.*

OTHER DATABASE OBJECTS TABLES

We identify the following I_S tables as Table Objects. The first group of tables contain objects that can be created with various CREATE SQL commands:

➤ **ROUTINES**: Provides information on the stored procedures and stored functions that are defined. It does not include UDF functions. This table shows the full code of these stored routines in the ROUTINE_DEFINITION column.

➤ **VIEWS**: Provides information on the views defined with the database. It includes the canonical definition in the VIEW_DEFINITION column. This may be different from the actual CREATE VIEW command provided.

➤ **TRIGGERS**: Defines the details of database triggers. Unlike other tables, access to view this table requires the TRIGGER user privilege.

➤ **EVENTS**: Provides information on all defined events and includes the full event code in the EVENT_DEFINITION column.

The remaining tables contain details on nonstandard objects that are defined at compile or execution time:

➤ **PLUGINS**: Shows details of the currently installed plug-ins.

➤ **ENGINES**: Shows details of the currently installed and available storage engines that can be used for tables.

➤ **FILES**: Provides information on disk-based files for the MySQL Cluster NDB storage engine.

A good overall query to keep regular statistics is the number of user-defined objects in the MySQL database instance. This can be used as a very approximate way of determining the creation of unauthorized schema objects.

This query will not operate in MySQL 5.0 due to the EVENTS table.

LISTING 13-3: objects.sql

Available for download on Wrox.com

```
SELECT 'Tables', COUNT(*) AS cnt FROM INFORMATION_SCHEMA.TABLES
WHERE TABLE_SCHEMA NOT IN ('INFORMATION_SCHEMA','MYSQL')
UNION SELECT 'Views', COUNT(*) AS cnt FROM INFORMATION_SCHEMA.VIEWS
UNION SELECT 'Procedures', COUNT(*) AS cnt FROM INFORMATION_SCHEMA.ROUTINES
WHERE ROUTINE_TYPE = 'PROCEDURE'
UNION SELECT 'Functions', COUNT(*) AS cnt FROM INFORMATION_SCHEMA.ROUTINES
WHERE ROUTINE_TYPE = 'FUNCTION'
UNION SELECT 'Events', COUNT(*) AS cnt FROM INFORMATION_SCHEMA.EVENTS
UNION SELECT 'Triggers', COUNT(*) AS cnt FROM INFORMATION_SCHEMA.TRIGGERS;
```

```
+------------+-----+
| Views      | cnt |
+------------+-----+
| Tables     | 431 |
| Views      |   0 |
| Procedures |  10 |
| Functions  |   0 |
| Events     |   0 |
| Triggers   |   0 |
+------------+-----+
```

MYSQL STATUS TABLES

It is also possible to obtain database system status information from the INFORMATION_SCHEMA through the tables presented in the following sections:

PROCESSLIST (5.1)

This table provides the same information as the command SHOW PROCESSLIST, except with INFORMATION_SCHEMA, you can run queries and find out specific user processes. The columns of this table are:

➤ **ID**: The connection ID for a given process.

➤ **USER**: The name of the database user that a given process is running as.

➤ **HOST**: The host from where the process is being run.

➤ **DB**: The name of the schema for which the process is running.

➤ **COMMAND**: The command being run (QUERY, CONNECT, and so on).

➤ **TIME**: The amount of time the process has been running in seconds.

➤ **STATE**: The process state of the command (that is, executing, creating table, writing to net, and so on). There are a large number of possible different thread states.

➤ **INFO**: Lists the actual query being run for this process.

The code is as follows:

```
select * from information_schema.processlist where USER = 'patg'\G
*************************** 1. row ***************************
     ID: 6016
   USER: patg
   HOST: localhost
     DB: test
COMMAND: Query
   TIME: 0
  STATE: creating table
   INFO: create table bench_1224 (i int NOT NULL,d double,f float,
         s char(10),v varchar(100),primary key (i))
1 row in set (0.19 sec)
PROFILING
```

The MySQL profiler was originally written by Jeremy Cole from Proven Scaling (`http://www`
`.provenscaling.com/`). This is an invaluable diagnostic utility that allows you to analyze the exact
steps of the internal server execution of your queries. This can allow you to find any inefficiencies
with your queries and in turn tune those queries to have better performance. The columns for this
table are listed in Table 13-2:

TABLE 13-2: Profiling Table Columns

COLUMN	DESCRIPTION
QUERY_ID	The ID for the given query being profiled
SEQ	The sequence or step number of the listed execution
STATE	The process state of the command
DURATION	The time the listed execution took, in seconds
CPU_USER	The amount of time spent on the execution of the command (user CPU time)
CPU_SYSTEM	The amount of time the CPU spends on system calls for the kernel on behalf of the process
CONTEXT_VOLUNTARY	Not currently implemented
CONTEXT_INVOLUNTARY	Not currently implemented
BLOCK_OPS_IN	Not currently implemented
BLOCK_OPS_OUT	Not currently implemented
MESSAGES_SENT	Not currently implemented
MESSAGES_RECEIVED	Not currently implemented
PAGE_FAULTS_MAJOR	Not currently implemented
PAGE_FAULTS_MINOR	Not currently implemented
SWAPS	Not currently implemented
SOURCE_FUNCTION	The source code function the particular execution was issued by.
SOURCE_FILE	The source file from where the particular execution originated
SOURCE_LINE	The line in the source file from where the particular execution originated

To use the profiler and be able to utilize this table, you must first issue:

```
set profiling = 1;
```

From this point on, any queries you issue for your session will be captured by the profiler and hence viewable via the PROFILING table. You can issue queries against this table, such as how long it takes for a given query to execute:

```
select sum(duration), sum(cpu_user), sum(cpu_system)
from   information_schema.profiling where query_id = 3;
+---------------+---------------+----------------+
| sum(duration) | sum(cpu_user) | sum(cpu_system) |
+---------------+---------------+----------------+
|      0.795895 |      0.000362 |       0.003601 |
+---------------+---------------+----------------+
```

You can also use the profiler to find out how MySQL processes a query and gain insight into how MySQL works:

```
select distinct(source_function), source_file
from   information_schema.profiling where query_id = 3;
+----------------------+----------------+
| source_function      | source_file    |
+----------------------+----------------+
| NULL                 | NULL           |
| open_tables          | sql_base.cc    |
| mysql_lock_tables    | lock.cc        |
| mysql_select         | sql_select.cc  |
| optimize             | sql_select.cc  |
| exec                 | sql_select.cc  |
| mysql_execute_command | sql_parse.cc  |
| mysql_parse          | sql_parse.cc   |
| log_slow_statement   | sql_parse.cc   |
| dispatch_command     | sql_parse.cc   |
+----------------------+----------------+
```

When you are done with using the profiler, you can of course run:

```
set profiling = 0;
```

SESSION_STATUS/GLOBAL_STATUS (5.1)

These tables contain values of MySQL status variables for the given session or system, respectively. Their columns are:

➤ **VARIABLE_NAME**: Name of the status variable.

➤ **VARIABLE_VALUE**: Value of the status variable.

For instance, you can find out the SQL commands that have been executed on your MySQL instance:

```
select * from information_schema.global_status
where   variable_name like 'COM%'
and     variable_value > 0;
+----------------------+----------------+
| VARIABLE_NAME        | VARIABLE_VALUE |
+----------------------+----------------+
| COM_ALTER_TABLE      | 191            |
```

```
| COM_CREATE_INDEX     | 8        |
| COM_CREATE_TABLE     | 30043    |
| COM_DELETE           | 10147    |
| COM_DROP_INDEX       | 8        |
| COM_DROP_TABLE       | 60083    |
| COM_INSERT           | 554780   |
| COM_INSERT_SELECT    | 2        |
| COM_SELECT           | 1740554  |
| COM_SET_OPTION       | 6022     |
| COM_SHOW_DATABASES   | 4        |
| COM_SHOW_FIELDS      | 107      |
| COM_SHOW_PROCESSLIST | 1        |
| COM_SHOW_STATUS      | 10       |
| COM_SHOW_TABLES      | 11       |
| COM_UPDATE           | 450773   |
+----------------------+----------------+
```

Or you could find out index status variables for your given session:

```
select * from information_schema.session_status
where  variable_name like 'KEY%';
+-----------------------+----------------+
| VARIABLE_NAME         | VARIABLE_VALUE |
+-----------------------+----------------+
| KEY_BLOCKS_NOT_FLUSHED | 0             |
| KEY_BLOCKS_UNUSED     | 7245           |
| KEY_BLOCKS_USED       | 7245           |
| KEY_READ_REQUESTS     | 119528769      |
| KEY_READS             | 1197779        |
| KEY_WRITE_REQUESTS    | 7783921        |
| KEY_WRITES            | 3869884        |
+-----------------------+----------------+
```

SESSION_VARIABLES/GLOBAL_VARIABLES (5.1)

These tables contain the values of MySQL system variables for the given session or system, respectively. The columns are:

➤ **VARIABLE_NAME**: The name of the variable.

➤ **VARIABLE_VALUE**: The value of the variable.

For instance, one query you could perform to find out what features and/or storage engines are supported would be the following:

```
select * from information_schema.global_variables
where  variable_name like 'have_%';
+-----------------------+----------------+
| VARIABLE_NAME         | VARIABLE_VALUE |
+-----------------------+----------------+
| HAVE_CRYPT            | YES            |
| HAVE_OPENSSL          | NO             |
| HAVE_SYMLINK          | YES            |
| HAVE_CSV              | YES            |
| HAVE_GEOMETRY         | YES            |
```

```
| HAVE_PARTITIONING       | NO         |
| HAVE_QUERY_CACHE        | YES        |
| HAVE_DYNAMIC_LOADING    | YES        |
| HAVE_SSL                | NO         |
| HAVE_NDBCLUSTER         | NO         |
| HAVE_COMMUNITY_FEATURES | YES        |
| HAVE_INNODB             | NO         |
| HAVE_RTREE_KEYS         | YES        |
| HAVE_COMPRESS           | YES        |
+-------------------------+------------+
```

You could also find out the location of various system directory locations by the following query:

```
select * from information_schema.global_variables
where  variable_name like '%DIR%';
+--------------------+-----------------------------------------+
| VARIABLE_NAME      | VARIABLE_VALUE                          |
+--------------------+-----------------------------------------+
| CHARACTER_SETS_DIR | /usr/local/maria/share/mysql/charsets/  |
| BASEDIR            | /usr/local/maria/                       |
| SLAVE_LOAD_TMPDIR  | /var/tmp/                               |
| TMPDIR             | /var/tmp/                               |
| MARIA_SYNC_LOG_DIR | NEWFILE                                 |
| DATADIR            | /usr/local/maria/var/                   |
| PLUGIN_DIR         | /usr/local/maria/lib/mysql/plugin       |
+--------------------+-----------------------------------------+
```

MYSQL META DATA TABLES

The INFORMATION_SCHEMA provides several tables that provide metadata information particularly having to do with character sets and collation:

CHARACTER_SETS

This table lists the character sets that are available on your instance of MySQL. The columns are:

➤ **CHARACTER_SET_NAME:** The name of the character set. This is the value you would specify when creating a table.

➤ **DEFAULT_COLLATE_NAME:** The default name of the collation of the character set. You will see that collation names can end in _cs or _ci. This corresponds to **case-sensitive** or **case-insensitive**.

➤ **DESCRIPTION:** A canonical description of the character set.

➤ **MAXLEN:** The length of the character set in bytes.

The code is as follows:

```
select * from information_schema.character_sets;
+-----------+----------------------+---------------------------+--------+
| CHARACTER_| DEFAULT_COLLATE_NAME | DESCRIPTION               | MAXLEN |
+-----------+----------------------+---------------------------+--------+
| dec8      | dec8_swedish_ci      | DEC West European         |      1 |
```

```
| cp850    | cp850_general_ci    | DOS West European          |    1 |
| hp8      | hp8_english_ci      | HP West European           |    1 |
| koi8r    | koi8r_general_ci    | KOI8-R Relcom Russian      |    1 |
| latin1   | latin1_swedish_ci   | cp1252 West European       |    1 |
| latin2   | latin2_general_ci   | ISO 8859-2 Central European|    1 |
| swe7     | swe7_swedish_ci     | 7bit Swedish               |    1 |
| ascii    | ascii_general_ci    | US ASCII                   |    1 |
| hebrew   | hebrew_general_ci   | ISO 8859-8 Hebrew          |    1 |
| koi8u    | koi8u_general_ci    | KOI8-U Ukrainian           |    1 |
| greek    | greek_general_ci    | ISO 8859-7 Greek           |    1 |
| cp1250   | cp1250_general_ci   | Windows Central European   |    1 |
| latin5   | latin5_turkish_ci   | ISO 8859-9 Turkish         |    1 |
| armscii8 | armscii8_general_ci | ARMSCII-8 Armenian         |    1 |
| utf8     | utf8_general_ci     | UTF-8 Unicode              |    3 |
| cp866    | cp866_general_ci    | DOS Russian                |    1 |
| keybcs2  | keybcs2_general_ci  | DOS Kamenicky Czech-Slovak |    1 |
| macce    | macce_general_ci    | Mac Central European       |    1 |
| macroman | macroman_general_ci | Mac West European          |    1 |
| cp852    | cp852_general_ci    | DOS Central European       |    1 |
| latin7   | latin7_general_ci   | ISO 8859-13 Baltic         |    1 |
| cp1251   | cp1251_general_ci   | Windows Cyrillic           |    1 |
| cp1256   | cp1256_general_ci   | Windows Arabic             |    1 |
| cp1257   | cp1257_general_ci   | Windows Baltic             |    1 |
| binary   | binary              | Binary pseudo charset      |    1 |
| geostd8  | geostd8_general_ci  | GEOSTD8 Georgian           |    1 |
+----------+---------------------+----------------------------+------+
```

COLLATIONS

This table lists the collations for the character sets available on your instance of MySQL. The columns are:

➤ **COLLATION_NAME:** The name of the collation.

➤ **CHARACTER_SET_NAME:** The character set name.

➤ **ID:** The collation ID.

➤ **IS_DEFAULT:** Specifies if the collation is default for the character set.

➤ **IS_COMPILED:** Specifies whether the collation is compiled into your MySQL instance.

➤ **SORTLEN:** The amount of memory required for sorting strings using the character set.

For instance, a query that lists the default collations that are latin related character sets is as follows:

```
select character_set_name, collation_name
from   information_schema.collations where is_default = 'Yes'
and    character_set_name like 'latin%';
+--------------------+-------------------+
| character_set_name | collation_name    |
+--------------------+-------------------+
| latin1             | latin1_swedish_ci |
| latin2             | latin2_general_ci |
| latin5             | latin5_turkish_ci |
| latin7             | latin7_general_ci |
+--------------------+-------------------+
```

COLLATION_CHARACTER_SET_APPLICABILITY

This table specifies what character sets are applicable for what collation. The columns are:

➤   **COLLATION_NAME**: The name of the collation.

➤   **CHARACTER_SET_NAME**: The name of the applicable character set.

For instance, to find out what collations are available for the latin1 character set, you would issue the following query:

```
select collation_name
from   information_schema.collation_character_set_applicability
where  character_set_name = 'latin1';
+-------------------+
| collation_name    |
+-------------------+
| latin1_german1_ci |
| latin1_swedish_ci |
| latin1_danish_ci  |
| latin1_german2_ci |
| latin1_bin        |
| latin1_general_ci |
| latin1_general_cs |
| latin1_spanish_ci |
+-------------------+
```

MYSQL ACL PERMISSIONS TABLES

The INFORMATION_SCHEMA has a number of privilege tables that provide information about which objects given users have access to.

USER_PRIVILEGES

This table specifies the global privileges of users and is derived from the mysql.user system schema table. The columns are:

➤   **GRANTEE**: The user to which the privilege is granted. This is in user@host format.

➤   **TABLE_CATALOG**: This specifies the catalog of the privilege, but is not used and is NULL.

➤   **PRIVILEGE_TYPE**: The type of privilege (INSERT, SELECT, DELETE, and so on).

➤   **IS_GRANTABLE**: If the privilege was given with WITH GRANT OPTION.

An example of displaying which global privilege the *sakila* user connecting on *localhost* is granted would be:

```
select grantee,privilege_type
from   information_schema.user_privileges
where  grantee like '%sakila%';
+-----------------------+----------------+
| grantee               | privilege_type |
+-----------------------+----------------+
| 'sakila'@'localhost'  | USAGE          |
+-----------------------+----------------+
```

SCHEMA_PRIVILEGES

This table specifies privileges on a given schema to which a user has been granted access. The columns are:

➤ **GRANTEE**: The user to which the privilege is granted. This is a user@host format.

➤ **TABLE_CATALOG**: This specifies the catalog of the privilege, but is not used and is NULL.

➤ **TABLE_SCHEMA**: The schema name on which the privilege is granted.

➤ **IS_GRANTABLE**: If the privilege was given with the WITH GRANT OPTION specified.

An example of listing the privileges and schema name of what the *sakila* user has been granted would be:

```
select table_schema,privilege_type
from   information_schema.schema_privileges
where  grantee = "'sakila'@'localhost'";
+--------------+-------------------------+
| table_schema | privilege_type          |
+--------------+-------------------------+
| sakila       | SELECT                  |
| sakila       | INSERT                  |
| sakila       | UPDATE                  |
| sakila       | DELETE                  |
| sakila       | CREATE                  |
| sakila       | DROP                    |
| sakila       | REFERENCES              |
| sakila       | INDEX                   |
| sakila       | ALTER                   |
| sakila       | CREATE TEMPORARY TABLES |
| sakila       | LOCK TABLES             |
| sakila       | EXECUTE                 |
| sakila       | CREATE VIEW             |
| sakila       | SHOW VIEW               |
| sakila       | CREATE ROUTINE          |
| sakila       | ALTER ROUTINE           |
| sakila       | EVENT                   |
| sakila       | TRIGGER                 |
+--------------+-------------------------+
```

TABLE_PRIVILEGES

This table specifies the privileges granted to specific tables to a given user. The columns are:

➤ **GRANTEE**: The name of the grantee to which the privilege has been granted. This is in user@host format.

➤ **TABLE_CATALOG**: Not used, NULL.

➤ **TABLE_SCHEMA**: The schema name of the table on which the privilege is granted.

➤ **PRIVILEGE_TYPE**: The type of privilege (SELECT, INSERT, DELETE, and so on).

➤ **IS_GRANTABLE**: If the privilege was given with the WITH GRANT OPTION specified.

For instance, if you had granted the user *sally@localhost* all privileges on the *film* table of the *sakila* schema:

```
grant all privileges on sakila.film to 'sally'@'localhost'
identified by 'sakila';
```

You could in turn view this privilege with the following query:

```
select table_schema,table_name,privilege_type
from   information_schema.table_privileges
where  grantee = "'sally'@'localhost'";
+--------------+------------+----------------+
| table_schema | table_name | privilege_type |
+--------------+------------+----------------+
| sakila       | film       | SELECT         |
| sakila       | film       | INSERT         |
| sakila       | film       | UPDATE         |
| sakila       | film       | DELETE         |
| sakila       | film       | CREATE         |
| sakila       | film       | DROP           |
| sakila       | film       | REFERENCES     |
| sakila       | film       | INDEX          |
| sakila       | film       | ALTER          |
| sakila       | film       | CREATE VIEW    |
| sakila       | film       | SHOW VIEW      |
| sakila       | film       | TRIGGER        |
+--------------+------------+----------------+
```

COLUMN_PRIVILEGES

This table specifies the privileges granted on a column of a specific table to a given user. The columns are:

➤ **GRANTEE:** The name of the grantee to which the privilege has been granted. This is in user@ host format.

➤ **TABLE_CATALOG:** Not used, NULL.

➤ **TABLE_SCHEMA:** The schema name of the table to which the privilege is granted.

➤ **TABLE_NAME:** The name of the table on which the privilege is granted.

➤ **COLUMN_NAME:** The name of the column on which the privilege is granted.

➤ **PRIVILEGE_TYPE:** The type of privilege (SELECT, INSERT, DELETE, and so on).

➤ **IS_GRANTABLE:** If the privilege was given with the WITH GRANT OPTION specified.

For instance, if you granted select access to the user *jason@localhost* the film_id and *title* columns of the *film* table in the *sakila* schema with the following:

```
grant select (film_id,title) on sakila.film
to 'jason'@'localhost' identified by 'sakila';
```

You could in turn view these grants with the following query:

```
select table_schema,table_name,column_name,privilege_type
from   information_schema.column_privileges
```

```
where  grantee = "'jason'@'localhost'";
+---------------+-------------+-------------+-----------------+
| table_schema  | table_name  | column_name | privilege_type  |
+---------------+-------------+-------------+-----------------+
| sakila        | film        | title       | SELECT          |
| sakila        | film        | film_id     | SELECT          |
+---------------+-------------+-------------+-----------------+
```

INFORMATION_SCHEMA EXTENSIONS

MySQL provides the ability for software developers to extend the INFORMATION_SCHEMA. This requires C programming skills and requires patching the MySQL source code. MySQL community member Roland Bouman provides a detailed technical article at http://rpbouman.blogspot .com/2008/02/mysql-information-schema-plugins-best.html.

Some examples of extensions included in current products are detailed in Table 13-3.

TABLE 13-3: Examples of Extensions

PRODUCT	EXTENSION	FOR MORE INFORMATION
InnoDB Plugin	INNODB_CMP INNODB_CMP_RESET INNODB_CMPMEM INNODB_CMPMEM_RESET INNODB_TRX INNODB_LOCKS INNODB_LOCK_WAITS	Refer to http://www.innodb.com/ doc/innodb_plugin-1.0/innodb- information-schema.html.
Falcon	FALCON_RECORD_CACHE_SUMMARY FALCON_SYSTEM_MEMORY_DETAIL FALCON_TABLESPACE_IO FALCON_SYSTEM_MEMORY_SUMMARY FALCON_VERSION FALCON_TRANSACTION_SUMMARY FALCON_SERIAL_LOG_INFO FALCON_SYNCOBJECTS FALCON_TRANSACTIONS FALCON_RECORD_CACHE_DETAIL	For more information refer to http:// dev.mysql.com/doc/refman/6.0/ en/se-falcon-stats.html.

SHOW CROSS REFERENCE

MySQL provides a set of SHOW commands (see Table 13-4) that give valuable information. The SHOW command was available before version 5.0 when the INFORMATION_SCHEMA was introduced. The disadvantages of the SHOW commands are they do not follow an ANSI SQL standard syntax, and also do not allow for any restriction or subset of information, which is possible via a WHERE clause when selecting data from tables.

TABLE 13-4: Show Command Cross Reference

SHOW COMMAND	INFORMATION_SCHEMA TABLE(S)
SHOW CHARACTER SETS	CHARACTER_SETS
SHOW COLLATION	COLLATIONS
SHOW COLUMNS	COLUMNS
SHOW CREATE DATABASE	SCHEMATA
SHOW CREATE EVENT	EVENTS
SHOW CREATE FUNCTION	ROUTINES
SHOW CREATE PROCEDURE	ROUTINES
SHOW CREATE TABLE	TABLES, COLUMNS
SHOW CREATE TRIGGER	TRIGGERS
SHOW CREATE VIEW	VIEWS
SHOW DATABASES|SCHEMAS	SCHEMATA
SHOW ENGINES	ENGINES
SHOW EVENTS	EVENTS
SHOW FUNCTION CODE	ROUTINES
SHOW FUNCTION STATUS	ROUTINES
SHOW INDEX	TABLE_CONSTRAINTS, KEY_COLUMN_USAGE, STATISTICS
SHOW PLUGINS	PLUGINS
SHOW [GLOBAL|SESSION] STATUS	SESSION_STATUS
SHOW TALBLE STATUS	TABLES
SHOW TABLES	TABLES
SHOW TRIGGERS	TRIGGERS
SHOW [GLOBAL|SESSION] VARIABLES	GLOBAL_VARIABLES, SESSION_VARIABLES

SUMMARY

This chapter covered the various tables in the INFORMATION_SCHEMA and showed how you can utilize each to obtain useful information about your MySQL instance — such as information that you can use to learn more about how MySQL works, where system files are located, and how to identify performance issues.

14

Security

WHAT'S IN THIS CHAPTER?

➤ Identifying the limitations of default MySQL security

➤ Learning best practices for providing a more secure MySQL installation

➤ Identifying the ideal privileges for client access to the database

➤ Encrypting and decrypting data using PHP

➤ Creating secure hash values using PHP

➤ Preventing common exploits including cross-site scripting, SQL injection, as well as some lesser-known exploits

Security is a critical component of any application software. It's often overlooked and implemented insufficiently due to lack of time or commitment which can translate into a less robust and secure option. Yet it only takes one weak link to destroy a site or brand's reputation.

To ensure that best practices are part of the solution to a secure product, adequate data security must be a prerequisite to commencing development. In fact, it's imperative that applications follow all the rules and best practices outlined in this chapter. This chapter creates a path to securing an application; you'll looks at hardening your MySQL server, encrypting and decrypting data in PHP, and some techniques for overcoming common vulnerabilities.

HARDENING YOUR MYSQL SERVER

A default MySQL installation fails to provide adequate best practices in database security. This section discusses these limitations and then various means of improving security including:

➤ Operating system security

➤ MySQL security permissions

➤ Database privileges

➤ Other security options

Installation Defaults

When installed, MySQL enables any user with physical permissions to the server to connect to MySQL as an unauthenticated users. MySQL also provides complete access to all SUPER user privileges via the 'root' user with no default password.

The following lists the default users for a new installation:

```
$ mysql -uroot
mysql> SELECT host,user,password FROM mysql.user;
+--------------+------+------------------------------------------+
| host         | user | password                                 |
+--------------+------+------------------------------------------+
| localhost    | root |                                          |
| server.local | root |                                          |
| 127.0.0.1    | root |                                          |
| localhost    |      |                                          |
| server.local |      |                                          |
+--------------+------+------------------------------------------
```

What you see here are two types of users.

➤ The 'root' user which has MySQL super user privileges for your server or 'localhost' connections with no password.

➤ Unauthenticated users indicated by the blank 'user' column.

MySQL does, however, provide an optional command for immediate improvements in default security with mysql_secure_installation command. When running this command, you're prompted for the following options — the output has been trimmed for presentations purposes.

```
$ mysql_secure_installation

Enter current password for root (enter for none):
Set root password? [Y/n] y
New password:
Re-enter new password:
Remove anonymous users? [Y/n] Y
Disallow root login remotely? [Y/n] Y
Remove test database and access to it? [Y/n] Y
Reload privilege tables now? [Y/n] Y
```

If you revisit permissions now, you'll see what you would expect from a more initially secure installation.

```
mysql> SELECT host,user,password FROM mysql.user;
+-----------+------+------------------------------------------+
| host      | user | password                                 |
+-----------+------+------------------------------------------+
| localhost | root | *FDAF706717E70DB8DDAD0C5214B13770E1A80B0E |
+-----------+------+------------------------------------------+
```

Operating System Security

Having performed the most basic improvements to accessing MySQL, it's time to present the operating system security process with the following recommendations:

➤   Install software as 'root' OS user. The file permissions of all MySQL binary and support files are to be owned by 'root'.

➤   Restrict access to the 'root' OS user via sudo privileges. Be diligent by only granting access in limited form.

➤   Configure an OS 'mysql' user, but do not allow direct login access to this user. The mysqld process does not run as the 'root' OS user.

➤   Set permissions of the MySQL data directory to OS 'mysql' user for example:

```
chmod 700/mysql/datadir
```

➤   Ensure the MySQL data directory only contains data, and InnoDB transactional logs only.

➤   The MySQL error, slow and general logs should be in a separate directory. This allows for permissions of the 'mysql' group to view logs. Grant group 'mysql' access when necessary.

➤   The MySQL socket file needs to be in a world readable directory. The pid file does not.

➤   You can provide additional constraints on the MySQL port, e.g. 3306 at a firewall level. Ideally, your database should not be world accessible. Access should be restricted to the application or monitoring servers only.

These can be best achieved when using the MySQL tar binary installation rather than an Operating System packaged version. However, the same rules can apply.

MySQL Security Permissions

After securing MySQL at the Operating System level, you can improve security for MySQL client access with the following recommendations:

➤   Always set a MySQL 'root' user password.

➤   Change the MySQL 'root' user id to a different name, e.g. 'dba'.

➤   Only enable SUPER privileges to dba accounts, and only ever for 'localhost'.

➤   Application user permissions should be as restrictive as possible.

➤   Never use '%' for a hostname.

➤   Never use ALL TO *.*.

➤   Ideally the application should have at least two types of users, a read/write user and a read user.

About the MySQL Security Model

MySQL users have three attributes for the identification component. These are:

➤ username

➤ password

➤ host identifier

A user is then granted permissions to objects. The valid types of objects include:

➤ database schemas

➤ schema tables

➤ table columns

The list of valid permissions for MySQL 5.1 are:

➤ `ALTER, ALTER ROUTINE`

➤ `CREATE, CREATE ROUTINE, CREATE TEMPORARY TABLES, CREATE USER, CREATE VIEW`

➤ `DELETE, DROP, EVENT, EXECUTE, FILE, INDEX`

➤ `INSERT, LOCK TABLES, PROCESS, RELOAD`

➤ `REPLICATION CLIENT, REPLICATION SLAVE`

➤ `SELECT, SHOW DATABASES, SHOW VIEW, SHUTDOWN`

➤ `TRIGGER, UPDATE, USAGE`

➤ `SUPER`

➤ `ALL`

➤ `GRANT OPTION`

This chapter discusses the users, objects and privileges in more detail as it reviews the commands used to manage MySQL security.

You use the `CREATE USER` command to define the username, password and host for a user. It is possible to create a user without a password; however you should never do this.

The host component defines the accessible connection options for the given username and password. This may be either DNS names or IP addresses. MySQL also allows the use of the `'%'` wildcard to provide a greater mask of security. Some examples include:

```
CREATE USER nopass@localhost;
CREATE USER withpass@localhost IDENTIFIED BY 'password';
CREATE USER userbyhostname@%.example.com IDENTIFIED BY 'password';
CREATE USER userbyip@192.168.100.% IDENTIFIED BY 'password';
```

Improving performance involves using IP addresses because it eliminates the need to perform an internal DNS lookup. This can be user configured with the `--skip-name-resolve` my.cnf or mysqld startup option because it tells MySQL to not perform DNS lookups.

 Using a host of `'%'` is not recommended because it provides global access from any accessible server that can see the MySQL server. For a publically accessible server, this provides opportunity for a brute force password attack on your server.

You can optionally create a user. It is possible to grant permissions to a user that does not exist and this results in the user being created by default.

When you refer to a user for subsequent commands, a user represents a given username, password and host.

GRANT

You use the GRANT command to give permissions to a specific user. The grant command is broken down into four components:

> privilege(s)
> database objects
> user
> WITH GRANT OPTION

Some example GRANT commands include:

```
GRANT SELECT,INSERT,UPDATE,DELETE ON db.* TO appuser@192.168.100.%;
GRANT SELECT ON db.* TO appreadonly@192.168.100.%;
GRANT CREATE,CREATE VIEW, DROP ON db.* TO appdba@localhost;
```

The SHOW GRANTS command can be run to provide a GRANT compatible syntax for permissions for specified users. You can also query the `mysql.user` table for specific details.

REVOKE

The REVOKE command, as the name indicates, removes privileges given by the GRANT command. For example:

```
REVOKE DELETE ON db.* FROM appuser@192.168.100.%;
```

As you can see, it is possible to provide a subset of granted permissions.

DROP USER

You can remove a user and all permissions with the DROP USER command.

It is possible to manipulate the MySQL security model manually via normal DDL commands against the mysql meta data schema. While this is possible, it is strongly recommended you refrain from this historical process and use the GRANT and REVOKE commands.

Now that you understand how to manage permissions, the rest of this section discusses the MySQL security recommendations.

The Security Backdoor

You need to restrict shutdown and restart permissions on the mysql server because the mysql server can be started with the --skip-grants option. This option not only bypasses all security, it lets you change existing security. There is no way to remove this functionality from the mysql server.

Change Default 'root' User

MySQL provides a feature over other commercial database products because you can replace the default supplied super user 'root' with any user you define. The advantage here is to reduce any brute force password attempts on a publically accessible mysql server. You have two ways to achieve this, the correct GRANT way, and the hack mysql security way.

For example, if you want to replace the 'root' user with a 'dba' user, you would use the following SQL statements:

```
$ mysql -uroot -p
CREATE USER dba@localhost IDENTIFIED BY 'somepass';
GRANT ALL on *.* TO dba@localhost WITH GRANT OPTION;

$mysql -udba -p
SHOW GRANTS;
+---------------------------------------------------------------------------
| Grants for dba@localhost
+---------------------------------------------------------------------------
| GRANT ALL PRIVILEGES ON *.* TO 'dba'@'localhost' IDENTIFIED BY PASSWORD
  '*13883BDDBE566ECECC0501CDE9B293303116521A' WITH GRANT OPTION
+---------------------------------------------------------------------------

DROP USER root@localhost;
SELECT host, user,password
FROM mysql.user
WHERE super_priv='Y' OR grant_priv='Y';
+-----------+------+-----------------------------------------------+
| host      | user | password                                      |
+-----------+------+-----------------------------------------------+
| localhost | dba  | *13883BDDBE566ECECC0501CDE9B293303116521A |
+-----------+------+-----------------------------------------------+
```

The incorrect way is as follows.

```
$ mysql -uroot -p
mysql> (before "UPDATE") UPDATE mysql.user SET user='dba' WHERE user='root';
mysql> (before "FLUSH") FLUSH PRIVILEGES;
```

Using Privileges Appropriately

The lazy approach is to grant the ALL privilege for a single application user. Permissions should always be restricted to the purpose of the user only. There should also be multiple users for the different roles, further allowing for greater security. By default, application users would fall into at least two categories:

➤ Those operations that require permissions to read and write application data

➤ Those operations that require read only permissions to application data

You should only grant the SELECT, INSERT, UPDATE, DELETE privileges when needed. Only add additional privileges when needed, for example EXECUTE for stored routines, or CREATE VIEW for dba's.

Defining User Host Permissions

The lazy approach is to grant user permissions to a '%' host. Ideally hosts should be restricted to specific IP address or submask, e.g. 192.168.100.1 or 192.168.100.%. You may use DNS names or IP addresses; however, MySQL can elect to ignore DNS entries based on configuration options.

A DBA account with SUPER privileges should be restricted to a host string of 'localhost' especially when WITH GRANT OPTION is also specified. This requires a DBA to physically connect to the database server first and provides a separate level of security that you can manage better via OS specific user security such as LDAP, yellow pages or RSA tokens, for example.

 Be careful when you add multiple permissions to varying host strings when using wildcards. There is an order of precedence and adding more restrictive global permissions may override other permissions. Refer to the MySQL Reference Manual for specific details at http://dev.mysql.com/doc/refman/5.1/en/privilege-system.html.

Ideal Application Security

What is an ideal permission model for your application? Ideally you should have the following:

➤ A dba user for database administration operations only. This includes operations such as creating users, schemas and permissions for daemon administration. This user is restricted to the host of 'localhost'.

➤ An app_dba user for a different level of DBA administration that only has permission on the respective application schemas to create and drop objects. Ideally this is restricted to the host of 'localhost'.

➤ An app_rw user that has INSERT, UPDATE, DELETE, SELECT privileges to the respective application schemas.

➤ An app_readonly user that has SELECT privileges to the respective application schemas.

 You need to realize that MySQL security is checked for every executed SQL statement. Having a complex privilege model increases the overhead of validation for every SQL statement. While security is important, you should use a moderated approach as detailed in this chapter.

Additional Database Security

In addition to MySQL user security there are other practical approaches to hardening your MySQL environment and the data recorded.

➤ When the application server accessing the database resides on the same server as your database, disable access externally with the --skip-networking option.

➤ MySQL by default will bind to all IP addresses of the server and accept connections on the specified port, the default of 3306. You can restrict MySQL to a specified IP address with the --bin-address option. This can also enable you to run multiple versions of MySQL on the same default port of 3306 on the same server with the use of multiple IP addresses.

➤ You can configure MySQL to operate with SSL keys; however, this only provides encryption of the communication between the client and the server.

➤ The use of sql_mode=NO_AUTO_CREATE_USER to ensure that users must always have passwords.

➤ The use of Referential Integrity, e.g. Foreign Keys.

➤ The use of check constraints such as NOT NULL, UNSIGNED and ENUM.

➤ Don't store passwords in clear text in the database.

Auditing

MySQL provides no means of system auditing. This is a significant shortcoming in important security environments such as financial and banking.

Your only option is to enable binary logging. This provides the only audit trail option of SQL commands possible with a standard mysql installation that logs all DML and DDL by default. It is possible to configure the binary log to ignore operations on a per schema and table basis which negates its complete view of all operations.

You also have the option to disable commands from being reported in the binary log, but this only further highlights this method as insufficient as a true audit trail. The process only works for honest people.

You can monitor the occurrence of any admin, alter, or drop commands via SHOW GLOBAL STATUS variables. You can then use the mysqlbinlog tool to review these commands.

ENCODING DATA

Encoding data so that it cannot be easily read or guessed is one of the key tenets of security. A properly designed system not only takes measures to prevent data from being exposed but also makes sure that the damage is limited should the worst happen and the data is compromised. The MySQL portion of the chapter covered precautionary steps that you can take on the MySQL side. This section covers the PHP side of things.

Two types of encoding are covered in this section:

➤ **Bi-directional** methods encode the data in such a way as to make it possible to retrieve the original value as long as you know the key.

➤ **Single-directional** or **one-way** methods calculate values that you can then compare against a known pre-calculated value.

Both methods have their place in security. The bi-directional methods are covered first.

Bi-directional Encoding

Two types of bi-directional encoding are available to you, one being a subset of the other:

➤ The superset, simply referred to here as **encoding**, is the process of changing the representation of data to another equivalent but distinct representation. Some basic encoding methods include base-conversion in numbering systems, URL encoding, Json encoding (the process of converting an object to JavaScript Object Notation), serialization and others. Such methods provide convenient ways to use the same data across multiple mediums but do not provide any security.

➤ One subset of encoding is referred to as encryption. **Encryption** encodes the data in such a way that it cannot be easily decoded without a key that both the encoder and the decoder know.

The XOR Cipher

There are numerous very basic forms of encryption. The simplest involves a lookup table of keys and values and translating every value in a string. Another basic encoding method is referred to as an XOR Cipher. XOR encoding is easy to do in PHP and can be used in applications where weak encryption is sufficient (more on why, later). PHP does not provide a single function to XOR encode data but it does provide the binary manipulation method (XOR — short for **Exclusive OR** — or sometimes Exclusive Disjunction) needed to produce the encoded string.

A cipher is a reproducible set of instructions used to encode and decode the data. XOR may be confusing for developers who do not have a computer science background.

XOR is a logical bitwise operation, which means that it is performed on a single bit and always produces the same results. XOR is represented in computer science as a plus sign (the symbol for OR) surrounded by a circle. The rules are simple:

$A \oplus 0 = A$

$0 \oplus 1 = 1$

$1 \oplus 1 = 0$

In simplest terms: the result will be one iff (if and only if) exactly one of the bits is 1.

In the XOR Cipher the application has a single shared key. The key can be any length. Performing an XOR operation on every byte in the source data generates the encrypted data. For example:

```
  01000011 01110101 01110010 01101001 01101111 01110011 01101111
⊕ 01000001 01101110 01100100 01110010 01100101 01110111
  00000010 00011011 00010100 00011011 00001010 00000100 00101110
```

Note the bolded byte. If there are not enough bytes in the shared key (if the key is shorter than the source string) then the key will wrap around. The last byte in the encrypted data is the last byte in the source data XORed with the first byte in the key. Longer keys are more secure. The code to perform the encryption in PHP looks like this:

```php
Function xorCipher( $source, $key="sample-key!" ) {
  $source = "Expert PHP and MySQL";
  $output = "";
  for( $i=0; $i<strlen($source); ) {
    for( $j=0; $j<strlen($key); $j++,$i++ )
      $output .= $source{$i} ^ $key{$j};
  }
  return $output;
}
```

The data returned can be binary; as such it is not suitable for screen display. Encoding the data in base-64 using `base64_encode()` is a good solution.

Because of the nature of XOR it is possible to decode data using the exact same function used to encode it. This feature is simultaneously the thing that makes XOR Ciphers very easy to implement and the thing that makes them easy to decipher by malicious users. Mathematically it is possible, given any two parts, to easily get the third part. So if someone has both the encoded and decoded value they can easily get the key.

In theory, a method called **one-time pad** encryption can be used along with XOR to create a near unbreakable encryption system. However, one-time pads are difficult to implement because they require that both the sender and the receiver agree to a series of one-time use keys. Then the question arises on how to securely agree on the keys. The easy availability of public/private key encryption has made such methods largely unnecessary. However, XOR Ciphers are still useful in the event that security is not one of the primary business goals and it has the added benefit of the encrypted version not taking up any more space than the original string.

Using the mcrypt Extension

The PHP mcrypt extension is compiled into many installations of PHP and provides an easy way to encrypt and decrypt data. Although mcrypt supports many different ciphers, they are typically more secure than a cipher like XOR because the key cannot be easily determined even if a malicious user has both the encrypted and decrypted values to use as reference.

Note that the mcrypt library will not be reviewed in detail in this chapter (it contains over 20 functions) but the basics of encrypting and decrypting data with the library are. For a practical example of using mycrpt refer back to Chapter 12.

In addition to the key and the source data, it is also necessary to decide on a cipher to use, a mode of encoding, and occasionally an **initialization vector** depending on the cipher used. The mycrypt library (on which the extension is built) supports many different encryption methods. This book does not go into each one in-depth; however, they include those shown in Table 14-1.

TABLE 14-1: Encryption Methods That mycrypt Library Supports

cast-128	gost	rijndael-128
cast-256	loki97	rijndael-192
blowfish-compat	serpent	xtea
des, rijndael-256	rc2	tripledes
twofish	blowfish	wake
saferplus	arcfour	enigma

Each has different benefits and disadvantages when it comes to speed, security, and interoperability. The classes later on in this chapter use RIJNDAEL-246 as the default. Sometimes the encryption method may be predetermined by the application but sometimes the choice does not make much of a difference.

The mcrypt manual page can be useful for finding a complete list of supported methods on a particular system as well as descriptions. Simply type **man mcrypt** on a system that has mcrypt installed. Mycrpt also supports eight modes of encryption:

➤ **STREAM:** Similar to the XOR cipher and as such you should avoid using the same key twice (since, again, having any two parts to an XOR Cipher can lead to the third part being easily determined). The difference is that the key string for the XOR is generated using the cipher chosen from the previous list. It does have the benefit of having an output that is equal in length to the input.

➤ **ECB (Electronic Code Book):** The simplest block encryption mode. It also has weaknesses largely because it does not require an initialization vector.

➤ **CBC (Cipher Block Chaining):** Created blocks that are dependent on previous blocks. The first block is the initialization vector. Subsequent blocks are the result of an XOR or the initialization vector and the previous block.

➤ **CFB (Cipher-Feedback Mode):** A stream cipher and therefore does not use block encoding. It does, however, require an initialization vector, which primes the XOR string.

➤ **OFB (Output-Feedback Mode):** Similar to CFB only it uses blocks instead of a stream. Both methods use 8-bit so they are not usually the best choice. The manual pages for mcrypt explicitly say that OFB was included just for completeness.

➤ **nCFB** and **nOFB:** Similar to CFB and OFB. The difference is in the number of bits used for the encryption. The **n** stands for the block size.

➤ **CTR (Counter Mode):** A block-mode encryption method that uses the initialization vector to start the counter. The counter is then incremented for each block and XORed with each block.

Using these methods is easy. An example of using the encryption and decryption functions was already seen in Chapter 12. However, Listing 14-1 is a simple encryption and decryption class:

LISTING 14-1: SimpleEncryption.class.php

```php
<?php
class SimpleEncryption {
  protected $mode;
  protected $cipher;
  protected $secret = "tHiS-1s-a-SeCret!";

  public function __construct( $cipher=MCRYPT_RIJNDAEL_256,
                               $mode=MCRYPT_MODE_CBC ) {
    $this->cipher = $cipher;
    $this->mode = $mode;
  }

  public function getIV() {
    static $iv = false;
    if ( $iv !== false ) return $iv;
    $iv_size = mcrypt_get_iv_size($this->cipher, $this->mode);
    srand();
    $iv = mcrypt_create_iv($iv_size, MCRYPT_RAND);
    return $iv;
  }

  public function encrypt( $source ) {
    return mcrypt_encrypt($this->cipher, $this->secret,
                          $source, $this->mode, $this->getIV());

  }

  public function decrypt( $data ) {
    return mcrypt_decrypt( $this->cipher, $this->secret, $data,
```

```
                                $this->mode, $this->getIV() );
    }
};
?>
```

Depending on the method of encryption that you use, the mcrypt library may pad extra white space onto the end of the string before encoding. The purpose of the padding is to make the string length into a multiple of the block side. When you decode the string, that extra padding is still there. In most cases it is a null character so you can get rid of it with: `rtrim( $string, "\0" )`.

Keep in mind that in the modes that use the initialization vector (CBC, CFB, and OFB), you must use the same initialization vector for both encryption and decryption. Because the initialization vector does not need to be a secret (it can safely be transmitted over the network) it can be stored in a cookie-like in the authentication example or stored in the database. It is not a good idea to use the same initialization vector for everything. Instead, the application should generate a new random one for everything it encrypts.

 Although this chapter covers many types of strong encryption, the methods presented may not meet certain military or governmental requirements. Make sure to check the appropriate regulations before attempting encryption at that level.

There is much more that can be done with the mcrypt library. Read through the PHP documentation for more information. Sometimes it is not necessary to use bi-direction encoding (and sometimes it is also undesirable) but it is still important to protect the application information. In those cases, single directional encoding can be used instead.

Single-Directional Encoding

Single directional encoding is often known as **hashing** because it produces a non-unique but reproducible output given a set input (useful for hash tables). It is very useful under two main circumstances, both covered in Chapter 12, and they are:

➤ Storing a value against which you need to test and which is sensitive, but never needs to be retrieved — such as a password.

➤ Comparing a calculated value on multiple nodes based on a shared secret. For example, when you test to see if a value is valid without ever actually sending the value over the network.

Basic hashing is simple: `md5($value)`. However, a basic hash is not very secure. An attacker can — through various means, such as rainbow tables — find another value that calculates to the same hash. If the hash is used for something like a password — which it often is — that calculated value can be used as if it were the actual password. Using a salt creates a part of the source data that cannot be controlled through user input.

For example, say that hash of the password is stored in $x and a malicious user determined that for `md5($y)` `==` $x he or she can use $y as if it were the password. But when a salt is introduced it becomes md5($y.$salt). Because the malicious user does not know the salt it is impossible to guess a value of y that would generate the correct hash. Even if the value of $salt is compromised it is still less likely to find a collision value than it is with a hash that does not use a salt. There isn't any excuse for an application to not salt the hashes.

PHP also provides a hashing function that can be used for other forms of hashes (MD5 has been broken and is considered weak but is still widely used). The complete list of hashing functions can be retrieved using `hash_algos()`. Some of the basic ones are:

➤ md5 as well as the deprecated md2 and md4. md5 and md3 should not be used for anything other than verifying data integrity. Likewise, md5 allows for predictable collisions and, as described earlier, is not ideal for security because of that. However, md2 and md4 can be useful when dealing with legacy protocols and formats.

➤ sha1, sha256, sha384 and sha512 are significantly stronger hashes than md5. sha1 is by far the most widely adopted of the sha family of hash functions. However, the other functions are mandatory for some military and governmental applications. It is worth noting that the sha() function will behave in the same way as passing sha1 to the hash function.

➤ The crc32 and crc32b hashes (cyclic redundancy check) are useful for providing lightweight checks for data integrity. They are absolutely not suitable for things like password checking; however, they are useful for checking to make sure that data has not been tampered with.

➤ Other alternative hashing functions include whirlpool (an open and free algorithm), gost, adler32, as well as the ripemd, tiger, and haval family of hashes. The variety of hash functions allows for an appropriate hash for most applications (legacy and otherwise).

It is most common to see sha, md5, and crc32; however it is important to take time to choose the right one.

PHP SECURITY RECIPES

This chapter closes with some examples of real-world security situations starting with the mandatory SQL injection and then continuing with other methods of exploitations. Security is only as strong as the weakest link and the best encryption in the world is useless if bypassing the encryption or executing functions on the user's behalf can compromise the data.

Protecting against SQL Injection

SQL injection is the exploit that everyone knows about and everyone knows how to prevent so it will be covered only briefly here.

SQL injection always starts with some form of user input either through forms, query strings (or data passed to query strings via rewrite rules), or even in uploaded files. Every place that accepts user input (directly or indirectly), which is then passed into the database, is fair game for a malicious user.

One form of SQL injection involves terminating the current query and executing a new one. For example:

```
# The original query
SELECT * FROM `users` WHERE `id`= USER INPUT
```

```
# The user input
0; DROP `users`
# The resulting query
SELECT * FROM `users` WHERE `id`=0; DROP `users`;
```

However, any of the libraries that use `prepare()` will auto-escape the data. The standard MySQL functions do not, but they won't execute multiple semicolon separated queries (`mysql_query()` needs to be executed multiple times) so that type of injection isn't possible under most circumstances. However, you can also use sub-queries for injection as well as to bypass authentication and ACL. For example, take this SQL statements:

```
SELECT * FROM `reports` WHERE `user_id`= USER INPUT
```

Given the proper user input they can become:

```
SELECT * FROM `reports` WHERE `user_id`= 1234 OR true
```

A simple page that lists all reports from a user suddenly lists all reports by any user anywhere in the system. The bottom line is to escape all input with `mysql_real_escape_string()` before passing it into a query.

 The `mysql_escape_string()` *function is deprecated and will be removed from later versions of PHP. Always use* `mysql_real_escape_string()`, *which requires a database connection but also takes into account the character encoding on the MySQL server.*

Protecting against Replay Attacks

A **replay attack** is when an intruder takes a packet that a user sends and then retransmits it to the server. The end result is that if the captured packet contained authentication information, the intruder can then masquerade as that user, thus compromising the user's data.

What Do Replay Attacks Look Like?

When done right replay attacks look exactly like the original request from the user. An application that does not take precautions can easily fall victim to an attack. Worse, it is difficult to know if an attack ever took place.

HTTP does provide a method, known as **Digest Authentication**, for authentication that prevents replay attacks. Digest Authentication is covered in great detail in Chapter 12 on authentication. The basic elements of a replay attack are this:

➤ The user sends a request that requires authentication.

➤ Another system on the network sniffs that request and stores it for later.

➤ Later comes and the attacker replays the packet, thus gaining access to the authenticated data any time that they want.

Replay attacks have symptoms very similar to a common accidental action that can be taken by the user: duplicate form submittal. Incidentally, the steps to protect against it are the same. Although duplicate form submittal is not a security risk it does provide a bad user experience (not limited to duplicate posts on a forum or a credit card being charged twice!).

Protecting against replay attacks will not prevent the attacker from stealing the actual password if it is transited over plain text. Thus, it is important to always perform login over an encrypted connection where sensitive user data is involved.

The Code

Preventing replay attacks was already covered briefly in Chapter 12. A **nonce** or "number used once" is a way to prevent a replay attack. The server will create a nonce and then send it to the client. The client then creates a hash that includes both the nonce and a shared secret that the user provides (the password).

There are two types of nonce values. Those that:

➤ Expire immediately after use

➤ Are good only for a short period of time

Both have benefits and drawbacks.

Immediately expiring a nonce can be implemented in one of two ways:

➤ One requires a database of nonces that have been previously used. However, the database can be pruned periodically. That is the way that OAuth and OpenID work.

➤ A second way can be used in HTTP based connections. A session can be used to store the current nonce for the user, which is updated on each use.

In essence, they are the same. However, sessions remove the need for manually managing the nonce. A session-based nonce may look like Listing 14-2.

LISTING 14-2: SessionNonce.class.php

```php
<?php
class SessionNonce {
  private $salt;

  public function __construct( $salt = "abc123" ) {
    session_start();
    $this->salt = $salt;
    if ( !array_key_exists('nonce',$_SESSION) )
      $this->generate();
  }

  public function consume( $nonce ) {
    if ( $nonce == $_SESSION['nonce'] )
      $this->generate();
```

```
      else
        throw new Exception("Invalid nonce");
    }

    private function generate() {
      $_SESSION['nonce'] = MD5(uniqid().$salt.rand(1,1000));
    }

  }
  ?>
```

The problem with this method is that the user cannot submit more than one form simultaneously. The first form will succeed while the second will fail. An advanced system might generate multiple nonce values depending on the content.

However, this "defect" can also be an advantage. For example, if the application is a wiki, this kind of nonce prevents not only replay attacks but also helps protects the user from overwriting content with an older version.

A time-based nonce requires no storage overhead because it is decoded at validation time but it does create a period where replay attacks can occur. It is also not practical when user input is involved because giving more time for the user to enter their input also means giving more time for an attack to happen.

In a time-based expiring nonce, instead of calculating a random nonce, the current time is used. A time-based nonce can then be decoded to determine the time that the nonce was created. If the nonce is older than a set time then it is considered stale. At that point the client would have to resubmit the request.

Both the immediately expiring and time-based methods involve inserting the nonce into a form that is submitted by the user. The function that accepts the form would then consume the nonce. If the nonce is invalid, an exception is thrown. Both methods also have disadvantages. One opens up a window in which attacks can occur and the other cannot manage multiple simultaneous requests from the same session without some additional hacking.

Nonces also have the added disadvantage of inhibiting both automated unit testing and load testing. Unit tests need to be able to handle session cookies. The load-testing problem is more difficult. In most situations a load test is indistinguishable from a replay attack since it does exactly the same thing as a replay attack (records sessions then retransmits them to the server. The load testing problem needs to be considered on a per-application basis.

Again, for more information on preventing replay attacks be sure to go back and re-read the chapter on authentication.

Protecting against XSS

Cross-site scripting attacks (XSS) are very common and there have been several high-profile cases where they were executed on websites with huge user-bases. Unlike some other attacks in this chapter: XSS attacks are exclusive to web-based PHP applications and have little bearing on types of PHP applications that are not accessible via the Internet.

What Does XXS Look Like?

An XSS attack is very closely related to SQL injection. Both occur because user input is not properly sanitized. SQL injection occurs when a field includes malicious SQL while XSS occurs when a field contains malicious scripts. The scripts are then run on the client's computer. Any tag that can load content from a remote source is vulnerable; the three most common are: `<script>`, `<img>`, and `<embed>`. Alternatively, you can use `<meta>` for cookie manipulation and `<base>` to rewrite every embedded image or script on a page.

XSS can range from the basic to the extremely complex. The most basic form is to just include a `<script>` tag in the form input:

```
<script src="http://example.com/attack.js"></script>
```

Other forms of attack include executing a code that is obfuscated in order to avoid automatic detection by poorly written XSS detection scripts. There are several things to remember when trying to detect an XSS attack:

➤ Parameters in HTML do not need to be enclosed in quotes. Alternatively they can be enclosed in: single quotes, double quotes, or grave accents. That last one is lesser known and therefore not checked by many detection scripts. It is the back tick used to enclose tables and columns in MySQL queries.

➤ Embedded content can have `AllowScriptAccess` set to true, which allows Flash and SVG images to access JavaScript.

➤ HTML comments can be in most places in a document and can easily confuse XSS detection.

➤ URLs can contain JavaScript and VBScript.

You can find many resources on the Internet for learning more about XSS attacks. Preventing XSS attacks could cover several chapters. Be sure to check out this book's web page on www.wrox.com for more information on XSS.

The Code

Because XSS is so complicated there is really only one easy way to prevent it. That is to encode all HTML using `htmlentities()` which will cause any HTML in the user's input to be displayed verbatim on the output page. The second best approach is to strip all HTML from the input entirely, thus avoiding the ugly raw output.

Both methods have their flaws. The largest one is that neither will work in applications where HTML is actually allowed (such as when the input is rich text). The second method (stripping the HTML) is also flawed because there are numerous techniques to trick code into leaving HTML in the data. A good HTML stripping function will know about and try to prevent all of them. A good alternative is a combination of them both:

```
$html = preg_replace(
        '/<script(?:\s(?:(["`\']) (?:\\\1|[^\1])*?\1|[^>])*)?'.
        '>(?:.*?<\/script\s*>)?/g'
        '', $html);
$html = preg_replace('/<[^\s>]+(?:\s(?:(["`\']) (?:\\\1|[^\1])*?\1|[^>])*)?>/g',
        '',$html);
```

```
$html = htmlentities($html);

// Input:
//    <script type="text/javascript">alert('hello');</script>
//    <strong>world ></strong>
// Output:
//     world &gt;
```

In this code, the first regular expression replaces all script tags as well as the content inside of them. The second expression replaces all other tags while preserving the content inside of them. Alternatively, the second expression can replace all but a special white list of tags. The new `preg_replace()` call may look something like this:

```
$whitelist = array('strong','b','i','u','s','em','del','p','br','br\/');
$html = preg_replace(/<(?!\/?(?:'.implode('|',$whitelist).
      '))[^\s>]+(?:\s(?:(["`'])(?:\\\1|[^\1])*?\1|[^>])*)?>/,'',$html);
```

The <br> tag is included twice because it is the only one on the list that can be self-closing. The script uses a negative lookahead to make sure that none of the white listed tags are used. Lookaheads are covered in-depth in Chapter 1. If the white list includes any tag that has a `src` or `href` such as <img>, be sure to make sure that the source does not have the "`javascript:`" prefix.

Another popular approach to preventing XSS is to entity encode the entire string and disallow HTML altogether but also provide an alternative means of formatting. Such systems include wiki syntax and BBCode. It is likely that most developers have seen one of the other at some point. Here is an example of bolded text in each method. First BBCode then wiki code:

```
[b]Bolded text[/b]
'''Bolded text'''
```

 Wiki syntax is not standardized. Different wikis use different formatting rules. It is highly likely that if the XSS prevention code is treated as a side-project and not a dedicated task, there will be exploits. For that reason, it is recommended that applications use third party libraries for XSS prevention and/or HTML cleansing.

One of the most common uses of XSS attacks is to steal a user's authentication information by reading the cookie with JavaScript. The `setcookie` function in PHP offers one final level of protection against that type of XSS attacks. The last parameter to the function is the often-overlooked `httpOnly`. Setting the cookie to use HTTP only means that JavaScript cannot read it. Do not rely on this option though; it is not supported in all browsers.

Protecting against CSRF

One of the most overlooked security vulnerabilities is the **cross-site request forgery**. It is abbreviated as **CSRF** and often pronounced as "sea-surf" and can have devastating effects on users' data. This type of attack is HTTP specific (but independent of format) and is unfortunately quite common because when developers design forms, they often don't think of the fact that an HTTP request can come from anywhere.

What Does a CSRF Look Like?

A CSRF attack works on the premise that users remain logged into web pages via cookies. As such, any form submission to the website will appear to come from the currently logged in user. A would-be attacker tricks the user's browser into requesting a site that requires authentication.

The attacker has no way of knowing if the person has an account on the target site. So the probability of an attack being successful grows as the number of visitors to your website increases as a percentage of the total number of people with Internet access.

However, it is also possible to target individuals specifically by tricking them into visiting a link that contains an attack. Social networks have played a role in spreading an attack by acting as a traffic driver for the malicious website.

Things that seemed harmless in HTML suddenly take on new meaning when dealing with CSRF. For example, one vector of attack is when a site allows for embedded images or HTML.

The first rule of preventing CSRF attacks is: never use a GET request to modify data. Consider this hypothetical situation. A website allows users to delete their account by going to the URL: /users/delete.php?confirm=yes. That page can then be invoked from an attacker's website (or the site itself if the site allows embedding of remote images!) using any of the following:

```
<img src="http://www.example.com/users/delete.php?confim=yes" />
<script src="http://www.example.com/users/delete.php?confim=yes"></script>
<iframe src="http://www.example.com/users/delete.php?confim=yes"></iframe>
<link rel="stylesheet" type="text/css"
      href="http://www.example.com/users/delete.php?confim=yes" />
<embed src="http://www.example.com/users/delete.php?confim=yes" />
```

Other methods include actual frames or JavaScript to write any of the above tags. An alternative method that allows for the POST method looks like this:

```
<form method="POST" id="csrf_form" action="http://www.example.com/users/delete">
  <input type="hidden" name="confirm" value="yes" />
</form>
<script type="text/javascript" language="javascript">
  settimeout( function() { document.getElementById("csrf_form").submit(); }, 500 );
</script>
```

A more elaborate script might put the form inside of an iframe where it can be submitted without the user ever knowing a thing. Deleting an account is one example of an action that could be taken. Other actions may include transferring money from one bank account to another, changing a password then using the site's private messaging service to send a note to the attacker alerting them of the compromise, or any number of actions that can be done via forms or via clicking a link.

It is worth noting that CSRF is not click-jacking. **Click-jacking** is an attack that is possible now that most web-browsers have robust support for DHTML and iframes. It involves one of two techniques:

➤ Making a submit button look like it is part of the website when it's actually a cleverly placed iframe.

➤ Positioning an iframe with a button so that it is always directly below a user's cursor but setting the opacity to zero so that the user cannot see it until they've already clicked.

The security measures in this chapter cannot prevent click-jacking.

The Code

There are two methods for preventing CSRF attacks. Make sure to use both, although either one will do. One good thing about CSRF attacks is that they are relatively easy to track back to their origin. This is because most modern browsers send a referrer string that contains either the page in which the content is embedded, the page that the user was linked to the content from, or the page where the form was embedded.

The first method of prevention, checking the referrer, relies on this fact. It is very simple. In each page that modifies data (which should only be post requests!), include this:

```
define(SITE,example.com');
$referer = $_SERVER['HTTP_REFERER'];
if ( $referer != "" &&
     !preg_match('/^https?:\/\/([^/]+\.)?'.preg_replace('.','\.',SITE).'(\/|$)/') )
  die('Invalid referer!');
```

At this point, it might also be a good idea to log the attempted attack. The regular expression seems a little bit more complicated than it needs to be. A few reasons for that are:

➤ It needs to account for secure and non-secure connections.

➤ It needs to make sure that the site is at the start of the string and is followed by either a slash or the end of the string.

Otherwise one or both of these may match:

```
http://example.com.example.org
http://example.org/example.com
```

In both the previous examples, the site `example.org` is the attacker's website. As an added bonus, the regular expression also allows for forms submitted from any (or no) sub-domain of the main site. However, a close look at the code reveals the check to make sure that the referrer is not empty. If the referrer is empty, the security check passes. This is not ideal, but it prevents legitimate users from being rejected. After all, not all browsers send referrer strings.

The second preventative measure is to use a token. The **token** is similar to the nonce discussed earlier. However, it is not necessary to keep the token a secret and it doesn't need to change as often. The most efficient way to use the token is store it in a cookie. Checking that the token is valid is as simple as comparing it with the cookie. In this system the page that renders the form looks something like this:

```
<?php
if ( !array_key_exist("form_token",$_COOKIE) ) {
  $_COOKIE['form_token'] = uniqid().rand(1000);
  set_cookie('form_token', $_COOKIE['form_token']);
}
?>
<form method="POST" action="/doAction.php">
  ...
```

```
        <input type="hidden" name="form_token"
               value="<?php echo $_COOKIE['form_token'] ?>" />
        ...
    </form>
```

The page that accepts the form request looks like this:

```
<?php
if ( $_COOKIE['form_token'] != $_POST['form_token'] )
    die( "Invalid token" );
...
```

Again, now might be a good time to log the potential attack. Using a combination of the two methods above all but guarantees that the site is protected from CSRF attacks. Just remember the three basic rules: always change data with POST and never GET, check the referrer, and use a token.

Automation Attacks

Automation attacks or exploits occur when a website is accessed by something other than a human. Everyone knows what these attacks look like and how they are typically prevented.

A **Turing Test** is designed to determine if someone or something is a person or machine. It generally involves putting the person/computer in one room and a person in the other. The person then goes to ask whatever/whoever is in the next room a series of questions. The computer passes the test if it can answer all the questions so well that the person on the other end cannot tell the difference between it and a human.

A web version of this is known as **CAPTCHA (Completely Automated Public Turing test to tell Computers and Humans Apart)**, which is an attempt to take the person asking the questions out of the picture. After all, it would be inefficient to have a person on staff all day administering non-automated Turing Tests.

The problem is that as CAPTCHAs become more complicated the computer programs that read them get more and more sophisticated. A lot of money is to be had, particularly by spammers wanting to create thousands of free email accounts, by breaking CAPTCHAs. The result is that most tests are almost completely unreadable to humans while the computers seem to continue to have no problem.

Other test method such as "click on the three dogs in this 6x6 grid of fluffy animals" or "answer this simple math problem" have failed to gain adoption. The latter is a very effective way of making sure only smart humans can use your website and the first is an effective way of locking out visually impaired individuals.

Since CAPTCHAs are such a difficult problem and their use is a constantly evolving field, the official stance in this book is that developers should use a third party library or distributed solution (such as reCAPTCHA) rather than try to roll their own. However, this section creates a really quick CAPTCHA just to show the basics. The form for the CAPTCHA could look like this:

```
<form method="POST" action="signup.php">
  <p>
    Username: <input type="text" name="username" /><br />
```

```
        Password: <input type="password" name="password" /><br /><br />

        <img src="captcha.php" /><br />
        <input type="text" name="captcha" /><br /><br />

        <input type="submit" name="Sign Up" />
    </p>
</form>
```

The file captcha.php then uses the GD library to generate the CAPTCHA image (see Listing 14-3):

LISTING 14-3: captcha.php

Available for
download on
Wrox.com

```php
<?
    session_start();

    $img = imagecreate(400,100);
    $captcha = "";
    for ( $i=rand(5,7); $i >= 0; $i-- )
      $captcha .= chr(rand(ord('A'),ord('Z')));

    $white = imagecolorallocate($img, 255, 255, 255);
    $black = imagecolorallocate($img, 0, 0, 0);

    imagestring($img, 5, 3, 3, $captcha, $black);

    header("Content-type:image/jpeg");
    imagejpeg($img);

    $_SESSION['captcha'] = $captcha;
?>
```

The form processing page then checks the value of $_SESSION['captcha'] against the value given in the form.

The system has a few flaws, not the least of which is that it is impossible to have more than one form with a CAPTCHA open at once and still have them both work. The other thing that should become glaring once the code is executed is that this CAPTCHA is extremely easy to read with traditional OCR (Optical Character Recognition) techniques. It is meant to serve only as an example.

Some really easy ways to improve the example include:

➤   Using a True Type Font (TTF) instead of the default GD font.

➤   Making the letters touch and/or put non-straight lines through some of the letters to make it more difficult to pick the letters out from each other.

➤   Adding some color.

➤   Varying the font size and position on the Y-axis on a per-letter basis.

SUMMARY

You can take various steps to harden a MySQL server. The most important is to only grant necessary permissions to users. You should never see, for example:

➤   Application users with SUPER permissions.

➤   Application users with CREATE permissions.

➤   Anybody with access to mysql meta schema.

➤   MySQL user hostname of '%' allowing access from the world.

Additionally, there are many features of PHP that allow for better security in applications including strong support for encryption and many different hashing algorithms. However, none of that is any use if the site is not protected against common (and even uncommon) exploits. Some of the exploits covered in this chapter are:

➤   SQL injection

➤   Replay attacks

➤   Cross-site scripting (XSS)

➤   Cross-site request forgeries (CSRF)

➤   Automation

It is important to understand each of the exploits. However, the most important thing to understand is that it is not always the best path to develop security custom to an application. Some problems such as CAPTCHAs and XSS attack prevention are solved problems and libraries provide easy ways to implement features and fixes without reinventing the wheel or writing tons of code.

15

Command-Line and Web Services

WHAT'S IN THIS CHAPTER?

➤ Building command-line services

➤ Creating recurring jobs

➤ Describing web services with WSDL

➤ Building RESTful web services

➤ Building a web service with SOAP

There is more to PHP and MySQL than just consumer-facing web sites. They are capable of so much more. To this point, this book has covered using PHP as a Gearman worker and as a tool for rewriting URLs. This chapter explores some more of the less traditional uses of PHP, expanding on topics expressed in previous chapters.

This chapter also talks about using PHP to create *web services*, which are endpoints for communication between two parties. Those parties can be the application and another server, the application and the user, or even the application and any third party that could benefit from gaining access to some of the application information.

CREATING COMMAND-LINE SCRIPTS

PHP is not the first language that comes to mind when the subject of command-line scripts comes up. Although it's as common to use PHP for this purpose as it is to use other languages, PHP is extremely powerful. This section covers how to create a command-line script using the PHP CLI (Command Line Interface). The chapter focuses mostly on UNIX/Linux; however, many of the concepts do translate well to Windows.

The first step in creating command-line scripts is to create a stand-alone executable file. This was covered in Chapter 11 when you created a dynamic rewrite map. The CLI doesn't care if the filename ends in PHP so the file can have any extension (a common aproach is to have no extension at all). What is important is that the file is launched one of two ways:

➤ **Via a parameter to php:** `php ./filename`

➤ **Directly:** `./filename`

Although the second method is preferred, it is more work to set up due to two requirements. The first is that the top line of the file must be a *shebang* — an instruction to the shell to use a specific program to execute the file. The shebang for PHP usually looks like:

```
#!/usr/bin/php
```

The shebang will never be read if the shell does not know that the file is executable. Thus the second requirement is that the file has the correct permissions. On UNIX/Linux that is as simple as:

```
chmod +x ./filename
```

Most file versioning systems will maintain the executable state. Once that is done, the file can be executed just by typing `./filename` from the command line. It might be a good idea to put `<?= "hello world"; ?>` or something in there. Otherwise it will just launch and immediately exit.

This section builds a command-line class that can be extended for any command-line application. Each piece of functionality extends the base class. At the end of the command-line section, you will have a listing of the completed base class. But first, the application must be able to read user input.

Reading Command-Line Input

The base class does most of the difficult work of handling parameters. The descendant class registers each of the parameters. The Using registration method means you do not act on the parameters directly, ensuring that you can have multiple levels of inheritance that all work together.

Chapter 14 covered encryption and security, which is used again in this very simple application and which will accept data to be encoded. The data is read from the command line. Additionally, you can specify a cipher, secret, encoding mode, and initialization vector.

The registration function in the new class takes several parameters:

➤ The short version of the option flag

➤ The long version of the option flag

➤ A Boolean specifying whether the flag is supposed to be followed by a value

➤ A help string for that flag

➤ A validation callback function

Only the short flag is actually required. The first registration function looks like this:

```
$this->registerParameter("c", "cipher", true,
        "The cipher to use. Use the -1 option to list all valid ciphers.",
        array($this,"isValidCipher"));
```

The preceding registration line would accept input that takes either of these two forms:

```
./phpcrypt -c=DES "text to encrypt"
./phpcrypt --cipher=DES "text to encrypt"
```

It validates the input using the member method, `isValidCipher()`. For more on using callback functions, see Chapter 1. A good place to register all these switches is in the constructor. The constructor for your new class looks like this:

```
public function __construct() {

  parent::__construct();

  $this->registerParameter("c", "cipher", true,
          "The cipher to use. Use the -l option to list all valid ciphers.",
          array($this, "isValidCipher"));

  $this->registerParameter("m", "mode", true, "The encoding mode to use.",
          array($this, "isValidMode"));

  $this->registerParameter("I", "iv", true, "The initialization vector to use.",
          array($this, "isValidIV"));

  $this->registerParameter("s", "secret", true, "The secret key to use.",
  "strlen");

  $this->registerParameter("i", "interactive",false, "Use interactive
  encryption.");

  $this->registerParameter("l", "list", false, "Lists all valid encoding modes.");

}
```

The order of the registration does matter for validation. For instance, to make sure the initialization vector is valid, it's important to first have the encryption cipher set because different ciphers require different length vectors.

The validation methods look like this:

```
public function isValidIV( $iv ) {
   return ( strlen($iv) != mcrypt_get_iv_size($this->cipher, $this->mode) );
}

public function isValidCipher( $cipher ) {
   return in_array($cipher, mcrypt_list_algorithms());
}

public function isValidMode( $mode ) {
   return in_array($mode, mcrypt_list_modes());
}
```

Behind the scenes, it is accessing the parameters via the variables `$argc` and `$argv`. The `$argc` variable contains the number of arguments passed via the command-line. The variable `$argv` contains an array of those arguments. The filename of the script is always counted as the first argument so at a minimum there will always be one argument when executing a script via the CLI.

The base class takes care of validating the input as well as displaying the help if the input is invalid. The utility also calls for an interactive mode that will prompt the user for input. To accomplish that, it's necessary to read from standard input.

Prompting for Input

Two types of input can come into an application from the standard input stream. The first is piped data and the second is direct user input. The base class takes care of the piped data so for now it is just necessary to handle the interactive mode (for when the user types ./phpcrypt --interactive or ./phpcrypt -i).

PHP automatically opens a handle to the standard input stream, standard output stream, and standard error stream when using PHP CLI. They are referenced via the STDIN, STDOUT, and STDERR, respectively. Alternatively the stream can be manually opened. For example, to get a handle to standard input:

```
$stdin = fopen('php://stdin', 'r');
```

Reading a line from standard input is as easy as $this->readln() when using the base class in this chapter. To help out even further, the base class has a method called prompt() that asks for input and then reads a line or sets a default if the input is empty. Interactive mode reads the values of the cipher, secret, mode, and source string from standard input. The resulting run() method (the method called when executing the command-line application) looks like this:

```
public function run() {
  parent::run();

  if ( $this->interactive )
    $this->runInteractiveMode();
  else
    echo $this->crypt();
}

private function runInteractiveMode() {
  $defaultCipher = $this->cipher;
  do {
    $this->cipher = $this->prompt("Choose a cipher",$defaultCipher);
  } while ( !$this->isValidCipher( $this->cipher ) );

  $defaultMode = $this->mode;
  do {
    $this->mode = $this->prompt("Choose an encoding mode",$defaultMode);
  } while ( !$this->isValidMode( $this->mode ) );

  $defaultSecret = $this->secret;
  do {
    $this->secret = $this->prompt("Choose an encryption key/secret",
                          $defaultSecret);
  } while ( strlen( $this->secret ) == 0 );

  while ( count($this->data) == 0 ) {
    $data = $this->prompt("Enter the data that you would like to encrypt: ");
    if ( $data ) $this->data = array($data);
```

```
        }

        $this->crpyt();
    }

    private function crypt() {
        if ( $this->iv == null ) {
            $iv_size = mcrypt_get_iv_size($this->cipher, $this->mode);
            srand();
            $this->iv = mcrypt_create_iv($iv_size, MCRYPT_RAND);
        }

        if ( $this->decrypt ) return $this->doDecrypt( $this->data );
        else return $this->doEncrypt( $this->data );
    }

    private function doEncrypt( $source ) {
        return mcrypt_encrypt($this->cipher, $this->secret,
                              $source, $this->mode, $this->getIV());

    }

    private function doDecrypt( $data ) {
        return mcrypt_decrypt( $this->cipher, $this->secret, $data,
                               $this->mode, $this->iv );
    }
```

The base class automatically puts anything that is not part of a flag into the $data member variable as an item in an array. Just like the command line, data can also be enclosed in quotes to keep it all in one piece.

Chapter 11, "Rewrite Rules," uses a command-line application to constantly read values and spit out the results. This class would be useful for that but because of the simplicity of the application (no command-line parameters, no interactivity, and so on) it is more efficient to just write it from scratch.

Completed Classes

Two complete classes are defined in this section:

➤ **The base class:** Defines basic functionality of a command-line application.

➤ **The application class:** You use this to do the encryption and decryption.

The base class needs to perform two functions: input and high-level output. To facilitate input, the class has utility functions that make it easy to read and register command-line options as well as prompt for input. The class first reads in all the command-line parameters and then calls the run() method.

The base class is too large to list inline in the book. It is also probably unnecessary to review basic string parsing and array handling. However, here are some key concepts to remember:

➤ The $argv variable, as mentioned earlier, stores a vector (array) of arguments, passed through the command line. The first argument at index zero is always the path to the script.

The variable $argc stores the count of the arguments. PHP CLI takes care of all the hard work of dealing with quotations, but it is up to the script to gain meaning from the command line.

➤ php://stdin can be read from and written to like any other file on the system. It benefits from a concept called *protocol wrappers*, which allow different protocols to act as a standard file handle in PHP.

The next step is to take a command-line program, which is already quite useful, and make it even more useful by running it on a schedule.

Setting Up Cron Jobs

A *cron job* is a recurring task on a Linux/UNIX server and is very useful for cleanup operations, messaging, or any number of actions that you periodically need to take care of. It can be set up to run at specific intervals ranging from once a minute to annually. You cannot create jobs that run more frequently than a minute — for that, it's probably best to set up a daemon.

> A daemon, besides being a supernatural being, is a program on a UNIX/Linux system that runs in the background. Usually that means that it runs indefinitely until it is shut down or restarted. Although not covered in this chapter, it is possible to write a daemon in PHP. The Rewrite Map code from earlier acted as a type of daemon. The key is one line of code:
>
> ```
> set_time_limit(0);
> ```

The list of cron jobs is edited by a program called *crontab* (again, the system must be UNIX or Linux). To enter the crontab editor, type:

```
crontab -e
```

Once there, it's possible to create cron jobs. There can be one job per line, which consists of two main parts: the timing indicators and the command to be executed. The command should be a PHP file that is set up properly with executable permissions and a shebang in place. A job that runs every hour on the hour would look like this:

```
0 * * * *    /some/php/script
```

The five dots, in order, represent minutes, hours, day of month, month, and day of week. Minutes, hours, and day of week are zero-based. Day of month and the month itself are one-based. So, if a job were to run once a year at the very start of the year, it would look like this:

```
0 0 1 1 *    /happy/new/year
```

The last star is intentionally left in this code. A star indicates *every time*. For instance, a star for minutes means that the script will run once per minute. If that last star were changed to a 0 it means the script will only execute if the first day of the year also happens to align with the first day of the week.

It is also possible to have a job run only at specific increments, for example once every fifteen minutes. To do this it's necessary to represent the time as a fraction (an asterisk over the delta):

```
*/15 * * * *   /some/php/script
```

Bonus: Output in Color

Command lines are not all black and white (or black and green, or whatever your settings may be). They come in a range of colors. Colors are useful for providing emphasis or for design but they are only easily accessible in Bash-compatible shells (which is fine for most Linux but not Windows users). The section shows how to switch colors on the fly.

You create colored text using special escape sequences (called *ANSII control codes*) in the output. They always start with a null byte, followed by an ASCII 33 and then the color number (in decimal) followed by the letter m. For example, to make text red:

```
echo "\033[31mThis text will be red";
```

Why the number 31? That is the code for a red foreground. Table 15-1 shows the complete color table:

TABLE 15-1: Output Color Table

COLOR	FOREGROUND VALUE	BACKGROUND VALUE
Black	30	40
Red	31	41
Green	32	42
Brown	33	43
Yellow	33	43
Blue	34	44
Purple	35	45
Cyan	36	46
Grey	37	47

It doesn't take much to notice a pattern in the colors. The background color code is always exactly 10 higher than the foreground color code. You can combine multiple color codes by separating them with a semicolon. For instance, to get gray text on a black background:

```
echo "\033[37;40mThis text will grey on a red background";
```

There are also several codes that have special effects on the text. The text can start blinking just by adding a ";5" to the end. Normal (0) returns the text back to its default state (including color and background). Light or bold (1) make the text stick out compared to other text. There are more but they are less useful and not honored by all console emulators and terminals.

Once you've implemented the command-line services to modify and access the data, it may become necessary to create services that allow third parties to access the content. The next section covers web services.

CREATING WEB SERVICES

Web services provide a standard way for third parties to access and potentially modify data on the application server. They are also useful for communicating between application servers. This section covers the two most common types of web services: RESTful and SOAP. Both have distinct advantages and disadvantages. Which method an application uses is up to the developer.

RESTful Web Services

REST stands for *Representational State Transfer* and it is more than just a service protocol, it is a software architecture. It is based on two main concepts: resources (subjects) and verbs. A client application can request that an action be executed on a resource and then "rest" for a while as the user consumes that resource before the application optionally makes another request. The application does not maintain a constant connection between client and server but it can store data to send with each request (cookies). An application that follows this model is often referred to as *RESTful*.

Millions of users use RESTful systems every day. The most common one is HTTP. If developers are not familiar with rest they will still likely recognize the terms *GET* and *POST*, which are the two main verbs for HTTP. Although a RESTful service does not have to be based on HTTP, PHP and HTTP do make a natural pair, so it's only fitting to build a restful service on top of the two.

HTTP has several RESTful verbs and each is associated with a specific action on a resource. It is best practice to obey these guidelines:

➤ **GET:** Used solely for retrieving data. A GET request should never modify any of the data on the server. Doing so both violates the architecture conventions and opens the application up to security holes (see Chapter 14, specifically regarding CSRF attacks).

➤ **HEAD:** The corresponding verb HEAD can be used to retrieve just the header information but none of the content. It too should never modify content.

➤ **PUT:** The opposite of GET. It should only be used to do inline editing of a resource. A client might "PUT" new data onto the server. A similar, but different, verb called **POST** can be used to both edit and create new resources.

➤ **DELETE:** This is fairly self-explanatory. It removes a resource.

OPTIONS, TRACE, and ECHO are less common and are not well supported. They are not covered in this book. With the exception of PUT, DELETE, and POST, none of the methods should modify any data at all. They are the "safe" methods.

There are a few steps that are common when creating any RESTful system with PHP:

➤ Define the resources.

➤ Define and create a controller to handle requests.

➤ Test to make sure everything works.

➤ Write the first consumer of the RESTful service using PHP.

Defining Resources

Each resource must have a unique identifier (its URN). In most RESTful systems the resource URN is the type of resource followed by the username. For example, to access a company named MyVBO you would use the URL: `http://www.example.com/`**`companies/myvbo.xml`**.

The highlighted part is the URN. Performing a GET request on that URL might return a resource in the XML format that contains the company name and address. POSTing data to that URL with a company name and address will modify it (if the user has the proper permission).

It is typical for a RESTful system to have numerous supported data formats. They are usually represented using mime-types in the "content-type" header variables. Some common content encoding formats for REST are Json, XML, and RDF (based on XML). However, it is possible to use any format. It wouldn't make much sense to have a company resource defined by an image mime-type (the logo would be a different resource) but it might make sense to provide the company information via HTML.

At a bare minimum the application should support Json (JavaScript Object Notation) and XML. Those two formats are both widely recognized; however, in some systems one is more accessible than the other, so the best bet is to provide both.

Defining the Controller

This chapter does not attempt to create a full MVC design pattern but rather implements a simple controller that handles a request and passes it to a class. However, it is extremely easy to implement a RESTful system in most MVC frameworks. For example, in CakePHP you can simply add one line to the route:

```
Router::mapResources('company');
```

After that, all GET, POST, and DELETE requests are forwarded to the appropriate method. The example in this chapter does something similar. The first job of the controller is to detect the request type. In this example, you define the controller as `RestController` and place the methods into it.

Detecting the type of request is relatively easy. It is stored in the `REQUEST_METHOD` server variable. The `RestController` class can use that variable to dispatch to the appropriate method. It is sometimes desirable to emulate REST requests so the constructor will take parameters and the application can use a `getInstance()` method to retrieve an instance using automatically detected parameters. The new constructor and method to get an instance looks like this:

```
public function __construct( $method, $urn, $query, $post ) {
    $this->_method = $method;
```

```php
    $this->_urn = $urn;
    $this->_query = $query;
    $this->_post = $post;

    $matches = array();
    preg_match('/([^\/]+)(?:\/([^.])\.(json|xml))?/', $urn, $matches);
    $this->resource = new $parts[1]($parts[2]);
    $this->_format = $parts[3];
}

public static function getInstance() {
    $method = $_SERVER['REQUEST_METHOD'];
    $urn = $_GET['_urn'];
    return new RestController( $method, $urn, $_GET, $_POST );
}
```

This approach makes testing easier without having to resort to generating fake requests. The particular class in this chapter only accepts Json and XML requests. Once the request method and data are determined they must be dispatched to the appropriate object. You can do this in an `execute()` command:

```php
public function execute() {
    $parameters = array();

    switch ( $this->_method ) {
        case 'GET':
            $method = 'view';
            break;
        case 'DELETE':
            $method = 'delete';
            break;
        case 'POST':
        case 'GET':
            $method = 'edit';
            $parameters = array( $this->_post );
            break;
        default:
            header('HTTP/1.1 404 Method Not Allowed');
            header('Allow: GET, POST, PUT, DELETE');
            exit;
    }

    try {
        $response = call_user_func_array( array($this->resource, $method),
                                          $parameters );
        return $this->resource->format( $response, $this->_format );
    } catch ( RestException $e ) {
        header("HTTP/1.1 {$e->code} {$e->string}");
        echo $e->message;
        exit;
    } catch ( Exception $e ) {
        header('HTTP/1.1 500 Internal Server Error');
        exit;
    }
}
```

The execute method expects that the resource class has a `view()`, `delete()`, `edit()`, and `format()` method. It first gets the response to the specific action in a display-neutral format and then passes it to the formatting method. In this case, the formatting method should also output the appropriate status code. The status codes should be familiar to any web developer, but they are covered here as a refresher in Tables 15-2 through 15-4. The remaining status codes are somewhat less useful although they can be used in extremely complete implementations of a RESTful service. The implementation in this book uses only a few of the status codes.

TABLE 15-2: The 200 Range — Success

RESPONSE	DESCRIPTION
200 OK	Returns in response to a successful GET request or a POST request that modified existing data.
200 Created	The data was created using a POST or PUT request.
202 Accepted	The request was received but has not been acted on yet. It is useful for things such as video transcoding that could take a while.
203 Non-Authoritative	The resource being served is made up of a copy of the original data set and a more authoritative set does exist.
204 No Content	The response does not have a body and the client should not change the view from the one originally used to submit the request.
205 Reset Content	This is related to the 204 No Content response. It indicates that the client should reset the form and prepare to make another request of the same type.
206 Partial Content	Only a range of the response is being returned. The 206 message is rarely useful for REST.

TABLE 15-3: The 300 Range — Valid URN with the Actual Resource Existing Elsewhere

RESPONSE	DESCRIPTION
200 Multiple Choices	May be given if the clients do not specify the format in which they want the result. The body of the response would include the URI of all possible formatting choices.
301 Moved Permanently 307 Moved Temporarily 302 Found 303 See Other	All ways of indicating that the client should redirect the user. With the exception of the 303 they all mean that the resource is no longer at the location specified. 303 indicates that the request was successful but there is another resource that the client should be directed to afterwards. All four differ greatly in how caching is handled.

continues

TABLE 15-3 *(continued)*

RESPONSE	DESCRIPTION
304 Not Modified	Useful in REST to return the appropriate response if GET request is made contingent on the resource having changed.

305 Use Proxy	Useful to force the client to use a proxy to make the call. Now is a good time to go over how to send HTTP statuses:
	
	`<?php`
	`header("HTTP 1.1 301 Moved Perminently");`
	`header("Location: /new/uri.xml");`
	`?>`

If a header is sent more than once, only the most recent one is used. Just like cookies in PHP, the headers cannot be sent after any output has been sent to the client. That is the nature of HTTP.

TABLE 15-4: 400 Range — Request Cannot Be Fullfilled

RESPONSE	DESCRIPTION
404 File Not Found	Very familiar.
405 Method Not Allowed	The controller class uses this to respond to requests that are not one of the four allowed methods for the controller.
401 Unauthorized	Denies access to a resource. This response has a dedicated response code, which is covered in detail in the authentication chapter.
402 Payment Required	This has been "reserved for future use" for quite some time and it is not clear whether it is acceptable to use.

Once a RESTful application is set up (see the example code for this chapter for an example implementation) it becomes necessary to test requests. To do that, you can use a command-line utility called cURL.

Testing Using cURL

cURL is a command-line tool that is useful for making HTTP/S requests. It can also perform requests over several other protocols (including FTP and LDAP), which are not covered here. cURL also runs on all major operating systems, which makes testing universal across all systems.

The simplest kind of request is a GET request. It is a good start for demonstrating the basic syntax for cURL. The first step is to get the company from earlier. Type this into the terminal/console:

```
curl http://www.example.com/companies/myvbo.xml
```

Remember, the GET request should never modify any data. To delete the data it is as simple as setting the -x argument, which specifies the method (verb) to use. DELETE does not take any parameters so it is barely more complicated than before:

```
curl -X DELETE http://www.example.com/companies/myvbo.xml
```

You can also attach data to the request. The particular controller from earlier did not distinguish between PUT and POST. When using either method it is necessary to URL-encode the data. So to edit the company MyVBO it would be as simple as:

```
curl -X POST -d "name=MyVBO&website=http%3A%2F%2Fwww.myvbo.com%2F" \
             http://www.example.com/companies/myvbo.xml
```

Changing it to a PUT request should be self-explanatory. To switch the response from XML to Json it is only necessary to change the extension. It should be noted that PUT and POST requests are expected to return the new object. Usually this is the same as the original object but with missing fields filled in (either default values — on create — or values from the database on edit) as well as any primary key fields. The latter is particularly necessary when creating new data because the client will need the ID in order to reference the object later. Alternatively, the POST data can come from a file instead of the command line:

```
curl -X POST -d "@/path/to/file.txt"
```

The important part to notice is that at (@) symbol in front of the path. The contents of the file must be URL encoded prior to being passed into cURL the same was as if they were passed via the command line.

cURL has functionality for authentication as well as cookies. It can also spoof the user agent. These factors together make it the only tool needed to test RESTful applications.

Making REST Requests from PHP

PHP has functionality to use libcurl (the library that is used by the cURL command-line utility) from within any PHP script. The ease of posting data makes it a natural choice for consuming RESTful APIs. But first, PHP has a very simple way of making GET requests without libcurl, which is sometimes useful when just a quick proof of concept is needed:

```
$data = json_decode(
  file_get_contents("http://www.example.com/companies/myvbo.json")
);
```

For security reasons URL protocol wrappers are sometimes disabled. This most commonly happens on a shared hosting environment. The reasoning is that developers don't always know about the wrapper functionality and may inadvertently allow a user to trick the script into making a request to a remote server or worse — executing code that came from a remote server.

The bottom line is, always keep this in mind when you're passing any variable from user input to any file I/O functions. And always filter user input.

The previous example won't work on servers that explicitly disable the URL opening behavior.

This is made possible by using PHP's protocol wrappers to load content via HTTP as if it were a local file. This, of course, is only useful for making GET requests and it does not provide much more than BASIC authentication. For a more complete request it becomes necessary to use libcurl. The equivalent libcurl commands look like this:

```php
<?php
$ch = curl_init();
curl_setopt($ch, CURLOPT_URL, "http://www.example.com/companies/myvbo.json");
curl_setopt($ch, CURLOPT_HEADER, false);
curl_setopt($ch, CURLOPT_RETURNTRANSFER, true);
$data = json_decode(curl_exec($ch));
curl_close($ch);
?>
```

The CURLOP_RETURNTRANSFER option causes the data to be returned by the curl_exec() function. An alternative option is to write the output to a file. It is also possible to return the headers as well as the body of the response. This can be particularly useful to auto-detect output formats and other functions. These simple examples only require retrieving the body of the response.

Posting data is also simple; cURL accepts several ways to post data, the easiest being as an array of key/value pairs, which avoids the need to URL-encode the values. The PHP version of the POST request from the previous section is as follows:

```php
<?php
$postData = array(
  "name" => "MyVBO",
  "website" => "http://www.myvbo.com/"
);

$ch = curl_init();
curl_setopt($ch, CURLOPT_URL, "http://www.example.com/companies/myvbo.json");
curl_setopt($ch, CURLOPT_HEADER, false);
curl_setopt($ch, CURLOPT_POST, true);
curl_setopt($ch, CURLOPT_POSTFIELDS, $postData);
curl_setopt($ch, CURLOPT_RETURNTRANSFER, true);
$data = json_decode(curl_exec($ch));
curl_close($ch);
?>
```

The DELETE request is slightly different. The PHP interface to libcurl only has options explicitly for GET and POST. It can, however, create any type of request by specifying a custom type. In this case, the DELETE action doesn't add much more complexity:

```php
<?php
$ch = curl_init();
curl_setopt($ch, CURLOPT_URL, "http://www.example.com/companies/myvbo.json");
curl_setopt($ch, CURLOPT_HEADER, false);
curl_setopt($ch, CURLOPT_RETURNTRANSFER, true);
curl_setopt($ch, CURLOPT_CUSTOMREQUEST, "DELETE");
$data = json_decode(curl_exec($ch));
curl_close($ch);
?>
```

Although it is not difficult to use REST through PHP and libcurl, it is useful to create a class to do all the hard work. The four basic events (create, edit, get, and delete) can be called from a wrapper class. The new class can then be reused in any application.

```php
<?php

class RESTRequestProxy {

  public $service;
  public $resource;

  public function __construct($service_url, $resource) {
    $this->service = $service_url;
    $this->resource = $resource;
  }

  public function create($data) {
      return $this->exec(null, "POST", $data);
  }

  public function edit($id, $data) {
      return $this->exec($id, "PUT", $data);
  }

  public function delete($id) {
      return $this->exec($id, "DELETE");
  }

  public function get($id) {
      return $this->exec($id, "GET");
  }

  private function exec($id=null, $method="GET", $post=false) {
    $ch = curl_init();
    curl_setopt($ch, CURLOPT_URL,
      "{$this->service}/{$this->resource}/".($id? "$id.json" : "") );
    curl_setopt($ch, CURLOPT_HEADER, false);
    curl_setopt($ch, CURLOPT_RETURNTRANSFER, true);
    curl_setopt($ch, CURLOPT_CUSTOMREQUEST, $method);
    curl_setopt($ch, CURLOPT_POSTFIELDS, $post);
    $data = json_decode(curl_exec($ch));
    curl_close($ch);
    return $data;
  }

};
?>
```

REST, although popular, is not the only type of service. SOAP is an extremely popular, but heavier weight, solution to web services.

SOAP Web Services

SOAP is a standard messaging protocol for accessing objects over an existing application protocol such as HTTP. It was previously an acronym for *Simple Object Access Protocol* but is now referenced as a single technology. The stated goals of SOAP — according to the W3C recommendation — are "simplicity and extensibility," and as such you can get SOAP up and running quickly but you can also build on it and thus perform many complex tasks.

Unlike REST, the SOAP protocol is designed as an *RPC* (*Remote Procedure Call*) protocol and is not resource-oriented by default. As such, an "object" in SOAP will have an endpoint on the server and any number of procedures can be called on that endpoint. The methods do not have to be the read, update, insert, and delete actions from REST.

For example, a SOAP application might perform simple math operations. The request is always wrapped in an *envelope* and is broken into two parts: the header and the body. A multiplication operation may look like this:

```
<?xml version="1.0"?>
<soapenv:Envelope
    xmlns:soapenv="http://schemas.xmlsoap.org/soap/envelope/"
    xmlns:xsi="http://www.w3.org/2001/XMLSchema-instance"
    xsi:schemaLocation="http://schemas.xmlsoap.org/soap/envelope/
                        http://schemas.xmlsoap.org/soap/envelope/">
  <soapenv:Body>
    <math:multiply xmlns:req="http://example.com/services/math/">
      <math:terms>
        <math:term>123</math:term>
        <math:term>456</math:term>
      </math:terms>
    </math:multiply>
  </soapenv:Body>
</soapenv:Envelope>
```

Because the request is XML, it requires that XML conventions must be followed. Specifically, it is possible to define a new XML namespace within the request. However, make certain that the namespace is properly described and documented. The response might look like this:

```
<?xml version="1.0"?>
<soapenv:Envelope
    xmlns:soapenv="http://schemas.xmlsoap.org/soap/envelope/"
    xmlns:xsi="http://www.w3.org/2001/XMLSchema-instance"
    xsi:schemaLocation="http://schemas.xmlsoap.org/soap/envelope/
                        http://schemas.xmlsoap.org/soap/envelope/">
  <soapenv:Body>
    <math:multiply xmlns:req="http://example.com/services/math/">
      <math:result>56088</math:result>
    </math:multiply>
  </soapenv:Body>
</soapenv:Envelope>
```

Of course doing math with SOAP isn't very practical (unless of course the math problem is very complex and difficult to calculate client-side). This section uses the simplified company data set from before and translates it over to SOAP.

One last thing: RESTful systems based on HTTP have a built-in set of error codes. SOAP, on the other hand, is intentionally ignorant of the way HTTP works. After all, the two are independent of each other. Instead, SOAP has carefully crafted fault messages that tell the client exactly what went wrong. For example, if the client tries to use the math service from before and one of the terms is not a number, the result may look like this:

```
<env:Envelope xmlns:env="http://www.w3.org/2003/05/soap-envelope"
              xmlns:math="http://www.example.org/math"
              xmlns:xml="http://www.w3.org/XML/1998/namespace">
  <env:Body>
    <env:Fault>
      <env:Code>
        <env:Value>env:Sender</env:Value>
        <env:Subcode>
          <env:Value>math:NaN</env:Value>
        </env:Subcode>
      </env:Code>
      <env:Reason>
        <env:Text xml:lang="en">Term is not a number.</env:Text>
      </env:Reason>
    </env:Fault>
  </env:Body>
</env:Envelope>
```

The preceding envelope is the bare minimum SOAP fault plus the optional sub-code for the fault. More complex faults can be defined by adding node, role, and detailed information. Notice how the main code value is in the SOAP-envelope namespace whereas the sub-code is in the custom math namespace. See the W3C recommendation for more information.

Rather than try to parse SOAP natively using the PHP DOM object (which is, indeed, easily achieved but unnecessary) this book uses a SOAP client and server library.

Getting Started with the SOAP Library

There is a lot to worry about in a typical SOAP server so the best choice is to let a library do all the work. PHP ships with a SOAP extension but it is enabled only if PHP is compiled with the `--enable-soap` option. Most servers are likely to already have this configuration.

The SOAP library can also be used as a client. This chapter goes over both. But first, it is desirable to define a WSDL for the service.

Defining the WSDL

WSDL is the *Web Service Descriptor Language*. It is not specific to SOAP; however, it does work best with SOAP. There are two versions of WSDL: version 2.0 and version 1.1. Unfortunately, PHP's SOAP extension only supports the older of the two and they are not backwards compatible. For that reason, this book covers WSDL 1.1.

Even though it is not supported by the PHP SOAP implementation it is useful to learn the WSDL 2.0 format. The two formats are not compatible but it is easy to detect which one is used. WSDL 2.0 can be found as a WSC recommendation.

WSDL files are written in XML. It is not strictly necessary to have a WSDL file, but it makes consuming the service easier.

The WSDL is broken up into five parts:

➤ The first part defines the data types used by the web service.

➤ The second defines messages, which effectively describe the type of data that the service expects.

➤ The third part is port types that can be used to describe what methods the service has.

➤ The final two sections consist of bindings, which tell the client how to execute a specific request, and a service description.

A typical WSDL file will follow this structure:

```
<definitions xmlns="http://schemas.xmlsoap.org/wsdl/"
             xmlns:soap="http://schemas.xmlsoap.org/wsdl/soap/"
             xmlns:xsd="http://www.w3.org/2001/XMLSchema"
             xmlns:tns="http://example.com/companies"
             targetNamespace="http://example.com/companies">
  <types>
    ...
  </types>

  <message>
    ...
  </message>

  <portType>
  ...
  </portType>

  <binding>
  ...
  </binding>

  <service>
  ...
  </service>

</definitions>
```

A fair number of namespaces are also involved in the document. The main ones are:

➤ **XSD:** An XML schema language used to define XML document content. It is used in the "types" section to define each data type that can be found in any of the requests. It can also be used in the messages section for primitive data types.

➤ **TNS:** The target namespace, which should be the same as the `targetNamespace` attribute of the root element. It is a namespace that, by convention, refers to the current document.

➤ **SOAP:** This is not the namespace for SOAP itself but rather one specific to the WSDL. The SOAP namespace is used when defining bindings. As mentioned earlier, bindings are what expose the method calls to the outside world. If the endpoint is not written to use SOAP, that namespace will be different.

WSDL Types

First, the "types." The company type is rather simple because the examples in this chapter include only a name and web site. But it is ironically defined as a *complex type* inside of the WSDL file. This means it's a type that consists of more than one part. It may be useful to look at it as an object:

```
<types>
  <xsd:schema>
    <xsd:complexType name="company">
      <xsd:all>
        <xsd:element name="name" type="xsd:string"/>
        <xsd:element name="website" type="xsd:anyURI"/>
      </xsd:all>
    </xsd:complexType>
  </xsd:schema>
</types>
```

XSD is extremely flexible. Both examples in this section use <xsd:all> to specify that each element must occur once (unless specified otherwise like it is next). Other possibilities include:

➤ **<xsd:sequence>** which means that all elements must appear in the order that they are defined.

➤ **<xsd:choice>** indicates that either one element or the other must be present (not both/all).

➤ **<xsd:group>** can be used to create logical groupings of elements, which can be combined with any one of the previous indicators.

Of course, there can be more than one type in a schema. Each type must have a unique name, in this case the one and only type is "company." In a different example case it might be useful to define a schema that allows for more than one of an element. The math example from before, which can have multiple terms, would look like this:

```
<types>
  <xsd:schema>
    <xsd:complexType name="terms">
      <xsd:all>
        <xsd:element name="term" type="xsd:decimal"
                     minOccurs="1" maxOccurs="unbounded" />
      </xsd:all>
    </xsd:complexType>
  </xsd:schema>
</types>
```

You can use many types with XSD in addition to the ones listed here. A quick look at the XSD specification should clarify. The data types that are most common are string, integer, decimal, date, and time. The company example also uses anyURI, which indicates that the value can be any valid URI.

Other possible numeric values include byte, int, long, negativeInteger, nonNegativeInteger, nonPositiveInteger, positiveInteger, short, unsignedLong, unsignedShort, unsignedByte, float, and double.

A few things to remember about the numeric types:

➤   In XSD the number zero (0) is neither negative nor positive. So `positiveInteger` starts at zero and `nonNegativeInteger` outwardly sounds like the same thing but starts at one (1) instead.

➤   `Byte`, `short`, `int`, and `long` (and their unsigned counterparts) are limited by size. A `byte` is the largest integer that can fit in 8-bits; `short` is 16-bits; `int` is 32-bits; and `long` is 64-bits.

➤   The maximum value of an unsigned `byte` is $2^8 - 1$ or 255. The signed variation uses the highest order bit to indicate whether the variable is positive or negative so it loses a bit but gains the ability to have negative numbers. Signed bytes range from –127 to +127.

Additional data types are `boolean`, `base64Binary`, and `hexBinary`. Several other types of strings aren't covered here because they are rarely used in SOAP requests. However, when using XSD to define arbitrary documents they may come in handy. Just don't forget to append the namespace to the front of the type like so: `xsd:boolean`.

Defining the Message

Now that the data types/schema is defined it is time to specify the messages. In WSDL 2.0, the messages element no longer exists in favor of referring directly to the schema. The 1.1 specification is significantly more complex.

Messages define what parts are needed for the request and response. In the context of an RPC it may be helpful to think of them as parameter lists and responses. Alternatively, you might want to think of the message as something that goes into the envelope. Only four message types are needed to handle all the company examples in this section:

```
<message name="CompanyInputOutput">
  <part name="id" type="xsd:integer"/>
  <part name="company" type="tns:company"/>
</message>

<message name="ReferenceCompanyInput">
  <part name="id" type="xsd:integer"/>
</message>

<message name="CreateCompanyInput">
  <part name="company" type="tns:company"/>
</message>

<message name="DeleteCompanyOutput">
  <part name="result" type="xsd:boolean"/>
</message>
```

Remember the custom complex type that was defined earlier in the chapter? It is used here in the first two message definitions.

Both deletion and retrieval operations take the same input so only one message is needed for them both. Likewise, creating and editing the company both use the same output format.

Specifying Ports

Once the messages are defined it is time to specify the ports. *Ports* define the input and the output in terms of what type of messages they produce or consume and as such are the function definitions. The two types of operations that are commonly used are one-way and request-response. All the functions defined in the company WSDL file are request-response although a one-way function would just exclude the "output" tag.

Because all the functions are somewhat similar, it is unnecessary to list each one. The completed WSDL file in the example code has each port (function) defined. The definition for the `GetCompany` port is as follows:

```
<portType name="CompanyPortType">
  <operation name="GetCompany">
    <input message="tns:ReferenceCompanyInput"/>
    <output message="tns:CompanyInputOutput"/>
  </operation>
</portType>
```

It is possible and desirable to define multiple operations inside of a single port. However, keep in mind that the port type is used next as the type attribute for the bindings and there can only be one type per binding.

Defining Bindings

The next step is to define the bindings. When doing so, remember that HTTP is not the only protocol that SOAP can be transmitted over so the first step is to define the transport type and style of the binding. The examples in this chapter all use RPC style, which is the most common:

```
<binding name="CompanyBinding" type="tns:CompanyPortType">
    <soap:binding style="rpc" transport="http://schemas.xmlsoap.org/soap/http" />
    <operation name="GetCompany">
      <soap:operation soapAction="http://example.com/GetCompany" />
      <input><soap:body use="literal"/></input>
      <output><soap:body use="literal"/></output>
    </operation>
</binding>
```

The `soapAction` attribute of the binding tag is one of the most confusing in the SOAP world because it seems completely redundant. After all, the type of action is specified in the body of the SOAP request. To better illustrate, here is the request that is made using the preceding binding (with the headers included at the top):

```
Content-Type: text/xml
Soapaction: http://example.com/GetCompany
Host: example.com


<?xml version="1.0" encoding="UTF-8"?>
<soap:Envelope xmlns:xsd="http://www.w3.org/2001/XMLSchema"
    xmlns:xsi="http://www.w3.org/2001/XMLSchema-instance"
```

```
        xmlns:soap="http://schemas.xmlsoap.org/soap/envelope/">

    <soap:Body>
      <companies:GetCompany xmlns:companies="http://example.com/companies">
        <id xsi:type="xsd:integer"></id>
      </companies:GetCompany>
    </soap:Body>
  </soap:Envelope>
```

The two bolded areas both indicate which action is being taken. In fact, the PHP SOAP extension
ignores the soap-action header. Likewise, the soap-action is not used unless the transport protocol is
HTTP. So why is it there? Three reasons:

➤ It is possible to use SOAP in a more RESTful way that does not necessarily have the action in
the body.

➤ The HTTP header can be read by network appliances and used for optimization (load balancing, caching, and so on). It is much easier to read and filter based on the header than to
parse the SOAP request.

➤ The action can also be included in web server logs. In Apache using the CustomLog directive
does this. For example: CustomLog logs/soap_log "%t %f $a > %{Soapaction}i".

The soap-action is required to be passed as-is to the client. Although it takes the form of a URI, it is
not required to be resolvable. The client shouldn't make any attempts at transforming the action at
all. That includes, but is not limited to, expanding relative URNs to be fully-qualified.

Defining the Endpoint

The final step in creating the WSDL is to define a service. You can use the service to group similar
functionality or to define an endpoint for the service. Unlike with soap-action, the endpoint for the
service must be a valid URI because the client uses it to connect.

```
    <service name="CompanyService">
      <port name="CompanyPort" binding="tns:CompanyBinding">
        <soap:address location="http://example.com/companies/"/>
      </port>
    </service>
```

By combining everything explained in the previous six sections it is possible to make a valid WSDL
1.1 file, which can be read by any SOAP client.

Setting up a SOAP Server

Once you have the WSDL, setting up the SOAP server in PHP is very easy with the SOAP library.
Indeed, creating the WSDL for the first time can seem like more work than actually implementing
the procedure calls in PHP.

Two approaches exist to creating a SOAP server. Both require creating a new PHP file (in the same
location as the endpoint) and initializing a new server object. One is object oriented and the other is

procedural. For the sake of dealing with legacy systems, the procedural method is detailed first. The procedural code for the GetCompany function looks like this:

```php
<?php
$server = new SoapServer('company.wsdl');

$companyConnection = mysql_connect("localhost", "username", "password");
mysql_select_db("companies", $companyConnection);

function GetCompany( $id ) {
  global $companyConnection;

  $res = mysql_query("SELECT * FROM `companies` WHERE `id`=".(int)$id,
                        $companyConnection);

  if ( $row = mysql_fetch_assoc($res) ) {
    $company = new Company();
    $company->name = $row["name"];
    $company->website = $row["website"];

    return array( $id, $company );

  } else {
    throw new SoapFault("Server", "Company not found.");
  }
}

$server->addFunction("GetCompany");
$server->handle();

?>
```

The call to handle() at the end actually processes the SOAP request. It does all the tedious work of reading in the standard input and HTTP headers. The code also throws a SoapFault exception when the company is not found. The SoapFault class extends from Exception so it can be used like any other type of exception.

Of course, it would be better to create a class to handle the procedure calls instead. It would de-clutter the main variable scope, making the code more readable. Fortunately, the PHP SOAP extension provides a way to register a class. Every public method in the class is then automatically added to the interface. Private and protected methods are kept private and protected. The new object-oriented code looks like this:

```php
<?php
$server = new SoapServer('company.wsdl');

class CompanySoap {

  protected function _getDatabase() {
    static $conn = false;
    if ( $conn === false ) {
      $conn = mysql_connect("localhost", "username", "password");
```

```
        mysql_select_db("companies", $conn );
    }
    return $conn;
}

function GetCompany( $id ) {
    $res = mysql_query("SELECT * FROM `companies` WHERE `id`=".(int)$id,
                        $this->_getDatabase());

    if ( $row = mysql_fetch_assoc($res) ) {
        $company = new StdClass();
        $company->name = $row["name"];
        $company->website = $row["website"];

        return array( $id, $company );

    } else {
        throw new SoapFault("Server","Company not found.");
    }
  }
}

$server->setClass("CompanySOAP");
$server->handle();
?>
```

That is all there is to creating a SOAP server in PHP. Once again, the completed classes are part of the sample code that comes with this book. The next step is to set up a SOAP client.

Setting Up a Soap Client

Setting up a soap client in PHP is even more straightforward than setting up a server — assuming, of course, that the WSDL is valid. Setting up a client takes two steps: instantiating the object and making the request.

The `SoapClient` class acts as a proxy (referring all the way back to Chapter 1). Calling a method on the client class is the same as calling it on the server. Thus, making a call to `GetCompany` is intuitive:

```
<?php
$client = new SoapClient("company.wsdl");
$company = $client->GetCompany( $id );
?>
```

The output for the SOAP call should seem familiar. It is an associative array that looks like this:

```
Array
(
    [id] => 123
    [company] => stdClass Object
        (
            [name] => MyVBO
            [website] => http://www.MyVBO.com/
        )

)
```

It is almost the same as the return value from the procedure call on the PHP server. The main difference is that the server put in the key values for "id" and "company" automatically. Incidentally, it is possible to manually specify those keys on the server as well.

Passing an object (such as the one that is needed for `CreateCompany` and `EditCompany`) is easy as well. Simply create an instance of `StdClass` and set the appropriate variables. Of course, it is possible to create a new predefined class and instantiate that instead.

The PHP SOAP extension is designed to be object oriented from the ground up. For that reason, it has some significant benefits, not the least of which is that the server class, client class, and fault classes can all be extended to create brand new classes. The PHP manual has an excellent class that extends `SoapClient` and can be used to call procedures on a local SOAP server without needing to go over the network. Here are some other things that you can do by extending the client or the server:

➤ Use memcached or APC to transparently cache the output of the server so that the result does not need to be recalculated every time.

➤ Cache the response from the server on the client-side to reduce load on the server and lessen the delays caused by high latency between the client and server.

➤ Log SOAP requests.

➤ Perform access control and authentication across the board.

There are numerous ways to create robust SOAP services. However, if the PHP SOAP extension is lacking for a particular job, you have multiple alternatives. The two more popular alternatives are NuSOAP and the SOAP Pear library. However, the packaged PHP Extension should be enough to get started using all the services on the Internet that make use of SOAP and create useful SOAP services.

SUMMARY

This chapter covered creating applications with PHP and MySQL that go above and beyond what you normally use them for. Because you're nearing the end of the book, hopefully you won't find it difficult to think up exciting and novel uses for the technologies in this chapter and the chapters leading up to it.

For example, using the technologies covered in this book, you could possibly create a service that takes input via SOAP and then passes the processing of the input off to Gearman. The client can then make periodic requests to see if the job has finished running.

Hopefully, at this point, it's also obvious how important security is. The techniques in the authentication and security (Chapters 12 and 14) can and should be applied to anything that changes data. That includes the services in this chapter.

So, as a quick review, this chapter covered:

➤ Creating command-line scripts that can read from user input

➤ Turning those scripts into cron jobs

- ➤ Creating RESTful web services
- ➤ Defining a WSDL to describe a web service
- ➤ Writing a SOAP client
- ➤ Writing a SOAP server

SOAP and REST both have their benefits and disadvantages. SOAP is lightweight but not as lightweight as REST. A RESTful application also focuses more on resources and less on procedure. The benefits of each can also be disadvantages in some situations. You should choose the one that best fits the application. If the application deals mainly with storing, editing, and retrieving resources, REST is probably the best bet. If the application provides a service that does calculations or lookups and returns the result directly to the user, SOAP is a good choice.

An application can always support both.

Be sure to download the code that comes with this book for completed RESTful and SOAP controllers and clients as well as more examples of how to use cURL.

16

Optimization and Debugging

WHAT'S IN THIS CHAPTER?

➤   Using PHP back-traces

➤   Learning what you need to review SQL performance

➤   Understanding how to review SQL statements with EXPLAIN

➤   Learning about different index optimizations

No matter how well thought out or planned an application is, there are always problems and they can creep up at any moment. Ranging from performance issues to functionality flaws, you may feel it's completely impossible to find and diagnose them.

Fortunately PHP and MySQL have tools to help deal with such situations. This chapter covers the tools of the trade and best practices for debugging and optimizing PHP and MySQL. It starts with advanced PHP debugging — including ways to find hidden performance bottlenecks — and then gets into the details on how to make slow queries run fast.

DEBUGGING PHP

For simple applications it is possible to get away with just basic debugging techniques. Some of the most common are using print_r() to recursively display the contents of an array or class or var_dump() when a little bit more information is needed.

For more complex applications, basic debugging is simply not enough. It becomes necessary to closely inspect the state of the application. This section reviews methods for inspecting state, injecting code into the application at run time, and profiling the application to achieve performance boosts.

Creating Stack Traces

One of the most basic forms of PHP debugging is the *debug back-trace*, which produces an associative array of information about the current state of the application. Also, it provides information about the application's stack.

The stack is the method of storing the state of the application. Every time a function call is made, the current scope is pushed onto the stack and a new scope is created, which is why *stack overflow* errors can occur, particularly when you use recursive functions. When the function returns, the current scope is popped off the end of the stack and the application returns to the previous scope.

The debug back-trace is a way to inspect the application stack. It provides a wealth of information including the line numbers and filenames all the way down the stack. It is very useful for tracking where a function call came from.

The code for doing a debug back-trace is one line:

```
$debug = debug_backtrace();
```

The return value is an array of associative arrays. The first item in the array (index 0) is the current state of the stack, and subsequent items are states that are further down the stack. One of the most useful times to do a back-trace is when an exception is thrown. It is possible to isolate specific information from the back-trace and use it in the error logs.

The array items format changes depending on the context that the back-trace function is called in. You may encounter four basic types of output depending on the context. The possible contexts are:

> The global scope

> Inside of an included file

> Inside of a function call

> Inside of a method call (function inside of a class)

Depending on the scope and context, one or more of the following keys may be present:

> **function**: Contains the function name as a string. It is only present if the current scope is inside of a function call.

> **args**: Contains an array used to store the arguments passed to the current function. If the scope is not inside of a function call then `args` is not present. In the case of a file inclusion, you'll have one argument: the function name used to include the file.

> **class**: Contains the name of the current class (if any). If there is a class, there may also be an `object` key, which is a reference to the instance of the class. However, it is possible that the method call was static, in which case you won't have any object.

> **type**: A more reliable way to test if a method call was static or invoked on an object. The type variable will be `->` for a normal method call or `::` for static. Of course, if current scope is not within a class, it will not be present.

> **file** and **line**: contain the current file and line number. They are always present.

It is important to note that each of the keys is relative to the scope at that point in the stack. Backtraces are useful for producing custom logs and even auto-recovering from errors.

OPTIMIZING QUERIES

Whereas designing your database tables and writing SQL statements are important for your application's functionality, optimizing your queries is necessary for your application's operation and performance. This section discusses the various options of optimizing your SQL queries.

Reducing SQL

Surprisingly the best way to optimize a query is actually quite simple. Eliminate it. When reviewing your SQL statements, identify if the statement is indeed required; can the query be combined with another query or can the query be cached?

The next step is to try and reduce SQL statements, especially statements that are repeated. Are you running the same query multiple times in the page request? In a well-tuned high-performance application, it is not the slow query that is difficult to address, it is the very quick queries that are executed at a high frequency. Can these queries be combined?

The longest component of a SQL statement execution can be the network latency to pass the SQL statement from the application server to the database server, and to then return the packets of information back to the application server. Reducing the number of SQL statements can improve performance. Reducing the amount of necessary information, for example unnecessary columns, can improve performance. Stored procedures are an option here.

Identifying SQL Statements

Before optimization can really begin, you need to identify the SQL statements that you need to optimize. In a well-engineered development practice, you may like to apply the following principles to all SQL statements.

The focus of SQL statements to review should include a balance of slow SQL statements, SQL statements from important business logic, and SQL statements from high frequency business functionality in use with your application.

Capturing all SQL statements can be more complex than necessary. Though all DML statements are easily obtained from the MySQL binary log when enabled, capturing all SELECT statements in a production environment can be hard.

The default MySQL option is the general query log. Prior to MySQL 5.1 the only way to enable this was to define the log option in your my.cnf configuration file and to restart your MySQL server. You would then need to repeat this to turn the option off. In a production environment, this is impractical. Starting with MySQL 5.1, you can enable and disable logging dynamically with the following syntax.

```
SET GLOBAL general_log = ON;
SET GLOBAL general_log = OFF
```

With MySQL 5.1, you also have the ability to define the output of the general query log to a file, table or both when you specify with the configuration file option `log-output=TABLE,FILE`.

Although this helps to gather all SQL statements, it's a broadsword approach with the only granularity being on and off. The other disadvantage with the general query log is that the granularity of time may not be sufficient.

The following alternative options are more advanced and do not require you to restart MySQL; however, they require other components to be installed for use and analysis:

➤ **MySQL proxy is a great option.** It is very flexible, and using the supplied `histogram.lua` example with MySQL proxy and a PHP application, you can effectively enable `iptables` rules to capture SQL for any time slice, for example, 2 seconds, 1 minute, and so on. You can then have access to the captured information in an aggregated manner as well as get microsecond execution granularity. You can refer to the MySQL Proxy download page at `http://dev.mysql.com/downloads/mysql-proxy/` and the MySQL forge information page at: `http://forge.mysql.com/wiki/MySQL_Proxy` for more detailed information about MySQL Proxy.

➤ **Another option, requiring no moving parts, is the monitoring of the TCP/IP packets sent to the MySQL server directly.** Historically, it's been a black art to understand these network packets; however, the Maatkit `mk-query-digest` available from `http://maatkit.org` is an excellent option to provide valuable human-readable information and aggregated information and this also can provide microsecond execution granularity. For more information on example usage see `http://ronaldbradford.com/blog/take-a-look-at-mk-query-digest-2009-10-08`.

Having gathered your SQL statements to optimize, you can now start analyzing.

Optimizing SELECT

When optimizing `SELECT` SQL statements, the following is a checklist of information that you should ideally gather:

➤ The Query Execution Plan (QEP)

➤ The table structures, including indexes

➤ Index cardinality

➤ The query execution time

➤ The number of rows returned

➤ The total size of the result set

You should also consider additional information that can affect your results over time, including:

➤ The date and time

➤ The MySQL variables

➤ The database table data and index size

The essential command you will use is `EXPLAIN`. The syntax is to include this keyword before the SQL statement you want to analyze.

For the following examples, you're going to use the sakila test database that is provided by MySQL. Refer to the MySQL documentation at `http://dev.mysql.com/doc/` for instructions to download and install this database.

The EXPLAIN syntax

To use EXPLAIN, add the command as a prefix to a SELECT statement. For example:

```
mysql> EXPLAIN SELECT id FROM example_table WHERE id=1\G
*************************** 1. row ***************************
           id: 1
  select_type: SIMPLE
        table: example_table
         type: const
possible_keys: PRIMARY
          key: PRIMARY
      key_len: 4
          ref: const
         rows: 1
        Extra: Using index
```

The most efficient EXPLAIN plan is one that uses an index defined in the key column, uses 1 row, and specifies in the Extra column the value Using Index as shown above.

```
mysql> EXPLAIN SELECT * FROM example_table\G
*************************** 1. row ***************************
           id: 1
  select_type: SIMPLE
        table: example_table
         type: ALL
possible_keys: NULL
          key: NULL
      key_len: NULL
          ref: NULL
         rows: 59
        Extra:
```

Conversely, a query that uses no key, and that processes a large number of rows is the worst case. This is referred to as a full table scan.

The following list describes the more important columns in the EXPLAIN output.

➤ **key:** This column defines the index that is used for the given table. By default, MySQL uses only one index per table. There are a small number of exceptions; however, it is best to design your queries to use one optimal index per table.

➤ **type:** The type of index match that is being used. A few common values include:

   ➤ **const:** An exact index match

   ➤ **ref:** An index reference scan

   ➤ **range:** An index range scan

   ➤ **ALL:** A full table scan

> ➤ `eq_ref`: An equals reference on join tables
>
> ➤ `unique_subquery`: A subquery

➤ `extra`: This includes various pieces of information including:

> ➤ `Using index`: This actually means that the index is all that is needed to satisfy the resultant columns of the SELECT. This is the most optimal solution.
>
> ➤ `Using temporary`: This indicates that MySQL needed to create an internal temporary table. It does not indicate a memory or on disk table.
>
> ➤ `Using filesort`: This indicates that MySQL has to internally sort the results.

After gathering information on the QEP you need to know the details of the indexes that exist for the table, and also the cardinality of indexes. You obtain this information with the following commands:

➤ `SHOW CREATE TABLE [tablename];`

➤ `SHOW INDEXES FROM [tablename];`

Example Queries

The sakila schema which is available for download from `http://dev.mysql.com/doc` is highly optimized for indexes. The following query may not be an ideally executed query; however, it's used as an example to show missing indexes:

```
EXPLAIN SELECT a.first_name, a.last_name
FROM    actor a
INNER JOIN film_actor fa USING (actor_id)
INNER JOIN film f USING (film_id)
WHERE a.first_name = 'JOE'
AND f.release_year=2008\G

*************************** 1. row ***************************
           id: 1
  select_type: SIMPLE
        table: a
         type: ALL
possible_keys: PRIMARY
          key: NULL
      key_len: NULL
          ref: NULL
         rows: 200
        Extra: Using where
*************************** 2. row ***************************
           id: 1
  select_type: SIMPLE
        table: fa
         type: ref
possible_keys: PRIMARY,idx_fk_film_id
          key: PRIMARY
      key_len: 2
```

```
         ref: sakila.a.actor_id
        rows: 1
       Extra: Using index
*************************** 3. row ***************************
          id: 1
 select_type: SIMPLE
       table: f
        type: eq_ref
possible_keys: PRIMARY
         key: PRIMARY
     key_len: 2
         ref: sakila.fa.film_id
        rows: 1
       Extra: Using where
```

In this query, you see that the actor table has a full table scan with key = NULL and type = ALL.

You can review the actual indexes of the table with the SHOW CREATE TABLE command.

```
mysql> SHOW CREATE TABLE actor\G
*************************** 1. row ***************************
       Table: actor
Create Table: CREATE TABLE `actor` (
  `actor_id` smallint(5) unsigned NOT NULL AUTO_INCREMENT,
  `first_name` varchar(45) NOT NULL,
  `last_name` varchar(45) NOT NULL,
  `last_update` timestamp NOT NULL DEFAULT CURRENT_TIMESTAMP
                           ON UPDATE CURRENT_TIMESTAMP,
  PRIMARY KEY (`actor_id`),
  KEY `idx_actor_last_name` (`last_name`)
) ENGINE=InnoDB AUTO_INCREMENT=201 DEFAULT CHARSET=utf8
```

Identifying Indexes

After finding a table within a query that does not include an index or an efficient index, you add or change the index with the ALTER TABLE command. In the preceding SELECT example, you are selecting based on first_name, yet no index exists. You could consider an index on first_name; the best way to confirm is to test and verify:

```
ALTER TABLE actor ADD INDEX (first_name);
```

If you rerun the EXPLAIN, you'll now observe the index is used on the actor table:

```
explain SELECT a.first_name, a.last_name
FROM   actor a
INNER JOIN film_actor fa USING (actor_id)
INNER JOIN film f USING (film_id)
WHERE a.first_name = 'JOE' AND f.release_year=2008\G
*************************** 1. row ***************************
          id: 1
 select_type: SIMPLE
       table: a
        type: ref
possible_keys: PRIMARY,first_name
```

```
          key: first_name
      key_len: 137
          ref: const
         rows: 1
        Extra: Using where
```

In this example, you may be able to further improve this index by defining a multi-column index on `first_name` and `last_name` that is also called covering index. For example:

```
ALTER TABLE actor DROP INDEX first_name, ADD INDEX (first_name, last_name);

explain SELECT a.first_name, a.last_name
FROM    actor a
INNER JOIN film_actor fa USING (actor_id)
INNER JOIN film f USING (film_id)
WHERE a.first_name = 'JOE' AND f.release_year=2008\G
*************************** 1. row ***************************
           id: 1
  select_type: SIMPLE
        table: a
         type: ref
possible_keys: PRIMARY,first_name
          key: first_name
      key_len: 137
          ref: const
         rows: 1
        Extra: Using where; Using index
. . .
```

Adding an index does not mean the performance of your system will improve. Looking at SQL statements in isolation and not looking at all SQL statements against the tables in question could produce a loss of performance elsewhere. Adding indexes to tables also increases the time to perform writes. In a high write environment, adding an index to improve a query, which is not executed frequently, may not offset the loss in performance of writes.

About Cardinality

As previously mentioned, the SHOW INDEXES command can be used to provide an estimation of index cardinality. *Cardinality* is a measure of the uniqueness of values tracked by an index. A higher cardinality number indicates a greater level of uniqueness. In the following example you will see that the higher number of the cardinality shows a higher uniqueness of values. The PRIMARY key is the best cardinality.

```
mysql> SHOW INDEXES FROM rental;
```

Table	Non_unique	Key_name	Seq	Column_name	Cardinality
rental	0	PRIMARY	1	rental_id	16291
rental	0	rental_date	1	rental_date	16291

```
| rental |            0 | rental_date          | 2 | inventory_id |        16291 |
| rental |            0 | rental_date          | 3 | customer_id  |        16291 |
| rental |            1 | idx_fk_inventory_id  | 1 | inventory_id |        16291 |
| rental |            1 | idx_fk_customer_id   | 1 | customer_id  |         1253 |
| rental |            1 | idx_fk_staff_id      | 1 | staff_id     |            3 |
+--------+-------------+----------------------+---+--------------+--------------+
```

 This output has been trimmed for presentation style.

As you can see, the `staff_id` index has very poor cardinality.

Better Index Types

The following are some tips on improving your indexes:

➤ **Define index columns where possible as NOT NULL:** If the column does not contain NULL values, change the data type to NOT NULL to avoid possible double scans of a nullable column index.

➤ **Use UNIQUE INDEX:** If the column contains unique values, you can define a unique key to both improve relational integrity and improve the optimizer to not require an index range scan in comparison to a regular index.

➤ **Use PRIMARY KEY:** A primary key is a specific form of UNIQUE KEY. In InnoDB, for example, a PRIMARY KEY is a clustered index — that is, an index where data is ordered on disk. This can be a great improvement when data is retrieved in primary key order.

➤ **Too many indexes can be detrimental:** If `possible_keys` lists more than three indexes, for example, the MySQL optimizer has too much information to determine the best index to use. This is also an indication of possible ineffective or unused indexes.

➤ **Use the smallest data type possible for in index:** For instance, the author has seen cases where a schema was created by developers who created an index on a VARCHAR(100) (or even greater!) column. One improvement to this would be creating an additional column and index on an additional CHAR(32) column that contains an MD5 of the larger VARCHAR(100) column. Even better is to use a BIGINT column that contains a numeric representation of the MD5 value, giving you an even more efficient numeric index using the following tip demonstrated by a Flickr developer at the 2008 MySQL user's conference:

```
select conv(substr(md5('this is a test'),1,16),16, 10);
+--------------------------------------------------+
| conv(substr(md5('this is a test'),1,16),16, 10)  |
+--------------------------------------------------+
| 6102594702268822184                              |
+--------------------------------------------------+
```

Flickr certainly has a requirement of great uniqueness, so this is a great way to obtain a numeric representation of the MD5 value of text for a column you would rather not create an index on!

Optimizing Indexes

While creating an index on a single column can generally improve performance of certain SQL statements, optimizing indexes can provide additional improved in performance. The following are three popular tips to multiple your index performance:

➤ **When possible, define indexes with multiple columns if these columns can be used.** When an index has multiple columns, and you use multiple columns in your SELECT statements, your goal is to get the best cardinality on the first column; that is, the greatest number of unique rows is generally the best.

➤ **A covering index is an ideal index.** A covering index includes all required columns and does not require individual data pages to be read. What exactly does a covering index mean? Well, it means that the values specified in the WHERE clause of the query result in MySQL comparing the values contained in the index are used to locate the record or records versus reading the values of the data store. For MyISAM table types, this means that only the index file is read to obtain the record in question. For InnoDB, the indexes and data are in the same file, yet this is still more efficient because only the index is read.

➤ **A partial index is optimized for performance.** Rather than defining an index on a large character column, you define a smaller left portion of the index. Though a query may need to scan the index for additional rows, the reduction in index size can dramatically improve performance.

These index descriptions are described in greater detail in the following post at http://ronald-bradford.com/blog/understanding-different-mysql-index-implementations-2009-07-22/.

When Indexes Are Not Used

Two common problems where an index should have been used but is not are when your starting character is a wildcard meta character or when you use a scalar function on the indexed column. For example:

```
SELECT * FROM actor WHERE last_name LIKE '%smith';
SELECT * FROM actor WHERE UPPER(last_name) = 'SMITH';
```

In more recent versions of MySQL, the use of scalar functions can utilize a defined index; however this requires a full index scan.

Common INDEX Mistakes

In the years of reviewing schemas for performance improvements, the authors have seen some common mistakes, or assumptions, about how indexes are used. One is when too many single column indexes are created for each column specified in a WHERE clause that would otherwise be better served by utilizing a multi-column index. Always use EXPLAIN to make sure you have created a table with a covering index on the columns that are specified in the WHERE clause of the query. For instance, if your query is:

```
SELECT *  FROM geeks WHERE username = 'sakila' AND state = 'CA' WHERE age < 30;
```

you would want to have a covering index on (username, state, age) versus each column separately. Now, if your query were:

```
SELECT * FROM geeks WHERE state = 'CA';
```

that query would not utilize the multi-part index because the column in the WHERE you are specifying was the second column specified (this is called a *key-part*). In this case, if both queries were the ones most commonly used, you would want to have the covering index specify state first (state, username, age). The rule is this: for a covering index to be used, the first column specified in the covering index is the only column you can specify by itself in a WHERE clause and has to be contained in the WHERE clause specifying the other two indexes for those to be covered by the multi-column index. The following EXPLAIN listing hammers this concept home. In the first example, all columns are listed in the WHERE clause and the covering index age_state_name is used:

```
explain select *
from users
where name = 'Chaintanya Mahaprabhu'
and age = 28
and state = 'HI'\G
*************************** 1. row ***************************
           id: 1
  select_type: SIMPLE
        table: users
         type: ref
possible_keys: age_state_name
          key: age_state_name
      key_len: 50
          ref: const,const,const
         rows: 1
        Extra: Using where
```

Next, only the first column of the name_state_age index is used, resulting in the index being used:

```
explain select * from users where name = 'Chaintanya Mahaprabhu'\G
*************************** 1. row ***************************
           id: 1
  select_type: SIMPLE
        table: users
         type: ref
possible_keys: age_state_name
          key: age_state_name
      key_len: 42
          ref: const
         rows: 1
        Extra: Using where
1 row in set (0.00 sec)
```

Only the age and state columns are specified in the WHERE clause, but the index is *not* used:

```
mysql> explain select * from users where age = 28 and state = 'HI'\G
*************************** 1. row ***************************
           id: 1
  select_type: SIMPLE
```

```
          table: users
           type: ALL
  possible_keys: NULL
            key: NULL
        key_len: NULL
            ref: NULL
           rows: 8
          Extra: Using where
```

In this case, you would want another covering index but only on (age, state). So, whenever in doubt, use EXPLAIN.

Other Commands

This chapter doesn't go into great detail about the SHOW PROFILE command; however this can also be a valuable and fine-grained tool for query analysis. This can show micro-second breakdown of SQL statements by individual components within the MySQL kernel, and can provide some hints as to where to tune your query. To use profiling, all you have to do is set profiling to true with the following statement:

```
mysql> set profiling=1;
```

The following code shows the breakdown of the internal operations for executing a query:

```
SELECT user,host,password FROM mysql.user;
SHOW PROFILE;
+--------------------+----------+
| Status             | Duration |
+--------------------+----------+
| starting           | 0.000078 |
| Opening tables     | 0.000015 |
| System lock        | 0.000007 |
| Table lock         | 0.000008 |
| init               | 0.000031 |
| optimizing         | 0.000016 |
| statistics         | 0.000062 |
| preparing          | 0.000018 |
| executing          | 0.000005 |
| Sending data       | 0.000075 |
| end                | 0.000006 |
| query end          | 0.000004 |
| freeing items      | 0.000031 |
| logging slow query | 0.000004 |
| cleaning up        | 0.000005 |
+--------------------+----------+
```

For the source code savvy developer, the SOURCE option even provides the source file and line number so you can delve into the MySQL source code (if available) to review the code. If you add to the previous query SOURCE, you can see what source file and line the particular operation originated from:

```
SELECT user,host,password FROM mysql.user;
SHOW PROFILE SOURCE\G
```

```
*************************** 1. row ***************************
       Status: starting
     Duration: 0.000078
Source_function: NULL
  Source_file: NULL
  Source_line: NULL
*************************** 2. row ***************************
       Status: Opening tables
     Duration: 0.000015
Source_function: open_tables
  Source_file: sql_base.cc
  Source_line: 4501
*************************** 3. row ***************************
       Status: System lock
     Duration: 0.000007
Source_function: mysql_lock_tables
  Source_file: lock.cc
  Source_line: 258
. . .
```

In this example, the \G ending is used because there are so many columns in the output that it's easier to view this way, as well as a LIMIT 3 put on the query to save a couple trees! You can be more selective of the columns you want to display by simply using the INFORMATION_SCHEMA, PROFILING table which contains the same exact data that the SHOW command does:

```
select state, source_file, source_line, duration
from information_schema.profiling
limit 1;
+--------------------+---------------+-------------+----------+
| state              | source_file   | source_line | duration |
+--------------------+---------------+-------------+----------+
| starting           | NULL          |        NULL | 0.000078 |
| Opening tables     | sql_base.cc   |        4501 | 0.000015 |
| System lock        | lock.cc       |         258 | 0.000007 |
| Table lock         | lock.cc       |         269 | 0.000008 |
| init               | sql_select.cc |        2386 | 0.000031 |
| optimizing         | sql_select.cc |         781 | 0.000016 |
| statistics         | sql_select.cc |         963 | 0.000062 |
| preparing          | sql_select.cc |         973 | 0.000018 |
| executing          | sql_select.cc |        1657 | 0.000005 |
| Sending data       | sql_select.cc |        2226 | 0.000075 |
| end                | sql_select.cc |        2431 | 0.000006 |
| query end          | sql_parse.cc  |        4915 | 0.000004 |
| freeing items      | sql_parse.cc  |        5942 | 0.000031 |
| logging slow query | sql_parse.cc  |        1648 | 0.000004 |
| cleaning up        | sql_parse.cc  |        1615 | 0.000005 |
+--------------------+---------------+-------------+----------+
```

By using a query from the INFORMATION_SCHEMA, you can display information in any arrangement while with the SHOW command you are restricted to a set format.

Optimizing UPDATE

To optimize an UPDATE, look at the WHERE clause. If you are using the PRIMARY KEY, no further analysis is necessary. If you are not, it is of benefit to rewrite your UPDATE statement as a SELECT statement and obtain a QEP as previously detailed to ensure optimal indexes are used. For example:

```
UPDATE t
SET     c1 = 'x',
        c2 = 'y',
        c3 = 100
WHERE   c1 = 'x'
AND     d  = CURDATE()
```

You can rewrite this UPDATE statement as a SELECT statement for using EXPLAIN:

```
EXPLAIN
SELECT c1, c2, c3
FROM    t
WHERE   c1 = 'x'
AND     d = CURDATE()
```

You should now apply the same principles as detailed in optimizing SELECT statements.

Optimizing DELETE

You should refer to the "Optimizing UPDATE" section and apply the same principles to optimize DELETE statements. The next example shows that is a common delete query run on a table (child table) that has a relation to a parent table where there are "orphaned" records — which means that some records exist in the child table without a corresponding parent record.

For instance, if you have a parent table with four parent records:

```
mysql> select * from parent;
+----+---------+
| id | name    |
+----+---------+
|  1 | parentA |
|  2 | parentB |
|  3 | parentC |
|  4 | parentD |
+----+---------+
```

and a child table with some orphaned records (those with parent_id values not existing in the parent table):

```
mysql> select * from child;
+-----------+----------+
| parent_id | child_id |
+-----------+----------+
|         1 |        1 |
|         2 |        2 |
|         3 |        3 |
|         1 |        4 |
```

```
|         1 |        5 |
|         2 |        6 |
|         0 |        7 |
|         0 |        8 |
|        10 |        9 |
|         5 |       10 |
+-----------+----------+
```

one common way to delete these orphaned records is to use a subselect in the DELETE statement:

```
delete from child where parent_id not in (select id from parent);
Query OK, 4 rows affected (0.00 sec)
```

But a more efficient way to do this is to use a join because it avoids the subquery, which is an extra query the deletion must internally perform to obtain the list of parent_id values to in turn find which of the child records don't have matches. You can test this idea before you actually run the delete statement by using a join query. This query obtains a list of orphaned records to verify what you want to delete. The following code shows how to use profiling, which utilizes a join and results in faster execution and fewer internal operations:

```
set profiling = 1;
select *
from child
where parent_id not in (select id from parent);
+-----------+----------+
| parent_id | child_id |
+-----------+----------+
|         0 |        7 |
|         0 |        8 |
|        10 |        9 |
|         5 |       10 |
+-----------+----------+
select parent_id, child_id
from child
left join parent on (parent.id = child.parent_id)
where parent.id is NULL;
+-----------+----------+
| parent_id | child_id |
+-----------+----------+
|         0 |        7 |
|         0 |        8 |
|        10 |        9 |
|         5 |       10 |
+-----------+----------+
select query_id,count(*) as '# ops', sum(duration)
from information_schema.profiling
group by query_id;
+----------+-------+---------------+
| query_id | # ops | sum(duration) |
+----------+-------+---------------+
|        1 |    18 |      0.000725 |
|        2 |    15 |      0.000535 |
+----------+-------+---------------+
```

The preceding code shows that both queries give the same results; however, the optimizer shows that the second query uses fewer operations and executes faster. With this list, you can now delete these records using the join in a DELETE statement:

```
delete from child using child left join parent on (parent.id = child.parent_id)
where parent.id is NULL;
Query OK, 4 rows affected (0.00 sec)
```

And the four rows were deleted!

Optimizing INSERT

Generally, no optimization is necessary for an INSERT because the result of your SQL is one inserted row. You can, however, optimize multiple INSERT statements on the same table using multiple VALUES clauses, otherwise known as a *bulk insert*. This can actually save you time when you insert multiple records in a single operation. For example:

```
INSERT INTO t1(c1,c2,c3,d) VALUES ('a','b','c',CURDATE());
INSERT INTO t1(c1,c2,c3,d) VALUES ('1','2','3',CURDATE());
INSERT INTO t1(c1,c2,c3,d) VALUES ('x','y','z',CURDATE());
```

This is actually three individual INSERT statements, which incur three network round trips to the database. If you rewrite as shown in the previous code, you actually reduce this network communications from three to one network round trip. The other benefit of this optimization is that MySQL only needs to produce one execution plan for the INSERT statement. It can then utilize that same execution plan for multiple values. One caveat when you work with bulk inserts: if the single insert fails, all the records specified in the multiple VALUES clauses will also fail to be inserted.

```
INSERT INTO t1(c1,c2,c3,d) VALUES
('a','b','c',CURDATE()),
('1','2','3',CURDATE()),
('x','y','z',CURDATE());
```

Optimizing REPLACE

The MySQL REPLACE command is actually implemented internally as a DELETE and an INSERT. The REPLACE command, however, can cause fragmentation at the disk data level due to the unexpected DELETE operation. If possible, you should consider using alternative means of inserting or updating your data, as shown next with the INSERT ... ON DUPLICATE KEY UPDATE statement.

INSERT ... ON DUPLICATE KEY UPDATE

As stated, REPLACE is inefficient because it is internally implemented using a DELETE and INSERT. You have another way to have a replace-like functionality when you use the INSERT ... ON DUPLICATE KEY UPDATE statement. This statement results in a record being updated if the record exists for the primary key value *and* any of the record's columns' values are different than the existing specified record. If the record does not yet exist, it is inserted. If the record exists but none of the values have changed, nothing happens. This behavior is preferable to using REPLACE which deletes the record and then re-inserts it.

Using the sakila database, which — to say the least — contains interesting geek-humor for data, and, in particular, the `film` table — which contains records for films — an existing record demonstrates the use of the `INSERT ... ON DUPLICATE KEY UPDATE` statement:

```
mysql> select * from film where film_id = 500\G
*************************** 1. row ***************************
          film_id: 500
            title: KISS GLORY
      description: A Lacklusture Reflection of a Girl And a Husband who must
                   Find a Robot in The Canadian Rockies
     release_year: 2006
      language_id: 1
original_language_id: NULL
  rental_duration: 5
      rental_rate: 4.99
           length: 163
 replacement_cost: 11.99
           rating: PG-13
  special_features: Trailers,Commentaries,Behind the Scenes
      last_update: 2006-02-15 05:03:42
```

In the following query, you see what appears to be a regular insert, but with the additional specification to update the record if the unique key (the primary key `film_id`) is a value of an existing record, you will see that this record is updated:

```
INSERT INTO film (film_id, description, title)
VALUES (500,
'Epic story featuring Krishna and Arjuna on the battlefield of Kurukshetra',
'Mahabarata')
ON DUPLICATE KEY UPDATE
film_id = 500,
title = 'Mahabarata',
description = 'Epic story featuring Krishna and Arjuna on the Battlefield
of Kurukshetra';
Query OK, 2 rows affected, 1 warning (0.01 sec)
```

Note that two rows have been affected and a warning issued. This is because a `SET` value for `language_id` was not specified and `language_id` does not have a default value specified in the table definition, as the `SHOW WARNINGS` output shows in the following code.

```
mysql> show warnings;
+---------+------+----------------------------------------------------+
| Level   | Code | Message                                            |
+---------+------+----------------------------------------------------+
| Warning | 1364 | Field 'language_id' doesn't have a default value   |
+---------+------+----------------------------------------------------+
```

Next, a query shows that the record was indeed updated:

```
mysql> select * from film where film_id = 500\G
*************************** 1. row ***************************
          film_id: 500
            title: Mahabarata
      description: Epic story featuring Krishna and Arjuna on the Battlefield
                   of Kurukshetra
```

```
       release_year: 2006
        language_id: 1
original_language_id: NULL
    rental_duration: 5
        rental_rate: 4.99
             length: 163
   replacement_cost: 11.99
             rating: PG-13
    special_features: Trailers,Commentaries,Behind the Scenes
        last_update: 2009-11-23 16:40:56
```

DEBUGGING MYSQL

You can debug MySQL in a number of ways. In this section, you see that when you use the various logs, view process lists, and use the Gnu Debugger, gdb, you can receive all the information you could ever need to debug a problem. You can get useful information in order to report a crash to the developer community.

Error Log

Whenever you have an issue, you first want to view the error log. This is specified by the `log-error` directive in the `my.cnf`, or if not specified, you'll most likely find the error log in your data directory where the data files for MySQL are stored, and the error log is often named using the hostname of your server:

```
ls /usr/local/mysql/var/*err
/usr/local/mysql/var/patrick-galbraiths-macbook-pro.local.err
```

In this log file, you can see normal operations such as startup and shutdown as well as possible problems. The startup and shutdown messages appear as:

```
091119  1:54:28 [Note] /usr/local/mysql/libexec/mysqld: Normal shutdown
091119 01:54:34 mysqld_safe mysqld restarted
091119  1:54:34 [Warning] Setting lower_case_table_names=2 because file system for
                /usr/local/maria/var/ is case insensitive
091119  1:54:34 [Note] Event Scheduler: Loaded 0 events
091119  1:54:34 [Note] /usr/local/mysql/libexec/mysqld: ready for connections.
Version: '5.1.35-maria-beta1'  socket: '/tmp/mysql.sock'
port: 3306  Source distribution
```

You'll also see various errors from time to time. For example, the following output shows an error loading the Memcached Functions for MySQL (UDFs). The particular problem is due to the UDF plugin shared library not being installed correctly, resulting in this error message:

```
091118 10:56:53 [ERROR] Can't open shared library
'libmemcached_functions_mysql.so' (errno: 0 dlopen(/usr
/local/maria/lib/mysql/plugin/libmemcached_functions_mysql.so, 2): Symbol not
found: _memcached_pool_behavior_get
```

Or in the case of a crash, you can see this unwanted but useful message:

```
091023  8:54:34 - mysqld got signal 11 ;
This could be because you hit a bug. It is also possible that this binary
```

or one of the libraries it was linked against is corrupt, improperly built,
or misconfigured. This error can also be caused by malfunctioning hardware.
We will try our best to scrape up some info that will hopefully help diagnose
the problem, but since we have already crashed, something is definitely wrong
and this may fail.

```
key_buffer_size=8384512
read_buffer_size=131072
max_used_connections=1max_threads=153
threads_connected=0
It is possible that mysqld could use up to
key_buffer_size + (read_buffer_size + sort_buffer_size)*max_threads = 342071 K
bytes of memory
Hope that's ok; if not, decrease some variables in the equation.

thd: 0x0
Attempting backtrace. You can use the following information to find out
where mysqld died. If you see no messages after this, something went
terribly wrong...stack_bottom = 0x0 thread_stack 0x48000
0    mysqld                         0x0032db8d my_print_stacktrace + 40
1    mysqld                         0x000ce0c1 handle_segfault + 10252
         libSystem.B.dylib              0x932bf2bb _sigtramp + 43
3    ???                            0xffffffff 0x0 + 4294967295
4    ha_federatedx.so               0x00d4cd08 _ZN13ha_federatedx5closeEv + 72
5    mysqld                         0x0012d464 _Z8closefrmP8st_tableb + 244
6    mysqld                         0x00127181 _Z11lock_tablesP3THDP10TABLE_LIS
                                    TjPb + 1809
7    mysqld                         0x003232ee my_hash_delete + 711
8    mysqld                         0x00129c9c
                    _Z19close_cached_tablesP3THDP10TABLE_LISTbbb + 588
9    mysqld                         0x0012a10c _Z16table_cache_freev + 76
10   mysqld                         0x000cbee4 print_signal_warning + 324
11   mysqld                         0x000d3609
                    _Z34create_thread_to_handle_connectionP3THD + 2121
12   mysqld                         0x000d3632 kill_server_thread + 18
13   libSystem.B.dylib              0x93284155 _pthread_start + 321
14   libSystem.B.dylib              0x93284012 thread_start + 34
The manual page at http://dev.mysql.com/doc/mysql/en/crashing.html contains
information that should help you find out what is causing the crash.
```

As much as you don't want to see a message like this, it is very useful because it contains a crash
trace that you can send to MySQL developers.

Slow Query Log

If you turn on the slow query log, any slow queries — queries that take an excessive amount of
time — are logged to this file, which is extremely useful to identify badly written queries — potential queries to optimize. To specify the slow query log, you can add to your my.cnf:

```
log-slow-queries  = /var/log/mysql/mysql-slow.log
long_query_time = 2
log-queries-not-using-indexes
```

Notice here that you specify the log, as well as the `long_query_time`, which is the number of seconds a query takes to execute, as well as logging any queries where indexes aren't used. The entries in the log contain useful information about these slow queries:

```
# Query_time: 3  Lock_time: 0  Rows_sent: 140  Rows_examined: 280
SELECT acl_actions .*, acl_roles_actions.access_override
                 FROM acl_actions
                 LEFT JOIN acl_roles_users ON acl_roles_users.user_id = ''
AND  acl_roles_users.deleted = 0
                 LEFT JOIN acl_roles_actions ON acl_roles_actions.role_id =
acl_roles_users.role_id AND acl_roles_actions.action_id = acl_actions.id AND
acl_roles_actions.deleted=0
                 WHERE acl_actions.deleted=0  ORDER BY category,name;
# Time: 091125 11:23:07# User@Host: root[root] @ localhost []
# Query_time: 2  Lock_time: 0  Rows_sent: 0  Rows_examined: 67
select * from leads where account_name like '%foo%';
```

This code shows how long a query took, how long the table was locked, and the number of rows sent from the query, as well as the number of rows examined to produce the result.

Processlist

Some tools you will want in your arsenal are SHOW PROCESSLIST and the even more verbose SHOW FULL PROCCESSLIST, which gives you a listing of the queries running within MySQL. The listing includes the following:

➤ Query id

➤ Username running the query

➤ Host the query is initiated from

➤ Database/schema the query is running against

➤ Command

➤ Time the command has been running

➤ Query being executed and full text of the query if FULL is specified

The following shows the output:

```
mysql> show full processlist\G

*********************** 1. row ***************************
     Id: 1
   User: system user
   Host:
     db: NULL
Command: Connect
   Time: 650731
  State: Waiting for master to send event
   Info: NULL
*********************** 2. row ***************************
     Id: 139282
```

```
     User: dbuser
     Host: 192.168.0.99:62623
       db: NULL
  Command: Binlog Dump
     Time: 595445
    State: Has sent all binlog to slave; waiting for binlog to be updated
     Info: NULL
*************************** 3. row ***************************
       Id: 184194
     User: system user
     Host:
       db: NULL
  Command: Connect
     Time: 2
    State: Has read all relay log; waiting for the slave I/O thread to update it
     Info: NULL
 < output truncated to save trees >
*************************** 122. row ***************************
       Id: 14608817
     User: exporter
     Host: 192.168.0.50:22012
       db: export?
  Command: Query
     Time: 130
    State: NULL
     Info: LOAD DATA LOCAL INFILE 'data/data_info99.txt' REPLACE?INTO TABLE
carexport.extraint_results_sets  FIELDS TERMINATED BY '|' (          rcust_id,
     user_id,        dept_id,         all_constraints,         passed,
failed,          addedby ) SET dateadded = NOW()  ***************************
123. row ***************************         Id:
       Id: 14160644
     User: uioda
     Host: 192.168.1.5:42241
       db: ioda?
  Command: Query
     Time: 0
    State: Sending data
     Info: SELECT count(distinct books.book_id) from books.publish_queue pbq
WHERE books.book_id = '8953' AND (book.status = 'review' OR book.status =
'sold' ) AND book.type = 'technical' AND (book_id IS NULL OR book_id !=
'30497')
```

As you can see, the output shows a lot of useful information to spot a troublesome query that's taking a lot of time to execute, which in some cases would affect the PHP application's overall performance. Whenever an application is taking a while to display or load data, you want to display the processlist to see if there's something obvious that you can fix. Also, if a process is hung, you can kill it:

```
*************************** 7. row ***************************
       Id: 1245
     User: cacti
     Host: localhost
       db: cacti
  Command: Sleep
     Time: 93
```

```
    State:
     Info: NULL
7 rows in set (0.00 sec)

mysql> kill 1245;
Query OK, 0 rows affected (0.00 sec)
```

which in this case killed a sleeping process. But in some cases it could be a query that has been running for minutes resulting in a blank page for one of your users!

Other Commands

You have a number of other commands at your disposal but detailing them is beyond the scope of this book. Here a quick list:

➤ **SHOW STATUS/SHOW GLOBAL STATUS:** Shows the complete status of a given session or database as a whole, and provides a wealth of information pertaining to the running status of your MySQL instance.

➤ **SHOW TABLE STATUS:** Shows the status of tables on your MySQL instance.

➤ **SHOW INNODB STATUS:** Shows the status of the InnoDB storage engine. For any tables where you are using InnoDB, this provides information pertaining to how those tables function.

➤ **SHOW MASTER STATUS:** Shows you the status of your binary log, if turned on.

➤ **SHOW SLAVE STATUS:** Shows you the status of the slave — information such as which relay log the SQL slave thread is reading and which binary position the IO slave thread is reading on the master, and the lag that exists between the slave and master, as well as other information pertaining to the running state of replication.

Do remember that you can find all SHOW commands information in the INFORMATION_ SCHEMA database. For more complete information, please consult with the MySQL user's manual at http://dev.mysql.com/.

Using a Debugger with MySQL

Another tool that really shows how MySQL functions as well as tracks down the cause of bugs (if you want to become a MySQL hacker yourself!) is GDB — the GNU Debugger. To really make use of this, you need to install GDB and the source distribution of MySQL. For more information, refer to your operating system information and the MySQL user's manual. You can also find information by joining mailing lists and IRC channels #mysql, #mysql-dev on Freenode.

To use GDB to track down a crash, you would find the process id of your running MySQL instance as root or the mysql user:

```
yourhost:~ root# ps auxww|grep mysqld|grep -v mysqld_safe|grep -v grep
_mysql   26456  0.0  0.3   109232  14624 s003  S   10:18AM   0:00.08
/usr/local/mysql/libexec/mysqld --basedir=/usr/local/maria
--datadir=/usr/local/mysql/var --user=mysql
--log-error=/usr/local/mysql/var/yourhost.local.err
--pid-file=/usr/local/mysql/var/yourhost.local.pid
```

In this case, the process ID is 26456. You can attach to this process with GDB:

```
yourhost:~ root# gdb /usr/local/maria/libexec/mysqld 26456
<extra text removed>
Attaching to program: `/usr/local/maria/libexec/mysqld', process 26456.
Reading symbols for shared libraries ++++....
(gdb)
```

At the (gdb) prompt, you type **continue** to tell MySQL to continue running:

```
(gdb) continue
Continuing.
```

If, for instance, there's a query that's causing MySQL to crash, you run that query in another window. Then you will see something like this appear in GDB:

```
Program received signal SIGUSR1, User defined signal 1.
[Switching to process 26456 thread 0x2507]
0x932532ce in semaphore_wait_signal_trap ()
To see what caused the problem and have something you could submit to a mailing
list, you can run backtrace:
(gdb) backtrace
#0   0x932532ce in semaphore_wait_signal_trap ()
#1   0x9325ada5 in pthread_mutex_lock ()
#2   0x0032e74f in thr_end_alarm ()
#3   0x0025b437 in mysql_real_connect ()
#4   0x00d53ef0 in federatedx_io_mysql::actual_query ()
#5   0x00d54846 in federatedx_io_mysql::query ()
#6   0x00d4da3d in test_connection ()
#7   0x00d4fcf9 in ha_federatedx::create ()
#8   0x001d1610 in ha_create_table ()
#9   0x0019512c in rea_create_table ()
#10  0x001ddc39 in mysql_create_table_no_lock ()
#11  0x001de1be in mysql_create_table ()
#12  0x000e6cde in mysql_execute_command ()
#13  0x000e7626 in mysql_parse ()
#14  0x000e8135 in dispatch_command ()
#15  0x000e9079 in do_command ()
#16  0x000d7834 in handle_one_connection ()
#17  0x93284155 in _pthread_start ()
#18  0x93284012 in thread_start ()
(gdb)
```

The code shows that there is something wrong with the FederatedX storage engine. This is the type of trace you could provide the developer of the FederatedX storage engine (one of the authors of this book, Patrick Galbraith!). Or if you feel adventurous and greatly hailed in the open source community, you could even fix this bug!

SUMMARY

Performance is a key characteristic of a successful application. By using the techniques to optimize your queries and inspecting state in your PHP code, your application will operate faster and more efficiently and lead to higher throughput.

This chapter detailed a number of great tools that you can use to analyze the status of and debug MySQL. You have many different ways to debug MySQL — many more than could fit in this book — but this chapter should point you in the right direction to diagnose any MySQL problem.

Understanding and knowing the EXPLAIN output and PHP profiling output are essential skills for an expert PHP and MySQL developer.

Using these skills and the other skills outlined in this book, you can create finely tuned and robust applications with PHP and MySQL.

INDEX

[ ] (square brackets) in regular expressions, 50

A

abstract keyword, 3
abstract methods, 353
access permissions, views, 223–224
aCFB encryption, 504
ACID, 238
  atomicity
      non-transactional tables, 238–239
      transactional tables, 239–240
  consistency, 240–241
  durability, 247–250
  foreign keys, 38
  isolation, 242
      levels, 247
      READ_COMMITTED, 244–245
      READ_UNCOMMITTED, 245–246
      REPEATABLE_READ, 242–244
      replication, 247
      SERIALIZABLE, 246–247
  relational integrity, 35
ACLs (Access Control Lists), 473–474
Aksyonoff, Andrew, 369
algorithms, UDFs, 277
aliases, MySQL, 22
ALTER ROUTINE privilege, 230
alternation in regular expressions, 51
AND operator (MySQL), 33
anonymous functions, 78
ANSII control codes, 523
APC (Alternative PHP Cache), 132
  configuration, 132–133
  installation, 132–133
  serialization, 135
  when to use, 138
appending, memcached, 166–167
application sample view, 67–69

Archive storage engine, 109–110
args key, 544
arguments
  checking for string, 285
  functions, in extensions, 331–334
  type, checking, 274
  UDFs, 192
ArrayAccess interface, 77–78
arrays
  accessing, 347–349
  associative, 70, 348
  building, 347–349
  tracking unlinks, 77
associative arrays, 70, 348
atomicity (ACID)
  non-transactional tables, 238–239
  transactional tables, 239–240
auditing, 500–501
authorization, memcached, 140
autoconf, 292
  macros, 292
automation attacks, 514–515

B

b-tree indexes, 365
back-references in regular expressions, 53
basic authentication, 461–463
Beanstalk, 442
bi-directional encoding
  mycrypt extension, 503–505
  XOR Cipher, 501–503
binary, definition, 327
binary logging, 500
  file analysis, 256–257
  replication and, 251
bindings (SOAP), 537–538
bison, 308
Blackhole storage engine, 108–109

E

Q

X

Y

Z